D0354303

ACCOUNTING DESK BOOK

The Accountant's Everyday Instant Answer Book

TENTH EDITION

TOM M. PLANK

PRENTICE HALL
Paramus, New Jersey 07652

Library of Congress Cataloging-in-Publication Data

Plank, Tom M.
    Accounting desk book: the accountant's everyday instant answer
book / Tom M. Plank—10ed.
      p. cm.
    Includes index.
    ISBN 0-13-366980-7
    1. Accounting. II. Title.
HF5635.B668   1995   88-39352
657′.02′02—dc19   CIP

© *1995 by Prentice-Hall, Inc.*

All rights reserved. No part of this book may be reproduced in any form or by any means, without permission in writing from the publisher.

Printed in the United States of America

10   9   8   7

This publication is designed to provide accurate and authoritative information in regard to the subject matter covered. It is sold with the understanding that the publisher is not engaged in rendering legal, accounting, or other professional service. If legal advice or other expert assistance is required, the services of a competent professional person should be sought.
—*From the Declaration of Principles jointly adopted by a Committee of the American Bar Association and a Committee of Publishers and Associations*

ISBN 0-13-366980-7

9 780133 669800   90000

ATTENTION: CORPORATIONS AND SCHOOLS

Prentice Hall books are available at quantity discounts with bulk purchase for educational, business, or sales promotional use. For information, please write to: Prentice Hall Special Sales, 240 Frisch Court, Paramus, New Jersey 07652. Please supply: title of book, ISBN number, quantity, how the book will be used, date needed.

PRENTICE HALL PRESS
Paramus, NJ 07652

On the World Wide Web at http://www.phdirect.com

About the Author

Tom M. Plank is a specialist in SEC Accounting Rules and Regulations, new security issues registration, and annual report filings with the SEC. He holds his degrees from the Graduate School of Management, University of California at Los Angeles.

Mr. Plank has served on the accounting and finance faculties of various major universities in Chicago and Los Angeles. His business experience includes that of an officer and economist for a larger commercial bank, a securities analyst for an investment banking firm, an account executive for one of the largest brokerage firms in the world, and a consultant for various corporations.

Mr. Plank has published many articles in various journals and is the author of many business books: *SEC Accounting Rules and Regulations, The Age of Automation, The Science of Leadership,* and more than ten accounting books, including the seventh, eighth, ninth, and tenth editions of this volume—the *Accounting Desk Book*—as well as five supplements to the ninth edition. He also edited the *Encyclopedia of Accounting Systems.*

Introduction

This tenth edition of the *Accounting Desk Book* has its origins in two sources. First, the passage of time has required the updating and substantive revision of the material from prior editions. We have merely to cite the continuing inundation of the accounting and other professions with new accounting rules, Generally Accepted Accounting Principles (GAAP) and tax legislative modifications and changes occurring annually.

Second, the inclusion of new topics in this edition is necessary because accounting and associated disciplines—e.g. finance, management, taxes, etc.—are dynamic areas of business administration with an increasing number of new practices, standards, rules, regulations, technical terminology and knowledge. Accordingly, several new chapters have been added.

Objectives. The objective of the *Desk Book* continues to be to provide a reference manual useful in meeting the specific and varied needs of accountants, attorneys, controllers, financial officers, bankers, credit analysts, securities analysts, government administrators, business managers generally, and others who require accuracy and clarity. Equally important, this volume is for those who want—and need instantly while working at their desks—a *succinct* clarification of significant responsibility areas in a minimum of time for the information they are seeking.

Structure of the book. To further the objective and contribute to the quality, application, and usefulness of accounting and financial principles, the book's coverage is broad in scope, and is organized for quick and convenient access by the user. Each of the 23 chapters, and 8 appendixes, is formatted in a topical arrangement. Each topic is titled; many are further subdivided into sub-topics which also are titled. The discussions of the material have been developed from a *user* approach. They are concise in substance and applicable to all types of business enterprises, both manufacturing and service industries.

Users of the book are urged to review the Index for the topical presentation and instant location of the material in the book.

Timeliness. The author recognizes the importance of current information to keep pace with the fast moving states-of-the-art. The coverage of the topics, applications, illustrations, examples, and definitions of terms (where necessary because of the unique vernacular in many of the specialized topics) are consistent with the contemporary literature in accounting and finance. Care has been taken to avoid confusing abstract theory, technical jargon, complex "legalese," or textbook type of dissertations. All topics have been covered in as straightforward a presentation as possible.

It should be emphasized that the *Desk Book* is not a textbook. Rather, it is essentially a reference manual to provide the user with immediate answers to a large number of practical accounting, finance, tax, and other management questions. The discussions for the most part are largely self-contained; e.g., an explanation of a topic does not require any reference to other sources, nor is it linked to a topic treated elsewhere in the book.

Contents

CHAPTER 3   47
WHO DETERMINES STANDARDS?

CHAPTER 4   60
PRINCIPLES OF FINANCIAL STATEMENTS, DISCLOSURE, ANALYSIS INTERPRETATION

CHAPTER 5   95
STATEMENT OF CASH FLOWS

CHAPTER 6   107
CURRENT AND NON-CURRENT ASSETS

CHAPTER 15   300
THE SECURITIES AND EXCHANGE COMMISSION— ORGANIZATION AND THE ACTS

CHAPTER 16   341
THE SECURITIES AND EXCHANGE COMMISSION INTEGRATED DISCLOSURE SYSTEM AND FILING REQUIREMENTS

CHAPTER 17   390
BUSINESS COMBINATIONS

CHAPTER 18   410
MANAGEMENT PRINCIPLES

CHAPTER 19   463
EMPLOYEE BENEFITS

CHAPTER 20   496
TAX ACCOUNTING

CHAPTER 21   540
TAX TERMINOLOGY

CHAPTER 22   566
TAX REGULATIONS

CHAPTER 23   607
BUSINESS TOPICS

APPENDIX A   641
INDEX TO JOURNAL ENTRIES

APPENDIX B   668
THE GOING CONCERN CONCEPT

APPENDIX C   670
GOODWILL

Chapter 1
The Accountant
and Accounting

WHAT ACCOUNTING IS ALL ABOUT

The definition in the AICPA Professional Standards for Accounting ("The Environment of Financial Accounting") was superseded as follows (October 1970):

> Accounting is a service activity. Its function is to provide quantitative information, primarily financial in nature, about economic entities that is intended to be useful in making economic decisions, in making reasoned choices among alternative courses of action. Accounting includes several branches, for example,
>
>
> Financial Accounting
> Managerial Accounting
> Governmental Accounting
>

CONCEPTUAL FRAMEWORK

Six Statements of Financial Accounting Concepts have been adopted by the Financial Accounting Standards Board. These concepts form the basis for financial accounting standards from the standpoint of the nature, function, and limits of financial accounting.

Accounting Information

Accounting information can be classified into two categories—financial accounting and managerial accounting. Financial accounting is information for the users of financial statements, i.e., creditors, stockholders, financial analysts, governmental regulatory agencies, trade associations, customers. (This is not to say, however, that the same information is not of interest to management.) Financial accounting, then, concerns the financial position, earnings, liquidity, and operating performance generally of the enterprise.

Managerial accounting is primarily for internal control purposes: cost-volume-profit analysis, efficiency, productivity, planning and control, pricing decisions, operating and capital budgets, and a variety of specialized reports which management needs for the decision-making process.

Accounting Principles

Accounting can be thought of as a system—a system of assumptions, doctrines, tenets, and conventions, all included in the concept "Generally Accepted Accounting Principles" commonly referenced by the acronym GAAP. These principles developed by a process of evolution over a long period of years much in the same way that the common law developed, by way of an analogy. Very few accounting rules are embodied in statutory law, as government has for the most part deferred the promulgation of accounting standards to the private sector of the economy. Let's examine a few of the fundamental notions (concepts) that underlie accounting principles and practices as they exist today.

For the financial accounting standards required for external reporting, GAAP encompasses the conventions, rules, and procedures necessary to define accepted accounting practices at a particular time, and includes not only broad guidelines of general application, but also detailed practices and procedures. The conventions, rules, and procedures provide a standard by which to measure financial presentations.

The significant principles are that accounting information be relevant, reliable, comparable, and consistent. Relevant information helps users to predict events, or to confirm or correct prior expectations. Reliable information can be verified, is accurate and objective. Comparable information is measured and reported in a similar manner for different enterprises, particularly in the same industry. Consistent information is reported in the same manner from period-to-period, i.e., the same accounting methods are consistently applied.

Accounting Concepts

The *matching principle* requires that the revenues of the accounting period be precisely matched with the expenses of that same period that were incurred to generate the revenues.

The *accrual principle* considers revenues and expenses to be an inflow and outflow of *all* assets, not just the flow of cash in and out of the enterprise.

The *historical cost principle* requires that economic resources be entered into the system at cost, when the transaction occurs. The price paid is, on the face of it, considered to be the value of the asset.

The *realization* notion means economic events are accounted for only when the enterprise has been a party to one side of a *bona fide* transaction. For example, if a parcel of land has appreciated in value, the gain cannot be recognized until the land has been sold.

Associated with the realization concept is the idea of *substance-over-form* standard. All transactions must have "economic substance" as opposed to "sham" transactions entered into for some "creative accounting" purpose.

The *entity* concept concerns any person or group of persons having a name, common purpose, and *transactions with outsiders*. A relationship between the entity and external parties must be clearly established. The form of organization of the enterprise is not relevant with respect to the entity being an *accounting unit*.

The *going-concern* assumption considers the entity as one that will operate indefinitely.

The *consistency* standard requires the accounting procedures applied during a given accounting period be the same procedures that were applied in previous periods. The purpose of the consistency principle is to ensure that the statements of the enterprise for the current and prior periods are comparable.

The *conservative doctrine* directs that when the enterprise is exposed to uncertainty and risk that are material, accounting measurement and disclosure should be approached with a high degree of caution and in a prudent manner, until evidence develops that there is a significant reduction or elimination of the uncertainty.

Finally, the all-important *disclosure* principle. The financial statements must present for the users all the relevant information that is necessary in order *not* to be misleading. This includes not only errors of commission, but also errors of omission of material information.

FASB Concepts Statements

1) *Objectives of Financial Reporting by Business Enterprises* covers information useful to anyone (whether externally or internally) needing to review financial statements, including creditors and investors.

Thus, the aims of this statement are twofold: to provide a general purpose external financial reporting method by business enterprises, and at the same time satisfy the needs of internal users who are not in a position to provide the information necessary to carry out their responsibilities, but must rely upon the information that management has chosen to furnish them.

2) The *Qualitative Characteristics of Accounting Information Statements* provides step-by-step guidelines for acceptable accounting methods, including the amount and types of information to be disclosed, and the appropriate form for that information. The FASB emphasizes that relevance and reliability are the key words in providing useful accounting information. Only slightly less vital qualities are consistency and the ease with which the relevant information can be verified or used in comparison studies.

3) *Elements of Financial Statements of Business Enterprises* is superseded by Concept No. 6.

4) *Objectives of Financial Reporting by Nonbusiness Organizations.* The Statement prescribes the external financial reporting by nonbusiness organizations, such as governmental entities and government-sponsored entities, including hospitals, universities, and utilities.

5) *Recognition and Measurement in Financial Statements of Business Enterprises.* This Statement specifies what information should be included in financial statements and when that information should be collected and reported. It deals with four basic assumptions relevant to financial accounting:

  1) A going concern
  2) A monetary unit
  3) An economic entity
  4) Periodicity

6) *Elements of Financial Statements.* Ten elements germane to financial statements are defined and described in this Statement. Included are economic terms used in financial reporting relevant to investment, credit, and other resource allocation decisions. These ten interrelated key words vital to financial statements are:

  1) Assets
  2) Liabilities
  3) Equity
  4) Investments by Owners
  5) Distributions to Owners
  6) Comprehensive Income
  7) Revenues
  8) Expenses
  9) Gains
  10) Losses

NOTE: The concepts are not a rigid outline for specific accounting procedures or disclosure practices required by GAAP, but attempt to provide a broad perspective useful in setting up acceptable accounting standards and procedures, as well as in evaluating and/or improving existing ones.

ECONOMIC PERFORMANCE RULE

All-events test. In determining whether an amount for any item has been incurred during a taxable year, the *all-events test* will not be deemed to have been met before economic performance of the item occurs. The all-events test is adjudged to have been met with respect to any item if all events have occurred which determine the fact of liability, and it is possible to determine the amount of liability with a reasonable degree of accuracy.

The time frame in which economic performance takes place can be determined under the following principles:

1) When the liability of the taxpayer originates with services provided for the taxpayer by another person, economic performance occurs when the services have in fact been provided.
2) When the liability of the taxpayer is the result of another person providing *property* to the taxpayer, economic performance occurs at the time the person provides the property.
3) When the liability of the taxpayer results from the *use* of property by the taxpayer, economic performance occurs when the taxpayer uses that property. An item is treated as incurred during any taxable year if:
   a) The all-events test when applied to that item is met during the taxable year.
   b) The economic performance occurs:
      1) Within a reasonable period after the close of the taxable year; or
      2) 8 1/2 months after the close of the taxable year, whichever is shorter;
   c) It is a recurring item and the taxpayer consistently treats said items as incurred in the taxable year in which the requirements of the all-events test relating to them are met.

Also, the all-events test can be considered met if either the item is not a material item, or the accrual of the item in the taxable year in which the requirements of the all-events test are met results in costs more closely matching income than in accruing the item in the taxable year in which economic performance occurs.

Under the accrual method of tax accounting, an expenditure is taken into account for deduction or capitalization purposes in the year in which all events have occurred that determine the *fact* of the liability, and its amount can be estimated with reasonable accuracy.

The *Economic Performance Rule* establishes an additional standard for determining when an expenditure may be taken into account—the *economic performance test.* Expenditures of a recurring nature may be taken into account in advance of economic performance if the taxpayer adopts a special method applicable to qualifying items, provided that economic performance for the expenditure occurs within a stated period after year-end.

The economic performance rule could have a deleterious effect upon the taxpayer. For example, deductions for accrued property taxes prior to payment are prohibited unless a special method appropriate for recurring expenditures has been adopted in reference to the time in question and the relevant taxes are paid usually within 81/2 months after the end of the year in which they become due, or would have become due. The rule also provides for the timing of the income recognition of taxpayers who are subject to the long-term contract rules. Under the percentage-of-completion method, the portion of the contract price on a long-term contract is to be recognized income as a percentage of estimated total income:

1) That actual costs bear to total costs after giving effect to recent estimates of costs to complete.
2) As indicated by other appropriate measures of progress to completion.

Under the percentage-of-completion method, current assets may include costs and recognized income not yet filled for certain contracts. Liabilities (usually current liabilities) may include billings in excess of costs and recognized income with regard to other contracts.

The regulations provide that economic performance on costs associated with long-term contracts has occurred 1) if at the earlier time, payment is made, or 2) at the time at which the taxpayer *actually receives* the related property or services. Thus, income recognition can be accelerated if the taxpayer must pay for property or services before delivery.

To illustrate, assume the total cost of building 25 houses at the same fixed price in a development includes $500,000 for required costs at the end of the project in five years. Under prior law, if four of the houses were finished and sold during the first year, the costs of building the four houses, as well as $100,000 (20% x $500,000) could be applicable to the future costs. Now, the application of the economic performance rule would result in a deferral of any deduction for the future costs until the end of the construction when the entire development is completed.

ACCOUNTING PRINCIPLES BOARD (APB) OPINIONS

Omnibus Opinion

(*NOTE:* Portions of this Opinion are superseded by APB 14, which immediately follows.)

APB 12 requires allowances for depreciation and depletion to be deducted from the assets to which they specifically relate. In line with this rule, the following disclosures should be made:

1) Depreciation expense for the period.
2) Balances of the major classes of depreciable assets should be according to the function of the assets being depreciated.
3) Depreciation should be accumulated either by classes or in total.
4) The accounting procedures used in computing depreciation for all the major classes.

Deferred compensation contracts. When a deferred compensation contract is involved, the following steps should be taken:

1) The estimated amounts to be paid under each contract should be accrued in a systematic manner extending over the entire period of actual employment from the time the contract becomes effective.

2) Some deferred compensation contracts provide for periodic payments to employees or surviving spouses for life with provisions for a minimum lump sum settlement in the event of the early death of one or all of the beneficiaries. However, in estimating future payments, calculations should be based on life expectancy of each individual concerned or on the estimated cost of an annuity contract rather than on the minimum amount paid in the event of early death(s).

3) Amounts relating to deferred compensation contracts with active employees which have not been accrued as stated in item 1) should be accrued over the employees' remaining term of employment.

In noting *capital changes,* when both financial position and the results of operations are presented, changes in stockholders' equity accounts and changes in the number of shares outstanding should be disclosed either in separate statements or in the basic financial statements.

Accounting for Convertible Debt and Debt Issued with Common Stock Warrants

APB 14 covers GAAP for the issuance of convertible debt and debt issued with stock purchase warrants. When warrants to purchase stock are issued with bonds but are detachable, that portion of the proceeds that may be allocated to the warrants should be accounted for as paid-in capital. Any bond discount or premium resulting should be accounted for by the same procedure. The allocation should be based on the relative values of the two securities at the time of issue. If the warrants are not detachable, the bonds are convertible debt.

In addition:

1) No portion of the proceeds from the convertible debt issue should be accounted for as associated with the conversion feature.
2) The inseparability of the debt and the conversion feature are the principal reason for accounting for convertible debt solely as debt.

Other reasons are:

1) Both choices cannot be consummated.
2) The monetary value of the conversion option presents problems because the market values are not established.
3) Material adjustments which result from retroactive adoption of this option should be treated as a prior period adjustment.

Intangible Assets

APB 17 reviews GAAP in accounting for intangibles. A company should record as assets the costs of those intangibles acquired from outside sources:

1) Cost of developing, maintaining, or restoring intangible assets which a) are not specifically identifiable, b) have indeterminate lives, or c) are inherent in a continuing business and related to an enterprise as a whole and should be deducted from income at the time the expense is incurred.
2) Individually acquired intangible assets should be recorded at cost at the time of acquisition. Cost is measured by:
   a) The amount of cash disbursed;
   b) The fair value of other assets distributed;
   c) The present value of amounts to be paid for liabilities incurred; or
   d) The fair value of consideration received for any stock issued.

Intangible assets in this category, including those acquired as a part of a major acquisition, should also be recorded at cost at the time of acquisition. Cost is calculated in a different manner for specifically identifiable intangible assets and those which cannot be specifically identified. Since the cost of identifiable intangible assets is an assigned part of the total cost of the group of assets or enterprise acquired, usual procedure is to base the cost on the stated fair values of the specific, individual assets. On the other hand, the cost of unidentifiable intangible assets is measured by the difference between the cost of the group of assets or enterprise acquired and the sum of the assigned costs of individual tangible and identifiable assets acquired less liabilities assumed. Costs should be assigned to all specifically identifiable intangible assets; cost of identifiable assets should not be included in goodwill.

Because the value of intangible assets eventually disappears, the recorded costs of those assets should be amortized by systematic charges to income over a period during which they are deemed to have a beneficial effect. Elements which must be kept in mind when estimating the useful lives of intangible assets include:

1) Legal, regulatory, or contractual provisions may set maximum limits upon them.

2) Provisions for renewal or extension may alter a stated limit.

3) Results of obsolescence, demand, competition, and other economic factors may shorten the anticipated useful period.

4) A useful life may be tied to the service-life expectancies of key individuals or groups of employees.

5) Anticipated actions and/or reactions of competitors and others may reduce existing competitive advantages.

6) An apparently unlimited useful life may be so indefinite that benefits cannot be reasonably projected with any degree of accuracy.

The cost of each type of intangible asset should be amortized on the estimated life of that specific asset and should not be written off at the time it is acquired. After critical analysis, most intangible assets can be assigned a reasonably accurate useful life. Even when this approach proves to be overly subjective, a reasonable estimate of the useful life may at times be based on upper and lower limits. However, the period of amortization should not exceed an upper limit of 40 years. Analysis may show that the indeterminate lives of some of the intangible assets will probably exceed 40 years. In such cases, at the time of acquisition, it should be established that the cost of these assets will be amortized over 40 years, not a shorter period of time.

Unless a company can show that another amortization method is more appropriate, the straight-line method should be applied. The method and period of amortization should be disclosed in the financial statements. A timing difference is not created by the amortization of acquired goodwill and of other acquired intangible assets not deductible in computing income taxes payable. An allocation of income taxes is inappropriate.

Disclosure of Accounting Policies

APB 22 covers *Disclosure of Accounting Policies*. A description of all significant accounting policies of the reporting entity should be included as an integral part of all financial statements. Whether these statements are issued in presenting the entity's financial position, changes in the financial position, or in showing results of operations in accordance with GAAP, a description of all significant accounting policies, methods and practices of the reporting entity should be included as an integral part of all financial statements. When it is appropriate to issue one or more basic financial statements without the others, these statements should also comprise the pertinent accounting policies. Not-for-profit entities should also present details of their accounting policies as an integral part of their financial statements.

Content and Format of Disclosures

1) Disclosure of accounting policies should identify and describe the accounting principles employed by the reporting business and the methods of applying those principles which are important in the determination of financial position, changes in financial position, or results of operations. The disclosure should include decisions concerning applicability of principles relating to recognition of revenue and allocation of asset costs to current and future periods. The disclosure statement should comprise all the reasoning behind the choice of, or an explanation of, the accounting principles and methods employed that involve any of the following:
   a) Selection of one practice over another from existing acceptable alternatives.
   b) Principles and methods peculiar to the industry of the reporting firm, even when such principles and methods are characteristically followed in that industry
   c) Unusual or innovative applications of generally accepted accounting principles or of practices and methods peculiar to that industry.
2) Examples of disclosures commonly required in regard to accounting policies include those relating to basis of consolidation, depreciation methods, amortization of intangibles, inventory pricing, accounting for research and development costs and the basis for amortization thereof, translation of foreign currencies, recognition of profit on long-term con-

struction-type contracts, recognition of revenue from franchising and leasing operations, and any other items deemed pertinent to give a complete picture of a firm's financial status.

3) The format follows a plan of having a separate *Summary of Significant Accounting Policies* preceding the notes to the financial statements or, in some cases, as the initial note of the statement.

Early Extinguishment of Debt

APB 26 covers the extinguishment of *all* debt other than debt that has been extinguished through a troubled restructuring and convertible debt that is converted to equity securities of the debtor.

The reacquisition of any form of debt security or debt instrument before the scheduled maturity date, other than through conversion by the holder of the said debt obligation, is classified as early extinguishment. This is true whether the debt is considered as terminated or is held as so-called treasury bonds. All open-market or mandatory reacquisitions of debt securities in order to meet sinking fund requirements are considered to be extinguishments. Three definitions which may be helpful in understanding APB 26 are:

1) *Difference* as used in this opinion is the excess of the reacquisition price over the net carrying amount or the excess of the net carrying amount over the acquisition price.

2) *Net carrying amount of debt* is the amount due at maturity, adjusted for unamortized premium, discount and cost of issuance.

3) *Reacquisition price of debt* is the amount paid on early extinguishment including a call premium and miscellaneous costs of reacquisition. If early extinguishment is achieved by a direct exchange of new securities, the reacquisition price is the total present value of the new securities.

All extinguishments of debt before their scheduled maturity dates are basically the same. Therefore, accounting for these transactions is the same despite differing methods used to bring about extinguishments. Any difference between the reacquisition price and the net carrying amount of the extinguished debt should be recognized in income for the period during which extinguishment occurs. That difference is to be recorded as losses or gains and recorded as a separate item.

The extinguishment of convertible debt before maturity does not change its nature in relation to its classification as debt or equity at that time. Hence, any difference between the cash acquisition price of the debt and its net carrying amount is to be recognized in income during the period of extinguishment as a loss or gain, as the case may be.

FINANCIAL ACCOUNTING STANDARDS BOARD (FASB) STATEMENTS

FASB Statement 4, *Reporting Gains and Losses from Extinguishment of Debt*

I.   FASB Statement No. 4 specifies that gains and losses from extinguishment of debt should be aggregated and, if material, classified as an extraordinary item in the income statement.

II.   Statement 4 requires the following disclosures in financial statements in which debt extinguishments are reported as extraordinary items:

   A) A description of the extinguishment transaction, including the sources of any funds used to extinguish debt.

   B) The income tax effect in the period of extinguishment.

   C) The per share amount of the aggregate gain or loss, net of related income tax effect.

III. Paragraph 8 of FASB Statement No. 4 says, in part:

   Gains and losses from extinguishment of debt that are included in the determination of net income shall be aggregated and, if material, classified as an extraordinary item, net of related income tax effect. That conclusion shall apply whether an extinguishment is early or at scheduled maturity date or later.

   This portion of the Statement amends APB Opinion No. 30 in that material gains and losses from extinguishment of debt are to be classified as an extraordinary item in the income statement.

IV.   *Types of Extinguishment of Debt:*

   A) Retirement of debt serially—includes serial bonds as well as debt payable in periodic installments (e.g., term loans and notes payable to insurance company).

   B) Refinancing—replacing existing debt with new debt.

   C) Early extinguishment of debt at a discount.

   D) Early extinguishment of debt at a premium.

   E) Sinking-fund purchase.

V.   *Disclosure Requirements:* The Statement concludes that gains or losses from extinguishment of debt that are reported as extraordinary items should be described sufficiently to enable users of financial statements to evaluate their significance. The following disclosures are required:

   A) A description of the extinguishment transactions, including the sources of any funds used to extinguish debt.

   B) The income tax effect in the period of extinguishment.

C) The per share amount of the aggregate gain or loss, net of related income tax effect.

FASB Statement 5, *Accounting for Contingencies*

FASB Statement No. 5 establishes new accounting criteria for an estimated loss from a contingency and carries forward existing criteria for an estimated gain from a contingency. To comply with the Statement, many companies which have made accruals for contingent losses will be required to reverse the accruals and credit the balance to income in the year of change. Other companies will be required to begin accruing for loss contingencies and charge income in the year of change.

I. The key provisions of the Statement are:

    A) An estimated loss from a contingency should be charged to income only if *both* of the following conditions are met.

        1) It is *probable* that a future event or events will occur confirming the likelihood that an asset had been impaired or a liability had been incurred as of the balance sheet date;

        2) The amount of the loss can be *reasonably estimated.*

    B) Contingencies which might result in gains usually are not recorded prior to realization.

    C) Reserves for catastrophic losses, general contingencies (i.e., general or unspecified business risks), and self-insurance reserves or accruals for workers' compensation and other employment-related costs which are excluded from the scope of the Statement.

II. *Disclosure:*

    A) For accrued loss contingencies, disclosure of the nature of the accrual and, in some circumstances, the amount accrued may be necessary for the financial statements not to be misleading.

    B) For contingencies which represent at least a "reasonable possibility" of loss, but which are not accrued because both conditions for accrual (probable and reasonable estimate) are not met, the Statement requires disclosure of:

        1) The nature of the contingency;

        2) An estimate of the possible loss or range of loss or a statement that an estimate cannot be made.

III. *Contingency:* An existing condition, situation, or set of circumstances involving uncertainty as to possible gain or loss to an enterprise that will ultimately be resolved when one or more future events occurs or fails to occur. Resolution of the uncertainty may confirm the acquisition of an asset, or the reduction of a liability, or the loss or impairment of an asset, or the incurrence of a liability.

IV. In determining whether an accrual is required for a loss contingency, it is first necessary to assess the outcome of the contingency in terms of the likelihood of occurrence of the future event or events that will confirm the loss.

A) The Statement uses three terms in discussing the likelihood of occurrence:

    1) *Probable*—The future event (or events) is likely to occur.

    2) *Reasonably possible*—The chance of the future event or events occurring is more than remote but less than likely.

    3) *Remote*—The chance of the future event or events occurring is slight.

B) If it is probable that a loss will result from a contingency and the amount of the loss can be *reasonably estimated*, the estimated loss should be accrued by a charge to income. *Both* conditions must be met if a loss contingency is to be accrued.

C) Companies which currently have contingency reserves that do not meet both conditions for accrual (e.g., general contingencies, self-insurance, catastrophic losses) will be required to reverse the reserves; other companies will be required to begin accruing for loss contingencies that meet both conditions (e.g., warranty obligations).

V. *Examples of Loss Contingencies*—loss related to:

A) Collectibility of receivables.

B) Obligations related to product warranties and product defects.

C) Risk of loss or damage of enterprise property by fire, explosion, or other hazards.

D) General or unspecified business risks.

E) Risk of loss from catastrophies assumed by property and casualty insurance companies including reinsurance companies.

F) Threat of expropriation of assets.

G) Pending or threatened litigation.

H) Actual or possible claims and assessments.

I) Guarantees of indebtedness of others.

J) Obligations of commercial banks under "standby letters of credit."

K) Agreements to repurchase receivables (or the related property) that have been sold.

VI. *Examples of Items Not Affected by the Statement:*

A) Pension costs.

B) Deferred compensation contracts.

C) Capital stock issued to employees.

D) Group insurance.

E) Vacation pay.

F) Workers' compensation.

G) Disability benefits.

VII. The Statement continues existing accounting and disclosure requirements for the following items:

A) Net losses on long-term, construction-type contracts.

B) Write-down of carrying amount of operating assets because questionable recovery of cost.

C) Unused letters of credit.

FASB Statement 91, *Accounting for Nonrefundable Fees and Costs Associated with Originating or Acquiring Loans and Initial or Direct Costs of Leases*

FASB Statement 91 prescribes accounting for nonrefundable fees and costs associated with lending, committing to lend, or purchasing a loan or group of loans. The Statement also details the accounting methods to be used for initial direct costs connected with leasing.

Loan fees may be deferred and recognized over the life of the loan as an adjustment of yield. Also, some organization costs are to be deferred and amortized over the life of the loan and appear as a reduction in yield. Deferred fees and costs are customarily figured using the interest method.

Costs which may be deferred are spelled out in the Statement and must be related to an actual loan or commitment. The new rules do away with the practice of deferring all or some portion of costs related to a particular lending activity or unit, such as the mortgage loan department, regardless of the volume of business generated. Payroll and other costs related to unsuccessful, rejected applications, or idle time, are considered as current expense. Fees and costs must normally be accounted for on a loan-by-loan basis, but under specified conditions, fees and costs can be grouped.

Although not mentioned in Statement 91's title, the Statement also covers the accounting procedures for discounts and premiums related to purchased debt securities, such as corporate bonds.

FASB Statement 92, Regulated Enterprises—Accounting For Phase-In Plans

What Is A Phase-In Plan?

The usual rate-making procedure gives a utility the authority to increase consumer rates to allow for recovery of the costs of newly constructed utility plants that have been placed in service. In recent years, the high costs of construction, particularly for nuclear plants, and at times the high cost of capital have resulted in *rate spikes*, which are an unusually high one-time increase in the usual rates of a regulated enterprise. *Phase-in-plans* have been developed to solve the problems caused by rate spikes, principally to reduce their impact by deferring a portion of the initial rate increase to future years and providing the regulated enterprise with a return on the amounts deferred. Phase-in plans are an approach that replaces the usual pattern of increases in costs for utility plants in the early years of a plant's service life, followed by decreasing costs after the plants have been placed in service.

FASB Statement 92 outlines procedures for regulated enterprises to recover allowable cost of construction of a new plant under a phase-in plan adopted by regulators. Further, it specifically relates to allowable costs deferred for future recovery under phase-in plans for plants completed before January 1, 1988, or plants on which substantial physical construction was performed prior to that date.

The allowable costs usually permit a regulated enterprise to charge the rates required to include actual or estimated costs that are incurred to provide products and services, and include a return on investments to compensate investors in long-term debt and equity capital. The authorized rates are set to produce total revenue for a regulated enterprise that is approximately equal to new plant costs.

The terms of any phase in-plan in effect during the current year (or ordered for future years) must be disclosed in the financial statements. If costs for future recovery have been deferred for rate-making purposes, but *not* for financial reporting purposes, the net amount of such allowable costs that have been deferred for future recovery must be disclosed. Also, the disclosure of the net change in the related deferrals for those plants during the year is required. Also, required is disclosure about the nature and amounts of any allowance for earnings on shareholders' investment that have been capitalized for rate-making purposes, but not capitalized for financial reporting purposes.

Capitalization of construction costs is required if each of the following criteria is met:

1) The regulators have agreed to the plan.
2) The plan specifies recovery time.
3) Allowable costs that are deferred will be recovered within ten years of beginning the deferral.
4) The percentage increases in scheduled rates for each succeeding year are less than, or equal to, the percentage increases in rates of the prior year.

If *all* of these criteria are not met, capitalization of the allowable costs deferred under the plan is not permitted for financial reporting purposes.

Statement 92 applies to phase-in plans that do not meet the criteria for capitalization of deferred allowance costs set forth in the Statement. The costs can be deferred if the regulated enterprise has filed, or plans to file, a rate application to amend the phase-in plan to meet the criteria for capitalization, and it is reasonably possible regulators will change the phase-in plan. If regulators amend, or refuse to amend a plan, the Statement should be applied.

FASB Statement 97, *Accounting and Reporting by Insurance Enterprises for Certain Long–Duration Contracts and for Realized Gains and Losses from the Sale of Investments*

FASB Statement 97 amends Statement 60 by concluding that the accounting methods required by Statement 60 are not appropriate for insurance contracts in which the insurer can vary amounts charged or credited to the policyholder's account or the policyholder can vary the amount of premium paid.

The Statement outlines the accounting methods for three different classifications of long-duration life and annuity products. These classifications are:

1) Universal life-type policies
2) Limited payment policies
3) Policies not covering significant mortality or morbidity risks

Universal life-type policies.   Universal life-type policies must utilize a retrospective deposit method. The liability for this type of policy will be equal to the gross account balances before deduction of surrender charges. Revenues reported will be made up of charges assessed against the policy for mortality, expenses, and surrenders. These charges are presumed to be earned in the period during which they were assessed; however, charges, such as front-end fees, for example, assessed a limited number of times are deferred as unearned revenue.

For universal life-type policies, acquisition costs will be deferred and amortized in relation to present value of estimated future gross profits. Interest accrues to the unamortized balance of the deferred acquisition costs. The estimated gross profits are computed from estimated future mortality charges minus the estimated benefit claims exceeding:

1) The related account balances.
2) Expense charges minus the policy's estimated administration costs.

3) Estimated surrender charges.

4) Estimated future earnings based on investment yields of the policyholder's account balances, minus the estimated interest to be credited to account balances.

When the estimates of future gross profits are reevaluated, the amortization of deferred acquisition costs accrued to date must be adjusted and recognized in current operations. Any deferred revenues, including deferred front-end fees, are recognized as income on the same basis as the amortization of deferred acquisition costs.

Limited-payment policies.   Limited-payment policies consist of life insurance and annuity policies with fixed and guaranteed terms having premiums that are payable over a period shorter than the period during which benefits are paid. The premiums for this type of policy are reported as revenues (reserves are computed in accordance with rulings set forth in Statement 60). However, the accumulated profit, formerly shown as a percentage of premiums, is deferred. The amount of coverage must be related to life insurance in force or expected future annuity benefit payments.

Policies not covering significant mortality or morbidity risk.   Policies not covering significant mortality or morbidity risks, such as *guaranteed investment contracts* (GICs) and some types of annuities, are shown as interest-bearing or other financial instruments, rather than as insurance contracts. Therefore, the accounting for these policies would show the account balance as a liability, and premiums as deposits rather than as revenues. Deferred acquisition costs would primarily be amortized in relation to future interest margins.

Policies including accident and health insurance not falling under one of these three classifications remain within the requirements of Statement 60.

Statement 97 also requires that property/casualty and stock life insurance companies must provide one-step income statements for realized investment gains or losses instead of the currently required two-step statement. The latter shows operating income after taxes but before net realized investment gains or losses. The one-step income statement presents realized investment gains or losses on a pretax basis with revenues, investment income, and expenses to show income before taxes.

FASB Statement 101, *Accounting for Regulated Enterprises (Discontinuation of FASB Statement 71)*

FASB Statement 101 specifies that an entity that no longer meets the criteria for application of FASB Statement 71, *Accounting for the Effects of*

Certain Types of Regulation, to all or part of its regulated operations, should discontinue application of Statement 71 and adjust the affected items and amounts reported in its balance sheet to reflect what they would have been if Statement 71 had never been applied.

However, the carrying amounts of plant, equipment, and inventory measured and reported in line with provisions of Statement 71 should not be adjusted unless they would be impaired. In that eventuality, the carrying amounts of the assets should be reduced to reflect the impairment. The net effect of these adjustments would be included in income during the transition period and classified as an extraordinary item. The Statement takes into consideration that reasonable estimates may be used when determining the effect resulting from discontinuing the provisions of Statement 71, as long as the results would be in line with those that would result from a detailed application of the Statement.

FASB Statement 113, *Accounting and Reporting for Reinsurance of Short-Duration and Long-Duration Contracts*

Definitions. The following definitions of terms relate to this Statement. They will be helpful in understanding their exact meaning in this Statement.

Amortization—The act or process of extinguishing a debt, usually by equal payments over a specific period of time. The liquidation of a financial obligation on an installment basis.

Assuming Enterprise—The receiving company in a reinsurance contract. The assuming enterprise (or reinsurer) receives a reinsurance premium and, in turn, accepts an obligation to reimburse a ceding enterprise under specified terms; reinsures on a risk or exposure.

Ceding Enterprise—The company seeking a reinsurance contract. The ceding enterprise exchanges a reinsurance premium for the right to reimbursement from the assuming enterprise under specified terms. The insurer that cedes all or part of the insurance or reinsurance it has written to another insurer. Also known as the *direct writer.*

Contract Period—The length of time over which the specified terms are covered by the reinsured contracts.

Covered Period—Same as contract period (above).

Fronting Arrangements—Reinsurance provisions in which the ceding enterprise issues a policy to the assuming enterprise to reinsure all or substantially all of the insurance risk.

Incurred but Not Reported (IBNR) —Refers to losses that have occurred but have not been reported to the insurer or reinsurer.

Indemnification—Action of compensating for the actual loss or damage sustained; the fact of being compensated; the payment made for loss or damage.

Insurance Risk—The risk caused by the uncertain nature of the underwriting risk relating to the amount of net cash flows from premiums, commissions, claims, and claim settlement expenses paid as a result of contract specifications and the equally uncertain nature of the timing risk, which involves the timing of the receipt and payment of those cash flows. Actual or imputed investment returns are not an element of insurance risk. An insurance risk encompasses the possibility of adverse events occurring outside the control of the insured.

Long-Duration Contract—A contract expected to cover a prolonged period of time; in contrast to a short-duration contract (*see* Short-Duration Contract). While the time element is obvious from the long/short descriptive terms applied, the nature of the services rendered and the degree of control by the insurance company also differ. Along with insurance coverage, the long-duration carrier provides additional services and functions for the policyholder, including loans secured by the insurance policy, various options for payment of benefits, etc. The contract is usually not unilaterally controlled as is the short-duration type. It is customarily noncancellable, guaranteed renewable, and has fixed contract terms.

Most life and title insurance policies are considered long-duration contracts, while accident and health insurance policies depend on the expected term of coverage for the determination of long- or short-duration.

Offsetting—Showing a recognized asset and a recognized liability as a net amount on a financial statement. As a result of offsetting the assets and liabilities in reinsurance contracts, pertinent information could be lost and financial statement relationships altered.

Prospective Reinsurance—Reinsurance in which an assuming enterprise agrees to reimburse a ceding enterprise for losses that may be incurred as a result of future insurable events covered under contracts subject to the reinsurance. A reinsurance contract may include both prospective and retroactive reinsurance provisions.

Reinsurance—A device whereby an insurance company lessens the catastrophic hazard in the operation of the insurance mechanism; insurance for the insurer.

Reinsurance Receivables—All amounts recoverable from reinsurers for past and unpaid claims and claim settlement expenses, including estimated amounts receivable for unsettled claims, claims incurred but not reported, or policy benefits.

Reinsurer—*See* Assuming Enterprise.

Retroactive Reinsurance—Reinsurance in which an assuming enterprise agrees to reimburse a ceding enterprise for liabilities incurred as a result of past insurable events covered under contracts subject to reinsurance. A reinsurance contract may include both prospective and retroactive reinsurance provisions.

Retrocession—The process by which the reinsurer, or assuming enterprise, in turn, becomes a party in a reinsurance contract with still other reinsurers.

Settlement Period—The estimated period over which a ceding enterprise expects to recover substantially all amounts due from the reinsurer under the specified terms of the reinsurance contract.

Short-Duration Contract—An insurance policy not expected to cover an extended period of time. A carrier primarily provides insurance for a short, fixed period. The insurance carrier has more one-way control than in the long-duration contract (*see* Long-Duration Contract). The various specified terms of the contract, including amount of premiums and coverage, may be altered or canceled at the end of any contract period by the insurance company. Short-duration contracts include most property and liability policies and, to a lesser extent, some short-term life policies.

Statutory Accounting—The accounting system followed by insurance companies as required by the statutes of the various states. These procedures are geared to the National Association of Insurance Commissioners' (NAIC's) standardized reporting format. Differs in some instances from GAAP, but because the principal emphasis is on reflecting the ability of the insurer to meet its contract commitments, tends to be conservative.

FASB Statement 113, *Accounting and Reporting for Reinsurance of Short-Duration and Long-Duration Contracts* amends FASB Statement 60, Accounting and Reporting by Insurance Companies, and is effective for fiscal years starting after December 15, 1992. The new rule eliminated the former practice of reporting assets and liabilities related to insurance contracts net of the effects of reinsurance. Statement 60, which is the basic document dealing with specialized insurance accounting and reporting practices, had continued the statutory accounting practice of offsetting reinsurance assets and liabilities. However, this procedure is now considered inconsistent with the generally accepted criteria for offsetting. Under this rule, the practice is eliminated for general-purpose financial statements.

Beginning in 1993, reinsurance receivables and prepaid reinsurance premiums must be reported as assets. Reinsurance receivables include amounts related to a) claims incurred but not reported and b) liabilities for future policy benefits. Estimated reinsurance receivables are to be recognized in a manner consistent with the related liabilities.

Statement 113 also sets up a method of determining whether a specific contract qualifies for reinsurance accounting. The accounting standard revolves around determination of whether the reinsurance is long-duration or short-duration, and, if short-duration, whether it is prospective or retroactive insurance. A contract must result in a reasonable possibility that the reinsurer may realize a significant loss from assuming insurance risk, or the contract does not qualify for reinsurance accounting, but must be accounted for as a deposit. All reinsurance contracts prohibit the reinsurance from recognizing immediately a gain if there remains a chance of liability to the policyholder by the ceding enterprise.

To further clarify the financial picture, the reinsurer is required to provide footnote disclosures explaining all facets of the terms, nature, purpose, and effect of ceded reinsurance transactions. In addition, disclosures of concentrations of credit risk associated with reinsurance receivables and prepaid premiums are also required under the provisions of FASB 105, *Disclosures of Information About Financial Instruments with Off-Balance-Sheet Risk and Financial Instruments with Concentrations of Credit Risk.*

A portion of the impetus for consideration, or reconsideration, of the accounting and reporting for reinsurance has evolved from the general concern about the highly visible failure of some insurance companies. Risk relating to reinsurance has been considered germane to some of the failed enterprises.

Among the concerns voiced in regard to reinsurance were:

1) The effect of reinsurance accounting relating to contracts that did not provide indemnification for the ceding party against loss or liability.

2) The fact that FASB Statement 60 did not provide sufficient guidance relating to reinsurance accounting. Among other weaknesses, this led to acceleration of the recognition of income relating to reinsurance contracts.

3) The absence of requirements for disclosure of reinsurance transactions. The policyholder was seldom aware of any reinsurance arrangement.

4) The inconsistency between the widespread use of *net* accounting for reinsurance-related assets and liabilities in spite of not meeting the established criteria for offsetting.

Therefore, the thrust of the Statement is: a) as already noted, to address these perceived problems; b) to provide guidance in the determination of whether specific reinsurance contracts actually make provision for indemnification of the ceding enterprise to qualify for reinsurance accounting; and c) to establish the necessary accounting methods.

Statement 113 does *not* change present practice in accounting for reinsurance *assumed* other than to require certain disclosures relating to reinsurance by all insurance companies.

For short-duration contracts to qualify for reinsurance accounting, there should be a positive answer to the following questions:

1) Does the reinsurer assume significant insurance risk under the reinsurance provisions of the underlying insurance contracts?

2) Is there a reasonable possibility that the assuming enterprise may be faced with a significant loss as a result of this contract?

3) Is there a possibility of a significant variation in the amount or timing of payments by the reinsurer?

A ceding company's evaluation of whether it is reasonably possible for a reinsurer to realize a significant loss should be based on a present value analysis of cash flows between the ceding and assuming enterprises under reasonably possible outcomes. When the ceding company reaches the conclusion that the reinsurer is not exposed to the possibility of significant loss, the ceding company can decide that it is indemnified against loss or liability related to insurance risk only if *substantially all* of the insurance risk relating to the reinsured portion of the specific underlying insurance policy has been assumed by the reinsurer. Thus, any insurance risk remaining with the ceding company must be of little or no importance or of a trivial nature if the ceding company decides to consider itself indemnified against loss or liability.

For a long-duration contract to qualify for reinsurance accounting, there must be a reasonable probability that the reinsurer may realize significant loss from assuming the insurance risk. FASB Statement 97, *Accounting and Reporting by Insurance Enterprises for Certain Long-Duration Contracts and for Realized Gains and Losses from the Sale of Investments*, defines long-duration contracts that do not subject the insurer to mortality or morbidity risks as investment contracts. Consistent with that definition, if a contract does not subject the reinsurer to the reasonable possibility of significant loss from the events insured by the underlying insurance contracts, it does not indemnify the ceding enterprise against insurance risk.

FASB 113 mandates that reinsurance contracts can lead to recognition of immediate gains only if the reinsurance contract is a legal replacement of one insurer by another and the ceding company's liability to the policyholder is extinguished.

Amounts paid for prospective reinsurance of short-duration insurance contracts must be accounted for as prepaid reinsurance premiums. They are to be amortized over the remaining contract period in proportion to the amount of insurance protection provided.

Amounts paid for retroactive reinsurance of short-duration insurance contracts must be reported as insurance receivables to the extent those amounts do not exceed the recorded liabilities relating to the reinsured contracts. If the recorded liabilities exceed the amount paid, reinsurance receivables should be increased to reflect the difference and the resulting gain should be deferred. The deferred gain is to be amortized over the estimated remaining settlement period. If the amount paid for retroactive reinsurance exceeds the recorded related liabilities, the ceding company must increase the related liabilities or reduce the reinsurance receivable, or both, at the time the reinsurance contract is entered into. The excess is charged to earnings.

If, when both prospective and retroactive provisions are included in a single short-duration reinsurance transaction and it is deemed impracticable to account for every provision separately, retroactive short-duration reinsurance contract accounting must be used. Amortization of the estimated costs of insuring long-duration insurance contracts depends on whether the reinsurance contract is long- or short-duration. These costs should be amortized over the remaining life of the underlying insured contracts if the contract is long-duration, or over the reinsurance contract period if the reinsurance contract is short-duration. Determining whether a contract that reinsures a long-duration insurance contract is long- or short-duration is a matter of judgment.

The financial statements of all insurance companies must now disclose the following information:

1) The nature, purpose, and effect of ceding and reinsurance transactions on the insurance company's operations.

2) The ceding company must disclose the amount of earned premiums ceded and recoveries recognized under reinsurance contracts in footnotes to the financial statement, unless these are reported separately in the statement of earnings.

3) Premiums from direct business, reinsurance assumed, and reinsurance ceded, on both a written and earned basis, must be disclosed for short-duration contracts.

4) For long-duration contracts, premiums and amounts assessed against policyholders from direct business, reinsurance assumed and ceded, and premiums and amounts earned must be disclosed.

5) Companies must detail the methods used for income recognition on their reinsurance contracts.

FASB Statement 115, *Accounting for Certain Investments in Debt and Equity Securities*

Statement 115 covers the accounting and reporting for certain investments in debt securities and for equity securities that have readily determinable fair value. It applies to financial assets in security form, but not to loans or liabilities. It supersedes Statement 12, *Accounting for Certain Marketable Securities,* and is basically effective for fiscal years beginning after December 15, 1993. The use of fair value accounting is expanded for those securities mentioned above, but the Statement retains the use of the amortized cost methods for investments in debt securities which the reporting organization intends to and can realistically retain until they reach their maturity date. FASB 115 is intended as at least a stopgap measure in market value accounting and in reporting for a portion of those investments which contributed to the problems of the failed banks and savings and loans.

It is definitely not the end of the search for valid, all-encompassing methods of accounting for financial instruments which gained impetus with the deregulation of interest rates several years before the debacle involving thrift and bank failures—and now the fiasco surrounding derivatives.

The Securities and Exchange Commission (along with the AICPA, Congress and other outspoken groups and individuals) has been pressuring for more definitive answers to some of the problems. While Statement 115 moves away from the traditional historical cost approach and closer to a fair value approach, it appears to have been viewed favorably by no one. Those who were against change and prefer to retain the status quo regard it as going too far while those who want comprehensive market value accounting feel that it is not the giant step forward they envision. Many view it as changing GAAP only minimally and merely reworking various suggestions advanced to an unenthusiastic audience in the last few years.

Two dissenting members of the seven-member board raised several objections to the provisions stipulated in FASB 115 on the grounds that:

1) Similar securities could be accounted for using three different approaches.
2) The Statement does not eliminate gains trading by selectively selling securities.
3) Classification of securities was based upon management *intent.*

They argued that these problems could only be resolved by reporting all securities covered by FASB 115 at their fair value and including unrealized changes in fair value in earnings.

It can be said that the fair *value* of an equity security can be *readily determinable* if one or more of the following criteria can be met:

1) The sales price or bid/asked price can be obtained from an SEC registered exchange or an OTC quotation if reported by the National Association of Securities Dealers or the National Quotation Bureau.
2) Although it is sold only in a foreign market, said market is comparable to one of the U.S. exchanges.
3) It is an investment in a mutual fund in which the unit price of the fund is available and being used in ongoing sales transactions.

Statement 115 does *not* apply to:

1) Investments in equity securities accounted for under the equity method.
2) Investments in consolidated subsidiaries.

3) Enterprises with specialized accounting practices that include accounting for investments in debt and equity securities at either market value or fair value where changes in value are recognized either in earnings or in a change in net assets.

4) Not-for-profit organizations.

5) Unsecured loans. However, when mortgage loans are converted to mortgage-backed securities, they come under rulings of this Statement and are placed in the trading category described below. This provision amends FASB 65, *Accounting for Certain Mortgage Banking Activities*, by removing the mortgage-backed securities from its requirements.

Within this framework, the focus of Statement 115 is on identifying and categorizing three classes of debt and equity securities and in providing guidelines for accounting for them. Those guidelines are:

1) Held-to-Maturity. These are debt securities which the entity expects to and is reasonably capable of holding to maturity. These investments will be measured at amortized cost in the financial statements.

2) Trading. These are both debt and equity securities obtained for the purpose of gaining a quick profit from selling at a change in the market price rather than from holding them for a longer period to realize gains from capital appreciation. Their worth is stated at fair value in the financial statement.

3) Available-for-Sale. This is a catchall designation for those securities that do not quite fit into either of the other categories. They are found in portfolios of investors who use them to manage interest rate risk, meet other business objectives, comply with legal requirements or take advantage of market opportunities. As with trading securities, this category is measured only at fair value for financial reporting.

Transfers among the three categories should not be undertaken lightly. The trading classification is for those securities that are frequently and actively bought and sold; the held-to-maturity classification refers to just that, not to investments that are being held only for an indefinite period. However, Statement 115 does give some specific guidelines to instances wherein it is/is not permissible to transfer/ sell held-for-maturity investments, and gives the appropriate accounting procedures to recognize the changed situation.

Other important accounting procedures addressed by the Statement relate to reporting changes in fair value in the three categories:

1) In all categories, the dividend and interest income, including amortization of premium and income, continues to be accounted for in earnings.

2) Methods used for recognizing and measuring the dividend and interest earnings remain the same.

3) Realized gains/losses of available-for-sale and held-to-maturity securities continue being reported in earnings.

4) Unrealized holdings gains/losses in the trading category are accounted for in earnings, but those in the-available-for-sale category are excluded from earnings and must be reported as a separate component of shareholders' equity.

In addition, when either an available-for-sale or a held-to-maturity security's fall in fair value below the amortized cost appears to be permanent, the cost basis of that particular security must be written down to a new cost basis. The amount of the write-down is to be accounted for as a realized loss in earnings. The entry may not be reversed should there be a recovery in fair value. Disclosure requirements identified in FASB 115 include:

1) Separate disclosure for the two securities categories held-to-maturity and available-for-sale are:

a) Aggregate fair value.

b) Gross unrealized holding gains/losses.

c) Amortized cost basis of the major types of securities held.

2) Information about the contractual maturities of all investments in debt securities in the held-to-maturity category and separately for available-for-sale category. Fair value and amortized cost must be disclosed based on four maturity groups.

a) one year or less

b) one to five years

c) five to 10 years

d) more than 10 years

3) Proceeds from sale of available-for-sale securities and the gross realized gains/losses.

4) Basis used in determining cost to compute gain/loss.

5) Gross gains/gross losses included in earnings resulting from transfers from available-for-sale category to the trading category.

6) Change in net unrealized holding gain/loss on trading securities included in earnings during the period reported.

7) Change in net unrealized holding gain/loss in available-for-sale investments included in shareholders' equity during the reporting period.

8) Explanation in the notes to the financial statement regarding sale of/transfer from the held-to-maturity category. This should include the amortized cost of the security; the realized/unrealized gain/loss; the reasoning behind the decision to sell or transfer.

Chapter 2
Information Systems

THE FLOW OF DOCUMENTS

Paper. The forest primeval—milled and pressed to industrial use.

Contracts, certificates, invoices, correspondence, memos, rules, ledgers, machine-tapes, flow charts, advertising catalogs, computer runs, time-cards, checks, statements, tags, cards, sheets, rolls—scratch paper—envelopes, boxes, cartons. Unused paper supplies; paper-in-process; paper filed. Microfilm. Tax returns. Tape and red tape.

An avalanche, if uncontrolled.

Logic, purpose and usefulness, when held in check. A systematized schematic designed to control the economic current which generates the power of the business entity. Periodically to be monitored and tested for resistance, weakness, stability and storage capacity.

The aim—the goal—is to focus all paper into a group picture—one still-life, the photo at a given moment in time—the year-end for the financial statements, as posed by the figures in the general ledger, adjusted and dressed for that split-second closing moment. The numerical characters in a tableau, arranged and described in narration in conformity with professional standards.

Throughout the year, the numerical characters which will ultimately be stilled for one moment—to be counted and accounted for—to be placed in proper perspective for that financial statement group photograph—these characters keep moving, refusing to stand still, adding, accumulating, building, sometimes detracting and withdrawing—darting in and out of the books of account.

A firm hand is needed to guide these figures, to direct their movements, to prevent the inanimate from taking on life of its own, to stop the machine before it becomes the master.

The chart of the anatomical business blood-line, in terms of recorded circulation, must be clearly directed, delineated and controlled:

The veins: through which information flows to the heart—
The books of original entry:

1) General Journal
2) Cash Receipts Book
3) Cash Disbursements Book
4) Sales Book with its corollary Accounts Receivable sub-ledger
5) Purchases Book with its corollary Accounts Payable sub-ledger
6) Payroll Register and Summaries

The heart: which stores and pumps out the information—
The general ledger (with its associated valves):

7) General Ledger and Subsidiaries:
   Inventory Control
   Fixed Assets Ledger
   Cost Sub-Ledger Control
   Schedules to supplement

The arteries: which take that flow for digestion to the body and members of the community—owners, bankers, creditors, government, the general public—
The financial statements:

8) Balance Sheet
9) Income Statement
10) Statement of Changes in Stockholder's Equity
11) Statement of Cash Flows
12) Financial notes

The following pages outline an approach to the development of an information system, which is sufficiently broad in its components, so that the accountant can apply it as a starting point for a study. Following this general outline are the components of an accounting system in detail.

AN ACCOUNTING INFORMATION SYSTEM OUTLINE

What is an Information System?

A network of *procedures* for processing raw data in such a way as to generate the information required for management use.

1) Procedures—the logical steps for accomplishing a job.
2) System—a network of related procedures, the sum of which result in the accomplishment of the objective.

Objective of an Information System

To reduce the range of uncertainty in the decision-making process.

The Nature of Information

I.   Understanding the nature of information.
  A) What is information?
      1) Information includes *all* the data and intelligence—financial and nonfinancial—that management needs to plan, operate and control a particular enterprise.
      2) Information is not just the accounting system and the forms and reports it produces. An efficient information system must move beyond the limits of classical accounting reports, and conceive of information as it relates to two vital elements of the management process—planning and control.
          a) Information about the future.
          b) Data expressed in nonfinancial terms, e.g., share of market, performance of personnel, adequacy of customer service.
          c) Information dealing with external conditions as they might bear on a particular company's operations.
  B) Data is not information. Information *is* data presented in a useful form.
      1) A report is a device which communicates information, not data.
II. Information is quantitative (statistical) or qualitative (nonstatistical).
  A) Quantitative—concerns selected data; data selected with respect to the problem, the user, time, place and function.
  B) Qualitative—concerns information that can be expressed in non-statistical terms; i.e., adequacy of customer service, environmental conditions.

The Economics of Information

I.   Information is a *resource* used in a way that improves the organization's other resources—its personnel and physical facilities. Proper information can help to achieve the goals of the organization in the most efficient manner.

II. Like any other resource, information is not a free commodity. Accordingly, the same criteria should be applied to the development of an information system as to the development of any other resource.

- Will the additional benefits expected from an information system justify the additional costs of developing and implementing the system (marginal cost vs. marginal utility)?

III. In regard to paragraph 2, information is available to the organization at some cost. Generally, the initial information is of great value. However, as more and more information is "bought," it becomes increasingly difficult to make use of these incremental units. Therefore, the utility of additional information decreases as more and more information becomes available.

IV. As more information is searched for, the cost of each *additional* unit of information tends to increase.

V.   *The Problem:* Determining the amount of information you needed from an information system becomes a balancing act. The maximum amount of information that the system can provide is not necessarily the best. The additional costs of *one* more unit of information should be *exactly* equal to the assigned monetary value of the last unit of information provided.

Impact of the Information System on Organizational Structure

I.   The system must tie together information requirements of the organizational structure.

II. The information system will produce changes in personnel working environment.

III. Usually, there is a gap created by a changing organization structure and a static information system.

Three Elements of an Information System

I.   Syntheses of three subsystems of an information system.

   A) The computer

   B) Data processing

   C) The language

Approach

I.   Cornerstone for developing a management information system is the determination of the organization's information needs.

 Requires a clear understanding of each decision-maker's role in the organization. This includes responsibilities, authority, and relationships with other executives.

 A) This cannot be accomplished by the open approach of simply asking an executive what information he or she requires.

 B) Information systems analyst must help management determine its information needs.

 C) Must be related to the manager's planning and control functions.

II.   Analyze and evaluate the system *currently* in use.

 A) Procedures

 B) Forms used

 C) Costs

Planning Information

I.   Planning means setting objectives, formulating strategies, and deciding among alternative courses of action.

 The information required to do planning is of three basic types.

 A) *Environmental Information.* Describes the social, political, and economic aspects of the climate in which a business operates, or may operate in the future.

 B) *Competitive Information.* Explains the past performance, programs, and plans of competing companies.

 C) *Internal Information.* Indicates a company's own strengths and weaknesses.

II.   Planning information.

 A) The strategic (as opposed to operating) information about critical business problems.

 B) Flows to the top executive level.

 C) The information required for executive-level decisions, e.g., policies.

 D) Policy maker will be faced with less uncertainty, in the sense that he or she is better informed about what is going on.

 E) Organization discipline is tightened as operating methods and results come under instantaneous observation of top management.

III. Determine the decision-making levels in the organization. How many "tiers" are to be included in the information system?

IV. Is the current system adequate?

Twenty tests to determine if the current system is adequate.

1) Does the current system produce useful reports, or just listings of numbers?

2) Do all individuals, or stations, who receive reports use them for decision-making purposes, or do they receive them because they are interesting, or because it is ego-satisfying to be on the distribution list?

3) Does the same report go to different levels of decision makers? Does the information system take into account the different needs for information at the different organizational levels?

4) If an organization has automated, is the data processing subsystem simply a bookkeeping tool of the conventional accounting system? Is the automatic data processing system being used for information purposes, or merely as computing hardware?

5) Are the managing officers completely familiar with the current system? Are they devoting personal interest and talent to this area?

6) Is the system viewed as a decision-making resource, or narrowly as only a means to reduce accounting costs?

7) Is the fact realized that conventional accounting systems fail to provide *all* the information necessary for the decision-making process?

8) When was the system last analyzed?

9) Is the information system centralized or decentralized? If the latter, is there a duplication of information processing?

10) Can stored information be retrieved efficiently by users?

11) How good are the internal data for planning purposes?

12) How do costs behave in response to volume changes?

13) Are the factors that condition success in the organization explicitly stated and widely communicated among the management group?

14) Has the organization's structure remained *unchanged* during the past 15 years?

15) Does the organization regularly collect and analyze information about population, price level, labor, and other important trends affecting the general profitability of the organization?

16) What analyses are currently reported to operating management? Are they reported in a manner that permits their utilization in the planning process?

17) Is significant information about competitors regularly collected and analyzed?

18) How is current information "factored into" the planning process?

19) To what extent are decisions based upon fact vs. belief and opinion?

20) How is current information communicated? In a formal or informal manner?

V.   Steps in analyzing the current system to discover weaknesses.

A)   Analysis of the flow of information through the system.

B)   Analysis of the operations (termed "events") performed by individuals (or stations) in the system.

C)   Combination of (A) and (B) by locating the *origin* of documents, and determining the effort needed to produce them, data needed for correct preparation, number of individuals, or stations, in the system that need copies, and the events that cause documents to be prepared.

1) Comparison of the output that results with the output desired.

2) Consideration of modifications that can reduce input, or will result in more desirable output, or both.

D)   Study of all the operations of the business in order to understand clearly the *processes* within the company.

Use of Linear Programming

I.   Linear programming can be used to maximize resource allocation.

A)   Linear programming is a systematic way of finding the best course of action when many variables and many conditions must be taken into consideration.

B)   An approach to maximizing an objective (profits) which is subject to many restrictions—legal, safety, service, and policy.

C)   Four advantages of using linear programming:

1) Construction of the model will give management additional insight into its everyday operations.

2) The model gives management a way of testing and quantifying the effects of policy decisions.

3) Linear programming stimulates the setting of goals and criteria for evaluating performance.

4) Linear programming is an effective technique for long-range planning in the face of uncertainty.

Feedback Control

I.   Controls involve *techniques* such as financial controls, costs, and other types of controls.

II. Based on pertinent and timely information.

III. Information for feedback control:

  A) Provides a constant check on day-to-day results to be compared with expected or forecasted standards.

  B) Fulfills most of the decision-making information for middle and lower echelons of operating personnel.

  C) The information provided is usually historical in nature—deals with money, materials, people, performance.

  D) Introduces management by exception techniques.*

  1) Establishes criteria, standards, forecasted or expected performance.

  2) Directs management attention *only* to off-target performance. Keeps useless information from the top. Only relevant facts, as they arise, will reach management, enabling control of circumstances as they are developing.

  3) Reduces volume of information needed, because on-target performance can proceed without further action. Relieved of unnecessary data-gathering and other unproductive routines, the manager is freed for other work—particularly where human abilities are needed, such as working with and helping employees he or she supervises.

Sub-Ledgers And Schedules

Some accounts in the general ledger are by their very nature *summaries* of important supplemental data which, because of bulk alone, would, if not entered in summary form, make the physical ledger too huge to handle. Items such as individual accounts receivable and payable, inventory units, machin-

---

*Incidentally, this technique is hardly new in concept. See Exodus XVIII, Jethro to Moses, ". . . every great matter they shall bring to you, but any small matter they shall decide themselves."

ery and equipment— though each represents an individual asset or liability— are best displayed in one or more summary accounts, with full details being maintained in a separate book or ledger, individually tended, the total of which ties to the control account.

Some, like accounts receivable and accounts payable, are automatic products of the internal system. (The computer updates the accounts receivable file with sales and with payments received, with the monthly summaries of changes going to the general ledger control account.) Sometimes, a one-write system updates subsidiaries simultaneously. Others must be maintained manually, like the fixed asset ledger or the manual inventory control card-system. Others may be generated by outside sources, like payroll records and summaries. Others are as basic as a petty cash summary.

SYSTEMS—MANUAL, MECHANIZED OR COMPUTERIZED

The number of different methods used for keeping records is almost as varied as the personalities of the people designing, operating and maintaining the system. With the exception of those larger entities where work is so divided that each employee performs only one small function in a huge system overviewed by few, except top management and outside auditors, few businesses use a standard text-book approach.

Most private systems are the result of accumulations of changing bit-by-bit adaptions to the needs and demands of the business itself and outside influences (taxes, AICPA and SEC guides and requirements, state and federal laws, competitive practices, advanced technology, market conditions, good-bad sales/profit results, etc.). Except where the availability of funds and skills is unlimited (practically nowhere), most systems in use today are evolvements and combinations of good old basic handwritten techniques, now partitioned into piecemeal refinements, combining mechanical, electronic and manual skills.

Complete automation of the *entire* accounting process is a rarity.

Ultimately, the nature of the system depends upon one or more of these factors:

Time and expediency
Skill required
Cost
Facilities and space available
The degree of in-depth coverage *wanted* by owners/management.

Note the emphasis on the word "wanted." Many weaknesses need correction for better tax-review backup or for more efficient reporting, but management, in weighing the costs involved, wisely chooses not to refine. For example, if the *cost* of instituting a highly complex standard costing system outweighs the advantages to be gained from it, management may choose to retain its current, less complex, less specific costing system, which has understandable, but controllable tolerances of error.

The Evolutionary Process of the Machine

The evolutionary process of systematized accounting record maintenance might use the following piecemeal add-on progression:

All Manual System

1) The *"shoebox" system.* The owner transacts all business in cash—buying, selling, paying expenses—and tosses invoices, documents, and receipts into a box.

2) The *checkbook.* The owner stops paying bills with cash, now pays by check. Still uses shoebox for receipts for sales. Notes deposits in checkbook.

3) *Cash disbursements book.* Has now hired someone to do the payroll tax reporting. Lists each check in a book, from which a columnar breakout distribution of each type of expense can be obtained.

4) *Payroll register.* Supplements the above by transferring the weekly payroll items to separate sheets for each employee where total earnings and deductions are accumulated as required for payroll tax reports.

5) *Cash receipts book.* Owner now lists each day's receipts separately and distributes to columns by type of sale or income.

6) *General ledger.* Owner sets up a ledger sheet for each column category in the disbursements and receipts book. "Posts" summary totals periodically.

7) *General ledger expanded.* The owner goes back to the old shoebox and digs out the cost information needed to set up the value of permanent items bought then (assets: equipment, fixtures, etc.) sets up asset accounts, long-term liabilities and a balancing net worth account.

8) *Sales book/accounts receivable ledger.* To get more sales, owner finds he or she must start giving credit. Owner uses sequentially numbered invoices, lists charge sales daily in numerical order in Sales Book. Makes a separate page for each customer in an accounts receivable subsidiary

ledger, using a carbonized two-part preprinted statement, which is updated manually every day or so.

In the Cash Receipts Book, owner adds a column for "received on account" from customers. Line-by-line, these credits are posted to the above subsidiary ledger statement. Also, owner includes a column for cash discounts and allowances taken by customers. At month-end, he mails original to customer and keeps the copy of the statement as the ledger sheet and starts a new sheet for the new month with the balance from the old sheet.

9) *Periodic financial statements.* Owner now wishes to see how he progresses. Finds he needs further information for an accurate statement. He must, in a side computation, compute or estimate:

Any unpaid bill to creditors

Inventory on hand

Taxes due to date on payrolls, etc.

Possible bad debts among his stated receivables

Depreciate his equipment

At this point, he probably seeks outside assistance.

10) *Purchase book/accounts payable ledger.* As business expands, his debts accumulate, and he wants to know the exact status of when and to whom payments are due. He adds these books to the system. In the Cash Disbursements Book, he puts a column for payment on account to accounts payable and another for cash discounts taken.

11) *Perpetual inventory cards.* The on-hand stock of unsold items grows daily, and he can no longer trust his memory to recall the exact cost of items in stock, nor the quantities on hand. He sets up one card for each type of merchandise on hand, goes to the storage area, counts and lists everything, checks his purchase invoices and assigns a cost to each item. On the card, he provides all the details pertaining to that item, so that he knows what's on hand and what cost it represents. Periodically, he takes a physical count to verify the perpetual cards.

12) *General journal.* He rounds off the system by putting in here any entry which does not appropriately go in the other books of original entry. He posts from here and the other books directly to the General Ledger.

13) *Worksheet entries and worksheet trial balance.* As an adjunct to the preparation of the now monthly financial statements, accruals, recurrent adjustments and accrual reversals (when necessary) are made to the bal-

ances taken from the ledger—all on workpapers—to determine monthly position and progress.

14) *Imprest petty cash system.* Adds this to tighten up on loose expenditures.

15) *Fixed asset subsidiary ledger.* To better detail them for depreciation investment tax credit, gains or losses on dispositions, and basis on trade-ins.

Mechanizing

16) *A one-write system for check disbursements.* Here the old check book and the Cash Disbursements Book are combined into one writing process, instead of two. Owner also opens a separate bank account for the payroll and uses a onewrite system for it also. At month-end, owner summary posts to the General Ledger.

17) *A billing machine.* Rented or bought. Mechanizes invoices, customer statements, sales book and subsidiary receivable ledger.

18) *Service bureau.* Owner assigns numbers to the general ledger accounts in an ascending series covering assets, liabilities, equity, income, costs and expenses in that order. Is assisted in setting up framework numbers for captioning and totaling functions so the computer-produced financial statement conforms with the special format desired. Monthly, owner sends to the service bureau:

- A copy of one-write check listing, with account numbers assigned for the debiting (in lieu of the columnar distribution spread);
- Manual summary entries for each other book of original entry;
- Manual entries for accruals, adjustments, recurrent monthly entries, reversals of accruals.

All this is submitted in a simple debit/credit style with account numbers indicated. Owner adds each page, gets totals for debits, credits and *account numbers,* and gets an overall batch control total for each. The Service Bureau cross-checks the inputting to the batch totals, and posting to wrong accounts is virtually eliminated.

Owner receives from the Service Bureau a printed Cash Disbursements listing, a General Ledger with alpha description (brief, as inputted), and financial statements with detailed supporting schedules.

19) *Computer terminal.* A typewriter-like console, which is hooked via telephone lines into an outside-owned computer. An owner may put sales and receivables on it, check-processing and disbursements run, his purchase-vendor invoices and purchase book, inventory, the payroll, or general ledger—practically anything desired, depending upon the programming availability and the costs. The techniques used are compatible with those learned in the use of the service bureau, with the addition of a few typewriter-input techniques.

20) *Video scope.* May supplement the computer terminal, providing for almost instantaneous display of that off-premises storage in the central processor's electronic file. A printout may be requested for later delivery.

21) *The in-house computer.* The final decision is made. Owner rents or buys a computer for total in-house use. The extent of options available is vast. Basically, the type of in-house computer obtained should depend upon the more important of the following features:

The output wanted.

The capacity of the central processing unit for permanent program storage.

The additional adjunct program storage possibilities.

The type of storage—cassette, disc, tape, and on down to magnetic cards or punched-paper tape, with each having advantages in terms of cost or access.

The type of input—punched cards, direct input from console, intermediate from console-to-tape-to-computer, etc.

The extent of printout capabilities and demands (speed, size of paper, etc.).

The adaptation of video screens at the console or remote locations—branches, warehouse.

The cost factor—initial investment, machine and programs, maintenance, personnel needed, space necessitated.

The extent of skill needed.

The imagination of the owner or management—willingness to learn, try, develop new methods, new talents.

PAYROLLS AND PAYROLL TAXES

Legal requirements have made the maintenance of accurate earnings records a mandatory function of any financial accounting system. The preparation of payrolls is now, in many companies, a segregated division of duty. Regular periodic summary information from detailed payroll records is needed for entry into the general ledger.

Details of each payroll are usually summarized monthly in a general journal entry and posted to the general ledger with distribution of the debits going to various salary-expense areas (for the gross salary) and the credits going to various withholding accounts (sometimes netted against corresponding employer-expense accounts, such as unemployment insurance) and the cash account upon which the net payroll checks are drawn.

The employer later pays the amounts withheld (hopefully as due) to the various taxing or other authorities, including the employer's added share (expense) as determined in the preparation of the required form for filing.

To support the filings, each payroll item must be isolated and collated for *each* individual employee to accumulate that individual's record of earnings as required for these quarterly, semi-annual and annual reports to federal, state and city taxing arms. The Fair Labor Standards Act and state laws also set standards of minimum pay for work hours and overtime for some or all employees.

Many payrolls are now prepared by outside processors, such as banks and service bureaus. Controls should be as strong as possible to assure accurate, protected input and output. All voided checks, for example, should be surrendered to the employer and accounted for in bank reconciliations.

Individual personnel permanent files should be maintained and would probably include:

Name and address, Social Security number, date of birth, date hired, occupation, work week, regular and overtime rates, basis of pay (day, week, month), authorization increases, vacation time, bonuses, injuries and compensation claims and settlements, pension and profit-sharing information (deductions, rights, and vested interests), W-4 and other withholding authorizations, references and correspondence, educational transcripts, unemployment claims and reports, medical records, health claims, expense-account authorizations, separation information (date, circumstances, etc.) and other information.

Time cards are usually filed separately and tied to specific payrolls by reference identification.

Payroll tax reports usually required are:

Federal:
Card-form 501 for payroll tax deposits with local bank
Quarterly 941 for withholding and FICA
W-2's
W-3
Annual 940 (Federal Unemployment)
1099—information returns with summary 1096

State:

Withholding tax—interim and annual

Unemployment insurance—usually quarterly

Disability insurance—usually quarterly, sometimes combined with unemployment report

Annual reports covering individual earnings; possibly annual information returns also.

The entire process of payroll preparation is an area which is conducive to effective statistical sampling techniques. Management (as well as outside auditors) should periodically sample all phases of the payroll routine, from initial authorization through to the canceled-check returns. The discovery of one flaw might prove significant.

The General Ledger, Chart Of Accounts And Trial Balance

In the world of mechanical figures uniformity offers many advantages, especially the one of eliminating hard-knock costly errors experienced by forerunners in the field of experimentation. One such area of "uniformity" in standard usage, which is most beneficial, is the conventional layout of the general ledger.

As shown below, accounts in the general ledger are most useful if arranged and numbered in the order sequence indicated. Any firm which has gone to an outside computer service or installed its own in-house computer for the generation of machined financial statements will attest to the necessity for this format. The machines, unthinking as they are, can easily be programmed to add, subtract, combine, sub-total, balance, and print these accounts according to numerically sequential instructions each step of the way down the line-by-line financial balance sheet and income statement. (Moreover, sub-ledgers can be added as needed.)

Assets:
    Current
    Non-current
    Other
Liabilities:
    Current
    Long-term
Equity:
    Capital stock
    Retained earnings

Income—revenue from operations
Cost of sales items
Expenses:
Selling
Administrative
Non-operating income and expense
Federal income tax
Extraordinary items:
Less applicable income tax
Net income

Limitations and definitions of the entries into each account should be spelled out for anyone with responsibility for booking entries into the general ledger. Most large firms have drawn up internal "charts of accounts" which pinpoint exactly which accounts should be debited or credited and the sources from which the entry might come. At the least, someone should be charged with the responsibility of making the decision, and written authorizations (sometimes, voucher-type general journal entries) should be prepared and signed by that authority.

Many modern systems call for the manual booking of summaries of all the books of original entry, recurrent monthly journal entries, adjustments, accruals and reversals onto loose-leaf-type numbered journal sheets, batch-totaled, with a copy going to the computer department for processing to monthly hard-copy ledger cards. Sometimes, a yearly re-run is made showing all the action in each account for the entire year. A trial balance is usually a by-product of the computer-run general ledger.

Summary entries may be bypassed for cash disbursements, sales or purchases, if the input of this material is programmed for direct summation of monthly activity, being stored and posted to the general ledger when run with the other input from the summary general journal sheets.

Some systems in use today even bypass the use of a general ledger, producing all the same pertinent information and references in comprehensive, detailed financial statements. Controls here should assure proper input, output and traceable audit trails.

LONG-TERM CONSTRUCTION CONTRACTS

Revenue is usually recognized at the time of exchanges in which cash is received or new claims arise against other entities. However, exceptions are made, for example . . . for long-term construction-type contracts.

There are two methods available to commercial organizations engaged wholly or partly in the contracting business for handling long-term construction contracts:

1) The completed-contract method; and
2) The percentage-of-completion method.

These contracts generally entail the construction of a specific project.

The Completed-Contract Method

The completed-contract method recognizes income only when the contract is completed or substantially completed. Costs of contracts in process and current billings are accumulated, but there are no charges or credits to income except for provisions for losses. If remaining costs are not significant in amount, a contract may be regarded as substantially completed.

General and administrative expenses are not charged off to periodic income but are allocated to the contract. This is especially important when no contracts are completed in a year in which there are general and administrative expenses. It is not as important when there are numerous contracts. However, there should be no excessive deferring of overhead costs which might occur if total overhead was assigned to few or small contracts in process.

Even though the completed-contract method does not permit recording any income before completion, provision should be made for expected losses. Any excess of accumulated costs over related billings should be shown in the balance sheet as a current asset. Excess of accumulated billings over related costs should be shown in most cases as a current liability. Where there are many contracts, and costs exceed billing on some and billings exceed costs on others, the contracts should be segregated so that the figures on the asset side include only those contracts in which costs exceed billings and on the liability side, only those in which billings exceed costs. The assets should be described as "costs of uncompleted contracts in excess of related billings" rather than as inventory or work in process. On the liability side, the item should be described as "billings and uncompleted contracts in excess of related costs." The standards state that the excess accumulated billings over related costs should be shown as a current liability in *most cases*. Noncurrent classification is discouraged, but would nevertheless be within GAAP.

The advantage of the completed-contract method is that, since it is based on results as finally determined, it is generally more accurate than if it were based on estimates for unperformed work which could involve unforeseen costs or other possible losses. It is generally used for contracts lasting less than one year. But where accurate estimates of completion costs aren't available, it may be used for longer term contracts. The disadvantage of the completed-contract method is that in a period where no contract has been completed, current performance is not reflected. This results in showing high profits one year and little or no profits in other years.

Percentage-of-Completion Method

The percentage-of-completion method recognizes income as work on a contract goes along. Recognized income should be *that percentage of estimated total income* that either a) incurred costs to date *bear to total costs* after giving effect to estimates of costs to complete based upon most recent information or b) which may be indicated by such other measures of progress to completion as may be appropriate (see illustration). Under the percentage-of-completion method current assets may include costs and recognized income not yet billed for certain contracts, and liabilities (usually current liabilities) may include billings in excess of costs and recognized income with regard to other contracts.

The principal advantages of the percentage-of-completion method are 1) periodic recognition of income instead of the irregular recognition of income on completed contracts, and 2) the reflection of the status of the uncompleted contracts through the current estimates of costs to complete or of progress toward completion. In the *completed-contract method* there is no reflection of status of uncompleted contracts.

ILLUSTRATION
Income reflected under percent-of-completion method:

	Accumulated Percent Completed (1)	Expenses allocable to contract (2)	Year's assigned portion of contract (1)	Net income to report
Year 1	30%	$ 305,000	$ 300,000	$ (5,000)
Year 2	75%	385,000	450,000	65,000
Year 3	100%	210,000	250,000	40,000
Totals		$ 900,000	$ 1,000,000	$ 100,000

Total contract price is $1,000,000.

1) A Percentage of completion is a certified percentage furnished by the architect. The percent increases each year until 100% is completed. The difference between one year and the next is that year's completed portion.

2) Includes supplies used during year, with consideration given to opening and closing inventories. Expenses are those ascertainable as incurred to bring the contract to the stage of completion.

The chief disadvantage of the percentage-of-completion method is that it depends upon estimates of ultimate costs and, consequently, of currently accruing income which is subject to uncertainties inherent in long-term contracts.

Note that *billings* are not shown because reportable income is *not* predicated on them, though in some cases billings may coincide with the percentage completed.

Income under the "Completed Contract" Method

Using the same example above, the net income of $100,000 would be reported only in the final year (Year 3), together with details. No reflection of partial completion is shown on the income statement for the first and second years.

Chapter 3
Who Determines Standards?

AMERICAN INSTITUTE OF CERTIFIED PUBLIC ACCOUNTANTS (AICPA)

In society at large, citizens are not praised for *upholding* laws; they are condemned or punished for *breaking* laws or *failure* to conform to the laws. On a smaller scale, the professional accountant is not applauded for adhering to standards; he or she is, or may be, criticized, reprimanded, ostracized or faced with monetary or criminal penalties for noncompliance with the standards or for *failure* to conform with accounting standards.

Most professional accountants will agree that, despite criticism for certain actions or nonactions, the AICPA is the one dominant organization of accountants. The Institute speaks with recognized authority for the *entire* profession of accounting (for members and nonmembers alike). When the AICPA speaks "officially," on-the-record, adherence is compulsory for members. When the AICPA speaks "unofficially," off-the-record, adherence is *not* compulsory. BUT— (and to emphasize it)— *but*— a member who violates an *unofficial* pronouncement had best have a good defense for an alternate position if it conflicts even with this *unofficial* AICPA position.

The AICPA is the national organization of certified public accountants in the United States. Its membership is made up of thousands of certified public accountants engaged in one or more of every conceivable phase of the accountant's function in society.

There are two requirements for membership:

1) Possession of a valid certified public accountant certificate issued by a state, territory or territorial possession of the United States or the District of Columbia, and

2) Passing an examination in accounting or other related subjects, satisfactory to the Board of Directors of the AICPA.

Members are governed by *four* sets of standards:

1) The Bylaws of the AICPA; (not discussed)
2) The Code of Professional Ethics; (discussed briefly)
3) Auditing Standards; (discussed briefly)
4) Financial Accounting Standards (discussed and enlarged in this entire section of the book).

FINANCIAL ACCOUNTING STANDARDS

Financial accounting standards, since May 7, 1973, have been determined by the Financial Accounting Standards Board (the FASB), which, by action of the Council of the AICPA, was designed to replace the old Accounting Principles Board (the APB).

> *Status of FASB interpretations.* Council is authorized under Rule 203 to designate a body to establish accounting principles and has designated the Financial Accounting Standards Board as such body. Council also has resolved that FASB Statements of Financial Accounting Standards, together with those Accounting Research Bulletins and APB Opinions which are not superseded by actions of the FASB constitute accounting principles as contemplated in Rule 203.
>
> In determining the existence of a departure from an accounting principle established by a Statement of Financial Accounting Standards, Accounting Research Bulletin or APB Opinion encompassed by Rule 203, the division of professional ethics will construe such Statement, Bulletin or Opinion in the light of any interpretations thereof issued by the FASB.

The FASB is *not* a division of the AICPA or a committee thereof. It is an autonomous organization in which the AICPA has representation. It is one part of a three-part rule-making process, with each part performing important and distinct functions in the process of setting accounting standards:

The Financial Accounting Foundation is governed by a nine-member board of trustees comprised of five CPAs, two financial executives, one financial analyst, and one accounting educator. The president of the AICPA is a trustee. The trustee's primary duties are to appoint members of the Standards Board and the Advisory Council, to arrange financing, to approve budgets and periodically to review the structure of the organization.

The Financial Accounting Standards Board (FASB) is an independent body with seven full-time, salaried members, at least four of whom are CPAs drawn from public practice; the other members are persons well versed in financial reporting. The FASB's primary duty is to issue statements on financial accounting standards, including interpretations of those standards.

The Financial Accounting Standards Advisory Council comprises not fewer than 20 members who are experts in the field. The Council works closely with the FASB in an advisory capacity, consulting with the Board to identify problems, set agenda priorities, establish task forces, and react to proposed financial accounting standards.

The net result of the recognition of the new FASB was to make the following designated pronouncements the *official,* binding standards to be observed:

Those *prior* pronouncements of the *old* Accounting Principles Board (the APB) which were *not* changed by the new FASB:

1) APB Opinions

2) APB Statements

3) Accounting Research Bulletins:

Plus the new pronouncements (rules) of the FASB:

4) FASB Statements

5) FASB Interpretations

An Important Distinction

The (old) "Accounting Interpretations" (that is the terminology used) were prepared by the AICPA staff and were *not,* when issued, considered to be official. They were answers to practitioners' questions. These "Accounting Interpretations" are *still* in effect, still unofficial, but recommended for use, with the burden of departures on the individual accountant. There will no longer be any new "Accounting Interpretations"— at least not under that title.

The new terminology for these unofficial answers to practitioners' questions (since June 1973) is *"Technical Practice Aids."* These have been added to the body of *unofficial* interpretations of standards.

Note that the "interpretations" issued by the FASB, however, carry the title, "FASB Interpretations" and, under Rule 203 cited previously, *are official* pronouncements.

Unofficial Pronouncements

The following are the unofficial pronouncements issued by the AICPA as guidance for members (who might have to explain departures therefrom):

The Accounting Interpretations (up to June 1973)

The Technical Practice Aids (from June 1973 on)

Terminology Bulletins

Guides on Management Advisory Services

Statements on Responsibility in Tax Practice

Statements of Position of the Accounting Standards Division

Accounting Research Studies (these are different from "Accounting Research Bulletins" which *are* official)

Industry Audit Guides

Most other publications of the AICPA, unless clearly specifying their official nature. (Reference here is to *accounting* publications.)

Reiterating the concept of the first paragraph of this chapter, the responsibility to know the standards and to follow them rests with the individual accountant.

The whole body of compulsory rules and interpretations (though some are unofficial) is suprisingly small in terms of printed material.

GENERALLY ACCEPTED ACCOUNTING PRINCIPLES (GAAP)

GAAP represents the accounting profession's efforts to establish a body of theory and practice that provides a guide in the form of a common set of standards and procedures. The term *generally accepted* has two meanings: 1) an accounting rulemaking authority has developed a principle of financial reporting for specific areas and 2) an accounting practice has been accepted as appropriate for a given procedure or standard because of its widespread application over a long period of time. In both cases the established principles are said to have "substantial authoritative support."

The primary sources of authoritative pronouncements are the Financial Accounting Standards Board *Statements* and *Interpretations,* the Accounting Principles Board, Committee on Accounting Procedures, and Accounting Research Bulletins, (for rules that have not been superseded by FASB Statements), AICPA Statements of Position, AICPA Industry Accounting and Auditing Guides, and FASB Technical Bulletins.

The importance of the accountant complying with GAAP is set forth in Rule 203 of the Code of Professional Ethics, which prohibits an accountant from stating in an opinion that financial statements conform with

GAAP if the statements in fact contain a significant departure from a principle.

The substance of GAAP concerns two areas of accounting; i.e., measurement and disclosure principles. Conservatism, verifiability, and objectivity are the primary attributes of the rules that govern the preparation and disclosure of financial statements.

There are other areas of accounting specialization, such as income taxes, cost accounting, SEC filings, statistical sampling, computers, mathematical "decisionmaking," etc., which require unique education and research. Though peripheral and adjunct, they are guided by the main body of standards, but not explicitly spelled out by them.

The FASB has developed a series of Statements of Financial Accounting Concepts:

1) Objectives of Financial Reporting by Business Enterprises
2) Qualitative Characteristics of Accounting Information
3) Elements of Financial Statements
4) Recognition and Measurement in Financial Statements of Business Enterprises

PRELUDE TO GAAP OUTLINE

Standards and Regulations

Until 1973, accounting principles had been established by the American Institute of Certified Public Accountants. In 1973, the Financial Accounting Standards Board was organized as an independent standard-setting body, with the AICPA continuing to set the standards for auditors. Corporations whose securities are publicly held must conform to rules set by the Securities and Exchange Commission, a federal government agency. The Internal Revenue Service administers the tax statutes and regulations at the federal level. There is no standard-setting authority for managerial accounting, but there is a program available for accountants to qualify for a certificate in management accounting (CMA). The Institute of Internal Auditors administers an examination for an accountant to be designated a certified internal auditor (CIA).

A well-defined body of knowledge and precise, for the most part, methodology have been developed for accounting procedures over a long period of time. Existing techniques and new approaches continue to be studied by the authorities in an effort to keep accounting standards consistent with changes and innovations in business practices, legislative changes, and socio-economic changes in our society.

The following is an outline of Generally Accepted Accounting Principles (GAAP):

I. Objectives of Financial Accounting
II. Basic Features and Basic Elements of Financial Accounting
   A) Basic Features—The Environment
   B) Basic Elements—The Individual Company
      1) Economic resources— obligations and residual interests
      2) Changes in those resources events that cause them to increase or decrease
      *3) GAAP—for recording and reporting them:
         *a) The Pervasive Principles
         *b) The Broad Operating Principles
            • Selection and measurement
            • Financial statement presentation
         c) Detailed Operating Principles

The starred items are covered in the outline below. They pertain to the practical application of the principles, which are described in more theoretical and historical-development terms in the prior sections of the outline.

THE PERVASIVE MEASUREMENT PRINCIPLES

Six principles establish the basis for implementing *accrual* accounting:

1) *Initial Recording:* of assets and liabilities, income determination, revenue and realization.
2) *Realization:*
   Revenue —when earning process is complete.
            —when an exchange has taken place.
   Expenses —gross decreases in assets.
            —gross increases in liabilities.
   Classes of expenses:
   Costs of assets used to produce revenue—cost of goods sold, selling—administrative expense, interest expense.
   Expenses from non-reciprocal transfers—taxes, thefts, floods.
   Costs of assets other than product disposed of—plant, equipment.
   Costs of unsuccessful efforts.
   Declines in market prices of inventories.

Does *not* include repayments of borrowings, expenditures to acquire assets, distributions to owners (including treasury stock) or adjusting prior period expenses.

3) *Associating Cause and Effect.*

4) *Systematic and Rational Allocation.*

5) *Immediate Recognition:*

Costs of the current period which provide no future benefits (those which have been incurred *now* or *prior*) or when allocating serves no useful purpose.

Measurement is based on its own exchanges: contracts not recorded until *one* party fulfills commitment; not all changes are recorded, not internal increases and not price changes in productive resources.

Assets usually are recorded at cost, or unexpired portion of it. When sold, difference increases the firm's net assets. The cost principle: use acquisition price (historical cost). Cost also refers to how asset was originally recorded, regardless of how determined.

6) *The Unit of Measure*—U.S. Dollar—no change is recognized for change in general purchasing power of the dollar.

The Pervasive Principles—Modifying Conventions

Modifying conventions are applied because too rigid adherence to the measurement principles might produce undesirable results, exclude other important events, or even at times be impractical.

The modifying conventions are:

1) *Conservatism*

2) *Emphasis on the importance of income* (LIFO is an example)

3) *Judgment of the accounting profession as a whole* with regard to:

The usual revenue recognition rule—recognition of contracts in progress.

Segregation of extraordinary items.

Avoiding undue effect on net income in one single period (installment sales).

Broad Operating Principles

Two broad principles are:

1) The Principles of Selection and Measurement.

2) The Principles of Financial Statement Presentation.

THE PRINCIPLES OF SELECTION AND MEASUREMENT

These principles guide the selection of the *events* to be accounted for; they determine *how* the selected *events* affect items; and they guide the *assignment of dollars* to the effects of the *events*.
The types of *events,* classified, are:

I. External Events
   A) *Transfers* to or from *other* entities
      1) Exchanges (reciprocal transfers)
      2) Non-reciprocal transfers
         a) With owners
         b) With outsiders
   B) *Other-than-transfers*
II. Internal Events
   A) Production of goods or services
   B) Casualties

The outline presented next breaks down each of the types of events above and briefly highlights, where appropriate:

When to record the transaction
How it is *measured*—what value to use
Some *discussion* and/or *examples*

In that order: when to record, how to value, discussion, examples. In addition to the events themselves (above), there are:

III. *Additional* principles which relate to the *changes* in events, which determine their effects.
IV. Principles governing assets and liabilities that are not resources or obligations (such as deferred taxes).

1A External Events—Transfers To or From Other Entities

1) Exchanges (reciprocal transfers)
Assets—Acquisitions: Record as acquired (some not carried forward are expenses); cost, face amount, sometimes discounted value; sometimes fair value in non-cash exchanges (allocate fair values for individual assets in group)—excess in goodwill. Cash, accounts receivable, short-term receivables at discounted amount when no or low interest stated.

Assets—Dispositions: When disposed of, at cost adjusted for amortization and other changes; in partial dispositions value is based on detailed principles (FIFO, LIFO, average).

Liabilities—Increases: When obligation to transfer assets or provide services is incurred in exchanges; value is established in the exchange, sometimes discounted (long-term)—pension obligations, loans under capitalized long-term leases, bonds, notes bearing little or no interest (the difference is amortized over period to maturity).

Liabilities—Decreases: When discharged through payments or otherwise; use recorded amounts. If partial, may have to apportion to recorded amount.

Commitments—Not recorded when unfulfilled on both sides, unless: one party fulfills its part: some leases are recorded: *losses* on firm commitments are recorded. Long-term leases are recorded as assets by the lessee, with the corresponding liability.

*Revenue from Exchanges—*When product is sold, service performed, resource used by others, and when asset is sold producing gain (or loss); recorded at price in the exchange, sometimes reduced for discounts or allowances. Exceptions: long-term construction contracts, revenue not recognized on purchases, certain products with an *assured* selling price—sometimes recorded over long periods without reasonable assurance of collection (installment method; cost recovery method). (Under the installment method, proceeds collected measure the revenue, but expense is measured by multiplying cost by ratio of collection to sales price. In cost recovery method, use all proceeds collected until all costs are recovered.)

*Expenses—*Directly associated with revenue from exchanges—use costs of assets sold or services provided, recorded when related revenue is recognized. If other than a product, the remaining *undepreciated* cost is subtracted from the revenue obtained.

2) Non-reciprocal transfers:

    a) *With owners:* Investments and withdrawals recorded as they occur:

Increases—by amount of cash received; the discounted value of money claims received or liabilities canceled; fair value of non-cash assets received (often, the fair value of *stock issued*).

Decreases—cash paid; recorded amount of non-cash assets transferred; discounted present value of liabilities incurred.

In "pooling," assets and liabilities are combined as on books (no change); "purchase" method entails use of fair value.

Investments of non-cash assets recorded when made; sometimes measured at cost to founder (rather than fair value).

b) *With outsiders:* assets, when acquired, when disposed of, when discovered; for non-cash assets given, usually use fair value; liabilities, at face value, sometimes discounted.

1B External Events—Other Than Transfers

Examples are: Changes in prices of assets, changes in interest rates, technological changes, damage caused by outside influences.

Favorable events—Generally not recorded, except at time of later exchange. Retained *on* books at recorded amounts until exchanged (assets) or until satisfied (liabilities). Exceptions are: When using the equity method; foreign currency translations; marketable securities under new rules, written down to market, up to cost, as fluctuates; obligations under warranties.

Unfavorable events—Decreasing market price or utility of asset, adjusted to lower market price or recoverable cost, usually governed by specific rules such as cost or market for inventories. A loss is recognized when utility is no longer as great as its cost, obsolescence; adjust write-offs or write-off entirely currently if it is completely worthless, or down to recoverable cost. Damage caused by others, record when occurs or discovered—to recoverable cost. Increases in amounts currently payable because of higher interest rates only generally not recorded until liquidated. Increases in non-U.S. Dollar liabilities are recorded in terms of U.S. Dollar because of currency translation.

2A Internal Events—Production of Goods or Services

Production is the input of goods and services combined to produce an output of product which may be goods or services. It includes: manufacturing, merchandising, transporting and holding goods.

Recorded at historical or acquisition costs (previously recorded) as used in the production process during the period; deducted from revenue to which related in the period sold. Costs are usually shifted or allocated from initially recorded asset accounts to other accounts in a *systematic* and *rational* manner.

Costs of manufacturing or providing services—Costs of assets completely used plus allocated portions of assets partially used; allocations are assumed, based on relationship between assets and activities; note that "costs" refers to amounts charged initially to assets—they become "expenses" when allocated to expense as follows:

If benefit only one period—expense then.

If benefit several periods—expense over periods involved (depreciation, depletion, amortization).

Expenses—Some items are recognized as expenses immediately and charged directly thereto. Enterprises never "acquire" expenses, as they acquire assets. Costs may be charged as expenses immediately under the principle of immediate recognition when they pertain to the period involved and cannot be associated with any other period, such as officer salaries and advertising.

Revenue—Under certain conditions and special standards, revenue may be recognized at completion of production or as production progresses (precious metals industry; long-term construction contracts). Ratio of performance to date must be capable of being reasonably estimated and collection *reasonably* assured. Take losses *immediately*. Revenue is measured by an allocated portion of a predetermined selling price, less product or service costs as they progress.

2B Internal Events Casualties

Sudden, substantial, unanticipated reductions in assets *not* caused by other entities, such as:

Fires, floods, abnormal spoilage.

Recorded when they occur or when they are discovered.
Measured by writing them down to recoverable costs and a *loss is* recorded.

3 Additional Principles Which, Related to the Changes in Events, Determine Their Effects

Dual effect—Every recorded event affects at least *two* items in the records. *The double-entry system is based on this principle.*

Increases In Assets Arise From:

A) Exchanges in which assets are acquired
B) Investments of assets by owners
C) Non-reciprocal transfers of assets by outsiders
D) Shifts of costs during production
E) External events (equity method)
F) Increases ascribed to produced assets with *opposite effect* of:
　　1) Decrease in other assets
　　2) Increase in liability
　　3) Revenue recognition
　　4) Sometimes, neutral effect—production costs shifted.

Decreases In Assets Arise From:

A) Exchanges in which assets are disposed of
B) Withdrawals of assets by owners
C) Non-reciprocal transfers to outsiders
D) External events which reduce market price
E) Shifts and allocations
F) Casualties with *opposite effect* of:
    1) Increase in other assets
    2) Decrease in liabilities
    3) Increases in expenses:
       Immediately, if used up:
       Or if future benefit cannot be determined.

Increases In Liabilities Arise From:

A) Exchanges in which liabilities are incurred
B) Transfers with owner (dividend declaration)
C) Non-reciprocal transfers with outsiders with opposite effect of:
    1) Decrease in other liabilities
    2) Increase in assets
    3) An expense.

Decreases In Liabilities Arise From:

A) Exchanges in which liabilities are reduced
B) Transfers with owners
C) Non-reciprocal transfers with outsiders (forgiveness of indebtedness) with *opposite effect* of:
    1) Increases in other liabilities
    2) Decreases in assets
    3) Revenue.

Increases In Owners' Equity Arise From:

A) Investments in enterprise
B) *Net* result of all revenue and expenses in a period
C) Non-reciprocal transfers with outsiders (gifts)
D) Prior period adjustments.

Decreases In Owners' Equity Arise From:

A) Transfers to owners (dividends)

B) Net losses for a period

C) Prior period adjustments.

Revenue Arises:

A) Primarily from exchanges

B) Occasionally from production

C) Rarely from transfers or external events with *opposite effect* of:
1) Usually an asset increase
2) Decrease in liability (called "unearned revenue").

Expenses Arise From:

A) Exchanges—costs directly associated with revenue are recognized when assets are sold or services provided

B) Non-reciprocal transfers with outsiders

C) External events other than transfers

D) Production:
1) Costs of manufacturing products and providing services *not* included in product costs (example—overhead)
2) Expenses from systematic and rational allocation, excluding those assigned to product costs of manufacturing
3) Expenses recognized immediately on the acquisition of goods or services
4) Costs of products for which revenue is recognized at *completion* of production or as *production* progresses (precious metals, percent-of-completion contracts).

Principles Governing Assets and Liabilities That Are Not Resources or Obligations

Certain items are shown as assets that are not in reality resources, such as deferred charges for income taxes; and certain items are shown as liabilities that are not in reality liabilities, such as deferred credits for income taxes.

Accounting for them is governed by detailed principles, such as accounting for deferred federal income taxes.

The effect of recording these items is an increase or a decrease in assets or liabilities, with a corresponding decrease or increase in expenses on the income statement.

Chapter 4

Principles of Financial Statements, Disclosure, Analysis, and Interpretation

The general objective is to provide reliable information on resources, obligations and progress. The information should be useful for comparability, completeness and understandability. The basic features involved in financial accounting are: the individual accounting entity, the use of approximation and the preparation of fundamentally related financial statements.

The financial statements—balance sheet, income statement, change in stockholders' equity and statement of cash flows, as well as segment reports and interim reports—will summarize a firm's operations and ending financial position. Analysts, investors, creditors and potential investors and creditors will analyze these documents in their decision-making processes.

Fair Presentation in Conformity with GAAP

1) GAAP applicable in the circumstances have been applied in accumulating and processing the accounting information; and

2) Changes from period to period in GAAP have been properly disclosed; and

3) The information in the *underlying* records is properly *reflected* and *described* in the financial statements in conformity with GAAP; and

4) A proper balance has been achieved between:

   a) The conflicting needs to disclose the important aspects of financial position and results of operation in conformity with conventional concepts, and to

b) Summarize the voluminous underlying data with a limited number of financial statement captions and supporting notes.

12 PRINCIPLES OF FINANCIAL STATEMENT PRESENTATION

1) Basic Financial Statements—minimum requirements:
   a) Balance Sheet
   b) Statement of Income
   c) Statement of Changes in Stockholders' Equity
   d) Statement of Cash Flows
   e) Disclosure of Accounting Policies
   f) Disclosure of Related Notes
   Usually presented for two or more periods.
   Other information may be presented, and in some cases required, as supplemental information: price-level statements; information about operations in different industries; foreign operations and export sales; major customers (segment reporting).

2) A Complete Balance Sheet
   a) All Assets
   b) All Liabilities
   c) All classes of Stockholders' Equity.

3) A Complete Income Statement
   a) All Revenues
   b) All Expenses

4) A Complete Statement of Cash Flow
   Includes and describes all important aspects of the company's financing and investing activities.

5) Accounting Period
   Basic time period is one year
   An interim statement is for less than one year.

6) Consolidated Financial Statements
   They are presumed to be more meaningful than separate statements of the component legal entities
   They are *usually* necessary when one of the group owns (directly or indirectly) *over 50 percent* of the outstanding voting stock
   The information is presented as if it were a *single enterprise.*

7) The Equity Basis

For unconsolidated subsidiaries (where over 50 percent is owned) *and for investments in 50 percent or less* of the voting stock of companies in which the investor has significant influence over investees, 20 percent or more ownership presumes this influence, unless proved otherwise. The investor's share of the net income reported by the investee is picked up and shown as income and an adjustment of the investment account—for all earnings subsequent to the acquisition. Dividends are treated as an adjustment of the investment account.

8) Translation of Foreign Branches

Translated into U.S. Dollars by conventional translation procedures involving foreign exchange rates.

9) Classification and Segregation:

(Must separately disclose these important components)

a) *Income Statement*—Sale (or other source of revenue); Cost of Sales; Depreciation; Selling Administration Expenses; Interest Expense; Income Taxes.

b) *Balance Sheet*—Cash; Receivables; Inventories; Plant and Equipment; Payables; and Categories of Stockholder's Equity:

- Par or stated amount of capital stock; Additional paid-in capital
- Retained earnings: (affected by—
    1) Net income or loss,
    2) Prior period adjustments,
    3) Dividends, or
    4) Transfers to other categories of equity).
- Working Capital—current assets and current liabilities should be classified as such to be able to determine working capital—useful for enterprises in: manufacturing, trading, some service enterprises.
- Current assets—include cash and other that can reasonably be expected to be realized in cash in one year or a shorter business cycle.
- Current liabilities—include those that are expected to be satisfied by the use of those assets shown as current; or the creation of other current liabilities; or expected to be satisfied in one year.
- Assets and liabilities should *not* be offset against each other unless a legal right to do so exists, which is a rare exception.
- Gains and Losses—arise from other than products or services, may becombined and shown as one item. Examples: write-downs of inventories, receivables, capitalized research and development costs, *all sizable*. Also, gains and losses on: temporary investments,

non-monetary transactions, currency devaluations are a few typical items.

- Extraordinary items or gain or loss—should be shown separately under its own title, distinguished by unusual nature and infrequent occurrence should be shown net of taxes.
- Net Income—should be separately disclosed and clearly identified on the income statement.

10) Other disclosures: (Accounting policies and notes)

    a) Customary or routine disclosures:

- Measurement bases of important assets
- Restrictions on assets
- Restriction on owners' equity
- Contingent liabilities
- Contingent assets
- Important long-term commitments not in the body of the statements
- Information on terms of equity of owners
- Information on terms of long-term debt
- Other disclosures required by AICPA

    b) Disclosure of changes in accounting policies.

    c) Disclosure of important subsequent events—between balance sheet date and date of the opinion.

    d) Disclosure of accounting policies ("Summary of Significant Accounting Policies").

11) Form of Financial Statement Presentation:

No particular form is presumed better than all others for all purposes. Several are used.

12) Earnings Per Share:

Must be disclosed on *the face of the Income Statement.*

Should be disclosed for:

a) Income before extraordinary items

b) Net Income.

Should consider:

a) Changes in number of shares outstanding

b) Contingent changes

c) Possible dilution from potential conversion of:

- Preferred stock
- Options
- Warrants

Materiality

There have been attempts by authoritative rule-making bodies, scholars of accounting, users of fnanicial statements, and others to develop quantitative criteria for determining the materiality of items in the financial statements. They postulate that if Item A is X percent of a total, Item A is material. If Item B is Y percent of a total, then Item B is material, but . . .. All efforts have proved fruitless, and there are no accepted quantitative standards that can be wholly relied upon for an unquestioned determination of whether an item is material or immaterial (and can be omitted from the financial statements or notes thereto).

The courts to some extent have helped. However, it should be cautioned that different jurisdictions in different geographic areas of the country have established many different opinions and definitions of materiality. For example, the Tenth Circuit Court of Appeals ruled that information is material if ". . . the trading judgment of reasonable investors would not have been left untouched upon receipt of such information." (*Mitchell v. Texas Gulf Sulphur Co.*) In the "landmark" *Bar Chris* case the judge said that a material fact is one ". . . which if it had been correctly stated or disclosed would have deterred or tended to deter the average prudent investor from purchasing the securities in question" (*Escott et al. v. Bar Chris Construction Corporation et al.*).

Principally because the U.S. Supreme Court defined materiality in the *TSC Industries Inc. v. Northway Inc.* case, the following statement of the Court is considered to be an authoritative basis upon which to render a judgment of materiality:

"An omitted fact is material if there is a substantial likelihood that a reasonable shareholder would consider it important in deciding how to vote. This standard is fully consistent with the general description of materiality as a requirement that the defect have a significant *propensity* to affect the voting process."

(Note: This decision dealt with omissions of material information.)

"The Securities and Exchange Commission defines *material information: 'The term* material *when used to qualify a requirement for the furnishing of information as to any subject, limits the information required to those matters as to which an average prudent investor ought reasonably to be informed.'"*

What's Material? The accountant must decide precisely what information requires disclosure. The accountant must exercise judgment according to the circumstances and facts concerning material matters and their conformity with Generally Accepted Accounting Principles. A few examples of material matters are:

1) The form and content of financial statements.
2) Notes to the statements.
3) The terminology used in the statements.
4) The classification of items in the statements.
5) Amount of detail furnished.
6) The bases of the amounts presented, i.e., for inventories, plants, liabilities, etc.
7) The existence of affiliated or controlling interests.

A clear distinction between materiality and disclosure should be noted. Material information involves both quantitative (data) and qualitative information. Additionally, the information must be disclosed in a manner that enables a person of "average" comprehension and experience to understand and apply it to an investment decision. Contra speaking, information disclosed in a manner that only an "expert" can evaluate is not considered within the meaning and intent of disclosure requirements.

Materiality should be thought of as an abstract concept. Many efforts to define the term can be found in the literature, e.g., accounting and auditing books, law books, and Regulation S-X. Nevertheless, in the final analysis, judgments with respect to what is material resulting from court decisions, SEC actions, accountants' interpretations, and corporate and financial officers' judgments have ultimately evolved into the subjective judgment of individuals (accountants and management) responsible for deciding what is and is not material.

DISCLOSURES REQUIRED IN FINANCIAL STATEMENTS

Below is an outline of the most important disclosures required in financial statements with a brief comment on the substance of each requirement.

Accounting Policies.   APB Opinion No. 22 "Disclosure of Accounting Policies" is the applicable GAAP. The disclosure should set forth the accounting principles underlying the statements that materially affect the determination of financial position, changes in financial position, and results of operations. Also included are the accounting principles relating to recognition of revenue, allocation of asset costs to current and future periods, the selection from existing acceptable alternatives, such as the inventory method chosen, and any accounting principles and methods unique to the industry of the reporting entity.

As a general rule, the preferred position of the review of accounting policies is footnote No. 1, but a section summarizing the policies preceding the footnotes is acceptable.

Who decides what information is material? This decision is the responsibility of management working with the company's accountant. Listed below are a few items considered material that *must* be recognized. As a generalization, the *causes* for material changes in financial statement items must be noted to the extent necessary for users to understand the business as a whole. This requirement applies to all financial statements, not just to the income statement.

1) Sales and revenues. Increases or decreases in sales and revenues that are temporary or nonrecurring and their causes.

2) Unusually increased costs.

3) Informative generalizations with respect to each important expense category.

4) Financial expenses. Changes in interest expenses (and interest income); changes in the company's cost of borrowing; changes in the borrowing mix, e.g., long-term vs. short-term.

5) Other income and expense items. These may include dividend income from investees; the equity in the income or losses of investees or of unconsolidated subsidiaries.

6) Income taxes. The effective tax rate paid by corporations should be reconciled to the statutory rates. The reconciliation provides the basis for a description of the reasons for year-to-year variations in the effective tax rate to which a business is subject. Changes caused by the adoption of new or altered policies of tax-deferred accounting are considered material.

7) Material changes in the relative profitability of lines of business.

8) Material changes in advertising, research and development, new services, or other discretionary costs.

9) The acquisition or disposition of a material asset.

10) Material and unusual charges or gains, including credits or charges associated with discontinuance of operations.

11) Material changes in assumptions underlying deferred costs and the plan for the amortization of such costs.

12) The cost of goods sold, where applicable. The gross margin of an enterprise can be affected by important changes in sales volume, price, unit costs, mix of products or services sold, and inventory profits and losses. The composition of cost among fixed, semi-variable and variable elements influences profitability. Changes in gross margins by an analysis of the interplay between selling prices, costs, and volume should be explained.

13) Cash flow information.
14) Dilution of earnings per share.
15) Segmental reporting.
16) Rental expense under leases.
17) Receivables from officers and stockholders.

FULL DISCLOSURE

Full Disclosure is an attempt to present all essential information about a company in the following reports:

1) Balance Sheet
2) Income Statement
3) Statement of Changes in Stockholders' Equity
4) Statement of Cash Flows
5) Accompanying Footnotes

The objectives of financial reporting are set forth in *FASB Concepts Statement No. 1*. The financial statements, notes to the financial statements, and necessary supplementary information are governed by FASB standards. Financial reporting includes other types of information, such as *Management's Discussion and Analysis*, letters to stockholders, order backlogs, statistical data, and the like, commonly included in reports to shareholders.

The Full Disclosure Principle

Financial facts significant enough to influence the judgment of an informed person should be disclosed. The financial statements, notes to the financial statements, summary of accounting policies, should disclose the information necessary to prevent the statements from being misleading. The information in the statements should be disclosed in a manner that the intended meaning of the information is apparent to a reasonably informed user of the statements.

DISCLOSURE IN FINANCIAL REPORTING

Disclosure. The heart of the compilation and disclosure of financial information is *accounting*. Yet, the idea of "adequate disclosure" stands alone as the one concept in accounting that involves all of the good things and all of the dangers inherent in the professional practice of accounting and auditing. Probably the use of the colloquialism "disclosure" best describes the all-embracing nature of the concept. That is to say, *disclosure is the name of the financial reporting game.*

For decades the profession has been inundated with disclosure literature, rules, regulations, statements, government agencies' accounting regulations, court decisions, tax decisions, intellectualizing by academics, books and seminars, all concerning what disclosure is all about.

Yet nobody has answered precisely what continues to remain the essential question: Disclosure of *what*, by *whom*, for *whom?*

The lack of definitive qualitative and quantitative criteria for what information must or need not be disclosed forces upon the independent accountant the responsibility to decide what constitutes a matter requiring disclosure, requiring an exercise of judgment in light of the circumstances and facts available at the time. The *accountant's* responsibility is confined to the expression of an opinion based upon an examination. The representations made through the statements are *management's* responsibility.

What is a material fact, and for whom does a disclosed fact have material significance? What substantive standards of disclosure must the accountant maintain? Who is to promulgate these standards? The profession? One or all of the governmental regulatory agencies? A federal board of accounting? The courts? The Congress?

One conclusion is clear, however. There is an unmistakable trend toward increasing demands upon the accounting profession for more financial information. What better evidence can be cited than the conclusion of the AICPA Study Group on the Objectives of Financial Statements? The group's report said that" . . . financial statements should meet the needs of those with *LEAST* ability to obtain information."

The confusion between what is and is not *material* is caused by a widely held concept—different facts have different meanings for the individual user of financial information. Information that is important to one user may be insignificant to another.

> "All information must adapt *itself* to the perception of those towards whom the information is intended."
>
> -Anonymous

It is neither possible nor economically feasible, however, for an accountant to cover in the statements every single small detail concerning a client's business. Where should the accountant draw the line? (Not many years ago, a large accounting firm had to defend a lawsuit up to the U.S. Supreme Court at a cost of several million dollars because the accountant did not question the company's chief executive officer's policy that he, alone, open the company's mail.)

Recent trends in financial reporting reflect an increase in the amount of disclosure found in financial statements. The information is communicated in the footnotes, which are an integral part of the financial statements. Although the footnotes are usually drafted in somewhat technical language, they are the accountant's means of amplifying or explaining the items present in the main body of the statements. Footnote information can generally be classified as follows:

1) *Disclosure of Accounting Policies Applied*. This information is required in order to inform the user of the statements of the accounting methods used in preparing the information that appears in statements.

2) *Disclosure of Gain or Loss Contingencies.* Because many contingent gains or losses are not properly included in the accounts, their disclosure in the footnotes provides relevant information to financial statement users.

3) *Examination of Credit Claims.* A liability, such as a bank loan, may have numerous covenants that are not conveniently disclosed in the liability section of the balance sheet.

4) *Claims of Equity Holders.* The rights of various equity security issues along with certain unique features that may apply to certain issues are commonly disclosed in footnotes to the statements.

5) *Executory Commitments.* These refer to contract obligations undertaken by the company that have not been performed, or have been only partially performed at the statement date.

In some cases a company is faced with a sensitive issue that requires disclosure in a footnote. Some examples are:

1) related party transactions
2) errors
3) irregularities
4) illegal acts

DISCLOSURES ITEMIZED

Following is an alphabetic listing of items requiring disclosure including short comments if applicable.

Accelerated Depreciation Methods—when methods are adopted.
Accounting Policies see "Summary of Significant Policies Accounting" in Chapter 1, in the discussion of APB 22.

Allowances (depreciation, depletion, bad debts)—deduct from asset with disclosure .

Amortization of Intangibles—disclose method and period.

Amounts Available for Distribution—note the needs for any holdback retention of earnings.

Arrangements with Reorganized Debtor—disclose if a subsequent event.

Arrears on Cumulative Preferred Stock—the rights of senior securities must be disclosed on the face of balance sheet or in the notes.

Assets (interim changes in)—only significant changes required for interims.

Business Segments.

Cash-Basis Statements—fact must be disclosed in the opinion with delineation of what would have been had accrual basis been used, its significant variance.

Change in Stockholders' Equity Accounts—in a separate schedule. This does not include the changes in retained earnings statement, which is also a basic requirement.

Change to Declining Balance Method—disclose change in method and effect of it.

Changes, Accounting—see text.

Commitments, Long-Term—disclose unused letters of credit, assets pledged as security for loans, pension plans, plant expansion or acquisition; obligations to reduce debt, maintain working capital or restrict dividend.

Commitments to Complete Contracts—only the extraordinary ones.

Consolidation Policy—method used.

Construction Type Contracts—method used.

Contingencies—disclose when reasonable possibility of a loss, the nature of, and estimated loss. Threats of expropriation, debtor bankruptcy if actual. Those contingencies which might result in gains, but not misleading as to realization. Disclosure of uninsured risks is advised, but not required. Gain contingencies should be disclosed, but not reflected in the accounts.

Contingencies in Business Combinations—disclose escrow items for contingencies in the notes.

Control of Board of Directors—disclose any stock options existing.

Corporate Officer Importance—disclose if a major sales or income factor to the company.

Current Liabilities—disclose why, if any, omitted (in notes).

Dating (Readjusted) Earned Surplus—no more than 10 years is the term now required.

Deferred Taxes—disclose and also see Timing Differences in this text.

Depreciation and Depreciable Assets—disclose the following:

1) Depreciation expense for the period

2) Balances of major classes of depreciable assets by nature or function

3) Accumulated depreciation by classes, or in total

4) A general description of the methods used in computing depreciation.

Development Stage Enterprises—are required to use the same basic financial statements as other enterprises, with certain additional disclosures required. Special type statements are not permissible.

Discontinued Operations—disclose separately below continuing-operating income, net of tax, but before extraordinary items. Show separate EPS.

Diversified Company's Foreign Operations.

Earnings per share—see discussion in this text, but the following is also required in addition to the data stated there (does not apply to non-public enterprises):

1) Restatement for a prior period adjustment

2) Dividend preference

3) Liquidation preference

4) Participation rights

5) Call prices and dates

6) Conversion rates and dates

7) Exercise prices and dates

8) Sinking fund requirements

9) Unusual voting rights

10) Bases upon which primary and fully diluted earnings per share were calculated

11) Issues which are common stock equivalents

12) Issues which are potentially dilutive securities

13) Assumptions and adjustments made for earnings per share data

14) Shares issued upon conversion, exercise, and conditions met for contingent issuances

15) Recapitalization occurring during the period or before the statements are issued

16) Stock dividends, stock splits or reverse splits occurring after the close of the period before the statements are issued

17) Claims of senior securities entering earnings per share computations

18) Dividends declared by the constituents in a pooling

19) Basis of presentation of dividends in a pooling on other than a historical basis

20) Per share and aggregate amount of cumulative preferred dividends in arrears.

Equity Method—as follows:

1) Financial statements of the investor should disclose in the notes, separate statements or schedules, or parenthetically:

    a) The name of each investee and percent of ownership

    b) The accounting policies of the investor, disclosing if, and why, any over 20 percent holdings are not under the equity method

    c) Any difference between the carrying value and the underlying equity of the investment, and the accounting treatment thereof;

2) Disclose any investments which have quoted market prices (common stocks) showing same—do not write down;

3) Present summary balance sheet and operating information when equity investments are material;

4) Same as above for any unconsolidated subsidiaries where ownership is majority;

5) Disclose material effects of contingent issuances.

Extinguishment (Early) of Debt—gains or losses should be described, telling source of funds for payoff, income tax effect, per share amount.

Extraordinary Items—describe on face of income statement (or in notes), show effect net of tax after income from continuing operations, also after business disposals if any, show EPS separately for extraordinary item. May aggregate immaterial items.

Fiscal Period Differences (in Consolidating)—disclose intervening material.

Fiscal Year Change—disclose effect only.

Foreign Items—Assets, must disclose any significant ones included in U.S. statements; gains or losses shown in body of U.S. statement; disclose significant "subsequent event" rate changes; operations, adequate disclosure to be made of all pertinent dollar information, regardless of whether consolidating or not (for foreign subsidiaries).

Headings and Captions—may be necessary to explain.

Income Taxes (and Deferred Taxes)—(see Timing Differences in this text.)

Income Taxes of Sole Proprietor or Partnership—may be necessary to disclose personal taxes to be paid if the money will come from and put a drain on the firm's cash position.

Infrequent Events—show as separate component of income and disclose nature of them.

Interim Statements—(see discussion in this text.)

Inventories—disclose pricing policies and flow of cost assumption in "Summary of Significant Accounting Policies"; disclose changes in method and effect on income. Dollar effect based upon a change should be shown separately from ordinary cost of sales items.

Investment Tax Credits—disclose method used, with amounts if material. Also, disclose substantial carryback or carryforward credits.

Leases—See Non-current Assets in this text.

Legal Restrictions on Dividend Payments—put in notes.

Liability for Tax Penalties—if significant, disclose in notes. May have to take exception in opinion.

Market Value of Investments in Marketable Securities—should be written down to market value and up again, but not to exceed cost for entire portfolio per classification.

Non-Cumulative Preferred Stock—should disclose that no provision has been made because it is non-cumulative.

Obligations (Short-Term)—disclose in notes reason any short-term obligations not displayed as current liabilities.

Partnerships, Limited—disclose fact that it's a limited partnership.

Patent Income—disclose if income is ending.

Pension Plans—must disclose the following:

1) Describe and identify employee groups covered by plan
2) The accounting and funding policy
3) The provision for pension cost for the period
4) Excess, if any, of vested benefits over fund total; any balance sheet deferrals, accruals, prepays
5) Any significant matters affecting comparability of periods presented.

Political Contributions—must disclose if material or not deductible for taxes, or if they are beneficial to an officer.

Pooling of Interests.

Price-level Restatements.

Prior Period Adjustments—must disclose with tax effects. Must disclose in interim reports.

Purchase Commitment Losses—should be separately disclosed in dollars in income statement.

Purchase Method. (See Business Combinations.)

Purchase Option Cancellation Costs—yes, disclose.

Real and Personal Property Taxes—disclose if using estimates, and if substantial. All adjustments for prior year estimates should be made through the current income statement.

Real Estate Appraisal Value—for development companies, footnote disclosure might be useful.

Receivables, Affiliated Companies, Officers and Employees—should be segregated and shown separately from trade receivables.

Redemption Call of Preferred Stock—disclose in the equity section.

Renegotiation Possibilities—use dollars if estimable or disclose inability to estimate.

Research and Development Costs—disclosure must be made in the financial statements of the total research and development costs charged to expenses in each period for which an income statement is presented. Government-regulated enterprises should disclose the accounting policy for amortization and the totals expensed and deferred, but not the confidential details of specific projects, patents, new products, processes or company research philosophy. Applies the above provision for disclosure to business combinations.

Restricted Stock Issued to Employee—disclose circumstance and the restrictions.

Retained Earnings Transferred to Capital Stock—arises usually with "splitups effected as dividends" and with stock dividends; must disclose and include schedule showing transfers from retained earnings to capital stock. Also, must disclose number of shares for EPS; must show subsequent event effects.

Sale and Leaseback.

Seasonal Business (Interim Statements)—must disclose, and advisable to include 12-month period, present and past.

Stock Dividends, Split-up—must disclose even if a subsequent event and use as if made for and during all periods presented.

Stock Options—disclose status. (See Equity chapter in this text.) Has effect on EPS.

Stockholders Buy/Sell Stock Agreements—disclose.

Subleases—(See Leases in Non-Current Assets in this text.).

Termination Claims (War & Defense Contracts)—shown as current receivable, unless extended delay indicated; usually shown separately and disclosed if material, in income statement.

Treasury Stock—(See Index of this text.) Shown in body of balance sheet (equity section ordinarily); should, in notes, indicate any legal restrictions.

Unconsolidated Subsidiaries—if using cost method, should also give independent summary information about position and operations.

Undistributed Earnings of Subsidiaries—(See disclosures required when not accruing deferred taxes under Indefinite Reversal Criteria in this text.).

Unearned Compensation—(See Stock Options in this text.).

Unremitted Taxes—disclose only if going concern concept is no longer valid.

(See next section for those disclosures which require Restatement.)

(Also, see sections on Timing and Permanent Differences—Income Taxes, and Timing Differences.)

RESTATEMENTS

The following alphabetic listing indicates those areas which *require* a restatement (with disclosure) for all prior periods presented in the comparative financial statements:

Appropriations of Retained Earnings—any change made for the reporting of contingencies requires retroactive adjustment.

Changes in Accounting Principle Requiring Restatement:
  1) Change from LIFO to another method.
  2) Change in long-term construction method.
  3) Change to or from "full cost" method in the extractive industries.
  4) Must show effect on both net income and EPS for all periods presented.

Change in Reporting Entity—must restate.

Contingencies—restate for the cumulative effect applying the rules for contingencies.

Earnings Per Share—the effect of all restatements must be shown on EPS, separating as to EPS from continuing operations, EPS from disposals, EPS from extraordinary items and EPS from net income.

Equity Method—restatement required when first applying the method, even though it was not required before.

Extraordinary Items—if a similar one in prior period was not classified as extraordinary, but is now, reclassify now for comparison.

Foreign Currency Translations—restate to conform with adoption of standards; if indeterminable, use the cumulative method. Disclose nature of restatement and effect (or cumulative effect) on income before extraordinary items, on net income, and on related per share amounts.

Income Taxes (Equity Method)—restate to comply.

Interim Financial Statements—restate for changes in accounting principle and for prior period adjustments. If it's a cumulative type change, the first interim period should show the entire effect; if in later period, full effect should be applied to the first period and restated for other periods.

Leases—(see Non-Current Assets in this text.)

Oil and Gas Producing Companies—in conforming with standards, restatement is not required, but it is permissible.

Pooling of Interests

1) A change in accounting method for pooled unit should be applied retroactively.

2) In initial pooling, combine year-to-date, restate prior periods presented, show separate information for independent operations and positions. Purchase method shows pro forma combine.

3) Until pooling is consummated, include the proportion of earnings in ordinary financials; but also present statements (retroactively applied) as if pooling had occurred.

Prior Period Adjustments—must restate the details affected for all periods presented, disclose and adjust opening retained earnings. Must also do it for interim reports.

Refinancing Short-Term Obligations—restatement is permitted, but not required.

Research and Development Costs—In conforming with standards, apply retroactively as a prior period adjustment.

(*No* retroactive recapitalization of costs is permissible. Applies to *purchase* combinations also. Basic rule: expense as incurred.)

Statistical Summaries (5 years, 10 years, etc.)—restate all prior years involved in prior period adjustments.

Stock Dividends and Splits—must restate earnings per share figures and number of shares to give effect to stock dividends and splits *including* those occurring after close of period being reported on (for all periods presented).

Revision based on FASB Opinions—retroactive restatement is not required *unless* the new standard *specifically* states that it is required.

(Note that restatements are *not* required for a change from FIFO to LIFO, nor for a change in the method of handling investment tax credits.)

Timing And Permanent Differences—Income Taxes

Those which will not reverse or "turn around" in other periods:

1) Specific *revenues exempt* from taxability (examples):
Dividend exclusions interest on tax-exempt securities
Life insurance proceeds
Negative goodwill amortization
Unrealized gains on marketable securities
Unrealized gains on foreign currency translations
Tax benefits arising from stock-option compensatory plans (when booked as income)

2) Expenses which are *not* tax deductible:
Depreciation taken on appraisal increases or donated property
Goodwill amortization
Premiums on officer life insurance
Tax penalties and fines
Unrealized losses on securities or currency translations

3) Those expenses which are predicated upon different bases for financial and tax purposes:
Depreciation on trade-ins
Statutory depletion vs cost depletion
Business combinations which treat purchase as "pooling for tax return or pooling as purchase."

Timing Differences

Those which *will* turn around or reverse in one or more subsequent periods. Four broad categories:

1) Income—for Accounting NOW—for Taxes LATER

2) Expenses—for Accounting NOW—for Taxes LATER

3) Income—for Accounting LATER—for Taxes NOW

4) Expenses—for Accounting LATER—for Taxes NOW

Below is an explanation of these four categories

1) Items of *income* included for accounting financial statement purposes NOW not taken on the tax return until a LATER time (examples):

  a) Gross profit on installment method date of sale/when collected on tax return.

  b) Percentage of completion method on books/completed contract method for tax return.

  c) Leasing rentals on books under financing method/actual rent less depreciation for tax return.

  d) Subsidiary earnings reported now/as received for tax return.

2) Items of *expense* taken on financial statements NOW, not taken on tax returns until LATER (examples):

  a) Accelerated depreciation used for financials/not for tax return.

  b) Contributions on financials over 5 percent limit/carried over for taxes.

  c) Deferred compensation accruals/taken when paid on tax return.

  d) Estimated costs of various kinds/taken when cost or loss becomes actual and known, such as: guarantees, product warranties, inventory losses, legal settlements, segment disposals, major repairs.

  e) Depreciation based on shorter life for books than for tax return.

  f) Organization costs taken now/amortized for tax return.

3) Items of *income* taken into financial books LATER, but reported as income NOW on tax returns:

  a) Rents and royalties deferred until earned/reported when collected for tax return.

  b) Deferred fees, dues, services contracts/reported when collected for tax returns.

  c) Intercompany consolidation gains and losses/taxed now if filing separate return.

  d) Leaseback gains, amortized gains over lease-term/date of sale for tax return.

4) Items of *expense* taken into financial books LATER, but taken NOW on tax returns:

  a) Depreciation; shorter lives used for tax purposes accelerated rates on tax return/straight-line on books;certain emergency facility amortization taken on tax returns/later on books.

b) Bond discount, premium costs taken on return/amortized on books.

c) Certain costs which are taken for tax purposes/but deferred for financial purposes, as:

d) Incidental costs of property acquisitions

e) Preoperating costs

f) Certain research and development costs (deferred for financial purposes).

Other Considerations Regarding Income Taxes

Interperiod tax allocation should be followed under the deferred method. Timing differences may be considered individually or grouped by similarity. Tax carryback losses (including investment tax credit carrybacks) should be recognized in the loss period in which the carryback originated. Carryforwards should not be recognized until realized (then show as *extraordinary* item) unless there is no doubt of realization (then show as part of operating profit or loss).

Balance Sheet Presentation of Income Taxes

Tax accounts on the balance sheet should be classified separately as to:

1) Taxes estimated to be paid currently.

2) *Net* amount of current deferred charges and deferred credits related to timing differences.

3) *Net* amount of noncurrent deferred taxes related to timing differences.

4) Receivables for carryback losses.

5) When realization is beyond doubt, show an asset for the benefit to be derived from a carryforward of losses.

6) Deferred investment credits, when this method is employed.

Income Statement Presentation of Income Taxes

All taxes based on income, including foreign, federal, state and local, should be reflected in income tax expense in the income statement.

The following components should be disclosed separately and put on the income statement before extraordinary items and prior period adjustments:

1) Taxes estimated to be payable.

2) Tax effects of timing differences.

3) Tax effects of operating losses.

In addition, the following general disclosures are required:

1) Amounts of any operating loss carryforwards not recognized in the loss period, with expiration dates and effect on deferred tax accounts;

2) Significant amounts of any other unused tax deductions or credits, with expiration dates;

3) Any reasons for significant differences between taxable income and pretax accounting income.

4) Deferred income taxes related to an asset or liability are classified the same as the related asset or liability. A deferred tax charge or credit is related to an asset or liability if reduction of the asset or liability would cause the underlying timing difference to reverse. Deferred income taxes that are not related to an asset or liability are classified according to the expected reversal date of the timing difference.

FINANCIAL STATEMENT ANALYSIS AND INTERPRETATION

Analysis techniques applied to financial statements are of interest to the corporate financial officer of any entity for a number of reasons. For one thing, that particular company's financial statements will be subject to analysis by creditors, credit grantors, and investors. Furthermore, the financial officer will want to analyze the company's statements for internal management use as well as analyze other companies' financial statements for credit purposes and perhaps for investment purposes (where an acquisition is being considered).

The financial statements are a systematic and convenient presentation of the financial position and operating performance of a business entity. The question is: What can be learned by analyzing and interpreting the information available in the statements?

There is much valuable information to be learned, as ratio analysis answers questions concerning the financial facts of a business:

1) GAAP permits a variety of accounting procedures and practices that significantly affect the results of operation reported in the statements. Statement analysis helps to evaluate the choices of alternative accounting decisions.

2) The statements for a number of successive years can be compared by the use of ratios and unusual trends and changes can be noted.

3) A company's statements can be compared with those of other similar companies in the same industry.

4) Statement analysis is the basis for estimating, or projecting, potential operating results by the development of pro forma statements.

5) The effects of external economic developments on a company's business can be applied to results as shown in the statements.

6) The balance sheet valuations can be related to the operating results disclosed in the income statement, since the balance sheet is the link between successive income statements.

7) Since ratios are index numbers obtained by relating data to each other, they make comparisons more meaningful than using the raw numbers without relating an absolute dollar figure to another statement item.

FOUR GROUPS OF RATIOS

Ratios are usually classified into four groups:

1) *Liquidity Ratios:* Measures of the ability of the enterprise to pay its short-term obligations.
2) *Profitability Ratios:* Measures of the profits (losses) over a specified period of time.
3) *Coverage Ratios:* Measures of the protection for the interest and principal payments to long-term creditors and investors.
4) *Activity Ratios:* Measures of how efficiently the company is employing its assets.

The ratios in the following discussion are those most commonly applied to measure the operating efficiency and profitability of a company. (There are hundreds of possible relationships that can be computed and trends identified.) The discussion includes an explanation of the answers that each ratio provides; each ratio's application to a specific area of a business will be noted.

ACCOUNTANT'S RESPONSIBILITY

In evaluating the ratios, the accountant must be mindful that the ratios are simply a measuring tool, not the final answers nor the end in themselves. They are one of the tools for evaluating the *past* performance and providing an indication of the future performance of the company. Ratios are a *control* technique and should be thought of as furnishing management with a "red flag" when a ratio has deviated from an established norm, or average, or predetermined standard.

Accordingly, ratio analysis is meaningless without an *adequate feedback* system by which management is promptly informed of a problem demanding immediate attention and correction.

While accountants are concerned primarily with the *construction* of the financial statements, particularly their technical accuracy and validity, the accountant is also relied upon by the many different users of the statements for assistance in the interpretation of the financial information. The accountant must use experience and technical skill to evaluate information and to contribute to management decisions that will maximize the optimum allocation of an organization's economic resources.

Basic Analysis Techniques

Much of the analytical data obtained from the statements is expressed in terms of ratios and percentages. (Carrying calculations to one decimal place is sufficient for most analysis purposes.) The basic analysis technique is to use these ratios and percentages in either a *horizontal* or *vertical* analysis, or both.

Horizontal analysis. Here, similar figures from several years' financial statements are compared. For example, it may be useful to run down two years' balance sheets and compare the current assets, plant assets, current liabilities, long-term liabilities, etc., on one balance sheet with the similar items on the other and note the amount and percentage increases or decreases for each item. Of course, the comparison can be for more than two years. A number of years may be used, each year being compared with the base year or the immediate preceding year.

Vertical analysis. Here, component parts are compared to the totals in a single statement. For example, it can be determined what percentage each item of expense on the income statement is of the total net sales, or, what percentage of the total assets the current assets comprise.

Ratios. Customarily, the *numerator* of the equation is expressed first, then the denominator. For example, fixed assets to equity means fixed assets *divided by* equity. Also, whenever the numerator is the larger figure, there is a tendency to use the word "turnover" for the result.

As indicated above, these techniques are widely used, generally in the course of one analysis.

BALANCE SHEET ANALYSIS

The significance of the balance sheet is that it shows relationships between classes of assets and liabilities. From long experience, businessmen have learned that certain relationships indicate the company is in actual or potential trouble or is in good financial shape. For example, these relationships may indicate that the business is short of working capital, is undercapitalized generally, or has a bad balance between short- and long-term debt.

It must be emphasized that there are no fixed rules concerning the relationships. There are wide variations between industries and even within a single industry. It is often more valuable to measure these relationships against the past history of the same company than to use them in comparison with other businesses. If sharp disparities do show, however, it is usually wise not to ignore them. Many of the so-called "excesses" that in the past have led to recessions often show up in the balance sheets of individual companies. The most important balance sheet ratios and their implications for the business are discussed below.

Ratio of Current Assets to Current Liabilities

The *current ratio* is probably the most widely-used measure of liquidity, i.e., a company's ability to pay its bills. It measures the ability of the business to meet its current liabilities. The current ratio indicates the extent to which the current liabilities are covered. For example, if current assets total $400,000 and current liabilities are $100,000, the current ratio is 4 to 1.

Good current ratios will range from about 2 to almost 4 to 1. However, the ratio will vary widely in different industries. For example, companies which collect quickly on their accounts and do not have to carry very large inventories can usually operate with a lower current ratio than those companies whose collections are slower and inventories larger.

If current liabilities are subtracted from current assets, the resulting figure is the *working capital* of the company; in other words, the amount of free capital which is immediately available for use in the business. One of the most significant reasons for the failure of small businesses is the lack of working capital, which makes it difficult or impossible for the business to cope with sudden changes in worsening economic conditions. Conversely, lack of a comfortable amount of working capital may prevent a small business from taking advantage of opportunities to expand in a growing economy.

The details of working capital flow are presented in the two-year comparative Statement of Cash Flows, a mandatory part of the financial statements.

An important feature of the ratios to remember is that when both factors are decreased by the same amount, the ratio is increased:

	Old	Change	New
Current Assets	$100,000	$(25,000)	75,000
Current Liabilities	50,000	(25,000)	25,000
Working Capital	50,000	—0—	50,000
Ratio	2 to 1		3 to 1

By paying off $25,000 worth of liabilities (depleting Cash), you have increased the ratio from 2 to 1 to 3 to1. Note that the *dollar* amount of *working capital* remains the same $50,000.

Conversely, should you borrow $50,000 on short-terms (increasing Cash and Current Liabilities), you would *reduce* the ratio to *11/2 to 1* ($150,000/ 100,000), again with the dollar amount of working capital remaining at $50,000.

A variation of the current ratio is the *acid test*. This is the ratio of *quick assets* (cash, marketable securities, and accounts receivable) to *current liabilities*. This ratio eliminates the inventory from the calculation, since inventory may not be readily convertible to cash.

Acid Test Ratio

The current ratio does not disclose the fact that a portion of the current assets may be tied up in slow-moving inventories, which leaves the question of how long it will take to transform the inventories into finished product and how much will be realized on the sale of the merchandise. Elimination of inventories and prepaid expenses from the current assets will give better information for short-term creditors. A *quick* or *acid-test ratio* relates total current liabilities to cash, marketable securities, and receivables. If this total is $150 divided by current liabilities of $100, the acid-test ratio is 11/2 to 1 which is low compared to an industry average of 3 to 1. This means a company would have difficulty meeting its short-term obligations and would have to obtain additional current assets from other sources.

Defensive-Interval Ratio

The defensive-interval ratio is computed by dividing defensive assets— cash, marketable securities, and receivables—by projected daily expenditures from operations. This ratio measures the time span a firm can operate with present liquid assets without resorting to revenues from next year's sources. Projected daily expenditures are computed by dividing cost of goods sold plus selling and administrative expenses and other ordinary expenses by 365 days. Assuming a company has a defensive-interval measure of 150 days and an industry average of 75 days, the 150 days provides a company with a high degree of protection, and can offset the weakness indicated by low current and acid-test ratios that a company might have.

Ratio of Current Liabilities to Stockholders' Equity

This ratio measures the relationship between the short-term creditors of the business and the owners. Excessive short-term debt is frequently a danger sign, since it means that the short-term creditors are providing much or all of the company's working capital. If anything happens to concern the short-term creditors, they will demand immediate repayment and create the risk of insolvency. Short-term creditors are most often suppliers of the business, and the company's obligation to them is listed under accounts payable. However, short-term creditors may also include short-term lenders.

A general rule occasionally cited for this ratio is that for a business with a tangible capital and earnings (net worth) of less than $250,000, current liabilities should not exceed two-thirds of this tangible net worth. For companies having a tangible net worth over $250,000, current liabilities should not exceed three-fourths of tangible net worth.

Tangible net worth is used instead of total net worth because intangible assets (such as patents and copyrights) may have no actual market value if the company is forced to offer them in distress selling.

Ratio of Total Liabilities to Stockholders' Equity

The ratio differs from the preceding one in that it includes only long-term liabilities. Since the long-term creditors of a company are normally not in a position to demand immediate payment, as are short-term creditors, this ratio may be moderately greater than the preceding one without creating any danger for the company. However, the ratio should never exceed 100 percent in an industrial company. If it did, this would mean that the company's creditors have a larger stake in the enterprise than the owners themselves. Under such circumstances, it is very likely that credit would not be renewed when the existing debts matured. Utilities and financial companies can operate safely with much higher ratios because more of their liabilities are long-term.

Ratio of Fixed Assets to Stockholders' Equity

The purpose of this ratio is to measure the relationship between fixed and current assets. The ratio is obtained by dividing the book value of the fixed assets by the tangible value of stockholders' equity. A rule sometimes used is that if tangible net worth is under $250,000, fixed assets should not exceed two-thirds of tangible net worth. If tangible net worth is over $250,000, fixed assets should not exceed three-fourths of tangible net worth.

Ratio of Fixed Assets to Long-Term Liabilities

Since long-term notes and bonds are often secured by mortgages on fixed assets, a comparison of the fixed assets with the long-term liabilities reveals what "coverage" the note or bondholders have—i.e., how much protection they have for their loans by way of security. Furthermore, where the fixed assets exceed the long-term liabilities by a substantial margin, there is room for borrowing additional long-term funds on the strength of the fixed asset position.

Ratio of Cost of Goods Sold to Inventory —Inventory Turnover

One of the most frequent causes of business failure is lack of inventory control. A firm that is optimistic about future business may build up its inventory to greater than usual amounts Then, if the expected business does not materialize, the company will be forced to stop further buying and may also have difficulty paying its creditors. In addition, if a company is not selling off its inventory regularly, that item, or part of it, is not really a *current* asset. Additionally, there may be a considerable amount of unsalable inventory included in the total. For all these reasons, a business is interested in knowing how often the inventory "turns over" during the year. In other words, how long will the current inventory be on the shelves, and how soon will it be turned into money?

To find out how often inventory turns over, the average inventory is compared to the cost of goods sold shown on the income statement. (Typically, average is computed by adding opening and closing inventories and dividing the total by two.) For example, if average inventory is $2 million and cost of goods sold adds up to $6 million, during the course of the year, the company has paid for three times the average inventory. Therefore, it can be said that the inventory turned over three times, and at year-end there remained about a four months' supply of inventory on hand.

Because information about cost of goods sold and average inventory may not be readily available in published reports, another way to measure the same results is by using the ratio of net sales to inventory. In this ratio, net sales is substituted for cost of goods sold. Since net sales will always be a larger figure (because it includes the business's profit margin), the resulting inventory turnover will be a higher figure.

How large an inventory should a company carry? That depends upon many factors within a particular business or industry. What may be large or small may vary with the type of business or the time of year. An automobile dealer with a large inventory at the beginning or middle of a model year will be in a strong position. A large inventory at the end of the season places him in a weak financial position.

Ratio of Inventory to Working Capital

This is another ratio to measure over- or under-inventory. Working capital is current assets minus current liabilities. If inventory is too high a proportion of working capital, the business is short on quick assets—cash and accounts receivable. A general rule for this ratio is that businesses of tangible net worth of less than $250,000 should not have an inventory which is more than three-fourths of net working capital. For a business with tangible net worth in excess of $250,000, inventory should not exceed net working capital. The larger-size business can tolerate a condition where there are no quick assets because its larger inventory can be borrowed against; in addition, it presumably has fixed assets which can be mortgaged if necessary.

Inventory as a percentage of current assets may indicate a significant relationship when comparison is made between companies in the same industry, but not between different types of companies because of other variables.

Receivables Turnover

An important consideration for any business is the length of time it takes to collect its accounts receivable. The longer accounts receivable are outstanding, the greater the need for the business to raise working capital from other sources. In addition, a longer collection period increases the risk of bad debts. A general rule for measuring the collection period is that it should not be more than one-third greater than the net selling terms offered by the company. For example, if goods are sold on terms of 30 days net, the average collection period should be about 40 days, though this varies from industry to industry. Special rules apply in the case of installment selling.

Another way of measuring the collection rate of accounts receivable is to divide the net sales from the income statement by the average accounts receivable. This gives the accounts receivable turnover; i.e., how many times during the year the average accounts receivable were collected. A comparison with prior years reveals whether the company's collection experience is getting better or worse. The faster the turnover, the more reliable the current and acid-test ratios are for financial analytical purposes.

Asset Turnover

This ratio indicates how efficiently a company utilizes its assets. If the turnover rate is high, the indication is that a company is using its assets efficiently to generate sales. If the turnover ratio is low, a company either has to use its assets more efficiently or dispose of them. The asset turnover ratio is affected by the depreciation method used. If an accelerated method of depreciation is used, the results would be a higher turnover rate than if the straight-line method is used, all other factors being equal.

Book Value of the Securities

This figure represents the value of the outstanding securities according to the values shown on the company's books. This may have little relationship to market value—especially in the case of common stock. Profitable companies often show a low net book value, but report very substantial earnings. Railroads, on the other hand, may show a high book value for their common stock, but have such low or irregular earnings that the stock's market price is much less than the book value. Insurance companies, banks and investment companies are exceptions. Since most of their assets are liquid—cash, accounts receivable, marketable securities—the book value of their common stock may well present a fair approximation of the market value.

Nevertheless, book value is an important test of financial strength. It is computed by simply subtracting all liabilities from total assets. The remaining sum represents the book value of the equity interest in the business. In computing this figure, it is a good idea to include only tangible assets—land, machinery, inventory, etc. A patent right or other intangible may be given a large dollar value on the balance sheet, but in the event of liquidation may not be salable at all. The theory underlying the measurement of book value is that it is a good measure of how much cash and credit the company may be able to raise if it comes upon bad times. Book value is usually expressed per share outstanding.

Book value is also an important measure for the bondholders of the company. For them, the value has the significance of telling them how many dollars per bond outstanding the company has in available assets. Since they have a call on the company's assets before either the preferred stockholders or the common stockholders, a substantial book value per bond in excess of the face amount of the bond offers relative assurance of the safety of the bond—assurance that funds will be available to pay off the bonds when they become due. To find the book value of the bonds, add together the total stockholders' equity and the amount of the bonds outstanding.

For example, stockholders' equity totals $5 million. Bonded indebtedness is $2 million. From this $7 million total we subtract $1 million of intangibles. That leaves $6 million of net tangible assets. This represents a coverage of three times the total bond indebtedness, usually a fairly substantial coverage.

INCOME STATEMENT ANALYSIS

Just as with the balance sheet, most of the figures obtained from the income statement acquire real meaning only by comparison with other figures, either with similar figures of previous years of the same company or with the corresponding figures of other companies in the same or similar business.

For example, comparisons can be made between each significant item of expense and cost and net sales to get a percentage of net sales (vertical analysis) which can then be compared with other companies. Percentages are more meaningful to compare than absolute dollar amounts, since the volume of business done by one company in the same industry may vary substantially from the volume of another company.

Comparison can also be made of each of the significant figures on the income statement with the same figures for prior years (horizontal analysis). Here, too, comparisons of percentages rather than absolute dollar amounts might be more meaningful if the volume of sales has varied substantially from year to year.

Other significant comparisons are covered in the following paragraphs.

Ratio of Long-Term Debt to Equity

This ratio measures the leverage potential of the business; that is, the varying effects which changes in operating profits will have on net profits. The rule is that the higher the debt ratio, the greater will be the effect on the common stock of changes in earnings because of increased interest expenses.

Many security analysts feel that in an industrial company equity should equal at least half the total of all equity and debt outstanding. Railroads and utilities, however, are likely to have more debt (and preferred stock) than common stock because of the heavy investments in fixed assets, much of which is financed by the use of debt and preferred stock.

A stock is considered to have high leverage if the issuing company has a high percentage of bonds and preferred stock outstanding in relation to the amount of common stock. In good years, this will mean that after bond interest and preferred stock dividends are paid, there will be an impressive earnings per share figure because of the small amount of common stock outstanding.

On the other hand, that same high leverage situation could cause real difficulty with even a moderate decline in earnings. Not only would the decline eliminate any dividends for the common stock, but also could even necessitate drawing from accumulated earnings to cover the full interest on its bonds.

Earnings Per Share (EPS)

Probably, the most important ratio used today is the earnings per share (EPS) figure. It is a *mandatory* disclosure on all annual financial (income) statements (for public companies) and mandatory for all interim statements (though unaudited) for public companies. Moreover, the EPS must be broken out separately for extraordinary items. The standards of calculation are quite complex where preferred stock, options and convertibility are involved.

The factors involved in the computation and disclosure of EPS for corporations with complex stock structure are discussed elsewhere in this book under "Reporting Earnings Per Share."

Basically, the EPS is the net income divided by the number of outstanding shares (including equivalent shares which are treated on an "as-if-issued" basis).

Investor reaction to the EPS figure—how it compares with other companies, with its own prior history, with the other investment choices (bonds, commodities, bank accounts, treasury notes, etc.)—is considered to be one of the significant factors in setting the market price of the stock, second only to dividends actually paid.

Sales Growth

The raw element of profit growth is an increase in sales (or revenues when the company's business is services). While merely increasing sales is no guarantee that higher profits will follow, it is usually the first vital step; therefore, in analyzing a company, the sales figures for the past four or five years are important. If they have been rising and there is no reason to believe the company's markets are near the saturation point, it is reasonable to assume that the rise will continue.

When a company's sales have jumped by the acquisition of another firm, it is important to find out if the acquisition was accomplished by the issuance of additional common stock, by the assumption of additional debt, or for cash. If the company was paid for by common stock and if the acquired firm's earnings are the same on a per-share basis as those of the acquiring firm, the profit picture remains exactly as it was before. The additional sales growth is balanced by the *dilution of the equity*—that is, the larger number of shares now sharing in the earnings.

The situation is quite different if the purchase was for cash or in exchange of bonds or preferred stock. Here, no dilution of the common stock has occurred. The entire profits of the new firm (minus the interest which must be paid on the new debt or the interest formerly earned on the cash) benefit the existing shareholders.

In any event, acquisitions of new companies often require a period of consolidation and adjustment, frequently followed by a decreased rate of sales growth.

Consideration should be given to the effect of inflation on sales. A situation can exist where the increase in sales may be caused by the increase in prices. The result may be that unit sales have dropped in relation to the previous year's, but the dollar sales have increased. Comparing unit sales may be a better method of ascertaining the sales increase under certain circumstances.

Computing Operating Profit

A company's costs of operations fall into two groups: *cost of goods sold* and *cost of operations*. The first relates to all the costs of producing the goods or services matched to the revenues produced by those costs. The second includes all other costs not directly associated with the production costs, such as selling and administrative costs (usually called period expenses).

Subtracting both of these groups of costs from sales leaves *operating profit*. Various special costs and special forms of income are then added or subtracted from operating income to get *net income before taxes* After deducting state and federal income taxes, the final figure (which is commonly used for computing the profit per share) is *net income*. When analyzing a company, however, you will often be most interested in the operating profit figure, since this reflects the real earning capacity of the company.

The best way to look at cost figures is as a percentage of sales. Thus, a company may spend 90 cents out of every dollar in operating costs. We say its cost percentage is 90 percent or, more commonly, its *operating profit margin* is 10 percent. Profit margins vary a great deal among industries, running anywhere from 1 percent to 20 percent of sales; thus comparisons should not be made between companies in different industries. The trend of the operating profit margin for a particular company, however, will give an excellent picture of how well management is able to control costs. If sales increases are obtained only by cutting prices, this will immediately show as a decrease in the margin of profit. In introducing a new product it is sometimes necessary to incur special costs to make initial market penetration, but this should be only temporary.

The most used, examined and discussed ratio within a company is the *gross profit ratio*. More significance is probably attached to this ratio than to any other because increases usually indicate improved performance (more sales, more efficient production) and decreases indicate weaknesses (poor selling effort, waste in production, weak inventory controls).

When comparing a company with others in the same field, if the company's profit margin is low by comparison, it signals troubles ahead; if it is high, the company appears to be a worthy competitor.

The terminology in the gross profit percentages is sometimes confusing and misinterpreted, especially when the word "markup" is used. As an example:

	$	%
Sales	$ 100	100%
Cost of Sales	80	80%
Gross Profit	$ 20	20%

In conventional usage, there is a 20 percent gross profit or margin on the sale (20/100). However, to determine the *markup*, the cost of sales is the denominator and the gross profit is the numerator (20/80 equals a 25 percent markup).

Starting with gross profit *percentage desired*, to gross 20 percent, what should the selling price be? (The only known factor is cost.)

	%	Known	As calculated
Selling price	100%	?	$ 150
Cost	80%	$ 120	120
Gross Profit	20%	?	$ 30

Selling price is always 100 percent. If cost is $120 and is equal to 80 percent of the selling price (it must be 80 percent because a gross of 20 percent was set), divide $120 by 80 percent to get the 100 percent selling price of $150.

Ratio of Net Sales to Stockholders' Equity

A company acquires assets in order to produce sales which yield a profit. If tangible assets yield too few sales, the company is suffering from underselling: i.e., the underutilization of its assets. On the other hand, the company may suffer from overtrading; i.e., too many sales in proportion to its tangible net worth. In other words, there is too heavy a reliance on borrowed funds to generate sales.

Another way of measuring the effective utilization of assets is to determine the ratio of net sales to total assets (excluding long-term investments).

In either case, comparisons of these ratios with similar ratios of other companies in the same industry can indicate the relative efficiency in utilization of assets of the company being analyzed.

Ratio of Net Sales to Working Capital

This is similar to the preceding ratio, since it measures the relationship between sales and assets. In this case, however, the ratio measures whether the company has sufficient net current assets to support the volume of its sales or, on the other hand, if the capital invested in working capital is working hard enough to produce sales.

Profit Margin on Sales

The profit margin on sales is obtained by dividing net income by net sales for the period. A ratio of 7.5 percent compared to an industry average of 4.6 percent indicates a company is achieving an above-average rate of profits on each sales dollar received.

The profit margin on sales does not indicate how profitable a company is for a given period of time. Only by determining how many times the total assets turned over during a period of time is it possible to ascertain the amount of net income earned on total assets. The rate of return on assets is computed by using net income as the numerator and average total assets as a denominator. An average of 6.2 percent compared to an industry average of 4.9 percent is above the average of an industry and results from a high profit margin on sales.

Rate of Return on Common Stock Equity

This ratio is defined as net income after interest, taxes, and preferred stock dividends (if any) divided by average common stockholders' equity. When the rate of return on common stock equity is higher than the rate of return on total assets, the company is considered to be trading on the equity. Trading on the equity increases a company's financial risk, but it increases a company's earnings.

Dividend Yield

The dividend yield is the cash dividend per share divided by the market price of the stock at the time the yield is determined. This ratio gives the rate of return that an investor will receive at the time on an investment in a stock or bond.

Times Interest Earned

This ratio is computed by dividing income before interest charges and taxes by the interest charge. The ratio indicates the safety of a bondholder's investment. A company that has an interest earned ratio of 5 to 1 shows a significantly safer position for meeting its bond interest obligations than a company with a lower ratio.

STATEMENT OF CHANGES IN STOCKHOLDERS' EQUITY

This statement presents an equity analysis of changes from year to year in each shareholder's account, records any additional shares issued, foreign currency translation gains/losses, dividends per share (if paid), retained earnings. This last figure indicates how well the company itself is doing by revealing how much of the profits it can retain to finance further growth opportunities. In an era of corporate raiding and takeovers, management may be wise to be sure that retained earnings are not too high, but are put to good use in increasing total earnings per share for the benefit of current stockholders.

Return on Equity

This ratio is another method of determining earning power. Here, the opening equity (capital stock plus retained earnings, plus or minus any other equity section items) is divided into the net income for the year to give the percentage earned on that year's investment.

Return to Investors

This is a relatively new ratio used mostly by financial publications, primarily for comparison of many companies in similar industries. The opening equity is divided into the sum of the dividends paid plus the market price appreciation of the period. In addition, the ratio is sometimes extended to cover five years, ten years or more.

Dividend Payout Ratio

The *dividend* per common share is divided by the *earnings* per common share to get the *percentage* of dividend payout.

The dividends on common stock will vary with the profitability of the company but other considerations also affect the percent of payout:

1) the relative stability of the earnings
2) the need for new capital
3) the directors' judgment concerning the outlook for earnings
4) the general views of management relating to the advisability of
   a) plowing back a large part of earnings into the business, or
   b) raising additional funds from outside sources

Dividends on the preferred stock are not subject to a year-to-year fluctuation. If the fixed dividend on *cumulative* preferred stock for any year cannot be met, the payments would accumulate and be paid before any dividends could be declared on the common stock.

Chapter 5
Statement of Cash Flows

The term "cash flow" refers to a variety of concepts, but its most common meaning in financial literature is the same as "funds derived from operations." The *concept* of cash flow can be used effectively as one of the major factors in judging the ability to meet debt retirement requirements, to maintain regular dividends, to finance replacement and expansion costs.

In no sense, however, can the amount of cash flow be considered to be a substitute for, or an improvement upon, the net income as an indication of the results of operations or the change in financial position.

IMPORTANCE OF CASH FLOW

The concept of cash flow was originated by security analysts. It has been stated that in evaluating the investment value of a company, cash flow is frequently regarded as more meaningful to them than net income.

Cash flow from operations data in financial summaries shows the liquid or near-liquid resources generated from operations which may be available for the discretionary use of management. Analysts have suggested that this is a useful measure of the ability of the entity to accept new investment opportunities, to maintain its current productive capacity by replacement of fixed assets, and to make distributions to shareholders without drawing on new external sources of capital.

While information about cash flow from operating activities is useful, it should be considered carefully within the framework of the complete statement of cash flows. This statement reflects management's decisions as to the

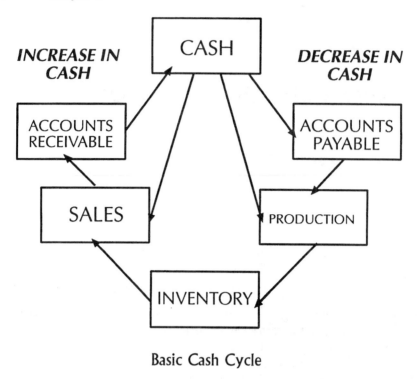

Basic Cash Cycle

use of these cash flows and the external sources of capital used relating to investing and financing activities. The implication of considering or analyzing only the cash flows generated from the operations portion of a cash flows statement is that its use is entirely at the discretion of management. In fact, certain obligations (e.g., mortgage payments) may exist even if replacement of nondepreciating assets is considered unnecessary.

In using cash flow as an analytic tool, care is required. For example, Corporation X has been capitalized with straight common stock. Corporation Y, the same size as Corporation X and comparable in other respects, has been capitalized 25 percent with common stock and 75 percent with debt. A cash flow equivalent to, say, 20 percent of each corporation's gross sales will seem to be four times as large in relation to Corporation Y's stock when compared with the common stock of Corporation X. Cash flow as a meaningful tool, therefore, will have more significance when related to industries and companies in which long-term debt is limited.

One valid point in using cash flow is to put the profit margin squeeze into proper perspective. One of the most rapidly increasing costs is the depreciation charged against newly acquired plants and equipment. The use of accelerated methods of depreciation has created huge depreciation deductions which reduce profits. At the same time, accelerated depreciation creates additional cash flow and encourages further spending for facilities. In the opinion of some financial authorities, a showing of relatively high cash flow per dollar of capitalization is some compensation for a poor showing of net income per dollar of capitalization.

High cash flow is also the reason that some companies with relatively poor earnings per share are able to continue paying cash dividends per share, sometimes in excess of earnings. The SEC has noted situations where investors were misled by these cash distributions in excess of net income when not accompanied by disclosure indicating clearly that part of the distribution represented a return of capital.

In addition to profits, the extractive industries get cash flow through depletion allowances, drilling write-offs, and amortization of development costs and depreciation.

Cash flow also helps analysts judge whether debt commitments can be met without refinancing, whether the regular cash dividend can be maintained despite ailing earnings, whether the extractive industries (i.e., oils and mining) will be able to continue exploration without raising additional capital, or whether additional facilities can be acquired without increasing debt or present capital.

Relative cash flow is an important factor in deciding whether to buy or lease. But it is not necessarily true that owning property creates funds for use in expansion. The cash made available to a corporation through operations will be similar whether the business property is owned or leased. Owned property acquired by borrowed capital will require periodic payments on the debt which will have to be met before funds are available for expansion.

FASB STATEMENT NO. 95

Statement of Cash Flows.   Financial Accounting Statement No. 95 was issued in November, 1987. The Statement establishes the standards for reporting cash flows in the financial statements. It. supersedes APB Opinion No. 19, *Reporting Changes in Financial Position*, and supersedes or amends prior pronouncements.

Specifically, the Statement requires disclosure of cash flows to be included in the full set of financial statements, replacing the *Statement of Changes in Financial Position*.

Business enterprises are encouraged to report cash flows from operating activities *directly* by disclosing the major sources of operating cash receipts and disbursements (the *direct* method). Enterprises can elect not to show operating cash receipts and disbursements, but will be required to disclose the same amount of net cash flow from operating activities *indirectly* by adjusting net income to reconcile the net cash flow from operating activities (the *indirect* reconciliation method) by eliminating the effects of:

1) all deferrals of past operating cash receipts and payments,
2) all accruals of expected future operating cash receipts and payments,
3) all items that are included in net income that do *not* affect operating cash receipts and payments.

It should be noted that if the direct method is applied, a reconciliation of net income and net cash flow from operating activities is required to be provided in a separate schedule.

If a reporting company has foreign business operations, the cash flows statement must disclose the currency equivalent of foreign currency cash flows, applying the current exchange rate at the time of the cash flow. The effect of changes in the exchange rates is disclosed as a separate item in the reconciliation of beginning and ending balances of cash and cash equivalents.

Information about investing and financing activities not resulting in cash receipts or payments is to be disclosed separately.

Terminology.   Precise definitions to clarify the meaning of the terms related specifically to FASB 95 can be helpful to an understanding of the requirements.

Cash. Includes currency on hand, demand deposits with banks, and accounts with financial institutions that have the general characteristics of demand deposits; e.g., a depository that accepts deposits and permits withdrawals without prior notice or penalty.

Cash Equivalent. Short-term, highly liquid investments that are 1) readily convertible into known amounts of cash, and 2) near enough to maturity (see *Original Maturity*) that a change in the interest rate structure presents an insignificant risk of changes in the value of the investment.

Cash Flow. Cash receipts and cash payments resulting from investing, financing, or operating activities.

Direct Method. Shows the principal components to be operating cash receipts and payments; e.g., cash received from accounts receivable; cash paid to suppliers.

Financing Activities. Borrowing money; paying borrowings; long-term credit. In general, transactions to acquire and repay capital.

Indirect Method. Computation starts with net income that is adjusted for revenue and expense items *not* resulting from operating cash transactions (e.g., noncash transactions) to reconcile to net cash flow from operating activities. This method does not disclose operating cash receipts and payments.

Investing Activities. Making loans; collecting loans; acquiring and disposing of debt; acquiring and disposing of equity; acquiring and disposing of productive assets (e.g., plant and equipment).

Net Cash Flow. The arithmetic sum of gross cash receipts and gross cash payments which results in the net cash flow from operating activities.

Noncash And Investing Activities. Investing and financing activities which affect assets or liabilities, but do not result in cash receipts or cash payments.

Operating Activities. All transactions and other events that are not defined as investing or financing activities. Cash flows from activities which generally result from transactions and other events that enter into the determination of net income.

Original Maturity. An investment *purchased* three months from the maturity date.

NOTE: An investment *purchased more than three months from maturity is not* a cash equivalent, even though its remaining maturity on financial statement date is within the three months' rule.)

Summary

The summary that follows brings together in columnar format the significant requirements of the Statement that are scattered throughout the FASB manual.

1) The objective of FASB 95 is to provide detailed information about the cash receipts and cash payments of an enterprise during a specified accounting period.

2) The statement of cash flows reports the cash effects of any enterprise's operations, investing transactions and financing transactions.

3) Related disclosures detail the effects of investing and financing transactions that affect an enterprise's financial position, but do not directly affect cash flows.

4) Net income and net cash flow from operating activities are reconciled to provide information about the *net* effects of operating transactions, other events, and financial activities.

5) The cash flows statement should explain the change during specified accounting period in cash and cash equivalents.

6) FASB 95 requires enterprises with foreign currency transactions (e.g., cash receipts and payments) to report the currency equivalent of foreign currency cash flows applying the exchange rates in effect at the time of the cash flows. (A weighted average exchange rate for the period for translation is permissible as specified in FASB 52, Para. 12.)

7) Noncash transactions have a significant effect on the cash flows of a company and should be disclosed. (Reference APB Opinion 29, *Accounting for Nonmonetary Transactions*.)

CLASSIFICATION OF CASH RECEIPTS AND CASH PAYMENTS

Resulting from Operating Activities

Cash Inflows

Receipts from sale of goods and services.

Collections on accounts.

Collections on short- and long-term notes and other credit arrangements.

Interest and dividend receipts.

Other cash receipts that do not originate from investment or financing activities.

Generally , the cash effects of transactions that enter into the determination of net income.

Cash Outflows

Payments to suppliers.

Payments on accounts.

Principal payments on short- and long-term payables.

Interest payments.

Other cash payments that do not originate from investment or financing activities.

Payments to employees, tax payments, etc.

Resulting from Investing Activities

Cash Inflows

Principal collections on loans

Sale of equity securities of other enterprises.

Sale of plant, equipment, property, and other productive assets.

Cash Outflows

Loans made. Payment for debt instruments of subsidiaries.

Purchases of equity securities of other enterprises.

Purchases of plant, equipment, property, and other productive assets.

Resulting from Financing Activities

Cash Inflows

Proceeds from new securities issues.

Bonds, mortgages, notes, and other indebtedness.

Cash Outflows

Repurchase of enterprise's equity securities.

Debt repayments; dividend payments.

Direct Method-Discussion and Illustration

The direct method requires reporting the three major classes of gross cash receipts and gross cash payments, as well as their arithmetic sum to disclose the *net cash flow* from operating activities.

The Rule allows reporting entities to detail cash receipts and payments to any extent considered to be meaningful. For example, payments to suppliers might be divided between raw material purchases and other major supplies used in the business. Wage and salary payments might be divided between manufacturing, selling, and administrative expenses. Sales receipts could be divided among different sources, with an "other" operating cash receipts, if any.

The reconciliation of net income to net cash flow from operating activities must be provided in a separate schedule.

Statement of Cash Flows
Increase (Decrease) in Cash and Cash Equivalents

(Direct Method)
Year Ended December 31, 19xx

Cash flows from *operating* activities:		
Cash received from customers	$435,000	
Interest received	5,000	
Cash provided by operations		440,000
Cash paid to employees and suppliers	(382,000)	
Interest paid	(13,000)	
Taxes paid	(20,000)	
Cash disbursed by operations		(415,000)
Net cash flow from operations		$ 25,000
Cash flows from *investing* activities:		
Marketable securities purchases	$(32,500)	
Proceeds-marketable securities sales	20,000	
Loans made	(8,500)	
Loan collections	6,000	
Plant purchase	(80,000)	
Proceeds-sale of plant assets	37,500	
Net cash used in investing activities		$(57,500)
Cash flows from *financing* activities:		
Loan proceeds	$ 22,500	
Debt repayment	(27,500)	
Proceeds-Bond issue	50,000	
Proceeds-Common Stock issue	25,000	
Dividends paid	(20,000)	
Net cash provided by financing activities		$50,000
Net increase (decrease) in cash		$17,500

The following is a more comprehensive Statement of Cash Flow from operations applying the *direct* method. This approach includes the disclosure of noncash transactions in a separate schedule formatted beneath the statement.

Statement of Cash Flows
Increase (Decrease) in Cash and Cash Equivalents

(Direct Method)
Year Ended December 31, 19xx

Cash flow from operations:		
Cash from receivables	$10,000,000	
Dividend receipts	700,000	
Cash provided		10,700,000
Cash paid to suppliers	2,000,000	
Wage and salary payments	4,000,000	
Interest payments	750,000	
Taxes	1,000,000	
Cash disbursed		7,750,000
Net cash flow from operations		$2,950,000
Cash flow from investing activities:		
Property and plant purchases	(4,000,000)	
Proceeds from sale of equipment	2,500,000	
Acquisition of Corporation X	(900,000)	
Securities purchases	(4,700,000)	
Securities sales	5,000,000	
Borrowings	(7,500,000)	
Collections on notes receivable	5,800,000	
Net cash outflow from investments		$(3,800,000)
Cash flow from financing activities:		
Increase in customer deposits	1,100,000	
Short-term borrowings (increase)	75,000	
Short-term debt payments	(300,000)	
Long-term debt proceeds	1,250,000	
Lease payments	(125,000)	
Common stock issue	500,000	
Dividends to shareholders	(450,000)	
Net cash provided by financing		$2,050,000
Foreign exchange rate change		100,000
Net increase (decrease) in cash		$1,300,000
Schedule—Noncash Investing and Financing Activities:		
Incurred lease obligation	$ 750,000	
Acquisition of Corporation X:		
Working capital acquired (except cash)	(100,000)	
Property and plant acquired	3,000,000	
Assumed long-term debt	(2,000,000)	
Cash paid for acquisition	$ 900,000	
Common stock issued in payment		
of long-term debt	$ 250,000	

INDIRECT METHOD—DISCUSSION AND ILLUSTRATION

The indirect method (also termed the *reconciliation method*) requires *net cash flow* to be reported indirectly with an adjustment of net income to reconcile it to net cash flow from operating activities. The adjustment requires:

1) The removal from net income of the effects of all deferrals of past operating cash receipts and payments.
2) The removal from net income of the effects of all accruals of expected future operating cash receipts and payments.
3) The removal from net income of the effects of items of all investing and financing cash flows.

The reconciliation can be reported *either* within the statement of cash flows *or* in a separate schedule, with the statement of cash flows reporting only the net cash flow from operating activities. However, if the reconciliation is disclosed in the cash flow statement, the adjustments to net income must be identified as reconciling items.

Statement of Cash Flows
Increase (Decrease) in Cash and Cash Equivalents

(Indirect Method)
Year Ended December 31, 19xx

Cash flows from *operating* activities:		
Net cash flow from operating activities*		$ 25,000
Cash flows from *investing* activities:		
Marketable securities purchases	$(32,500)	
Proceeds-marketable securities sales	20,000	
Loans made	(8,500)	
Loan collections	6,000	
Plant purchase**	(80,000)	
Proceeds-sale of plant assets	37,500	
Net cash used in investing activities		$(57,500)
Cash flows from *financing* activities:		
Loan proceeds	$ 22,500	
Debt repayment	(27,500)	
Proceeds-Bond issue	50,000	
Proceeds-Common Stock issue	25,000	
Dividends paid	(20,000)	
Net cash provided by financing activities		$50,000
Net increase (decrease) in cash		$17,500

*See supplemental schedule A. (Details operating activity.)

**See supplemental schedule B. (Details investing and financing activity.)

The following is a more comprehensive Statement of Cash Flow from operations applying the *indirect* method. This approach includes the disclosure of noncash transactions in a separate schedule formatted beneath the statement.

BANKERS' USE OF FINANCIAL STATEMENTS

The accountant needs to know how financial information is used and interpreted by different kinds of statement users who have different needs for credit information. The following review concerns accountants' relationships with banker clients and specific items in financial statements that bankers emphasize in their analysis of financial statements that accompany loan applications.

Of specific concern to a banker are the *trends*, both short-term and long-term, in the prospective borrower's operating results. Sales, liquidity, earnings, and the equity accounts give significant evidence of a company's operating performance since it has been in business and in the near-term trends in those indicators. Banks lend money; a business has inherent risks. The more complete

Statement of Cash Flows

(Indirect Method)
Year Ended December 31, 19xx

Net cash flow from operations		$2,950,000
Cash flow from investing activities:		
Property and plant purchases	(4,000,000)	
Proceeds from sale of equipment	2,500,000	
Acquisition of Corporation X	(900,000)	
Securities purchases	(4,700,000)	
Securities sales	5,000,000	
Borrowings	(7,500,000)	
Collections on notes receivable	5,800,000	
Net cash outflow from investments		$(3,800,000)
Cash flow from financing activities:		
Increase in customer deposits	1,100,000	
Short-term borrowings (increase)	75,000	
Short-term debt payments	(300,000)	
Long-term debt proceeds	1,250,000	
Lease payments	(125,000)	
Common stock issue	500,000	
Dividends to shareholders	(450,000)	
Net cash provided by financing		$2,050,000
Foreign exchange rate change		100,000
Net increase (decrease) in cash		$1,300,000
Schedule—Earnings to net cash flow reconciliation from operations:		
Net income	$3,000,000	
Noncash expenses, revenues, losses, and gains included in income:		
Depreciation and amortization	1,500,000	

(Indirect Method), *Con't*
Year Ended December 31, 19xx

Deferred taxes	150,000	
Net increase in receivables	(350,000)	
Net increase in payables	(200,000)	
Net increase in inventory	(300,000)	
Accrued interest earned	(350,000)	
Accrued interest payable	100,000	
Gain on sale of equipment	(600,000)	
Net cash flow from operations		$2,950,000

Schedule of noncash investing and financing activities:

Incurred lease obligation	$ 750,000

Acquisition of Corporation X:

Working capital acquired (except cash)	$(100,000)
Property and plant acquired	3,000,000
Assumed long-term debt	(2,000,000)
Cash paid for acquisition	$ 900,000

Common stock issued in payment of long-term debt	$ 250,000

and accurate the financial statements of the borrower are, the more acceptable are the borrower's statements in a risk-evaluation examination by a banker.

The acceptability of financial statements and the verifiability of the information in the financial reports that accountants certify give the banker confidence in a borrower's accountant and in the integrity of the financial information furnished by the borrower. There should not be any deficiencies in the auditor's certificate, no violations of accounting principles (GAAP), no AICPA and SEC disclosure deficiencies, and no lack of accuracy and consistency with previous years' reports.

Evaluation of Financial Ratios

While most ratios are valuable in measuring the financial excellence of a business, certain ratios, such as the current ratio, are emphasized for particular purposes. The following discussion covers the more common purposes for which ratios are used by bankers.

With respect to those commonly used by bankers, no one ratio can be said to be the most important, as they are all related to one another. For bank loan officers, one of the particular single items in the balance sheet is the *current ratio*, which is important because the nature of the banking business—deposits available upon demand—requires bank lending activity to be concerned predominantly with furnishing short-term loans, i.e., working capital loans. Banks as creditors attach importance to the *debt-to-net-worth ratio* and the borrower's ability to generate sufficient cash flow to service any current debt load.

Management Evaluation

Management's primary interest is efficient use of the company's assets. Management is particularly interested in the turnover ratios, such as the inventory turnover and the relationship of working capital to total sales. To the extent that assets are not being used efficiently, the company is overinvesting and realizing a smaller return than possible on its equity. On the other hand, excessive turnover is dangerous because it puts the company in a vulnerable position. Bankers are also particularly interested in trend relationships shown in the income statements for the past years. Excessive selling expenses may indicate that commissions or other payments are out of line with the market. Bank creditors will also make a comparison between a loan applicant and its competitors in all areas to indicate where improvements in operations should be expected.

Short-Term Creditors

As was stated earlier, a loan officer making short-term loans is particularly interested in the current ratio, since this is a measure of the borrower's working capital and ability to meet current debt obligations. Also discussed was the importance of the net-worth-to-debt ratio, which shows the relationship of the stockholders' investments to funds furnished by trade creditors and others, and shows a borrower's ability to stand up under pressure of debt. The sales-to-receivables ratio (net annual sales divided by outstanding trade receivables) shows the relationship of sales volume to uncollected receivables and indicates the liquidity of the receivables on the balance sheet. Another ratio important to a short-term lender is cost of sales to inventory, which shows how many times a company turns over its inventory, which shows whether-inventories are fresh and salable and helps evaluate its liquidating value.

Long-Term Creditors

Since the long-term lender is looking far into the future, a banker wants to be convinced that the company's earnings will continue at least at the current level. In addition, a lending officer will study the various working capital ratios to determine if the company will have sufficient cash when needed to amortize the debt. The ratio of total liabilities to the stockholders' equity is important because the long-term lender wants to be sure that the shareholders have a sufficient stake in the business. One ratio which is used virtually solely by long-term lenders is the number of times fixed charges are earned. Fixed charges represent the interest payments on the lender's debt as well as any debt which has priority over it. When total earnings of the company are divided by total fixed charges (including preferred stock dividends, if any) the resulting figure represents the number of times fixed charges are earned.

Chapter 6

Current and Non-Current Assets

CLASSIFICATION OF CURRENT ASSETS

Classification of current assets is important since the more the current assets exceed the current liabilities, the higher becomes the working capital. There is considerable variation and inconsistency among companies in the way assets are classified in financial statements.

For accounting purposes, the term "current assets" is used to designate cash and other assets or resources which are reasonably expected to be realized in cash, sold or consumed during the normal operating cycle of the business.

Here are some examples:

1) Cash available for current operations and items which are the equivalent of cash; 2) inventories of merchandise, raw materials, goods in process, finished goods, operating supplies, and ordinary maintenance materials and pans; 3) trade accounts, notes and acceptances receivable; 4) receivables from officers, employees, affiliates and others if they are collectible in the ordinary course of the business within one year; 5) installment or deferred accounts and notes receivable if they conform generally to normal trade practices and business terms; 6) marketable securities representing the investment of cash available for current operation; and 7) prepaid expenses, such as insurance, rent, taxes, unused royalties, current paid advertising services not yet received, and operating supplies.

Prepaid expenses are not current assets in that they will be converted into cash, but in the sense that, if not paid in advance, they would require the use of current assets otherwise available during the operating cycle

The operating cycle is defined as the average time between the acquisition of materials or services until the time that cash is finally realized on sale of the materials or services. Where there are several operating cycles occurring within a year, a one-year time period is used as the criterion for a current asset. Where the operating cycle is more than 12 months (i.e., in the tobacco, distillery, and lumber businesses), a longer period is used. Where a business has no clearly defined operating cycle, a one-year period is used.

Assets Excluded from "Current Assets"

The following types of items are to be excluded from the current asset classification:

1) Cash and claims for cash which are a) restricted as to withdrawal or use for other than current operations, b) earmarked for expenditure in the acquisition or construction of noncurrent assets, or c) segregated for the liquidation of long-term debts. Even though funds may not actually be set aside in separate accounts, funds that are clearly to be used in the near future for the liquidation of long-term debt, sinking fund payments, or other similar purposes should be excluded from current assets, unless the maturing portion of debt is being shown as a current liability.

2) Investments in securities (marketable or not), or advances which have been made for the purposes of control, affiliation, or other continuing business advantage.

3) Receivables arising from unusual transactions (e.g., sale of capital assets, loans or advances to affiliate companies, officers or employees) not expected to be collected within a one-year period.

4) Cash surrender value of life insurance policies.

5) Land and other natural resources.

6) Depreciable assets.

7) Long-term prepayments which are chargeable to the operations of several years or deferred charges, such as bonus payments under a long-term lease and costs of rearranging a factory or removal to a new location.

Accounts and notes receivable due from officers, employees or affiliated companies should not be included under the general heading "Accounts Receivable." They should be shown separately. The basic reasoning behind this is that accounts receivable are classified as a current asset presuming they will be convened into cash within one year. Except in the case where goods have actually been sold to them on account, for collection according to the regular credit terms, amounts due from officers, directors and stockholders are not likely to be collected within one year. Therefore, they should be shown under a noncurrent caption.

The same is true of accounts receivable from affiliated companies. These amounts are not likely to be paid off currently and are usually of a more permanent nature. Showing them as current assets is misleading. Also, there is an overstatement of current assets and consequently of working capital.

Sometimes current assets are carried at values which do not represent realizable values. For example, accounts receivable should be net of allowances for uncollectible accounts or net of earned discounts when discounts are expected to give an *estimated* receivable value.

Also, some current assets should now reflect *unrealized* gains or losses. (See both Marketable Securities and Foreign Currency Translations in this Accounting Section.)

Assets and liabilities in the balance sheet should not be offset unless a legal right of setoff exists.

Inventory is valued at cost unless its utility value has diminished to a lower market replacement cost. Standard costing is acceptable, if it reasonably approximates actual cost. The flow of inventory costs may be predicated upon FIFO, LIFO, or average assumptions.

CASH

GAAP requires accounting for cash to include money that is represented by actual coins and currency on hand or demand deposits available without restriction. It must be management's intention that the cash be available for current purposes. Cash in a demand deposit account that is being held for retirement of long-term debts not currently maturing should be excluded from current assets and shown as a noncurrent investment.

Another common restriction on a company's cash balance is in borrowing arrangements with banks. A business entity will be required to maintain a minimum amount of cash on deposit, usually an agreed upon percentage of the cash balance. This requirement is termed a *compensating balance*. The compensating balance is not available to the company for unrestricted use as it would be a violation of the loan contract with the lender. The compensating balance must be disclosed as a noncurrent asset, if the related borrowing is a noncurrent liability. If the borrowing is a current liability, it is permissible to show the compensating balance as a separately captioned current asset to enable other creditors, suppliers for instance, to see that a portion of the cash balances of their customer is unavailable.

Cash in a savings account subject to statutory notification before withdrawal and cash in certificates of deposits maturing during the current operating cycle or within one year can be included as current assets, but should be separately captioned in the balance sheet to avoid the misleading disclosure that the funds are available immediately upon demand. Such items usually are disclosed in the *short-term investments* caption, but they can also be labeled *Time Deposits or Restricted Cash Deposits.*

INVENTORY

The term "inventory" is used to designate tangible personal property which is: 1) held for sale in the ordinary course of business, 2) in the process of being produced for later sale, or 3) currently consumed directly or indirectly in the production of goods or services to be available for sale.

Manufacturing firms have many types of inventory: for example, finished goods, work in process, raw materials and manufacturing supplies. Finished goods of a manufacturing company are comparable to the merchandise of a non-manufacturing company. Excluded from inventory are long-term assets subject to depreciation and depreciable fixed assets retired from regular use and held for sale. Raw materials which become part of a finished product become part of that inventory cost. Trade practices and materiality are usually the determining factors in either inventorying production supplies on hand or expensing them as part of product costs.

In accounting for inventories we try to match appropriate costs against revenues. This gives a proper determination of realized income. Another way of putting it is to say that by applying the best method of costing inventory, we are measuring out "cost of goods sold," by associating cause and effect.

Inclusion of Goods in Inventory Should Follow the Legal Rule of Title

Whatever the location of goods, if title is legally held by the company, the goods should be included in inventory. If title to the goods has passed to a customer, the goods should not be included in inventory.

Cost of Inventory

The primary basis of accounting for inventories is cost. This means the sum of the expenditures and charges, directly or indirectly, incurred in bringing the inventory to its existing condition and location.

As applied to inventories, cost means acquisition and production costs. However, there are many items which, although related to inventory, are not included in the cost of the inventory: for example, idle facility expense, excessive spoilage, double freight, rehandling costs. If these costs are abnormal, they should be treated as expenses of the current period rather than carried forward as part of the inventory cost. General and administrative expenses should be treated as expenses of the period. Likewise, selling expenses should not be included in inventory. The cost of inventory, however, should include an applicable portion of manufacturing overhead. The exclusion of *all* overhead from inventory cost is not an acceptable accounting procedure.

Cost, however, *must not* be used when the market value of inventory items is lower than the cost.

Flow of Cost Assumptions

Costs for inventory may be determined under any one of several assumptions as to the flow of costs; for example, FIFO, average, and LIFO. The method selected should be the one which most clearly reflects periodic income.

The "flow of costs" and "flow of goods" are usually not the same. But we use a "flow of cost"—such as FIFO, average, or LIFO—because to identify the cost of a specific item sold is often impossible, impractical, or even misleading. Where similar goods are purchased at different prices at different times, it would be difficult to identify specific goods sold except in a case of valuable jewelry, automobiles, pianos or other large items. Even perpetual inventory records would not make identification possible. Therefore, an assumption is made with respect to the flow of costs in order to provide a practical basis for measuring period income.

LIFO is considered an appropriate method for pricing inventory during extended inflationary periods, when costs continue accelerating. When the economy is deflationary or relatively stable, the FIFO or average methods is usually preferred by management. Practices of the other companies in the same industry should also be considered. Financial statements would be more useful if all companies within a given industry used uniform methods of inventory pricing.

The method used must be consistently applied and disclosed in financial statements. (See Disclosures and Restatements in this text.)

LIFO TERMINOLOGY

The accounting terminology for LIFO inventory accounting is unique to the topic. The appropriate definitions of terms follow.

Base Year: The year in which LIFO was adopted for a particular item or pool of items.

Base-Year Cost Of An Item: The average cost of the item at the beginning of the base year.

Base-Year Cost Of a Pool: The current year quantity of all items in a pool, priced at base-year cost.

Curent Costs: The cost basis of items may be determined by reference to actual cost of goods purchased or produced:

- Most recently in the year.
- Earliest in the year.
- Throughout the year.
- Any method which in the Commissioner's opinion clearly reflects income.

Decrement: A decrease in an inventory pool at base-year prices.

Dollar-Value Method: A method for pricing inventory that uses comparison of total dollars in inventory adjusted for price level changes, rather than a comparison of specific items. This method applies the double-extension technique, the link-change technique, and the LIFO retail method (these methods defined below).

Double-Extension Index: When applied to a pool, as used in the dollar-value method, is a measure of the change in the value of the ending inventory between the base year and the current year. The index is obtained by dividing the current year by the base year.

Double-Extension Technique: The approach by which an index is developed by double pricing the ending inventory at base-year cost and at current-year cost.

Double Pricing: The procedure of costing items in the ending inventory pool of a given year at both current-year cost and the cost of a prior year, either the base year or immediately prior year.

Increment: An increase in a pool at base-year prices.

Index-Method: The use of a LIFO index by reference to outside sources or by double pricing a statistical or judgmental sample.

Item: A classification of either an inventoriable product or the raw material cost component of the LIFO inventory.

LIFO Cost Layer: An increase in the LIFO value of a pool in a given year resulting from an increase in total base-year cost multiplied by the current-year LIFO index.

LIFO Reserve: The difference between the FIFO cost and LIFO cost of an item or pool.

LIFO Retail Method: This method combines the LIFO dollar-value method with the retail inventory method resulting in the determination of LIFO inventory increments or decrements in terms of base-year retail value rather than base-year cost.

Link-Chain Technique: The technique of developing a cumulative index by double pricing the ending inventory at current-year costs and beginning-of-year costs instead of base-year costs as for the double-extension techniques.

Natural Business Unit: A manufacturer or processor ordinarily engaged in the entire production of one product line, or two or more related product lines.

Pool: A group of similar items of inventory accounted for as a unit under the dollar-value method.

Raw Materials Content Pool: A pool of raw materials, including raw materials in work-in-process and finished goods.

Specific Indentification Method: A comparison of the quantity of a specific item in the ending inventory with the quantity of the same item in the beginning inventory. This is also called the *Unit Method.*

First-In, First-Out (FIFO)

This is probably the most common method of valuing inventories. The latest costs are assigned to the goods on hand; thus, the earliest costs become the costs of the goods sold. The theory here is that goods are disposed of in the same order as acquired.

Here is a simple illustration of FIFO. Opening inventory and purchases during the year were as follows:

Opening inventory	1,000 units at $10, or	$10,000
First purchase	800 units at $11, or	8,800
Second purchase	500 units at $14, or	7,000
Third purchase	400 units at $12, or	4,800
Fourth purchase	300 units at $13, or	3,900
Totals	3,000	$34,500

The closing inventory consists of 1,100 units. Under the FIFO method of costing, the closing inventory is considered to be made up of:

300 units of the fourth purchase (at $13)	$3,900
400 units of the third purchase (at $12).	4,800
400 units of the second purchase (at $14).	5,600
Cost of 1,100 units in closing inventory	$14,300

Last-In, First-Out (LIFO)

In recent years, LIFO has become a very popular method. In years of rising prices and high taxes, the LIFO method keeps profits (and taxes) down. It has the virtue of applying the current price structure to the cost of goods sold, thus matching the high price structure of the sales with the high price structure of costs.

The basic approach to LIFO costing is to assign the *earliest* costs to the *closing* inventory, as if the latest-acquired items were the first sold. For example, if we use the figures set forth above in the FIFO illustration, the costs of our closing inventory of 1,100 units under the LIFO costing approach would be:

1,000 units of the opening inventory (at $10).	$10,000
100 units of the first purchase (at $11)	1,100
Cost of 1,100 units in closing inventory	$11,100

Note that the 100-unit incremental increase over the inventory might, in the LIFO method, have been valued under *any* one of the following four options:

1) In the order of acquisition (as illustrated)
2) At the most recent purchase cost
3) At an average cost for the year
4) At the "dollar-value" method which converts the incremental increase by means of an index based on the LIFO base year prices.

Average Costs

A weighted average is sometimes used to determine the cost of the closing inventory. This method is generally not approved for tax purposes. Under the weighted average method, you determine an average unit cost and then multiply that average unit cost by the number of units in the closing inventory. To get the weighted average, the number of units in each purchase is multiplied by the unit price for that purchase. And the total units purchased and the total of all purchase costs are added to the units and costs in the opening inventory. Then the total of all the costs is divided by the total of all the units. The resulting figure is the average cost per unit.

For example, in the FIFO illustration above, the total number of units involved in the opening inventory plus the four purchases was 3,000. The total cost of the 3,000 units was $34,500. Dividing $34,500 by 3,000, results in an average cost per unit of $11.50. Since our closing inventory consisted of 1,100 units, if we priced it at average cost (1,100 × $11.50), the cost of our closing inventory would be $12,650.

Thus, depending on the method of cost used, our closing inventory could have been $11,100, $12,650, or $14,300.

The Retail Inventory Method

This method of inventory pricing is sometimes most practical and appropriate. It is used principally by retail establishments. This inventory valuation has as its initial starting point the retail or selling price of the merchandise rather than the cost. It arrives finally at the cost valuation entirely on the basis of average relationships of retail and cost figures over the period involved.

When merchandise is purchased, the retail selling price is placed on the price tag attached. At inventory time, the inventory is taken at the selling price. The cost is then arrived at by multiplying the inventory by the cost complement percentage, which is the difference between the mark-up % and 100%. It is arrived at as follows:

	Cost	Retail	Mark-up	Mark-up %	Cost Complement %
Beginning inventory	$ 50,000	$ 75,000	$ 25,000	33⅓%	66⅔%
Purchases	72,000	120,000	48,000	40 %	60 %
Total to Date	122,000	195,000	73,000	37.4%	62.6%
Markdowns		3,000	3,000		
Total to Date	$122,000	$192,000	$ 70,000	36.5%	63.5%
Sale for period		95,000			
Ending inventory		$ 97,000			

At the end of the period, the retail inventory of $97,000 will be reduced to cost by applying the cost complement percent of 63.5. Thus, the inventory figure at cost is $61,595.

The gross margin tabulation follows:

Sales		$ 95,000
Opening inventory	$ 50,000	
Purchases	72,000	
	122,000	
Closing inventory	61,595	
Cost of sales		60,405
Gross margin		$ 34,595

Lower of Cost or Market

A departure from cost basis of pricing inventory is *required* when the disposal of the goods in the ordinary course of business will be at less than cost. This calls for valuing the inventory at the lower of cost or market.

As used in the phrase, "lower of cost or market," market means current replacement cost (by purchase or reproduction) with the exception that: 1) market is not to exceed the net realizable value which is the estimated selling price in the ordinary course of business less reasonably predictable costs of completion and disposal, and 2) market should not be less than net realizable value reduced by an allowance for a normal profit margin. Here, for example, are the prices to be used in carrying out the lower of cost or market concept (the price to be used in each case is the one in boldface):

		1	2	3	4	5
1)	Cost	**.82**	.95	.95	**.78**	.94
2)	Market-cost to replace at inventory date	.86	**.90**	.80	.75	.94
3)	Selling price less estimated cost to complete and sell	.92	.92	.92	.92	**.92**
4)	Selling price less estimated cost to complete and sell and normal profit margin	.83	.83	.83	.83	.83

In applying the cost or market rule, no loss should be recognized unless the evidence indicates clearly that a loss has been sustained. Where evidence indicates that cost will be recovered with a normal profit margin upon the sale of merchandise, no loss should be recognized even though replacement cost is lower. It should also be remembered that pricing goods at the lower of cost or market is not to be followed literally in all cases. Rather, it is to be applied realistically with regard to the form, content, and composition of the inventory.

There are three ways of applying the lower-of-cost-or-market rule: The rule may be applied on 1) each item in the inventory, 2) the total cost of the major categories in the inventory, or 3) the cost of the entire inventory.

Each of these methods would produce different results, and all of them are considered acceptable for financial statement purposes. The method used should be the one which most clearly reflects periodic income. For example, if there is only one product, rule 3) would seem to have the greatest significance. Where there is more than one major product, rule 2) would seem to be the most useful. Rule 1), application of the lower of cost or market to each item of inventory, is the most common in practice.

When substantial and unusual losses result under the cost or market rule, it is desirable to disclose them separately from normal cost of goods sold.

Any procedure adopted for the treatment of inventory items should be applied consistently and disclosed in the financial statement. Without such consistency there is no basis with which to compare the results of one year with another. Any change in the basis of stating inventories will probably have an important effect on the statements, and full disclosure of such a change should be made.

There are some instances when inventories are properly stated above cost. Exceptions are made in the case of precious metals (e.g., gold and silver), agricultural or mineral products or the packing industry.

Where a company has firm purchase commitments for goods in inventory, losses which are expected to arise from such uncancellable and unhedged commitments for future purchase of inventory should be reflected in the current period in the same way as losses on inventory.

LIFO CONFORMITY RULE (IRS TITLE: "REPORT RULE")

If a company adopts LIFO for tax purposes, then LIFO *must* be applied for determining income, profit (or loss) for financial reporting purposes. IRS regulations do permit a few exceptions to the conformity rule:

1) The use of an inventory method other than LIFO when the taxpayer is presenting information as a supplement, or an explanation of the taxpayer's primary presentation of income in financial reports to outside parties. The supplemental information must be in notes to the financial statements, not in the body of the income statement.

2) An inventory method other than LIFO can be used to determine the value of the taxpayer's inventory for reporting the value of the inventory as an asset on the balance sheet.

3) An inventory method other than LIFO can be used for information reported in internal management reports.

4) The application of an inventory method other than LIFO for financial reports for a period of less than one year.

5) The use of LIFO lower-of-cost-or-market valuation of inventories when applying LIFO for tax purposes.

The Code also includes a rule covering related corporations. All members of the same group of *financially* related corporations shall be treated as a single taxpayer when applying the conformity rule. Formerly, the rule enabled taxpayers to circumvent the conformity rule by having a subsidiary on LIFO, while the non-LIFO parent presented combined non-LIFO financial statements. The Code considers this treatment a violation of the conformity requirement. One exception resulting from a Tax Court case is allowable for tax and reporting purposes. Parent corporations can convert their inventories to the *moving-average method* in the consolidated annual report to shareholders. The Court ruled that the conformity rule is satisfied because the financial report is *not* attributable to the subsidiaries, so the right of the subsidiaries to use the LIFO method in a consolidated tax return is allowable.

The IRS permits companies on LIFO to explain the inventory amount on the balance sheet and the primary presentation of income by disclosing what income would have been had another inventory method been used.

Example:	Inventory on FIFO method	$1,000
	Less adjustment to LIFO method	500
		$ 500

When a company discloses what its income would have been under an alternative inventory valuation method, the company should state the reasons for the disclosure. One reason, for example, might be to enable users of the financial statements to compare the company's reported income with that of other companies in the industry.

During the period of double-digit inflation there was widespread adoption of the LIFO inventory method, changing from FIFO and other methods. The objective is to charge the most current inventory costs against sales revenues, or closer compliance with the matching principle. The Code provides taxpayers with an election to account for inventories under the LIFO method, the essence of which is the requirement that companies electing LIFO for tax purposes cannot use another method of inventory valuation for purposes of reporting income, profit or loss in credit statements, financial reports to shareholders, partners, or other proprietors or beneficiaries. This is the essential requirement of the conformity rule.

There are a number of exceptions permitted by the Code where another method of inventory valuation can be used without violating compliance with the conformity rule.

1) As a supplement to or explanation of the primary presentation in statements of income for a taxable year, *but not on the face of the income statement.*

2) To ascertain the value of inventory of specified goods on hand for purposes of reporting such value on the balance sheet.

3) For purposes of information reported in internal management reports.

4) Market value may be used each year in lieu of the LIFO cost assigned to inventory items for federal income tax reporting when the market value is *less than* the LIFO cost.

In defining what will be considered supplemental or explanatory information, and therefore allowed to be shown, the regulations provide that information reported on the face of the income statement cannot be included in order to eliminate all parenthetical information being considered supplemental by the user of the statements. Hence, the regulation explicitly spells out that the footnotes to the statement are not a part of the face of the statement. This allows another method of inventory valuation to be used and disclosed in a footnote, but cost of goods sold using the FIFO method cannot be disclosed parenthetically. The footnote disclosures should be issued with the income statement as part of a single report.

A company that changes to LIFO is required to explain the change and its effect on earnings. The following is a sample of a footnote:

> "In order not to overstate profits as a result of inflation during the year, the company changed its method of accounting for inventory from First-in, First-out to Last-in, First-out. This was necessary because of the rapid increase in prices in recent years which caused inventories sold to be replaced at substantially higher prices. The effect of the change was to decrease reported earnings by $XXX,XXX, or $X.XX per share."

Another example:

> "The company has changed its method of accounting for inventories to Last-in, First-Out (LIFO) method. This was done because the rapid increase in prices during the year would result in an overstatement of profits if use of the First-in, First-out (FIFO) method were continued since inventories sold were replaced at substantially higher prices. The effect on reported earnings of the change for the year was a decrease of $XXX,XXX, or $X.XX per share."

It is worth repeating that any supplementary information on the face of the income statement *other than footnotes* is a violation of the conformity rule. For column format, for example, one for LIFO earnings and the other for FIFO earnings for comparative purposes would be a violation.

Earnings information on a FIFO basis is more representative of actual performance than LIFO-based information. This is of special concern when a company has recently changed to LIFO under the presumption that LIFO is the preferable method for this particular situation. An addition to the above footnote could read

> "Many of the company's competitors use the FIFO method of inventory valuation. Had the company reported its LIFO inventories under the FIFO method, and had a 44 percent tax rate been applied to changes in income, *and had no other assumptions been made as to changes in income* (emphasis added), net income for 19XX would have been $XXX,XXX ($X.XX per share) and for 19XX $XXX,XXX ($X.XX per share)."

This addition to the footnote disclosure is informative because items in the financial statements other than just income tax expense could change as a result of the difference in earnings using FIFO rather than LIFO. Accordingly, the point specified in the phrase "and had no other assumptions been made as to changes in income" is a significant qualification.

Under the current rule, companies are encouraged, but are not required, by the conformity rule to disclose on a pro forma basis the effect on earnings that LIFO would have had if applied in the year prior to the actual change to LIFO. The reason is there was no conformity problem since LIFO was not used for tax purposes in the year preceding its adoption.

MARKETABLE SECURITIES

The traditional precept of stating assets at historical costs has, in the area of marketable equity securities, been changed by the AICPA. Effective for statements ending on or after December 31, 1975, marketable securities are to be shown at the *lower* of historical cost or current market value (statement date), through the use of offsetting valuation allowance accounts (separated as to current and noncurrent).

There are several ramifications to be considered in accomplishing this periodic write-down (or possible write-up) to historical costs:

1) Management decides whether to classify securities as current or noncurrent assets, *generally* basing the classification upon its intent or non-intent of one-year disposition.

2) All current equity securities held are considered to be a single portfolio. All noncurrent equity securities are considered to be another single portfolio.

3) In unclassified balance sheets, securities are considered to be noncurrent.

4) Entire portfolios are considered to be *one unit* for the purpose of determining the overall lump-sum value to be shown. This entails an *item-by-item comparison* between *cost* and *market price* for each holding. When an *entire* portfolio's market value sinks *below* its cost (some holdings may be *over* cost), a valuation allowance account is *credited* for the difference (and serves as an offsetting asset account for net balance sheet display purposes)-with the *debit* for the unrealized loss going to:

   a) An *income* statement unrealized loss account for those securities in the *current* portfolio;

   b) An *equity section* unrealized loss account for those securities in the *noncurrent* portfolio. This account is a separate (debit) component of retained earnings and is shown in the Statement of Retained Earnings, or in the more expansive Statement of Stockholders' Equity.

5) At each subsequent year end, the new market values are compared again with cost, and the valuation allowance accounts for the entire portfolios are adjusted for:

   a) Further declines, or

   b) Increases up to, but not exceeding, cost.

6) When securities are sold, the difference between *cost* and *selling price* becomes an income statement *realized* gain or loss, the asset cost being deleted from the portfolio and the valuation allowance account at year end being subsequently adjusted to reflect the temporary decline in the market value of the remaining securities held.

7) Permanent declines should be reflected immediately upon discovery as an income statement realized loss and a reduction of the asset cost account. The newly reflected written-down cost-basis becomes the portfolio value, and it should not be changed for later recoveries in market value.

8) When reclassifying portfolios from one category to another (current to noncurrent or vice-versa), permanent entries should be made to reflect the change as of the date of reclassification.

9) Timing differences should be recognized unless there is reasonable doubt that unrealized losses will be offset by subsequent capital gains.

10) Disclosure is required.

11) *No* restatement of prior year is necessary.

12) *Not* mandatory for not-for-profit organizations, except investor-owned hospitals.

13) *Not* applicable to immaterial items.

14) Equity securities do not include bonds, treasury stock, or redeemable preferred stock.

15) Does *not* pertain to those holdings treated under the equity method.

16) See illustrative journal entries in Appendix A.

Marketable securities are securities that can be sold readily because of an established market, i.e., securities listed on a national securities exchange or traded regularly in the over-the-counter market. The Marketable Securities classification (a current asset) in a statement of financial condition includes U.S. government securities and corporate stocks and bonds. The accounting entries when an investment is made are:

Marketable Securities	XXX	
Cash		XXX

If the securities are sold at a gain:

Cash	XXX	
Marketable Securities		XXX
Gain on Sale of		
Marketable Securities		XXX

If the securities are sold at a loss:

Cash	XXX	
Loss on Sale of Marketable		
Securities	XXX	
Marketable Securities		XXX

CLASSIFICATION OF NON-CURRENT ASSETS

Noncurrent assets are assets which have a useful life of more than one accounting period. Equipment, land and buildings are examples of this category.

EQUIPMENT AND PLANT—ACQUISITIONS AND DISPOSITIONS

Acquisitions

Assets acquired in exchanges are measured at the exchange price, that is, acquisition cost. Money and money claims are measured at their face amount or sometimes at their discount amount.

In exchanges in which neither money nor promises to pay money are exchanged, the assets acquired are generally measured at the fair value of the assets given up. However, if the fair value of the assets received is more clearly evident, the assets acquired are measured at that amount.

Under the above standards, equipment and plant are therefore valued:

1) At cost, if purchased for cash or its equivalent, or
2) If an exchange of non-cash property is involved (wholly or partially), preferably at the fair value of the asset acquired, or, if that is not clearly evident, of the asset surrendered (an example of the latter would be the use of the market price of the company's own stock given in exchange for an asset whose fair value cannot reasonably be determined), or
3) If a group of assets is acquired in one exchange, the total price is allocated to the individual assets based on their relative fair values. Excess

paid over fair value is treated as goodwill. In the opposite case, any excess of fair value of the assets acquired over the exchange price is used to reduce the value of the non-current assets (except investment securities) proportionately.

Dispositions

Decreases in assets are recorded when assets are disposed of in exchanges.

Decreases in assets are measured by the recorded amounts that relate to the assets. The amounts are usually the historical or acquisition costs of the assets (as adjusted for amortization and other charges).

The disposal of equipment and plant assets usually results in a gain or loss and is reported as such on the financial statements. In an exchange, for financial purposes, losses should be recognized, but gains should be used to adjust the basis of the new acquisition.

On straight dispositions, depreciation is usually calculated to the date of disposal (approximately) and both the accumulated depreciation and the asset account are then netted to the amount recovered to arrive at the gain or loss, which, for tax purposes may require special consideration, such as recapture of depreciation and investment tax credits.

Other Considerations

Self-constructed assets should not be depreciated while under construction. The cost basis should be determined not only by the material and labor expended, but also by apportionment of overhead items, such as depreciation on any fixed assets used in that construction process (which application in turn reduced the depreciation expense for that particular fixed asset).

Detailed sub-ledgers or worksheets should be maintained for all fixed assets, showing date acquired, cost or basis, investment tax credit, estimated life, salvage value (if any), depreciation taken by year, accumulated depreciation and gains or losses on dispositions or trade-in information.

Appraisal write-ups are contrary to generally accepted accounting principles, but when circumstances necessitate write-ups, the offset goes to "appraisal surplus" and becomes part of the equity capital. Depreciation then must be based on the higher, appraisal values.

DEPRECIATION

If an asset provides benefit for several periods, its cost is allocated to the periods in a systematic and rational manner in the absence of a more direct basis for associating cause and effect . . . . This form of expense recognition always involves assumptions about the pattern of 'matching costs to benefits' because neither can be conclusively demonstrated.

Depreciation is the term applied to the allocation of a fixed asset's cost over its beneficial useful life. It is a method of accounting which aims to distribute the cost or other value of tangible or capital assets, less salvage (if any), over the estimated useful life of the asset (which may be a single asset or a group of assets in a single account) in a systematic and rational manner. It is a process of allocation, not of valuation, applied on a consistent basis.

Rather than increasing expenses immediately, depreciation might also *increase* other asset values temporarily, such as in the application of overhead depreciation to inventory or to self-constructed assets.

From a tax viewpoint, the deduction for depreciation (which requires no annual cash outlay) reduces the amount of tax to be paid. This has the effect of increasing the accumulation of cash available—i.e., the "cash flow."

Before determining the amount of depreciation deductions, the following three elements must be known: 1) the method of depreciation used, 2) the amount recovered (depreciable basis), and 3) the period over which deductions (useful life) can be taken.

The depreciation is usually applicable only to property which approaches, by wear and tear, business ineffectiveness. "Depreciation" and "repairs and maintenance" are not the same. It is necessary to distinguish between repairs and maintenance costs to keep the asset in operation and repairs which are capital expenditures and increase the life of the asset. The former are expense deductions in the year incurred; the latter must be amortized over the life of the asset. What repairs increase the life of the asset and what repairs are necessary for its operation is often a matter of judgment. Examples of repairs which are classified as capital expenditures are the costs of remodeling or reconditioning a building.

The determination, or estimation of useful life, may be based on: 1) IRS guidelines, such as in Bulletin F or ADR rules, basically determined by estimated physical durability, longevity or unit-productive capability; 2) statutory law, as in the case of a patent; 3) contract, as in the case of some leases; 4) utility, as in the case of an airport built for military training during war.

Although write-up of fixed assets to reflect appraisal, market or current values is not in accordance with GAAP, where such appreciation has been recorded, depreciation should be based on the written up amounts for financial statement purposes

Methods of Depreciation

Following the passage of the Internal Revenue Act of 1954, which permitted the use of the declining-balance and similar accelerated methods of depreciation, the AICPA stated such methods met the requirement of being systematic and rational and could be used for general accounting purposes, with appropriate disclosure to be made of any change in method when depreciation is a significant factor in determining net income.

The declining-balance and the sum-of-the-year-digits methods of depreciation are appropriate and most used in those cases where the expected productivity or revenue-earning power of an asset is greater during earlier years of life or when maintenance charges tend to increase during later years.

Accounting methods of depreciating assets may differ from tax methods used. It is the practice of many firms to use straight-line depreciation for accounting purposes and an accelerated one for tax purposes. When this happens, disclosure should be made of the timing differences.

Straight-line method. The depreciation expense is the same from period to period. The formula followed for this method is:

$$\text{Depreciation expense} \quad = \quad \frac{(\text{Cost} - \text{Salvage Value})}{\text{Estimated Life}}$$

For example, if the asset costs $10,000, has a salvage value of $100, and an estimated life of ten years, the depreciation expense for the year would be computed as follows:

$$\frac{(\$10,000 - \$100)}{10} \quad = \$990$$

The straight-line method depends upon the hypothesis that depreciation will be at a constant rate throughout the estimated life.

200%-Declining-balance method. Under this method (also called the double-declining-balance method), the amount of depreciation expense decreases from period to period. The largest depreciation deduction is taken in the first year. The amount then declines steeply over succeeding years until the final years of estimated useful life when the depreciation charge becomes relatively small. Code § 167 restricts the taxpayer to a rate not in excess of twice the straight-line rate if the straight-line method had been employed.

While true declining-balance method requires the application of a complex formula, if the maximum declining-balance depreciation is used—i.e., the 200% method—these mathematical computations are not needed. It is necessary to: 1) determine the straight-line percentage rate; 2) double it; 3) apply it against the full basis (undiminished by salvage value) to get the first year's deduction. In the second year it is necessary to: 1) reduce the basis by the previous year's depreciation deduction; 2) apply the same percentage rate to the new basis arrived at in step 1). In the third year and later years, the same process is repeated.

Example: A truck is bought for the business. It costs $5,500 and has a five-year useful life. Assume it is bought January 1, 1979. Since it has a five-year life, the percentage of depreciation by the straight-line method is 20%. Using 200%-declining-balance, a 40% rate is used. So, for 1979, the deduction is $2,200 (40% of $5,500). For 1980, the $5,500 basis (original cost) is reduced by the $2,200 1979 depreciation deduction. That gives a basis for 1980 of $3,300. For 1980, the depreciation deduction would be 40% of that $3,300, or $1,320. That cuts the basis for 1981 to $1,980 and the depreciation deduction for that year becomes $792 (40% of $1,980). This process continues on for the future years of holding this truck.

Sum-of-years-digits method. Here, diminishing rates, expressed fractionally, are applied to the total depreciable value (cost—salvage).

Under sum-of-the-digits, the annual depreciation charge decreases rapidly; since maintenance charges, on the other hand, increase rapidly, the effect is to level off the annual costs of depreciation and maintenance.

To use sum-of-the-digits, proceed as follows. Using, for purposes of illustration, a depreciation account of $5,500 with a 10-year life and ignoring salvage, add the numbers of the years: $10 + 9 + 8 + 7 + 6 + 5 + 4 + 3 + 2 + 1 = 55$. Depreciation the first year will be 10/55 of $5,500, or $1,000. For the remaining years, follow one of two practices. Either continue to base depreciation on original cost, using 55 as the denominator of the fraction and the number of the year as the numerator—9/55 of $5,500, 8/55 of $5,500, and so on, or apply a fraction with a diminishing denominator to unrecovered cost—9/45 of $4,500, 8/36 of $3,600, and so on.

Note that in the second method, the amount by which the denominator for a given year diminishes is always the amount of the numerator for the preceding year. Denominator 45 in the second year is denominator 55 for the first year, less numerator 10 for the first year; denominator 36 for year 3 is denominator 45 for year 2, less numerator 9 for year 2.

Regardless of which method is used, annual depreciation will be the same: 9/55 of $5,500 and 9/45 of $4,500 both give $900 of depreciation; 8/55 of $5,500 and 8/36 of $3,600 both give depreciation of $800.

Sinking-fund method. The sinking-fund method of computing depreciation has been generally preferred by independent businesspeople. An imaginary sinking fund is established by a uniform end-of-year annual deposit throughout the useful life of the asset. The assets are assumed to draw interest at some stated rate, e.g., 6%, sufficient to balance the fund with the cost of the asset minus estimated salvage value. The amount charged to depreciation expense in any year consists of sinking fund plus the interest on the imaginary accumulated fund. The book value of the asset at any time is the initial cost of the asset minus the amount accumulated in the imaginary fund.

Assume that an asset costs $1,000 and has no salvage value but has an estimated life of 25 years. The interest rate is assumed to be 6%. By using conversion tables, the sinking fund deposit is $1,000 x .01823 or $18.23. In the second year, the depreciation charge will be $18.23 + ($18.23 x .06) = $19.32; in the third year, it will be $18.23 + ($18.23 + $19.32) x .06 = $20.48, and so forth. The $18.23 represents the sinking fund deposit and remains the same for the period of depreciation. In other words, under this method the businessman or woman anticipates earnings and profits on capital investment and thus increases capital.

This method is permissible for Federal income tax purposes provided it does not exceed the rate as computed under the declining-balance method, during the first two-thirds of the asset life.

Units-of-production method. This method is used for the depreciation of assets used in production. Under this method, an estimate is made of the total number of units the machine may be expected to produce during its life. Cost less salvage value, if any, is then divided by the estimated total production to determine a depreciation charge for each unit of production. The depreciation for each year is obtained by multiplying the depreciation charge per unit by the number of units produced. Here's how it works on a $10,600 machine good for 300,000 units of output:

$$R = \frac{\text{Cost - Salvage Value}}{\text{Estimated Units}}$$

$$R = \frac{\$10,600 - \$600}{300,000}$$

$$R = \$.03 \tfrac{1}{3}$$

Units produced for 1 year = 24,000
Depreciation = 24,000 × $.03 $\tfrac{1}{3}$ = $800

A severe obstacle to the use of this method is the difficulty of ascertaining the total number of units which the asset will produce. The production method is most applicable to fixed assets like airplane engines, automobiles, and machinery where wear is such an important factor. It is useful for fixed assets that are likely to be exhausted prematurely by accelerated or abnormal use.

BASIS

Normally, the basis for depreciation (i.e., the capital amount on which depreciation deductions are figured) is what was paid for property. To the cost of the property itself is added the cost of transporting the property to the premises, the cost of installation, and acquisition related costs.

For tax purposes, the basis for depreciation can be different from the basis used for financial reporting purposes. This difference often arises when there are trade-ins involved. According to GAAP, the entity paying any monetary consideration on a trade-in should recognize losses immediately, but, for gains, should adjust the basis of the acquisition to the extent of the gain. For tax purposes, neither gain nor loss is usually recognized, with neither serving to adjust the basis of the new acquisition. Hence, there may be a timing difference with respect to the different bases used for depreciation.

Allocation of Basis

When property is acquired, it is often necessary to allocate basis. These are the instances when allocation is necessary:

1) When improved real estate is purchased, there must be an allocation made as to land (nondepreciable, because land doesn't wear out) and buildings;
2) When more than one asset is purchased for a lump sum;
3) When a group of assets (or possibly a business) is purchased for a single sum involving depreciable and nondepreciable assets.

Improved real estate. Whenever a piece of improved real property is acquired, there is an immediate need for an allocation. Land is not depreciable; and in order to determine the basis for depreciating the building, the overall basis is reduced by an amount which represents a reasonable basis for the land. The usual method of making the allocation is in proportion to the respective fair market values.

If proportionately more has been paid for the building for some special reason and the fact can be established, the higher amount can be used as the depreciation basis. The best way to secure such an advantage, however, is by specific allocation in the contract which spells it out in detail.

If any of the contents of the building are included in the purchase transaction, further allocation is needed between the structure and the contents. Then the amount allocated to the contents must be further broken down among the various items which are included in the sale.

This latter allocation may require all parties to consider the investment credit and depreciation recapture provisions of the tax law.

Acquisition of more than one asset. In the purchase of more than one asset (mixed assets) the same rules which have been discussed above apply. The cost of a group of assets which is stated as a single sum must be broken down and allocated among the separate items or groups. This permits the proper allocation of useful lives to different assets or groups, and separates depreciable from nondepreciable assets. Again, the possible effects of the investment credit and depreciation recapture provisions must be watched.

Appraisal

Accounting for an appraisal write-up
   Building 350,000
      Appraisal Capital 350,000
      (Equity Section. Raises building from
      cost of 400,000 to appraised value of 750,000)

Year 2
Depreciation Building $21,667
      Accumulated Depreciation-Building $21,667
Depreciation based on *appraised value:* $400,000 for
40 years; $350,000 for 30 years. Building 10 years old
at time of appraisal.

What can be depreciated?   Depreciable property is property for which a depreciation deduction is allowed. Many different kinds of property can be depreciated; for example, machinery, buildings, vehicles, patents, copyrights, furniture, and equipment. Property is depreciable if it meets the following requirements:

1) It must be used in business or held for the production of income.
2) It must have a determinable life, and that life must be longer than one year.
3) It must be something that wears out, decays, gets used up, becomes obsolete, or loses value from natural causes.

If property does not meet all three of these conditions, it is not depreciable.

Depreciable property can be tangible or intangible. Tangible property is any property that can be seen or touched. Intangible property is property, such as a copyright or franchise, that is not tangible. Depreciable property can be *real* or *personal*. Personal property is property, such as machinery or equipment, that is not real estate. Real property is land and generally anything that is erected on, growing on, or attached to land. However, land itself is never depreciable.

Depreciation can be deducted on tangible property only if it can wear out, decay, or lose value from natural causes; be used up; or become obsolete. Intangible property can be depreciated if its useful life can be determined. The straight-line method must be used. Patents and copyrights are two kinds of intangible property that can be depreciated. The useful life is granted by the government for a patent or copyright. If a patent or copyright becomes valueless in any year before it expires, the undepreciated cost or other basis can be deducted in that tax year.

It should be noted that *goodwill* is not depreciable because its useful life cannot be determined.

When to claim depreciation.   A business can begin to claim depreciation on property when it is placed in service in a trade or business or for the production of income. Depreciation of property is continued until the basis in the property is recovered, disposed of, or use of the property for business or investment purposes has stopped.

Depreciation not deducted.   If, in an earlier year, depreciation was not claimed for property for which deduction could have been taken, the basis of the property must be reduced by the amount of the depreciation that was not deducted. The unclaimed depreciation cannot be deducted in the current year, or in any later tax year. However, the depreciation for an earlier year can be claimed on an amended return. The amended return must be filed within three years from the date the original return was filed, or within two years from the time the tax was paid, whichever is later.

Section 179 deduction.   All or part of the cost of certain qualifying property can be treated as an expense rather than as a capital expenditure. The taxpayer decides for each item of qualifying property whether to deduct, subject to the yearly limit, or capitalize and depreciate a property's cost. If an election is made for a deduction, a limited amount of the cost of qualifying property purchased for use in a trade or business is deductible in the first year the property is placed in service. For the 179 deduction, property is considered placed in service in the tax year in which the property is first placed in a condition or state of readiness and availability for a specifically assigned function, whether in a trade or business, in the production of income, in a tax-exempt or personal activity.

The determination of whether property is qualifying property is made in the first year the property is placed in service. Therefore, if property is placed in service in a tax year and the property does not qualify for the Section 179 deduction, no 179 deduction is ever allowed on the property even though the property becomes qualifying property in a later tax year.

Example: In 1989 a new car is purchased and used entirely for personal purposes. In 1994 the car is used in a trade or business. No Section 179 deduction is allowed for the car. The car was placed in service in 1989 when it was used for personal purposes.

Qualifying property.   A Section 179 deduction can be claimed on depreciable property that is Section 38 property and that is purchased for use in the active conduct of a trade or business. Property held merely for the production of income cannot be deducted. The following property does not qualify for a Section 179 deduction:

1) Property acquired by one member of a controlled group from another component member of the same group.

2) Property acquired from another person and the basis in that property is determined in whole or in part by reference to the adjusted basis of the property in the hands of the person from whom the property was acquired, or under the stepped-up basis rules for property acquired from a decedent.

3) Property acquired from a related person if the relationship to the related person would result in the disallowance of losses.

Section 38 property.   Section 38 property is property with a useful life of at least three years. It includes:

1) Tangible personal property (except heating or air-conditioning units).

2) Other tangible property, except most buildings and their structural components.

3) Elevators and escalators built or acquired new.

4) Single purpose livestock or horticultural structures.

5) Storage facilities (excluding buildings and their structural components) that are used in connection with distribution of petroleum or any primary product of petroleum.

Tangible personal property.   Tangible personal property is tangible property *other than* real property. Machinery and equipment are examples of tangible personal property.

Land and land improvements, such as buildings and other permanent structures and their components, are real property and, therefore, do not qualify as tangible personal property. For the same reason, swimming pools, paved parking areas, wharfs, docks, bridges, fences, and similar property also do not qualify as tangible personal property.

All business property, other than structural components, contained in or attached to a building is tangible personal property. Some property that is tangible personal property under local law may not qualify as tangible personal property for Section 179 purposes, and some property that may be real property under local law, such as fixtures, may be considered tangible personal property for Section 179 purposes. Transportation and office equipment, printing presses, testing equipment, and signs are tangible personal property. A car or truck used in a business also qualifies.

Section 38 property *does not* include:

1) Buildings and structural components.
2) Property used for lodging.
3) Certain property used predominantly outside the United States.
4) Property used by a tax-exempt organization other than a farmer's cooperative unless it is used predominantly to produce unrelated business taxable income which is subject to tax.
5) Certain property completed outside the United States or property for which less than 50% of the basis is attributable to value added within the United States.
6) Property used primarily for lodging. This includes most property used in the operation of an apartment house and most other facilities where sleeping accommodations are provided and rented (property used by a hotel, motel, inn, or similar establishment that primarily serves *transient guests*, i.e., the rental period is normally less than 30 days) or property used in nonlodging commercial facilities, such as a restaurant.

MACRS—Assets Placed in Service After 1986

The *modified accelerated cost recovery system* (MACRS), also referred to as the General Depreciation System or (GDS), applies to all tangible property placed in service after 1986. A business could have made a property-by-property election to use MACRS for tangible property placed in service after July 31, 1986, and before January 1, 1987.

Transition property.   Transition property must have a class life of at least 7 years or be residential rental or nonresidential real property that is placed in service *before*:

- 1989 if it has a class life of at least 7 but less than 20 years.
- 1991 if it has a class life of 20 years or more, or is residential rental or nonresidential real property.

To qualify it must be:

1) Property constructed, reconstructed, or acquired under a written contract that was binding on March 1, 1986.
2) Property constructed or reconstructed by the taxpayer if:
   a) The lesser of $1,000,000, or 5% of the cost of the property had been incurred or committed by March 1, 1986; *and*

b) The construction or reconstruction of the property began by March 1, 1986;

3) An equipped building or plant facility if construction was started by March 1, 1986, under a written specific plan and more than one-half of the cost had been incurred or committed by March 1, 1986.

A *plant facility* is a facility that does not include any building, or for which buildings are an insignificant portion, and that is:

1) A self-contained single operating unit or processing operation.

2) Located on a single site.

3) Identified as a single unitary project as of March 1, 1986.

Property classes under MACRS.   Each item of property depreciated under MACRS is assigned to a property class. The property classes establish the recovery periods over which the basis of items in a class are recovered. The classes of property are:

- 3-year property.
- 6-year property.
- 7-year property.
- 10-year property.
- 15-year property.
- 20-year property.
- Nonresidential real property.
- Residential rental property.

The class to which property is assigned is determined by its class life. The class life of an item of property determines its recovery period and the method of depreciation that is used. Class lives for most assets are listed in a table labeled *Table of Class Lives and Recovery Periods*. The table has a description of assets included in each asset class. At the end of each asset class description are listed the class life, the MACRS recovery period, and the alternate MACRS recovery period for the property described.

The asset class is first determined for an item of property by reading the description for the assets included in the asset class. Once the asset class into which the property fits has been determined, the MACRS recovery period assigned to that asset class is used. If the property does not fit into any of the asset classes, the property has not been assigned a class life. Property without a class life is assigned to the 7-year property recovery class

Example: X is a building contractor. In 1994 X purchased and placed a tractor in service in the business. Reading the tables, X's accountant comes to asset class 15.0 for construction assets. Since the class life is six years, the tractor is in the 5-year property class. The MACRS recovery period for the tractor is five years and the alternate MACRS recovery period is six years.

Recovery periods.   Under MACRS, tangible property that is placed in service after 1986, or after July 31, 1986, if elected, falls into one of the following classes:

- **3-year property.** This class includes property with a class life of four years or less. It includes tractor units for use over-the-road.
- **5-year property.** This class includes property with a class life of more than four years but less than ten years. It includes taxis, buses, heavy general purpose trucks, computers and peripheral equipment, and office machinery (typewriters, calculators, copiers, etc.), and any automobile, light general purpose trucks, and any property used in connection with research and experimentation.
- **7-year property.** This class includes property with a class life of ten years or more but less than 16 years. It includes office furniture and fixtures and any property that does not have a class life and that has not been designated by law as being in any other class.
- **10-year property.** This class includes property with a class life of 16 years; or more; but less than 20 years. It includes vessels, barges, tugs, and similar water transportation equipment and any single purpose agriculture or horticultural structure and any tree or vine bearing fruits or nuts.
- **15-year property.** This class includes property with a class life of 20 years or more but less than 25 years. It includes roads, shrubbery, wharves (if depreciable), and any municipal wastewater treatment plant.
- **20-year property.** This class includes any property with a class life of 25 years or more. It includes farm buildings and any municipal sewers.
- **Nonresidential property.** This class includes any real property that is not residential rental property and any real property that is section 1250 property with a class life of 27.5 years or more. This property is depreciated over 31.5 years.
- Residential rental property. This class includes any real property that is a rental building or structure (including mobile homes) for which 80% or more of the gross rental income for the tax year is rental income from dwelling units. If any part of the building or structure is occupied by the taxpayer, the gross rental income includes the fair rental value of the part the taxpayer occupies. This property is depreciated over 27.5 years.

A *dwelling unit* is a house or an apartment used to provide living accommodations in a building or structure, but does not include a unit in a hotel, motel, inn, or other establishment where more than half of the units are used on a transient basis.

For depreciation purposes, property is considered *placed in service* when it is in a condition or state of readiness and availability for a specifically assigned function whether in a trade or business, in the production of income, in a tax-exempt activity, or in a personal activity. However, depreciation applies only to property placed in service in a trade or business or in production of income. For example, if property is placed in service in a personal use, no depreciation would be allowable. If the use of the property is changed to a business or income producing activity, depreciation would begin at the time of the change in use.

Example 1: On November 22, 1989, Smith purchased a machine for his business. The machine was delivered on December 7, 1989. However, the machine was not installed and in operation until January 3, 1990. Since the machine was not operational until 1990, it is considered placed in service in 1990. If the machine had been ready for use when it was delivered in 1989, it would be considered placed in service in 1989, even if not actually used until 1990.

Example 2: On April 6, 1989, Jones purchased a house to use as residential rental property. Jones made extensive repairs to the house and had the house ready for rent on July 5, 1989, at which time Jones began to advertise the house for rent. Jones began to rent the house on September 1, 1989. The house is considered placed in service in July when it was ready and available for rent. Jones can begin to depreciate the house in July.

Computing MACRS deductions.   The MACRS deduction can be computed in one of two ways. It can actually be computed using the applicable depreciation method and convention over the recovery period. In the alternative, the MACRS percentage table can be used. One deduction is the same under both methods.

Depreciation methods.   For property in the 3-, 5-, 7-, or 10-year class, use the double (200%) declining balance method over 3, 5, 7, or 10 years and a half-year convention. For property in the 15- or 20-year class, use the 150% declining balance method over 15 or 20 years and a half-year convention. For these classes of property, change to the straight-line method for the first tax year for which that method when applied to the adjusted basis at the beginning of the year will yield a larger deduction. Always use the straight-line method and a midmonth convention for nonresidential real property and residential rental property.

Instead of using the declining balance method, the *straight-line method* can be elected with a half-year or midquarter convention over the recovery period. The election to use the straight-line method for a class of property applies to all property in that class that is placed in service during the tax year of the election. Once made, the election to use the straight-line method over the recovery cannot be changed.

Half-year convention.   Under MACRS, the half-year convention treats all property placed in service, or disposed of, during a tax year as placed in service, or disposed of, on the midpoint that tax year.

A half-year of depreciation is allowable for the first year property is placed in service, regardless of when the property is placed in service during the tax year. For each of the remaining years of the recovery period, a full year of depreciation can be taken. If the property is held for the entire recovery period, a half-year of depreciation is allowable for the year following the end of the recovery period. If the property is disposed of before the end of the recovery period, a half-year of depreciation is allowable for the year of disposition.

Midquarter convention.   If during any tax year the total basis of depreciable property placed in service during the last 3 months of that year exceed 40% of the total basis of all depreciable property placed in service during that tax year (whether or not all of the property is subject to MACRS) a midquarter convention is used instead of a half-year convention. In determining the total basis of the property, do not include basis of either:

- Residential rental property.
- Nonresidential real property.
- Property placed in service and disposed of in the same tax year.

Under a midquarter convention, all property placed in service, or disposed of, during any quarter of a tax year is treated as placed in service, or disposed of, on the midpoint of the quarter. To figure a MACRS deduction for property subject to the midquarter convention, first calculate the depreciation for the full tax year and then multiply by the following percentages for the quarter of the tax year the property is placed in service.

Quarter of the Tax Year	Percentage
First	87.5%
Second	62.5%
Third	37.5%
Fourth	12.5%

For nonresidential real and residential rental property, a midmonth convention is used in *all* situations. Under a midmonth convention all property placed in service, or disposed of, during any month is treated as placed in service, or disposed of, on the midpoint of that month.

ACRS—Assets Placed in Service After 1980 and Before 1987

ACRS (*accelerated cost recovery system*) was mandatory for most tangible depreciable assets placed in service after 1980 and before 1987. MACRS must be used for assets placed in service after 1986, except for transition property and certain excluded property.

ACRS allows a recovery of the unadjusted basis of recovery property over a recovery period. The property's recovery period is determined by the class life of the property. The class life of the property places it in a 3-, 5-, 10-, 15-, 18-, or 19-year class. A recovery percentage for each year of the recovery period is prescribed for figuring the ACRS deduction. The deduction is figured by multiplying the unadjusted basis of the property by the applicable recovery percentage.

ACRS cannot be used for property placed in service before 1981 or after 1986. ACRS also cannot be used for intangible depreciable property. For depreciation purposes, property is considered placed in service when it is in a condition or state of readiness and availability for a specifically assigned function whether in a trade or business, in the production of income, in a tax-exempt activity, or in a personal activity.

Depreciation-dispositions. A *disposition* is the permanent withdrawal of property from use in a trade or business or in the production of income. A withdrawal may be made by sale, exchange, retirement, abandonment, or destruction. A gain or loss is usually recognized on the disposition of an asset by sale. If property is physically abandoned, a loss can be deducted on the adjusted basis of the asset at the time of its abandonment. There must be an *intent* to discard the asset so that it will not be used again, retrieved for sale, exchange, or other disposition.

If an asset is disposed of before the end of its specified recovery period, it is referred to as an *early disposition*. When an early disposition occurs, the depreciation deduction in the year of disposition depends on the method of depreciation used for the property and the class of property involved. If depreciated under MACRS, a depreciation deduction for the year of disposition is allowed. The depreciation deduction for the year of disposition is determined by using a half-year, midquarter, or midmonth convention.

For residential rental and nonresidential real property, a midmonth convention is always used. For all other depreciated property under MACRS, either a half-year or midquarter convention is used depending on the convention that was used when the property was placed in service.

For property for which a half-year convention was used, the deduction for the year of disposition is half of the depreciation determined for the full year.

For property for which the midquarter convention was used, first determine the depreciation for the full year and then multiply by the following percentages for the quarter of the tax year in which the property was disposed of.

Quarter of the Tax Year	Percentage
First	12.5%
Second	37.5%
Third	62.5%
Fourth	87.5%

Depreciated recapture. All gain on the disposition of property, other than residential rental and nonresidential real property, depreciated under MACRS is recaptured as ordinary income to the extent of previously allowed depreciation deductions. For purposes of this rule, any Section 179 deduction claimed on the property is treated as depreciation. For residential rental and nonresidential real property, there is no recapture of previously allowed depreciation.

Property Under ACRS. A gain or loss will generally be recognized for property disposed of that is Section 1245 recovery property and depreciated under ACRS. Gain on the disposition is ordinary income to the extent of prior depreciation deductions taken. This recapture rule applies to all personal property in the 3-, 5-, and 10-year classes.

If Section 1250 real property is disposed of at a gain, the property is treated as Section 1245 recovery property; gain will be recognized as ordinary income to the extent of prior depreciation deductions taken. This rule applies to all Section 1250 real property *except*:

1) 15-, 18-,19-year real property that is residential rental property.
2) 15-, 18-, 19-year real property for which depreciation was elected using the ACRS method.
3) 15-, 18-, 19-year real property that is subsidized low-income housing.

For purposes of these recapture rules, the Section 179 deduction and 50% of the investment credit which reduced the basis are treated as depreciation.

Before the ACRS method was enacted, other depreciation methods were used. If property placed in service before 1981 does not qualify for

ACRS or MACRS, the methods in place must continue to be used; however, those methods cannot be used for property that qualifies for ACRS or MACRS.

There are many different methods of figuring depreciation that are acceptable. Any method is acceptable that is reasonable and applied consistently. The two most common methods used are the straight line method and the declining balance method. If ACRS or MACRS does not apply, either of these methods can be used. For both of these methods, three factors must first be determined:

1) The property's basis.
2) The property's useful life.
3) The property's estimated salvage value at the end of its useful life.

The amount of the depreciation deduction in any year will depend on which method of depreciation is applied. If the method of depreciation is changed, the change is usually the result of a change in accounting method. IRS approval of a change must be obtained, except a change from the declining balance method to the straight-line method at any time during the useful life of the property can be made without permission from the IRS. Once the change to the straight-line method is made, a change back to the declining balance method, or to any other method of depreciation, cannot be made for a period of 10 years without written permission from the IRS.

INTANGIBLE ASSETS

Intangible assets are a group of long-term assets that do not have physical existence or tangible form, but are considered to have value to the entity. Examples are patents, copyrights, trademarks, and goodwill.

Intangible assets are categorized into two classes:

1) Identifiable intangible assets—those having specific identity and usually a known limited life. The limitation may be a legal regulation, a contractual agreement or the nature of the intangible itself—for example, a patent, copyright, franchise, trademark and the like.
2) Unidentifiable intangible assets—those having no specific identity and an unknown life. Goodwill is the most notable example.

Identifiable intangible assets should be recorded at their cost. If the asset is acquired in a transaction other than a purchase for cash, it is to be valued at its fair value or the fair value of the consideration given, whichever is more definitely determinable. If several identifiable intangible assets are acquired as a group, a separate cost should be established for each intangible asset. The cost or assigned basis should be amortized by systematic charges to income over the expected period of economic benefit usually set by law or by contract. If it becomes apparent that the period of economic benefit will be shorter or longer than that originally used, there should be an appropriate decrease or increase in annual amortization charges.

The costs of *unidentifiable* intangible assets (such as goodwill) are normally amortized on a straight-line basis over a period not exceeding forty years. Arbitrary shorter periods are not to be used unless specific factors pinpoint a shorter life.

Unidentifiable intangible assets are usually measured as the excess paid over the identifiable assets.

The cost of an intangible asset, including goodwill acquired in a business combination, should not be written off to income in the period of acquisition nor charged as a lump sum to capital surplus or to retained earnings, nor be reduced to a nominal amount at or immediately after acquisition.

The question of whether other costs of internally developed identifiable intangible assets are to be capitalized or expensed is not delineated by the Standards Board. Questions have arisen regarding the capitalization of the cost of a large initial advertising campaign for a new product or capitalizing the cost of training new employees. The interpretation is that there is no encouragement to capitalize these costs under existing standards.

Expected Period of Benefit. Some intangibles have the length of their beneficial lives set by law, or contract. Patents have a beneficial life of 17 years. Copyrights are granted for the life of the creator plus 50 years. Trademarks have a legal life of 20 years, but can be renewed an indefinite number of times. A franchise can be for a definite period of time specified in a contract, as is a lease.

Separability from the Enterprise. Patents, copyrights, licenses, franchises, etc., are salable and therefore are separable from the business entity. Goodwill is a part of the enterprise and therefore is not separable.

RESEARCH AND DEVELOPMENT COSTS (AND PATENTS)

Under the latest standards of financial accounting and reporting for research and development costs adopted in October, 1974 (and the subsequent extensions of that section to cover applicability to business combinations accounted for by the "purchase" method, and applicability to computer software) research and development costs are to be *charged as expenses when incurred.* Note that this is diametrically opposed to the old system of deferral and amortization. Note also that in changing to the direct expense method, previously amortized "R & D" costs should be treated as prior period adjustments.

Research is planned search or critical investigation aimed at discovery of new knowledge with the hope that such knowledge will be useful in developing a new product or service or a new process or technique or in bringing about a significant improvement to an existing product or process.

Development is the translation of research findings or other knowledge into a plan or design for a new product or process or for a significant improvement to an existing product or process whether intended for sale or use. It includes the conceptual formulation, design and testing of product alternatives, construction of prototypes, and operation of pilot plants. It does not include routine or periodic alterations to existing products, production lines, manufacturing processes, and other on-going operations even though those alterations may represent improvements; and it does not include market research or market testing activities.

Typical activities which would be included in research and development costs (excluding those done for others under contract) are:

1) Laboratory research aimed at finding new knowledge.
2) Searching for applications of findings.
3) Concepts-forming and design of new product or processes.
4) Testing of above.
5) Modifications of above.
6) Design, construction and testing of prototypes.
7) Design of new tools, dies, etc, for new technology.
8) Pilot plant posts not useful for commercial production.
9) Engineering activity to the point of manufacture.

Certain activities, however, are *excluded* from the definition of research and development and are either expensed or amortized depending upon the apparent periods benefited:

1) Engineering costs during early commercial production.
2) Quality costs during commercial production.
3) Break-down trouble-shooting costs during production.
4) Routine efforts to improve the product.
5) Adapting to a customer's requirement, if ordinary.
6) Existing product change-costs for seasonal reasons.
7) Routine designing of tools and dies, etc.
8) Costs of start-up facilities other than pilot plant or those specifically designed only for research and development work.
9) Legal work involved in patent applications or litigation, and the sale or licensing of patents.

In the following list, the *italicized* portions represent those elements of research and development costs and expenditures which should be *capitalized* and not expensed immediately. The non-italicized items are those which should be expensed immediately:

1) Materials, Equipment And Facilities: *The costs of materials (whether from the enterprise's normal inventory or acquired specially for research and development activities) and equipment or facilities that are acquired or constructed for research and development activities and that have alternative future uses (in research and development projects or otherwise) shall be capitalized as tangible assets when acquired or constructed.* The cost of such materials consumed in research and development activities and the depreciation of such equipment or facilities used in those activities are research and development costs. However, the costs of materials, equipment, or facilities that are acquired or constructed for a particular research and development project and that have no alternative future uses (in other research and development projects or otherwise) and therefore no separate economic values are research and development costs at the time the costs are incurred.

2) FASB No. 86, *Accounting for the Costs of Computer Software to be Sold, Leased, or Otherwise Marketed*, requires all costs associated with the development of a computer software product to be sold, leased, or otherwise marketed to be charged to expense as required by FASB No. 2, *Accounting for Research and Development*. The costs of maintenance and customer service are charged to expense when the related revenue is recognized, or when these costs are incurred, whichever occurs first.

3) Personnel: Salaries and wages and other related costs of personnel engaged in research and development activities shall be included in research and development costs.

4) Tangibles Purchased From Others: *The costs of intangibles that are purchased from others for use in research and development activities and that have alternative future uses (in research and development projects or otherwise) shall be capitalized and amortized as intangible assets in accordance with Section 5141.* The amortization of those intangible assets used in research and development activities is a research and development cost. However, the costs of intangibles that are purchased from others for a particular research and development project and that have no alternative future uses (in other research and development projects or otherwise) and therefore no separate economic values are research and development costs at the time the costs are incurred.

5) Contract Services: The costs of services performed by others in connection with the research and development activities of an enterprise, including research and development conducted by others in behalf of the enterprise, shall be included in research and development costs.

6) Indirect Costs: Research and development costs should include a reasonable allocation of indirect costs. However, general and administrative costs that are not clearly related to research and development activities should not be included as research and development costs.

Research and development costs should *not* be charged as part of factory overhead because this handling would result in partial deferral to closing inventory. The standard requires expensing as incurred.

Writing Off a Patent

A patent has a legal life of 17 years. However, most companies write off patents in much shorter periods for the following reasons, since their useful lives are generally shorter than 17 years.

1) The patent could have been purchased many years after issuance.
2) The patent is for a current-fad-type item and sales can be expected to last for only a year or two.
3) A newer patented item appears on the market which puts an end to the economic usefulness of the patent.
4) The legal costs to defend a patent must be capitalized.

Some companies buy a patent just to protect an older patent they have from becoming outmoded. The cost of the new patent purchase should be written off over the remaining life of the old patent.

Copyrights

A copyright has a legal life of 50 years after author's death, with those prior to December 31, 1977, renewable for 47 years. However, here, as in the case of patents, copyright costs are usually written off in a much shorter period since the economic usefulness of a copyright usually is only a few years. Since the cost of obtaining a copyright usually is nominal (unlike a patent), the amount is usually not amortized but is written off immediately to income. Publisher-held copyrights last 75 years, unless reassigned to the author.

Franchises

Franchises are identifiable intangibles and, by contract, have a certain number of years to run. They should be written off over that contractual period. Sometimes, a franchise can be terminated by the will of the licensor. In such case, an immediate write-off may be justified.

Trademarks

A trademark is an identifiable intangible, usually with an indeterminable life and should, therefore, be written off over forty years unless a shorter life can be determined with reasonable certainty.

In the same category are trade names, brand names, secret formulas and processes, designs, and the right to use certain labels.

ORGANIZATION EXPENSES

When a corporation is created, numerous expenses are involved such as legal fees. stock certificate costs, underwriters' fees, corporation fees, commissions, promotion expenses, etc.

Under Section 248 of the tax law, organization expenses are to be written off over a minimum five-year period. This is the factor which causes many corporations to write organization costs off over that period, though the standards permit immediate write-off.

SECRET FORMULAS AND PROCESSES

A formula or process known only to a specific producer may be a valuable asset even though there is no patent involved. Such property usually has economic benefit which continues indefinitely instead of for a limited period.

In those instances in which the life is indeterminate, the forty-year period should be used, amortizing on a straight-line basis, as long as benefit continues and cannot be reasonably pinpointed or rejected.

Chapter 7
Liabilities and Long-Term Debt

IDENTIFICATION OF CURRENT LIABILITIES

The category of current liabilities normally consists of obligations which must be paid within one year. Some other current liabilities are as follows:

1) Obligations whose liquidation is reasonably expected to require the use of existing current assets or the creation of other current liabilities.

2) Obligations for items such as payables incurred in the acquisition of material and supplies which are to be used in the production of goods, or in providing services which are offered for sale.

3) Collections received in advance pertaining to the delivery of goods or the performance of services which will be liquidated in the ordinary course of business by delivery of such goods or services. But note that advances received which represent long-term deferments are not to be shown as current liabilities. An example of this would be a long-term warranty or the advance receipt by a lessor of rentals for the final period of a ten-year lease as a condition to the execution of the lease.

4) Debts which arise from operations directly relating to the operating cycle. Examples are accruals for wages, salaries, commissions, rentals, royalties, and income and other taxes; short-term debts which are expected to be liquidated within a relatively short period of time, usually one year; short-term debts arising from acquisition of capital assets; the current portion of a serial note; amounts required to be expended within one year under a sinking fund; loans accompanied by a pledge of

a life insurance policy which by its terms is to be repaid within one year. When the intent is to repay a loan on life insurance from the proceeds of the policy received upon maturity or cancellation, the obligation should not be included as a current liability.

5) Amounts which are expected to be required to cover expenditures within the year for known obligations, the amount of which can only be approximately determined. An example is a provision for accruing bonus payments. When an amount is expected to be required to be paid to persons unknown (for example, in connection with a guarantee of products sold), a reasonable amount should be included as a current liability.

It does not include debts to be liquidated by funds accumulated in non-current assets, or long-term obligations incurred to provide working capital for long periods. A contractual obligation falling due within a one-year period which is expected to be refinanced on a long-term basis should also be excluded from current liabilities. Bonds maturing within a one-year period which are to be refinanced by the issuance of new bonds should not therefore be included as current liabilities. Doing so would give a wrong impression of the company's working capital. The bonds should remain among long-term liabilities, with a footnote indicating the maturity date and the contemplated refinancing.

6) Accounts payable for goods purchased before the end of the accounting period and for which title has passed but which have not been received.

7) Liabilities for services rendered to your company before the end of the period but not yet billed.

8) Dividends which have been declared but have not yet been paid.

9) Liabilities to be liquidated in merchandise arising from the issuance of due bills, merchandise coupon books, and gift certificates.

10) A liability must be accrued for employees' rights to receive compensation for future absences under certain conditions:

   a) If the employees' right to compensation for future absences is related to services already rendered to the company.

   b) The obligation relates to accumulated or vested rights.

   c) Payment of the compensation is probable.

   d) The amount of the compensation can be reasonably estimated.

Vacations, illness, and holidays are examples of liabilities to be accrued, if compensation is expected to be paid.

This rule does not apply to such items as termination pay, deferred compensation, stock (or stock options) issued to employees, nor to such fringe benefits as group insurance or longterm disability pay.

LONG-TERM DEBT

Bond Premium or Discount

Liabilities are measured at amounts established in exchanges, usually the amounts to be paid, sometimes discounted. Conceptually, a liability is measured at the amount of cash to be paid discounted to the time the liability is incurred . . . Bonds and other long-term liabilities are in effect measured at the discounted amount of the future cash payments for interest and principal.

The difference between the face amount of the liability to be paid in the future and the actual net proceeds received in the present for incurring of this debt is amortized over the period to the maturity due-date. When this amount of periodic calculated interest is combined with the nominal face-amount of interest actually paid to debt-holders, the difference is amortized, giving a level, "effective" rate, and is called the "interest" method of amortization and is an acceptable method to be used.

Statement presentation. Unamortized discount or premium or debentures or other long-term debt should be shown on the balance sheet as a direct deduction or addition to the face value. It should *not* be shown as a deferred item. The amortized portion of either premium or discount should be shown as an interest item on the income statement. Issue costs should be treated as deferred charges.

The accounting method for bonds issued at a premium follows.

Year 1		
Cash	2,025,000	
Unamortized Bond Issue Costs	15,000	
Bonds Payable (8%, 10 years)		2,000,000
Unamortized Premium on Bonds		40,000
(Entries for the face value of the bonds,		
issue costs, and net cash proceeds received)		

Year 2		
Unamortized Premium on Bonds	4,000	
Unamortized Bond Issue Cost		1,500
Interest Expense (difference)		2,500
Interest Expense	160,000	
Cash		160,000

Early Extinguishment of Debt

Bonds and other long-term obligations often contain provisions giving the bond issuer an option to retire the bonds before their maturity date. This option is often exercised in connection with the issuance of new bonds at favorable rates (a refunding).

Usually, the amount paid for early extinguishment will be different from the face amount due and also different from the "net carrying value" of the debt. The "net carrying value" is the sum due at maturity plus or minus the remaining unamortized premium or discount (and cost of issuance).

On January 1, 1973, standards were adopted for the treatment of this early extinguishment of debt:

1) The difference between the reacquisition price and the *net carrying amount* of the debt (face value plus/minus unamortized items) should be recognized currently *in income* as gain or loss and shown as a separate item, and, if material, shown as an *extraordinary item*, net of related income tax effect.

2) Disclosure of pertinent details should be made.

3) Gains or losses should not be amortized to future periods. A gain or loss from the early extinguishment of debt made to satisfy sinking fund requirements that must be met within one year of the date of extinguishment is an ordinary item.

4) The extinguishment of *convertible* debt before maturity should be handled in the same manner.

5) The criteria of "unusual nature" and "infrequency of occurrence" do *not* apply here for the classification of the early extinguishment of debt as extraordinary. The determining factor for classification is *"materiality."*

These existing standards, in effect, prohibit the old practice of applying gains or losses on debt refunded to any new issues of similar obligations.

Troubled Debt Restructurings

A restructuring of debt constitutes a troubled debt restructuring if the creditor, for economic or legal reasons related to the debtor's financial difficulties, grants a concession to the debtor that it would not otherwise consider. That concession stems either from an agreement between the creditor and debtor, or is imposed by law or a court.

Debtors. A debtor that transfers its receivables from third parties, real estate, or other assets to a creditor to settle fully a payable, shall recognize a gain on restructuring of payables. The gain shall be measured by the excess of 1) carrying amount of payable settled (the face amount increased or decreased by the applicable accrued interest and applicable unamortized premium, discount finance charges or issue costs), over 2) the face value of the assets transferred to the creditor. This difference is a gain or loss on the transfer of assets. The debtor shall include that gain or loss in measuring net income for the period of transfer, reported as provided in APB #30 (section 2012) "Reporting Results of Operations."

A debtor that grants an equity interest to a creditor to settle fully a payable shall account for the equity interest at its fair value. The difference between fair value of the interest granted and the carrying amount of the payable is recognized as a gain on restructuring of payables. Gains on restructuring of payables shall be aggregated and, if material, shall be classified as an extraordinary item, net of related income tax effect.

Creditors. When a creditor receives from a debtor in full satisfaction of a receivable, either 1) receivables from third parties, real estate, or other assets, or 2) shares of stock, the creditor shall account for those assets at their fair value at the time of restructuring. The excess of the recorded investment in receivables satisfied, over the fair value of assets received, is a loss to be recognized and included in net income for the period of restructuring and reported according to APB #30 (section 2012).

A creditor shall disclose the following information pertaining to troubled debt restructurings:

1) For outstanding receivables whose terms have been modified, by major category:
   a) the aggregate recorded investment,
   b) the gross income that would have been recorded in the period then ended, if those receivables had been current in accordance with their original terms and had been outstanding throughout the period, or since origination, if held for part of the period, and
   c) the amount of interest income on those receivables that was included in net income for the period.
2) The amount of commitments to lend additional funds to debtors using receivables whose terms have been modified in troubled debt restructurings.

Commitments that are associated with a supplier's financing arrangements which involve an unconditional purchase obligation must be disclosed. These obligations are termed "take-or-pay" contracts.

The following must be disclosed:

1) The nature of the obligation.

2) The amount of the fixed and determinable obligation in the aggregate and for each of the next five years.

3) A description of the obligation that is variable, and the purchases in each year for which an income statement is presented.

Disclosure of future payments on long-term borrowings and redeemable stock must also be disclosed. The maturities, sinking fund requirements (if any), and redemption requirements for each of the next five years must be shown.

For additional situations and more detailed information, see FASB Statement No. 15, *Accounting by Debtors and Creditors for Troubled Debt Restructuring*, June, 1977.

Chapter 8

Revenue, Expenses, Earnings per Share

REVENUE (INCOME)

The principles upon which net income is determined derive from the pervasive measurement principles, such as realization, and the modifying conventions, such as conservatism.

The entire process of income determination ("matching") consists of identifying, measuring and relating revenue and expenses for an accounting period. Revenue is usually determined by applying the realization principle, with the changes in net asset value interrelated with the recognition of revenue. Revenue arises from three general activities:

1) Selling products;
2) Rendering services or letting others use owned resources, resulting in interest, rent, etc;
3) Disposing of other resources (not products), such as equipment or investments.

Revenue does not include proceeds from stockholders, lenders, asset purchases or prior period adjustments.

Revenue, in the balance sheet sense, is a gross increase in assets or a gross decrease in liabilities recognized and measured in conformity with GAAP, which results from those profit-directed activities that can change owners' equity.

Revenue is considered *realized* when:

1) The earning process is complete or virtually complete, and
2) An exchange has taken place.

The objectives of accounting determination of income are not always the same as the objectives used for tax purposes.

There are various acceptable ways of determining income, all of which are discussed in other parts of this book:

Revenue (see three general activities above):

1) Accrual method—this is financial accounting and GAAP.
2) Cash method—this is *not* considered financial accounting, and not GAAP, since one of the characteristics of GAAP is the *accrual* of appropriate items.
3) Installment sales method—generally for retail stores.
4) Completion of production method—used for precious metals.
5) For long-term construction contracts:
   a) Completed contract method.
   b) Percentage-of-completion method.
6) For leasing activities:
   a) The direct financing method.
   b) The operating method.
   c) The sales method.
7) The cost recovery method (used for installment sales).
8) Consolidation method—for majority-owned subsidiaries (over 50%).
9) Equity method—for non-consolidated subsidiaries and for controlled non-subsidiaries.

Other types of income requiring special determination:
1) Extraordinary items of income.
2) Unrealized income arising from:
   a) Foreign currency holdings or transactions.
   b) Ownership of marketable securities shown as current assets.

A *shareholder* in a corporation does *not* have income when that corporation earns income (except for a Sub-S corporation). The shareholder has, and reports for tax purposes, income only upon *distribution* of that income in the form of dividends. Generally, distributions of stock—stock dividends and stock splits—are *not* income to the shareholder, but merely an adjustment of the number of shares he holds (for the same original cost plus token costs, if any). However, there are some situations which call for the stockholder to report stock dividends as income.

If a buyer has a right of return to the seller, revenue is recognized if *all* of the following criteria are met:

1) Buyer is obligated to pay (and not contingent upon resale of the product) or has paid the seller.

2) Buyer's obligation would not be changed by theft, damage, or destruction of the product.

3) Seller does not have any significant obligation to buyer related to resale of the product by the buyer.

4) Buyer's business must have economic substance separate from the seller's business.

If these criteria are met, sales revenue and cost of sales reported in the income statement are reduced to reflect estimated returns; expected losses are accrued.

EXPENSES

Expenses are one of the six basic elements of financial accounting, along with assets, liabilities, owners' equity, revenue and net income.

> Expenses are determined by applying the expense recognition principles on the basis of relationships, between acquisition costs [the term "cost" is commonly used to refer to the amount at which assets are initially recorded, regardless of how determined], and either the independently determined revenue or accounting periods. Since the point in time at which revenue and expenses are recognized is also the time at which changes in amounts of net assets are recorded, income determination is interrelated with asset valuation.

All costs are not expenses. Some costs are related to later periods, will provide benefits for later periods, and are carried forward as assets on the balance sheet. Other costs are incurred and provide no future benefit, having expired in terms of usefulness or applicability—these expired costs are called "expenses." All expenses, therefore, are part of the broader term "cost." These expired costs are not assets and are shown as deductions from revenue to determine net income.

> Expenses are gross decreases in assets or gross increases in liabilities recognized and measured in conformity with GAAP that result from those types of profit-directed activities that can change an owner's equity.

Recognizing Expenses

Three pervasive principles form the basis for recognizing expenses to be deducted from revenue to arrive at net income or loss:

1) Associating cause and effect ("matching"):

For example, manufacturing cost of goods sold is measured and matched to the *sale* of the product. Assumptions must be made as to how these costs attach to the product—whether on machine hours, space used, labor expended, etc. Assumptions must also be made as to how the costs flow out (LIFO, FIFO, average costs).

2) Systematic and rational allocation:

When there is no direct way to associate cause and effect and certain costs are known (or presumed) to have provided benefits during the accounting period, these costs are allocated to that period in a systematic and rational manner and to appear so to an unbiased observer. The methods of allocation should be consistent and systematic, though methods may vary for different types of costs. Examples are: Depreciation of fixed assets, amortization of intangibles, interperiod allocation of rent or interest. The allocation referred to here is not the allocation of expired manufacturing costs with the "cost" area to determine unit or job costs; it is rather the broader area of allocation to the manufacturing area from the unexpired asset account: Depreciation on factory building, rather than overhead-depreciation on Product A, B, or C.

3) Immediate recognition (period expenses):

Those costs which are expensed during an accounting period because:

a) They cannot be associated on a cause-and-effect basis with revenue, yet no useful purpose would be achieved by delaying recognition to a future period, or

b) They provide no discernible future benefits, or

c) They were recorded as assets in a prior period and now no longer provide discernible future benefits.

Examples are: Officer salaries, most selling expenses, legal fees, most general and administrative expenses.

Other Expenses (and Revenue)

Gains and losses. Expenses and revenue from *other* than sales of products, merchandise or services may be separated from (operating) revenue and disclosed net separately.

Unusual items. Unusual items of expense or income not meeting the criteria of "extraordinary" should be shown as a separate component of income from continuing operations.

Extraordinary items. Extraordinary items are discussed elsewhere in this book. They should be shown separately—net of applicable taxes—*after* net income from continuing operations. If there are any disposals of business segments, they should be shown immediately prior to extraordinary items—also with tax effect.

Imputed Interest on Notes Receivable or Payable

Accounting Considerations

The AICPA sets forth the appropriate accounting when the face amount of certain receivables or payables ("notes") does not reasonably represent the present value of the consideration given or received in certain exchanges. The objective of these rules is to prevent the form of the transaction from prevailing over its economic substance.

(*Present value* is the sum of future payments, discounted to the present date at an appropriate rate of interest.)

APB Opinion No. 21 states that:

1) When a note is received or issued solely for cash, the note is presumed to have a present value equal to the cash received. If it is issued for cash equal to its face amount, it is presumed to earn the stated rate of interest.

2) When a note is received for cash and some other rights or privileges, the value of the rights or privileges should be given accounting recognition by establishing a note discount or premium account, with the offsetting amount treated as appropriate. An example is a five-year noninterest-bearing loan made to a supplier in partial consideration for a purchase of products at lower than prevailing market prices. Under such circumstances, the difference between the present value of the receivable and the cash lent to the supplier is regarded as a) an additional cost of the purchased goods, and b) interest income, amortized over the life of the note.

3) When a note is exchanged for property, goods, or services and a) interest is not stated, or b) it is stated but is unreasonable, or c) the stated face amount of the note is materially different from the current cash sale price of goods (or services), the note, the sales price, and the cost of the property (goods or services) should be recorded at their fair value, or at an amount that reasonably approximates the market value of the note, whichever is more clearly determinable.

Any resulting discount or premium should be regarded as interest expense or income and be amortized over the life of the note, in such a way as to result in a constant effective rate of interest when applied to the amount outstanding at the beginning of any given period.

Opinion No. 21 also provides some general guides for determining an "appropriate" interest rate and the manner of amortization for financial reporting purposes.

IMPUTED INTEREST: When a sale is made for an amount that is collectible at a future time giving rise to an account receivable, the amount is regarded as consisting of a sales price *and* a charge for interest for the period of the payment deferral. APB Opinion No. 21 requires that in the absence of a stated rate of interest, the present value of the receivable should be determined by reducing the face amount of the receivable by an interest rate that is approximated under the circumstances for the period that payment is deferred.

This rate is the *imputed rate*. It is determined by approximating the rate the supplier pays for financing receivables, or by determining the buyer's credit standing and applying the rate the borrower would have to pay if borrowing the sum from, say, a bank.

The process of arriving at the present value of the receivable is referred to as *discounting* the sum. If the total present value of the receivable (face amount plus the imputed interest) is less than the face amount, the difference between the face value of the receivable and its present value is recognized as a discount. If the present value exceeds the face amount of the receivable, the difference is recognized as a premium.

The sale is recorded as a debit to a receivable account, a credit to a discount on the receivable, and a credit to sales at the present value as reported for the receivable. The discount is amortized as a credit to interest income over the life of the receivable. On the balance sheet any unamortized discount at the end of the accounting period is reported as a direct subtraction from the *face amount* of the receivable.

Example: Seller ships merchandise totaling $10,000 to a customer with payment deferred for five years. Seller and customer agree to impute an interest charge of 10 percent for the $10,000. The journal entries follow.

Accounts Receivable	10,000	
Sales (Present value at 10%)		6,209
Unamortized Discount		3,791
(To record the sale of merchandise		
at the present value of the receivable)		

The *interest method* is applied to amortize the discount.

End of Year 1		
Unamortized Discount	620.90	
Interest Income		620.90
(10% of $6,209.00)		
End of Year 2		
Unamortized Discount	682.99	
Interest Income		682.99
(10% of $6,829.90)		
End of Year 3		
Unamortized Discount	751.29	
Interest Income		751.29
(10% of $7,512.89)		
End of Year 4		
Unamortized Discount	826.42	
Interest Income		826.42
(10% of $8,264.18)		
Unamortized Discount	909.06	
End of Year 5		
Unamortized Discount	909.06	
Interest Income		909.06
(10% of $9,090.60)		

At the end of five years full amortization of the discount has been recorded and the face amount of the receivable results. (*Note:* Opinion No. 21 does not require the imputed interest method when ". . . receivables and payables arising from transactions with customers or suppliers in the normal course of business which are due in customary trade terms not exceeding approximately one year.")

CLASSIFYING AND REPORTING EXTRAORDINARY ITEMS

Income statement presentation requires that the results of *ordinary operations* be reported first, and applicable provision for income taxes provided for.

In order, the following should then be shown:

1) Results of discontinued operations:

   a) Income or loss from the operations discontinued for the portion of the period until discontinuance—shown net of tax, with the tax shown parenthetically;

   b) Loss (or gain) on disposal of the business segments, including provision for phase-out operating losses—also shown net of tax parenthetically.

2) Extraordinary items.

Should be segregated and shown as the last factor used in arriving at net income for the period. Here, the caption is shown net of applicable income taxes, which are shown parenthetically.

Note that extraordinary items do *not* include disposal of business segments as such, because they are segregated and shown separately prior thereto (as above).

An example of the reporting of the above:

	1994		1993
Income from continuing operations before income taxes	$ xxx		$ xxx
Provision for income taxes	xx		xx
Income from continuing operations		$ xxx	xxx
Discontinued operations (Note):			
Income from operations of discontinued Division B (less applicable taxes of $xx)	$ xx		
	1994		1993
Loss on disposal of Division B, including provision for phase-out operating losses of $xx (less applicable income taxes of $xx)	xx	xx	
Income before extraordinary items		xxx	
Extraordinary items (less applicable income taxes of $xx)			
(Note)		xx	
Net Income		$ xxx	$ xxx
Earnings per share:			
Income from continuing operations		$ x.00	$ x.00
Discontinued operations		x.00	x.00
Extraordinary items		x.00	x.00
Net Income		$ x.00	$ x.00

Note that earnings per share should be broken out separately for the factors of discontinued operations and extraordinary items, as well as for income from (continuing) operations.

The criteria for classifying a transaction or event as an "extraordinary item" are as follows:

Extraordinary items are events and transactions that are distinguished by their unusual nature *and* by the infrequency of their occurrence. Thus, *both* of the following criteria should be met to classify an event or transaction as an extraordinary item:

1) *Unusual nature*—the underlying event or transaction should possess a high degree of abnormality and be of a type clearly unrelated to, or only incidentally related to, the ordinary and typical activities of the entity, taking into account the environment in which the entity operates.

2) *Infrequency of occurrence*—the underlying event or transaction should be of a type that would not reasonably be expected to recur in the foreseeable future, taking into account the environment in which the entity operates.

Items which are *not* to be reported as extraordinary, because they may recur or are not unusual, are:

1) Write-downs of receivables, inventories, intangibles, or leased equipment.
2) Effects of strikes.
3) Gains or losses on foreign currency translations.
4) Adjustment of accruals on long-term contracts.
5) Gains or losses on disposal of business segments.
6) Gains or losses from abandonment or sale of property, plant or equipment used in the business.

Note that some highly unusual occurrence might cause one of the above types of gains or losses and should be considered extraordinary, such as those resulting from: major casualties (earthquake), expropriations, and legal restrictions. Disposals of business segments, though not extraordinary in classification, should be shown separately on the income statement, just prior to extraordinary items, but after operations from continuing business.

Miscellaneous data pertaining to extraordinary items:

Bargain sales of stock to stockholders are *not* extraordinary items, but they should be shown separately.

A gain or a loss on sale of coin collections by a bank is *not* an extraordinary item.

PRESENT VALUE COMPUTATION AND APPLICATION

The procedure of computing interest on principal *and interest on interest* underlies the concept of *compounding*. There are a number of accounting procedures (accounting for bonds, accounts receivable, accounts payable, and leases, for example) to which the compound interest formula (and variations) can be applied.

1) The *future value* of a sum of money. If $1,000 (the principal P) is deposited in a bank today, what will be the balance (S) in the account in n *years* (or *periods*) if the bank accumulates interest at the rate of i percent per year?

2) The *present value* of a sum of money due at the end of a period of time. What is the value *today* of the amount owed if $1,000 has to be paid, say to a creditor, n years from today?

3) The *future value of an annuity* which is a series of *equal* payments made at *equal* intervals. If $1,000 a year is deposited for n years, how much will have accumulated at the end of the n-years period if the deposits earn interest at the rate of i percent per year?

4) The *present value of an annuity* which is a series of *equal* payments made at *equal* intervals. If we are to be paid $1,000 a year for n years, how much is this annuity worth today, given i percent rate of interest?

The formula for the future value of a sum of money is the familiar compound interest formula. In the four examples to follow let:

S = The future worth of a sum of money invested today.

P = Principal, or the sum of money that will accumulate to S amount of money.

i = The rate of interest (r may be substituted).

n = Number of periods of time.

It is important to understand that a "period of time" is not necessarily one year, even though rates of interest in the United States are always understood to mean the rate for a period of one year. A period can be any length of time—i.e., day, week, month, year, second, minute, hour. Time is a *continuous*, not a *discrete* function.

With compound interest the total amount accumulated (S in the formula) at the end of one period earns interest during the subsequent period, or "interest on interest." The formula is:

$$S = P(1 + i)^n$$

At this point it should be emphasized that the user no longer must do the arithmetic. Not only can the problem types be solved by the use of tables, but now inexpensive hand calculators will perform the computations and give the answers. The user has simply only to enter the numbers that represent the letters in the formula. Users with computers can, of course, program the formulas for permanent storage and simply "call out" whichever formula applies to the problem at hand. With respect to the arithmetic, however, three of the variables in the equation are always known quantities; therefore, finding the value of the fourth and *un*known variable follows.

A word of caution.   Computational errors caused by entering the wrong value for n are not uncommon. If $i = 12\%$ and the compounding period is every six months, n in the formula is 6. If the compounding period is quarterly n is 3. If the compounding period is daily (as is the case in many financial institutions savings policies) n becomes i/360—360 days in the year are applied in this country for interest calculations instead of 365. This is because the *smaller* the denominator, the bit more interest the *lender* collects. However, if the formula applies to a problem involving U.S. Government bonds, a 365-day year must be assumed because it enables the government to borrow a bit cheaper, relatively.

Annuities

The previous discussion considers the accumulation of interest on a *single* payment, however the single payment may be invested. *Annuities* apply to problems that involve a series of *equal payments* (or investments, savings, etc.,) made at *equal intervals* of time. The period of time between payments is called the *payment period*. The period of time between computation of the interest accumulation is called the *interest-conversion period*. When the payment period exactly equals the interest-conversion period, the annuity is an *ordinary annuity*. The equal payments are termed rents, which are spread over equal periods of time, the first rent payment made at the *start* of the annuity, and the last payment made at the *end* of the annuity.

The *future worth* of the annuity is the sum of the future worths of each of the separate rents. Assuming $100 invested we have $100 at time 1. At time 2 we have the $100 invested that day, plus the $100 invested at time 1, plus the interest earned during the period between time 1 and time 2. At time 3 another $100 is deposited; we now have the $100 deposited that day, the $100 deposited at time 2 plus the interest earned for one period, and the $100 deposited at time 1 plus the interest earned during the period between time 1 and time 2.

The formula for the future worth of an annuity of $1 is:

$$S = \frac{(1 + i)^n - 1}{i}$$

Note that the formula for the accumulation of interest on an ordinary annuity has the same variables as the compounding formula for a single payment.

To obtain S for any amount more than $1, multiply both sides of the equation by the amount invested, by P. In this case multiply both sides of the equation by 100. As above the amount for $1 can be found in tables (or by the use of a hand calculator).

The *present worth* of an annuity concerns the same question as the present worth of a single payment for n years at i rate of interest. How much would we pay today for an annuity in order to receive a given number of equal payments at equal intervals for a given number of periods in the future?

The formula for $1 is:

$$S = \frac{1 - (1 + i)^{-n}}{i}$$

The method for accounting for the premium or discount on bonds payable are compound interest procedures. The resultant interest charges are the product of the net balance of bonds payable and the effective interest rate at the time the bonds were issued. For bonds issued at a premium, the computed interest charges will *decrease* each year as the bonds approach maturity because the net balance of the liability decreases each year due to the amortization of the premium. Conversely, for bonds issued at a discount, the computed interest charges will *increase* each year as the bonds approach maturity because of the accumulation of the discount.

A straight-line method is used for the amortization of premiums or accumulation of discounts which involves simply dividing the original premium or discount by the number of years until maturity to determine the constant annual amount of amortization or accumulation.

The most frequent application of the above formula for accounting procedures is the present value formula. For example, when a company issues bonds, cash is debited for the proceeds of the bond issue and a liability account is credited for the amount. The entries will be the present value of the bonds. Assume a bond issue sold at a premium, or for more than the typical $1,000 par value, the present value of which we assume to be $1,200. The entries at the time of the sale of the bonds are:

Cash	$1,200	
Bonds Payable		$1,200

An alternative treatment is permissible by rule:

Cash	$1,200	
Bonds Payable		$1,000 (par)
Premium on Bonds		200

The Premium Account is an adjunct account (an addition) to Bonds Payable. The interest charge each year is computed by multiplying the bond liability *at the end of each year* by the effective rate of interest (see the definition). The adjunct account at the end of each period is debited for the amount of interest which reduces the liability each period. *The interest charge calculation is computed on the reduced amount of the liability that occurs each year as the adjunct account is debited.* At maturity the Premium Account has a zero balance and the liability will be reduced to the maturity, or face amount (the par value of $1,000) of the bond.

Assume the bond is sold at a $200 *discount*, i.e., $200 less than the $1,000 par value. The journal entry is:

Cash	$800	
Bond Discount	200	
Bonds Payable		$1,000

The Bond Discount account is a *contra* account to bonds payable with the liability at time of issue $800. Again, for an amount deposited for the annuity of more than $1 multiply both sides of the equation by that amount. Also, again note the same variables as in the compound interest formula.

REPORTING EARNINGS PER SHARE

APB 15, *Earnings per Share*, provides the basic guidelines for following the mandate that earnings per share (EPS) data be shown in conjunction with the presentation of financial statements, annual or interim, and that such data be shown on the face of the income statement. However, these requirements no longer apply to nonpublic enterprises. A nonpublic enterprise, as defined in FASB 21, *Suspension of the Reporting of Earnings per Share and Segment Information by Nonpublic Enterprises*, is an enterprise other than an entity a) whose debt or equity securities trade in a public market, on a foreign or domestic stock exchange, or in the over-the-counter market including securities quoted only locally or regionally, or b) that is required to file financial statements with the Securities and Exchange Commission.

When reporting for companies that are considered to be public enterprises, such amounts should be presented for:

1) Income before extraordinary items, and
2) Net income.

It is customary to show the earnings per share for the extraordinary items also. There are basically two types of capital structure involved in the calculation of EPS:

1) A simple capital structure, or

2) A complex capital structure.

Corporations with complex capital structures must present two types of earnings per share data for what is termed dual presentation:

1) *Primary earnings per share*, based on outstanding common shares and those securities that are in substance equivalent to common shares (CSE); and

2) *Fully diluted earnings per share* which reflect the *dilution* of earnings per share that would have occurred if all contingent issuances of stock had taken place. Reduction of less than three percent is not deemed sufficient to cause dilution.

Dilution shows a reduction in earnings per share resulting from securities having been converted, options or warrants exercised, or other shares issued under conditions that would reduce EPS. Securities that have the potential for diluting EPS include convertible securities such as bonds and preferred stock, stock options, warrants, contingent shares, purchase contracts, and the like, that enable the holder to become a common shareholder by exchanging or converting the security. Essentially, dilutive securities are considered to be only one step short of the common stock because their value relates directly to it; therefore, CSEs are included with outstanding common stock in figuring primary EPS. Thus, the primary EPS is calculated by dividing the earnings for the year not only by the number of shares of common outstanding, but by the sum of those shares plus the common stock equivalents of dilutive securities.

Convertible preferred stock and convertible bonds give the holder either a specified dividend rate or interest return, or the option of participating in increased earnings on the common stock through conversion. They do not actually have to be converted to common stock, nor even necessarily be expected to be converted in the near future to qualify as CSE.

The reasoning underlying this is that they are in substance equivalent to common shares, enabling the holder at his or her discretion to bring about an increase in the number of common shares through exchange or conversion at the shareholder's discretion. Thus, the idea behind the CSE is an application of the principle of substance over form which in effect mandates that the accountant cut through any verbiage to discover the actual economic substance of a business arrangement or financial instrument.

A convertible security is considered a common stock equivalent if its effective yield at the date of issuance is less than two-thirds of the then current average of Aa corporate bond yield.

It should be clearly understood that CSE shares are included in computing EPS only if the effect of conversion is dilutive. Thus dilution occurs when earnings per share decrease, or loss per share increases. CSE are not included when the financial picture improves with the inclusion of CSE.

As discussed above, the primary earnings per share include common stock and common stock equivalents in figuring EPS. The more conservative fully diluted earnings per share take into consideration the maximum dilution potential to affect earnings of all issuance of common stock as if they had been effective at the beginning of the year.

This is calculated by dividing the earnings for the year by the total of the common stock, common stock equivalents, and all other securities that are convertible even though they do not qualify as CSE.

In addition to APB 15 and FASB 21, two other GAAP pronouncements relate to EPS. FASB 55, *Determining Whether a Convertible Security is a Common Stock Equivalent* establishes the criteria for computing the yield test for determining whether a convertible security is a common stock equivalent. The Statement replaced the prime interest rate with the average Aa corporate bond yield as the basis, and a later rule, FASB 85, *Yield Test for Determining Whether a Convertible Security is a Common Stock Equivalent* changed the cash yield test to an effective yield test.

Therefore, as noted earlier, a convertible security is considered a CSE if its effective yield at the date of issuance is less than two-thirds of the then current average Aa corporate bond yield. The average bond yield used on the date of issuance is obtained from the average Aa corporate bond yield for a very brief period, usually the week preceding issuance of the convertible security. The annual interest or dividend payments plus any original call premium or discount are included in arriving at the effective yield of a convertible security.

Earnings per share should be presented for all periods covered by the income statement. If a prior period has been restated, the earnings per share should also be restated for that period.

The underlying simple basic formula for calculating EPS is:

Net income (earnings) *divided by* number of shares outstanding (common only)

$$\frac{\text{Earnings (net income)}}{\text{Number of common shares outstanding}} = \text{EPS}$$

The *dollars* are always the numerator; the *number* of shares the *denominator*.

The complexity of determining either factor in the formula increases as the corporate's capital structure expands into more exotic types of equity security and potential types of equity security.

Refer now to the *Fact Sheet* presented next and to the illustrations which follow based on that fact sheet:

FACT SHEET FOR EARNINGS PER SHARE ILLUSTRATIONS

	(in thousands of dollars)		
INCOME STATEMENT	1994	1993	1992
Income before extraordinary item	$12,900	$ 9,150	$7,650
Extraordinary item—net of tax	900	900	—
Net Income	$13,800	$10,050	$7,650
SHARE INFORMATION			
Common stock outstanding:	(in thousands of shares)		
Beginning of year	3,300	3,000	3,000*
Issued during year	—	300(3)	—
Conversion of preferred stock(1)	500	—	—
Conversion of debentures(2)	200	—	—
End of year	4,000	3,300	3,000
Common stock reserved under employee stock options granted	7	7	—
Weighted average number of shares (see calculations): 1992—3,000,000 shares weighted average 1993—3,150,000 shares weighted average 1994—4,183,333 shares weighted average			

*issued at 1/1/92.

(3) issued at 7/1/93.

1) *Convertible preferred stock:* 600,000 shares issued at the beginning of the second quarter of 1993. Dividend rate is 20 cents per share. Market value was $53 at time of issue with a cash yield of 0.4 percent as opposed to bank prime rate of 18 percent. Warrants to buy 500,000 shares of common stock at $60 per share for a period of five years were, in addition, issued along with this convertible preferred. Each share of the convertible stock was convertible into one common share (exclusive of the warrants).

During 1994, 500,000 shares of the preferred stock were converted because the common dividend exceeded the preferred. But *no warrants were exercised* during the year.

2) *Convertible debentures:* 10 percent with a principal amount of $10,000,000 (due 2000) were sold at 100 in the last quarter of 1992. Each $100 debenture was convertible into two shares of common stock. The entire issue was converted at the beginning of the third *quarter* of 1994, when called by the company. (None were converted in 1992 or 1993.)

The prime rate at issue in 1992 was 12 percent. The coupon face rate of the bonds was 10 percent. The bonds had a market value of $100 when issued.
Additional information:
Market price of the common stock: (average prices)

	1994	1993	1992
1st quarter	50	45	40
2nd quarter	60	52	41
3rd quarter	70	50	40
4th quarter	70	50	45
Dec 31 closing price	72	51	44
Cash dividends on common stock:			
Declared and paid *each* quarter	$1.25	$ .25	$ .25

ILLUSTRATIONS (BASED ON THE FACT SHEET)

1992—SIMPLE CAPITAL STRUCTURE
The simplest computation involves those companies with:

1) Only common stock issued, and
2) No change in outstanding number during the year, and
3) Net income arising without any extraordinary items.

For 1992, the first year of the company's operation on the fact sheet, the EPS would be:

$$\frac{\text{Income}}{\text{\# shares outstanding}} \quad \text{or} \quad \frac{\$7,650,000}{3,000,000} \quad \text{or } \$2.55 \text{ per share.}$$

1993—EXPANDED SIMPLE CAPITAL STRUCTURE
The significant changes in 1993 affecting EPS:

1) The extraordinary item of income of $900M, requiring separate disclosure; and
2) The 300,000 shares issued during the year, requiring the computation of a weighted average.

Computing the weighted average—determine the number of shares outstanding at the end of each quarter and divide by four:

1st quarter	3,000,000
2nd quarter	3,000,000
3rd quarter	3,300,000
4th quarter	3,300,000
	12,600,000 divided by 4, or 3,150,000 shares

The employee stock options are *under* 3% of the aggregate outstanding, so they are not considered dilutive and are ignored in the EPS calculation.

Proper *disclosure* for the 1993 EPS would be:

Earnings per common share:	1993	1992
Income before extraordinary items	$2.90(4)	$2.55
Extraordinary item	.29(5)	—
Net Income	$3.19	$2.55
$9,150,000 divided by 3,150,000		
900,000 divided by 3,150,000		

(In the above example, the dilution factors used *below* are not applicable, appearing on the fact sheet merely for use in the complex structure example next.)

1994—COMPLEX CAPITAL STRUCTURE

The significant changes in 1994 affecting EPS:

1) The number of common shares (equivalents) represented by the warrants; and

2) The number of common share equivalents represented by the 600,000 shares of convertible preferred stock, issued in 1991; and

3) The additional EPS computation required for the full dilution assumption.

1) The number of common shares (equivalents) represented by the warrants.

$60 exercise price × 500,000 warrants of $30,000,000	
$30,000,000 divided by $70 share market price	428,572
	(shares)
500,000 shares minus 428,572	71,428
	(shares)

Weighted average of the warrant shares: Not applicable for any quarter prior to the third quarter of 1992 because the market price did not exceed the exercise price:

First quarter 1994	—
Second quarter 1994	—
Third quarter 1994	71,428
Fourth quarter 1994	71,428
	142,856 divided by 4
Warrant share equivalents—or 35,714 shares	

2) The number of common share equivalents represented by the convertible preferred stock:

	1994	1993
Number of shares of preferred stock issued in 1991	600,000	450,000*
Less the number of shares of common stock issued on conversion in 1994 (500,000). But, these shares were issued at various times during the year. Based on even issuance, the weighted average is ½ or	(250,000)	—
The equivalent shares with potential issue factor	350,000	450,000

	1992	1991
The weighted average number of common shares and equivalents is therefore:		
Shares outstanding at beginning (incl. 7/1/93 issue)	3,300,000	3,150,000
Shares issued on conversion of preferred stock (as above)	250,000	—

*Based on weighted average from start of second quarter

	1992	1991
Shares issued on conversion of the debentures—200,000 at 7/1/94 weighted average is 100,000	100,000	
Equivalents for the warrants (as prior)	35,714	
Equivalents for the convertible preferred stock above	350,000	450,000
Total weighted average (primary)	4,035,714	3,600,000

3) Additional share calculation to determine full dilution:

Remaining shares applicable to convertible debentures	100,000	200,000
Shares applicable to warrants	(35,714)	—
Shares applicable to warrants based on yearend price of $72—$60 × 500,000 divided by $72, with result subtracted from 500,000	83,333	
Add primary weighted shares above	4,035,714	3,600,000
Shares for full-dilution EPS	4,183,333	3,800,000

Proper disclosure of EPS for 1994 would then be:

	1994	1993
Primary earnings per common share and common equivalent shares (Note _):		
Income before extraordinary item	$ 3.20(1)	$ 2.54(1A)
Extraordinary item	.22(2)	.25(2A)
Net Income	$ 3.42(3)	$ 2.79(3A)

Fully diluted earnings per common share (Note _):

	1994	1993
Income before extraordinary item	$ 3.11(4)	$ 2.46(7)
Extraordinary item	.21(5)	.24(8)
Net income	$ 3.32(6)	$ 2.70(9)

1)	$12,900,000 divided by 4,035,714 or	$3.20
2)	900,000 divided by 4,035,714 or	.22
3)	13,800,000 divided by 4,035,714 or	$ 3.42
1A)	9,150,000 divided by 3,600,000 or	$ 2.54
2A)	900,000 divided by 3,600,000 or	.25
3A)	10,050,000 divided by 3,600,000 or	$ 2.79
4)	13,004,000 divided by 4,183,333 or	$ 3.11
(above includes $104,000 addback for debenture interest)		
5)	900,000 divided by 4,183,333 or	.21
6)	13,904,000 divided by 4,183,333 or	$ 3.32
7)	9,358,000 divided by 3,800,000 or	$ 2.46
(includes $208,000 for interest or debentures)		
8)	900,000 divided by 3,800,000 or	.24
9)	$10,258,000 divided by 3,800,000 or	$ 2.70

The illustrations here do *not* cover the following topics:

1) Disclosure requirements for financial notes.
2) Handling of dividends paid or unpaid on convertible stocks.
3) Subsequent events which require supplemental calculations.
4) Anti-dilution.
5) The test for common stock equivalent status (including the treasury stock method).
6) Details of calculating dilution under the treasury stock method.
7) Effect of stock splits or stock dividends on number of shares.
8) EPS in business combinations.
9) Discussion of the "if converted" method of computation.
10) Discussion of the "cashyield" test for the consideration of equivalents.
11) Effect of contingencies involved in share issuance.
12) Securities of subsidiaries.

Some of the above topics may be illustrated best in financial statements issued by prominent public corporations.

The investment community generally recognizes the relevance of "earnings per share" as a measure of the historically achieved earning power of an economic entity in terms of a unit which is bought, sold and quoted in the market place, the share of common stock. The earning power represented by that share has generally been considered a significant element in the determination of its worth. Net income, as a measure of ultimate result, may reasonably be interpreted on a per share basis since no significant claims stand between it and the common stock owner. Where there are senior equity claims, these are deducted before computing the per share figure. In a similar manner, dividends are logically presented in terms of the individual share, as are net assets.

However, per share data other than that relating to these three items—net income, net assets and dividends—should not be used in reporting financial results.

It is possible, even probable, that within the near future GAAP for disclosing primary earnings per share will be replaced by a requirement to report *basic earnings per share.*

Basic earnings per share are figured by dividing net income after deducting minority interest and preference dividends by the weighted average common stock outstanding during that particular period. There is no adjustment made for CSEs.

The FASB's decision is motivated by two basic considerations:

1) To simplify the admittedly convoluted U.S. earnings per share calculations, and

2) To bring GAAP for EPS more in line with international standards and thus improve the quality of financial reporting by improving international comparability.

At present both the International Accounting Standards Committee (IASC) and the FASB are working independently in this direction. There is no plan to make this a joint effort.

However, the aims appear to be closely allied and both will probably recommend continuation of the use of fully diluted EPS.

Chapter 9
Stockholders' Equity

"Stockholders' equity" is the most commonly used term to describe the section of the balance sheet encompassing the corporation's capital and retained earnings. Other terms used are "net worth" or "capital and surplus." Stockholders' equity consists of three broad source classifications:

1) Investments made by owners: Capital Stock (Common and/or Preferred)—at par value (legal value) or stated amount. Additional Paid-In Capital—"In Excess of Par," "Capital Surplus," etc.

2) Income (loss) generated by operations: Retained Earnings—the accumulated undistributed annual profits (losses), after taxes and dividends

3) Appraisal Capital—resulting from the revaluation of assets over historical cost (not in conformity with GAAP)

Changes in shareholders' equity, primarily in retained earnings, are caused by:

1) Periodic net income (loss) after taxes
2) Dividends declared
3) Prior period adjustments of retained earnings
4) Contingency reserves (appropriations of retained earnings)
5) Recapitalizations:
   a) Stock dividends and split-ups
   b) Changing par or stated value

    c) Reducing capital

    d) Quasi-reorganizations

    e) Stock reclassifications

    f) Substituting debt for stock

6) Treasury stock dealings

7) Business combinations

8) Certain unrealized gains and losses

CAPITAL STOCK

Capital stock is the capital contributed by the stockholders to the corporation.

Common Stock

The common stockholders are the residual owners of the corporation; that is, they own whatever is left after all preceding claims are paid off. By definition, common stock is "a stock which is subordinate to all other stocks of the issuer."

When a corporation has a single class of stock, it is often called "capital stock" instead of "common stock." The three aspects of stock ownership are 1) dividends, 2) claims against assets on liquidation, and 3) shares in management. As to these aspects of ownership, common stockholders have the following rights: 1) The amount of any/all dividend payments depends upon the profitability of the company. 2) Common stockholders have no fixed rights but, on the other hand, are limited to no maximum payment. 3) Their claim against the assets of the corporation on liquidation is last in the order of priority, following all creditors and all other equity interests. 4) The common stockholders, by statute, must have a voice in management. Their voice is often to the exclusion of all other equity interests, but they may also share their management rights with other classes of stock.

Common stock may be classified:

1) Par and no-par stock. Par stock is stock with a stated, legal dollar value, whereas no-par stock lacks such a given value. The distinction today is largely an academic one. However, state laws regarding stock dividends and split-ups and the adjustments of par value may affect the accounting treatment of such dividends.

2) Classes of common stock. Common stock may be divided into separate classes, e.g., class A, class B, etc. Usually, the class distinction deals with the right to vote for separate directors, or one class may have the right to vote and one class may not. Class stock is a typical technique used where a minority group wishes to maintain control.

Preferred Stock

The second major type of capital stock is preferred stock, that which has some preference with regard to dividend payments or distribution of assets on liquidation. In the usual situation, preferred stock will have a preference on liquidation, to the extent of the par value of the stock. In addition, its right to dividends depends on the following classification:

1) Participating and nonparticipating right.   If the preferred has a right to a fixed dividend each year but has not the right to share in any additional dividends over and above the stated amount, it is nonparticipating preferred. If it is entitled to a share of any dividends over and above those to which it has priority, it is called participating. For example, a preferred may have the right to a 5 percent annual dividend and then share equally with the common stock in dividends after a dividend (equal to the preferred per-share dividend) has been paid to the common stockholders.

2) Convertible preferred stock.   Convertible preferred is stock which may, at the holder's option, be exchanged for common. The terms of the exchange and the conversion period are set forth on the preferred certificate. Thus one share of $100 par preferred may be convertible beginning one year after issue into two shares of common. The preferred stockholder who converts will own two shares of common at a cost of $50 per share (this assumes the purchase of the preferred at par). A company will issue a convertible security at a time when it needs funds but for one reason or another cannot or does not wish to issue common stock. For example, in a weak stock market, common may be poorly received while a convertible preferred can be privately placed with a large institutional investor. The conversion privilege, from the point of view of the purchaser, is a "sweetener" since it affords the opportunity to take a full equity position in the future if the company prospers. The issuer may be quite satisfied to give the conversion privilege because it means that (assuming earnings rise) the preferred stock, with a prior and fixed dividend claim, will gradually be eliminated in exchange for common shares.

Accounting for a convertible preferred issue follows the usual rules. That is, when the preferred is first issued, a separate capital account will be set up, to which will be credited the par value of the outstanding stock. When conversion takes place, an amount equal to the par of the converted stock is debited to the preferred account. The common stock account will be credited with an amount equal to the par or stated value of the shares issued in exchange for the preferred. Any excess will go to capital surplus.

Both participating 1) and convertible 2) preferred stocks above must be taken into consideration when computing earnings per share.

3) Cumulative and noncumulative.   A corporation which lacks earnings or surplus cannot pay dividends on its preferred stock. In that case, the question arises whether the past dividend must be paid in future years. If past dividends do accumulate and must be paid off, the stock is cumulative; otherwise, noncumulative.

The preferred may share voting rights equally with the common stock; it may lack voting rights under any circumstances; or it may have the right to vote only if either one or more dividend is passed. In the latter case, the preferred may have the exclusive right to vote for a certain number of directors to be sure that its interests as a class are protected.

For cumulative stock, the dividends must be accrued each year (even if unpaid), unless issued with an "only as earned" provision. The effect on earnings per share is the extent of the reduction of net income for this accrual.

Par Value, Stated Capital, and Capital Stock Accounts

The money a corporation receives for its stock is in a unique category. It is variously referred to as "a cushion for creditors," "a trust fund," and similar expressions. The point is that in a corporation which gives its stockholders limited liability, the only funds to which the creditors of the corporation can look for repayment of their debts in the event the corporation suffers losses is the money received for stock, which constitutes the stated capital account. Consequently, most state corporation statutes require a number of steps to be taken before a corporation can reduce its stated capital. These steps include approval by the stockholders and the filing of a certificate with the proper state officer, so that creditors may be put on notice of the reduction in capital.

Stated capital is actually divided into separate accounts, each account for a particular class of stock. Thus, a corporation may have outstanding a class A common, a class B common, a first preferred, a second preferred, etc. Each class would have its own account, which would show the number of shares of the class authorized by the certificate of incorporation, the number actually issued and the consideration received by the corporation.

It is at this point that the distinction between par and no-par stock becomes important. Par stock is rarely sold for less than its par value, although it may be sold for more. In many states, it is illegal to sell stock at a discount from par, and even when not illegal, there may be a residual stockholder liability for that original discount to the creditors. In any case, an amount equal to the par value of the stock must be credited to its capital account, with any excess going into a surplus account.

In the case of no-par stock, the corporation, either through its board of directors or at a stockholders' meeting, assigns part of the consideration received as stated capital for the stock and treats the rest as a credit to a capital surplus account. Treating part of the consideration received as stated capital is the equivalent of giving the stock a par value.

Capital Stock Issued for Property

Where capital stock is issued for the acquisition of property in a non-cash transfer, measurement of owners' investment is usually determined by using the fair market value of the assets (and/or the discounted present value of any liabilities transferred).

When the fair value of the assets transferred cannot be measured, the market value of the stock issued may be used instead for establishing the value of the property received.

When the acquisition is an entire business, the principle of "fair value" is extended to cover each and every asset acquired (other than goodwill). If the fair value of the *whole* business is considered to be *more* than the individual values, that excess is considered to be goodwill.

The difference between fair value put on the assets received and the *par value* (stated) of the stock issued goes to the Capital-in-Excess of Par Value account (or Additional Paid-in Capital, etc.) as either a positive or negative (discount) amount. Note that this does *not* pertain to any "negative" goodwill which might have been created; said negative goodwill, if any, should be used to reduce, immediately, the noncurrent assets (except investment securities) proportionately to zero, if necessary, with any remaining excess to be deferred and amortized as favorable goodwill is amortized.

Capital in Excess of Par or Stated Value (Capital Surplus)

The term "capital surplus" is still widely used, although the preferred terminology is "capital in excess of par" or "additional paid-in capital."

The capital in excess of par account is credited with capital received by the corporation which is not part of par value or stated capital. It is primarily the excess of consideration received over par value or the amount of consideration received for no-par stock which is not assigned as stated capital.

In addition, donations of capital to the corporation are credited to this account. If stated capital is ever reduced as permitted by law, the transfer is from the capital stock account to this capital surplus account.

This account is also credited for the excess of market value over par value for stock dividends (which are not split-ups) and for the granting of certain stock options and rights.

Retained Earnings

Terminology bulletins do not have authoritative status; however, they are issued as useful guides. Accounting Terminology Bulletin No. 1 recommended the following:

1) The abandonment of the term "surplus";

2) The term "earned surplus" be replaced with such terms that indicate the source such as:

   a) Retained Earnings
   b) Retained Income
   c) Accumulated Earnings
   d) Earnings Retained for Use in the Business

Retained earnings are the accumulated undistributed past and current years' earnings, net of taxes and dividends paid and declared.

Portions of retained earnings may be set aside for certain contingencies, appropriated for such purposes as possible future inventory losses, sinking funds, etc. A Statement of Changes in Retained Earnings is one of the basic financial statements *required* for fair presentation of results of operation and financial condition to conform with GAAP. It shows net income, dividends, prior period adjustments. A Statement of Changes in Stockholders' Equity shows additional investments by owners, retirements of owners' interests and similar events (if these are few and simple, they may be put in the notes).

Regardless of how a company displays its undistributed earnings, or the disclosures thereof, for tax purposes, the actual earnings and profits which could have been or are still subject to distribution as "dividends" *under IRS regulations* may, under some circumstances, retain that characteristic for the purpose of ordinary income taxation to the ultimate recipient. There is no requirement for this disclosure other than normal requirement for the "periods presented," which would usually show the activity in retained earnings for only two years and not prior.

Prior Period Adjustments

Only the following rare types of items should be treated as prior period adjustments and *not* be included in the determination of current period net income:

1) Correction of an error (material) in prior financial statements; and

2) Realization of income tax pre-acquisition operating loss benefits of *purchased* subsidiaries.

Corrections of errors are *not* changes in accounting *estimates*. Error corrections are those resulting from:

1) Mathematical errors;
2) Erroneous application of accounting principles;
3) Misuse of, or oversight of, facts existing at a prior statement period.

Changes in accounting *estimates* result from *new* information or developments, which sharpen and improve judgment.

Litigation settlements and income tax adjustments *no longer* meet the definition of prior period adjustments. However, for *interim periods only* (of the current fiscal year), material items of this nature should be treated as prior interim adjustments to the identifiable period of related business activity.

Goodwill cannot be written off as a prior period adjustment.

Retroactive adjustment should be made of all comparative periods presented, reflecting changes to particular items, net income and retained earnings balances. The tax effects should also be reflected and shown. Disclosure of the effects of the restatement should be made.

Prior period adjustments must be charged or credited to the opening balance of retained earnings. They cannot be included in the determination of net income for the current period.

Beginning Retained Earnings		$1,000
Correction Depreciation Error		
$300 x .50 (net of tax)		150
Adjustment Beginning Retained Earnings		1,150
Net Income		400
Ending—Retained Earnings		$1,550
Accumulated Depreciation	$300	
Taxes Payable		150
Retained Earnings		150

CONTINGENCY RESERVES

A "contingency" is defined as "an existing condition, situation, or set of circumstances involving uncertainty as to possible gain or loss to an enterprise that will ultimately be resolved when one or more events occur or fail to occur." Loss contingencies fall into three categories:

1) Probable
2) Reasonably possible
3) Remote

In deciding whether to accrue the estimated loss by charging income or setting aside an appropriation of retained earnings, or merely to make a disclosure of the contingency in the notes to the financial statement, the following standards have been set:

A charge is accrued to income if *both* of the following conditions are met at the date of the financial statements:

1) Information available *before* the issuance of the financial statements indicates that probably the asset will be impaired or a liability incurred; and

2) A *reasonable* estimate of the loss *can* be made.

   (When a contingent loss is probable but the reasonable estimate of the loss can only be made in terms of a range, the amount shall be accrued for the loss. When some amount within the range appears at the time to be a better estimate than any other amount within the range, that amount shall be accrued. When no amount within the range is a better estimate than any other amount, the minimum amount in the range shall be accrued.)

If discovery of the above impairment occurs *after* the date of the statements, disclosure should be made and pro-forma supplementary financial data presented giving effect to the occurrence as of the balance sheet date.

When a contingent loss is only *reasonably possible* or the probable loss cannot be estimated, an estimate of the *range* of loss should be made or a narrative description given to indicate that *no* estimate was possible. Disclosure should be made; but no accrual.

When the contingency is *remote*, disclosure should be made when it is in the nature of a guarantee. Other remote contingencies are not required to be disclosed, but they may be, if desired, for more significant reporting.

General reserves for unspecified business risks are not to be accrued and no disclosure is required.

Appropriations for loss contingencies from retained earnings must be shown with the stockholders' equity section of the balance sheet, and clearly identified as such.

Examples of loss contingencies are:

1) Collectibility of receivables.
2) Obligations related to product warranties and product defects.

3) Risk of loss or damage of enterprise property by fire, explosion, or other hazards.

4) Threat of expropriation of assets.

5) Pending or threatened litigation.

6) Actual or possible claims and assessments.

7) Risk of loss from catastrophes assumed by property and casualty insurance companies including reinsurance companies.

8) Guarantees of indebtedness of others.

9) Obligations of commercial banks under "standby letters of credit."

10) Agreements to repurchase receivables (or to repurchase the related property) that have been sold.

Handling of these loss contingencies depends upon the nature of the loss probability and the reasonableness of estimating the loss. (Gain contingencies are not booked, only footnoted.)

RECAPITALIZATIONS

Essentially, a recapitalization means changing the structure of the capital accounts. It can also mean a reshuffling between equity and debt. A recapitalization may be done voluntarily by the corporation; or it may be part of a reorganization proceeding in a court, pursuant to a bankruptcy or a reorganization petition filed by the corporation or its creditors.

In almost all cases of recapitalizations, stockholder approval is required at some point during the process. This is because a recapitalization may affect the amount of stated capital of the corporation or change the relationships between the stockholders and the corporation or between classes of stockholders. The different categories of recapitalizations are discussed in the following paragraphs.

Stock Split-Ups

A split-up involves dividing the outstanding shares into a larger number, as, for example, two for one in which each stockholder receives a certificate for additional shares equal to the amount of shares already held. The split-up is reflected in the corporate books by reducing the par value or the stated value of the outstanding shares. Thus if shares with a par value of $10 are split two for one, the new par becomes $5. No entry is necessary, other than a memo entry. The stockholder adjusts his or her basis for the unit number of shares.

Reverse split. The opposite of a split-up is a reverse split, which results in a lesser number of outstanding shares. Stockholders turn in their old certificates and receive a new certificate for one-half, for example, of former holdings. The par value or stated value is adjusted to show the higher price per share. A reverse split is sometimes used in order to increase the price of the stock immediately on the open market.

Stock Dividends

As far as the stockholder is concerned, a stock dividend is the same as the stock split; the stockholder receives additional shares, merely changing the unit-basis of holding. But the effect is quite different from the point of view of the corporation. A stock dividend requires a transfer from retained earnings of the *market value* of the shares. Capital stock is credited for the par value and capital in excess of par value is credited for the excess of market price over par. (The stockholder who has the option of receiving cash must report the dividend as ordinary income.)

Stock Split-up Effected in the Form of a Dividend

Usually, a stock distribution is either a dividend or a split-up. However, there is another type of distribution, which, because of certain state legal requirements pertaining to the minimum requirements for or the changing of par value, necessitates a different nomenclature.

In those instances where the stock dividend materially reduces the market value, it is by nature and AICPA definition a "split-up." However, because certain states require that retained earnings must be capitalized in order to maintain par value, those types of transactions should be described by the corporation as a "split-up effected in the form of a dividend." The entry would then be a reduction of retained earnings and an increase in capital stock for the *par value* of the distribution. For income tax purposes, the corporation may be required to show this reduction of retained earnings as a Schedule M adjustment and may technically still have to consider it as available for ordinary rate ultimate distribution.

Changing Par or Stated Value of Stock

This type of recapitalization involves changing from par to no-par or vice versa. This is usually done in conjunction with a reduction of stated capital. A corporation, for example, may decide to change its stock from par stock to no-par stock in order to take advantage of lower franchise fees and transfer taxes.

Or no-par shares may be changed to shares having par value to solve legal problems existing under particular state statutes. A par value stock which is selling in the market at a price lower than its par must be changed if the corporation intends to issue new stock. This is necessary because of some state laws which prohibit a corporation from selling its par value stock for less than par value. In such a case, the corporation may reduce par value or may change the par to no-par; thereby, the new stock can be given a stated value equivalent to the price it can bring in the open market.

QUASI-REORGANIZATIONS

Current or future years' charges should be made to the income accounts instead of to capital surplus. An exception to this rule (called "readjustment") occurs when a corporation elects to restate its assets, capital stock and retained earnings and thus avail itself of permission to relieve its future income account or retained earnings account of charges which would otherwise be made. In such an event, the corporation should make a clear report to its shareholders of the restatements proposed to be made, and obtain their formal consent. It should present a fair balance sheet as at the date of the readjustment, in which the readjustments of the carrying amounts are reasonably complete, in order that there may be no continuation of the circumstances which justify charges to capital surplus.

As an example of how this readjustment might occur, suppose that a company has a deficit in its retained earnings (earned surplus) of $100,000. By revaluing its assets upward, it is possible for this company to create a capital surplus account for the write-up to fair value, then write off the deficit in retained earnings to that account. From then on, a new retained earnings account should be established and the fact be disclosed for ten years.

STOCK RECLASSIFICATIONS

Another category of stock recapitalization involves reclassifying the existing stock. This means that outstanding stock of a particular class is exchanged for stock of another class. For example, several outstanding issues of preferred stock may be consolidated into a single issue. Or, common stock may be exchanged for preferred stock, or vice versa. The objective in this type of reclassification is to simplify the capital structure, which in many cases is necessary in order to make a public offering or sometimes to eliminate dividend arrearages on preferred stock by offering a new issue of stock in exchange for canceling such arrearages.

SUBSTITUTING DEBT FOR STOCK

One form of recapitalization that has become popular in some areas involves substituting bonds for stock. The advantage to the corporation is the substitution of tax-deductible interest on bonds for nondeductible dividends on preferred stock. Of course, where dealing with a closely-held corporation, substituting debt for stock in a manner to give the common stockholders a pro rata portion of the debt may be interpreted for tax purposes as "thin" capitalization, and the bonds may be treated as stock, regardless.

Also, to attract new money into the corporation, it is advantageous to consider the issuance of convertible debt securities bonds—to which are attached the rights (warrants) to buy common stock of the company at a specified price. The advantages of this type of security are:

1) An interest rate which is lower than the issuer could establish for non-convertible debt;
2) An initial conversion price greater than the market value of the common stock;
3) The conversion price which does not decrease.

The portion of proceeds from these securities which can be applied to the warrants should be credited to paid-in capital (based on fair value of both securities) and discounts or premiums should be treated as they would be under conventional bond issuance.

TREASURY STOCK

Treasury stock is stock which has previously been issued by a corporation but is no longer outstanding. It has been reacquired by the corporation and, as its name implies, held in its treasury. Treasury stock is not canceled because cancellation reduces the authorized issue of corporation stock. In some circumstances, it is permissible to show treasury stock as an asset if adequately disclosed.

Treasury Stock Shown at Cost

When a corporation acquires its own stock to be held for future sale or possible use in connection with stock options, or with no plans or uncertainty as to future retirement of that stock, the cost of the acquired stock can be shown separately as a deduction from the total of capital stock, capital surplus and retained earnings. Gains on subsequent sales (over the acquired-cost price) should be credited to capital surplus and losses (to the extent of prior gains) should be charged to that same account, with excess losses going to retained earnings. State law should be followed if in contravention.

Treasury Stock Shown at Par or Stated Value

When treasury stock is acquired for the purpose of *retirement* (or constructive retirement), the stock should be shown at par value or stated value as a reduction in the equity section; the excess of purchase cost over par (stated) value should be charged to capital surplus to the extent of prior gains booked for the same issue, together with pro-rata portions applicable to that stock arising from prior stock dividends, splits, etc. Any remaining excess may be applied pro-rata to either common stock or to retained earnings.

Treasury Stock as an Asset

If adequately disclosed, it is permissible in some circumstances to show stock of a corporation held in its own treasury as an asset. For example, pursuant to a corporation's bonus arrangement with certain employees, treasury stock may be used to pay the bonus, and, in accordance with the concept of a current asset satisfying a current liability, that applicable treasury stock might be shown as current asset. However, dividends on such stock should not be treated as income while the corporation holds the stock.

Treasury stock has neither voting rights nor the right to receive dividends. (Note: treasury stock remains *issued* stock, but not *outstanding* stock). Treasury stock can either be retired or resold. Treasury stock is an owners' equity account and is deducted from the stockholders' equity on the balance sheet.

When a company buys its own stock:		
Treasury Stock	XXX	
Cash		XXX
If the stock is resold:		
Cash	XXX	
Treasury Stock		XXX
(The credit is the amount paid for the stock when purchased by the corporation)		

If there is a difference between the corporation's acquisition of the stock and the resale price, the difference is debited or credited to an account Paid-In Capital from Treasury Stock Transactions for the amount of the difference between the proceeds of the resale and the amount paid by the corporation.

Under the cost method, treasury stock is shown as the last item before arriving at stockholders' equity, while under the par value method treasury stock reduces the common stock account directly under the capital stock section of stockholders' equity.

Chapter 10

Foreign Currency Translations and Derivative Disclosure

FASB STATEMENT 52, *FOREIGN CURRENCY TRANSLATION*

FASB 52 covers accounting for the translation of foreign currency statements and the gain and loss on foreign currency transactions. Foreign currency transactions and financial statements of foreign entities include branches, subsidiaries, partnerships and joint ventures, which are consolidated, combined, or reported under the equity method in financial statements prepared in accordance with U.S. generally accepted financial principles.

Why is translation necessary? It is not arithmetically possible to combine, add, or subtract measurements expressed in different currencies. It is necessary, therefore, to translate assets, liabilities, revenues, expenses, gains, and losses that are measured or denominated in a foreign currency.

Definitions

An understanding of this rather complex accounting rule can be aided by becoming familiar with the terms used in the Statement. The following list of definitions will enable the accountant to apply the accounting procedures and methods outlined below.

Attribute—For accounting purposes, the quantifiable element of an item.

Conversion—Exchanging one currency for another.

Currency Exchange Rate—The rate at which one unit of a currency can be exchanged or converted into another currency. For purposes of translation of financial statements, the current exchange rate is the rate at the end of the period covered by the financial statements, or the dates of recognition in the statements for revenues, expenses, gains and losses.

Currency Swap—An exchange between enterprises of the currencies of two different countries with a binding commitment to reverse the exchange of the two currencies at the same rate of exchange on a specified future date.

Current Rate Method—All assets and liabilities are translated at the exchange rate in effect on the balance sheet date. Capital accounts are translated at *historical exchange rates.*

Discount or Premium on a Forward Contract—The foreign currency amount of a contract multiplied by the difference between the contracted forward rate and the spot rate at the date of inception of the contract.

Economic Environment—The nature of the business climate in which an entity *primarily* generates and expends cash.

Entity—In this instance, a party to a transaction which produces a monetary asset or liability denominated in a currency other than its functional currency.

Exchange Rate—The ratio between a unit of one currency and the amount of another currency for which that unit can be exchanged at a particular time. The appropriate exchange rate for the translation of income statement accounts is the rate for the date on which those elements are recognized during the period.

Foreign Currency—A currency other than the functional currency of the entity being referred to. For example, the dollar could be a foreign currency for a foreign entity. Composites of currencies, such as the Special Drawing Rights (SDRs), used to set prices or denominate amounts of loans, etc., have the characteristics of foreign currency for purposes of applying Statement 52.

Foreign Currency Transaction—A transaction in which the terms are denominated in a currency other than an entity's functional currency. Foreign currency transactions arise when an enterprise buys or sells goods or services on credit at prices which are denominated in foreign currency; when an entity borrows or lends funds and the amounts payable or receivable are denominated in foreign currency; acquires or disposes of assets, or incurs or settles liabilities denominated in a foreign currency.

Foreign Currency Translation—Amounts that are expressed in the reporting currency of an enterprise that are denominated in a foreign currency. An example is the translation of the financial statements of a U.S. company from the foreign currency to U.S. dollars.

In the translation of balance sheets, the assets and liabilities are translated at the *current exchange rate*, e.g., rate at the balance sheet date. Income statement items are translated at the *weighted-average exchange rate* for the year.

There are two steps in translating the foreign country's financial statements into U.S. reporting requirements:

1) Conform the foreign country's financial statements to GAAP.

2) Convert the foreign currency into U.S. dollars, the reporting currency.

Foreign Entity—An operation (subsidiary, division, branch, joint venture, etc.) whose financial statements are prepared in a currency other than the currency of the reporting enterprise. The financial statements are combined and accounted for on the equity basis in the financial statements of the reporting enterprise.

Foreign Exchange Contract—An agreement to exchange, at a specified future date, currencies of different countries at a specified rate, which is the *forward rate.*

Functional Currency—The currency of the primary economic environment in which an entity operates; that is, the currency of the environment in which an entity primarily generates and expends cash.

Hedging—An effort by management to minimize the effect of exchange rate fluctuations on reported income, either directly by entering into an exchange contract to buy or sell one currency for another, or indirectly by managing exposed net assets or liabilities' positions by borrowing or billing in dollars rather than the local currency. An agreement to exchange different currencies at a specified future date and at a specified rate is referred to as *the forward rate.*

Highly Inflationary Economy—Economies of countries in which the *cumulative* local inflation rate over a three-year period exceeds approximately 100 per cent, or more.

Historical Exchange Rate—A rate, other than the current or a forward rate, at which a foreign transaction took place.

Inflation—Not defined by specific reference to a commonly quoted economic index. Management can select an appropriate method for measuring inflation. An annual inflation rate of about 20% for three consecutive years would result in a cumulative rate of about 100%.

Intercompany Balance—The foreign currency transactions of the parent, the subsidiary, or both. An intercompany account denominated in the local foreign currency is a foreign currency transaction of the parent. An intercompany account denominated in dollars is a foreign currency transaction of a foreign entity whose functional currency is a currency *other than* the U.S. dollar.

Local Currency—The currency of a particular country.

Measurement—Measurement is the process of measuring transactions denominated in a unit of currency (e.g., purchases payable in British pounds).

Remeasurement—Measurement of the functional currency financial statement amounts in other than the currency in which the transactions are denominated.

Reporting Currency—The currency used by an enterprise in the preparation of its financial statements.

Reporting Enterprise—An entity or group whose financial statements are being referenced. In Statement 52, those financial statements reflect a) the financial statements of one or more foreign operations by combination, consolidation, or equity accounting; b) foreign currency transactions; c) both a) and b).

Self-Contained Operations—Operations which are integrated with the local economic environment, and other operations which are primarily a direct or integral component or extension of a parent company's operations.

Speculative Contracts—A contract that is intended to produce an investment gain (not to hedge a foreign currency exposure).

Spot Rate—An exchange for *immediate delivery* of the currencies exchanged.

Transaction Date—The date at which a transaction, such as a purchase of merchandise or services, is recorded in accounting records in conformity with GAAP. A long-term commitment may have more than one transaction date; for example, the due date of each progress payment under a construction contract is an *anticipated transaction date* credited to shareholders' equity.

Transaction Gain or Loss—Gains or losses from a change in exchange rates between the functional currency and the currency in which a foreign transaction is denominated.

Translation Adjustment—Translation adjustments translate financial statements from the entity's functional currency into the reporting currency. The amount necessary to balance the financial statements after completing the translation process. The amount is charged or credited to shareholder's equity.

Unit of Measure—The currency in which assets, liabilities, revenues, expenses, gains and losses are measured.

Weighted Average Rates—Determined on a monthly basis by an arithmetic average of daily closing rates, and on a quarterly and an annual basis by an arithmetic average of average monthly rates.

Discussion of FASB Statement 52

The application of Statement 52 (the "Statement") is to the financial reports of most companies with foreign operations. The essential requirements of the Statements are:

1) Transaction adjustments arising from consolidating a foreign operation which do not affect cash flows are *not* included in net income.

Adjustments should be disclosed separately and accumulated in a separate classification of the equity section of the balance sheet.

2) Exchange rate changes on a foreign operation which directly affect the parent's cash flows must be included in net income.

3) Hedges of foreign exchange risks are accounted for as hedges without regard to their form.

4) Transaction gains and losses result from exchange rate changes on transactions denominated in currencies other than the functional currency.

5) The balance sheet translation uses the exchange rate prevailing as of the date of the balance sheet.

6) The exchange rate used for revenues, expenses, gains and losses is the rate on the date those items are recognized.

7) Upon sale (or liquidation) of an investment in a foreign entity, the amount accumulated in the equity component is removed and reported as a gain (or loss) on the disposal of the entity.

8) Intercompany transactions of a long-term investment nature are not included in net income.

9) Financial statements for fiscal years before the effective date of this Statement may be restated. If restatements are provided, they must conform to requirements of the Statement.

10) The financial statements of a foreign entity in a highly inflationary economy must be remeasured as if the functional currency were the reporting currency. A "highly inflationary economy" is defined in the Statement to be an economy that has had a cumulative inflation rate of 100%, or more, over a three-year period.

11) If material change in an exchange rate has occurred between year-end and the audit report date, the change should be reported as a subsequent event.

Background. The rapid expansion of international business activities of U.S. companies and dramatic changes in the world monetary system created the need to reconsider the accounting and reporting for foreign currency translation. In considering this topic, the FASB issued FASB Statement 52, which related to the following four areas:

1) Foreign currency transactions including buying or selling on credit goods or services whose prices are denominated in a foreign currency; i.e., currency other than the currency of the reporting entity's country.

2) Being a party to an unperformed foreign exchange contract.

3) Borrowing or lending funds denominated in a foreign currency.

4) For other reasons, acquiring assets or incurring liabilities denominated in foreign currency.

Statement 52 also applies to a foreign enterprise which reports in its currency in conformity with U.S. generally accepted accounting principles. For example, a French subsidiary of a U.S. parent should translate the foreign currency financial statements of its Italian subsidiary in accordance with Statement 52. The objective of translation is to measure and express in dollars, and in conformity with U.S. generally accepted accounting principles, the assets, liabilities, revenues, or expenses that are measured or denominated in foreign currency. In achieving this objective, translation should remeasure these amounts in dollars without changing accounting principles. For example, if an asset was originally measured in a foreign currency under the historical cost concept, translation should remeasure the carrying amount of the asset in dollars at historical cost, not replacement cost or market value.

The most common foreign currency transactions result from the import or export of goods or services, foreign borrowing or lending, and forward exchange contracts. Import or export transactions can be viewed as being composed of two elements—a sale or purchase and the settlement of the related receivable or payable. Changes in the exchange rate, which occur between the time of sale or purchase and the settlement of the receivable or payable, should not affect the measurement of revenues from exports or the cost of imported goods or services.

Foreign currency statements should be translated based on the exchange rate at the end of the reporting year. Translation gains and losses are presented in the stockholders' equity section. Also important is the accounting treatment of gains and losses resulting from transactions denominated in a foreign currency. These are shown in the current year's income statement.

Because of the proliferation of multinational companies, expanding international trade, business involvement with foreign subsidiaries, and joint ventures, FASB 52 was established, in effect, by popular demand. The stated aims of Statement 52 are to a) provide information that is generally compatible with the expected effects of a rate change on an enterprise's cash flows and equity, and b) reflect in consolidated statements the financial results and relationships of the individual consolidated entities as measured in their functional currencies, whether the U.S. dollar or a specified foreign currency, in conformity with U.S. generally accepted accounting principles.

The method adopted to achieve these aims is termed the *functional currency approach* which is the currency of the primary economic environment in which the entity carries on its business; in substance, where it generates and expends cash. The Statement permits a multiple measurement basis in consolidated financial statements (depending upon the country in which the sub-sidiary operates) because business enterprises made up of a multinational enterprise operate and generate cash flows in diverse economic environments, each with its own functional currency. When an enterprise operates in sever-al of these environments, the results of business transactions are measured in the functional currency of the particular environment. "Measured in the func-tional currency" has the specific meaning that gains and losses comprising income are determined only in relation to accounts denominated in the func-tional currency.

Mechanically, the functional currency approach calls for eventual trans-lation of all functional currency assets and liabilities into dollars at the current exchange rate. Under Statement 52, use of the current rate for all accounts resolves both the economically compatible results and operating margins dis-tortions. In the past, these distortions came about with the translation of non-monetary accounts at historical rates. The volatility of earnings distortions is alleviated by recording the translation adjustments directly into shareholders' equity.

The functional currency approach presumes the following:

1) Many business enterprises operate and generate cash flows in a number of different countries (different economic environments).

2) Each of these operations can usually be identified as operating in a sin-gle economic environment: the local environment or the parent compa-ny's environment. The currency of the principal economic environment becomes the functional currency for those operations.

3) The enterprise may be committed to a long-term position in a specific economic environment and have no plans to liquidate that position in the foreseeable future.

Because measurements are made in multiple functional currencies, deci-sions relating to the choice of the functional currency of a specific foreign operation will in all likelihood have a significant effect upon reported income. Even though the management of the business enterprise is entitled to a degree of latitude in its weighing of specific facts, the thinking behind adoption of this Statement is that the functional currency is to be determined based on the true nature of the enterprise and not upon some arbitrary selection which management feels might be of particular advantage to the reporting entity.

Determining the functional currency. Multinational companies are involved with foreign business interests either through transactions or invest-ments in foreign entities operating in a number of different economic envi-ronments. Each of these endeavors may be associated with one primary economic environment whose currency then becomes the functional currency for that operation. On the other hand, in a foreign country where the economic and/or political environment is so unstable that a highly inflationary economy is likely, it may be deemed wise to carry on the enterprise with the dollar as the functional currency. If the operations in situations of this nature are remeasured on a dollar basis, further erosion of nonmonetary accounts may be avoided.

When there is a reasonably stable economic situation, the national environment of each operation should be considered as the primary economic environment of the particular operation since national sovereignty is a primary consideration in relation to currency control.

Industry practice, on the other hand, may in some instances be instrumental in the determination of a primary economic environment and functional currency. If it is an industry-wide practice that pricing or other transaction attributes are calculated in a specific currency, such as prices set in dollars on a worldwide basis, that fact may be more of a determinant than local currency considerations.

The actual decisions in determining a functional currency depend to a large extent upon the operating policy adopted by the reporting company. Two broad classes of foreign operations are to be considered:

1) Those in which a foreign currency is the functional currency. This designation will have been made after receiving the facts and determining that this particular aspect of foreign business operations is largely autonomous and confined to a specific foreign economic environment. That is, ordinary operations are not dependent upon the economic environment of the parent company's functional currency, nor does the foreign operation primarily generate or expend the parent's functional currency.

2) When the workaday business of the foreign operation is deemed to be in actuality just an extension of the parent company's operation and dependent upon the economic environment of the parent company, the dollar may be designated as the functional currency. In substance, most transactions can reasonably be in dollars, thus obviating the need for foreign currency translation.

One of the objectives of Statement 52 is to provide information that is generally compatible with the expected economic effects of a rate change on an enterprise's cash flow and equity in a readily understood manner. If a foreign operation's policy is to convert available funds into dollars for current or nearterm distribution to the parent, selection of a dollar functional currency may be expedient.

Therefore, reporting for investments expected to be of short-term duration, such as construction or development joint ventures, the dollar should probably be designated the functional currency. If the nature of an investment changes over a period of time, future redetermination of the appropriate functional currency may become necessary. Such redetermination is permissible only when, in actual fact, significant changes in economic facts and/or circumstances have occurred. The operative functional currency cannot be redetermined merely because management has "changed its collective mind." It becomes evident that functional currency determination should be carefully considered with the decision weighted in favor of the long-term picture rather than short-term expectations.

In the event that redetermination is necessary, three procedures should be kept in mind:

1) When the functional currency has been changed, Statement 52 provides that the prior year's financial statement need not be restated for a change in functional currency.

2) When the functional currency change is from the local currency to the dollar, historical costs and exchange rates are to be determined from translated dollar amounts immediately prior to the change.

3) When the functional currency change is from the dollar to the local currency, nonmonetary assets are to be translated at current exchange rates, charging the initial translation adjustment to equity similar to that produced when Statement 52 was adopted.

Translation.   Translation is the process of converting financial statements expressed in one unit of currency to a different unit of currency (the reporting currency). In short, translation as used in Statement 52 is the restatement into the reporting currency (the U.S. dollar) of any/all foreign currency financial statements utilized in preparing the consolidated financial statements of the U.S. parent company.

Thus, the focus for the preparation and subsequent translation of the financial statements of individual components of an organization is, as previously stated, to:

1) Provide information that is generally compatible with the expected economic effects of a rate change on the enterprise's cash flows and equity, and

2) Reflect in consolidated statements the financial results and relationships of the individual consolidated entities as measured in their functional currencies in conformity with U.S. generally accepted accounting principles.

Measurement is the process of stating the monetary value of transactions denominated in a particular unit of currency (e.g., purchases payable in British pounds). These transactions may also be figured in a unit of currency other than that in which they are denominated. This process then becomes remeasurement and is accomplished by assuming that an exchange of currencies will occur at the exchange rate in effect at the time of the remeasurement. As is evident, should the exchange rate fluctuate between the date of the original transaction and the date of the exchange, a foreign exchange gain or loss will result. The gains or losses so recorded vary little from other trading activities and are, therefore, included in income.

It is important to note that while translations were formerly based on the premise that financial statements of a U.S. enterprise should be measured in a single unit of currency—the U.S. dollar—translation was under FASB 80, *Accounting for Futures Contracts*, a one-step process that included both remeasurement and reporting in dollars. In the newer context of the functional approach, multiple units of measure are permitted so that remeasurement is required only when 1) the accounts of an entity are maintained in a currency other than its own functional currency, or 2) an enterprise is invoiced in a transaction which produces a monetary asset or liability not denominated in its functional currency.

The subsequent translation to dollars under FASB 52 is the second step of a two-step process necessary to prepare U.S. dollar financial statements.

Foreign currency transactions.   Foreign currency transactions are those denominated in a currency other than the entity's functional currency. These transactions include:

1) Buying or selling goods priced in a currency other than the entity's functional currency.
2) Borrowing or lending funds (including intercompany balances) denominated in a different currency.
3) Engaging in an unperformed forward exchange contract.

As becomes evident, companies with foreign subsidiaries can readily become engaged in foreign currency transactions which must be considered when financial statements are prepared. But, in addition, companies which have no foreign branches may also in the everyday course of business become involved in foreign currency transactions.

Regardless of whether the company is entirely domestic-based or not at the transaction date, each resulting asset, liability, revenue, expense, gain, or loss not already denominated in the entity's functional currency must be so measured and recorded. At the close of each subsequent accounting period, all unsettled monetary balances are to be remeasured using the exchange rates in effect on the balance-sheet date. Gains and losses from remeasuring or settling foreign currency transactions are accounted for as current income. However, with certain restrictions, hedging losses and gains may be excluded from net current income.

Hedging.   Hedging, according to FASB 52, is planning to enter into a forward exchange contract to buy or sell one currency for another, or to manage an exposed net asset or liability position, such as borrowing or billing in dollars instead of in a local currency.

Hedging gains and losses can be excluded from net income when the transaction is *designated* as a hedge by management and is effective as such. Foreign currency transactions can be used in addition to, or in place of, forward exchange contracts to hedge a firm's foreign currency commitments. Formerly, the deferral of unrealized translation gains and losses was permitted only when the commitment was hedged by forward exchange contracts and they, in turn, had to match the commitment dates. On the other hand, FASB 52 permits maintenance of a hedge for any desired period of time. Furthermore, management now also has the option of removing a hedge and later reestablishing it. Qualifying as hedges are foreign currency cash balances and certificates of deposit, foreign currency loans, foreign currency swaps, and intercompany account balances.

Gains and losses from hedges of firm commitments in foreign currency, such as a contract to buy equipment, are deferred and included in the measurement of the related foreign currency transaction, e.g., the cost of the equipment at the date of the actual purchase. However, hedging losses may not be deferred if it appears likely that deferral will have the effect of recognizing losses in later periods. When a firm commitment is hedged, the translation gains or losses which are deferrable are limited to the amount that provides a hedge on an after-tax basis.

Derivative Accounting

FASB 52 and 80

Many investors and creditors have difficulty in their attempts to assess the effects of derivatives on the companies they follow. As a result, the FASB issued a new standard in 1994 expanding derivative financial instrument disclosure, and plans to issue another dealing with hedge accounting in the near future.

The following information summarizes accounting rules and practices which have preceded the newest rulings for the four basic derivative instruments—forward, futures, option, and swaps contracts. Since most complex derivatives are some combination of these four basic instruments, knowledge of the accounting for them should be of value in determining the appropriate accounting for more complex instruments. These even more sophisticated derivatives and derivative-like instruments run the gamut of exotic financial instruments including: interest rate caps, interest rate floors, fixed-rate commitments, variable rate loan commitments, commitments to purchase stocks and bonds, forward interest rate agreements, interest rate collars, and over 600 other imaginative creations which have been developed in the last few years.

Until the recently promulgated FASB 119, the basic U.S. accounting recognition and measurement rules for derivatives were limited to FASB 52 and 80. As we have seen, FASB 52 deals with accounting for foreign currency forwards and swaps; FASB 80 covers the accounting for exchange traded interest rate and commodity futures contracts. Between these two, there are inconsistencies particularly in the treatment of hedges of anticipated transactions and the definition of an effective hedge.

Two other FASB statements are relevant: FASB 105, *Disclosure of Information About Financial Instruments with Off-Balance Sheet Accounting Risk and Concentrations of Credit Risk* and FASB 107, *Disclosure About Fair Value of Financial Instruments.*

They have often been difficult to interpret and apply. The required disclosures are scattered among the notes to the financial statements, and some derivatives are excluded from the required disclosure because they are not subject to their coverage for one reason or another.

Hedge Accounting. All derivatives are accounted for at market but the basic question is under what conditions hedge accounting can be used. Hedge accounting recognizes the gains or losses on a hedging instrument in the same period as gains or losses on the hedged item are recognized.

1) If the hedged item is measured using mark-to-market accounting, the end of period unrealized gains and losses on the related hedging instrument are recorded in income.

2) If the hedged item is measured at the lower of cost or market, the end of period unrealized gains or losses on the related hedging instrument are recorded as an end of period adjustment to the hedged item's carrying value.

3) If the hedged item is measured at cost, the end of period unrealized gains and losses on the related hedging instrument are deferred until the gains or losses on the hedged item are recognized in some subsequent period.

The economics and purpose of a derivative transaction determine if it qualifies as an effective hedge and if hedge accounting is appropriate. Hedge accounting is usually thought to be appropriate when:

1) The item to be hedged is exposed to price, currency or interest rate risk.

2) The hedging instrument reduces the exposure to the risk associated with the item to be hedged.

3) The hedging instrument relates to a hedged item.

4) The hedging instrument is designated as a hedge of the hedged item.

Forward Contracts. Application of hedge accounting can be inconsistent and confusing, particularly since forwards accounting is handled differently in FASB 52 and 80 in several respects.

1) FASB 52 defines "risk" in terms of the sensitivity of the hedged item's exposure to risk. Consequently, in the case of foreign currency, the risk criterion is met if the foreign currency item is exposed to exchange rate risk regardless of possible offsetting positions the company may have. On the other hand, FASB 80 defines risk in terms of the sensitivity of the total enterprise's net income to risk. In the case of commodities and interest rates, possible offsetting positions of the total enterprise must be considered.

2) Statement 52 permits hedge accounting for foreign currency cross-hedges (using a hedge on one currency to hedge another) only if no direct foreign currency hedge is available. FASB 80 permits hedge accounting for commodities and interest rate cross hedges if there is a high correlation between the fair values of the various components of the positions that reduces risk exposure.

3) The accounting standards for forward contracts to hedge anticipated transactions that have not occurred or been committed to, but are expected to take place, also differ. The FASB's Emerging Issues Task Force (EITF) interpreted FASB 52 generally to disallow hedge accounting for forwards to hedge anticipatory transactions, except when the company's functional currency is the U.S. dollar or the transaction is intracompany. On the other hand, FASB 80 allows hedge accounting for forward commodity and interest rate contracts hedging anticipated transactions when:

a) The forward contract qualifies as a hedge.

b) The terms and characteristics of the anticipated future transaction can be identified.

c) It is probable that the anticipated future transaction will occur.

Futures Contracts.   Rules for hedge accounting when appropriate for futures are similar to those used in accounting for forwards.

Option Contracts.   Except for EITF and SEC pronouncements, there has been little authoritative guidance on accounting for options: FASB 52 does not mention them; FASB 80 is used as a guide when they are analogous to commodity and interest rate futures.

Statement 52 does not mention foreign currency options. The SEC and EITF have provided some guidance. EITF and the SEC permit hedge accounting for straight and tandem foreign currency options purchased to hedge anticipated transactions when both FASB 80's overall requirements for hedge accounting, including the standard's enterprise risk test, and FASB 52's transaction risk requirement are met.

Swap Contracts.   Currency swaps are covered by FASB 52. There is no comparable authoritative source of accounting standards for interest rate swaps. FASB 52 concluded that currency swaps are in substance equivalent to a series of forward foreign currency contracts. Thus, currency swaps may be accounted for in a manner similar to forward foreign currency contracts.

However, accounting for interest rate swaps is far from a settled issue. Some of the more common approaches followed include:

1) Swaps are executory contracts in which the contract is to be executed at or over some future period of time by the counterparts. They are covered by the general accounting standards for executory contracts. Swaps are not recognized on the face of financial statements as either assets or liabilities.

2) Up front organization and other similar fees paid by the counterparties are amortized over the life of the swap as an interest yield adjustment.

3) Unless the swap was accounted for as a hedge or an integral part of a borrowing arrangement, voluntary termination payments and receipts are included in income. If not, any gain or loss is spread over the remaining life of the related financial instrument.

4) Receivables and payables can be offset under swap arrangements.

5) Unrealized losses for changes in the market value of speculative swaps are recognized currently. Unrealized market value gains are generally not recognized.

6) Unrealized gains or losses for changes in the market value of swaps used either to hedge interest rate exposure or as an integral part of a borrowing arrangement are not recognized, except when the hedged item is accounted for at market.

FASB 119

In a continuing effort to make financial reporting more revealing and "user friendly" (to borrow a term from computer terminology), Statement 119 has been issued by the Financial Accounting Standards Board to apply to financial statements beginning with 1994. However, the provisions of the statement need not be applied to businesses and not-for-profit organizations with less than $150 million in assets until 1995.

FASB 119, *Disclosures about Derivative Financial Instruments and Fair Value of Financial Instruments*, addresses some of the many problems faced in providing investors with more in-depth information concerning the ever increasing area of derivative financial instruments held by the reporting entity. The statement requires complete disclosure to provide a clearer picture of an entity's position in this volatile several trillion dollar market.

As we have seen, derivatives are financial agreements including futures, forwards, swaps or option contracts, and the like, that "derive" their returns from other financial instruments to which they are linked. These may be commodities, bonds, or currencies, for example. Because of the complexity and volatility of such instruments, it is imperative that the financial statement simplify and clearly explain the ramifications (to the analyst and investor alike) of the very sophisticated as well as the very risky nature of these financial instruments. This pronouncement is certainly not the final word regarding derivatives. It is more than likely that the FASB will redouble its efforts to agree upon further requirements for control of disclosure about derivatives in light of the difficulties experienced by Orange County, California, in delving into this speculative type of investment.

The growing concern to gain better control of derivative activities is not confined to a select group of large organizations but extends to every level of those interested in financial markets both here and abroad. Because of the enormous leverage generated in the derivative market, a relatively modest investment can result in huge returns, but then there is always the other side of the coin and damaging losses can result. As the investors become more sophisticated and the disclosure picture becomes more revealing, these extremes should be modified. Informed investors as well as speculators have traded in options for many years and people have hedged foreign currency exposures routinely. It is the ever-expanding, more imaginative, more exotic form of derivative that needs to be defined and revealed.

FASB 119 amends some and expands upon other provisions of two previously enacted statements mentioned earlier and discussed below. FASB 105, *Disclosure of Information about Financial Instruments with Off-Balance Sheet Risk, and Financial Instruments with Concentrations of Credit Risk*, and FASB 107, *Disclosures about Fair Value of Financial Instruments*. Some, but not all, of these provisions are listed below. Neither of these two previous

Statements faced the issues of the measurement nor the recognition of financial instruments.

The principal features of the disclosure requirements for derivatives outlined in FASB 119 include the following:

1) Requires disclosures about amounts, nature, and terms including credit and market risk, cash requirements and accounting policy of derivative instruments not covered by FASB 105 because they do not result in off-balance-sheet risk of accounting loss.

2) Makes distinction between financial instruments held or issued for trading purposes and financial instruments held or issued for other purposes, including risk management.

3) Requires disclosures for derivatives held for trading purposes:
   a) average and end-of-period amounts of fair value in assets and liabilities,
   b) net trading gains or losses by class, business activity and risk and when reported.

4) Includes for derivatives held or issued for other than trading purposes:
   a) disclosure of their purposes and the plan to attain these objectives,
   b) the financial reporting treatment in the financial statement including recognition and measurement policies and when and where reported.

5) Includes for financial derivatives hedging anticipated transactions:
   a) description and time frame of the anticipated events to be hedged by derivatives,
   b) description of the anticipated hedge instruments,
   c) disclosure of the amount of hedging gains and losses deferred,
   d) the transactions or other events that will result in recognition of the deferred items in income,

6) Encourages, but does not require, quantitative disclosures about interest rate foreign exchange, commodity price or other market risks.

These disclosures may be on the face of the financial statement or in the accompanying notes.

FASB 105, Disclosure of Information about Financial Instruments with Off–Balance Sheet Accounting Risk and Concentrations of Credit Risk

One of the first responses to this now full-fledged derivatives market was the attempt to provide more information about off-balance-sheet items which carried the possibility of drastic accounting loss. FASB Statement 105, as its title states, requires disclosure about:

1) the nature, extent and terms of financial instrument with off-balance-sheet credit or market risk, and
2) significant concentration of credit risk for all financial instruments.

These provisions apply to not-for-profit organizations as well as to for-profit entities. However, as discussed below, some groups of financial instruments are excluded fully or partially from the requirements of this statement because they are already covered by other pronouncements.

Partially because of the almost "experimental" nature of some of the newly developed financial instruments and the lack of accounting standards applying to them, the recording and recognition of assets or liabilities resulting from these contracts may, at best, appear to only a limited extent in the financial statements.

In addition to a broad definition of financial instruments, FASB 105 specifically defined many of the newer types with off-balance-sheet risk of accounting loss including the derivatives already mentioned and also letters of credit, obligations to repurchase receivables sold, loan commitments, and various financial guarantees. They are defined as being instruments in which the risk of loss (even if remote) is greater than the amount recognized (if any) in the balance sheet. The accounting loss would result from credit or market risk attributable directly to conditional rights and obligations spelled out in the financial instrument's contract. The risks involved encompasses the failure of others to live up to terms of the contract, the vagaries of market prices, and actual theft or loss of the document.

In addition to a thorough discussion in the notes to the financial statement concerning the elements of risk listed above, an entity must delineate its nature and terms by type and specify any cash requirements and the accounting policies related thereto. The face, contract, notional or principal amount by type of instrument with off-balance-sheet risk must also be disclosed.

The portion of FASB 105 relating to *significant concentrations* of credit risk focuses on the specific business or industrial activity, the geographic area and/or the economic character of the situation which could endanger a portfolio of instruments that both do and do not run the risk of off-balance-sheet accounting loss.

Disclosure requires the following:

1) description of the activity, region or economic characteristics involved
2) figuring the maximum amount of damage resulting if the individual or group failed completely to live up to the terms of the contract and there was no other recourse

3) revealing the provisions and means for obtaining/requiring collateral or other security to support the financial instruments should the above occur.

Exempt from all of the disclosure requirements of FASB 105 are the following instruments:

1) Most insurance contracts because they are covered by FASB 60, *Accounting and Reporting by Insurance Enterprises* and FASB 97, *Accounting and Reporting by Insurance Enterprises for Certain Long-Duration Contracts and for Realized Gains and Losses from the Sale of Investments* (see elsewhere in this text.).

2) All long-term unconditional purchase obligations covered by FASB 47, *Disclosure of Long-Term Obligations.*

3) Employee benefit plans, pension, insurance, stock options, postretirement health-care, and other types of deferred compensation plans covered by myriad pronouncements including FASBs 87, 88 and 106 discussed elsewhere in this text.

4) Pension plan financial instruments, covered by FASB 87, *Employers'Accounting for Pensions.*

5) Extinguished debt covered by FASB 76, *Extinguishment of Debt.*

Exempt from some of the stipulations but required to disclose the concentration of credit risk in instruments with or without off-balance-sheet risk are the following:

1) lease contracts covered in FASB 13, *Accounting for Leases*

2) certain accruals denominated in foreign currency and translated in the balance sheet according to terms of FASB 52.

When there are instruments with off-balance-sheet risk other than from foreign exchange or which are foreign exchange forwards, options, swaps or futures, they are subject to FASB 105.

FASB Statement 107, Disclosure About Fair Value of Financial Instruments

Statement 107, *Disclosure About Fair Value of Financial Instruments*, defines fair value to mean the amount at which a financial instrument could be exchanged in a current transaction between willing parties, other than a forced or liquidation sale.

The rule is a broad approach to help issuers of financial statements understand what is required of them in meeting the newer, improved disclosure requirements, as well as to help minimize the costs of providing that information. Of course, the reasoning behind the stipulations in this Statement is to ensure a clearer, better defined picture of the fair value of financial instruments than has been provided in the past. This truer picture of an entity's financial activities should be of value to creditors, current and potential investors, and others in making informed decisions concerning granting credit to, investing in, or investigating more thoroughly, a particular entity.

Other impetus for enactment of this rule comes from a desire to provide another useful indicator of the solvency of a financial institution. A recent report issued by the U.S. Treasury Department has suggested that further market value information about various financial institutions could be of aid in regulatory supervision.

Since in many instances generally accepted accounting principles already necessitate disclosure, the term *fair value* use in FASB 107 in no way supersedes or modifies the set of figures obtained using *current value, mark-to-market*, or simply *market value*. It is simply an attempt to get more accurate information about financial instruments—both their assets and liabilities whether on or off the balance sheet—available for easy access.

For the purposes of this Statement, a financial instrument is cash, an ownership interest in an entity, or a contract that imposes on one entity a contractual obligation to deliver cash or another financial instrument to a second entity, or to exchange other financial instruments on potentially unfavorable terms with the second entity. The agreement gives the second entity a contractual right to receive cash or another financial instrument from the first entity, or to exchange other financial instruments on potentially favorable terms with the first entity.

If available, open-market prices are the best and easiest to obtain a measure of fair value of financial instruments. If quoted market prices or other established values are not available, estimates of fair value can be based on the quoted market price of a financial instrument with similar characteristics. Estimates can also be based on valuation techniques, such as the present value of estimated future cash flows using a discount rate commensurate with the risks involved, or using option pricing models. If it is not practicable to estimate the fair value of a particular financial instrument, reasons why it is not practicable must be thoroughly explained.

In all instances, descriptive material must be included detailing the method(s) and the basis for assumptions utilized in arriving at a stated fair value or in the failure to do so. In any event, failure to do so is not to be considered final. A continuing effort to arrive at a practicable (without incurring excessive cost) fair value should be carried out. Because the Board realizes that the cost of attempting to compute fair value in some instances would become excessive, certain types of financial instruments have been excepted from the requirements of Statement 107. These are:

1) Extinguished debt and assets held in trust in connection with a defeasance of that debt.
2) Insurance contracts, other than financial guarantees and investment contracts.
3) Lease contracts as defined in FASB Statement 13.
4) Warrant obligations and rights.
5) Unconditional purchase obligations.
6) Investments accounted for under the equity method.
7) Minority interests in consolidated subsidiaries.
8) Equity investments in consolidated subsidiaries.
9) Equity instruments issued by the entity and classified in stockholders' equity in the statement of financial position.
10) Obligations of employers and plans for pension benefits, other postretirement benefits including health care and life insurance benefits, employee stock option, and stock purchase plans.

Chapter 11

Internal Controls

When considering a topic of the magnitude of importance and complexity of internal control systems (ICS), it can be helpful first to understand what is being dealt with before getting into the technical aspects of the discussion. In the case of ICS it can be thought of as a "way of thinking." That is to say ICS involves the *evaluation* of both the methods and the application of those methods to an entity's controls system. Evaluation techniques require thoughtful consideration, rigorous study and research, and objective analysis. These three attributes are "ways of thinking," which in turn provide the guidance and direction of an orderly approach to a review of the techniques and procedures for the *judgmental* appraisal of the "adequacy" of an organizations's ICS.

The development of an internal accounting control system should be made in relation to the *objectives* of accounting controls as set forth in the Statements on Auditing Standards No. 1, Section 320.28:

> *Accounting control* comprises the plan of organization and the procedures and records that are concerned with the safeguarding of assets and the reliability of financial records and consequently are designed to provide reasonable assurance that:
>
> **a)** Transactions are executed in accordance with management's general or specific authorization.
>
> **b)** Transactions are recorded as necessary (a) to permit preparation of financial statements in conformity with generally accepted accounting

principles or any other criteria applicable to such statements and (b) to maintain accountability for assets.

c) Access to assets is permitted only in accordance with management's authorization.

d) The recorded accountability for assets is compared with the existing assets at reasonable intervals and appropriate action is taken with respect to any differences.

Two levels of objectives are implicit in the Statement. The primary objectives are the *safeguarding* of assets and the *reliability* of financial records.

THE FOREIGN CORRUPT PRACTICES ACT OF 1977

Primarily as a result of the enactment of the Foreign Corrupt Practices Act of 1977 (FCPA), internal accounting controls have become a significant point of concern for corporate management, the public accounting profession, and the Securities and Exchange Commission.

Section 102 of the FCPA titled *Accounting Standards* specifies that all corporations required to file with the SEC must:

Make and keep books, records, and accounts, which, in reasonable detail, accurately and fairly reflect the transactions and dispositions of the assets of the issuer.

The significance of this statutory requirement is that it represents the first time, historically, that the U.S. Congress has legislated an accounting Rule. The promulgation of accounting principles and practices (GAAP) has always been developed by "private sector" authorities, i.e., the AICPA, the FASB, the AAA (American Accounting Association), and "other authoritative sources." These are, essentially, highly specialized industries to which the general principles (GAAP) cannot be fully applied as it would be impractical to incorporate procedures unique to just one industry into GAAP. Banking, insurance, and financial institutional accounting is an example; railroad accounting is another as is the motion picture industry.

Accountant's Responsibility

Again, the significance of the Act is the explicit statutory recognition by the Federal Government given to accounting controls and control systems. The accountant's responsibility is to plan a system which constantly monitors for errors, irregularities, malfeasance, embezzlement, and fraudulent manipulation of the accounts. The accountant is in fact the "monitor" who must continually evaluate the effectiveness of the system and monitor compliance with the requirements of the statute. This, of course, also includes compliance with GAAP since the statute explicitly includes GAAP in the Act.

The fact that the statutory requirement applies to publicly-held corporations has led, initially, to the misunderstanding that it is of no concern to public accountants who are not involved in auditing public corporations. But auditors must be mindful of the *Statement on Auditing Procedure No. 1*, which applies to the scope of the examination of all companies, whether public or private corporations, partnerships, or other forms of business organizations. This Statement specifically references creditors, for example, who are a primary user of financial statements and to whom an auditor has a potential liability for materially misleading financial statements accompanying applications for credit to financial institutions, regardless of honest error or fraudulent intent.

Compliance Problems

What can an accountant do to ascertain compliance with the 1977 Act? Compliance can be demonstrated by an *intent* to comply, since neither the Act nor the professional literature specifies criteria for evaluating a system's adequacy or materiality levels. This makes it difficult for management, directors, independent auditors, and legal counsel to be sure of compliance with the Act.

The following suggestions may be helpful both to the accountant and to management for establishing intent to comply.

There should be:

1) Records of memos and minutes of meetings held by management, the board of directors, and the audit committee (if any) concerning internal accounting control concepts. The discussions should include legal counsel, internal auditors, and independent auditors.

2) Statements for the record of intention to comply.

3) A record of all meetings within the company of the accounting personnel and internal audit staff to ensure that they understand the importance of compliance and are able to monitor compliance.

4) A written program for continuing review and evaluation of the accounting controls system.

5) Letters from the independent auditors stating that no material weaknesses in internal accounting controls were discovered during the audit, or that suggested needed improvements have in fact been made. If necessary, the independent auditors' comments should include other deficiencies, and management's written plans to correct them should be included.

6) A record of periodic review and approval of the evaluation of the system by senior management, the audit committee, and the board of directors.

7) Instructional manuals for the development of methods and techniques for describing, testing, and evaluating internal controls.

8) Training programs conducted for internal auditors and other company personnel responsible for internal controls.

9) Changes in internal controls to overcome identified deficiencies that are initiated and documented.

10) A formal written code of conduct appropriately communicated and monitored. (Note: the SEC regards a corporate written code of conduct as imperative.)

11) Documentation that compliance testing was done by direct visual observations during the period being audited.

INTERNAL ACCOUNTING AND ADMINISTRATIVE CONTROL

Internal control according to the Professional Auditing Standards, is subdivided as follows:

a) Accounting control, which comprises the plan of organization and all methods and procedures that are concerned mainly with, and relate directly to, safeguarding assets and the reliability of the financial records.

b) Administrative control, which comprises the plan of organization and all methods and procedures that are concerned mainly with operational efficiency and adherence to managerial policies, such as sales policies, employee training and production quality control. This is usually only indirectly related to the financial records.

Administrative control includes, but is not limited to, the plan of organization and the procedures and records that are concerned with the decision processes leading to management's authorization of transactions. Such authorization is a management function directly associated with the responsibility for achieving the objectives of the organization, and is the starting point for establishing account control of transactions.

Accounting control comprises the plan of organization and procedures and records that are concerned with safeguarding assets and the reliability of financial records, and consequently are designed to provide reasonable assurance that:

a) Transactions are executed in accordance with management's general or specific authorization.

b) Transactions are recorded as necessary (a) to permit preparation of financial statements in conformity with generally accepted accounting principles or any other criteria applicable to such statements, and (b) to maintain accountability for assets.

c) Access to assets is permitted only in accordance with management's authorization.

d) The recorded accountability for assets is compared with the existing assets at reasonable intervals and appropriate action taken with respect to any differences.

Fundamentals of a System of Internal Accounting Control

1) Responsibility: There should be a plan or an organizational chart which places the responsibility for specified functions on specific individuals in the organization.

The responsibility for establishing and maintaining a system of internal accounting control rests with management. The system should be continuously supervised, tested and modified as necessary to provide reasonable (but not absolute) assurance that objectives are being accomplished, all at costs not exceeding benefits.

2) Division of duties: The idea here is to remove the handling and recording of any one transaction from beginning to end from the control of any one employee. Further, making different employees responsible for different functions of a transaction actually serves as a cross-check which facilitates the detection of errors, accidental or deliberate.

3) Use of appropriate forms and documents: Efficient design of forms and documents aids in the administration of the internal control system. Mechanical or electronic equipment can also be used to expedite the process of checking. Both of these methods provide control over accounting data.

4) Internal auditors: Periodic review of all the above elements of the internal control system should be carried out by an internal audit staff. The function of this staff would be to periodically check the effectiveness of above items 1), 2), and 3).

There is a relationship between the size of an organization and the development of its internal control system. Complete separation of functions and internal auditing department may not exist in smaller companies. The objective in these smaller companies is to divide the duties in the way that creates the greatest amount of internal check.

Elements of a Satisfactory System of Internal Accounting Control

The elements of a satisfactory system of internal control include:

1) A plan of organization which provides appropriate segregation of functional responsibilities.
2) A system of authorization and record procedures adequate to provide reasonable accounting control of assets, liabilities, revenues and expenses.
3) Sound practices to follow in the performance of duties and functions of each of the organizational departments.
4) Personnel of a quality commensurate with responsibilities.

One important element in the system of internal control is the independence of the operating, custodial, accounting and internal auditing functions. There should be a separation of duties in such a way that records exist outside each department to serve as controls over the activities within that department. Responsibilities for various functions and delegation of authority should be clearly defined and spelled out in organizational charts and manuals. Conflicting and dual responsibility is to be avoided. The function of initiation and authorization of an activity should be separate from the accounting for it. Custody of assets should be separated from the accounting for them.

Relationship of an Internal Control System to Outside Accountants

The efficiency of an internal control system becomes important to a company's outside, independent auditors. Before determining how much of an audit they should make, they must review the internal control system. An efficient system may do away with certain audit procedures which might otherwise be necessary. Conversely, a poor internal control system may necessitate greater checking on the part of the auditor at additional cost.

INTERNAL CONTROL FOR INVENTORIES

Some internal control procedures that can be used in conjunction with different types of inventories—finished goods, work in process, materials, goods for resale—are detailed in the paragraphs that follow.

Inventories of Merchandise Purchased for Resale and Supplies

1) The purchasing department approves the purchase orders for merchandise to be bought. In a small company, the owner or manager may be the one to approve these purchase orders which should be sequentially numbered and traced to final disposition.

2) After okays from purchasing manager have been received, requests for price quotations are usually sent out. These requests should go to various companies, and the company quoting the lowest price will be the one from which the purchases are made, unless there are other overriding considerations.

3) In the selling department, an updated individual quantity record for each type of unit is kept on perpetual inventory stock cards. It is usually the responsibility of inventory clerks to keep these cards up to date. These stock cards indicate the need for reorders and they should be checked against purchase requisition by the manager of the selling department or other person in control of the merchandise stock. In a business too small to have a separate selling department, the owner or manager is the one to perform these functions. The number of units of merchandise ordered is then entered on the inventory stock cards by one clerk. The number actually received is entered from the receiving list by another clerk. The number sold or used is entered on the stock cards by still another clerk from sales lists or salesperson's orders. After recording the number ordered, received and issued on the inventory stock, cards the balance represents the number of units actually on hand. A well-rounded perpetual card system usually includes detailed unit costs for ready computation under either LIFO, FIFO, or average methods.

4) In the receiving department, the receiving clerk should not be allowed to see purchase order records or purchase requisitions. Receiving reports are checked against the perpetual inventory stock records and a notation is made on these stock record cards indicating the date, order number and quantity received. Even where a business is too small to have a perpetual inventory, a receiving report should be made, which should then be checked against the purchase orders and a notation as to the day and quantity received made on those purchase orders.

5) In the accounts payable department, the receiving report is checked against the merchandise stock record, then sent to the accounts payable department where it is verified against the seller's invoice. The purchasing agent should have approved the price on the seller's invoice before that invoice was sent to the accounts payable department. A clerk in the accounts payable department should verify all extension totals on the invoice. If the vendor's invoice and receiving report are in agreement, the invoice is then entered into a purchase journal or voucher register for future payment. Any discrepancy between quantity received and quantity on the seller's invoice will hold up payment until an adjustment is made by the seller.

The departments involved in internal control in merchandise and supplies inventories are purchasing, sales, receiving, accounts receivable and accounts payable.

Finished Goods Inventories

1) It is necessary to: Ascertain the quantity of units which have been completed from the production record and transferred to the shipping department or warehouse. The daily report of finished goods units transferred to the warehouse or shipping department indicates the number of finished units available to the sales department.

2) Compute the unit cost of finished goods delivered to the sales department. This information is obtained from the unit cost sheet (for a process cost accounting system) or from the job-order cost card (in a job order cost accounting system).

3) Set up finished goods inventory cards and for each item record the quantity received at the warehouse, the quantity shipped on orders and the balance remaining at specified unit costs. The number of finished goods units in the warehouse or stockroom should tie in with this finished goods inventory file.

4) Periodically, physically count the finished goods inventory and see that it ties in with the finished goods inventory file.

The departments involved in internal control of finished goods inventories are manufacturing, cost accounting, accounts receivable and sales.

Raw Materials and Supplies Inventories

1) In the stores department, the storekeeper must safeguard the raw materials and supplies inventories—both physically and by accounting control. No raw materials or supplies can leave without a stores requisition. Quantity control at minimum levels is also the responsibility of the storekeeper.

The storekeeper should keep a stores record for each item, listing the maximum and minimum quantities, quantity ordered and number, quantity received, quantity issued, and balance on hand. When stores cards show minimum quantities, a stores ledger clerk pulls those cards from the file to make sure that materials or supplies are ordered to cover the minimum needs. Quantities shown on the stores record should be verified by making an actual count of the stores items which are to be ordered; then a purchase requisition is filled out from the stores records. The quantity of each item ordered is approved by the storekeeper who knows the average monthly consumption of each item. The ordering of special equipment by department heads also goes through the storeroom after having the necessary executive approval. The purchase requisition is then sent to the purchasing agent.

In the stores department, a receiving report is prepared in triplicate by the receiving clerk. One copy goes to the stores ledger clerk, another to the accounts payable department; the third is kept by the receiving clerk. The receiving clerk puts the stores items in proper places within the storeroom after preparing the receiving report. Sometimes, location numbers are used to facilitate ready accessing.

The stores ledger clerk gets a copy of the receiving report and makes a record of the quantity and the order number on the stores ledger card affected by the items received.

2) In the purchasing department, the purchase agent places the order for the quantity needed on the quantity requisition. If the agent feels the quantity ordered is excessive, he or she may look into the storekeeper's purchase requisition. The next step is to request price quotations from various supply companies, placing the order with the lowest bidder. The purchase agent also verifies the prices on the seller's invoices by comparing them with the price quotations.

3) In the accounts payable department, no bill should be approved for payment until materials ordered have actually been received, are in good condition, and the prices of the seller's invoice matched to the quotations.

4) In the manufacturing department, different individuals have authority to sign stores requisitions to withdraw materials from the storeroom. Usually, a foreman prepares a stores requisition where raw materials or supplies are needed in any of the manufacturing departments. This requisition contains the account name and number, department name and number, job order number, quantity of material issued, the stores item name and classification symbol, the name of the person to withdraw materials from the storeroom, the unit price of the item and the total cost of items withdrawn from the storeroom.

The departments involved in internal control for raw materials and supplies inventory are stores, purchasing, accounts payable and manufacturing.

Work-in-Process Inventory

1) In the manufacturing department, stores requisitions are prepared by shop foremen for materials which are to be charged to the work-in-process inventory account. Quantities of materials are obtained from engineering or administrative departments. Specifications for raw materials are usually shown on a bill of materials (a list of different items required to complete an order). The stores requisition will specify the quantity, price, cost of each item of raw material requisitioned and the job order number.

Time tickets are prepared by the workers and approved by a foreman in the department in which work is performed before it is charged to the work-in-process inventory account. Each labor operation may have a standard time to perform a certain operation which has been predetermined by the engineering department. There also may be a predetermined standard wage rate, determined by the head of the manufacturing department and known by the payroll department. The cost accounting department is responsible for the amount of manufacturing expense charged to the work-in-process inventory account.

2) In the cost department, raw material cost is computed from sales requisitions, direct labor costs from time tickets, and manufacturing expense is estimated from prevailing overhead rates.

Internal control methods for the work-in-process inventory account depend on whether the firm has a process cost accounting or job-order cost accounting system.

The chief point of internal control for work-in-process inventories is computing costs. Product costs are analyzed by operations, departments and cost elements. This permits measurement of the cost of products at different stages of completion. The number of partly finished units when multiplied by a cost at a particular stage should come close to the value in the work-in-process inventory account.

The departments involved in internal control of work-in-process inventories are manufacturing and cost accounting.

Taking Count—The Physical Inventory

The two most significant factors of inventory control are:

1) Knowing what *should* be on hand, based on paper controls; and
2) Verifying *what actually is on hand*; by a physical count.

The Perpetual System—Knowing What Should Be on Hand

In many firms, not enough effort and emphasis are put into the timely keeping of detailed perpetual inventory stock records, thus ignoring the most basic control available.

The nature and extent of the records to maintain vary from company to company. At the least, there should be a constant updated record of the *units* handled—a card or a loose-leaf sheet to which are posted the "ins" and "outs" always showing the new morning's balance on hand—or rather, the balance which *should* be on hand. If expanded to the fullest, the system would also include unit-costs of acquisitions (or, in manufacturing, detailed material, labor and overhead costs assigned), unit-sales deleted at cost (based on the company's "flow-of-cost" assumption of LIFO, FIFO or average costs) and balance on hand extended at cost. Also, the individual record would show back-order positions, writedowns, destructions, and, most important, locations in the storage area (by location number or description). It may show the total sales income for that particular unit, displaying unit gross profits. Retail stores using the gross profit method of valuing inventories usually maintain controls over entire departments, or sections of departments, rather than by individual units, and extended values are at retail, showing markups and markdowns, as well as bulk cost figures.

The general ledger summary inventory asset account should (where the system provides cost-flowing movement) always tie to the total of the subsidiary perpetual system (at least monthly). They should be matched as often as possible and all differences traced to eliminate any weaknesses in the system.

The point is—know what *should be on hand!*

The Physical Count—Verifying What Is Actually on Hand

At least once a year, a physical count of the entire inventory should be taken, usually as of the balance sheet date. Management, not the auditor, is responsible for taking this physical inventory. The auditor is an *observer* of methods, count and valuation, who may help establish the system of counting, the tags to use, the methods of assuring a full count, the cutoff procedures, the pricing, etc., so as to be satisfied about the reasonability of the total value acceptable for attestation.

The method of tagging, counting, weighing or measuring, locating, recounting—the assignment of personnel—all the procedures should be set in advance and followed (unless properly authorized changes develop).

The auditor should become familiar with the nature of the products handled, the terminology, the packaging, the principles of measurement. Such "education" in the client's processes should not be obtained at the sacrifice of counting-time.

The auditor is concerned with the final evaluation of that *physical* inventory. The perpetual records, as such, and errors therein are not a necessary part of the audit process, though weaknesses should be commented upon in the management letter.

However, a history of *accurate* internal paper control of inventory can substantially reduce the extent of testing by the auditor. When it can be expected that variations from perpetual inventories will be small and within tolerable limits, the auditor may choose to use statistical random sampling in testing either an immediately prior physical count or in counting only those items *drawn by the auditor* (without advance notice) for random selection. If the sample then indicates an unacceptable rate of error, the auditor may request another (or full) physical count, or may, with management's consent, adjust the overall value of the inventory to an amount indicated by the sample (see Journal Entries in Appendix A), with management promising to investigate the error in the ensuing fiscal year.

When an effective perpetual inventory control is in use, management usually "cycle" counts the inventory once, or several times over, during the year, testing bits and pieces throughout the year, covering it entirely at least once.

There are often *portions* of an inventory which may require more time and effort to physically count than the relative merit of those portions warrants. Such items may be *reasonably* estimated (with joint approval of management and auditor), based on such elements as: last year's value, movement during the year, space occupied, weight, or, considering sales and purchases, using an estimated gross profit method.

Summary Thoughts

The accuracy of a physical inventory even with the most sophisticated computerized system, may always be in doubt if there is *no* perpetual record for comparison. A perpetual inventory is meaningless unless tested periodically to a physical count. A history of accurate perpetual records can be justification for an auditor's using statistical sampling for year-end evaluation. Moreover, management itself can use statistical sampling techniques for cycle counting. Tie-in to the general ledger asset account should be made regularly by management. The financial statement value of the inventory must be at cost or market, whichever is lower. Standards are *not* acceptable, unless approximating cost.

INTERNAL CONTROL FOR EXPENSES

Each of the various types of expenses requires special internal control procedures. These procedures are covered in the following paragraphs.

Manufacturing Expenses

1) In the manufacturing service and producing department, small tools which are not constantly being used should be kept in the toolroom. Each worker requiring such tools is given metal checks, each stamped with a personal number. The toolroom attendant will release a tool to a worker in exchange for a metal check bearing the worker's number. The check is kept in the toolroom until the tool is returned, at which time the check is returned.

The department supervisor has the responsibility for approving a requisition for a new tool when one wears out.

2) Charges for freight and shipping on incoming supplies should be charged to the account to which the supplies are charged. Copies of the freight or shipping bills should be attached to supply invoices. Supplies inventory is, therefore, charged for these freight and shipping charges instead of an expense account.

3) Numerous types of shop supplies, such as brooms, oil, waste, solder, wire, are part of the raw materials and supplies inventory. They should be kept in the storeroom and issued only by a stores requisition, signed by an authorized individual. The individual who indicates the need for such supplies (usually a supervisor) should indicate the job order number or departmental expense account number to which the material is to be charged on the stores requisition.

4) Workers categorized as indirect laborers should have an identification number when they work in a specific department. A time clock card should be kept and verified by a supervisor or timekeeper.

The departments involved in internal control of manufacturing expenses are factory production, factory service and accounts payable.

Selling Expenses

1) Salesperson's salaries should be okayed by the sales department manager before a summary is sent to the payroll department. The basis for the summary is the salesperson's daily report. Commissions earned are verified from duplicate sales invoices mailed to the customer. These are computed in the sales department and approved by the sales department manager.

2) To prevent padding of travel expenses, many companies allow flat rates or maximum amounts for each day of the week. Unusual amounts should require an explanation from the salesperson.

3) The office manager retains control over outgoing mail and postage. A mail clerk usually affixes the postage. A point to keep in mind as a control of postage expenses is not to permit every office worker access to stamps or a postage meter.

4) Telephone expenses can be controlled by having the switchboard operator record all outgoing calls by departments on a call report sheet. Long distance calls should be reported on a special form indicating the party making the call and where the call is going to. From the long distance call record, telephone expenses are distributed by departments.

5) Subscriptions to publications and dues of various organizations and professional societies should be approved by the sales manager before a voucher is prepared.

6) All bills approved by the sales manager are sent to the accounting department for payment.

The departments involved for internal control of selling expenses are sales and accounts payable.

Administrative Expenses

Internal control for administrative expenses is very similar to that for the sales department. Bills for administrative expense items should be approved by an administrative department executive before they are sent to the accounts payable department for payment.

The departments involved in internal control of administrative expenses are administrative and accounts payable.

Financial and Other Expenses

In corporations which have special departments to control financial problems in the company, a treasury department or similar department will handle expenses in the nature of interest, discount and dividends and may even supervise handling of cash. The financial department may also have the responsibility for authorizing credit extended to customers.

1) A credit manager in the financial department should have the responsibility for approving sales orders above a specific amount. The manager should be in constant touch with the accounts receivable department to determine whether or not a customer has been regular in payments. The treasurer has the responsibility for authorizing bad debt writeoffs. The writeoff itself should be made by someone in the accounts receivable department on the authority of the financial department executive—not the sales manager.

2) The financial department executive or office manager approves expenditures such as interest and bank discounts, office expenses and supplies. After approval of these items, invoices are sent to the accounts payable department.

The departments involved in internal control for factory payrolls are timekeeping, payroll, accounts payable and the particular manufacturing division.

Salaries and Wages

1) In the timekeeping department each worker is given an identifying number which will serve to identify his or her department. A badge with this number serves as identification when presence within the factory is checked each day.

2) It is the duty of a time clerk to check the presence of each worker once or twice a day, every day. This is to eliminate the possibility of one person punching the time clock for another who is absent. Absences are noted in a time book. These are then checked against the employee's time ticket, time clock card or payroll sheet at the end of each specific pay period.

3) Care should be taken to prevent one worker punching another worker's time clock card. The time clock card indicates the number of hours the worker is present each day in the plant and can be used to verify either daily or weekly the hours shown on daily time tickets.

4) In the manufacturing department, a time ticket which lists the worker's name, number of hours worked on different jobs and labor operations, and total hours worked is prepared. It must be approved by the foreman of the department in which work is performed.

5) In the payroll department, time tickets are verified against the time clock cards and the time keeper's time clock book. The time ticket is then given to a clerk who inserts the hourly or piece-work rate of each worker. Another clerk computes the earnings. The time tickets are then used for working up the payroll sheet. Then, the time tickets are sent to the cost accounting department to prepare a payroll distribution sheet. The payroll sheet becomes the record by which the worker is paid. After the payroll sheet has been completely okayed, it is sent to the accounts payable department for payment. Payment to each worker, either by check or cash, should be receipted.

In the accounts payable department the payroll sheet serves as the basis for payment.

The departments involved in internal control for factory payrolls are timekeeping, payroll, accounts payable and the particular manufacturing division.

Office Payroll

1) In the sales department, the sales manager approves the daily sales reports. From these reports, a record of the salesperson's days is prepared. The record is sent to the payroll department after approval by the sales manager. The manager in the sales department also approves the records of work performed by the sales office force before sending it to the payroll department.

2) In the administrative department, the office manager approves time worked by the office force and then sends it to the payroll department. Salaries of top executives are often placed on a special payroll. Their salaries are usually known by the paymaster who prepares their checks and sends them directly to the executives' offices.

3) The treasurer or financial department office manager similarly approves the work performed by the clerical personnel in his or her department.

4) Upon receiving these authorized reports from the various departments, the paymaster sets them up on a payroll sheet and after computing the applicable salary for each office worker, takes all applicable deductions and indicates a net salary for each employee.

5) In the accounts payable department, payment for these office workers' salaries is prepared from the payroll sheets.

INTERNAL CONTROL FOR CASH

Where currency is available, internal control is needed the most. Incoming checks may be used in manipulating accounts receivable and must be controlled. Accounts receivable control becomes part of cash control, and vice versa. Cash disbursements and petty cash also need special internal controls, for which details follow.

Cash Receipts

1) In the selling department, cash sales should be recorded in a register. A numbered sales slip should be made up for each sale. These slips should be used in numerical order.

2) In the cashier's department, an employee should count the cash in each register at the end of the day. Except for a small amount left to make change, all cash should be removed. The total daily cash receipts should be recorded on slips and placed in the same pouch as the cash itself. The pouch should then be turned over to a clerk (a different employee from the one who counted the cash in the register) who will make out a bank deposit slip. Still another clerk in the cashier's department should read the cash register totals of the day or remove the cash sales slips. The cash removed from the register must agree with the tape and the total of cash slips which are numbered sequentially (all numbers must have been accounted for). The sales readings are then compared with the amount of cash removed from the registers by the cashier. Small discrepancies are charged to a cash, short or over account. Larger discrepancies call for an explanation.

3) In the accounts receivable department, incoming mail should be opened by a bonded clerk. All checks, currency, money orders are listed by this clerk on a cash-received record. The cash-received record lists date of receipt, name of sender and amount. The record and totals are then sent to the accounts receivable department to be properly applied to the customers' accounts. The cash is sent to the cashier's office and subsequently given to the deposit clerk.

4) In the accounts receivable department, the record of cash received is used to credit against customers' accounts. This record then goes to the general accounting department where it is compared with daily deposit slips of cash received from customers before it is entered on the books.

The departments involved in internal control of cash receipts are selling, treasury or cashier's and accounts receivable.

Cash Disbursements

In the accounts payable department, purchase of any item must have prior approval from the authorized person in charge of the department in which the expenditure originates before it comes to the accounts payable department. Where a voucher system is in operation, vouchers are prepared for each expenditure. Information on the voucher matches that shown on the seller's invoice. Vouchers are entered in the voucher register after having been approved by the head of the voucher department and then placed in a pending file for future payments.

The departments involved in the internal control of cash disbursements are accounts payable and voucher.

Petty Cash

In any department where it is necessary to have a petty cash fund, at least two individuals should have the responsibility for handling petty cash. One individual inspects and approves the item for payment. The other has charge of the petty cash fund and pays the vouchers as they are presented. Each petty cash voucher should list the date, amount paid and name of the account to be charged. A bill or other receipt, if there is one, should be attached to the voucher. The employee who controls the petty cash fund should compare the receipts attached to the petty cash vouchers with the vouchers.

When the petty cash fund needs reimbursement, the person who controls the fund totals those petty cash vouchers which have been paid out and presents them to the accounts payable department, which then arranges for the necessary reimbursement.

The departments involved in the internal control of petty cash are selling, administrative, or others in which there is a need for such petty cash funds, and accounts payable.

Accounts Receivable

Copies of sales slips from the sales department are used to charge customers' accounts. Copies of any credits due customers come from the sales department. These records are sent to the accounts receivable department, where, if possible, one clerk should have the responsibility for entering only debits to customers' accounts and another for posting credits for returned merchandise, receipt of a note, etc. Still a third employee should enter the credit in the customer's account for cash received.

Sending statements at the end of each month is a good way to check the accuracy of the customer's accounts.

The departments responsible for internal control of accounts receivable are the accounts receivable and sales.

Notes Receivable

In the treasury department, a record of notes held from customers is made. A record is then sent to the accounts receivable division where a clerk makes the proper credits. A copy is sent to the general accounting department to reflect the charge to the control account—notes receivable. The treasurer keeps the notes until maturity date or until discounted with the bank. A subsidiary note register should be kept if the company receives a large number of such notes.

The departments responsible for internal control of notes receivable are treasury and accounts receivable.

Cash and Bank Reconciliations

Cash is the lifeblood of the company. It is the center upon which the whole circle of business activity is pivoted. Here is the reservoir into which all flows—in and out.

It is surprising to find that tests of cash receipts and cash disbursements are usually limited by management (through intermediaries) to monthly bank reconciliations.

Nothing is more effective than unannounced, non-routine, spot-tests of the cash-handling procedures (for that matter, *any* business procedure) by the highest authority within the company. Think of the impact made on an employee who *knows* there may be an impromptu test by the president of the company—at any time! Called in, for example, to explain the purpose of a canceled check the worker now holds; imagine the psychological impact if this is done periodically, but irregularly? A test of application of payments on account—receivables and payables—almost any awareness of constant high-level review has an alerting effect. Peak, honest, performance is encouraged.

Bank reconciliations by and of themselves cannot stand alone as proof of cash authenticity. They prove only the activity *within* that one period and serve to lend to prior reconciliations substantiation of then-listed outstanding checks. The current reconciliation is technically unproved until the outstanding checks and uncredited deposits in transit appear.

Reconciliations should be tested by someone other than the original preparer.

Block-proofs of cash should also be used occasionally to test an entire year's transactions. Here, all deposits are matched to all receipts recorded (in total); and all recorded disbursements are matched to total bank charges for cleared checks and minor items, with consideration given to opening and closing transit items.

The theory behind the mechanics of the bank reconciliation is to *update* the *bank* figures (on a worksheet) to reflect all transit items which have not yet cleared the bank, as follows:

Bank shows a balance of	$ 10,500
Add deposits in transit	2,000
	12,500
Less checks outstanding (itemized)	600
Adjusted bank balance	$ 11,900
Balance per books shows	$ 11,909
Difference	$ 9 (more on books)

Having taken the preliminary steps of determining the deposits in transit (by checking the bank credits against recorded receipts) and the outstanding checks (by checking off all returned canceled checks against the listing of those issued or carried over), we note a remaining difference of $9.

In the following *order*, the *most expedient* ways to find this difference is to:

1) Look at the bank statement for any bank charge (D/M's or combination)—not yet recorded in the general ledger;

2) Look at the books for any $9 debit (or combination) on the books and not on the statement;

3) $9 may be indicative of a transposition. Match the bank's opening pickup balance to the closing one on the last statement:

Match deposits to receipts recorded;

Check general ledger footings and subtraction;

Check summary postings into the general ledger from the original source;

Check footings in the books of original entry (Receipts, Disbursements, General Journal);

4) Having exhausted the above possibilities and still not having found the difference, check the face amount of each check to the amount charged by the bank (each check is canceled with a clearance date).

5) Now match the listing of the check to the actual check. (Steps 4 and 5 are interchangeable).

6) Not yet? Prove the bank's additions.

7) If still elusive, it probably has been missed above or a transposition error has been made in listing transit checks or deposits; or, it may be an error made last month which was missed.

FILE MAINTENANCE

One of the most important, yet least emphasized, facets of the business enterprise is the establishment and proper maintenance of an effective, accurate filing system. How costly is the time wasted in frustrating searches for misfiled data, when initial precautions and firm rules might have assured quick access to and retrieval of needed documents by competent, authorized personnel!

Suggestions

Establish firm rules for filing.

Provide adequate accessible filing space for current files.

Pinpoint responsibilities for filing and accessing files.

Follow legal requirements for record retention. Establish an annual policy of removing outdated files.

Utilize flow charts when appropriate.

Have sufficient copies of documents such as purchase orders, sales shipping papers, and all papers ultimately tied to a sales or vendor's invoice, to allow for a complete numerical file of each document.

A List of File Categories

Sales invoices to customers—both alphabetic and numeric files;

Vendor invoices—alphabetic, sometimes with copy of paid voucher check or numbered voucher. Some firms keep invoices segregated in an "unpaid" file until paid;

Canceled checks—keep by month in reconciled batches. Do not intermingle different batches;

Correspondence files—for customers, vendors, others;

Permanent files—organizational information, legal documents, leases, minutes, deeds, etc. Usually in fireproof areas, accessibility limited.

Other:

Tax files

Payroll and personnel files

Backup for journal entries

Investment files—security transactions

Petty cash voucher files

Purchasing department files—supplies, bids, etc. (costs)

Credit department files

Prior years' books of entry

Data from subsidiary companies owned

Advertising programs, literature, etc.

Computer Files—Considerations

1) Security protection—access, codes, permanent tapes/discs of programs, updated balance files for accounts receivables, payables, general ledger, payrolls. Keep enough of these changing files for re-runs or accumulation runs, as needed for emergencies.

2) Keep hard copy until sure replacement hard copy is accurate, or as necessary for continuous file.

3) Be prepared for manual emergency work, if computer goes down suddenly.

4) Pinpoint responsibility for keeping logs, storage, etc.

One of the most significant developments in public accounting in recent years is the provision in the Foreign Corrupt Practices Act of 1977 (FCPA). It requires publicly-held companies to develop and maintain a system of internal accounting controls sufficient to ensure:

1) That transactions are executed in accordance with management's general or specific authorization.

2) That transactions are recorded as necessary to permit preparation of financial statements in conformity with generally accepted accounting principles, or any other criteria applicable to such statements.

3) That the system maintains accountability for assets.

4) That access to assets is permitted only in accordance with management's general or specific authorization.

5) That the recorded accountability for assets is compared with existing assets at reasonable intervals, with appropriate action taken with respect to any difference.

Auditor's Objective: The significance of the Act, insofar as auditors are concerned, is the explicit statutory recognition given to accounting controls. The auditor's objective is to plan the examination to search for errors or irregularities that would have a material effect on the financial statements, and to use skill and care in the examination of the client's internal control system. While the independent auditor is not part of a company's internal accounting control system, the auditor must evaluate the effectiveness and monitor compliance of internal accounting control systems.

INTERNAL CONTROLS FOR A SMALL BUSINESS ENTERPRISE

There are many definitions of a "small business." The most commonly accepted one is the U.S. Department of Commerce classification of an enterprise of less than 500 employees as a small business concern. Using this definition there are millions of nonagricultural small business establishments in the United States.

In a small business organization of only a few people, little reliance can be placed on internal controls involving a segregation of duties such as among several persons in a large organization. However, that is no excuse to ignore the importance of some degree of internal controls; rather, limited personnel with a few wearing more than one hat and associated with the handling of a company's money can be the reason for a review of the need and the establishment of the control function.

A plan of organization which provides at least a limited segregation of functional responsibilities within the constraint of limited staff should be developed. In a small business the segregation is not so much between employees as between the owner and employees. An alert and able owner can provide about as much control as the segregation of duties does in a large organization.

The owner of a small business usually is the key person in its management. Different from a large organization, the small business person represents one of the effective components of a control system, e.g., that of *personal observation*. Principally, the owner can personally focus attention upon selective areas of the business. One example would be reconciling the bank statement—one of the prime areas of control for a manager with limited time.

The selection of a few areas for control is an important step. A tendency to over-control must be avoided in order to avoid a negative cost-benefit allocation of time and expense. There is no need to control pencils and paper clips; the effort should be directed toward areas where the risk of error and material loss are greatest. Careful evaluation can uncover areas over which no control is exercised, but which are significant enough for procedures to be established for their control.

The checklist which follows has been developed by the authors as an economic and simplified guide for the responsible person in a small business to conduct periodic internal audits for the implementation and continuous review of the activities in the various areas of the business. From this checklist, which includes the significant areas of any business, can be selected those areas most important to the individual user. While a small business does not need accounting controls as sophisticated and expensive as those of a large company, neither can a small business be lax and informal with respect to procedures that can prevent possible mismanagement of assets or even embezzlement or fraud. The checklist, itself, is a set of procedures that can be a suitable system.

AN INTERNAL CONTROLS CHECKLIST FOR SMALL BUSINESS

(After selecting the areas that are considered to be necessary for some degree of control, the user can refer a few pages back for additional detail for each item selected).

EMBEZZLEMENT—ITS PREVENTION

Definition: Embezzlement is the fraudulent appropriation of property by a person whom management has *trusted*. "Trusted" is the key word.

A company can be losing money before suspecting that an embezzlement might be taking place, because this crime is usually committed by someone in a position of trust. Losses can be a small amount taken from a cash register, or a large sum of money stolen through manipulating the books. A set of simple controls built into the accounting system can prevent an embezzling operation. At the least, proper controls can document incriminating evidence in the absence of which it would be difficult to estimate a loss for insurance purposes, or to prove in the courts that the losses resulted from a crime.

This discussion reviews procedures for the detection and prevention of dishonest practices. It can be helpful first to understand a few of the usual methods of embezzlers in diverting company funds to their own pockets. Such an understanding can be a framework for developing the record-keeping and control procedures to safeguard the company's money and other property vulnerable to misappropriation by an employee. (In general, however, an embezzler's methods are limited only by his or her creativity.)

1) By definition an embezzler is usually a trusted employee enjoying the complete confidence of his or her employer. Usually, the embezzler has authority in such important areas as managing the checkbook. The easiest

Question	Remarks	N/A	Yes	No
GENERAL				
1. Are accounting records kept up-to-date and balanced monthly?		——	——	——
2. Is a standard chart of accounts with descriptive titles in use?		——	——	——
3. Are adequate and timely reports prepared to insure control of operations?				
a. Daily reports		——	——	——
b. Monthly financial statements		——	——	——
c. Ratio analysis such as C/S or gross profit		——	——	——
d. Comparison of actual results with budget		——	——	——
e. Cash and other projections		——	——	——
4. Does the owner/Board take an active interest in the financial affairs and reports available?		——	——	——
5. Are personal expenses kept separate from business expenses?		——	——	——
6. Are employees who are in a position of trust bonded?		——	——	——
7. Are director/employees required to take annual vacations and are their duties covered by another?		——	——	——
8. Are monthly bank reconciliations reviewed by owner/director?		——	——	——
9. Do employees appear to be technically competent?		——	——	——
10. Are job descriptions prepared?		——	——	——
11. Are volunteers properly trained and supervised?		——	——	——
12. Is there any separation of duties?		——	——	——
13. Is there utilization of machine accounting and/or EDP in the preparation of financial reports, accounts receivable, etc.?		——	——	——
14. Are Minutes up to date and complete?		——	——	——
15. Are transactions with stockholders at arms' length?		——	——	——
16. Are governmental reporting requirements being complied with in a timely manner?		——	——	——
17. Is insurance maintained in all major cases and is this coverage reviewed periodically by a qualified individual?		——	——	——

Question	Remarks	N/A	Yes	No

Conclusions:

_____

_____

_____

_____

_____

CASH RECEIPTS

Question	Remarks	N/A	Yes	No
1. Is mail opened by director/owner or someone other than the bookkeeper?		___	___	___
2. Are receipts taped or listed prior to turning them over to the bookkeeper, and are they subsequently traced to the cash receipts journal?		___	___	___
3. Does the client have adequate documentation of cash receipts?		___	___	___
4. Are checks immediately endorsed for deposit only, deposited promptly and intact?		___	___	___
5. Are over-the-counter receipts controlled by cash register, prenumbered receipts etc., and are these reviewed by owner/director?		___	___	___
6. Are checks returned by the bank followed up for subsequent disposition?		___	___	___

Conclusions:

_____

_____

_____

_____

_____

INVENTORIES

Question	Remarks	N/A	Yes	No
1. Are perpetual inventories maintained?		___	___	___
2. Are they verified periodically by someone not normally in charge of inventories?		___	___	___
3. Where perpetual records are not in use:				
a. Are periodic physical counts taken by responsible employees?		___	___	___
b. Is owner exercising control by review of gross profit margins?		___	___	___

Question	Remarks	N/A	Yes	No
4. Are physical facilities such as to discourage pilferage by employees and others?		___	___	___
5. Are off-premises inventories controlled?		___	___	___
6. Is customers' merchandise on the premises physically segregated and under accounting control?		___	___	___
7. Are inventories reviewed periodically for old, obsolete, or excessive items?		___	___	___

ACCOUNTS RECEIVABLE & SALES

Question	Remarks	N/A	Yes	No
1. Are work orders, sales orders, shipping documents and invoices prenumbered and controlled?		___	___	___
2. Would the existing system disclose shipments being made without recording a sale? (Sales on consignment, samples, etc.)		___	___	___
3. Is a credit check approved by owner?		___	___	___
4. Are sales invoices reviewed for price, terms, extensions and footings?		___	___	___
5. Is an aged trial balance prepared monthly, reconciled to the general ledger, and reviewed by the owner?		___	___	___
6. Are monthly statements:				
a. Reviewed by owner?		___	___	___
b. Mailed to all accounts?		___	___	___
c. Are zero and credit balance statements mailed?		___	___	___
7. Are write-offs, credit memos and special terms approved by the owner/director?		___	___	___
8. Is there sufficient separation of the receipts function and the application of payments to the accounts receivable?		___	___	___
9. Are notes and other receivables under separate control?		___	___	___
10. If there are any pledges receivable:				
a. Are they properly recorded?		___	___	___
b. Is there collection follow-up?		___	___	___

Question	Remarks	N/A	Yes	No
c. Are write-offs properly approved?		___	___	___
11. Is pricing of sales invoices from standard price lists?		___	___	___
12. Are variations from standard prices approved by owner/director?		___	___	___
13. Do adequate controls exist to assure receipts from miscellaneous sales (scrap, fixed assets, rents, vending machines, etc.)?		___	___	___

Conclusions:

_____

_____

ACCOUNTS PAYABLE, PURCHASES, DISBURSEMENTS				
1. Are prenumbered purchase orders used and are these approved by owner/director?		___	___	___
2. Are competitive bids required above prescribed limits?		___	___	___
3. Are payments made from original invoices?		___	___	___
4. Are supplier statements compared with recorded liabilities?		___	___	___
5. Are all disbursements made by prenumbered checks?		___	___	___
6. Is the owner/director's signature required on all checks?				
a. Does owner/director sign checks only when they are accompanied by original supporting documentation?		___	___	___
b. Is the documentation adequately cancelled to prevent reuse?		___	___	___
7. Is there evidence that the following items have been checked before invoices are paid?				
a. Prices, discounts, sales tax		___	___	___
b. Extensions and footings		___	___	___
c. Receipt of goods or services		___	___	___
d. Account distribution		___	___	___

Question	Remarks	N/A	Yes	No
8. Are voided checks retained and accounted for?		___	___	___
9. Is there an imprest petty cash fund?		___		___
a. If so, is there a responsible employee designated as a custodian of the fund?		___	___	___

Conclusions:

_____

_____

INVESTMENTS

1. Does owner have sole access to certificates, notes, etc.?		___	___	___
2. In case of non-profit organizations:				
a. Is dual control exercised over certificates?		___	___	___
b. Is there a written investment policy?		___	___	___
c. Does the board approve sales and purchases?		___	___	___
d. Is the return on investment checked periodically by the board?		___	___	___
3. Is there effective utilization of temporary excess funds?		___	___	___
4. Is income from investments accounted for periodically?		___	___	___

Conclusions:

_____

_____

PROPERTY, PLANT & EQUIPMENT

1. Are there detailed, and updated records to support general ledger totals for assets and accumulated depreciation?		___	___	___
2. Is the owner/Board acquainted with assets owned, and is approval required for sale or acquisition?		___	___	___
3. Are there physical safeguards against theft or loss of small tools and other highly portable equipment?		___	___	___

Question	Remarks	N/A	Yes	No
4. Is there a policy distinguishing capital and expense items?		——	——	——

Conclusions:

_____

_____

PAYROLL

1. Is owner/director acquainted with all employees and does he or she approve all new hires and changes of pay rates? —— —— ——

2. Is there a folder for each employee that contains an employment application, W-4, authorizations for deductions, etc.? —— —— ——

3. Are there controls to prevent the payroll from being inflated without the knowledge of owner/ director either by fictitious employees or padded hours? —— —— ——

4. Does the owner/director sign all payroll checks? —— —— ——

5. If payroll is prepared by a bank or service bureau, does the owner/director periodically review each check and related journals prior to distribution to employees? —— —— ——

   a. Are unusable checks properly voided or redeposited? —— —— ——

6. Is the payroll bank reconciliation prepared by someone other than the bookkeeper? —— —— ——

7. Is the payroll paid from a separate imprest bank account? —— —— ——

Conclusions:

_____

_____

REVIEW OF THE CHECKLIST

Review the checklist and record below the items and comments that appear to need attention both with respect to increased control and improved efficiency.

1. _____

_____

2. _____
_____
_____
3. _____
_____
_____
4. _____
_____
_____
5. _____
_____
_____
_____

opportunity is sales for cash with no recording of the transaction in the books and no relevant paperwork. Prenumbered invoices or simply cash register receipts can be used for all sales with appropriate monitoring procedures to assure that cash sales are being recorded. Also, when employees know written records are maintained, the temptation to embezzle is lessened.

2) A complicated method of embezzlement is termed *lapping*. Lapping involves temporarily withholding receipts, such as payments by a customer on accounts receivable, and is a continuing process that usually starts with a small amount and runs into thousands of dollars before it is detected.

Example: An employee opens mail or receives cash and checks as payment on open accounts. The employee pockets a $100 cash payment by a customer named Paul. To avoid Paul complaining at a later time about failure for his account to be credited, $100 is next taken from a *$200* subsequent payment by a customer named Peter and credited to Paul's account and the embezzler pockets the $100 difference. (Note that the amount pyramids; it has to in order for the embezzler to continue to profit.) The lapping procedure continues with the employee absconding with increasingly larger amounts of money involving a steadily increasing number of customer accounts.

Prevention requires detailed recordkeeping procedures of invoices and other supporting working papers and periodic unscheduled audits of the accounts, along with confirmation of accounts receivables. Without adequate procedures, detection of lapping is difficult and can continue for years. One red flag, however, is the discovery that an employee is keeping personal records of transactions outside of the established accounting system. Another indication that is a common practice is for an embezzler to decline vacations, or to even leave the premises for lunch. Many companies require employees responsible for funds management to take regular vacations; it has occurred that the substitute employee has discovered irregularities.

3) *Check-kiting* is one of the most popular operations in small and large companies alike. For a successful check-kiting operation, the employee must be in the position both to write checks and to make deposits in two or more bank accounts. One account is the embezzler's personal account and the other is the business checking account.

The check-kiter plays the *float*: e.g., the number of days between the deposit of a check and collection of funds. There may be several days between the date when a check drawn on Bank A is deposited in Bank B and the date the check clears Bank A for payment. A simple kite is accomplished simply by cashing a check at Bank B, and covering the morning of the day the check is expected to reach Bank A. As the process is repeated the kited checks become increasingly large, more cash is withdrawn from Bank B and the kiting continues as long as the shortage is covered on time in Bank A. Finally, the kite "breaks"; this is when Bank A refuses to honor a check because the funds on deposit are insufficient to cover the kited check, or because the check reached Bank A a day earlier than usual.

A temporary kite can be used by a dishonest employee who has stolen cash in a separate operation. The cash shortage can be concealed at the end of an accounting period by depositing a kited check into the company account. This deposit brings the bank balance into reconciliation with the book balance on the statement date.

The best preventive measure against kiting (or to detect suspected kiting) is for the owner of the business to request "cut-off" statements from the bank at periodic intervals which, in turn, should be irregular intervals.

4) Payroll frauds are a frequent source of loss. The usual practice is to add the names of relatives or fictitious individuals to the company payroll, enabling the embezzler to draw several weekly paychecks instead of one. The best preventive measure is a policy that no person is added to the payroll without the personal authorization of the owner, or a responsible personnel manager in the organization. Also, frequent and regular payroll audits can reveal more pay checks being drawn than the company has employees.

5) A typical embezzling procedure is for the dishonest employee to open an account on the books for a dummy supplier and issue checks to the nonexistent supplier for fictitious purchases. Established purchase procedures and an inventory controls system can discourage an employee from using false vouchers to process purchases of nonexistent merchandise.

There are a number of clues that can alert the owner or manager of a business to suspect dishonest practices.

- An unusual increase in sales returns can conceal accounts receivable payments.
- Unusual bad-debt write-offs can cover a fraudulent practice.

- A decline in credit sales that is unusual can indicate possible unrecorded sales.
- Unexpected large drop in profits or increase in expenses can be a red flag.
- An increasing rate of slow collections of receivables can conceal an embezzlement.

In addition to an accounting system that incorporates a system of internal controls, there are a number of precautions an owner can take to reduce the possibility of fraudulent losses.

- Careful checks of prospective employees' background.
- Know the employees' personal lifestyles, insofar as possible.
- Have company mail addressed to a post office box, and only the owner has access to the box.
- Have only the owner or a key person collect and open company mail.
- The owner can be the only person to manage the funds, write checks, and make deposits.
- Examine periodically all canceled checks, especially the endorsements on them.
- Unusual discounts and bad-debt write-offs should be approved by the owner, or manager.
- All employees responsible for company funds should be bonded.
- If possible, the preparation of the payroll and payment of employees should be done by different persons, especially if cash is disbursed on payday.
- Avoid the *cardinal* sin—*Never sign blank checks!* Not even to your *Mother*.

Chapter 12

Budgeting for Profit Planning and Budgetary Control

A budget in its simplest terms is an estimate of future events A budget is not a purely random guess, but a forecast which is computed from historical data that has been verified and assumed with some degree of credibility. The volume of sales for the following year, for example, may be estimated by using data from past experience, present-day market conditions, buying power of the consumer and other related factors.

Merely preparing the annual budget, then leaving it unaltered for the remainder of the budget period, is not the purpose. Preparation is only the first step. The second step is for management to control the operations of the firm and to adhere to the budget. Budgetary control is the tool of management for carrying out and controlling business operations. It establishes predetermined objectives and provides bases for measuring performance against these objectives. If variations between performance and objective arise, management should alter the situation by either correcting the weakness in performance or modifying the budget. Firms that adopt budgetary control have a better control of operations and are better able to modify them to meet expectations.

In addition to a review of the rolling budgets based on previous years' expenditures and operations, two management tools related to budgeting will also be discussed: break-even analysis (BE) and zero-base budgeting (ZBB).

The objective of break-even analysis is to determine an approximation as close as possible to the changes in costs generated by changes in the volume of production. Determining the BE point is a technique that can be applied to the control of costs, in the evaluation of alternatives, in the allocations of a firm's resources, and in making decisions in virtually every phase of a company's business.

The value to budgeting in break-even analysis is that the approach can be applied to sales, profits, costs, and selling prices, to help make sound decisions for the utilization of idle plant capacity, for proposed advertising expenditures, and for proposed expansion in production levels.

ZBB is a logical process, combining many elements of management. The key components of ZBB are:

1) Identifying objectives.
2) Determining value of accomplishing each activity.
3) Evaluating alternative funding levels.
4) Establishing priorities.
5) Evaluating workload and performance measures.

What ZBB does is to recognize that the budgeting process is a management process, a decision-making process and a driving force.

Types of Budgets

There are two principal types of annual profit budgets: the operating or earnings budget, and the financial or cash budget. The earnings budget, as its name implies, is an attempt to forecast the earnings of a company for a future period. To make such forecast, other estimates must be made. Consequently, we have sales budgets, production budgets (which include labor budgets, materials budgets, manufacturing expense budgets), capital expenditure budgets, administrative expense budgets, distribution expense budgets and appropriation-type budgets (e.g., advertising, research). The accuracy of each of these budgets determines the accuracy of the earnings forecast.

The cash budget, on the other hand, tries to forecast the utilization of the company's cash resources. It estimates the company's anticipated cash expenditures and resources for a period of operation. Cash budget forecasts, like the earnings forecast, depend heavily on sales forecasts. The amount of sales determines the amount of cash the company has for purposes of its operation.

THE SALES BUDGET

The foundation of the entire budget program is the sales budget. If anticipated sales of a particular product (or project) do not exceed the cost to produce and market it by an amount sufficient to reward the investors and to compensate for the risks involved, the product (project) should not be undertaken. Sales forecasting must be continuous. Conditions change rapidly; in order to direct one's efforts into the most profitable channels, there must be a continuous review and revision of the methods employed.

Forecasting Sales

A sales forecast represents the revenue side of the earnings forecast. It is a prediction as to the sales quantity and sales revenue. Sales forecasts are made for both short and long periods.

Forecasting sales with any degree of accuracy is not an easy task. For example, a firm which estimates sales with the expectation that a patent which it holds will not become obsolete may be disappointed.

In general, the business forecaster has two situations: 1) those which he or she can to some extent control, and 2) those where conditions created by others can only be observed, recorded, interpreted and applied to his or her own situation. A firm that has a monopoly due to an important patent which it owns is an example of a company which controls the situation. Forecasts made by such a company may be very accurate. In most cases, however, a company has no such control. It must attempt to interpret general conditions, the situation in its own industry, and future sales of its particular company before making forecasts.

Making the forecast is the responsibility of the sales manager, who, with the help of the district managers and the individual salespersons, determines the primary sales objectives for the year. Corrections of the forecast are made by the heads of the firm so that sales estimates will better reflect expected economic conditions. Before an estimate of sales is made, there must be a reasonable expectation that the projection is attainable. It must be based on the best evidence available. As conditions change, the forecast is revised.

If a firm desires to sell more than in the past, an analysis of past sales performances must be supplemented by other analyses. Consideration must be given to general business conditions. The effects of political and economic changes throughout the world are quickly reflected on individual business communities. Some of these factors which affect sales are wars, government regulations, and technological developments. This information should be used in appraising the probable effect of these changes on the sales of the firm for the budget period.

Market Analysis

A sales manager needs to know if the firm is getting its full share of potential customer demand as indicated by a market analysis.

The questionnaire is a popular method of reaching consumers, retailers and jobbers. Data collected give the firm valuable information, essential in arriving at a forecast of sales possibilities.

A market analysis at a given time gives a picture of the present and potential consumption of a product. This picture provides only half the significant information. The other half can be obtained by continuing the survey over a period of time to discover market trends.

Pricing Policy

The sales budget is not complete until the firm decides on a practical policy as to what price can be secured for its product(s). Generally, estimates should be made to conform with the market prices during the budget period.

The next step is to formulate the sales policies of the firm. These policies should be established relative to such considerations as territorial expansion and selection, customer selection, types and quality of products and service, prices, terms of sales, and sales organization and responsibility.

Only after a firm has thoroughly analyzed past sales experience, general business conditions, market potentials, the product to be sold, determined the prices to be charged and formulated its sales policies is it ready to develop the sales program.

Measuring Individual Performance

As a basis for measuring individual performance, a rewarding-merit sales standard could be established. A sales standard is an opinion of the best qualified judgment of performance which may reasonably be achieved under ideal conditions. By comparing this standard with the budget estimate (the figure expected) under normal conditions, management has provided the most important tool of sales control.

An example of how a comparison between the standard and budget estimate may serve as a basis for reward is the following: A saleswoman may be told to produce sales of $150,000 (standard), but the firm may expect her to produce sales of only $125,000 (budget estimate). The saleswoman does not have to be told what the firm's budget figures are. In an endeavor to reach $150,000, she is trying to better what she believes is the budget figure. Depending on how close she comes to the $150,000, the firm may devise a method of rewarding her It should be kept in mind, however, that the standard should not be set too high, since it may have a reverse effect if the sales personnel feel it is unreachable.

THE PRODUCTION BUDGET

After the sales budget has been prepared, the next step is to prepare the production budget which specifies the quantity and timing of production requirements.

While the sales budget is prepared in anticipation of seasonal fluctuations, the production budget endeavors to smooth out the fluctuations and thus make most effective use of productive capacity. This is accomplished by manufacturing for stock over the slow periods and using the stock to cover sales during busy periods.

There are different problems for a firm that sells stock products and one that produces special-order goods. The objective for a stock-order-type firm is to coordinate sales and production to prevent excessive inventories, but at the same time to have enough stock to meet sales. A forecast of production in such a firm should enable the executive to arrange to lay out the factory so as to handle the anticipated volume most conveniently. Production in such a firm must be as evenly distributed as possible over the year. It is uneconomical to manufacture the whole period's requirements within a relatively short time at the beginning of the budget period. This involves unduly heavy capital costs of carrying the large inventory. Also, distributing the work over the entire period spreads the labor costs.

With special-order items, the production department must be prepared at all times to manufacture the goods as soon as possible after receiving the order. Production in this case has to be arranged for the best possible utilization of equipment and labor, so that idle time is reduced to a minimum.

Budgeting Production Costs

Production budgets should be rigid as long as conditions remain the same, but they should be capable of prompt adjustment when circumstances change. For example, if a company operates at 70 percent of capacity in a period and the budget was based on a production volume of 80 percent, the budget is of little use. The budget will have to be altered to show what production costs will be at the 70 percent level. It is prudent when planning production at a particular anticipated percentage level to indicate in the budget the estimates of possible production costs at different levels.

Preparing the Production Budget

The production budget period may vary in length. However, it is common practice among large corporations to use what is known as a "product year." As an example, the automobile industry will usually start with the introduction of new models. The budget year should include at least one complete cycle of operations so that money tied up in raw materials and work-in-process materials may undergo one complete liquidation. Another factor influencing the budget period is the stability of general business conditions. It is more difficult to budget operations during an unstable period, and it is advisable at these times to shorten the budget period.

The production budget should be expressed in terms of physical units. To compute the physical quantities is simple. For example, a simple computation to estimate production required is:

	Units
Estimated sales	250,000
Less opening inventory	150,000
Total requirements	100,000
Add: Closing inventory	100,000
Production required	200,000

Before computing the quantity to be produced, it is necessary to decide quantities to be in the inventory at the end of the period. This decision should be based on factors such as:

a) Adequate inventory to meet sales demands
b) Evenly distributed production to prevent shortage of material and labor
c) Danger of obsolescence
d) High costs of storing large inventories.

Available Facilities.   The production program must conform with the plant facilities available and should determine the most economical use of these facilities. The capacity of the plant is measured in two ways: optimum plant capacity and normal plant capacity. All other measurements are in percentages of optimum or normal capacity. Optimum capacity of course, can never actually be attained. There are many unavoidable interruptions, such as waiting for setup of machines; time to repair machines; lack of help, tools, materials; holidays; inefficiency; etc. However, these interruptions should be looked into to determine how they can be minimized.

Management should also consider whether additional equipment is needed just to meet temporary sales demands. Later, such equipment may be idle. The replacement of old machinery with new high-speed equipment should also be considered. A careful study should help determine which step would be more profitable in the long run.

Records for each product showing the manufacturing operations necessary and a record of each machine's capability and capacity, should be maintained. Estimates must be made of material to be used, number of labor hours and quantities of service (power) required for each product. These estimates are called "standards of production performance." The establishment of these standards is an engineering rather than an accounting task. In this respect, these standards are similar to those used in standard cost accounting.

Cost of Production.   The following illustrates how cost of production is determined: Assume a concern has a normal capacity of 100 units of product. Current production budget calls for 80 units. Only one product is made; and its production requires two operations, A and B. The standard costs are: variable costs per unit of product, one unit of direct material, $2; operation A (direct labor and overhead), $3; operation B (direct labor and overhead), $5; total $10. Fixed production costs for the budget period are $500, or $5 per unit based on normal capacity. This production cost budget would then be expressed as follows:

Variable cost (80 units @ $10)	$ 800
Fixed costs (80 units @ $5)	400
Costs chargeable to production	1,200
Cost of idle capacity (500 less 400)	100
Total budgeted costs	$1,300

There is a tie-in here between estimated costs, standard costs, and production budgets.

THE LABOR BUDGET

The labor budget deals only with direct labor. Indirect labor is included in the manufacturing expense budget. (The manufacturing expense budget includes the group of expenses in addition to indirect labor, expenses such as indirect material, repairs and maintenance, depreciation and insurance.)

The purpose of the labor budget is to ascertain the number and kind of workers needed to execute the production program during the budget period. The labor budget should indicate the necessary worker-hours and the cost of labor required for the manufacture of the products in the quantities shown by the production budget.

Preparation of the Labor Budget

The preparation of a labor budget begins with an estimate of the number of labor hours required for the anticipated quantity of products. Before this can be done, it is necessary to know the quantity of items to be produced, as in the production budget. If the products are uniform and standard labor time allowances have been established, it is just a matter of multiplying the production called for by the standards to determine the labor hours required. If the products are *not* uniform but there is uniformity of operations, it is first necessary to translate production into operation requirements. Operation standards then should be established in terms of worker- or machine-hours to ascertain the quantity of labor required. The next step in preparing the labor budget is to estimate the cost of direct labor. These estimates are computed by multiplying the number of units to be produced by the labor costs per unit. The problem then is to predetermine the unit labor costs. Some of the methods of determining these costs are:

1) Day rate system
2) Piece rate system.
3) Bonus system.

In firms where standard labor costs have been established for the products manufactured, it is necessary only to multiply the units of the product called for in the production budget by the standard labor costs.

A detailed analysis should frequently be made of the differences between actual and estimated labor costs to determine whether they are justified. An investigation may reveal inefficient workers, wasted time, defective materials, idle time, poor working conditions, high-priced workers, etc. Responsibility must be definitely placed and immediate action taken to correct those factors which are capable of being controlled.

The budgets for direct labor and manufacturing expenses are not complete until schedules of the final estimates are prepared. The form will vary, depending on the needs of the firm. The following is an example of a schedule of estimated direct labor costs where estimates are shown for each department of the firm:

X Corporation

Estimated Direct Labor Costs
for the Period 1/1/xx to 12/31/xx

Dept.	Quantity to Be Produced	Standard Labor Cost Per Unit	Total Estimated Labor Cost
1	127,600	$ .90	$115,000
2	127,600	1.60	204,000
3	127,600	1.12	143,000
		$3.62	$462,000

MATERIALS BUDGET

The purpose of the materials budget is to be sure that there are sufficient materials to meet the requirements of the production budget. This budget deals with the purchase of raw materials and finished parts and controls the inventory. How to estimate the material required depends on the nature of the individual company. A company manufacturing standard articles can estimate fairly accurately the amount of raw materials and the purchases required for the production program. Even where the articles are not standard, there is usually a reliable relationship between the volume of business handled and the requirements for the principal raw materials.

Tie-in to Standard Costs

In the preparation of the material budget, there is a tie-in to standard costs. Here is an example of how purchase requirements are computed:

Quantity required for production	300,000 units
Desired inventory at end of budget period	75,000 units
Total requirements	375,000 units
Less: Inventory at beginning of period	80,000 units
Purchase requirements	295,000 units

The next step is to express material requirements in terms of prices. Some firms establish standard prices based on what are considered normal prices. Differences between standard and actual purchase prices are recorded as price variance.

Factors Affecting Policy

These are:

1) The time it takes the material to be delivered after the purchase order is issued.
2) The rate of consumption of material as indicated by the production budget.
3) The amount of stock that should be on hand to cover possible delays in inventory of raw materials.

On the basis of these factors, the purchasing department working with the production department can establish figures of minimum stocks and order quantities of raw materials and parts for each product handled. Purchases in large quantities are advisable if price advantages can be obtained. Bulk purchases are advisable during periods of rising prices but not during periods of declining prices. The unavoidable time lag between order and delivery of the material is also a reason to buy in advance.

Buying in advance does not necessarily involve immediate delivery. The deliveries may be spread over the budget period in order to coordinate purchases with production and to control inventory. To control inventory, it is desirable to establish minimum and maximum quantities for each material to be carried. The lower limit is the smallest amount which can be carried without risk of production delays. If materials can be obtained quickly, the inventory can be held near the lower limit. The advantage of keeping inventory at this lower limit is that it minimizes the cost of storage and possible obsolescence. If materials cannot be obtained quickly, there is the possibility of a rise in prices, as well as an unforeseen delay in delivery which could hold up production and so it is advisable to carry more than minimum inventory.

Goods in Process

The time it takes for material to enter the factory and emerge as a finished product is frequently much longer than necessary for efficient production. Comparisons with other companies may reveal that a firm allows its goods to remain in process much longer than other firms. Investigations should be made to determine the causes of such delays and formulate remedies. These investigations are usually made in connection with the production budget.

Finished Goods

The budget of finished goods inventory is based on the sales budget. For example, if 100 units of an item are expected to be sold during the budget period, the problem is to determine how much must be kept in stock to support such a sales program. Since it is difficult to determine the exact quantity customers will demand each day, the finished goods inventory must maintain a margin of safety so that satisfactory deliveries can be made. Once this margin is established, the production and purchasing programs can be developed to replenish the stock as needed.

MANUFACTURING EXPENSE BUDGET

In preparing the manufacturing expense budget, estimates and probable expenses should be prepared by persons responsible to authorize expenditures. The general responsibility for variable expenses lies with the production manager. But the immediate responsibility for many of these expenses lies with the supervisors of the several departments. Generally, expenses are estimated by those who control them. Each person who prepares a portion of the manufacturing expense budget is furnished with data of prior periods and any plans for the budget period which may affect the amount of expenses. With these data decisions can be made about:

1) Which, if any, present expenses can be eliminated.
2) Probable effect of the sales and production forecasts on those expenses which must be incurred.

No plans for the elimination or reduction of variable expenses should be made unless it is certain that the plan can be enforced.

The responsibility for many fixed manufacturing expenses is with the general executives. Such fixed expenses include long-term leases, pension plans, patents, amortization, salaries of major production executives, etc.

In preparing the budget estimates of manufacturing expenses, a common practice is to use percentages. Each expense is taken as a percent of sales or production costs. For example, if a certain expense is estimated to be 5 percent of sales, this percentage is applied to the sales estimate to obtain the amount of this expense. The fallacy with this method is that all expenses do not vary proportionately with sales or production. A sounder method of estimating manufacturing expenses is to give individual expenses separate treatment.

In estimating the indirect labor expense, it is important to first analyze the expense for the period preceding the budget period. The requirements for additional help, or the possibility of eliminating some of the help, should be considered along with plans for increasing or decreasing any rates of compensation. Detailed schedules should be prepared, showing the nature of each job and the amount to be paid. By summarizing these schedules, an aggregate estimate can be determined.

Indirect materials expense should be estimated by first analyzing the amount consumed in prior periods. This, together with the production budget showing the proposed volume for the budget period, serves as a basis for estimating the quantities of the indirect material requirements. The probable cost of such requirements estimated by the purchasing department is the amount to be shown in the manufacturing expense budget.

Repairs and maintenance estimates are based on past experience data, supplemented by a report on the condition of the present equipment. If any additional equipment is to be installed during the budget period, recognition must be given to the prospect of additional repairs and maintenance charges. Electric power expense is in direct proportion to the production volume. The charges for depreciation of equipment can be estimated with considerable accuracy.

Insurance expense for the budget period is estimated on the basis of the insurance in force charged to production with adjustments made for contemplated changes in equipment, inventories, or coverage of hazard incident to manufacturing.

To budget manufacturing expenses effectively it is important to establish standard overhead rates.

At frequent intervals during the budget period, comparison should be made between the actual expenses in each department and the amount estimated to be spent for actual production during the period. Variations should be investigated and steps taken to correct weaknesses in the production program.

A distinction should be made between controllable and uncontrollable expenses so that the responsibility of individuals can be more closely determined. To facilitate the estimating of expenses, a further distinction is made between fixed and variable expenses. Fixed expenses are those which remain the same regardless of the variations in sales or production. Variable expenses are those which increase or decrease proportionally with changes in volume, sales or production. Maintenance is seldom treated in a separate budget. It is usually regarded as part of the manufacturing expense budget.

Following is an example of a Schedule of Estimated Manufacturing Expenses for each operation of a particular product:

Y Corporation
for the Year Ended 12/31/xx

	Total	Operation 1	Operation 2	Operation 3
Variable expenses:				
Indirect materials	$ 20,000	$ 5,000	$ 10,000	$ 5,000
Indirect labor	100,000	10,000	15,000	75,000
Light and power	30,000	5,000	13,000	12,000
Telephone	5,000	3,000	—0—	2,000

	Total	Operation 1	Operation 2	Operation 3
Fixed and semi-variable:				
Factory rent	50,000	14,000	18,000	18,000
Superintendence	100,000	30,000	35,000	35,000
Depreciation	100,000	20,000	60,000	20,000
General and				
administrative expense	50,000	12,000	17,000	21,000
Total	$455,000	$ 99,000	$168,000	$188,000

After estimates of materials, direct labor and manufacturing expenses have been prepared, a Schedule of Estimated Cost of Production may be prepared as follows:

Z Corporation
for the Year Ended 12/31/xx

	Total	Product A	Product B	Product C
Cost Element:				
Materials	$200,000	$ 80,000	$ 50,000	$ 70,000
Labor	340,000	100,000	80,000	160,000
Manufacturing expenses	70,000	30,000	30,000	10,000
Total	$610,000	$210,000	$160,000	$240,000

CAPITAL EXPENDITURES BUDGET

Since capital expenditures represent a large part of the total investment of a manufacturing concern, the capital expense budget is of great importance. Unwise capital expenditures can seldom be corrected without serious loss to stockholders. The purpose of the capital expenditures budget is to subject such expenditures to careful examination and so avoid mistakes that cannot easily be corrected.

A carefully prepared capital expenditures budget should point out the effect of such expenditures on the cash position of the company and on future earnings. For example, too large a portion of total assets invested in fixed plant and equipment sooner or later may result in an unhealthy financial condition because of the lack of necessary working capital.

Preparation of Capital Expenditures Budget

In preparing the capital expenditures budget, the following information is recorded:

1) The amount of machinery, equipment, etc., on hand at the beginning of the budget period;
2) Additions planned for the period;
3) Withdrawals expected for the period;
4) The amount of machinery, equipment, etc., expected at the end of the budget period.

Consideration should be given to estimates of additions planned for the period. Additions will be justified if they increase the volume of production and earnings, will reduce unit costs, and the money needed can be spared. Consideration should also be given to the percentage of investment for fixed assets as compared with net worth of the firm for a number of years. Various business authorities have realized that an active business enterprise with a tangible net worth between $50,000 and $250,000 should have as a maximum not more than two-thirds of its tangible net worth in fixed assets. Where the tangible net worth is in excess of $250,000, not more than 75 percent of the tangible net worth should be represented by fixed assets. When these percentages are greatly exceeded, annual depreciation charges tend to be too heavy, the net working capital too moderate, and liabilities expand too rapidly for the good health of the business; alternative leasing should be considered.

The capital expenditures budget should include estimates not only for the budget period, but long-range estimates covering a period of many years. The ideal situation occurs when machinery is purchased at a time when prices are low. A long-range capital expenditures budget will indicate what machinery will be of use in the future; then, machinery may be acquired when prices are considered low. Inefficient or obsolete machines can sometimes be made into satisfactory units by rebuilding. If it is estimated that gains derived from rebuilding machinery will exceed the costs, then provision should be made in the capital expenditures budget to incur these expenses. Such expenditures are frequently called betterments and prolong the useful life of the machines. The preparation of detailed and accurate records is an essential part of the capital expenditures budget. The following information should be included in such a record:

1) Description of machines;
2) Date of requisition;
3) Cost for depreciation rate.

From the above information, it is a simple matter to complete the depreciation for the budget period.

As with other budgets, actual expenditures should be compared with the estimates, and any variation should be analyzed. In addition, a statement should be prepared showing the extent to which actual results obtained from the use of certain capital expenditures are in line with expectations. This is particularly important where substantial investments are made in labor-saving equipment, new processes or new machines.

THE CASH BUDGET

The cash budget is a composite reflection of all the operating budgets in terms of cash receipts and disbursements. Its purpose is to determine the cash resources that will be available during the entire budget program so that the company will know in advance whether it can carry out its program without borrowing or obtaining new capital or whether it will need to obtain additional capital from these sources. Thus, the company can arrange in advance for any necessary borrowing, avoiding emergencies and, more important, a cash crisis caused by a shortage.

A knowledgeable financial person goes into the market to borrow money when there is the cheapest rate. The cash budget will tell the manager when there is the need to borrow so he or she can plan accordingly. In a like manner, the manager can foresee when there will be sufficient funds to repay loans.

A cash budget is very important to a firm which does installment selling. Installment selling ties up cash resources, and a careful analysis of estimated future collections is needed to forecast the cash position of the company.

Other purposes of the cash budget are: 1) to provide for seasonal fluctuations in business which make heavy demands on funds to carry large inventories and receivables; 2) to assist the financial executive in having funds available to meet maturing obligations; 3) to aid in securing credit from commercial banks (a bank is more likely to lend funds for a definite plan that has been prepared, indicating when and how the funds will be repaid) and 4) to indicate the amount of funds available for investments, when available and for what duration.

Preparation of the Cash Budget

The main difference between a cash budget and other budgets is that in the cash budget all estimates are based on the dates when it is expected cash will be received or paid. Other budgets are prepared on the basis of the accrual of the different items (for accrual-basis companies). Therefore, in the cash budget, the budget executive cannot base the estimate of cash receipts directly on the sales budget for the obvious reason that all the cash will not be received from such sales in the same month in which they are billed. This is not true in the case of a business on a strictly cash basis.

Depreciation is another item handled differently in the cash budget. Depreciation is a cost of doing business; it increases expenses and reduces net income for financial reporting purposes. It is not, however, a cash item and is ignored in preparing the cash budget, but the amount paid for a new plant or equipment in a single year or budget period is included in full in the cash budget.

Cash receipts of a typical firm come from cash sales, collections on accounts and notes receivable, interest, dividends, rent, sale of capital assets and loans. The cash sale estimate is taken from the sales budget. The estimate of collections on accounts should be based on the sales budget and company experience in making collections. With concerns whose sales are made largely on account, the collection experience should be ascertained with considerable care. As an illustration, assume the March account sales have actually been collected as follows:

Month	%
March	6.4
April	80.1
May	8.5
June	3.6
Cash Discount Taken	1.1
Bad Debts Loss	.3
Total	100.00

If the same experience is recorded for each month of the year, it is possible to resolve the sales estimates into a collection budget. It is sometimes desirable to develop the experience separately for different classes of customers for different geographical areas. Once these figures are ascertained, they should be tested from time to time.

Cash disbursements in a typical firm are made for payroll, materials, operating expenses, taxes, interest, purchases of equipment, repayment of loans, payment of dividends, etc. With a complete operating budget on hand, there is little difficulty in estimating the amount of cash that will be required and when it will be required. Wages and salaries are usually paid in cash and on definite dates. For purchases of material (from the materials budget), the purchasing department can readily indicate the time allowed for payments. Operating expenses must be considered individually. Some items, such as insurance, are prepaid. Others, such as commissions, are accrued. So, cash payments may not coincide with charges on the operating budget.

ZERO-BASE BUDGETING

A different approach to budgeting adopted by some industrial organizations as well as not-for-profit entities and governmental units is appropriately termed *Zero-Base Budgeting*. Whether adopted wholeheartedly on a yearly basis, as a review every few years, or merely as a mind-set tool, its precepts can be of value in the budgeting process.

Expenses for industrial organizations can be divided into two categories:

1) Direct manufacturing expense, for materials, labor, and overhead.
2) Support expense, for everything else.

It is the "everything else" that causes problems at budget time, when, for example, management is beset by rising costs and must decide between decreasing the budgetary allocation for a research and development project or cutting funds for executive development. Traditionally, problems like these boil down to one question: How should the company shift its allocations around? Rather than tinker with their existing budget, many companies have implemented this budgeting method that starts at base-zero.

This approach requires that the company view all of its discretionary activities and priorities afresh, and create a different and hopefully better set of allocations for the ensuring budget year. The base-zero procedure gives management a firm grip on support allocations of all kinds, a procedure for describing all support expense minutely, classifying the alternatives to each, and sorting them all according to their importance and priority.

This technique in budgeting differentiates between the basic and necessary operations and those of a more discretionary character, thus enabling management to focus specific attention on the optional group. The basic steps for effective zero-base budgeting require justification of every dollar spent on discretionary costs, and a prescribed order of approach to the final allocation of funds:

1) Describe each optional activity in a "decision" package.
2) Evaluate and rank these decision packages by cost/benefit analysis.
3) Allocate resources based on this analysis.

Where to Use Zero-Base Budgeting

Zero-base budgeting is best applied to service and support areas of company activity rather than to the basic manufacturing operation. Since a corporation's level of manufacturing activity is determined by its sales volume, the production level, in turn, determines how much the company should spend on labor, materials, and overhead. Hence, there is not the same simple relationship between costs and benefits here as there is in the service and support areas where management can trade off a level of expenditures on a given project against the direct returns on investment. Cost benefit analysis, which is crucial to zero-base budgeting, cannot be applied directly to decisions to increase or decrease expenditures in the manufacturing areas.

The main use of zero-base budgeting occurs when management has discretion to choose between different activities having different direct costs and benefits. Such areas normally include marketing, finance, quality control, personnel, engineering and other non-production areas of company activity.

Decision Package Concept

When implementing ZBB, a company must explain the "decision package concept" to all levels of management and then present guidelines for the individual manager to use in breaking the specific activities into workable packages. Next, higher management must establish a ranking, consolidation and elimination process. The decision package is the document that identifies and describes a specific activity in such a manner that management can 1) evaluate and rank that activity against other activities competing for limited resources, 2) decide whether to approve or disapprove expenditures in that area.

The specifications in each package must provide management with the information needed to evaluate the activity. Included should be 1) a statement of the goals of the activity; 2) the program by which the goals are to be attained; 3) the benefits expected from the program and methods of determining whether they have been attained; 4) suggested alternatives to the program; 5) possible consequences of not approving the package and expenditure of funds; 6) designation of personnel required to carry out the program.

There are two basic types of decision packages:

1) Mutually exclusive packages identify alternative means of performing the same function. The best alternative is chosen and the other packages are discarded.

2) Incremental packages reflect different levels of effort that may be expended on a specific function or program. One package, the "base package," may establish a minimum level of activity, and others identify increased activity or expenditure levels.

A logical starting point for determining next year's needs is the current year's operations. Each ground level manager who has the ultimate responsibility takes the areas's forecasted expense level for the current year, identifies the activities creating this expense, and calculates the cost for each activity. At this stage, the manager identifies each activity at its current level and method of operation and does not attempt to identify alternatives or increments.

After current operations have been separated into preliminary decision packages, the manager looks at requirements for the upcoming year. To aid in specifying these requirements, upper management should issue a formal set of assumptions on the activity levels, billings, and wage and salary increases for the upcoming year. These formal assumptions provide all managers with uniform benchmarks for estimating purposes.

At the conclusion of the formulation stage, the manager will have identified all of the proposed activities as follows:

1) Business-as-usual packages.
2) Decision packages for other ongoing activities.
3) Decision packages for new activities.

The ranking process forces management to face squarely the most basic decision: How much money is available and where should it be spent to obtain the greatest good? Management arrives at the decisions by listing, and then studying all the packages identified in order of decreasing benefit to the company, and eliminating those of least value.

It is possible for one ranking of decision packages to be obtained for an entire company and judged by its top management. While this one, single ranking would identify the best allocation of resources, ranking and judging the high volume of packages created by describing all of the activities of a large company would result in an unwieldy task for top management.

This problem can be resolved by grouping decision units which may correspond to a budget unit in organizations with detailed cost-center structures, or they can be defined on a project basis.

The initial ranking should occur at the cost-center or project level so that each manager can evaluate the relative importance of the segments and rank the packages accordingly.

The manager at the next level up the ladder then reviews these rankings with the appropriate managers and uses the resulting rankings as guides to produce a single consolidated ranking for all packages presented from below.

At higher levels of a large organization, the expertise necessary to rank packages is best obtained by committee. The committee membership should consist of all managers whose packages are being ranked with their supervisor serving as chairperson.

Each committee produces its consolidated ranking by voting on the decision packages presented by its members. As at the cost-center level, the most beneficial packages are ranked highest and the least important ranked lowest.

It is best to establish the cutoff line at the highest consolidation level first, and then for the lower levels. The most effective way to establish the first cutoff is for management at the highest consolidation level to estimate the expense that will be approved at the top level and then to set the cutoff line far enough below to allow trading off between the divisions whose packages are being ranked.

The ability to achieve a list of ranked packages at any given organization level allows management to evaluate the desirability of various expenditure levels throughout the budgeting process. This ranked list also provides management with a reference point to be used during the year to identify activities to be reduced or expanded if allowable expenditure levels change.

Zero-base budgeting can be a flexible and useful tool in simplifying the budgeting process and in bringing about better resource allocation by forcing meaningful consideration of varying priorities for available funds.

BREAK-EVEN POINT ANALYSIS

Definition. The break-even point (BE) is that amount of sales necessary to yield neither income nor loss.

If sales should be less than indicated by the BE point, a loss results. If the total cost of goods sold and other expenses is less than sales, and if this total varied in direct proportion to sales, operations would result in net income. BE analysis is not a budget, in itself, but is an approach in the budgeting process for dealing intelligently with the uncertainty of estimates for future operations that are based on statistical data. Breakeven analysis can be applied to sales, profit, costs, and selling price problems, and it can be used to help make sound decisions for employing idle plant capacity, planning advertising, granting credit, and expanding production. BE is a tool, and a useful one, with which to begin to approach decision problems.

BE Analysis, is an inexpensive method for analyzing the possible effects of decisions. Discounted cash flow techniques require large amounts of data expensive to develop. BE can help with the decision whether or not it is worthwhile to do more intensive, costly analysis.

BE provides a means for designing product specifications, which permits a comparison of different designs and their costs before the specifications for a specific product are accepted as the best choice cost-wise. For example, a new product with an uncertain volume is considered to be feasible if it's made with hand tools rather than with expensive capital equipment. The first method typically has higher variable costs, but lower fixed costs. This often results in a lower breakeven point for the project, and lower risks and potential profits. The fixed capital equipment approach raises the BE, but also raises the risks and profit potential for the manufacturer. BE helps to examine these trade-offs.

An important factor when using BE analysis is the nature of the user's cost structure. Some firms have a flexible labor force and standard cost analysis works well. In other businesses, however, management must treat labor costs differently. Certain skilled workers cannot be laid off when business is slow. BE analysis assumes a realistic definition of costs, both in amount and type. While fixed costs will not change with changes in revenue, variable and semi-variable costs do change with changes in sales, up or down. Product pricing can be significantly aided by using variations of breakeven analysis.

Break-Even Chart. A break-even chart presents a visual representation of sales volume, capacity, or output when expenses and revenues are equal, i.e., a volume level at which income equals expenses. A BE chart provides a projection of the impact of output upon expenses, income, and profits which makes the chart a useful tool for profit planning and control.

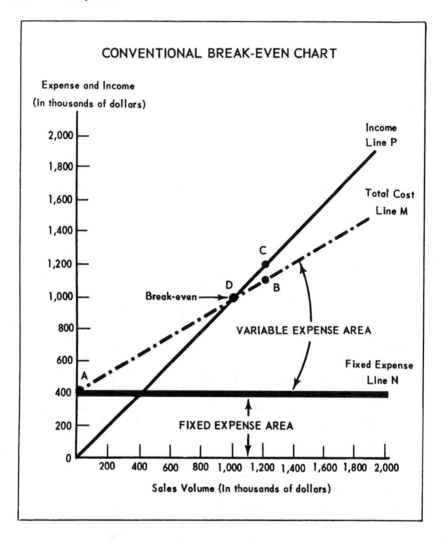

CONVENTIONAL BREAK-EVEN CHART

Expense and Income
(in thousands of dollars)

Income Line P

Total Cost Line M

Break-even

VARIABLE EXPENSE AREA

Fixed Expense Line N

FIXED EXPENSE AREA

Sales Volume (in thousands of dollars)

The BE chart assumes that selling prices do not change, total fixed expenses remain the same at all levels of output, and variable costs increase or decrease in direct proportion to sales. The N line remains the same regardless of sales volume; the point B on the chart is the total of the fixed and variable expenses on the list on the vertical axis. The area between line M and the fixed expense line N is the amount of variable expenses at different volumes of sales. The area between line M and the horizontal axis represents the total costs at various levels of sales. Line M can be considered a total cost line, since total costs for various volumes of sales can be readily determined from it. This can be done by starting at any point on the horizontal scale and measuring upward to line M and across to the vertical scale.

The income line P starts at zero and extends through point C, which is the point at which total sales and total income are shown on both scales, about $1,200. The profit area lies to the right of break-even point D where the revenue line P crosses the total cost line M. Revenue is greater than costs above—to the right—of the break-even point D; the loss area is below—to the left—of the break-even point D.

Break-Even is an inexpensive technique to determine whether or not it would be advisable to do more intensive and costly analysis of a proposed project. It provides a method for designing product specifications. Each design has costs which affect price and marketing feasibility by providing comparison of possible designs before the specifications are frozen by cash commitments. BE serves as a substitute for estimating an unknown factor in making project decisions. In deciding whether to go ahead with a project or to disband it, there are always variables to be considered such as costs, price, demand, and other miscellaneous factors. When most expenses associated with a proposed project can be determined, only two variables need be considered as variable items—profits (cash flow) and demand (sales). Demand is usually more difficult to estimate. By deciding that profit must at least be zero, the BE point, the demand is more easily estimated by determining what sales levels are needed to make the project a worthwhile undertaking. BE provides a way to attack uncertainty, to at least develop marketing targets for desired levels of income. One of the major problems of BE analysis is that no product exists in isolation; there are always alternative uses for an organization's funds. BE analysis helps decision makers to consider not only the value of an individual project, but how it compares to other uses of the funds and facilities.

Another problem is that BE analysis does not permit proper examination of cash flows. In considering financial commitments, the appropriate way to make investment or capital decisions is to consider the value of a proposed project's anticipated cash flows. If the discounted value of the cash flows exceeds the required investment outlay in cash, the project is acceptable. BE analysis makes restrictive assumptions about cost-revenue relationships; it is basically a negative technique defining constraints rather than looking at benefits; it is essentially a static tool for analyzing income and outflow for a single period of time.

The BE technique requires a realistic definition of costs, both in amount and type. A BE approach, therefore, should not be considered a technique to be used to make *final* investment decisions. It is a supplemental tool among the many factors a business decision maker must consider; it is an approach helpful to apply at the beginning of an analysis of a proposed solution of a business problem.

Although a complete and adequate budget may be developed without using a break-even analysis, its use adds to the understanding of estimates as shown in the following example.

Where the total cost of goods sold and other expenses is less than sales and if this total varied in direct proportion to sales, operations would always result in net income. For example, in a company in which the cost of goods sold and expenses amount to $1.80 per unit sold and the sale price is $2, on the first unit there would be net income of 20¢. On a million items, the net income would amount to $200,000.

As a practical matter, the simple example cited above is not realistic. Although some expenses may vary with volume of sales (e.g., salesperson's commissions, traveling expenses, advertising, telephone, delivery costs, postage, supplies, etc.), there are many other types of expenses which are not affected by the variations in sales. These expenses are the fixed expenses. Examples are depreciation, rent, insurance, heat, and so on.

If, going back to the above illustration, it is assumed that fixed costs and expenses amount to $40,000, at least $40,000 of costs and expenses are incurred before even one unit is sold. If a million units are sold, however, income before deducting fixed expenses is $200,000. After fixed expenses, net income is $160,000. So, the income picture goes from a loss of $40,000 (where no units are produced) to a profit of $160,000 (where one million units are produced). Somewhere between these, however, is a point represented by a certain number of units at which there will be neither income nor loss—the break-even point.

How to Compute the Break-Even Point

To determine the break-even point, let S equal the sales at the break-even point. Since sales at this point are equal to the total fixed costs and expenses ($40,000) plus variable costs and expenses ($1.80 per unit or 90 percent of sales):

$$S \quad\; = \$\ 40,000 + .9S$$
$$S - .9S \quad = \$\ 40,000$$
$$.1S \quad\; = \$\ 40,000$$
$$S \quad\; = \$400,000$$

Even the above illustration oversimplifies the problem. It makes the assumption that all costs and expenses can be classified as either fixed or *variable*. However, in actual operations, expenses classified as fixed expenses may become variable where sales increase beyond a certain point, and some variable expenses may not vary in direct proportion to the sales.

Rent expense, for example, may not always be a fixed expense. A substantial increase in sales may create a need for additional showroom or salesroom space or, perhaps, expenses for salesperson's offices, or salesperson's commissions may rise unexpectedly when they have gone above a certain quota.

Then, there are types of hybrid expenses which may be classified as *semifixed*. For example, executives' salaries, association dues, subscriptions to periodicals and many other expenses are not in proportion to sales. Another unreality in the above problem is that as sales increase, there is a likelihood that sale prices will decrease because of larger orders. Now let's take a look at another situation:

Net sales		$2,500,000
Costs and expenses:		
Fixed	$250,000	
Variable	$1,500,000	1,750,000
Net income		$750,000

This company currently has under consideration an investment in a new plant which will cause an increase in its fixed expenses of $200,000.

The present break-even point is as follows:

S	$= \$250,000 + .6S$
S-.6S	$= \$250,000$
.4S	$= \$250,000$
S	$= \$625,000$

If the company builds the plant, the break-even calculation will be:

S	$= \$450,000 + .6S$
S-.6S	$= \$450,000$
.4S	$= \$450,000$
S	$= \$1,125,000$

If the plant expansion is undertaken, then the sales must be increased by $500,000 for the company to maintain its net income of $750,000, as follows:

S	$= \$450,000 + .6S + \$750,000$
S - .6S	$= \$1,200,000$
.4S	$= \$1,200,000$
S	$= \$3,000,000$
Increase	$= \$500,000$ ($3,000,000 less $2,500,000)

The situation can be analyzed using two alternatives. The maximum production with the present plant is 1,500,000 units. At an average sale price of $2 per unit, sales would be $3,000,000. With the new plant, sales are estimated to hit $5,000,000 (2,500,000 units @ $2 per unit).

	Without New Plant	With New Plant
Net Sales	$3,000,000	$5,000,000
Less: Fixed costs and expenses	250,000	450,000
	2,750,000	4,550,000
Less: Variable costs		
and expenses (60% of sales)	1,800,000	3,000,000
Net income	$950,000	$1,550,000

If sales do not increase, the increase in fixed costs and expenses of $200,000 would cut the net income to $550.000. The break-even point will have been boosted $500,000, and the sales will have to be increased by this amount to produce the current $750,000 of income. Alternatively, the net income can be increased by $600,000 if the sales figure is increased by $2,000,000. Although these figures are based on an assumption that all costs and expenses are fixed or variable, the break-even analysis focuses attention on the factors involved in costs and income and provides a basis for consideration of various problems.

Chapter 13

Governmental Accounting and Not-For-Profit Organizations

DIFFERENCES BETWEEN GOVERNMENTAL AND COMMERCIAL ACCOUNTING

While both types of entities use double-entry bookkeeping procedures and either cash or accrual methods, and both prepare balance sheets and operating statements, there are many differences between commercial and governmental systems.

Governmental accounting is associated with: 1) an absence of a profit; 2) compliance with statutory and/or legal requirements; 3) a fundamental difference in the treatment of net worth. Commercial accounting provides accounting for preferred and common stock and retained earnings, with a paid-in capital account where appropriate. Governmental accounting treats "net worth" under account classifications *Reserve for Encumbrances or Unappropriated Surplus*; 4) characteristically, government accounts will include a *Reserve for Contingencies* account since the projected (budgeted) reserve may not materialize as the accounting year progresses.

LEGAL PROVISIONS

In governmental accounting, legal provisions relate to budgeting and to the disposition of assets. The preparation and implementation of the projected budget and related accounting procedures are governed by certain legal provisions expressed specifically in legislation (statutory) or restrictions imposed by a nonlegislative (regulatory) authority. The accounting system must have built-in safeguards that expenditures will comply with both types of restrictions. Governmental accounting must also include revenue and expense data which facilitates the preparation of budgets for the future.

As will be seen, certain *funds* are considered less flexible in their accounting treatment. The least flexible type is the one created by a state constitution or by legislation, because the accountant must keep the books as determined by law. The most flexible is the type established by executive authority, since such authority can make changes in a fund without prior legislative approval.

In fund accounting *estimated and actual revenues* and *expenditures* are compared on an ongoing basis, e.g., reviewed by the governing bodies approving the initial budget and the appropriation for the fund. Comparisons reveal the extent to which the "actuals" are in line with the estimates (the budget) and will show significant deviations, if any, during the fiscal year of actual revenues and expenditures from the budgeted amounts.

Assets and liabilities incurred by a fund are similar to those in a commercial enterprise. Asset accounts, for example, will include cash, accounts receivable, etc., while liabilities will show accounts or vouchers payable, notes payable, bonds payable, etc.

A separate *general ledger* must be maintained for each fund related to the governmental entity's budget. Each general ledger has a self-balancing account that brings the revenue and appropriation accounts into balance at the end of the fiscal year.

As a general rule independent auditors will insist on the entity using an *accrual* system, unless the financial authorities for that specific fund can demonstrate that the financial reports would not *materially* differ if a cash accounting system is used.

Is Governmental Accounting Complex? No!

While fund accounting is perceived to be complicated, it is not in the least any more difficult than commercial accounting. In fact, fund accounting is easier to understand if thought is given to the basic concept that underlies governmental accounting:

> Governmental accounting simply involves *two* sets of books instead of one set. There is a set of books for the projected budget for the upcoming fiscal year and a separate set of books for recording *actual* revenues and expenditures as the fiscal year progresses. The two sets of books are synchronized, so that as the actuals materialize and are recorded in the actual set, the complementary account in the budgeted set is appropriately debited or credited.

That's all there is to governmental accounting. Why then is it thought to be complicated? The answer is for the same reason that we initially think any totally new and unfamiliar discipline appears difficult—the *terminology* is the culprit. It is well-settled that learning the terminology of a new discipline is 50 percent or more of the learning battle of anything new that one endeavors to learn. Governmental accounting terminology is indeed entirely different from commercial accounting terminology; it has a vocabulary that is totally unique to governmental accounting; no governmental accounting term can be found in any other system of accounting, whether commercial, industrial, or otherwise.

The first step, then, to acquire an understanding of fund accounting procedures is to review and become familiar with the terms. The following list of definitions will enable the user to easily apply the accounting methods for the various types of funds which are covered in the material following the definitions.

TERMINOLOGY

Here is a listing of definitions applicable only to fund accounting:

Abatement. Cancellation of amounts levied or of charges made for services.

Accrued Assets. Assets arising from revenues earned but not yet due.

Accrued Expenses. Expenses resulting in liabilities which are either due or are not payable until some future time.

Accrued Revenues. Levies made or other revenue earned and not collected.

Allotment Ledger. A subsidiary ledger which contains an account for each allotment showing the amount allotted, expenditures, encumbrances, the net balance, and other related information.

Appropriation. An authorization granted by the legislative body to make expenditures and to incur obligations for specific purposes.

Appropriation Expenditure. An expenditure chargeable to an appropriation.

Appropriation Ledger. A subsidiary ledger containing an account with each appropriation.

Assessment. The process of making an official valuation of property for the purpose of taxation.

Authority Bonds. Bonds payable from the revenues of a specific public authority.

Betterment. An addition or change made in a fixed asset which prolongs its life or increases its efficiency.

Budget. A plan of financial operation embodying an estimate of proposed expenditures for a given period or purpose, and the proposed means of financing them.

Budgetary Accounts. The accounts necessary to reflect budget operations and condition, such as estimated revenues, appropriations, and encumbrances.

Capital Budget. An improvement program and the methods for the financing.

Clearing Account. An account used to accumulate total charges or credits for the purpose of distributing them among the accounts to which they are allocable, or for the purpose of transferring the net difference to the proper account.

Current Special Assessment. Assessments levied and due during the current fiscal period.

Current Taxes. Taxes levied and becoming due during the current fiscal period—from the time the amount of the tax levy is first established, to the date on which a penalty for nonpayment is attached.

Debt Limit. The maximum amount of gross or net debt legally permitted.

Debt Service Requirement. The amount of money necessary periodically to pay the interest on the outstanding debt and the principal of maturing bonded debt not payable from a sinking fund.

Deficit. The excess of the liabilities of a fund over its assets.

Delinquent Taxes. Taxes remaining unpaid on and after the date on which a penalty for nonpayment is attached.

Direct Debt. The debt which a governmental unit has incurred in its own name, or assumed through the annexation of territory.

Encumbrances. Obligations in the form of purchase orders, contracts, or salary commitments which are chargeable to an appropriation, and for which a part of the appropriation is reserved.

Endowment Fund. A fund whose principal must be maintained inviolate, but whose income may be expended.

Expendable Fund. A fund whose resources, including both principal and earnings, may be expended.

Expenditures. If the fund accounts are kept on the accrual basis, expenditures are the total charges incurred, whether paid or unpaid, including expenses, provision for retirement of debt not reported as a liability of the fund from which retired, and capital outlays.

Franchise. A special privilege granted by a government permitting the continuing use of public property.

Full Faith and Credit. A pledge of the general taxing body for the payment of obligations.

Fund Accounts. All accounts necessary to set forth the financial operations and financial condition of a fund.

Fund Group. A group of related funds.

Governmental Accounting. The preparation, reporting, and interpretation of accounts for governmental bodies.

Grant. A contribution by one governmental unit to another unit.

Gross Bonded Debt. The total amount of direct debt of a governmental unit, represented by outstanding bonds before deduction of sinking fund assets.

Indeterminate Appropriation. An appropriation which is not limited either to any definite period of time, or to any definite amount, or to both time and amount.

Inter-Fund Accounts. Accounts in which transactions between funds are reflected.

Inter-Fund Loans. Loans made by one fund to another fund.

Inter-Fund Transfers. Amounts transferred from one fund to another.

Judgment. An amount to be paid or collected by a governmental unit as the result of a court decision, including a condemnation award in payment for private property taken for public use.

Lapse. As applied to appropriations, this term denotes the automatic termination of an appropriation.

Levy. To impose taxes or special assessments.

Lump-Sum Appropriation. An appropriation made for a stated purpose, or for a named department, without specifying further the amounts that can be spent for specific activities or for particular expenditures.

Municipal. An adjective applying to any governmental unit below or subordinate to the state.

Municipal Corporation. A body or corporate politic established pursuant to state authorization, as evidenced by a charter.

Net Bonded Debt. Gross bonded debt less applicable cash or other assets.

Non-Expendable Fund. A fund the principal, and sometimes the earnings, of which may not be expended.

Non-Operating Income. Income of municipal utilities and other governmental enterprises of a business character, which is not derived from the operation of such enterprise.

Operating Expenses. As used in the accounts of municipal utilities and other governmental enterprises of a business character, the term means the costs necessary to the maintenance of the enterprise, or the rendering of services for which the enterprise is operated.

Operating Revenues. Revenues derived from the operation of municipal utilities or other governmental enterprises of a business character.

Operating Statement. A statement summarizing the financial operations of a municipality.

Ordinance. A bylaw of a municipality enacted by the governing body of the governmental entity.

Overlapping Debt. The proportionate share of the debts of local governmental units, located wholly or in part within the limits of the reporting government, which must be borne by property within such government.

Prepaid Taxes. The deposit of money with a governmental unit on condition that the amount deposited is to be applied against the tax liability of the taxpayer.

Proprietary Accounts. Accounts which show actual financial condition and operations such as actual assets, liabilities, reserves, surplus, revenues, and expenditures as distinguished from budgetary accounts.

Public Authority. A public agency created to perform a single function, which is financed from tolls or fees charged those using the facilities operated by the agency.

Public Trust Fund. A trust fund whose principal, earnings, or both, must be used for a public purpose.

Quasi-Municipal Corporation. An agency established by the state primarily for the purpose of helping the state to carry out its functions.

Refunding Bonds. Bonds issued to retire bonds already outstanding. The refunding bonds may be sold for cash and outstanding bonds redeemed in cash, or the refunding bonds may be exchanged with holders of outstanding bonds.

Related Funds. Funds of a similar character which are brought together for administrative and reporting purposes.

Reserve for Encumbrances. A reserve representing the segregation of surplus to provide for unliquidated encumbrances.

Revenue Bonds. Bonds the principal and interest on which are to be paid solely from earnings, usually the earnings of a municipally owned utility or other public service enterprise.

Revolving Fund. A fund provided to carry out a cycle of operations.

Special Assessment. A compulsory levy made by a local government against certain properties, to defray part or all of the cost of a specific improvement or service, which is presumed to be of general benefit to the public and of special benefit to the owners of such properties.

Special District Bonds. Bonds of a local taxing district, which has been organized for a special purpose—such as road, sewer, and other special districts—to render unique services to the public.

Suspense Account. An account which carries charges or credits temporarily pending the determination of the proper account or accounts to which they are to be posted.

Tax Anticipation Notes. Notes issued in anticipation of collection of taxes, usually retired only from tax collections as they come due.

Tax Levy. An ordinance or resolution by means of which taxes are levied.

Tax Liens. Claims which governmental units have upon properties until taxes levied against them have been paid.

Tax Rate. The amount of tax stated in terms of a unit of the tax base.

Trust Fund. A fund consisting of resources received and held by the governmental unit as trustee, to be expended or invested in accordance with the conditions of the trust.

Unencumbered Appropriation. An appropriation or allotment, or a part thereof, not yet expended or encumbered.

Utility Fund. A fund established to finance the construction, operation, and maintenance of municipally owned utilities.

Warrant. An order drawn by a legislative body, or an officer of a governmental unit, upon its treasurer, directing the treasurer to pay a specified amount to the person named, or to the bearer.

GOVERNMENTAL ACCOUNTING SYSTEMS

Governmental Accounting Standards Board (GASB)

The GASB was established in 1984, under the oversight of the Financial Accounting Foundation which, in turn, oversees the Financial Accounting Standards Board (FASB). Before the establishment of the GASB, the reports of governmental entities were criticized by the accounting community because they could not be interpreted in a manner consistent with the financial reports of private business organizations. The primary purpose of the GASB is to develop standards of reporting for state and local government entities; its organizational and operational structure is similar to that of the FASB, and its objective is to make the combined general purpose financial reports of governmental entities as comparable as possible to those of private business.

As a general rule the GASB will promulgate standards that parallel GAAP. However, there are instances that require a governmental entity to comply with a state law or regulatory accounting requirement that is in non-compliance with GAAP. Such reports are classified as *Special Reports or Supplemental Schedules*, which are not a part of the general purpose statements. In these cases governmental units can publish two sets of statements, one in compliance with legal requirements and one in compliance with GAAP. (An example of this problem is that it is not uncommon for some governmental entities to be required by law to apply the cash basis of accounting.)

Governmental accounting systems are developed on a *fund basis*. A fund is defined as an independent fiscal and accounting entity with a self-balancing set of accounts recording cash and other resources together with all related liabilities, obligations, reserves, and equities that are segregated for the purpose of carrying on specific activities or attaining specified objectives in accordance with applicable regulations, restrictions, and other statutory and regulatory limitations.

In addition to each fund's transactions within the fund itself, each fund in a governmental unit can have financial transactions with other funds in the same entity. The financial statements must reflect interfund transactions which result from services rendered by one fund to another.

The accrual basis of accounting is recommended for matching revenues and expenditures during a designated period of time which refers specifically to the time when revenues and expenditures are recorded as such in the accounting records.

Governmental revenues should be classified by fund and source. Expenditures should be classified by fund, function, organization unit, activity, character, and principal classes of objectives in accordance with standard recognized classifications. Common terminology and classifications should be used consistently throughout 1) the budget; 2) the accounts; and 3) the financial reports. These three elements of governmental financial administration are inseparable and can be thought of as the "cycle" of governmental financial transactions and final product of the accounting system.

Seven Types of Funds

1) The *General Fund* which accounts for all transactions not accounted for in any other fund.

2) *Special Revenue Fund* which accounts for revenues from specific sources or to finance specific projects.

3) *Debt Service Fund* which accounts for the payment of interest and principal on longterm debt.

4) *Capital Project Fund* which accounts for the receipt and disbursement of funds used for the acquisition of capital facilities.

5) *Enterprise Funds* which account for the financing of services to the public paid for by the users of the services.

6) *Fiduciary Funds: Trust and Agency Funds* which account for assets held by a governmental unit as trustee or agent for individuals, private organizations, or other governmental units.

7) *Internal Service Funds* which account for the financing of special projects and services performed by one governmental entity for an organization unit within the same governmental entity.

The accountant should:

- Maintain complete and adequate files for the initial documentation which established or restricted the fund, together with any special reporting requirements demanded.

- Keep separate detailed books of entry for each fund, separate bank account for that fund, separate identification of all property and securities.

- Under *no* circumstances should assets of separate funds be commingled. Transfers between funds should not be permitted without documentary authorization, and inter-fund receivables and payables should, in contra-effect, be equal and clearly identified, always maintaining the original integrity of each fund.

- Interest accruals, cooperative-share funding (example: government 80%—college 20% in Work Study Program), expense allowances or allocations—all should be made timely.

- Federal, state and local reporting requirements should be studied, met and reported as due to avoid stringent penalties, interest and possible loss of tax-exempt status. Options may exist regarding the handling of payroll and unemployment taxes; they should be studied and explored for money-saving possibilities.

- Independently audited annual financial statements by fund are usually required both by organizational charter and governmental departments (especially where grant-participation is involved). Publication of the availability of these statements is sometimes mandatory (foundations).

- One area of discussion and dispute is the "compliance" feature of audits involving certain governmental agency grants. Here, the independent auditor is called upon to measure the agency's compliance with certain non-accounting rules, such as eligibility of money-recipients, internal controls and other matters not ordinarily associated with a financial audit. The integrity of the auditor's financial opinion should never be compromised by peripheral compliance requirements. In most cases, the auditor should qualify any opinion indicating the results and *extent of tests* made for compliance. The AICPA, to some extent, has spelled out guidelines for "compliance" opinions in Section 9641 of its "Statements on Auditing Standards."

- Municipal accounting techniques, procedures, format and demands are not discussed here. Their overall application involves the use of fund accounting. The main distinction is the entering of the budget—the anticipated revenues and the appropriations thereof—directly on and as part of the books of account. Progress reports then show how actual compares with anticipated. The estimates are then zeroed out at year-end. The meaning and use of "encumbrances" should also be under-stood. Reports for some local subdivisions, such as school boards, usu-ally involve a strict accounting of each receipt and disbursement, includ-ing the detailing of outstanding checks.

Accounting for the General Fund (GF).   The General Fund is the type most frequently used as it accounts for revenues not allocated to specified activities by law or by contract. Every governmental entity *must* have a General Fund; none of the other types of funds are required, but are estab-lished as needed.

Entries in the GF system originally are made to Estimated Revenues and Appropriations and simultaneously a debit or credit, whichever is the case, is recorded in the Fund Balance account. For proper controls the encum-brance system is used with entries recorded when commitments are made or orders placed. This procedure has the effect of setting aside the money for the payment of future purchase orders and payment vouchers. When a purchase is actually made, the entries to an Encumbrances and Reserve for Encumbrances are reversed and those accounts cleared. (The later expendi-ture is not always the same as the encumbrance.) Simultaneously, the actual expenditure is recorded by a Debit to an Expenditures account and a credit to Vouchers Payable.

Taxes and service charges are budgeted in a Taxes-Receivable—Current Account. The estimated amounts should be recorded after the estimate and posting of uncollectibles, so the entries are a credit to Revenues and a credit to Estimated Uncollectible Taxes. When collections are actually received during the fiscal year, they are recorded with a debit to cash and a credit to Taxes Receivable—Current. Subsequently, it is determined that a certain amount of taxes will become delinquent as the year progresses. These amounts are recorded in a Taxes Receivable—Delinquent account (debit) and a credit to Taxes Receivable-Current. At this point an Interest and Penalties account should be opened for fees, penalties and other charges associated with the collection of delinquent taxes.

Taxes Receivable—Delinquent	xxx	
Estimated Uncollectible Current Taxes	xxx	
Taxes Receivable—Current		xxx
Estimated Uncollectible Delinquent Taxes		xxx
Interest and Penalties	xxx	
Estimated Uncollectible Interest and		
Penalties		xxx

At the end of the fiscal year, the accounts of the General Fund are closed out. Any differences are recorded for or against the Fund Balance.

Accounting for Special Revenue Funds (SRF). Special Revenue Funds account for revenues obtained via specific taxes or other designated revenue sources. They are usually mandated by statute, charter, or local ordinance to fund specific functions or activities. Examples are parks, museums, highway construction, street maintenance, business licensing.

Revenue Funds resources cannot be used for any purpose other than the purpose for which the bonds were sold.

Journal entries:		
Encumbrances	xxx	
Reserve for Encumbrances		xxx
Reserve for Encumbrances	xxx	
Encumbrances		xxx
Expenditures	xxx	
Vouchers Payable		xxx
Vouchers Payable	xxx	
Cash		xxx

Taxes and service charges are budgeted in a Taxes-Receivable—Current account. The estimated amounts should be recorded after the estimate and posting of uncollectibles, so the entries are a credit to Revenues and a credit to Estimated Uncollectible Taxes; e.g.,

Taxes Receivable—Current	xxx	
Estimated Uncollectible Current Taxes		xxx
Revenues		xxx

When collections are actually received during the fiscal year they are recorded with a debit to Cash and a credit to Taxes Receivable—Current.

Accounting for Debt Service Funds (DSF). Debt Service Fund accounts for the payment of interest and principal on long-term debt resulting from the sale of general obligation bonds. This fund does not include the accounting for special assessments and service debts of governmental enterprises.

There are three types of long-term debt:

- Term or sinking fund bonds.
- Serial bonds.
- Notes and time warrants having a maturity of *more than one year* after issuance.

The first entry in the accounting cycle for a bond fund is to record the bond authorization:

Bonds Authorized—unissued	xxx	
Appropriations		xxx
The bonds are sold:		
Cash	xxx	
Bonds Authorized—unissued		xxx

If the bonds are sold at a premium, a Premium on Bonds account is credited. If sold at a discount, a Discount on Bonds account is debited.

Accounting for the Capital Projects Fund (CPF). Capital Projects Funds are a set of accounts for all resources used to acquire *capital* facilities (except funds financed by special assessment and enterprise funds). There must be Capital Project Funds for each authorized project to ensure that the proceeds of a bond issue, for example, are expended only as authorized. There is also a separate budget for the CPF, usually labeled the Capital Budget.

The accounting process begins with project authorization which is in memorandum form; no entry is necessary. Assuming the project is financed by the proceeds of a bond issue (as most projects are), the proceeds of the borrowing is an entry to the Cash account and a credit to Revenues for the *par value* of the bonds. If the bonds were sold at a premium, there is a credit to a Premium on Bonds account for the amount of the premium. Since GAAP requires bond premiums to be treated as an adjustment to the interest costs, the premiums are transferred *to* the Debt Service Fund established to service the debt. The entry to record the transfer is:

Premium on Bonds	xxx	
Cash		xxx

If the bonds are sold at a discount, the discount is eliminated by a transfer of the amount of the discount *from* the Debt Service Fund *to* the Capital Projects Fund.

Accounting for Enterprise Funds (EF).   Enterprise Funds finance self-supporting (not taxpayers') activities of governmental units that render services on a user charge basis to the general public. Common enterprises are water companies, electricity, natural gas, airports, transportation systems, hospitals, port authority, and a variety of recreational facilities.

In most jurisdictions, utilities and other enterprises are required to adopt and operate under budgets in the same manner as non-enterprise operations of governmental units. A budget is essential for control of each enterprise's operating results and to ensure that the resources of one enterprise are not illegally or improperly utilized by another.

The accrual basis of accounting is the required method for Enterprise Funds. As customers are billed, Accounts Receivable accounts are debited and revenue accounts *by sources* are credited.

Four financial statements are required to disclose fully the financial position and results of operations of an Enterprise Fund:

- Balance Sheet
- Revenue and Expenses
- Changes in Financial Position
- Analysis of Changes in Retained Earnings

Accounting for Trust and Agency Funds (TAF).   Trust and Agency Funds are similar; the primary difference is that a Trust Fund is usually in existence for a long period of time, even permanently. Both have fiduciary responsibilities for funds and assets that are not owned outright by the funds.

There are two types of Trust Funds, i.e., expendable and nonexpendable funds. The former allows the principal and income to be spent on designated operations, while nonexpendable funds must be preserved intact. Pension and various retirement funds are examples of expendable funds; a loan fund from which loans are made for specific purposes and must be paid back, which requires maintaining the *original amount* of the fund, is a nonexpendable fund.

Trust Funds are operated as required by statutes and governmental regulations established for their existence. Accounting for Trust Funds consists primarily of the proper recording of receipts and disbursements. Additions are credited directly to the Fund Balance account and expenditures charged directly against the Fund Balance.

An Agency Fund can be thought of as sort of a clearinghouse fund established to account for assets received for and paid to others; the main asset is cash which is held only for a brief period of time, so is seldom invested because cash is usually paid out shortly after receipt.

An Agency Fund simplifies the complexities that can result from the use of numerous fund accounting entities; e.g., instances in which a single transaction affects several different funds. All Agency Fund assets are owed to another fund, a person, or an organization. The entries for receipts and disbursements in Agency Funds are easy:

Upon receipt:		
Cash	xxx	
Fund Balance		xxx
Upon disbursement:		
Fund Balance	xxx	
Cash		xxx

Accounting for Intergovernmental Service Funds (ISF).   ISF, also referenced as Working Capital Funds and Internal Service Funds, finances and provides accountability for services and commodities provided by a designated agency of a governmental unit to other departments, agencies, etc., of the same governmental entity. Examples are motor pools, centralized garages, central purchasing, storage, facilities, and central printing services.

Funds for the establishment of ISF usually originate from three sources:

- Contributions from another operating fund—e.g., the General Fund or an Enterprise Fund.
- The sale of general obligation bonds.
- Long-term advances from other funds, which are to be repaid over a specific period of time from the earnings of a revolving fund.

As cash is expended for the benefit of other fund-users, the users are charged with the cost of the materials or services furnished by the ISF and the ISF is then reimbursed by interdepartmental cash transfers from the departments of other funds to which materials or services have been furnished.

The accounting for ISF should include all accounts necessary to compile an accurate statement of the outcome of its financial operations, and of its financial position at any given time. These accounts will usually include the fixed assets owned by the fund, accounts for buildings financed from capital Project Funds, depreciation recorded on fixed assets to obtain an accurate computation of costs and to preclude depletion of the fund's capital. The accrual basis must be used for all ISF accounting, with all charges to departments of various funds billed at the time materials or services are rendered and expenditures are recorded when incurred. Encumbrances may or may not be formally recorded in the books of account; if they are the entries would be:

Encumbrances	xxx	
Reserve for Encumbrances		xxx

If encumbrances are not recorded in the accounts, memorandum records of orders and commitments should be maintained to preclude over-obligation of cash and other fund resources.

When an ISF is established, the entry to be made will depend upon the service the fund is to provide. If the fund's capital is obtained from the General Fund, the entry would be:

Cash	xxx	
Contribution from General Fund		xxx

If a general obligation bond issue is a source of the fund's capital:

Cash	xxx	
Contribution from		
General Obligation Bonds		xxx

If fund capital is obtained from another fund of the same governmental unit the entry is:

Cash	xxx	
Advance from (name of fund)		xxx

Accounting for the General Fixed Assets Account Group (GFA). The fixed asset accounts are maintained on the basis of original cost, or the estimated cost if the original cost is not available, as in the case of gifts. The appraised value at the time of receipt of the asset is an acceptable valuation. Otherwise, initial costs of fixed assets are obtainable from contracts, purchase vouchers, and other transaction documents generated at the time of acquisition or construction.

Depreciation on fixed assets should not be recorded in the general accounting records. Depreciation charges are computed for unit cost purposes, provided such charges are recorded in memorandum form and do not appear in the fund accounts.

Different from depreciation accounting for commercial enterprises, the depreciation of fixed assets is not recorded as an expense because there is no purpose in doing so. Property records should be kept, however, for each piece of property and equipment owned by the fund. The sum of the cost value of the properties—buildings, improvements, machinery, and equipment—should equal the corresponding balances of those accounts carried in the general ledger.

Accounting for the Long-Term Debt Group (LTD). General Obligation Bonds and other types of long-term debt supported by general revenues are obligations of the governmental unit as a whole, not of any of the entity's constituent funds individually. Additionally, the monies from such debt can be expended on facilities that are used in the operation of several funds. Accordingly, the total of long-term indebtedness backed by the "full faith and credit" of the government should be recorded and accounted for in a separate self-balancing group of accounts titled General Long-Term Debt Group of Accounts. Included in this debt group are general obligation bonds, time warrants, and notes that have a maturity date of *more than one year* from the date of issuance.

Long-term debt is recorded in the self-balancing accounts, so do not affect the liabilities of any other fund. The reason for these accounts is to record a governmental unit's long-term debt at any point in time from the date the debt is incurred until it is finally paid. Under GAAP the proper valuation for the long-term debt liability is the sum of 1) the present discounted value of the principal payable at the stipulated maturity date in the future and 2) the present discounted value of the periodic interest payments to the maturity date.

The entries to be made at the time the bonds are sold are:

Amounts to be Provided for the Payment of Term Bonds	xxx	
Term Bonds Payable		xxx

The proceeds of the bond issue are entered in a Capital Projects Fund account to be expended as authorized in the Authorized Capital Outlay account.

(Note: Not-for-profit accounting for other than governmental entities uses the accrual basis of accounting—e.g., colleges and universities, voluntary hospitals, health and welfare organizations, and so on.)

OBJECTIVES OF FINANCIAL REPORTING BY NONBUSINESS ORGANIZATIONS

The main distinguishing characteristics of nonbusiness organizations include:

1) Receipts of significant amounts of resources from resource providers who do not expect to receive either repayment or economic benefits commensurate with the resources provided.
2) Operating purposes for objectives other than to provide goods or services at a profit.
3) Absence of defined ownership interests that can be sold, transferred, or redeemed, or that convey entitlement to a share of a residual distribution of resources in the event of liquidation of the organization.

These characteristics result in certain types of transactions that are largely, although not entirely, absent in business enterprises, such as contributions and grants, and in the absence of transactions with owners, such as issuing and redeeming stock and paying dividends. General purpose financial reporting by nonbusiness organizations does not attempt to meet all the information needed by those interested parties or to furnish all of the different types of information that financial reporting can provide. It is not intended to meet specialized needs of regulatory bodies, donors or grantors, or others having the authority to obtain the information they need. The most important users in the nonbusiness environment are resource providers, such as members, taxpayers, contributors, and creditors. A full set of financial statements for a period should show:

1) Financial position at the end of the period.
2) Earnings for the period.
3) Comprehensive income for the period.
4) Cash flows during the period.
5) Investments by and distributions to owners during the period.

Financial statements result from simplifying, condensing, and aggregating masses of data. As a result, they convey information that would be obscured if great detail were provided.

Following are three FASB Statements relating specifically to not-for-profit organizations: FASB Statements 93, 116, and 117.

FASB STATEMENT 93: RECOGNITION OF DEPRECIATION BY NOT-FOR-PROFIT ORGANIZATIONS

FASB Statement 93 provides that all not-for-profit organizations must recognize depreciation on all long-lived, tangible assets in general-purpose external financial statements. Thus, the Statement eliminates previously allowed exemptions from depreciation accounting for landmarks, monuments, cathedrals, certain historical treasures, and structures such as churches or temples used primarily as houses of worship.

However, rare works of art and historical treasures that have exceptionally long lives will continue to be exempt from depreciation accounting; but to be in line for this exemption, these assets must have recognized cultural, aesthetic, or historical value, and normally will already have had a long existence, and be expected to retain this value far into the future. Statement 93 also requires not-for-profit organizations to disclose depreciation expense periodically. The financial statement is to include:

1) Depreciation expense for the current reporting period.
2) Balance of major classes reported by nature or function.
3) Accumulated depreciation by major class or in total.
4) Description of accounting methods employed in figuring depreciation.

FASB STATEMENT 116, ACCOUNTING FOR CONTRIBUTIONS RECEIVED AND CONTRIBUTIONS MADE

FASB STATEMENT 117, FINANCIAL STATEMENTS OF NOT-FOR-PROFIT ORGANIZATIONS

Two Statements dealing with not-for-profit organizations—Statements 116 and 117—are effective for financial statements issued after December 15, 1994, except for organizations whose total assets are less than $5 million and whose annual expenses run less than $1 million. The effective date for these NPOs is December 15, 1995, but they are encouraged to adopt the procedures earlier.

In the past, differing requirements, or deficient guidelines, have led divergent forms of not-for-profit enterprises to abide by various rulings promulgated for their particular type of organization, to follow lines of least resistance, or merely to perpetuate custom. This was true whether or not the organization or the external users were gaining insightful information from the various accounting and reporting procedures. The new rules supersede any/all inconsistencies or discrepancies with previous guides, announcements, or statements.

Statement 116 specifically addresses accounting standards for contributions of cash, assets, services or unconditional promises to provide these at some future time, made or received by any organization, whether it be a not-for-profit or a for-profit business concern:

1) Contributions *received*, including unconditional promises to give, are recognized at fair market value in the period received.

2) Contributions *made*, including unconditional promises to give, are recognized as expenses at fair market value in the period when given.

3) Conditional promises to give (whether received or made) are appropriately recognized when the conditions are substantially met.

This Statement acts to tighten some of the provisions relating to measurement and recognition of volunteer services and their relevancy. It specifies that before these services can be included in revenue, they must create or enhance nonfinancial assets, be of a specialized nature, and be provided by skilled individuals contributing services that would otherwise be purchased. Therefore, the services requiring little skill or training provided by the average volunteer will not be considered as revenue or gains. On the other hand, volunteer work by trained professionals and tradesmen, such as nurses, teachers, carpenters, plumbers may be measured at fair value and recognized in the financial report with explanatory notes describing the value of service rendered to various aspects of particular programs. Recognition of these services must also be deemed to be clearly relevant and clearly measurable. If practicable, the fair value of the ordinary volunteer services contributed but not recognized as revenue should also be disclosed even though not recognized as revenue.

Both Statements 116 and 117 take into consideration three classes of contributions:

1) permanently restricted net assets

2) temporarily restricted net assets

3) unrestricted net assets.

Statement 116 also requires accounting for the expiration of donor-imposed restrictions if/when said restrictions expire. It also establishes standards for accounting for disclosures relating to works of art, historical treasures, rare books and manuscripts—collections whether capitalized or not.

To be considered a "collection," the assets must be:

1) For the purpose of public exhibition, education or research, not an investment for financial gain.
2) Conserved, cared for, and remain unencumbered.
3) Protected by an organizational policy requiring that proceeds from the sale of any collection items be used to acquire other items for collections.

An organization is not required to recognize contributions if they are added to collections which meet the above criteria. However, when applying FASB 116, organizations are encouraged to capitalize previously acquired collections retroactively or to capitalize them on a prospective basis. One stipulation is that capitalization of selected collections or items is *not* permitted. If capitalized retroactively, these assets may be stated at their cost, at fair value at the time of acquisition, current cost or current market value.

When collections have been capitalized, additional contributed items are to be recognized as revenue or gains; if the collections have not been capitalized, these items are not recognized. There is, however, additional disclosure information required for them and for collections which have been capitalized prospectively.

1) On the face of the statement of activities, apart from revenues, expenses, gains and losses an organization that has not capitalized must report the cost of items purchased as a decrease in the appropriate class of net assets; or proceeds resulting from the sale of items; or from insurance recoveries as an increase in the appropriate class of net assets.
2) An organization that capitalizes prospectively must report proceeds from sales or insurance recoveries of items not previously capitalized separately.
3) Both those organizations that do not capitalize, or do so prospectively, must describe the collections and their significance, and the accounting conservatorship policies relating to them.
4) They must also describe and report the fair value of items lost or removed from collections for whatever reason.
5) A line in the body of the financial statement must refer directly to the note on collections.

In addition to the accounting functions which these stipulations provide, they would appear to help ensure the integrity of important collections.

The intent and purpose of FASB 117 is to begin to bring a measure of uniformity to the financial statements of NPOs, particularly for the benefit of external users. Emphasis is upon relevance and significance of the information provided, the ease with which it can be understood and interpreted, and the readiness with which financial reports can be compared with those of other not-for-profit entities.

FASB 117 stipulates that three financial statements with appropriate notes be included in all NPO financial reports:

1) statement of financial position
2) statement of activities
3) statement of cash flows.

This latter requirement is new for not-for-profit entities and thus amends FASB 95, *Statement of Cash Flows*, in which the requirements had previously applied only to business entities. Statement 117 also *requires* Voluntary Health and Welfare Organizations (*encourages* other NPOs) to prepare an additional financial statement showing expenses in natural classifications as well as the functional classifications required of all NPOs. Organizations may continue to present other financial reports if they have found them to be beneficial in demonstrating the handling of the service aspects of the particular type of NPO.

Most organizations will probably find that their accounting and reporting activities will not become more complicated and restrictive, but simplified, and at the same time, more meaningful once the initial changeover has been completed. This is particularly true if the organization has carried fund accounting to the extreme and attempted to fit everything into the pattern whether or not this proved to be appropriate or useful. Statement 117 does not tamper with fund accounting *per se* but does require that the emphasis on financial reporting be placed on the entity as a whole. Thus, organizations may continue to prepare their statement of financial position showing fund groups, but the groups must be aggregated into net asset classes.

In line with the aim to give a clear picture of an NPO's liquidity, FASB 117 requires that an organization must break down its net assets into the three classes mentioned above. Further, information about the amounts and/or conditions of the two restricted categories can be made in the statement itself if this is deemed sufficient, or it may be necessary to give detailed explanations in the notes. The latter could be more frequently necessary than not since the restrictions could range from a wealthy donor's desire to aid a "pet project" to a government grant funding a Congressional bill.

Much of the impetus for these statements was to bring about more readily usable full disclosure. Requirements will now make it more important than ever to distinguish between program and support activities and expenses. FASB 117 separates the latter into three classes:

1) Managements and general
2) Fund-raising
3) Membership development.

It is important for the preparer of the financial statement to be reminded that the focus should be on the *service* aspect of the NPO and how well this is being accomplished. Since it is doubtful if this information can be conveyed adequately in the body of the financial statement, the accompanying notes will be of particular relevance.

Below are some important points to keep in mind relating to the purpose of the three basic financial reports of not-for-profit entities.

Statement of Financial Position:

- Present assets, liabilities and net asset figures for the organization as a whole.
- Demonstrate credit status, liquidity, ability to meet service and financial obligations, need for outside financial aid.
- Distinguish between permanently restricted assets, temporarily restricted assets, unrestricted assets.
- Disclose donor-imposed restrictions and internally imposed restrictions relating to both time and purpose.

Statement of Activities (operating statement for NPOs):

- Report the changes in total net assets (equities).
- Present the changes in each of the three net asset classes (not fund balances): permanently restricted, temporarily restricted, unrestricted.
- Indicate total changes in net assets.
- Disclose expenditures by functional and/or natural classification as required/recommended for a particular type of NPO.

Statement of Cash Flows:

- Amends FASB 95 to require *all* NPOs to include a cash flow statement in their external financial reports.
- Present changes in cash and cash equivalents including certain donor-restricted cash used on a long-term basis.
- Present cash flow information utilizing either direct or indirect method.

Chapter 14

Cost Accounting Systems

What Is Cost Accounting? The cost accounting function in an organization is a system broadly defined in terms of procedures—i.e., the gathering, sorting, classifying, processing (computations), summarizing, reporting, and filing of information relevant to a company's costs, mostly in the form of data (numbers).

What is the function of a cost accounting system? Primarily, the system accepts disorganized, meaningless raw data (input) from the environment and processes (transforms) the data into understandable form. The information then leaves the system (output) in an organized form of reports required by management.

Specifically, cost accounting explicitly sets forth data which relate to the *costs* associated with the business. This includes the assignment of costs to a particular product, to a particular process, to a particular operation, or to a particular service, in the case of a service business.

The Objective of a Cost Accounting System. The primary objective of cost accounting is to provide information useful to management for the decisions necessary for the successful operation of the business. The system should be designed to achieve this objective by providing management with information concerning the efficiency and effectiveness of production and service processes in order that cost reduction and increased profits can be attained. An analysis of accurate cost data is the essence of profit planning—

285

what to produce, what *price* to charge, whether to *continue* producing a certain product.

Management should expect cost reports to show the results of past operations in terms of costs per unit of product, costs per unit of production in each operating department, or costs per unit of service in the case of a service organization. The system should provide immediate feedback information on changes in costs from accounting period to accounting period, and comparisons of costs with *predetermined estimates or norms.* With the proper cost information management can adjust operations quickly to changing economic and competitive conditions.

Developing a Cost Accounting System.

The task of developing a cost accounting system is to determine the specific needs of management, and the extent to which it is economically feasible to add detailed procedures to a basic system.

The system must be easily understood by all individuals in the organization who are involved in the use of control procedures, and flexible in its application. First, the system should be simple—i.e., must not include procedures that accumulate information that might be interesting, but *not particularly useful.* (A common pitfall is a cost system which, itself, is more expensive than the costs to be saved.) Second, the cost system must provide useful information in the most efficient manner. *Accurate* accounting records are particularly significant. Third, the cost accounting system must be flexible. Businesspeople often are required to adjust and adapt their operations to meet changing needs of customers, changes in production methods due to improved technology, changes in the economic and social environment in which the business operates, and changes in governmental regulations. Likewise, all businesses hope to grow and become larger. New cost accounting control requirements will appear by the nature of the growth process. Any system should be planned to meet changing needs with the least possible alteration of the present system.

There are fundamental cost control methods that apply to any business and include principles applicable to an individual business. The type of production, the number of products manufactured, the size of the business, the types of costs associated with the business, and the desires, capabilities, and attitudes of the individuals involved in the business will all have a part in determining the structure of the cost control system. Personnel responsible for the procedures within the business for the accounting and control techniques must be constantly aware of the unique characteristics of the particular business.

No Right Answer.

It is a rare instance that there is just one obviously right answer to any business problem. Certainly alternative choices for the allocation of an enterprise's limited resources confront the business manager every day. Information for selecting the "right" choice is provided by a cost accounting system. Is the product profitable? Is the product priced to yield a predetermined profit margin? What are the per unit costs of the product? Could it profitably be sold at a lower, more competitive price? Should production be expanded, reduced, discontinued? Are costs out of line? What are the controllable costs? Uncontrollable costs? These are only a few items of significant information that are furnished by a well-developed cost accounting system.

FOUNDATION OF A COST ACCOUNTING SYSTEM

What input does a cost accounting system accept?

There is an infinite amount of data within the business environment that can be entered into the system. It should be emphasized that the choice of data to be entered is not random; that is, chance or guesswork is not the determinant of the selection of data input. Rather, the selection of data is done within a carefully designed framework of the information needed to provide the required output (reports), with the framework continually subject to modification by a *feedback* system. The framework is governed by a set of *controls* to ensure compliance with the procedures, policies, and objectives which the system has been designed to carry out.

The elements of the framework of a set of books to track costs are briefly described as follows:

- The system is for a specific organization and accepts data relating only to that organization.
- Precautions should be taken against superfluous (and expensive) input.
- The system accepts information about transactions generated by events which have actually occurred, a purchase, for example.
- The system accepts information which has numbers assigned to it, with dollars and cents the most common measurement.
- The system accepts only information that has been predetermined to meet the needs of the users of the information.
- Information entered into the system should be completely free of bias; only absolutely objective information is acceptable.
- Information must be *verifiable*. Verifiability means transactions that are recorded in the same way by two or more qualified personnel acting independently of each other.
- Information entered into the system must be *consistent*. Consistency prevents manipulation of data in the accounts, as well as makes the financial information comparable from one period of time to another.

Four Group Classifications.   Most businesses of any size can be classified as to production activities into one of the following four groups:

1) *Jobbing Plants.* Jobbing plants specialize in products that are made to order, i.e., not conducive to a repetitive operation. Some examples are machine shops, printers, repair shops of all kinds, and custom made products of any kind, generally.

2) *Continuous Processing Plants.* Continuous processing is concentrated upon products that are produced for inventory and sold at a later date, instead of ordered in advance. The significant aspect of continuous processing is that the production of the product is adaptable to a *repetitive* operation which is sequential in steps in the conversion of raw materials into finished products, all the units of which are the same; mass production techniques apply. Examples are shoe manufacturers, food processors, glass, soap, paper, textiles, and automobiles.

3) *Assembly Plants.* Products are made up of many component parts, either manufactured by the assembler or purchased from other manufacturers. Aircraft manufacturers are one of the best examples, as they subcontract various parts of the aircraft to literally hundreds of subcontractors. Automobile production is an example of both continuous processing and assembling, as many parts for automobiles are purchased from other manufacturing suppliers.

4) *Service Establishments.* Service establishments include businesses that provide various services to the public, rather than manufactured products. Medical, legal, accounting, architectural, transportation, food, and recreational services are examples of service businesses.

The cost control problems of each of these groups are different. Control and cost procedures for each must be designed, as well as for individual businesses within a group.

Cost Accounting System—A Model
(An Outline)

Job Order Costs
    Need for a job order cost system.
    Use of journals and ledgers.
    Cost control reports.
    Recording job costs.

Process Costs
    Need for a process cost system.
    Advantages of a process cost system.
    Accuracy of data provided by the system.
    Characteristics of a process cost system.
    Production controls.
    Flow assumptions (FIFO or alternatives).
    Conversion cost components.
    Per unit cost information.
    Spoilage problems, shrinkage, breakage, theft, defective units, etc.
    Units of production.

Cost Accounting System—A Model
(An Outline) (cont.)

Accounting for Raw Materials
 Determining raw materials requirements.
 Purchasing.
 Recording materials' costs.
 Counting and pricing materials.
 Accounting for materials used.
 Materials control procedures—storing, issuing, etc.

Accounting for Labor Costs
 Labor and payroll records.
 Purpose for accounting for labor costs.
 Timekeeping.
 Allocating labor costs.
 By-products.
 Joint products.
 Distribution costs.
 Transfer pricing.
 Payroll preparation.
 Recording payrolls.
 Paying the payroll.
 Individual employee earnings' record.
 Salaried employees payroll records.
 Fringe benefits.

Responsibility Accounting
 Cost centers.
 Profit centers.

Accounting for Overhead Costs
 What is overhead? Manufacturing overhead?
  Administrative overhead?
 Overhead costs and tight control systems important.
 Allocating overhead costs.
 Overhead budgets (determining overhead rates).
 Administrative (nonmanufacturing) overhead, e.g., accounting and other support functions.

Cost Targets
 Predetermined costs.
 Determining cost estimates (the cost standards).
 Use of the standards in ledger accounts.
 Analyzing cost deviations from the standards.
 Standard costs for a job system.
 Standard costs for a process system.

Break-Even Analysis
 Cost-price-volume relationships.
 Fixed costs.
 Variable costs.
 Production capacity levels.
 Effects of changes in product price.
 Effects of changes in product costs.
 Unit costs.
 Total costs.

Cost Accounting System—A Model
(An Outline) (cont.)

Graphic method.
Incremental costs.
Single or multi-product firms.
Budgeting and Profit Planning
Various types of budgets, i.e., operating and capital budgets.
Cash flow planning.
Cash budget.
Cost Allocation Techniques
Direct costing and contribution approach.
Absorption costing.
Contribution approach.
Ratio Analysis for Control
The most commonly applied ratios, with the emphasis on the ratios for the expense elements of the income statement.
How to interpret and apply the ratios to business decisions.
Ratios as warning signals (red flags).
Summary of Operations
Promptness.
Accuracy.
Comparative reports, i.e., current vs. past trends highlighted.
Cost trends highlighted and explained.
Cost reports for areas of specific responsibility.
Report contents:
Direct labor hours and costs.
Indirect labor hours and costs.
Direct materials used.
Production overhead applied.
Actual overhead expense.
Variances.
Idle time costs, if any.
Overtime costs.
Spoilage costs.
Maintenance hours and costs.
Scrap costs.
Inventory status report.
New order book.
Orders shipped during the period.
New order bookings.
Interim expense and income statements. (For predetermined periods of time—week, month.
Actual versus budgeted costs for the period. Comparisons with prior determined periods of time. Year-to-date totals and comparisons with prior years).

The topics listed below are the essential elements of a cost accounting system; they are reviewed in the discussion that follows.

- Cost Accounting Terminology.
- Integrating a Cost System.

- Historical and Standard Cost Systems.
- Job and Process Cost Systems.
- Standard Costs—Illustration.
- Direct Costing.
- Effects of Costing on Financial Statements.
- Break-Even Point Analysis. (See Chapter 12.)
- Summary.

Cost Terminology (for quick reference).   Here are some brief definitions of various types of costs:

1) *Historical*—measured by actual cash payments or their equivalent at the time of outlay.
2) *Future*—expected to be incurred at a later date.
3) *Standard*—scientifically predetermined.
4) *Estimated*—predetermined.
5) *Product*—associated with units of output.
6) *Period*—associated with the income of a time period.
7) *Direct*—obviously tradeable to a unit of output or a segment of business operations.
8) *Prime*—labor and material directly traceable to a unit of output.
9) *Indirect*—not obviously traceable to a unit of output or to a segment of business operations.
10) *Fixed*—do not change in the total as the rate of output varies.
11) *Variable*—do change with changes in rate of output.
12) *Opportunity*—measurable advantage foregone as a result of the rejection of alternative uses of resources whether of materials, labor, or facilities.
13) *Imputed*—never involve cash outlays nor appear in financial records. Involve a foregoing on the part of the person whose costs are being calculated.
14) *Controllable*—subject to direct control at some level of supervision.
15) *Noncontrollable*—not subject to control at some level of supervision.
16) *Joint*—exists when from any one unit source, material, or process come products which have different unit values.
17) *Sunk*—historical and not recoverable in a given situation.
18) *Discretionary*—avoidable and unessential to an objective.
19) *Postponable*—may be shifted to future period without affecting efficiency.
20) *Out of pocket*—necessitate cash expenditure.

21) *Differential*—changes in cost that result from variation in operations.
22) *Incremental*—those added or eliminated if segments were expanded or discontinued.
23) *Alternative*—estimated for decision areas.
24) *Replacement*—considered for depreciation significance.
25) *Departmental*—production and service, for cost distributions.

HISTORICAL AND STANDARD COST SYSTEMS

Cost accounting systems vary with the type of cost (present or future) used. When present costs are used, the cost system is called an *historical* or *actual cost* system. When future costs are used, the cost system is called a *standard cost* system. In practice, combinations of these costs are used even in actual or standard systems. Where there is an intentional use of both types of costs, we sometimes refer to the system as a *hybrid cost* system.

Actual Cost System.   Since an actual cost system uses only those costs which have already been incurred, the system determines costs only after manufacturing operations have been performed. Under this system the product is charged with the actual cost of materials, the actual cost of labor, and an *estimated* portion of overhead (overhead costs represent the future cost element in an actual cost system).

Standard Cost System.   A standard system is based upon estimated or predetermined costs. There is a distinction between estimated and standard costs, however. Both are "predetermined" costs, but estimated costs are based upon average past experience, and standard costs are based upon scientific facts that consider past experience and controlled experiments. Arriving at standard costs involves careful selection of material, an engineering study of equipment and manufacturing facilities, and time and motion studies.

In either system, adjustment must be made at the financial statement date to the *closing inventory* so that it is shown at actual cost or reasonably approximate actual cost, or at market if lower. Also, the inventory must bear its share of the burden of overhead. "The exclusion of all overheads from inventory costs does not constitute an accepted accounting procedure."

For interim statements, estimated gross profit rates may be used to determine cost of goods sold during the interim, but this fact must be disclosed.

It must be emphasized that whatever cost accounting method is chosen by a company, its purpose is primarily an internal management tool directed at controlling costs, setting production goals, measuring efficiencies and variances, providing incentives and establishing realistic relationships between unit costs, selling prices and gross margins. Regardless of costing methods used, generally accepted accounting standards must be followed for the preparation of the financial statements, wherein the valuation must be cost or market, whichever is lower.

Also, either the FIFO or LIFO methods (or the average method) may be used under any cost system. These methods pertain to the assumption of the *flow* of costs, not to the actual costs themselves. Note that *both* methods may be used within one inventory, as long as the method is applied to that portion of the inventory consistently from period to period. Disclosures should be made of any change in method.

Integrating A Cost System.   It is not essential to integrate a cost system with the rest of the accounting system, but it is highly desirable. A cost system is really an extension of the regular system. With an integrated system, entries in the inventory account in the general ledger should represent the sums of figures taken from the cost accounting data. The general ledger inventory accounts (e.g., finished goods, work in process, and raw materials) are the control accounts and they should tie in with the amounts of physical inventories actually on hand. Discrepancies may result from errors, spoilage, or thievery.

Elements of Cost.   Production costs consist of three elements: direct materials, direct labor, and manufacturing (overhead) expenses:

Direct Materials: Those materials which can be identified with specific units of the product.

Direct Labor: That labor which can be identified with specific units of the product.

Manufacturing Expenses (Overhead): Those costs (including indirect material or labor) which cannot be identified with specific units of the product. These costs represent expenses for the factory and other facilities which permit the labor to be applied to the materials to manufacture a product.

Sometimes, overhead is further subdivided into:

Direct overhead—Those manufacturing costs, other than for material and direct labor, which specifically apply to production and require no allocation from other expense areas;

Indirect overhead—Those expenses which have been allocated into the manufacturing expense area from other more general areas.

For financial statement purposes, overhead should not include selling expenses or general or administrative expenses.

JOB ORDER OR PROCESS COST SYSTEMS

There are distinctions between cost systems other than the use of present or future costs.

A *job order system* compiles costs for a specific quantity of a product as it moves through the production process. This means that material, labor, and overhead costs of a specific number or lot of the product (usually identifiable with a customer's order or a specific quantity being produced for stock) are recorded as the lot moves through the production cycle.

A *process system* compiles costs as they relate to specific processes or operations for a period of time. To find the unit cost, these figures are averaged for a specified period and spread over the number of units that go through each process. Process costing is used when large numbers of identical products are manufactured, usually in assembly-line fashion.

Keep in mind that actual or estimated costs can be used with either a job order or process cost system.

Benefits and Drawbacks

Whether the job order or process system is used depends on the type of operation. The job order system is rarely used in mass production industries. It is invariably used when products are custom made. Process costing is used where production is in a continuous state of operation as for paper, baking, steel making, glass, rubber, sugar, chemicals, etc. Here are some of the relative merits and shortcomings of each method:

Advantages	
Job Order	*Process*
1) Appropriate for custom-made goods	1) It is usually only necessary to calculate costs each month
2) Appropriate for increasing finished goods inventory in desired quantities	2) Minimum of clerical work required
3) Adequate for inventory pricing	3) If there is only one type of product cost computation is relatively simple
4) Permits estimation of future costs	
5) Satisfies "cost-plus" contract requisites	

Disadvantages	
Job Order	*Process*
1) Expensive to use—a good deal of clerical work required	1) Use of average costs ignores any variance in product cost
2) Difficult to make sure that all materials and labor are accurately charged to each specific job	2) Involves calculation of stage of completion of goods in process and the use of equivalent units
3) Difficult to determine cost of goods sold when partial shipments are made before completion	

How to Use Standard Costs

Smith Company manufactures only one product, glubs—a household article made out of a certain type of plastic. Glubs are made from D raw material which goes through a single process. Glubs are turned out from D material in a fraction of a day. Smith Company has a process-type cost setup integrated with its other financial records. D material is charged to work in process through requisitions based upon actual cost. Direct labor is charged to work in process based upon payroll. Manufacturing expense is charged to work in process based upon the number of payroll hours. Each day a record of the number of glubs manufactured is kept. This is the responsibility of the production department.

Here's the way the Smith Company process cost system operates: Every month, total figures are worked up for raw material, payroll, factory expenses. Each of these figures is then divided by the total number of glubs produced for that month to arrive at a unit cost per glub. Here is what the unit cost accumulation for the four months shows (this example assumes no work-in-process inventory and no equivalent units):

Unit Cost per Glub Manufactured

	First Month	Second Month	Third Month	Fourth Month	Weighted Average
Material D	$ .94	$ .91	$ .97	$1.10	$ .95
Direct Labor	1.18	1.22	2.00	.70	1.29
Manufacturing Expenses	1.22	1.47	2.11	.82	1.42
	$3.34	$3.60	$5.08	$2.62	$3.66

Right now, glubs are being sold at $4.30, and the present profit appears sufficient. T.O. Smith, the president and major stockholder of the corporation, feels that if glubs were sold at $3.30 each, four times as many could be sold. He also reports that he has learned that Glubco, Inc., Smith's competitor, is going to market glubs for $3.60. Smith thinks that $3.30 is a good sales price since the cost records indicate that glubs were manufactured for as low as $2.62 in the fourth month. Smith Company's accountant says the president is incorrect. He points out that the average cost is somewhere in the area of $3.55 to $3.80 based upon the cost records for six months. Selling glubs for $3.30 would create losses. The factory foreman says that during the third and fourth months there was an error in calculating the number of glubs put into finished goods inventory. From the figures for the fourth month, it appears that the foreman is correct. The unit cost per glub is unusually low. Mr. Smith wants to know the lowest at which he can sell glubs and still make a reasonable profit. The accountant suggests setting up a cost system based upon standard costs. He outlines the following steps:

1) Purchasing department records indicate that material D should cost no more than 15¢ per pound. (According to the chief engineer, it takes approximately two pounds of D to produce one glub.) The 15¢ figure takes future market conditions into account.

2) A time study of half a dozen workers who produce glubs is made. The average time it takes each of these six workers to produce one glub is one-third of an hour. The average hourly wage of these workers is $3.00.

3) Based upon reasonable level of production for the following year, a departmental manufacturing expense or overhead is estimated to be 100% of direct labor.

Based upon the above determinations, the standard cost per glub is $2.30. It is calculated as follows:

Raw Material D: two pounds at 15¢ per pound	$ .30
Direct Labor: ⅓ hour at $3.00 per hour	1.00
Manufacturing Expense: 100% of direct labor	1.00
Total	$2.30

In order to produce glubs at this cost, the following points are agreed upon:

1) When more than 15¢ a pound is paid for raw material D, the excess is to be charged to a special variance account instead of the raw material account. These excesses are to be explained periodically by the purchasing department.

2) Requisitions for raw material D are to be limited to two pounds of D for each glub to be manufactured. If more than two pounds per glub is issued to meet scheduled production, the excess over two pounds is to be charged to a separate variance account. The reason for any excess will also have to be explained.

3) The daily number of direct labor hours spent making glubs is to be multiplied by three. This should equal the number of glubs produced that day. Any discrepancy here is probably due to inefficiency. The number of inefficient hours at the standard $3 rate times the 100% manufacturing expense rate is to be charged to a special variance account.

4) Payroll over $3 an hour is to be charged to a variance account. Only $3 an hour is to be charged to the work-in-progress account. The factory supervisor will have to explain hourly labor figures over $3 periodically.

5) Departmental variations in the 100% of direct labor manufacturing expense burden are to be charged or credited to separate variance accounts. This is to be done each month.

Here's what happened each month after this system was instituted:

Variance Accounts	Fifth Month	Sixth Month	Seventh Month	Eighth Month	Ninth Month
1) Material D Price	$ 2,100	$ 300	$ 750	$ 0	$ 0
2) Material usage	19,500	13,000	5,000	500	400
3) Labor efficiency	8,000	5,050	800	700	300
4) Labor rate	400	150	(50)	400	100
5) Mfg. Expense	0	5,000	1,000	300	(100)
	$ 30,000	$ 23,500	$ 7,500	$ 1,900	$ 700
Unit Manufactured	48,000	48,000	48,000	48,000	48,000
Variance per Unit	.63	.49	.16	.04	.01
Standard Unit Cost	2.30	2.30	2.30	2.30	2.30
Actual Cost	$ 2.93	$ 2.79	$ 2.46	$ 2.34	$ 2.31

Here is what was elicited from discussion with the persons responsible for the different variance accounts:

1) The purchase price for raw material D exceeded 15¢ per pound mainly because of the distance of Smith Company from where D is obtained in the South. The head of purchasing feels that D could be purchased for no more than 15¢ if there could be a small office in the South with one assistant who would remain there. It was decided to go ahead and provide the office and the additional employee.

2) The factory supervisor, together with the chief engineer, has been going over the requisitions of raw material D. More D was needed because some of the glubs had air holes in them and weren't usable. It seems that the pressure used to extrude them wasn't sufficient. The chief engineer says that he can replace the present air die channels with larger ones so that these defects do not recur. The supervisor knew that some glubs were scrapped in the past, but it wasn't until this switch to standard costs that he knew how much waste there really was.

3) The supervisor and the industrial engineer who performed the time and motion study discussed the labor efficiency loss. It was their opinion that there were more factory employees than needed to carry out various operations to convert D into finished glubs. It was also learned that some employees could use more training, while others were overskilled for their particular functions. Still others were not producing enough for some reason or other. Both felt that a training program instructing

employees in the efficient use of available tools would increase efficiency. Further time and motion studies on every phase of the production process were initiated.

4) There was not much variance in labor rate, but it was hoped that the training program would release more technically skilled and higher paid employees for use in the more complicated production steps.

At the end of the seventh month, it was obvious that the steps taken were beginning to pay off. The additional costs incurred in carrying out these steps (for example, the additional employee in purchasing and the southern office) created a manufacturing overhead variance where none had existed before; but the success in other areas outweighed this.

At the end of the ninth month, everyone agreed that the switch to standard costs had exceeded expectations. The new lower production cost would help expand the market for glubs. Smith Company was also in a good competitive position compared with Glubco since it probably could now undersell it.

This illustration shows the advantages of standard costs:

1) Control and reduction of costs;
2) Promotion and measurement of efficiencies;
3) Calculation and setting of selling prices;
4) Evaluation of inventories;
5) Simplification of cost procedures.

DIRECT COSTING

Another type of cost accounting which is used for internal purposes but not for financial or tax reporting purposes is "direct costing." This is a method in which only those costs which are a consequence of production of the product are assigned to the product—direct material cost, direct labor cost, and only variable manufacturing overhead. All fixed manufacturing costs are treated as expenses of the period.

The methods of recording costs for direct material and direct labor are similar under direct costing and conventional costing. It is in the method of reflecting manufacturing overhead that the systems differ. In a direct costing system, overhead costs are classified as fixed or variable. In conventional costing, only one overhead control account is used. In direct costing, two control accounts are used—a direct overhead account and an indirect overhead account. The direct overhead account is for variable expenses—those that vary with the volume of production. The indirect overhead account is for fixed expenses—those that do not vary with production. These are charged as expenses of the period rather than as costs of the finished product. Research costs, some advertising costs, and costs incurred to keep manufacturing and nonmanufacturing facilities ready for use are considered expenses of the period. Under direct costing, direct labor, direct material, and overhead costs that vary with production find their way into the inventory. The other manufacturing overhead expenses are charged off currently against income. The important reason behind direct costing is not to value inventories, but to segregate expenses.

Effect of Direct Costing on Financial Statements

Direct costing, if used on the financial statements (for internal use), would produce the following results:

1) Where the inventory of manufactured goods does not fluctuate from one accounting period to the next, there should be no difference between net income using direct costing or net income using conventional costing.

2) Where the inventory does fluctuate and is increased, net income under direct costing will be lower. *Reason*: Fixed overhead costs under direct costing will have been charged to the current period instead of deferred by increasing the value of inventory. Under conventional costing, the value of the ending inventory will have been increased by these fixed overhead costs.

3) Where inventory decreases, net income under direct costing will be higher than conventional costing. *Reason*: Fixed overhead costs included in the value of the inventory under conventional costing will now increase the cost of goods sold, thereby reducing income.

SUMMARY

When a business enterprise becomes as operationally and financially complex as even most small and medium-sized companies are today, fairly sophisticated control and evaluation techniques must be developed to ensure an adequate level of operational efficiency and financial stability.

The historical essence of cost accounting systems has been upon the *flow* of financial resources *into*, *through*, and *out* of the business. It cannot be overemphasized that the ultimate objective of cost accounting is to provide relevant, valid, and timely information of the cost of manufactured products, or to the cost of services provided by service organizations.

Chapter 15

The Securities and Exchange Commission— Organization and the Acts

In today's world of regulated business, it is important for accountants to have a working knowledge of the rules and regulations influencing SEC accounting.

In the late 1920s there was widespread speculation in the stock market. When the market crashed in 1929, the public demanded protective action by their legislators. Congressional committees held hearings into all phases of the securities industry, investment banking, and commercial banking activities prior to the market crash. As a result of these hearings, eight Federal statutes were enacted between 1933 and 1940 (with a ninth in 1970), bringing the securities markets and the securities business under federal jurisdiction. These laws are referenced as the "truth in securities" statutes. They include the Securities Act of 1933, the Securities Exchange Act of 1934, the Public Utility Holding Company Act of 1935, the Maloney Amendment to the Securities Exchange Act of 1934, and the Federal Bankruptcy Code. Also included are the Trustee Indenture Act of 1939, the Investment Company Act of 1940, the Investment Advisers Act of 1940, the Securities Investor Protection Act (SPIC) of 1970, and the Securities Act Amendments of 1975.

SEC REGIONAL AND DISTRICT OFFICES

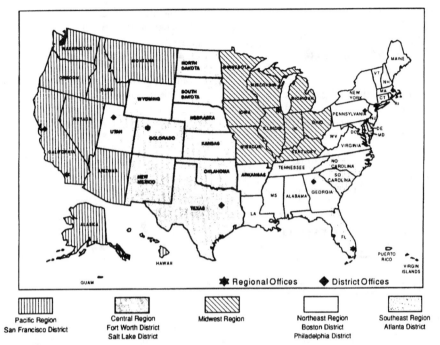

★ Regional Offices   ◆ District Offices

Pacific Region	Central Region	Midwest Region	Northeast Region	Southeast Region
San Francisco District	Fort Worth District		Boston District	Atlanta District
	Salt Lake District		Philadelphia District	

PREPARED BY THE SECURITIES AND EXCHANGE COMMISSION

REGION 1

Northeast Regional Office
7 World Trade Center
Suite 1300
New York, NY 10048
212-748-8000

Boston District Office
73 Tremont Street
Suite 600
Boston , MA 02108-3912
617-424-5900

Philadelphia District Office
The Curtis Center, Suite 1005 E.
601 Walnut Street
Philadelphia , PA 19106-3322
215-597-3100

REGION 2

Southeast Regional Office
1401 Brickell Avenue
Suite 200
Miami, FL 33131
305-536-4700

Atlanta District Office
3475 Lenox Road, N.E.
Suite 1000
Atlanta, GA 30326-1232

REGION 3

Midwest Regional Office
Citicorp Center
500 W. Madison Street
Suite 1400 Chicago, IL 60661-2511
312-533-7390

REGION 4

Central Regional Office
1801 California Street
Suite 4800
Denver, CO 80202-2648
303-391-6800

Fort Worth District Office
801 Cherry Street
Suite 1900 Fort Worth, TX 76102
817-334-3821

Salt Lake District Office
500 Key Bank Town
50 South Main Street
Suite 500
Box 79
Salt Lake City, UT 84144-0402
801-524-5796

REGION 5

Pacific Reginal Office
5670 Wilshire Boulevard
Suite 1100
Los Angeles, CA 90036-3648

San Francisco District Office
44 Montgomery Street
Suite 110
San Francisco, CA 94104
415-705-2500

THE SECURITIES AND EXCHANGE COMMISSION

The Commission is composed of five members: a Chairman and four Commissioners. Commission members are appointed by the President, with the advice and consent of the Senate, for five-year terms. The Chairman is designated by the President. Terms are staggered; one expires on June 5th of every year. Not more than three members can be of the same political party.

Under the direction of the Chairman and Commissioners, the SEC staff ensures that publicly held entities, broker-dealers in securities, investment companies and advisers, and other participants in the securities markets comply with federal securities laws. These laws are designed to facilitate informed investment analyses and decisions by the investment public, primarily by ensuring adequate disclosure of material significant information. Conformance with federal securities laws and regulations does not imply merit of securities. If information essential to informed investment analysis is properly disclosed, the Commission cannot bar the sale of securities which analysis may show to be of questionable value. Investors, not the Commission, must make the ultimate judgment of the worth of securities offered for sale.

The Commission's staff is composed of lawyers, accountants, financial analysts and examiners, engineers, investigators, economists, and other professionals. The staff is divided into divisions and offices, including eleven regional and district offices, each directed by officials appointed by the Chairman.

GLOSSARY OF SECURITY & EXCHANGE COMMISSION TERMINOLOGY

The Securities and Exchange Commission in Article 1, Rule 1-02, Title 17, Code of Federal Regulations (which is Accounting Regulation S-X), defines the meaning of terms used by the SEC in its Accounting Rules and Regulations. Also, many of the terms are defined as they appear in the Securities Act of 1933, the Securities Exchange Act of 1934, in Regulations S-K and D, and in the various Forms which publicly held corporations must file periodically with the SEC.

Occasionally, the Commission will use a term in a rule which in context will have a meaning somewhat different from its commonly understood meaning. Many of the definitions as they are written in the statutes and accounting regulations are lengthy and legalistic in style. The objective here is to "delegalize" the "legalese" in the interests both of clarity and brevity. The definitions are not, therefore, verbatim as developed by the Commission.

Accountant's Report. In regard to financial statements, a document in which an independent public accountant or certified public accountant indicates the scope of the audit (or examination) which has been made and sets forth an opinion regarding the financial statements taken as a whole, or an assertion to the effect that an overall opinion cannot be expressed. When an overall opinion cannot be expressed, the reasons therefore should be stated.

Accounting Principle, Change In. Results from changing one acceptable principle to another principle. A change in practice, or in the method of applying an accounting principle, or practice, is also considered a change in accounting principle.

Affiliate. One that directly or indirectly, through one or more intermediaries, controls or is controlled by, or is under common control with, the person specified (see **Person** below).

Amicus Curiae ("Friend of the Court"). An SEC advisory upon request of a court which assists a court in the interpretation of some matter concerning a securities law or accounting regulation.

Amount. When used to reference securities means:
a) The principal amount of a debt obligation if "amount" relates to evidence of indebtedness.
b) The number of shares if "amount" relates to shares.
c) The number of units if "amount" relates to any other type of securities.

Application for Listing. A detailed questionnaire filed with a national securities exchange providing information concerning the corporation's history and current status.

Assets Subject to Lien. Assets mortgaged, pledged, or otherwise subject to lien, and the approximate amounts of each.

Associate. When used to indicate a relationship with any person (see **Person** below), any corporation or organization, any trust or other estate, and any relative or spouse of such person, or any relative of such spouse.

Audit (or **examination**). When used in regard to financial statements, an examination of the statements by an accountant in accordance with generally accepted auditing standards for the purpose of expressing an opinion.

Audit Committee. A special committee of the board composed of directors who are *not* (if possible) officers of the company. The SEC wants the Audit Committee to assume the responsibility for arranging the details of the audit. In addition, an audit committee's major responsibilities include dealing with the company's financial reports, its external audit, and the company's system of internal accounting control and internal audit. The duties and responsibilities of audit committee members should be reasonably specific, but broad enough to allow the committee to pursue matters believed to have important accounting, reporting and auditing consequences.

Balance Sheet. Includes statements of assets and liabilities as well as statements of net assets unless the context clearly indicates the contrary.

Bank Holding Company. A person who is engaged, either directly or indirectly, primarily in the business of owning securities of one or more banks for the purpose, and with the effect of exercising control.

Blue Sky Laws. Terminology for State securities laws.

Broker. A person in the business of buying and selling securities, for a commission, on behalf of other parties.

Call. (see **Option** below.)

Censure. A formal reprimand by the SEC for improper professional behavior by a party to a filing.

Certificate. A document of an independent public accountant, or independent certified public accountant, that is dated, reasonably comprehensive as to the scope of the audit made, and states clearly the opinion of the accountant in respect to the financial statements and the accounting principles and procedures followed by the registrant (see **Registrant** below).

Certification. It is the accountant's responsibility to make a reasonably unqualified certification of the financial statements. It is important for the auditor to incorporate in the certificate an adequate explanation of the scope (see **Scope** below) of the audit.

Certified. When used in regard to financial statements, examined and reported upon with an opinion expressed by an independent public or certified public accountant.

Certiorari, Writ of. An order issued by a superior court directing an inferior court to deliver its record for review.

Chapter X Bankruptcy. Voluntary or involuntary reorganization of a corporation with publicly held securities.

Chapter XI Bankruptcy. Deals with individuals, partnerships and with corporations whose securities are not publicly held. Affects only voluntary arrangements of unsecured debts.

Charter. Includes articles of incorporation, declarations of trust, articles of association or partnership, or any similar instrument, as amended, affecting the organization of an incorporated or unincorporated person.

Civil Actions. Involves the private rights and remedies of the parties to a suit; actions arising out of a contract.

Class of Securities. A group of similar securities that give shareholders similar rights.

Closed-End Investment Company. A corporation in the business of investing its funds in securities of other corporations for income and profit. Investors wishing to "cash out" of the investment company do so by selling their shares on the open market, as with any other stock.

Closing Date. Effective date (see **Effective Date** below) of a registration statement.

Comment Letters (see **Deficiency Letter** below.)

Common Equity. Any class of common stock or an equivalent interest, including but not limited to a unit of beneficial interest in a trust or a limited partnership interest.

Compensating Balance. Restricted deposits of a borrower required by banks to be maintained against short-term loans. A portion of any demand, time, or certificate of deposit, maintained by a corporation, or by any person on behalf of the corporation, which constitutes support for existing borrowing arrangements of the corporation, or any other person, with a lending institution. Such arrangements include both outstanding borrowings and the assurance of future credit availability.

Consent Action. Issued when a person agrees to the terms of an SEC disciplinary action without admitting to the allegations in the complaint.

Consolidated Statements. Include the operating results of a corporation's subsidiary(ies) with inter-company transactions eliminated.

Control. (including the terms "controlling," "controlled by," "under common control with"). The possession, direct or indirect, of the power to direct or cause the direction of the management and policies of a person, whether through the ownership of voting shares, by contract, or otherwise.

Cooling-Off Period. The period between the filing and effective date (see **Effective Date** below) of a registration statement.

Criminal Action. Suits initiated for the alleged violation of a public law.

Dealer. A person in the business of buying and selling securities for his or her own account.

Deficiency Letter. A letter from the SEC to the registrant setting forth the needed corrections and amendments to the issuing corporations' registration statement.

Delisting. Permanent removal of a listed security from a national securities exchange.

Depositary Share. A security evidenced by an American Depositary Receipt that represents a foreign security or a multiple of or fraction thereof deposited with a depositary.

Development Stage Company. A company is considered to be in the development stage if it is devoting substantially all of its efforts to establishing a new business and either of the following conditions exists.

1) Planned principal operations have not commenced.

2) Planned principal operations have commenced, but there has been no significant revenue therefrom.

Disbarment. Permanent removal of a professional's privilege to represent clients before the SEC.

Disclosure. The identification of accounting policies and principles that materially affect the determination of financial position, changes in financial position, and results of operations.

Domiciled Corporation. A corporation doing business in the state in which its corporate charter was guaranteed.

Due Diligence Meeting. A meeting of all parties in the preparation of a registration statement to assure that a high degree of care in investigation and independent verification of the company's representations has been made.

Effective Date. The twentieth (20th) day after the filing date of a registration statement or amendment unless the Commission shortens or extends that time period.

Employee. Any employee, general partner, or consultant or advisor, insurance agents who are exclusive agents of the registrant, its subsidiaries or parents. It also includes former employees as well as executors, administrators or beneficiaries of the estates of deceased employees, guardians or members of a committee for incompetent former employees, or similar persons duly authorized by law to administer the estate or assets of former employees.

Equity Security. Any stock or similar security; or any security convertible, with or without consideration, into such a security, or carrying any warrant or right to subscribe to or purchase such a security, or any such warrant or right.

Examination. (See **Audit** above).

Exchange. An organized association providing a market place for bringing together buyers and sellers of securities through brokers.

Exempt Security. One that is not required to be registered with the SEC.

Exempt Transaction. A transaction in securities that does not require registration with the SEC.

Expert. Any specialist, accountant, attorney, engineer, appraiser, etc., who participates in the preparation of a registration statement. Broadly, any signatory to the registration statement is assumed to be an expert.

Fifty-Percent-Owned-Person. A person whose outstanding voting shares are approximately 50 percent owned by another specified person directly, or indirectly, through one or more intermediaries.

Filing. The process of completing and submitting a registration statement to the SEC.

Filing Date. The date a registration statement is received by the SEC.

Financial Statement. Includes all notes to the statements and all related schedules.

Fiscal Year. The annual accounting period or, if no closing date has been adopted, the calendar year ending on December 31.

Float. The difference on a bank's ledger and a depositor's books caused by presentation of checks and deposits in transit.

Footnote. Appended to financial statements as supplemental information for specific items in a statement.

Foreign Currency. Any currency other than the currency used by the enterprise in its financial statements.

Forms. Statements of standards with which registration statements and other filings must comply. Essentially, SEC forms are a set of instructions to guide the registrant in the preparation of the SEC reports to be filed; the forms are not required to be precisely copied.

Form S-1. A registration statement (see **Registration Statement** below) is filed on Form S-1 for companies issuing securities to the public. This form incorporates specified standards for financial statements and auditor's report.

Form 8-K. A report which is filed only when a reportable event occurs which may have a significant effect on the future of a company and on the value of its securities. Form 8-K must be filed not later than 15 days after the date on which the specified event occurs.

Form 10-K. The annual report to the SEC which covers substantially all of the information required in Form S-1. Form 10-K is due 90 days after a company's December 31 fiscal year, or by March 31 of each year.

Form 10-Q. A quarterly report containing *unaudited* financial statements. If certain types of events occur during the period, they must be reported on the Form. The 10-Q is due 45 days after the end of the first three fiscal quarters.

Going Private. The term commonly used to describe those transactions having as their objective the complete termination or substantial reduction of public ownership of an equity's securities.

Going Public. Registering a new issue of securities with the SEC. *Going public* is closely related to the process of applying for listed status on one or more of the exchanges, or registering for trading in the over-the-counter market.

Indemnification Provision. An agreement protecting one party from liability arising from the occurrence of an unforeseeable event.

Independent Accountants *(CPA)*. Accountants who certify financial statements filed with the SEC. Accountants must maintain strict independence of attitude and judgment in planning and conducting and audit and in expressing an opinion on financial statements. The SEC will not recognize any public accountant or certified public accountant that is not independent.

Information Statement. A statement on any pending corporate matters furnished by the registrant to every shareholder who is entitled to vote when a proxy is not solicited.

Initial Margin Percentage. The percentage of the purchase price (or the percentage of a short sale; see **Short Selling** below), that an investor must deposit with his/her broker in compliance with Federal Reserve Board margin requirements.

Injunction. A court order directing a person to stop alleged violations of a securities law or regulation.

Insurance Holding Company. A person who is engaged, either directly or indirectly, primarily in the business of owning securities of one or more insurance companies for the purpose, and with the effect, of exercising control.

Integrated Disclosure System (IDS). An extensive revision of the mandatory business and financial disclosure requirements applicable to publicly-held companies. It establishes a uniform and integrated disclosure system under the securities laws. The IDS adopted major changes in its disclosure systems under the Securities Act of 1933, and the Securities Exchange Act of 1934. The changes include amendments to Form 10-K and 10-Q, amendments to the proxy rules, amendments to Regulation S-K which governs the non-financial statement disclosure rules (see **Regulation S-K** below), uniform financial statement instructions, a general revision of Regulation S-X which governs the form, content, and requirements of financial statements (see **Regulation S-X** below), and a new simplified form for the registration of securities issued in business combinations.

Issuer. Any corporation that sells a security in a public offering.

Letter-of-Consent. Written permission from participating experts to include their names and signatures in a registration statement.

Line-of-Business Reporting. Registrants must report financial information regarding segments of their operations. The SEC does not define the term "line-of-business." Rather, the responsibility of determining meaningful segments that reflect the particular company's operations and organizational concepts is the responsibility of management. No more than ten classes of business are required to be reported.

Listed Status. Condition under which a security has been accepted by an exchange for full trading privileges. As long as a corporation remains listed on an exchange, it must file periodic reports to its stockholders.

Listing. A corporation applying to list its securities on an exchange must file a registration statement and a copy of the application for listing with the SEC.

Majority-Owned Subsidiary. A subsidiary more than 50 percent of whose outstanding voting shares is owned by its parent and/or the parent's other majority-owned subsidiaries.

Managing Underwriter. Underwriter(s) who, by contract or otherwise, deals with the registrant; organizes the selling effort; receives some benefit directly or indirectly in which all other underwriters similarly situated do not share in proportion to their respective interests in the underwriting; or represents any other underwriters in such matters as maintaining the records of the distribution, arranging the allotments of securities offered or arranging for appropriate stabilization activities, if any.

Margin Call. The demand by a broker that an investor deposit additional cash (or acceptable collateral) for securities purchased on credit when the price of the securities declines to a value below the minimum shareholder's equity required by the stock exchange.

Material. Information regarding any subject that limits the information required to those matters about which an average prudent investor ought reasonably to be informed.

Mutual Fund. Not legal terminology. It is a financial term commonly used in street jargon to mean an open-end investment company (see **Open-End Investment Company** below) as defined in the Investment Company Act of 1940.

National Association of Securities Dealers, Inc. (NASD). An association of brokers/dealers who are in the business of trading over-the-counter securities.

Net Sales. Income or loss from continuing operations before extraordinary items and cumulative effect of a change in accounting principle.

New York Stock Exchange (and **Regional Exchanges**). An association organized to provide physical, mechanical, and logistical facilities for the purchase and sale of securities by investors through brokers and dealers.

No-Action Letter. The SEC's written reply to a corporate issuer of securities stating its position regarding a specific filing matter.

Notification. Filing with the SEC the terms of an offering of securities that are exempt from registration.

Offering Date. The date a new security can be offered to the public.

Open-End Investment Company. A corporation in the business of investing its funds in securities of other corporations for income and profit. An open-end company continuously offers new shares for sales and redeems shares previously issued to investors who want to cash out.

Opinion. A required statement in the certification that the auditor believes the audit correctly reflects the organization's financial condition and results of operation.

Option. The contractual privilege of purchasing a security (Call) for a specified price, or delivering a security (Put) at a specified price.

Over-the-Counter Securities. Corporate and government securities that are not listed for trading on a national stock exchange.

Parent. A "parent" of a specified person(s) is an affiliate controlling such person(s) directly or indirectly through one or more intermediaries.

Pension Plan. An arrangement whereby a company undertakes to provide its retired employees with benefits that can be determined or estimated in advance.

Person. An individual, corporation, partnership, association, joint-stock company, business trust, or unincorporated organization.

Predecessor. A person from whom another person acquired the major portion of the business and assets in a single succession or in a series of related successions. In each succession the acquiring person acquired the major portion of the business and assets of the acquired person.

Prefiling Conference. A meeting of corporate officers and experts outlining the SEC requirements for the filing of a registration statement. Occasionally an SEC staff member will attend.

Previously Filed or Reported. Previously filed with, or reported in a definitive proxy statement or information statement, or a registration statement. Information contained in any such document will be assumed to have been previously filed with the exchange.

Principal Holder of Equity Securities. Used in respect of a registrant or other person named in a particular statement or report, a holder of record or a known beneficial owner of more than 10 percent of any class of securities of the registrant or other person, respectively, and of the date of the related balance sheet filed.

Promoter. Any person who, acting alone or in conjunction with one or more other persons, directly or indirectly takes initiative in founding and organizing the business or enterprise of an issuer. Any person is a promoter who, in connection with the founding and organizing of the business or enterprise of an issuer, directly or indirectly receives in consideration of services or property, or both services and property, 10 percent or more of any class of securities of the issuer or 10 percent or more of the proceeds from the sale of any class of securities. However, a person who receives such securities or proceeds either solely as underwriting commissions or solely in consideration of property shall not be deemed a promoter within the meaning of this paragraph if such person does not otherwise take part in founding and organizing the enterprise.

Prospectus. Document consisting of Part 1 of the registration statement filed with the SEC by the issuing corporation that must be delivered to all purchasers of newly issued securities.

Proxy. A power of attorney whereby a stockholder authorizes another person, or group of persons, to act (vote) for that stockholder at a shareholders' meeting.

Proxy Statement. Information furnished in conjunction with a formal solicitation in the proxy for the power to vote a stockholder's shares.

Put. (See **Option** above.)

Red-Herring Prospectus. Preliminary prospectus with a statement (in red ink) on each page indicating that the security described has not become effective, that the information is subject to correction and change without notice, and is not an offer to buy or sell that security.

Refusal. SEC action prohibiting a filing (see **Filing** above) from becoming effective.

Regional Exchanges. (See **New York Stock Exchange** above.)

Registrant. An issuer of securities for which an application, a report, or a registration statement has been filed.

Registration. Act of filing with the SEC the required information concerning the issuing corporation and the security to be issued.

Registration Statement. The document filed with the SEC containing legal, commercial, technical, and financial information concerning a new security issue.

Regulation S-K. An authoritative statement of disclosure standards under all securities acts. Regulation S-K establishes the standards of disclosure for non-financial information not included in financial statements, footnotes or schedules.

Regulation S-X. The principal document reporting for financial statements, footnotes and schedules' standards under all securities acts. No filing can be made without reference to Regulation S-X. It integrates all accounting requirements prior to February 21, 1940, into a single regulation.

Related Party. One that can exercise control or significant influence over the management and/or operating policies of another party, to the extent that one of the parties may be prevented from fully pursuing its own separate interests. Related parties consist of all affiliates of an enterprise, including its management and their immediate families, its principal owners and their immediate families, its investments accounted for by the equity method, beneficial employee trusts that are managed by the management of the enterprise, and any party that may, or does, deal with the enterprise and has ownership of, control over, or can significantly influence the management or operating policies of another party to the extent that an arms-length transaction may not be achieved. Transactions between related parties are generally accounted for on the same basis as if the parties were not related, unless the substance of the transaction is not arm's length. Substance over form is an important consideration when accounting for transactions involving related parties.

Replacement Cost. The lowest amount that would have to be paid in the normal course of business to obtain a new asset of equivalent operating or productive capability.

Restricted Security. Private offering of an issue that cannot be resold to the public without prior registration. Also called "investment letter" securities for the letter that the purchaser of such securities must submit to the SEC stating that the securities are being acquired for investment purposes, not for immediate resale.

Right. Provides current security holders the privilege of participating on a pro rata basis in a new offering of securities.

Roll-Up Transaction. Any transaction or series of transactions that, directly or indirectly through acquisition or otherwise, involves the combination or reorganization of one or more partnerships. The term includes the offer or sale of securities by a successor entity, whether newly formed or previously existing, to one or more limited partners of the partnership to be combined or reorganized, or the acquisition of the successor entity's securities by the partnerships being combined or reorganized.

Rules of Practice. Establishes standards of conduct for professionals practicing before the SEC.

Sale. Every contract of sale, disposition, or offer of a security for value (see **Security** below).

Schedule. Detailed financial information presented in a form prescribed by the SEC in Regulation S-X.

Scienter. Intent to deceive, manipulate, or defraud. Requires proof that defendant knew of material mistatements or omissions; that defendant acted willfully and knowingly.

Scope (of an Audit). A complete, detailed audit. The auditor includes in the certificate an adequate explanation of the extent of the audit.

Securities Act of 1933. Requires the disclosure of financial data for issues not exempted from registration and prohibits fraudulent acts and misrepresentations and omission of material (see **Material** above) facts in the issue of securities.

Securities Exchange Act of 1934 (The **Exchange Act**). Covers the regulation of stock market activities and the public trading of securities. The regulations covered are the disclosure of significant financial data, the regulation of securities market practices and operation, and control of credit (margin requirements) extended for the purchase and short sales of securities.

Security. Any instrument representing a debt obligation, an equity interest in a corporation, or any instrument commonly known as a security. In the Securities Act, security is defined to include by name or description many documents in which there is common trading for investment or speculation. Some, such as notes, bonds and stocks, are standardized and the name alone carries well settled meaning. Others are of a more variable character and were necessarily designated by more descriptive terms, such as transferable share, investment contract, and in general any interest or instrument commonly known as a security.

Selling Group. Several broker/dealers who distribute a new issue of securities at retail.

Share. A share of stock in a corporation or unit of interest in an unincorporated person.

Short-Selling. Selling a security that is not owned with the expectation of buying that specific security later at a lower market price.

Significant Subsidiary. A subsidiary (including its subsidiaries) in which the registrant's (and its other subsidiaries') investments in and advances to exceed 10 percent of the total assets of the registrant and its subsidiaries consolidated as of the end of the most recently completed fiscal year. For a proposed business combination to be accounted for as a pooling of interests, this requirement is also met when the number of common shares exchanged by the registrant exceeds 10 percent of its total common shares outstanding at the date the combination is initiated, or the registrant's (and its other subsidiaries') proportionate share of the total assets, after intercompany eliminations, of the subsidiary exceeds 10 percent of the total assets of the registrant and its subsidiaries consolidated as of the end of the most recently completed fiscal year.

Small Business Issuer. An entity that a) has revenues of less than $25,000,000; b) is a U.S. or Canadian issuer; c) is not an investment company; d) if a majority-owned subsidiary, the parent corporation is also a small business issuer.

Solicitation. Any request for a proxy or other similar communication to security holders.

Sponsor. The person proposing the roll-up transaction. (See **Roll-Up Transaction** above.)

Spread. The difference between the price paid for a security by the underwriter and the selling price of that security.

Stockholders' Meeting, Regular. The annual meeting of stockholders for the election of directors and for action on other corporate matters.

Stockholders' Meeting, Special. A meeting in which only specified items can be considered.

Stop Order. An SEC order stopping the issue or listing of a security on a stock exchange.

Subsidiary. An affiliate controlled by a specified person directly, or indirectly, through one or more intermediaries.

Substantial Authoritative Support. FASB principles, standards and practices published in Statements and Interpretations, AICPA Accounting Research Bulletins, and AICPA Opinions, except to the extent altered, amended, supplemented, revoked or superseded by an FASB Statement.

Succession. The direct acquisition of the assets comprising a going business, whether by merger, consolidation, or other direct transfer. This term does not include the acquisition of control of a business unless followed by the direct acquisition of its assets.

Successor. The surviving entity after completion of the roll-up transaction, or the entity whose securities are being offered or sold to, or acquired by, limited partners of the partnerships or the limited partnerships to be combined or reorganized.

Summary Prospectus. A prospectus containing specific items of information which subsequently will be included in the registration statement.

Suspension. An SEC order temporarily prohibiting the trading of a security on the stock exchange, usually invoked by the SEC when a news release is pending which may cause a disorderly market in that security. Trading is usually resumed shortly after the information has been publicly disseminated.

Totally Held Subsidiary. A subsidiary substantially all of whose outstanding securities are owned by its parent and/or the parent's other totally held subsidiaries. The subsidiary is not indebted to any person other than its parent and/or the parent's other totally held subsidiaries in an amount which is material in relation to the particular subsidiary, excepting indebtedness incurred in the ordinary course of business which is not overdue and which matures within one year from the date of its creation, whether evidenced by securities or not.

Underwriter. (See **Managing Underwriter** above.)

Unlisted Trading Privileges. A security issue authorized by the SEC for trading on an exchange without requiring the corporation to complete a formal listing application.

Voting Securities. Securities whose holders are presently entitled to vote for the election of directors.

Warrant. A security that grants the holder the right to purchase a specific number of shares of the security to which the warrant is attached at a specified price and usually within a stated period of time.

Wholly-Owned Subsidiary. A subsidiary substantially all of whose outstanding voting securities are owned by its parent and/or the parent's other wholly-owned subsidiaries.

SECURITIES ACT OF 1933

The *truth in securities* law has two main objectives:

1) To require that investors are provided with material information concerning securities offered for sale to the public.
2) To prevent misrepresentation, deceit, and other fault in the sale of securities.

The primary means of accomplishing these objectives is by requiring full disclosure of financial information by registering offerings and sales of securities. Securities transactions subject to registration are mostly offerings of debt and equity securities issued by corporations, limited partnerships, trusts and other issuers. Federal and certain other government debt securities are not. Certain securities and transactions qualify for exemptions from registration provisions. They are included in the discussion that follows.

REGISTRATION

Registration is intended to provide adequate and accurate disclosure of material facts concerning the company and the securities it proposes to sell. This enables investors to make a thorough appraisal of the merits of the securities and exercise informed judgment in determining whether or not to purchase them.

Registration requires, but does not guarantee, the accuracy of the facts represented in the registration statement and prospectus. However, the law does prohibit false and misleading statements under penalty of fine, imprisonment, or both. Investors who purchases securities and suffer losses have important recovery rights under the law if they can prove that there was incomplete or inaccurate disclosure of material facts in the registration statement or prospectus. If such misstatements are proven, the following could be liable for investor losses sustained in the securities purchase:

1) The issuing company.
2) Its responsible directors and officers.
3) The underwriters.
4) The controlling interests.
5) The sellers of the securities.
6) Others that are affiliated with the securities of the issuer.

Registration of securities does not preclude the sale of stock in risky, poorly managed, or unprofitable companies. Nor does the Commission *approve or disapprove* securities on their merits; and it is unlawful to represent otherwise in the sale of securities. The only standard which must be met when registering securities is adequate and accurate *disclosure* of required material facts concerning the company and the securities it proposes to sell. The fairness of the terms, the issuing company's prospects for successful operation, and other factors affecting the merits of investing in the securities have no bearing on the question of whether or not securities can be qualified for registration.

The Registration Process

To facilitate registration by different types of enterprises, the Commission has special forms that vary in their disclosure requirements, but generally provide essential facts while minimizing the burden and expense of complying with the law. In general, registration forms call for disclosure of information such as:

1) Description of the registrant's properties and business.
2) Description of the significant provisions of the security to be offered for sale and its relationship to the registrant's other capital securities.
3) Information about the management of the registrant.
4) Financial statements certified by independent public accountants.

Registration statements become public immediately upon filing with the SEC. After the registration statement is filed, securities can be *offered* orally or by summaries of the information in the registration statement, but it is unlawful to *sell* the securities until the *effective date* which is on the 20th day after filing the registration statement, or on the 20th day after filing the last amendment, if any. The SEC can issue a *stop order* to refuse or suspend the effectiveness of the statement if the Commission concludes that material deficiencies in a registration statement appear to result from a deliberate attempt to conceal or mislead. A stop order is not a permanent prohibition to the effectiveness of the registration statement, or to the sale of the securities, and can be lifted and the statement declared effective when amendments are filed correcting the statement in accordance with the requirements in the stop order decision.

There are exemptions to the registration requirements:

1) Private offerings to a limited number of persons or institutions who have access to the kind of information that registration would disclose and who do not propose to redistribute the securities.
2) Offerings restricted to residents of the state in which the issuing company is organized and doing business.
3) Securities of municipal, state, federal and other governmental instrumentalities, such as charitable institutions and banks.
4) Offerings not exceeding certain specified amounts made in compliance with regulations of the Commission.
5) Offerings of small business investment companies made in accordance with the rules and regulations of the Commission.

Regardless of whether or not the securities are exempt from registration, anti-fraud provisions apply to all sales of securities involving interstate commerce or the mails.

The small business exemption from registration provides that offerings of securities under $5 million can be exempt from full registration, subject to conditions the SEC prescribes to protect investors. Certain Canadian and domestic companies are permitted to make exempt offerings.

UNITED STATES
SECURITIES AND EXCHANGE COMMISSION
Washington, D.C. 20549

FORM 10

GENERAL FORM FOR REGISTRATION OF SECURITIES
Pursuant to Section 12(b) or (g) of The Securities Exchange Act of 1934

_____

(Exact name of registrant as specified in its charter)

_____

(State or other jurisdiction of incorporation or organization)   (I.R.S. Employer Identification No.)

_____

(Address of principal executive offices)   (Zip Code)

Registrant's telephone number, including area code _____

Securities to be registered pursuant to Section 12(b) of the Act:

Title of each class to be so registered	Name of each exchange on which each class is to be registered
_____	_____
_____	_____

Securities to be registered pursuant to Section 12(g) of the Act:

_____

(Title of class)

_____

(Title of class)

INFORMATION REQUIRED IN REGISTRATION STATEMENT

Item 1. Business.
Furnish the information required by Item 101 of Regulation S-K (§229.101 of this chapter).

Item 2. Financial Information.
Furnish the information required by Items 301 and 303 of Regulation S-K (§§229.301 and 229.303 of this chapter).

Item 3. Properties.
Furnish the information required by Item 102 of Regulation S-K (§229.102 of this chapter).

Item 4. Security Ownership of Certain Beneficial Owners and Management.
Furnish the information required by Item 403 of Regulation S-K (§229.403 of this chapter).

Item 5. Directors and Executive Officers.
Furnish the information required by Item 401 of Regulation S-K (§229.401 of this chapter).

Item 6. Executive Compensation.
Furnish the information required by Item 402 of Regulation S-K (§229.402 of this chapter).

Item 7. Certain Relationships and Related Transactions.
Furnish the information required by Item 404 of Regulation S-K (§229.404 of this chapter).

Item 8. Legal Proceedings.
Furnish the information required by Item 103 of Regulation S-K (§229.103 of this chapter).

Item 9. Market Price of and Dividends on the Registrant's Common Equity and Related Stockholder Matters.
Furnish the information required by Item 201 of Regulation S-K (§229.201 of this chapter).

Item 10. Recent Sales of Unregistered Securities.
Furnish the information required by item 701 of Regulation S-K (§229.701 of this chapter).

Item 11. Description of Registrant's Securities to be Registered.
Furnish the information required by Item 202 of Regulation S-K (§229.202 of this chapter).

Item 12. Indemnification of Directors and Officers.
Furnish the information required by Item 702 of Regulation S-K (§229.702 of this chapter).

Item 13. Financial Statements and Supplementary Data.
Furnish all financial statements required by Regulation S-X and the supplementary financial information required by Item 302 of Regulation S-K (§229.302 of this chapter).

Item 14. Changes in and Disagreements with Accountants on Accounting and Financial Disclosure.
Furnish the information required by Item 304 of Regulation S-K (§229.304 of this chapter).

Item 15. Financial Statements and Exhibits.
(a) List separately all financial statements filed as part of the registration statement.
(b) Furnish the exhibits required by Item 601 of Regulation S-K (§229.601 of this chapter).

SIGNATURES

Pursuant to the requirements of Section 12 of the Securities Exchange Act of 1934, the registrant has duly caused this registration statement to be signed on its behalf by the undersigned, thereunto duly authorized.

_____
(Registrant)

Date _____   By _____
                                                              (Signature)*
_____

*Print name and title of the signing officer under his signature.

GENERAL INSTRUCTIONS

A. Rule as to Use of Form 10.

Form 10 shall be used for registration pursuant to Section 12(b) or (g) of the Securities Exchange Act of 1934 of classes of securities of issuers for which no other form is prescribed.

B. Application of General Rules and Regulations.

(a) The General Rules and Regulations under the Act contain certain general requirements which are applicable to registration on any form. These general requirements should be carefully read and observed in the preparation and filing of registration statements on this form.

(b) Particular attention is directed to Regulation 12B [17 CFR 240.12b-1–240.12b-36] which contains general requirements regarding matters such as the kind and size of paper to be used, the legibility of the registration statement, the information to be given whenever the title of securities is required to be stated, and the filing of the registration statement. The definitions contained in Rule 12b-2 [17 CFR 240.12b-2] should be especially noted.

C. Preparation of Registration Statement.

(a) This form is not to be used as a blank form to be filled in, but only as a guide in the preparation of the registration statement on paper meeting the requirements of Rule 12b-12 [17 CFR 240.12b-12]. The registration statement shall contain the item numbers and captions, but the text of the items may be omitted. The answers to the items shall be prepared in the manner specified in Rule 12b-13 [17 CFR 240.12b-13].

(b) Unless otherwise stated, the information required shall be given as of a date reasonably close to the date of filing the registration statement.

(c) Attention is directed to Rule 12b-20 [17 CFR 240.12b-20] which states: "In addition to the information expressly required to be included in a statement or report, there shall be added such further material information, if any, as may be necessary to make the required statements, in light of the circumstances under which they are made, not misleading."

D. Signature and Filing of Registration Statement.

Three complete copies of the registration statement, including financial statements, exhibits and all other papers and documents filed as a part thereof, and five additional copies which need not include exhibits, shall be filed with the Commission. At least one complete copy of the registration statement, including financial statements, exhibits and all other papers and documents filed as a part thereof, shall be filed with each exchange on which any class of securities is to be registered. At least one complete copy of the registration statement filed with the Commission and one such copy filed with each exchange shall be manually signed. Copies not manually signed shall bear typed or printed signatures.

E. Omission of Information Regarding Foreign Subsidiaries.

Information required by any item or other requirement of this form with respect to any foreign subsidiary may be omitted to the extent that the required disclosure would be detrimental to the registrant. However, financial statements, otherwise required, shall not be omitted pursuant to this instruction. Where information is omitted pursuant to this instruction, a statement shall be made that such information has been omitted and the names of the subsidiaries involved shall be separately furnished to the Commission. The Commission may, in its discretion, call for justification that the required disclosure would be detrimental.

F. Incorporation by Reference.

Attention is directed to Rule 12b-23 [17 CFR 240.12b-23 which provides for the incorporation by reference of information contained in certain documents in answer or partial answer to any item of a registration statement.

SECURITIES EXCHANGE ACT OF 1934

The 1934 Act extends the disclosure doctrine of investor protection to securities that are listed and registered for public trading on U.S. national securities exchanges. In 1964 the SEC was authorized by Congress to include disclosure and reporting requirements to equity securities in the over-the-counter market. The object of the 1934 Act is to ensure *fair and orderly securities markets* by prohibiting certain types of activities and by setting forth rules regarding the operation of the markets and the participants.

Companies wanting to have their securities registered and listed or publicly traded on an exchange must file a registration application with the exchange and the SEC. Companies whose equity securities are traded over-the-counter must file a similar registration form. SEC rules prescribe the content of registration statements and require certified financial statements. After a company's securities have become registered, annual and other periodic reports to update information contained in the original registration statement must be filed.

The 1934 Act governs the solicitation of proxies (votes) from holders of registered securities, both listed and over-the-counter, for the election of directors and for approval of other corporate action. All material facts concerning matters on which shareholders are asked to vote must be disclosed. In 1970 Congress amended the Exchange Act to extend its reporting and disclosure provisions to situations where control of a company is sought through a tender offer to other planned stock acquisitions of over five percent of a company's equity securities by direct purchase or by a tender offer. Disclosure provisions are supplemented by other provisions to help ensure investor protection in tender offers.

INSIDER TRADING

Insider trader prohibitions are designed to curb misuse of material confidential information not available to the general public. Examples of such misuse are buying or selling securities to make profits or avoid losses based on material nonpublic information, or by telling others of the information before such information is generally available to all shareholders. The *Insider Trading Sanctions Act of 1984* allows imposing fines up to three times to profit gained or losses avoided by use of material nonpublic information. All officers and directors of a company and beneficial owners of more than ten percent of its registered equity securities must file an initial report with the SEC and with the exchange on which the stock is listed, showing their holdings of each of the company's equity securities. Thereafter, they must file reports for any month during which there was any change in those holdings, and any profits obtained by them from purchases and sales, or sales and purchases, of such equity securities within any six-month period can be recovered by the company or by any security holder on its behalf. Insiders are also prohibited from making short sales of their company's equity securities.

Margin Trading

The 1934 Act authorizes the Board of Governors of the Federal Reserve System to set limits on the amount of credit which can be extended for the purpose of purchasing or carrying securities. The objective is to restrict excessive use of credit in the securities markets. While the credit restrictions are set by the Board of Governors, investigation and enforcement is the responsibility of the SEC.

Division of Corporation Finance

Corporation Finance has the overall responsibility of ensuring that disclosure requirements are met by publicly held companies registered with the SEC. Its work includes: reviewing registration statements for new securities; proxy material and annual reports the Commission requires from publicly held companies; documents concerning tender offers, and mergers and acquisitions in general.

This Division renders administrative interpretations to the public of the Securities Act and the Securities Exchange Act, and to prospective registrants, and others. It is also responsible for certain statutes and regulations pertaining to small businesses and for the Trust Indenture Act of 1939. Applications for qualification of trust indentures are examined for compliance with the applicable requirements of the law and the Commission's rules. Corporation Finance works closely with the Office of the Chief Accountant in drafting rules and regulations which prescribe requirements for financial statements.

Truth in Securities Laws

The objectives of the laws are twofold. First is the protection of investors and the public against fraudulent acts and practices in the purchase and sale of securities. The second objective is to regulate trading in the national securities markets. For example:

1) "To provide full and fair disclosure of the character of securities sold in interstate and foreign commerce and through the mails, and to prevent fraud in the sale thereof, and for other purposes." (Securities Act of 1933.)

2) "To provide for the regulation of securities exchanges and the over-the-counter markets operating in interstate and foreign commerce and through the mails, to prevent inequitable and unfair practices on such exchanges and markets, and for other purposes." (Securities Exchange Act of 1934.)

3) "To provide for the registration and regulation of investment companies and investment advisers, and for other purposes." (Investment Company Act of 1940 and the Investment Advisers Act of 1940.)

DEVELOPMENT OF DISCLOSURE: 1933 AND 1934 ACTS

Two separate disclosure systems developed under the two principal securities laws. Generally, the Securities Act of 1933 regulates the *initial* public distribution of securities. The disclosure system developed under the 1933 Act emphasizes the comprehensive information about the issuer, because it was developed primarily for companies going public for the *first time* and about which the public had very little information.

The Securities Exchange Act of 1934 regulates the trading of securities in *publicly held companies* which are traded both on the exchanges and in the over-the-counter markets. The dual disclosure system developed under the 1933 and 1934 Acts deals primarily with the form and content of financial and business data in the annual reports to the SEC and to shareholders, and concerns proxy statements as well as the dissemination of interim data. The emphasis of this disclosure system is on periodic information concerning issuers already known to security holders, and the purpose is to keep the data up-to-date.

The dual system generated a large number of registration and periodic reporting forms, each with its own set of instructions. Many publicly-held companies filed numerous registration statements and distributed related reports to the public containing the same information produced several times in slightly different forms, repeating much information that was already available within the financial community.

In addition, the audited primary financial statements prepared in conformity with GAAP that were included in the annual reports to shareholders, were not explicitly covered by the very detailed disclosure requirements in S-X. These mandated the form and content of the audited primary financial statements that were included in documents filed with the SEC and in prospectuses. However, since the financial statements had to be in conformity with GAAP there were no essential differences between the two.

Financial statements that conformed to S-X included numerous additional technical disclosures to satisfy the needs of professional financial analysts and the SEC staff. Uniform financial disclosure requirements for virtually all documents covered by either the 1933 or the 1934 Acts as well as for nonfinancial disclosures under the 1934 Act and for a major portion of those required under the 1933 Act have been formulated. To reach the objective, where identical disclosures are included both in documents filed with the Commission and distributed to security holders in prospectuses, proxy statements and annual reports, the Commission has two basic regulations. These are Regulation S-X (See Chapter 16) which covers the requirements for audited primary financial statements, and Regulation S-K which covers most of the other business, analytical, and unaudited financial disclosures.

Regulation S-K covers analytical and unaudited supplementary financial disclosures under the 1934 Act and most disclosures under the 1933 Act. One of the key requirements in Regulation S-K is the *Management's Discussion and Analysis of Financial Condition and Results of Operations*. The discussion must cover the three years presented in the audited financials and treat not only results of operations, but also financial condition and changes in financial condition. Although the requirement is for three years, the SEC suggests that when trends are being discussed, references to five years of selected financial data are appropriate.

The discussion and analysis is filed under the Securities Acts, as well as included in all annual reports and prospectuses. Accordingly, companies should document the adequacy of their systems and procedures for analyzing past results to be sure that there is an adequate and reliable information base for the management discussion and analysis, including decisions as to scope and content. Since future plans and expectations, such as capital expenditure commitments, are important in formulating management's discussion and analysis, it may be prudent to reappraise internal financial forecasting procedures periodically.

Although forward-looking information is not mandated, the specifically required information is such that financial analysts will be able to work out a forecast of future operating results. As practice develops, managements may find it preferable simply to include formal financial forecasts and comply with the safe harbor rules, rather than rely solely on the forecasts analysts will make based on data presumed to be reliable.

Form S-15. When a company acquires a business that is relatively minor when compared to the acquiring company, a process that was difficult because of the complexity and cost of registration requirements is greatly simplified by the use of Form S-15 for the registration requirements. Form S-15 enables an issuer to provide an abbreviated prospectus accompanied by the issuer's latest annual report to shareholders instead of larger documents. This procedure is limited to cases where the acquiring company's key financial indices as specified in the regulations are not affected by more than 10% by the acquired company, and where State law applicable to the merger does not require a vote by the security holders of the company being acquired. There are other restrictions, however, and it is likely this simplified procedure will be most usable for mergers where the company to be acquired is closely-held and will not become a significant part of the combined company.

Three copies of Forms-15 must be filed with the SEC. One copy must be signed manually by an officer of the registrant, or by counsel, or by any other authorized person. The name and title of the person signing Forms-15 should be typed or printed under that person's signature.

Synopsis: The Securities Act of 1933

In 1933, the first Federal legislative act designed to regulate the securities business on an interstate basis was passed. Its expressed purpose was:

"To provide full and fair disclosure of the character of securities . . . and to prevent frauds in the sale thereof, and for other purposes." There are four things to note:

1) It related to newly-issued securities, not to those already in the hands of the public.
2) It called for full and fair disclosure of all the facts necessary for an intelligent appraisal of the value of a security.
3) It was designed to prevent fraud in the sale of securities.
4) This legislation led to the Securities Exchange Act of 1934 establishing the Securities and Exchange Commission which would administer both acts.

There are 26 sections to the Act:

Section 1. "This title may be cited as the Securities Act of 1933." Various court decisions have very liberally interpreted the meaning of "securities" as covered by the Act. One decision contains the following: ". . . that this statute was not a penal statute but was a remedial enactment . . . A remedial enactment is one that seeks to give a remedy for an ill. It is to be liberally construed so that its purpose may be realized." (SEC v Starmont, (1940) 31 F. Supp. 264.)

Section 2. Definitions. This section defines many of the terms used throughout the other sections of the Act. Importantly, it contains definitions of "security," "person," "sale," "offer to sell," and "prospectus," among many others. Several important Rules of the SEC are directly derived from this section, including Rule 134 (discussed in Section 5).

Section 3. Exempted Securities. Some securities, such as those issued or guaranteed by the United States, are exempted from the provisions of the Act.

Section 4. Exempted Transactions. Describes the transactions for which Section 5 does not apply.

Section 5. Prohibitions Relating to Intrastate Commerce and the Mails. It is unlawful to offer any security for sale "by any means or instruments of transportation or communication in interstate commerce or of the mails," unless a registration statement is in effect as to that security. It also prohibits the transportation by any means of interstate commerce or the mails of such a security for the purpose of sale or delivery after sale.

This Section further requires that any security that is registered cannot be sold without prior or concurrent delivery of an effective prospectus that meets the requirements of Section 10(a) of the Act.

There have been two important Rules promulgated by the SEC under this Section. The first, Rule 134, defines the types of advertising and of letters or other communications that can be used without prior or concurrent delivery of a prospectus. This Rule is frequently violated in letter form and also in telephone conversations. SEC Release 3844 of October 8, 1957, shows the importance of delivering a prospectus either before or at the same time that an attempt to sell is made. This Release states that a prospectus is defined to include any notice, circular, advertisement, letter, or communication, written or by radio or by television, which offers any security for sale except that any communication sent or given after the effective date of a registration statement shall not be deemed a prospectus if, prior to or at the same time with such a communication, a written prospectus meeting the requirements of Section 10 of the Act was sent or given.

Thus, any letter that gives more information than that allowed by Rule 134 becomes itself a prospectus, unless it is preceded or accompanied by the actual prospectus. A letter prospectus is in violation of Section 5 since it could not possibly comply with the requirements of Section 10.

The second, Rule 433, deals with the so-called "red-herring" prospectus which cannot be used as an offer to sell, but merely to disseminate information prior to the delivery of a regular prospectus which does offer the security for sale.

Section 6. Registration of Securities and Signing of Registration Statement. This Section details what securities may be registered and how such registration is to be done.

Section 7. Information Required on Registration Statement. This Section gives the SEC broad powers in regulating what must appear in a registration statement. In part, the section reads:

"Any such registration statement shall contain such other information, and be accompanied by such other documents, as the Commission may by rules or regulations require as being necessary or appropriate in the public interest or for the protection of investors."

Section 8. Taking Effect of Registration Statements and Amendments Thereto. Registration statements normally become effective on the twentieth day after filing, under this section. However, the SEC is empowered to determine whether or not the statement complies with the Act as to completeness and may refuse to allow the statement to become effective unless amended. If it appears to the SEC that untrue statements have been included, the Commission may issue a stop order.

Section 9. Court Review of Orders. As with any other act of Congress, provision is made so that any person who is aggrieved by an order of the administrative body (in this case the SEC) may obtain a review of the order in the Federal courts.

Section 10. Information Required in Prospectus. A prospectus must contain the same information as that contained in the registration statement. In addition, the SEC is given the authority to define the requirements for any additional material which that body considers necessary in the public interest. "Red herring" requirements and the manner of use of this type of preliminary prospectus are also detailed in this Section.

Note the application of Rule 134, discussed under Section 5, with respect to an "incomplete" prospectus.

One part of the Section, 10(3), relates to the length of time a prospectus may be used (that is, be considered an effective prospectus).

Under this Section of the Act, the SEC issued Rule 425, which requires the statement at the bottom of the first page of all prospectuses "These securities have not been approved or disapproved by the Securities and Exchange Commission nor has the commission passed upon the accuracy or adequacy of this prospectus. Any representation to the contrary is a criminal offense."

Section 11. Civil Liabilities on Account of False Registration Statement. Anyone directly connected with a company or signing the registration statement is subject to suit at law or in equity should the registration statement contain an untrue statement or fail to include a material fact necessary to make the statement not misleading.

Section 12. Civil Liabilities. If any person offers to sell or does sell a security in violation of Section 5, or uses any fraudulent means to sell a security, he or she is liable to civil suit for damages. This liability is in addition to any criminal liability arising under the Act.

Section 13. Limitation of Actions. Specified are the time limits within which civil suits may be instituted under Sections 11 and 12.

Section 14. Contrary Stipulations Void. Any provision in the sale of a security that binds the purchaser to waive the provisions of this Act or of the rules and regulations of the SEC is void. In other words, no one buying a security can relieve the seller from complying with the Act and with the rules issued under the Act.

Section 15. Liability of Controlling Persons. A dealer or broker is liable under Section 11 or 12.

Section 16. Additional Remedies. "The rights and remedies provided by this title (the Act) shall be in addition to any and all other rights and remedies that may exist at law or in equity."

Section 17. Fraudulent Interstate Transactions. As interpreted by the SEC, this section might be referred to as a "catch-all" section.

(a) "It shall be unlawful for any person in the offer or sale of any securities by the use of any means or instruments of transportation or communication in interstate commerce or by the use of the mails, directly or indirectly.

1) to employ any device, scheme or artifice to defraud, or

2) to obtain money or property by means of any untrue statement of a material fact or any omission to state a material fact necessary in order to make the statements made, in the light of the circumstances under which they were made, not misleading, or

3) to engage in any transaction, practice or course of business that operates or would operate as a fraud or deceit upon the purchaser."

Both TV and radio have been included by the SEC as "communication in interstate commerce" because it is impossible to control their area of reception.

While Section 17(a) refers only to the criminal courts in the term "unlawful," a court decision makes it clear that civil liability, in addition to criminal liability is incurred by violation of the section.

Court decisions also implement and amplify the language of the Act itself, with respect to the phrase "or by use of the mails." It would appear that Section 17 only applies to interstate mailings. However, the courts have ruled that if one used the mails *within one State* on an *intrastate* offering, and violated any provision in Section 17(a), that person is as guilty as if he or she had mailed across a state line.

Subparagraph (b) of Section 17 makes it illegal for anyone to publish descriptions of securities when the publisher is paid for such publicity, without also publishing the fact that compensation has been, or will be, received.

Section 17(c) makes the Section applicable to those securities exempted under Section 3. In other words, fraud is fraud whether in connection with exempt or other securities.

Section 18. State Control of Securities. "Nothing in this title (the Act) shall affect the jurisdiction of the Securities Commission . . . of any State . . . ." In other words, all the provisions of the Federal act *and* all the laws of the State in which business is being conducted must be complied with.

Section 19. Special Powers of Commission. The Commission has the authority to make, amend, and rescind such rules and regulations as may be necessary to carry out the provisions of the Act. Commissioners or their representatives are also empowered to subpoena witnesses and to administer oaths.

Section 20. Injunctions and Prosecution of Offenses. The SEC is empowered to make investigations and to bring criminal actions at law against persons deemed to have violated the Act. The wording of the section is interesting in that it gives the Commission power to act "whenever it shall appear ... that the provisions of this title (the Act) ... have been *or are about to be* violated ...."

Section 21. Hearings by Commission. "All hearings shall be public and may be held before the Commission or an officer or officers of the Commission designated by it, and appropriate records shall be kept."

Section 22. Jurisdiction of Offenses and Suits. Jurisdiction of offenses and violations and certain rules in connection with them, are defined in this section. Jurisdiction is given to the District Courts of the United States, the U.S. Court of any Territory, and the U.S. District Court of the District of Columbia.

Section 23. Unlawful Representations. The fact that the registration statement for a security has been filed or is in effect does not mean that the statement is true and accurate, or that the Commission has in any way passed upon the merits of the security. It is unlawful to make any representations to the contrary.

In short, the words in the registration statement (*and* the prospectus) have been made under the penalties of fraud. The registrants are liable, even though the Commission has not certified the truth and accuracy of the statements or of the worth of the security.

Section 24. Penalties. "Any person who willfully violates any of the provisions of this title (the Act), or the rules and regulations promulgated by the Commission under authority thereof ... shall upon conviction be fined not more than $10,000.00 or imprisoned not more than five years, or both."

Section 25. Jurisdiction of Other Government Agencies Over Securities. Nothing in the Act shall relieve any person from submitting to other U.S. Government supervisory units information required by any provision of law.

Section 26. Separability of Provisions. If any one section of the Act is invalidated, such findings will not affect other sections.

Schedule A. Sets forth the requirements for the registration of securities.

Schedule B. Sets for the registration requirements for securities issued by a foreign government or political subdivision thereof.

Synopsis: The Securities Exchange Act of 1934

The Securities Act of 1933 protects investors in the purchase of newly-issued securities. The Securities Exchange Act of 1934 concerns the regulation of trading in already issued securities.

The stated purpose of the 1934 Act is "to provide for the regulation of securities exchanges and of over-the-counter markets operating in interstate and foreign commerce and through the mails, to prevent inequitable and unfair practices on such exchanges and markets, and for other purposes."

The Act has been of importance in prohibiting abuses and manipulations through its creation of the SEC and later of the self-regulatory National Association of Securities Dealers, Inc.

The Act has 34 sections:

Section 1. Short Title. "This Act may be cited as the Securities Exchange Act of 1934."

Section 2. Necessity of Regulation. Citing that transactions in securities are affected with a national public interest, this section states that it is necessary to regulate and control such transactions and other matters in order to protect interstate commerce, the national credit, the Federal taxing power, to protect and make more effective the national banking system and Federal Reserve System, and to insure the maintenance of fair and honest markets in such transactions.

Parts of Sections 2(3) and 2(4) explain the effects of "rigged" markets and manipulative practices:

Section 2(3). Frequently, the prices of securities on such exchanges and markets are susceptible to manipulation and control, and the dissemination of such prices gives rise to excessive speculation, resulting in sudden and unreasonable fluctuations in the prices of securities which (a) cause alternately unreasonable expansion and unreasonable contraction of the volume of credit available for trade, transportation, and industry in interstate commerce . . . (c) prevent the fair valuation of collateral for bank loans and/or obstruct the effective operation of the national banking system and Federal Reserve System.

Section 2(4). "National emergencies, which produce widespread unemployment and the dislocation of trade, transportation, and industry, and which burden interstate commerce and adversely affect the general welfare, are precipitated, intensified, and prolonged by manipulation and sudden and unreasonable fluctuations of security prices and by excessive speculation on such exchanges and markets, and to meet such emergencies the Federal Government is put to such great expense as to burden the national credit."

Section 3. Definitions. In addition to defining 38 technical terms used in the Act, this Section gave the Securities Exchange Commission and the

Federal Reserve System the authority to define technical, trade, and accounting terms so long as such definitions are not inconsistent with the provisions of the Act itself.

Section 4. This Section established the Securities and Exchange Commission. Prior to the Commissioners' taking office, the Securities Act of 1933 was administered by the Federal Trade Commission.

Section 5. Transactions on Unregistered Exchanges. Under this Section, it became illegal for transactions to be effected by brokers, dealers, or exchanges on an exchange unless the exchange was registered under Section 6 of the Act.

Section 6. Registration of Exchanges. Combined with Section 5, this Section sets forth the requirements for exchanges to be registered and the method of registration. Exchanges file their rules and regulations with the SEC and must agree to take disciplinary action against any member who violates the Act or violates any of the rules and regulations issued by the SEC under the Act.

Section 7. Margin Requirements. The Board of Governors of the Federal Reserve System is given the power to set margin requirements for any securities, which requirements may be changed from time to time at the discretion of the Board. Under this authority, the Board issued Regulation T and Regulation U. Regulation T governs the extension and maintenance of credit by brokers, dealers, and members of national securities exchanges. Regulation U governs loans by banks for the purpose of purchasing or carrying stocks registered on a national securities exchange.

Section 8. Restrictions on Borrowing. In four parts, this Section (a) details from whom brokers or dealers may borrow money on listed securities, (b) lays the foundation for the SEC's "net capital rule," (c) deals with pledging and co-mingling of customers' securities, and (d) states no broker or dealer may lend or arrange for the lending of any securities carried for the account of a customer without the written consent of the customer.

Section 9. Prohibition Against Manipulation. Both this Section and Section 10 deal with manipulative practices that are intended to make money for those in the Securities business at the expense of the general public.

Section 9 makes it unlawful to do certain things that constitute manipulation, such as: (a) creating a false or misleading appearance of active trading in a security, (b) giving of information to potential investors as to the likelihood of a rise or fall in price solely for the purpose of causing the market price to react to purchases or sales by such potential investors, (c) making false or misleading statements about a security, (d) "pegging" or "fixing" prices, (e) improper use of puts, calls, straddles, or other options to buy or sell. Transactions in which there is no real change in ownership are also specifically prohibited.

Section 10. Regulation of Manipulative and Deceptive Devices. Section 10 first forbids the use of short sales or stop-loss orders that violate any rules or regulations the Commission may set to protect investors. Its wording, then, becomes much more inclusive than Section 9 or the first part of Section 10, since it forbids in general "any manipulative or deceptive device or contrivance . . . ."

Section 11. Trading by Members of Exchanges, Brokers, and Dealers. Authority is given to the Commission to set rules and regulations as to floor trading by members, brokers, or dealers for their own accounts and to prevent excessive trading off the floor of the exchanges. A part of this Section deals with the roles of the odd-lot dealers and the specialist on the floor of the exchange. Further, the Section places a limitation on certain customer credit extension in connection with underwritings.

Section 11A. National Market System for Securities; Securities Information Processors. Concerns the planning, developing, operating, or regulating of a national market system.

Section 12. Registration Requirements for Securities. It is unlawful for any broker or dealer to effect transactions in a security or a national securities exchange unless a registration statement is effective for that security. Information stating how such registration is to be accomplished is given here. The SEC is given authority to allow trading on one exchange in securities that are listed on another exchange (such securities are said to have "unlisted trading privileges").

Section 13. Reports. All companies whose securities are listed on a national securities exchange must file reports at such intervals and in such form as the SEC may require. The purpose of requiring such reports was to ensure that enough information was available on any company to enable an investor to make an intelligent decision concerning the worth of its securities.

Section 14. Proxies. Paragraph (a) of this Section gives the SEC the authority to make rules and regulations as to the solicitation of proxies and makes it illegal to solicit proxies other than in accord with such rules and regulations. Several rules have been issued under this Section which detail the manner in which proxies may be solicited and the information that must be given to shareholders whose proxies are being solicited. All of these rules are designated to ensure that the recipient of a proxy solicitation will understand what it is that he or she is being asked to sign and to give enough background on the matter in question so that the shareholder can make an intelligent decision about how to vote.

Paragraph (b) relates to the giving of proxies by broker or dealers in connection with securities held for the accounts of customers. It is standard practice for broker/dealers to vote proxies for shares held in their names for customers directly in accord with the wishes of the customers themselves.

Section 15. Over-The-Counter Markets. It is mandatory that all brokers and dealers who deal in the over-the-counter market (on other than an intrastate basis) be registered with the SEC. Further, the Section states that registration will be in accord with rules and regulations issued by the Commission. "Intrastate" means that the broker or dealer deals in intrastate securities as well as doing business only within his state. Here, as elsewhere in the Act,the "use of mails," even if within one State, places the user under the Act.

Section 15 also defines the grounds for denial of registration, for suspension, or for revocation of registration. Basically, these grounds are:

1) Making false or misleading statements in the application for registration.
2) Having been convicted within the last ten years of a felony or misdemeanor involving the purchase or sale of any security or arising out of the business of a broker or dealer.
3) Being enjoined by a court from engaging in the securities business.
4) Having willfully violated any of the provisions of the 1933 Act or of the 1934 Act. (After passage of the Investment Advisers Act of 1940 and the Investment Company Act of 1940, violation of those Acts also became grounds for suspension or revocation.)

Sections 9 and 10 dealt with manipulation with respect to securities listed on a national exchange. Section 15 adds a prohibition against over-the-counter manipulation as defined by the Commission. Some of the practices that have been so defined are:

1) Excessive prices that are not fairly related to the market.
2) False representations to customers.
3) Taking of secret profits.
4) Failure to disclose control of a market.
5) Creating false impression of activity by dummy sales.
6) "Churning," or unnecessary purchases and sales in a customer's account.

Another important rule of the SEC under Section 15 seeks to protect investors by forbidding certain practices in connection with pledging or comingling of securities held for the accounts of customers. This rule specifically applies to over-the-counter broker/dealers; a similar rule, under Section 8, applies to broker/dealers who are members of or do business through members of a national exchange.

Section 15A. Registration of National Securities Associations. Aided by the Maloney Act of 1938, which amended the original Act by adding this

Section, the formation of associations, such as the National Association of Securities Dealers, was authorized.

Section 15B. Concerns municipal securities dealers and transactions in municipal securities.

Section 15(c)(3) requires financial responsibility on the part of broker/dealers.

Sections 12 and 13 deal with registration and report requirements for listed securities. Section 15(d) is a corresponding list of requirements with respect to unlisted securities.

Section 16. Directors, Officers, and Principal Stockholders. Requires statements of ownership of stocks by "insiders" and other related information.

Section 17. Accounts and Records. Not only does this Section require that all brokers and dealers maintain records in accord with such rules and regulations as the SEC may set forth, but it also authorizes the SEC to make examinations of any broker's or dealer's accounts, correspondence, memoranda, papers, books, and other records whenever the Commission deems it in the public interest. Rules and regulations issued by the SEC under this Section state the types of records that must be kept. In practice, an SEC examiner may walk into a broker/dealer's office and ask that all files and books be opened for inspection. Under the law, no broker/dealer may refuse the examiner access to any and all correspondence and records. A broker/dealer can have his or her registration suspended or revoked by failure to keep copies of all correspondence or to keep books and records as required by the SEC.

Section 17A. Settlement of Securities Transactions. Concerns the clearance and settlement of securities transactions, transfer of ownership, and safeguarding of securities and funds. Congress directed the SEC to facilitate the establishment of a national system for securities clearings.

Section 18. Liability for Misleading Statements. In a rather unusual statement of law, this Section makes a person both criminally and civilly liable for any misleading statements made in connection with the requirements of Section 15 of this Act.

Section 19. Registration, Responsibilities, and Oversight of Self-Regulatory Organizations. The SEC has the power to suspend for 12 months or revoke the registration of any national securities exchange or of any security, if the Commission is of the opinion that such action is necessary or appropriate for the protection of investors. Further, authority is granted the SEC to suspend or expel from an exchange any member or officer who has violated any of the provisions of this Act.

Other provisions of this Section give the SEC broad powers in supervising the rules of national securities exchanges, which the Commission may require to be changed or amended. In other words, the SEC supervises the members of an exchange through the exchange itself as well as on an individual basis.

Section 20. Liabilities of Controlling Persons. In effect, this Section states that if A commits an illegal act under the direction of B, who controls A, then both A and B are equally liable under the law. Section 20 also makes it illegal for any "controlling person" to "hinder, delay, or obstruct" the filing of any information required by the SEC under this Act.

Section 21. Investigations; Injunctions and Prosecution. In the Securities Act of 1933, Sections 19 and 20 gave the SEC special powers in the areas of investigation, subpoenaing of witnesses, prosecutions of offenses and the like. Section 21 of this Act is similar in its provisions.

Section 22. Hearings. It is interesting to note the difference in wording with respect to hearings in the 1933 Act and in this Act. Section 21 of the 1933 Act states that "All hearings *shall* be public . . . ." Section 22 of the 1934 Act states "Hearings *may* be public . . . ."

Section 23. Rules and Regulations. Power to make rules and regulations under this Act is specifically given the SEC and the Board of Governors of the Federal Reserve System by this Section. Both bodies are required to make annual reports to Congress.

Section 24. Public Availability of Information. To protect those required to file under this Act, this Section makes it possible for certain information, such as trade secrets, to be made confidential and not a matter of public record. This Section also forbids any member or employee of the Commission to use information that is not public for personal benefit.

Section 25. Court Review of Orders and Rules. Like Section 9 of the 1933 Act, this Section reserves final judgment on any issue to the courts, rather than to the Commission itself.

Section 26. Unlawful Representations. It is unlawful to make any representation to the effect that the SEC or the Federal Reserve Board has passed on the merits of any issue. Also, the failure of either body to take action against any person cannot be construed to mean that that person is not in violation of the law.

Section 27. Jurisdiction of Offenses and Suits. Jurisdiction of violations of this Act is given to the district courts of the United States.

Section 28. Effect on Existing Law. "The rights and remedies provided by this title (the Act) shall be in addition to any and all other rights and remedies that may exist in law or at equity . . . ." The Section also leaves jurisdiction of offenses against a State law with the State.

Section 29. Validity of Contracts. No one can avoid compliance with the provisions of this Act by getting someone else to waive the requirements in any contract. Any contract that seeks to avoid the provisions of this Act are automatically void.

Section 30. Foreign Securities Exchange. It is unlawful to deal in securities whose issuers are within the jurisdiction of the United States on a foreign exchange in any manner other than that in which dealing in such securities would have to be handled in this country. In other words, the laws of the U.S. exchanges cannot be circumvented by placing business through a foreign exchange.

Section 31. Transaction Fees. Each national securities exchange is required to pay an annual fee to the Commission.

Section 32. Penalties. Individuals may be fined a maximum of $1,000,000 or sentenced to a maximum term of imprisonment of 10 years, or both, for violations of the Act.

Section 33. Separability of Provisions. An escape section that states that if any one section of the Act is found to be invalid, such findings shall have no effect on the other sections.

Section 34. Effective Date. July 1, 1934.

PUBLIC UTILITY HOLDING COMPANY ACT OF 1935

Interstate holding companies engaged through subsidiaries in the electric utility business or in the retail distribution of natural or manufactured gas are subject to regulation under the Act. These systems must register with the SEC and file initial and periodic reports. Detailed information concerning the organization, financial structure, and operations of the holding company and its subsidiaries is contained in these reports. If a holding company or its subsidiary meets certain specifications, the Commission can exempt it from part or all of the duties and obligations otherwise imposed by statute. Holding companies are subject to SEC regulations on matters such as structure of the system, acquisitions, combinations, and issues and sales of securities.

The most important provisions of the Act are the requirements for physical integration and corporation simplification of holding company systems. Integration standards restrict a holding company's operations to an *integrated utility system*. An integrated system is defined as one:

1) Capable of economical operation as a single coordinated system.
2) Confined to a single area or region in one or more states.
3) Not so large that it negates the advantages of localized management, efficient operation, and effective regulation.

The original structure and continued existence of any company in a holding company system must not necessarily complicate the corporate structure of the system or result in the distribution of voting power inequitably among security holders of the system.

The SEC can determine what action, if any, must be taken by registered holding companies and their subsidiaries to comply with Act requirements. The SEC can apply to federal courts for orders compelling compliance with Commission directives.

Acquisitions

To be authorized by the SEC, the acquisition of securities and utility assets by holding companies and their subsidiaries must meet the following standards:

1) The acquisition must not tend toward interlocking relations or concentrating control to an extent detrimental to investors or the public interest.
2) Any consideration paid for the acquisition, including fees, commissions, and remuneration, must not be unreasonable.
3) The acquisition must not complicate the capital structure of the holding company systems or have a detrimental effect on system functions.
4) The acquisition must tend toward economical and efficient development of an integrated public utility system.

Issuance and Sale of Securities

Proposed security issues by any holding company must be analyzed and evaluated by the SEC staff and approved by the Commission to ensure that the issues meet the following tests under prescribed standards of the law:

1) The security must be reasonably adapted to the security structure of the issuer, and of other companies in the same holding company system.
2) The security must be reasonably adapted to the earning power of the company.
3) The proposed issue must be necessary and appropriate to the economical and efficient operation of the company's business.
4) The fees, commissions, and other remuneration paid in connection with the issue must not be unreasonable.
5) The terms and conditions of the issue or sale of the security must not be detrimental to the public or investor interest.

Other provisions of the Act concern regulating dividend payments, inter-company loans, solicitations of proxies, consents and other authorizations, and insider trading.

TRUST INDENTURE ACT OF 1939

This Act applies to bonds, debentures, notes, and similar debt securities offered for public sale and issued under trust indentures with more than $7.5 million of securities outstanding at any one time. Even though such securities are registered under the Securities Act, they cannot be offered for sale to the public unless the trust indenture conforms to statutory standards of this Act. Designed to safeguard the rights and interests of the investors, the Act also:

1) Prohibits the indenture trustee from conflicting interests which might interfere with exercising its duties on behalf of the securities purchasers.
2) Requires the trustee to be a corporation with minimum combined capital and surplus.
3) Imposes high standards of conduct and responsibility on the trustee.
4) Precludes, in the event of default, preferential collection of certain claims owing to the trustee by the issuer.
5) Provides that the issuer supply to the trustee evidence of compliance with indenture terms and conditions.
6) Requires the trustee to provide reports and notices to security holders.

Other provisions of the Act prohibit impairing the security holders' right to sue individually for principal and interest, except under certain circumstances. It also requires maintaining a list of security holders for their use in communicating with each other regarding their rights as security holders.

In 1987 the Commission sent a legislative proposal to Congress which would modernize procedures under the Act to meet the public's need in view of novel debt instruments and modern financing techniques. This legislative proposal was adopted and enacted into law in 1990.

INVESTMENT ADVISERS ACT OF 1940

This law establishes a pattern of regulating investment advisers. In some respects, it has provisions similar to the Securities Exchange Act provisions governing the conduct of brokers and dealers. This Act requires that persons or firms compensated for advising others about securities investment must register with the SEC and conform to the statutory standards designed to protect investors.

The Commission can deny, suspend, or revoke investment adviser registrations if, after notice and hearings, it finds that grounds for a statutory disqualification exist and that the action is in the public interest. Grounds for disqualification include conviction for certain financial crimes or securities law violations, injunctions based on such activities, conviction for violating the mail fraud statute, willfully filing false reports with the SEC, and willfully violating the Advisers Act, the Securities Act, the Securities Exchange Act, the Investment Company Act, or the rules of the Municipal Securities Rulemaking Board. The SEC can recommend criminal prosecution by the Department of Justice for violations of the laws, fraudulent misconduct or willful violation of Commission rules.

The law contains antifraud provisions and empowers the Commission to adopt rules defining fraudulent, deceptive, or manipulative acts and practices. It requires that investment advisers:

1) Disclose the nature of their interest in transactions executed for their clients.
2) Maintain books and records according to SEC rules.
3) Make books and records available to the SEC for inspections.

TRUST INVESTMENT COMPANY ACT OF 1940

Activities of companies engaged primarily in investing, reinvesting, and trading in securities, and whose own securities are offered to the public, are subject to statutory prohibitions and to SEC regulations under this Act. Public offerings of investment company securities must be registered under the Securities Act of 1933. It is important that investors understand that the SEC does not supervise the investment activities of these companies and that regulation by the Commission does not imply safety of investment in them.

In addition to the registration requirement for investment companies, the law requires that they disclose their financial condition and investment policies to provide investors complete information about their activities. This Act also:

1) Prohibits investment companies from substantially changing the nature of their business or investment policies without stockholder approval.
2) Prohibits persons guilty of securities fraud from serving as officers and directors.
3) Prevents underwriters, investment bankers, or brokers from constituting more than a minority of the directors of the companies.
4) Requires that management contracts and material changes be submitted to security holders for their approval.
5) Prohibits transactions between companies and their directors, officers, or affiliated companies or persons, except when approved by the SEC.

6) Forbids investment companies to issue senior securities except under specific conditions and upon specified terms.

7) Prohibits pyramiding of such companies and cross-ownership of their securities.

Other provisions of the Act involve advisory fees, nonconformance of an adviser's fiduciary duty, sales and repurchases of securities issued by investment companies, exchange offers, and other activities of investment companies, including special provisions for periodic payment plans and face-amount certificate companies.

Investment companies must register securities under the Securities Act, and also must file periodic reports and are subject to the SEC proxy and insider trading rules.

CORPORATION REORGANIZATION

Reorganization proceedings in the U.S. Courts under Chapter 11 of the Bankruptcy Code are begun by a debtor voluntarily, or by its creditors. Federal bankruptcy law allows a debtor in reorganization to continue operating under the court's protection while the debtor attempts to rehabilitate its business and work out a plan to pay its debts. If a debtor corporation has publicly issued securities outstanding, the reorganization process may raise many issues that materially affect the rights of public investors.

Chapter 11 authorizes the SEC to appear in any reorganization case and to present its views on any issue. Although Chapter 11 applies to all types of business reorganizations, the SEC generally limits its participation to proceedings involving significant public investor interest, i.e., protecting public investors holding the debtor's securities, and participating in legal and policy issues of concern to public investors. The SEC also continues to address matters of traditional Commission expertise and interest relating to securities. When appropriate, the SEC comments on the adequacy of reorganization plan disclosure statements and participates where there is a Commission law enforcement interest.

Under Chapter 11, the debtor, official committees, and institutional creditors negotiate the terms of a reorganization plan. The court can confirm a reorganization plan if it is accepted by creditors for:

1) At least two-thirds of the amounts of allowed claims.

2) More than one-half the number of allowed claims.

3) At least two-thirds in amount of the allowed shareholder interest.

The principal safeguard for public investors is the requirement that a disclosure statement containing adequate information be transmitted by the debtor or plan proponent in connection with soliciting votes on the plan. In addition, reorganization plans involving publicly-held debt usually provide for issuing new securities to creditors and shareholders which are exempt from registration under Section 5 of the Securities Act of 1933.

Chapter 16

The Securities and Exchange Commission—Disclosure System and Filing Requirements

SEC REPORTING: THE INTEGRATED DISCLOSURE SYSTEM

Overview: In September, 1980, the SEC adopted rules implementing an Integrated Disclosure System (hereinafter "IDS"). SEC registrants must follow the new rules in their Form 10-K report, certain other SEC filings, and in their annual reports to shareholders (hereinafter "annual report").

The new rules are lengthy and involved an extensive revision of Regulation S-X and commonly used SEC formats. The result is symmetry and consistency of financial statements and other disclosures among many public reports and filings.

A Historical Note: For years, the SEC researched and studied ways by which a single comprehensive financial reporting system could be achieved, not only between the 1933 and 1934 Securities Act, but also between these Acts and the annual shareholder report. It is this effort which led to the IDS.

To understand why the need developed for an IDS, an understanding of SEC registration and reporting form genesis may be helpful. Many 1933 Act registration forms were spawned in response either to the nature of the offering (e.g., stock option plans on Form S-8), or by virtue of the status of the offeror (e.g., Form S-7). Financial statement periods and content varied considerably among the many filings (forms). These differences developed over a long period of time by an evolutionary process as different perceived needs arose, even though the 1933 Act relates simplistically to the same transaction—the public sale of securities. With the passage of time since the enactment of the 1933 Act, a proliferation of SEC regulations, rules, reports, registration statement forms, and amendments to the Act occurred.

In the first 30 years of the SEC's existence annual reports were exclusively a product of management decision. Until the early 1970's, the shareholder report financial statements were governed by Generally Accepted Accounting Principles (GAAP).

In the 1970s, however, the SEC added significantly to the shareholder report content by requiring disclosures such as a five-year summary of earnings and Management's Discussion and Analysis. Financial statements were expanded to include additional information such as quarterly operating data. Notwithstanding, the annual report to shareholders and the Form 10-K were typified as much by differences as by similarities. Since the differences were expanding and increasingly confusing, as well as compliance becoming increasingly expensive, an evaluation by the SEC of over 40 years of diverse rulemaking became necessary. The new IDS attempts to minimize these differences by achieving an interrelation among public financial reports.

For the SEC to achieve its goal of symmetry, a central framework of disclosure was necessary. SEC developed this framework only after evaluation of all elements of mandatory reporting (e.g., Regulation S-X, periodic filings, and shareholder reports) together with disclosures required by GAAP. This framework had to be adequate not only for annual reports, but also to meet the diverse disclosure requirements of the SEC—whether for the public sale of securities (1933 Act requirements) or for the Form 10-K annual report (1934 Act requirements).

Briefly, the IDS is based upon a "Basic Information Package" consisting of:

- Audited financial statements.
- Management's Discussion and Analysis.
- Selected income and balance sheet data.

This *Package* is common to the annual report, Form 10-K and most 1933 Act filings.

Changes Affecting Independent Auditors

The significant changes affecting the independent auditor concern the financial statements appearing in the annual report to shareholders. Formerly, the SEC had no authority over the annual report; the statements in the annual report, therefore, did not have to conform to Regulation S-X (but, of course, had to comply with GAAP). The new S-K requirements now govern the annual report. This was accomplished by the requirement that all financial statements presented in annual reports must conform to the S-X accounting and disclosure requirements.

For example, and among other major changes, a shareholder report requires the following:

- It must contain three-year comparative financial statements prepared in conformity with Regulation S-X.
- A majority of the Board of Directors must sign the Form 10-K.
- Management's Discussion and Analysis is expanded, materially.

There are two significant consequences resulting from the requirements of the IDS. *First*, the SEC financial statement disclosure requirements will in many instances add considerable volume and detail to the filings. *Second*, the prior distinction between GAAP and S-X compliance disclosures will be thoroughly submerged. Historically, GAAP has been conceptually oriented, and the SEC often applied GAAP concepts as a springboard to specific S-X disclosures by applying rigid materiality criteria (most of which have been retained). Formerly, any audited financial statement disclosures appearing only in an SEC filing presumptively were an S-X compliance disclosure and not a GAAP requirement. This distinction disappears. GAAP no longer will be pristinely visible.

Aging

The new aging requirements synchronize with the time frame for a 10-K filing (within 90 days after the end of the registrant's fiscal year). Continuous updating synchronizes with the quarterly report Form 10-Q, which must be filed with the SEC within 45 days after the end of each of the first three (but not the fourth) fiscal quarters.

Interim statement requirements closely follow 10-Q requirements.

For registration statements, the SEC adopted 135 days as the critical date for determining the aging of financial statements at the expected effective date of the registration statement, or proposed mailing date of a proxy statement, which includes financial statements. Registration statements which are filed and are to become effective 90 days after the end of the fiscal year, but *before* the 135th day, must include audited balance sheets for the last two fiscal years and the three-year income and changes in financial position statements. If the filing or expected effective date is 135 days *or more* after the end of the fiscal year, they must be updated with an unaudited interim balance sheet as of a date within 135 days of filing, and expected effective date and unaudited income and changes in financial condition statements for the interim period, and for the corresponding period of the preceding year must be included.

The Basic Information Package (BIP)

The new financial disclosure rule is termed the Basic Information Package (hereinafter BIP). The requirements of the BIP are common to Forms S-1, S-2, S-3, 10-K, and to the annual report to shareholders. The few differences are in the presentation of the financial information on the registration forms, i.e.:

> Form S-1. The Form requires complete disclosure to be set forth in the prospectus, and permits *no* incorporation by reference. Form S-1 is to be used by registrant in the Exchange Act reporting system for less than three years.
>
> Form S-2. Information can either be presented in the prospectus or in the most recent annual report, with the annual report delivered with the prospectus to shareholders. In the latter option, information is incorporated by reference *from* the annual report *into* the prospectus.
>
> Form S-3. Information can be incorporated by reference *from* the 10-K.

What Does the BIP Include?

Broadly, the Package requires information that the SEC considers to be essential for user decision making. Specifically, the following items constitute the substance of the BIP:

- Five years of comparative financial information.
- Management's Discussion and Analysis (MD&A) of the company's financial condition and results of operations.
- Information explaining the circumstances associated with a change in the registrant's independent auditor during the prior two fiscal years, if the change resulted from a disagreement on accounting practices and disclosure matters, or auditing scope or procedures.
- A description of the registrant's business and specified segmental information.
- Market and dividend record.
- Any material information necessary for a prudent investor to make an investment decision. Particularly, emphasis must be placed upon adverse information. "The SEC, in accord with the congressional purposes, specifically requires *prominent* emphasis be given in field registration statements and prospectuses to *material adverse* contingencies." (Italics provided).

Projections and Forward-Looking Information

Historically, the SEC has been opposed to projections and forecasts by registrants in their filings and annual reports. Over the years, however, there has been an increasingly widespread use of projections, estimates, forecasts, and other forward-looking information by private securities research organizations, with the projections based upon information originated with management in the first place.

Starting in 1963 with a *Special Study* reported to Congress, there have been a number of studies of this issue by various committees. Finally, in 1978, the SEC decided that as a practical matter the Commission should approve forward-looking information because such information had become widely used. Accordingly, Securities Act Release No. 5992 and Securities Exchange Act Release No. 15305, both dated November 7, 1978, read:

> "In light of the significance attached to projection information and the prevalence of projections in the corporate and investment community, the Commission has determined to follow the recommendation of the Advisory Committee and wishes to encourage companies to disclose management projections both in their filings with the Commission and in general."

The Safe Harbor Rule

Concurrently, with the adoption of the forward-looking rule, the Commission adopted a "safe harbor" rule which protects the registrant and independent auditor from lawsuits for a subsequently proved inaccurate projection *if* the projection was made in a:

> "good faith assessment of a registrant's performance" and that management "must have a reasonable basis for such assessment."

What is the significance of the safe harbor rule? It means that the plaintiff must carry the burden of proof to establish that the forecasts and projections did *not* have a reasonable basis, or were *not* disclosed in good faith. Heretofore, for the most part, the burden of proof was upon the defendants (the registrant, accountants, attorneys, and other signatories) to prove that they had, in fact, a reasonable basis for the projections, and had disclosed them in good faith.

The Information Covered by The Financial Forecasts Safe Harbor Rule

- Projections of revenues.
- Projections of earnings (losses).

- Projections of capital expenditures.
- Projections of dividend payments.
- Projections of capital structure and other financial items.
- Statements of management's plans and objectives.
- Statements of future economic performance in the MD&A.
- Disclosed assumptions underlying or relating to any of the projected financial information.

REGULATION S-X

Qualification of Accountants

The Securities Exchange Act gives the SEC the authority to establish accounting standards. To fulfill this requirement, the SEC issued Regulation S-X which is the authoritative source of SEC requirements regarding the form and content of financial statements and accompanying notes and schedules.

The SEC will not recognize any person as a *certified public accountant* who is not duly registered and in good standing under the laws of the place of residence or principal office, and also any person as a *public accountant* who is not in good standing and entitled to practice under the laws of the place of residence or principal office.

The term *member* means all partners, shareholders, and other principals in the firm, any professional employee involved in providing any professional service to the person, and the person's parents, subsidiaries, or other affiliates. The term *member* also includes any professional employee having managerial responsibilities and located in the engagement office or other office of the firm which participates in a significant portion of the audit.

The SEC does not approve of any certified public accountant or public accountant as independent who is not in fact independent. An accountant will be considered not independent with respect to any person or any of the person's parents, any of the firm's subsidiaries, or other affiliates during the period of the accountant's professional engagement to examine the financial statements being reported on, or at the date of the report, the accountant, his or her firm, or a member of that firm had, or was committed to acquire, any direct financial interest or any material indirect financial interest; also which, during the period of the professional engagement to examine the financial on the date of the accountant's report during the period covered by the financial statements, the accountant, his or her firm, or a member of that firm was connected as a promoter, underwriter, voting trustee, director, officer, or employee.

Accountant's Report. The accountant's report should:

1) Be signed manually.
2) Be dated.
3) Indicate the city and state where issued.
4) List the financial statements covered by the report.

The report should state whether the audit was made in accordance with GAAP. It should designate any auditing procedures which were omitted under the circumstances of a particular case and the reasons for their omission. The report should state the opinion of the accountant in respect of the financial statements, and also cover the consistency of the application of the accounting principles, as well as any changes in such principles which may have had a material effect on the financial statements.

Any matters to which the accountant takes *exception* should be clearly identified, the exception specifically and clearly stated, and the effect of each exception on the related financial statements.

General Instructions as to Financial Statements

The instructions specify the balance sheets and statements of income and cash flows to be included in disclosure documents filed in accordance with Regulation S-X. Other portions of this regulation govern the examination, form and content of financial statements, including the basis of consolidation and schedules to be filed.

Consolidated Balance Sheets

For the parent and its subsidiaries, audited balance sheets as of the end of each of the two most recent fiscal years should be filed with the SEC. If the filing is made within 45 days at the end of the registrant's fiscal year, and audited financial statements for the most recent fiscal year are not available, the balance sheets can be those as of the end of the two preceding fiscal years. The filing should include an additional balance sheet as of an interim date as current as at the end of the third fiscal quarter of the most recently completed fiscal year.

A Listing of Regulation S-X Topics that Should Be Reported in an SEC Filing

Qualifications and Reports of Accountants

- Qualifications of accountants.
- Accountants' reports.
- Examination of financial statements by more than one accountant.

General Instructions as to Financial Statements

- Consolidated balance sheets.
- Consolidated statements of income and changes in financial position.
- Instructions to income statement requirements.
- Changes in other stockholders' equity.
- Financial statements of businesses acquired or to be acquired.
- Financial statements covering a period of nine to twelve months.
- Separate financial statements of subsidiaries not consolidated.
- Financial statements of guarantors and affiliates whose securities collateralize an issue registered or being registered.
- Financial statements of an inactive company.
- Age of financial statements at effective date of registration statement or at mailing date of proxy statement.
- Filing of other financial statements in certain cases.
- Special instructions for real estate operations to be acquired.
- Special provisions as to real estate investment trusts.
- Reorganization of registrant.
- Financial statements of natural persons.
- Special provisions as to registered management investment companies required to be registered as management investment companies.
- Special provisions as to financial statements for foreign private issuers.
- Currency for financial statements of foreign private issuers.

Consolidated and Combined Financial Statements

- Consolidated financial statements of the registrant and its subsidiaries.
- Statement as to principles of consolidation or combinations followed.
- Intercompany items and transactions.
- Special requirements as to public utility holding companies.

Rules of General Application

- Form, order, and terminology
- Items not material.
- Inapplicable captions and omission of unrequired or inapplicable financial statements.
- Omissions of substantially identical notes.
- Current assets and current liabilities.
- Reacquired evidences of indebtedness.

- Discount on shares.
- General notes to financial statements.
- Financial accounting and reporting for oil and gas producing activities pursuant to the federal securities laws and the Energy Policy and Conservation Act of 1975.

Commercial and Industrial Companies

- Balance Sheets
- Income Statements
- Schedules to be filed.

Regulated Investment Companies

- Definition of certain terms.
- Special rules of general application to registered investment companies.
- Balance sheets.
- Statement of net assets.
- Statements of operations.
- Special provisions applicable to the statements of operations of issuers of face amount certificates.
- Statements of changes in net assets.
- Schedules to be filed.

Employee Stock Purchases, Savings and Similar Plans

- Special rules applicable to employee stock purchase, savings and similar plans.
- Statements of financial condition.
- Statements of income and changes in plan equity.
- Schedules to be filed.

Bank Holding Companies

- General requirement.
- Balance Sheets.
- Income statements.
- Foreign activities.
- Condensed financial information of registrant.
- Schedules to be filed.

Interim Financial Statements

- Interim Financial Statements.

Pro Forma Financial Information

- Presentation requirements.
- Preparation requirements.
- Presentation of financial forecast.

Form and Content of Schedules

- Marketable securities—other investments.
- Amounts receivable from related parties and underwriters, promoters, and employees other than related parties.
- Condensed financial information of registrant.
- Indebtedness of and to related parties—not current.
- Property, plant, and equipment.
- Accumulated depreciation, depletion, and amortization of property plant and equipment.
- Guarantees of securities of other issuers.
- Valuation and qualifying accounts.
- Short-term borrowings.
- Supplementary income statement information.
- Investments in securities of unaffiliated issuers.
- Investments—securities sold short.
- Open options contracts written.
- Investments other than securities.
- Investments in and advances to affiliates.
- Summary of investments—other than investments in related parties.
- Supplemental insurance information.
- Reinsurance.
- Supplemental information for property-casualty insurance underwriters.
- Investments in securities of unaffiliated issuers.
- Investment in and advances to affiliates and income from them.
- Mortgage loans on real estate and interest earned on mortgages.
- Real estate owned and rental income.
- Supplemental profit and loss information.
- Certificate reserves.
- Qualified assets on deposit.

- Real estate and accumulated depreciation.
- Mortgage loans on real estate.

REGULATION S-K

This regulation establishes disclosure standards under all securities acts. It sets standards of disclosure for financial information not presented in the financial statements, footnotes or schedules. For example, it establishes standards of disclosure for information presented in the section of various registration forms described in the registrant's *line-of-business*. Registrants have reported financial information regarding segments of their operations since 1969 when the SEC began line-of-business reporting in the Description of Business item of Form S-1. The requirement was subsequently extended to Form 10-K, and later line-of-business information was also made mandatory in the narrative section of the annual report to stockholders.

The SEC does not define the term, *line-of-business*. Rather, the responsibility of determining meaningful segments that reflect the particular company's operations and organizational structure is placed upon management. Line-of-business could be combined into one class when there were material intersegment transfers of goods or services. A class is reported upon if it contributes 10 percent or more to total sales and revenues in either of the most recent two fiscal years—15 percent for small companies. No more than ten classes of business are required to be reported.

What is considered to be the basic industry segment of a business is the profit center. Profit centers can be aggregated into groups until they cross industry lines, as defined by the government's *Standard Industrial Classification Manual*, at which point an industry segment is defined. Because the 10 percent materiality standard holds true for industry segments as well as for lines-of-business and the limit of ten reportable segments remains in effect, the definition of "industry" varies depending upon the registrant's operations. The industry segments of a highly diversified conglomerate are defined more broadly than a machinery manufacturer's, for example. In many cases, industry segments are identical to the registrant's lines-of-business because this is the approach that management had used originally to define lines-of-business.

Executive Officers' and Directors' Remuneration. Regulation S-K requires the inclusion of a table that discloses the remuneration of the five most highly compensated executive officers or directors of the registrant whose total cash and cash-equivalent remuneration exceeds $50,000. Required is the name of the individual, the capacities in which served, salaries, fees, directors' fees, commissions, and bonuses. Included in the requirement is the person's securities or property, insurance benefits or reimbursement, personal benefits, and aggregate of contingent forms of remuneration. The valuation of noncash items is determined by the actual incremental cost to the registrant unless such costs are significantly less than that the recipient would have to pay to obtain the benefits, in which case the aggregate value to the recipient should be disclosed in a footnote.

Form 10-K

Public companies prepare their annual reports to the SEC following the organization and specifications of Form 10-K. As with the annual report to stockholders, the interrelationships between authoritative sources that affect the 10-K are detailed. Form 10-K is due 90 days after the end of the fiscal year, but schedules can be filed in an amendment up to 120 days after fiscal year-end. The following is a list of information required:

- Business.
- Summary of operations.
- Properties.
- Parents and subsidiaries.
- Legal proceedings.
- Increases and decreases in outstanding securities and indebtedness.
- Changes in securities and changes in security for registered securities.
- Defaults on senior securities.
- Approximate number of equity security holders.
- Submission of matters to a vote of security.
- Executive officers of the registrant.
- Indemnification of directors and officers.
- Financial statements, exhibits filed, and reports on Form 8-K.
- Security ownership of certain beneficial owners and management.
- Directors of the registrant.
- Remuneration of directors and officers.
- Options granted to management to purchase securities.
- Interest of management and others in securities.

Financial Statements.   A balance sheet, income statement, and statement of changes in financial position must be filed as part of Form 10-K. Statements for the current fiscal year and prior year must be presented in comparative columnar form and be audited. The entities for which financial statements are required are:

- The consolidated entity, e.g., the parent and more than 50 percent owned affiliates.
- The registrant, that is, the parent company.
- Each majority-owned subsidiary not consolidated and each 50-percent-or-less-owned person for which the investment is accounted for by the equity method by the registrant or a consolidated subsidiary of the registrant. This requirement does not apply to holdings which represent ten percent or less of the registrant's total assets, sales and revenues, or income before income taxes and extraordinary items.
- Each affiliate whose securities constitute a substantial portion of the collateral securing any class of registered securities.

The financial statements of the parent company can be eliminated if it: 1) is primarily an operating company and the total minority interest of all consolidated subsidiaries does not exceed 5 percent of the total consolidated assets; 2) or the registrant's total assets, exclusive of investments in and advances to its consolidated subsidiaries, constitute 75 percent, or more, of total consolidated assets and the registrant's share of sales and revenues, exclusive of interest and dividends from the subsidiaries; 3) and equity in subsidiary income is 75 percent, or more, of the total consolidated amounts for sales, revenues and income.

Because Form 10-K must be filed at the end of every fiscal year, companies that change their fiscal year must file *short period* financial statements on an *interim* Form 10-K.

Form 10-K requirements for the contents of the results of operations include:

- Net sales or operating or other revenues.
- Cost of goods sold or operating or other expenses or gross profit.
- Interest expense.
- Income tax expense.
- Income from continuing operations.
- Discontinued operations, less applicable tax.
- Income or loss before extraordinary items.
- Extraordinary items, less applicable tax.
- Cumulative effects of changes in accounting principles.
- Net income or loss.
- Earnings per share, primary and fully diluted.
- Dividends per share.
- Any other information appropriate in the light of the issuer's circumstances.

If the company knows of any event that will cause a material change in the relationship between costs and revenues, it should be disclosed. For the three most recent fiscal years, the impact of inflation and changing prices on net sales and revenues and on income from continuing operations should be discussed.

If *interim period* financial statements are included, the financial condition of the company should be provided in order that changes between periods can be assessed. (The impact of inflation and changing prices on operations for interim periods need not be included in the discussion). Material changes in financial condition and results of operations from the end of the preceding fiscal year to the date of the most recent interim financial statement should be shown, as well as the corresponding year-to-date period of the preceding fiscal year.

Form 10-Q, The Quarterly Report To Stockholders

Form 10-Q is used for the quarterly report to be filed within 45 days after the end of *each* of the first three fiscal quarters of *each* fiscal year. No report need be filed for the fourth quarter of any fiscal year. A quarterly report to stockholders is not required, but a report is required by the exchanges on which the registrant's securities are sold.

The following is a list of the items required:

- Financial statements.
- Management's analysis of quarterly income statements.
- Other financial information.
- Review by independent public accountants.
- Exhibits.
- Legal proceedings.
- Changes in securities.
- Changes in security for registered securities.
- Defaults on senior securities.
- Increase or decrease in amount outstanding of securities or indebtedness.
- Submission of matters to a vote of security holders.
- Other materially important events.
- Exhibits and reports on Form 8-K.

The financial statements required by Form 10-Q are condensed and reported on a consolidated basis. A condensed income statement only is required for any subsidiary that is not consolidated or any 50 percent or less

UNITED STATES
SECURITIES AND EXCHANGE COMMISSION
Washington, D.C. 20549

(Mark One)

FORM 10-K

[ ] ANNUAL REPORT PURSUANT TO SECTION 13 OR 15(d) OF THE SECURITIES EXCHANGE ACT OF 1934 *[FEE REQUIRED]*

For the fiscal year ended_____

or

[ ] TRANSITION REPORT PURSUANT TO SECTION 13 OR 15(d) OF THE SECURITIES EXCHANGE ACT OF 1934 *[NO FEE REQUIRED]*

For the transition period from _____ to _____

Commission file number _____

_____
(Exact name of registrant as specified in its charter)

_____   _____
State or other jurisdiction of   (I.R.S. Employer
incorporation or organization   Identification No.)

_____
(Address of principal executive offices)   (Zip Code)

Registrant's telephone number, including area code _____

Securities registered pursuant to Section 12(b) of the Act:

Title of each class   Name of each exchange on which registered
_____   _____

_____   _____

Securities registered pursuant to section 12(g) of the Act:

_____
(Title of class)

_____
(Title of class)

Indicate by check mark whether the registrant (1) has filed all reports required to be filed by Section 13 or 15(d) of the Securities Exchange Act of 1934 during the preceding 12 months (or for such shorter period that the registrant was required to file such reports), and (2) has been subject to such filing requirements for the past 90 days.   ☐ Yes   ☐ No

Indicate by check mark if disclosure of delinquent filers pursuant to Item 405 of Regulation S-K (§ 229.405 of this chapter) is not contained herein, and will not be contained, to the best of registrant's knowledge, in definitive proxy or information statements incorporated by reference in Part III of this Form 10-K or any amendment to this Form 10-K. [ ]

State the aggregate market value of the voting stock held by non-affiliates of the registrant. The aggregate market value shall be computed by reference to the price at which the stock was sold, or the average bid and asked prices of such stock, as of a specified date within 60 days prior to the date of filing. (See definition of affiliate in Rule 405, 17 CFR 230.405.)

Note.--If a determination as to whether a particular person or entity is an affiliate cannot be made without involving unreasonable effort and expense, the aggregate market value of the common stock held by non-affiliates may be calculated on the basis of assumptions reasonable under the circumstances, provided that the assumptions are set forth in this Form.

owned person for which the investment is accounted for by the equity method and who files a separate annual income statement.

The balance sheets presented in Form 10-Q are dated as of the end of the most recent quarter and the comparative prior year's quarter. The income statement periods reported on, however, are: 1) The most recent fiscal quarter and the corresponding period of the preceding year; 2) The period between the end of the last fiscal year and the end of the most recent fiscal quarter and corresponding period of the preceding fiscal year; 3) The cumulative 12-month period ended during the most recent fiscal quarter and the corresponding fiscal year.

The financial statements need not be audited, but because interim data are required in the annual reports, these data are usually subject to a limited review. If a review has been conducted, the registrant must indicate whether all adjustments and disclosures proposed by the accountants have been reflected, and include a letter from the accountants commenting on the representations.

In addition to balance sheet and income statement information, the report requires comparisons to be made between three sets of periods in *Management's Analysis of Quarterly Income Statements*. For the most recent quarter and the comparable quarter immediately preceding it, management's report should include:

1) Unit sales volume.
2) Production levels.
3) Production cost variances.
4) Labor costs.
5) All adjustments necessary to present a fair statement of the results of the interim period.
6) Discretionary spending programs.
7) Changes in accounting principles.
8) Material prior period adjustments.
9) Pooling of interests, if any, during the current period.
10) Purchases of material business interests during the current year.
11) Disposal of a significant portion of the business during the current year.
12) Information regarding any matter that has been submitted to a vote of security holders during the period covered by the report.
13) Any material defaults in the payment of principal, interest, a sinking or purchase fund installment, or any other material default not settled within 30 days, with respect to any indebtedness of the registrant or any of its significant subsidiaries exceeding 5 percent of the total assets of the registrant and its consolidated subsidiaries. The amount of a default

in the payment of principal, interest, or a sinking or purchase fund installment, should be shown including the amount of the default and the total arrearage on the date of the filing of the 10-Q. This requirement refers only to events which have become defaults under the governing instruments, i.e., after the expiration of any period of grace and compliance with any notice requirements.

There should be reported any material arrearage in the payment of dividends or any material delinquency not corrected within 30 days, with respect to any class of preferred stock of the company which is registered or which ranks prior to any class of registered securities. The title of the class and the nature of the arrearage or delinquency should be indicated. In the case of an arrearage in the payment of dividends, the amount and the total arrearage on the date of filing the 10-Q must be shown.

Management's Discussion and Analysis of Financial Condition and Results of Operation.

For a full *fiscal year* the company's financial condition, changes in financial condition, and results of operations should be discussed. The discussion should provide information with respect to liquidity, capital resources, and results of operations, and also should provide any other information that the company believes to be necessary. Discussions of liquidity and capital resources can be combined whenever the two topics are interrelated. When a discussion of segment information or other subdivisions of the company's business would be appropriate to an understanding of the business, such information should be included.

Identification is necessary for any trends or any demands, commitments, events or uncertainties that will result in, or are reasonably likely to result in, the company's *liquidity* increasing or decreasing in any material way. If a material deficiency is identified, indication of the course of action that the company has taken or plans to take to remedy the deficiency is necessary. Also identification and separate descriptions of internal and external sources of liquidity, and any material unused sources of liquid assets must be made. The term *liquidity* as used in management's discussion means the ability of the company to generate adequate amounts of cash to meet the company's needs for cash. The enterprise should indicate any balance sheet condition or income or cash flow items which may be indicators of the liquidity condition. Liquidity should be discussed on both a long-term and short-term basis.

Discussion of the company's *capital resources*, including material commitments for capital expenditures as of the end of the latest fiscal period should be included along with the general purpose of the commitments and the anticipated source of funds required to fulfill the commitments. Any trends, favorable or unfavorable, in the company's capital resources should be outlined, as well as any expected material changes in the mix and relative cost

UNITED STATES
SECURITIES AND EXCHANGE COMMISSION
Washington, D.C. 20549

FORM 10-Q

(Mark One)

[ ] QUARTERLY REPORT PURSUANT TO SECTION 13 OR 15(d) OF THE SECURITIES EXCHANGE ACT OF 1934

For the quarterly period ended_____

or

[ ] TRANSITION REPORT PURSUANT TO SECTION 13 OR 15(d) OF THE SECURITIES EXCHANGE ACT OF 1934

For the transition period from_____ to_____

Commission File Number: _____

_____
(Exact name of registrant as specified in its charter)

_____
(State or other jurisdiction of incorporation or organization)   (I.R.S. Employer Identification No.)

_____
(Address of principal executive offices)   (Zip Code)

_____
(Registrant's telephone number, including area code)

_____
(Former name, former address and former fiscal year, if changed since last report)

Indicate by check mark whether the registrant (1) has filed all reports required to be filed by Section 13 or 15(d) of the Securities Exchange Act of 1934 during the preceding 12 months (or for such shorter period that the registrant was required to file such reports), and (2) has been subject to such filing requirements for the past 90 days.   ☐ Yes ☐ No

APPLICABLE ONLY TO ISSUERS INVOLVED IN BANKRUPTCY
PROCEEDINGS DURING THE PRECEDING FIVE YEARS:

Indicate by check mark whether the registrant has filed all documents and reports required to be filed by Sections 12, 13 or 15(d) of the Securities Exchange Act of 1934 subsequent to the distribution of securities under a plan confirmed by a court.
☐ Yes ☐ No

APPLICABLE ONLY TO CORPORATE ISSUERS:

Indicate the number of shares outstanding of each of the issuer's classes of common stock, as of the latest practicable date.

UNITED STATES
SECURITIES AND EXCHANGE COMMISSION
Washington, D.C. 20549

FORM 10-Q

GENERAL INSTRUCTIONS

A. **Rule as to Use of Form 10-Q.**

1. Form 10-Q shall be used for quarterly reports under Section 13 or 15(d) of the Securities Exchange Act of 1934, filed pursuant to Rule 13a-13 (17 CFR 240.13a-13) or Rule 15d-13 (17 CFR 240.15d-13). A quarterly report on this form pursuant to Rule 13a-13 or Rule 15d-13 shall be filed within 45 days after the end of each of the first three fiscal quarters of each fiscal year. No report need be filed for the fourth quarter of any fiscal year.

2. Form 10-Q also shall be used for transition and quarterly reports under Section 13 or 15(d) of the Securities Exchange Act of 1934, filed pursuant to Rule 13a-10 (17 CFR 240.13a-10) or Rule 15d-10 (17 CFR 240.15d-10). Such transition or quarterly reports shall be filed in accordance with the requirements set forth in Rule 13a-10 or Rule 15d-10 applicable when the registrant changes its fiscal year end.

B. **Application of General Rules and Regulations.**

1. The General Rules and Regulations under the Act contain certain general requirements which are applicable to reports on any form. These general requirements should be carefully read and observed in the preparation and filing of reports on this form.

2. Particular attention is directed to Regulation 12B which contains general requirements regarding matters such as the kind and size of paper to be used, the legibility of the report, the information to be given whenever the title of securities is required to be stated, and the filing of the report. The definitions contained in Rule 12b-2 (17 CFR 240. 12b-2) should be especially noted. See also Regulations 13A and 15D.

C. **Preparation of Report.**

1. This is not a blank form to be filled in. It is a guide copy to be used in preparing the report in accordance with Rules 12b-11 (17 CFR 240.12b-11) and 12b-12 (17 CFR 240.12b-12). The Commission does not furnish blank copies of this form to be filled in for filing.

2. These general instructions are not to be filed with the report. The instructions to the various captions of the form are also to be omitted from the report as filed.

D. **Incorporation by Reference.**

1. If the registrant makes available to its stockholders or otherwise publishes, within the period prescribed for filing the report, a document or statement containing information meeting some or all of the requirements of Part I of this form, the information called for may be incorporated by reference from such published document or statement, in answer or partial answer to any item or items of Part I of this form, provided copies thereof are filed as an exhibit to Part I of the report on this form.

2. Other information may be incorporated by reference in answer or partial answer to any item or items of Part II of this form in accordance with the provisions of Rule 12b-23 (17 CFR 240.12b-23).

3. If any information required by Part I or Part II is incorporated by reference into an electronic format document from the quarterly report to security holders as provided in General Instruction D, any portion of the quarterly report to security holders incorporated by reference shall be filed as an exhibit in electronic format, as required by Item 601(b)(13) of Regulation S-K.

E. Integrated Reports to Security Holders.

Quarterly reports to security holders may be combined with the required information of Form 10-Q and will be suitable for filing with the Commission if the following conditions are satisfied:

1. The combined report contains full and complete answers to all items required by Part I of this form. When responses to a certain item of required disclosure are separated within the combined report, an appropriate cross-reference should be made.

2. If not included in the combined report, the cover page, appropriate responses to Part II, and the required signatures shall be included in the Form 10-Q. Additionally, as appropriate, a cross-reference sheet should be filed indicating the location of information required by the items of the form.

3. If an electronic filer files any portion of a quarterly report to security holders in combination with the required information of Form 10-Q, as provided in this instruction, only such portions filed in satisfaction of the Form 10-Q requirements shall be filed in electronic format.

F. Filed Status of Information Presented.

1. Pursuant to Rule 13a-13(d) and Rule 15d-13(d), the information presented in satisfaction of the requirements of Items 1 and 2 of Part I of this form, whether included directly in a report on this form, incorporated therein by reference from a report, document or statement filed as an exhibit to Part I of this form pursuant to Instruction D(1) above, included in an integrated report pursuant to Instruction E above, or contained in a statement regarding computation of per share earnings or a letter regarding a change in accounting principles filed as an exhibit to Part I pursuant to Item 601 of Regulation S-K (§ 229.601 of this chapter), except as provided by Instruction F(2) below, shall not be deemed filed for the purpose of Section 18 of the Act or otherwise subject to the liabilities of that section of the Act but shall be subject to the other provisions of the Act.

2. Information presented in satisfaction of the requirements of this form other than those of Items 1 and 2 of Part I shall be deemed filed for the purpose of Section 18 of the Act; except that, where information presented in response to Item 1 or 2 of Part I (or as an exhibit thereto) is also used to satisfy Part II requirements through incorporation by reference, only that portion of Part I (or exhibit thereto) consisting of the information required by Part II shall be deemed so filed.

G. Signature and Filing of Report.

Three complete copies of the report, including any financial statements, exhibits or other papers or documents filed as a part thereof, and five additional copies which need not include exhibits shall be filed with the Commission. At least one complete copy of the report, including any financial statements, exhibits or other papers or documents filed as a part thereof, shall be filed with each exchange on which any class of securities of the registrant is registered. At least one complete copy of the report filed with the Commission and one such copy filed with each exchange shall be manually signed on the registrant's behalf by a duly authorized officer of the registrant and by the principal financial or chief accounting officer of the registrant. Copies not manually signed shall bear typed or printed signatures. In the case where the principal financial officer or chief accounting officer is also duly authorized to sign on behalf of the registrant, one signature is acceptable provided that the registrant clearly indicates the dual responsibilities of the signatory.

of such resources. Changes between equity, debt and any off-balance sheet financial arrangements should be discussed.

In the section of *results of operations*, any unusual or infrequent events or transactions or any significant economic changes that materially affect the amount of reported income from continuing operations are described. In each case, the extent to which income was affected should be explained. In addition, any other significant components of revenues or expenses that should be described in order to determine the results of operations are included here.

THE REGISTRATION STATEMENT—FORM S-1

When companies "go public"—issue securities to the public—a registration statement on Form S-1, the *general purpose form*, must be filed with the SEC. The registration statement, unlike reports filed under the 1934 Act, is required by the 1933 Act; it specifies certain standards for the financial statements and the auditor's consent and report incorporated in Form S-1. (See sample forms following.)

Financial information required in the registration statement follows:

- An audited balance sheet.
- Audited three-year comparative income statements.
- Audited three-year comparative statements of changes in financial position.
- Summary of Operations and Management's Analysis and Discussion.
- Supplementary income statement information.
- Summary of investments in securities, other than securities of affiliates.
- Supplementary information, e.g., a reorganization of the registrant, or a plan for reorganization in the future; a purchase or pooling of interests during the periods for which income statements are presented; pro forma information for intended purchases or pooling for all acquisitions not reported by the equity method.
- Historical material financial information.

Financial statements are required for the parent registrant and on a consolidated basis. If the parent meets certain conditions and if both its investment in its subsidiaries and the subsidiaries' sales and revenues are less than 25 percent of total assets, sales or revenues respectively, only consolidated statements need be presented. Financial statements also are required for subsidiaries not consolidated and 50-percent-or-less owned persons accounted for by the equity method that meet the criteria for inclusion in Regulation S-X.

UNITED STATES
SECURITIES AND EXCHANGE COMMISSION
Washington, D.C. 20549

FORM S-1

REGISTRATION STATEMENT UNDER THE SECURITIES ACT OF 1933

(Exact name of registrant as specified in its charter)

(State or other jurisdiction of incorporation or organization)

(Primary Standard Industrial Classification Code Number)

(I.R.S. Employer Identification Number)

(Address, including zip code, and telephone number,
including area code, of registrant's principal executive offices)

(Name, address, including zip code, and telephone number,
including area code, of agent for service)

(Approximate date of commencement of proposed sale to the public)

If any of the securities being registered on this Form are to be offered on a delayed or continuous basis pursuant to Rule 415 under the Securities Act of 1933 check the following box: ☐

Calculation of Registration Fee

Title of Each Class of Securities to be Registered	Amount to be Registered	Proposed Maximum Offering Price Per Unit	Proposed Maximum Aggregate Offering Price	Amount of Registration Fee

Note: Specific details relating to the fee calculation shall be furnished in notes to the table, including references to provisions of Rule 457 (§230.457 of this chapter) relied upon, if the basis of the calculation is not otherwise evident from the information presented in the table.

GENERAL INSTRUCTIONS

I.   Eligibility Requirements for Use of Form S-1

This Form shall be used for the registration under the Securities Act of 1933 ("Securities Act") of securities of all registrants for which no other form is authorized or prescribed, except that this Form shall not be used for securities of foreign governments or political subdivisions thereof.

II.   Application of General Rules and Regulations

    A. Attention is directed to the General Rules and Regulations under the Securities Act, particularly those comprising Regulation C (17 CFR 230.400 to 230.494) thereunder. That Regulation contains general requirements regarding the preparation and filing of the registration statement.

    B. Attention is directed to Regulation S-K (17 CFR Part 229) for the requirements applicable to the content of the non-financial statement portions of registration statements under the Securities Act. Where this Form directs the registrant to furnish information required by Regulation S-K and the item of Regulation S-K so provides, information need only be furnished to the extent appropriate.

III.   Exchange Offers

If any of the securities being registered are to be offered in exchange for securities of any other issuer, the prospectus shall also include the information which would be required by Item 11 if the securities of such other issuer were registered on this Form. There shall also be included the information concerning such securities of such other issuer which would be called for by Item 9 if such securities were being registered. In connection with this instruction, reference is made to Rule 409.

PART 1—INFORMATION REQUIRED IN PROSPECTUS

Item 1.   Forepart of the Registration Statement and Outside Front Cover Page of Prospectus.

    Set forth in the forepart of the registration statement and on the outside front cover page of the prospectus the information required by Item 501 of Regulation S-K (§229.501 of this chapter).

Item 2.   Inside Front and Outside Back Cover Pages of Prospectus.

    Set forth on the inside front cover page of the prospectus or, where permitted, on the outside back cover page, the information required by Item 502 of Regulation S-K (§229.502 of this chapter).

Item 3.   Summary Information, Risk Factors and Ratio of Earnings to Fixed Charges.

    Furnish the information required by Item 503 of Regulation S-K (§229.503 of this chapter).

Item 4.   Use of Proceeds.

    Furnish the information required by Item 504 of Regulation S-K (§229.504 of this chapter).

Item 5.   Determination of Offering Price.

    Furnish the information required by Item 505 of Regulation S-K (§229.505 of this chapter).

Item 6.   Dilution.

    Furnish the information required by Item 506 of Regulation S-K (§229.506 of this chapter).

Item 7.   Selling Security Holders.

    Furnish the information required by Item 507 of Regulation S-K (§229.507 of this chapter).

Item 8.   Plan of Distribution.

Furnish the information required by Item 508 of Regulation S-K (§229.508 of this chapter).

Item 9.   Description of Securities to be Registered.

Furnish the information required by Item 202 of Regulation S-K (§229.202 of this chapter).

Item 10.   Interests of Named Experts and Counsel.

Furnish the information required by Item 509 of Regulation S-K (§229.509 of this chapter).

Item 11.   Information with Respect to the Registrant.

Furnish the following information with respect to the registrant:

(a) Information required by Item 101 of Regulation S-K (§229.101 of this chapter), description of business;

(b) Information required by Item 102 of Regulation S-K (§229.102 of this chapter), description of property;

(c) Information required by Item 103 of Regulation S-K (§229.103 of this chapter), legal proceedings;

(d) Where common equity securities are being offered, information required by Item 201 of Regulation S-K (§229.201 of this chapter), market price of and dividends on the registrant's common equity and related stockholder matters;

(e) Financial statements meeting the requirements of Regulation S-X (17 CFR Part 210) (Schedules required under Regulation S-X shall be filed as "Financial Statement Schedules" pursuant to Item 15, Exhibits and Financial Statement Schedules, of this Form), as well as any financial information required by Rule 3-05 and Article 11 of Regulation S-X;

(f) Information required by Item 301 of Regulation S-K (§229.301 of this chapter), selected financial data;

(g) Information required by Item 302 of Regulation S-K (§229.302 of this chapter), supplementary financial information;

(h) Information required by Item 303 of Regulation S-K (§229.303 of this chapter), management's discussion and analysis of financial condition and results of operations;

(i) Information required by Item 304 of Regulation S-K (§229.304 of this chapter), changes in and disagreements with accountants on accounting and financial disclosure;

(j) Information required by Item 401 of Regulation S-K (§229.401 of this chapter), directors and executive officers;

(k) Information required by Item 402 of Regulation S-K (§229.402 of this chapter), executive compensation;

(l) Information required by Item 403 of Regulation S-K (§229.403 of this chapter), security ownership of certain beneficial owners and management; and

(m) Information required by Item 404 of Regulation S-K (§229.404 of this chapter), certain relationships and related transactions.

Item 12.   Disclosure of Commission Position on Indemnification for Securities Act Liabilities.

Furnish the information required by Item 510 of Regulation S-K (§229.510 of this chapter).

PART II—INFORMATION NOT REQUIRED IN PROSPECTUS

Item 13.   Other Expenses of Issuance and Distribution.

Furnish the information required by Item 511 of Regulation S-K (§229.511 of this chapter).

Item 14.   Indemnification of Directors and Officers.

Furnish the information required by Item 702 of Regulation S-K (§229.702 of this chapter).

Item 15.   Recent Sales of Unregistered Securities.

Furnish the information required by Item 701 of Regulation S-K (§229.701 of this chapter).

Item 16.   Exhibits and Financial Statement Schedules.

(a) Subject to the rules regarding incorporation by reference, furnish the exhibits as required by Item 601 of Regulation S-K (§229.601 of this chapter).

(b) Furnish the financial statement schedules required by Regulation S-X (17 CFR Part 210) and Item 11(e) of this Form. These schedules shall be lettered or numbered in the manner described for exhibits in paragraph (a).

Item 17.   Undertakings.

Furnish the undertakings required by Item 512 of Regulation S-K (§229.512 of this chapter).

SIGNATURES

Pursuant to the requirements of the Securities Act of 1933, the registrant has duly caused this registration statement to be signed

on its behalf by the undersigned, thereunto duly authorized in the City of _____,

State of _____, on_____, 19_____.

_____

(Registrant)

_____

By (Signature and Title)

Pursuant to the requirements of the Securities Act of 1933, this registration statement has been signed by the following persons in the capacities and on the dates indicated.

_____

(Signature)

_____

(Title)

_____

(Date)

Instructions.

1. The registration statement shall be signed by the registrant, its principal executive officer or officers, its principal financial officer, its controller or principal accounting officer and by at least a majority of the board of directors or persons performing similar functions. If the registrant is a foreign person, the registration statement shall also be signed by its authorized representative in the United States. Where the registrant is a limited partnership, the registration statement shall be signed by a majority of the board of directors of any corporate general partner signing the registration statement.

2. The name of each person who signs the registration statement shall be typed or printed beneath his signature. Any person who occupies more than one of the specified positions shall indicate each capacity in which he signs the registration statement. Attention is directed to Rule 402 concerning manual signatures and to Item 601 of Regulation S-K concerning signatures pursuant to powers of attorney.

INSTRUCTIONS AS TO SUMMARY PROSPECTUSES

1. A summary prospectus used pursuant to Rule 431 (§230.431 of this chapter), shall at the time of its use contain such of the information specified below as is then included in the registration statement. All other information and documents contained in the registration statement may be omitted.

    (a) As to Item 1, the aggregate offering price to the public, the aggregate underwriting discounts and commissions and the offering price per unit to the public;

    (b) As to Item 4, a brief statement of the principal purposes for which the proceeds are to be used;

    (c) As to Item 7, a statement as to the amount of the offering, if any, to be made for the account of security holders;

    (d) As to Item 8, the name of the managing underwriter or underwriters and a brief statement as to the nature of the underwriter's obligation to take the securities; if any securities to be registered are to be offered otherwise than through underwriters, a brief statement as to the manner of distribution; and, if securities are to be offered otherwise than for cash, a brief statement as to the general purposes of the distribution, the basis upon which the securities are to be offered, the amount of compensation and other expenses of distribution, and by whom they are to be borne;

    (e) As to Item 9, a brief statement as to dividend rights, voting rights, conversion rights, interest, maturity;

    (f) As to Item 11, a brief statement of the general character of the business done and intended to be done, the selected financial data (Item 301 of Regulation S-K (§229.301 of this chapter)) and a brief statement of the nature and present status of any material pending legal proceedings; and

    (g) A tabular presentation of notes payable, long term debt, deferred credits, minority interests, if material, and the equity section of the latest balance sheet filed, as may be appropriate.

2. The summary prospectus shall not contain a summary or condensation of any other required financial information except as provided above.

3. Where securities being registered are to be offered in exchange for securities of any other issuer, the summary prospectus also shall contain that information as to Items 9 and 11 specified in paragraphs (e) and (f) above which would be required if the securities of such other issuer were registered on this Form.

4. The Commission may, upon the request of the registrant, and where consistent with the protection of investors, permit the omission of any of the information herein required or the furnishing in substitution therefor of appropriate information of comparable character. The Commission may also require the inclusion of other information in addition to, or in substitution for, the information herein required in any case where such information is necessary or appropriate for the protection of investors.

Reports issued to the public cannot contain references by incorporation because they must be complete in and of themselves. Therefore, the annual report, quarterly report to stockholders, and the prospectus for public offerings cannot contain referenced information. Reports filed with the SEC, however, can contain references from reports to the public. Information, for example, from the annual report to stockholders can be referenced to the SEC in the Form 10-K, but information in the 10-K cannot be referenced in the report to stockholders.

GOING PUBLIC

"Going Public" is a significant step in the business life of any company. It is a step which should be taken only after a rigorous appraisal of the advantages, disadvantages, consequences, and other sources of financing. Going public is an expensive means of raising capital, so the benefits must more than outweigh the disadvantages.

When considering a public offering, planning should begin long in advance. Many of the decisions associated with a first stock offering require a long period of time to implement. A well-planned public offering, therefore, requires the preliminary studies and implementing procedures to begin sometimes years before the securities are offered to the investing public.

The listing that follows are some of the more common advantages and disadvantages of going public. Following the listing are brief generalizations of the requirements and procedures in a public offering of securities.

Advantages

1) Funds are obtained from the offering. When the securities are sold by the company, the money can be used for working capital, research and development of new products, plant and equipment expansion, retiring existing indebtedness, and for diversifying the company's operations.

2) Through public ownership of its securities, the company may gain prestige, become better known, and improve the business's operating results.

3) A company's customers and suppliers may become shareholders resulting in increased sales of the company's products or services.

4) Companies often consider expansion by the acquisition of other businesses. A company with publicly-traded stock is in a position to finance acquisitions with its own securities, instead of investing cash.

5) The business may be better able to attract and retain key personnel if it can offer stock having a public market (or options to purchase such stock).

6) A public offering of equity securities will usually improve a company's net worth, enabling the company to borrow capital on more favorable terms.

7) Once a public market is created for a stock and its price performs favorably, additional equity capital can be raised from the public, as well as privately from institutional investors on favorable terms.

8) Private ownership by one or a few persons of a fractional or even all of closely-held business is an asset with no ready market, usually no market at all. Once the company becomes publicly owned and the aftermarket becomes well developed, there will be a ready market for even a small number of the majority owners' shares.

Disadvantages

1) Public offerings are expensive, as registration with the SEC requires the retention of various professionals, i.e., investment bankers (underwriters), attorneys, accountants, and perhaps engineers, actuaries, and other experts.

2) Because of their responsibility to the public, the owners of a business lose some flexibility in management. There are practical, if not legal, limitations on salaries, fringe benefits, relatives on the payroll, and on operating procedures and policies. The authority to make decisions quickly may be lost, as many policies require prior approval by a board of directors, and in some instances by a majority of the shareholders.

3) There are many additional expenses and administrative problems for a publicly-owned company. Routine legal and accounting fees can increase materially. Recurring additional expenses include the preparation and distribution of proxy material and annual reports to shareholders, the preparation and filing with the Securities and Exchange Commission of reports required by the Securities Exchange Act of 1934, and the expenditure of fees for a transfer agent, registrar, and usually a public relations consultant. Added to the out-of-pocket costs is the cost in terms of executive time allocated to shareholder relations and public disclosures.

4) The owners of a privately-held business are often in so high a tax bracket that they prefer their company to pay either small dividends, or no dividends at all. The underwriters of an issue will usually require otherwise in order to increase the marketability and distribution of the first-time issue.

5) Once a company is publicly owned, research has demonstrated that management, some to a greater and some to a lesser extent, tends to consider the effect on the market price of its stock when considering

major decisions that will affect the profits. While it is generally acknowledged that management's preoccupation with day-to-day stock price fluctuations should be avoided, there are undoubtedly situations where a conscientious concern about the shareholders' investment quite properly should limit the decision-making alternatives for the management of a publicly-held company.

6) The one or few owners of a business possibly could be faced with a loss of control of the company if a sufficiently large proportion of the shares are sold to the public. Also, once a company's stock becomes publicly held, dilution of the prior owners' equity interest by subsequent public offerings, secondary financing, and acquisitions must be anticipated.

Evaluating a Company for Public Financing

In evaluating the advisability of going public, as well as pricing the company's stock, the underwriters will consider:

1) The amount and trend of sales and earnings.
2) Present and projected working capital and cash flow.
3) The experience, integrity and quality of the company's management.
4) The growth potential of the business.
5) The nature and number of the customers.
6) The company's suppliers.
7) The company's competitive position in the industry.

Selecting an Underwriter

Once the decision has been made to go public, one of the most important decisions to be made is the selection of an underwriter. Investment banking firms vary widely in prestige, financial strength, and ability to provide various services which the company needs. Some underwriters are not interested in first offerings; others specialize in that phase of the underwriting business. Some underwriters specialize in certain industries; the large investment banking firms will usually accept business in all of the major industries. The company's attorneys, auditors, and bankers can be helpful in selecting the underwriter.

The Underwriting Agreement

It is customary for the company going public to sign a "letter of intent" for the underwriter. If used, the letter outlines the details and proposed terms of the offering and the underwriter's compensation. It is explicitly written into the agreement that it is not binding upon either party, except there usually is a binding provision spelling out the payment of expenses if one party withdraws from the offering.

What Securities to Offer

Once a company has decided to go public, it must determine with the advice of the underwriter what class of securities to offer. Most first offerings are common stock issues. A first offering can consist of a package including other securities, such as debenture bonds which may or may not be convertible into common stock; warrants to purchase common stock can be "attached" to the new offering; preferred stock with a conversion privilege can be included in the package.

The Registration Statement

The registration statement is the disclosure document filed with the SEC that must accompany a registered offering of securities for sale to the public. This "filing" consists of two parts: Part I of the registration statement is the *prospectus*, which is the information that must be distributed to the offerees (the investors) of the securities. Part II contains supplemental information about the company of specific interest to the SEC, but which is available for public inspection at the office of the Commission.

Liabilities

It should be emphasized that management is responsible to determine that the factual information in the registration statement is accurate and complete. Management cannot assume a passive interest by relying entirely upon the attorneys and accountants to determine the information to be furnished, verify the information, and prepare the registration statement properly. It is reasonable, however, for management to rely upon counsel, accountants, and other experts associated with the registration for accuracy and completeness of the material in the statement, *assuming* management has properly disclosed factual information to the experts.

Under the Securities Act of 1933 (the governing statute for new security issues) and related statutes and regulations, civil and criminal liability can arise:

1) From material misstatements or omissions in a registration statement, including the final prospectus.
2) From failure to comply with applicable registration requirements.

Responsibilities of the Registration Team Members	
Member	*Responsibility*
Issuing company financial officer	Primary responsibility for all aspects of the offering. The SEC considers the registration statement to be the property of the issuing company.
Counsel for the issuer	Provides expert advice on compliance with state and federal securities laws. Helps issuer prepare the registration statement.
Underwriter	Also provides expert advice on financial matters. Manages the underwriting group composed of participating underwriters and distributes securities to retailers.
Independent accountant	Provides expert advice on accounting matters. Audits the financial statements of the issuer and provides an opinion as required by the SEC.

Annual Report Requirements of Rule 14a-3

Summary of operations and management's discussion and analysis
Description of business
Identity of directors and executive officers
Identity of principal market where voting securities are traded and high/low sales prices and dividends paid for past eight quarters
Statement that Form 10-K is provided without charge
Balance sheet
Income statement
Statement of security holders' equity
Footnote disclosure required by Regulation S-X
Reconciliation of differences between 10-K and financial statements
Schedule XVI, Supplementary Earnings Statement Information
Opinion letter
Other voluntarily disclosed information (including letter to shareholders; announcement of annual meeting and the year in brief)

Timetable for Preparation of Registration Statement		
Date	*Description of Procedure*	*General Responsibility*
Jan. 20	Hold board of directors meeting to authorize: issuance of additional amount of stock to be offered, preparation of registration statement for filing with SEC, negotiation of underwriting agreement.	Registrant
Jan. 25	Hold organizational meeting to discuss preparation of registration statement.	All parties
Jan. 26	Begin drafting registration statement.	Registrant and counsel
Jan. 30	Complete and distribute timetable for registration process.	Registrant's counsel
Feb. 10	Distribute first draft of underwriting agreement for review.	Underwriter counsel
Feb. 15	Distribute questionnaires to directors and	Registrant's counsel

	officers covering matters relating to registration requirements.	
Feb. 20	Distribute first draft of textual portion of registration statement of review.	Registrant and counsel
Feb. 25	Submit draft of financial statements to be included in registration statement.	Registrant and independent accountant
Feb. 27	Review draft of registration statement.	All parties
March 1	Send complete draft of registration statement to printer.	Registrant or counsel
March 10	Approve and submit final audited financial statements and related report for inclusion in registration statement.	Independent accountant
March 22	Receive and correct first printed proofs of registration statement.	All parties
	Distribute proof of registration statement to directors and officers.	Registrant or counsel
	Send revised draft of registration statement to printer.	Registrant or counsel
March 23	Hold board of directors meeting to approve and sign registration statement.	Registrant
March 24	File registration statement with SEC.	Registrant's counsel
	File listing application with stock exchange for common stock to be offered.	Registrant and counsel
	Distribute preliminary (red herring) prospectus.	Underwriters
April 15	Receive letter of comment from SEC regarding registration statement.	Registrant and counsel
April 16	Hold meeting to discuss letter of comment.	All parties
April 19	Complete draft of first amendment of registration statement and send to printer.	Registrant and counsel
April 20–21	Review printer's proof of amendment to registration statement.	All parties
	Send corrected proof to printer.	Registrant's counsel
April 22	File amendment to registration statement to cover SEC comments and to reflect any material developments since initial filing on March 24.	Registrant and counsel
	Notify SEC in writing that a final (price) amendment will be filed on May 2 and that the company requests "acceleration" in order that the registration statement may become effective as of the close of business on that date.	Registrant or counsel
	Receive approval from stock exchange of listing application subject to official notice of issuance and subject to effectiveness of registration statement.	Registrant and counsel
April 27	Resolve any final comments and changes with	Registrant and counsel

Timetable for Preparation of Registration Statement (*Continued*)		
	SEC by telephone.	
April 29	Hold due diligence meeting.	All parties
May 1	Finalize offering price.	Registrant and underwriters
May 2	Deliver first comfort letter to underwriters.	Independent accountant
	Sign underwriting agreement.	Registrant and underwriters
	File amendment to registration statement identifying price.	Registrant and counsel
	Receive notification that registration statement has become effective.	Registrant and counsel
	Notify stock exchange of effectiveness.	Registrant or counsel
May 7	Deliver second comfort letter to underwriters.	Independent accountants
	Complete settlement with underwriters—closing date.	Registrant, registrant's counsel, underwriters, and underwriter's counsel

3) From failing to supply a prospectus in connection with specified activities.

4) From engaging in fraudulent transactions.

Under various provisions of the Securities Act, company officers, directors, underwriters, controlling persons and experts who sign the registration statement are jointly and severally liable, and their civil liability can extend to the full sales price of the security; a criminal offense (fraud) can result in imprisonment for the signatory.

Preparation and Filing of a Registration Statement

Once it has been determined that a public offering of securities will take place, a corporate meeting involving the following parties is generally arranged:

1) A financial officer of the company (registrant).

2) Counsel for the issuer.

3) A representative of the underwriters.

4) Counsel for the underwriters.

5) The independent public accountant.

This group generally constitutes the *registration team.*

REGULATION D

Small Business Can Go Public

One of the primary sources of financing for small business public securities offerings is venture capital organizations. New venture capital investments have increased significantly in recent years, and the reduction in the capital gains rate in the Economic Recovery Tax Act of 1981 of the maximum tax on capital gains encourages risk-taking by venture capital firms. Small business enterprises are a significant investment for venture capital risk-takers. Access to venture capital financing, as well as to the money markets generally through investment bankers, has been made easier for the small entrepreneur by the *Small Business Issues' Simplification Act* passed by Congress in 1980. The objective of this legislation is to enable small business enterprises to raise funds in the public market, with reduced registration and reporting requirements of the SEC.

In response to the small business legislation, the SEC adopted new rules effective April 15, 1982, which significantly reduce the time and expense for small and new "start-up" enterprises to raise capital. Regulation D was promulgated by the SEC to simplify the procedures for small business enterprises to enter the capital markets.

The SEC points out in Release No. 33-6389:

> Regulation D is the product of the Commission's evaluation of the impact of its rules and regulations on the ability of small businesses to raise capital. This study has revealed a particular concern that the registration requirements and the exemptive scheme of the Securities Act impose disproportionate restraints on small issuers.

The important aspect of Regulation D concerns exemption from registration for small offerings and private placements. The Regulation is implemented by Rules 501–506.

Rule 501.   Defines 8 terms used in Regulation D.

1) Accredited investor.
2) Affiliate.
3) Aggregate offering price.
4) Business combination.
5) Calculation of number of purchasers.
6) Executive officer.
7) Issuer.
8) Purchaser representative.

Rule 502.   Sets forth the general conditions which apply to the three exemptions under Regulation D. The conditions relate to integration, information requirements, limitation on manner of offerings and limitations on resale.

Rule 503.   A uniform notice of sales form, designated Form D, is provided for in this rule. It is available for all offerings exempted by Regulation D. (Form D is reproduced immediately following the reprint of Regulation D.)

Rule 504.   Permits certain development stage companies, other than an investment company, an Exchange Act reporting company, or certain development stage companies to offer and sell a maximum of $1,000,000 of its securities to an unlimited number of persons during a twelve-month period.

Rule 505.   Provides a registration exemption for any noninvestment company issuer, *whether or not* a reporting company under the Exchange Act. An eligible issuer can offer and sell up to $5,000,000 during a twelve-month period without general advertising or general solicitation. An offering under this rule can be made to an unlimited number of accredited investors, and to a maximum of 35 nonaccredited investors.

Rule 506.   The transactional exemption provided by this rule does not restrict the dollar amount of securities offered. It is available to any issuer, whether or not a reporting company. A Rule 506 offering can be made to an unlimited number of sophisticated accredited investors.

REGULATION S-B

Regulation S-B is the source of disclosure requirements for small issuers. A small business issuer is defined as a company that meets all of the following four criteria:

1) Has revenues less than $25 million;
2) Is a U.S. or Canadian issuer;
3) Is not an investment company;
4) If a majority-owned subsidiary, the parent corporation is also a small business issuer.

Disclosure Requirements

1) Financial statements of a small business issuer, its predecessors, or any businesses to which the small business issuer is a successor should be

FORM D

UNITED STATES
SECURITIES AND EXCHANGE COMMISSION
Washington, D.C. 20549

FORM D

**NOTICE OF SALE OF SECURITIES
PURSUANT TO REGULATION D,
SECTION 4(6), AND/OR
UNIFORM LIMITED OFFERING EXEMPTION**

Name of Offering   (☐ check if this is an amendment and name has changed, and indicate change.)

Filing Under (Check box(es) that apply):   ☐ Rule 504   ☐ Rule 505   ☐ Rule 506   ☐ Section 4(6)   ☐ ULOE

Type of Filing: ☐ New Filing   ☐ Amendment

A. BASIC IDENTIFICATION DATA

1. Enter the information requested about the issuer

Name of Issuer   (☐ check if this is an amendment and name has changed, and indicate change.)

Address of Executive Offices (Number and Street, City, State, Zip Code)	Telephone Number (Including Area Code)

Address of Principal Business Operations (Number and Street, City, State, Zip Code) (if different from Executive Offices)	Telephone Number (Including Area Code)

Brief Description of Business

Type of Business Organization
  ☐ corporation   ☐ limited partnership, already formed   ☐ other (please specify):
  ☐ business trust   ☐ limited partnership, to be formed

Month   Year

Actual or Estimated Date of Incorporation or Organization: ☐☐ ☐☐   ☐ Actual   ☐ Estimated

Jurisdiction of Incorporation or Organization: (Enter two-letter U.S. Postal Service abbreviation for State: CN for Canada; FN for other foreign jurisdiction) ☐☐

GENERAL INSTRUCTIONS

Federal:

Who Must File: All issuers making an offering of securities in reliance on an exemption under Regulation D or Section 4(6), 17 CFR 230.501 et seq. or 15 U.S.C. 77d(6).

When To File: A notice must be filed no later than 15 days after the first sale of securities in the offering. A notice is deemed filed with the U.S. Securities and Exchange Commission (SEC) on the earlier of the date it is received by the SEC at the address given below or, if received at that address after the date on which it is due, on the date it was mailed by United States registered or certified mail to that address.

Where to File: U.S. Securities and Exchange Commission, 450 Fifth Street, N.W., Washington, D.C. 20549.

Copies Required: Five (5) copies of this notice must be filed with the SEC, one of which must be manually signed. Any copies not manually signed must be photocopies of the manually signed copy or bear typed or printed signatures.

Information Required: A new filing must contain all information requested. Amendments need only report the name of the issuer and offering, any changes thereto, the information requested in Part C, and any material changes from the information previously supplied in Parts A and B. Part E and the Appendix need not be filed with the SEC.

Filing Fee: There is no federal filing fee.

State:

This notice shall be used to indicate reliance on the Uniform Limited Offering Exemption (ULOE) for sales of securities in those states that have adopted ULOE and that have adopted this form. Issuers relying on ULOE must file a separate notice with the Securities Administrator in each state where sales are to be, or have been made. If a state requires the payment of a fee as a precondition to the claim for the exemption, a fee in the proper amount shall accompany this form. This notice shall be filed in the appropriate states in accordance with state law. The Appendix to the notice constitutes a part of this notice and must be completed.

ATTENTION
Failure to file notice in the appropriate states will not result in a loss of the federal exemption. Conversely, failure to file the appropriate federal notice will not result in a loss of an available state exemption unless such exemption is predicated on the filing of a federal notice.

SEC 1972 (1/94)

A. BASIC IDENTIFICATION DATA

2. Enter the information requested for the following:

- Each promoter of the issuer, if the issuer has been organized within the past five years;
- Each beneficial owner having the power to vote or dispose, or direct the vote or disposition of, 10% or more of a class of equity securities of the issuer;
- Each executive officer and director of corporate issuers and of corporate general and managing partners of partnership issuers; and
- Each general and managing partner of partnership issuers.

Check Box(es) that Apply: ☐ Promoter ☐ Beneficial Owner ☐ Executive Officer ☐ Director ☐ General and/or Managing Partner

Full Name (Last name first, if individual)

Business or Residence Address   (Number and Street, City, State, Zip Code)

Check Box(es) that Apply: ☐ Promoter ☐ Beneficial Owner ☐ Executive Officer ☐ Director ☐ General and/or Managing Partner

Full Name (Last name first, if individual)

Business or Residence Address   (Number and Street, City, State, Zip Code)

Check Box(es) that Apply: ☐ Promoter ☐ Beneficial Owner ☐ Executive Officer ☐ Director ☐ General and/or Managing Partner

Full Name (Last name first, if individual)

Business or Residence Address   (Number and Street, City, State, Zip Code)

Check Box(es) that Apply: ☐ Promoter ☐ Beneficial Owner ☐ Executive Officer ☐ Director ☐ General and/or Managing Partner

Full Name (Last name first, if individual)

Business or Residence Address   (Number and Street, City, State, Zip Code)

Check Box(es) that Apply: ☐ Promoter ☐ Beneficial Owner ☐ Executive Officer ☐ Director ☐ General and/or Managing Partner

Full Name (Last name first, if individual)

Business or Residence Address   (Number and Street, City, State, Zip Code)

Check Box(es) that Apply: ☐ Promoter ☐ Beneficial Owner ☐ Executive Officer ☐ Director ☐ General and/or Managing Partner

Full Name (Last name first, if individual)

Business or Residence Address   (Number and Street, City, State, Zip Code)

Check Box(es) that Apply: ☐ Promoter ☐ Beneficial Owner ☐ Executive Officer ☐ Director ☐ General and/or Managing Partner

Full Name (Last name first, if individual)

Business or Residence Address   (Number and Street, City, State, Zip Code)

(Use blank sheet, or copy and use additional copies of this sheet, as necessary.)

SEC 1972 (1/94)

prepared in accordance with generally accepted accounting principles (GAAP) in the United States.

2) Regulation S-X, Form and Content and Requirements for Financial Statements shall not apply to the preparation of financial statements.

3) The Commissions, where consistent with the protection of investors, may permit the omission of one or more of the financial statements or the substitution of appropriate statements of comparable character. The Commission by informal written notice may require the filing of other financial statements where necessary or appropriate.

4) Small business issuers must file an audited balance sheet as of the end of the most recent fiscal year, or as of a date within 135 days if the issuer existed for a period less than one fiscal year, and audited statements of income, cash flows and changes in stockholders' equity for each of the two fiscal years preceding the date of such audited balance sheet, or such shorter period as the registrant has been in business.

5) Interim financial statements, which can be unaudited, should include a balance sheet as of the end of the issuer's most recent fiscal quarter and income statements and statement of cash flows for the interim period up to the date of the balance sheet and the comparable period of the preceding fiscal year.

6) When the interim statement is more than one quarter, income statements must also be provided for the most recent interim quarter and the comparable quarter of the preceding fiscal year.

7) Cash flow statements should include cash flows from operating, investing and financing activities as well as cash at the beginning and end of each period and the increase or decrease in such balances.

8) The disclosure document is to inform investors. Therefore, information should be presented in a clear and understandable fashion. Unnecessary detail should he avoided, as well as repetition or the use of technical language.

9) Footnote and other disclosures should be provided as needed for fair presentation and to ensure that the financial statements are not misleading.

10) A company in the development stage must provide information that is cumulative from the inception of the development.

Financial Statements of Businesses Acquired or to be Acquired

1) Financial statements as specified in items 4 and 5 above should be provided if any of the following conditions exist:

a) Consummation of a significant business combination accounted for as a purchase has occurred or is probable. The term "purchase" encompasses the purchase of an interest in a business accounted for by equity method; or

b) Consummation of a significant business combination to be accounted for as a pooling is probable.

2) A business combination is considered significant if a comparison of the most recent annual financial statement of the business acquired or to be acquired and the small business issuer's most recent annual financial statements filed at or prior to the date of acquisition indicates that the business acquired or to be acquired meets any of the following conditions:

a) The small business issuer's and its other subsidiaries' (if any) investments in and advances to the acquiree exceed 10 percent of the total assets of the small business issuer and its subsidiaries consolidated as of the end of the most recently completed fiscal year. For a proposed business combination to be accounted for as a pooling of interests, this condition is also met when the number of common shares exchanged or to be exchanged by the small business issuer exceeds 10 percent of its total common shares outstanding at the date the combination is initiated, or

b) The small business issuer's and its subsidiaries' proportionate share of the total assets, after intercompany eliminations, of the acquiree exceeds 10 percent of the total assets of the registrants and its subsidiaries consolidated as of the end of the most recently completed fiscal year, or

c) The small business issuer's equity in the income from continuing operations before income taxes, extraordinary items and cumulative effect of a change in accounting principles of the acquiree exceeds 10 percent of such income of the small business issuer and its subsidiaries consolidated for the most recently completed fiscal year.

SHELF REGISTRATION

Historically, every new security issue by a corporation had to undergo the complete registration process, regardless of how short or long the intervening time period between issues, including new issues of the same security.

The registration and marketing of a new issue is expensive; for a large company the cost of a new issue runs into seven figures.

On March 3, 1982, the SEC issued ASR 306 announcing a temporary rule—Rule 415—which established a procedure permitting "delayed or continuous offerings." The procedure is termed "shelf registration." The essential element in the shelf-registration process gives public corporations permission to register a security whether or not the new issue is to be sold immediately. Subsequent issues of the *same* security can be sold without a new registration for each issue.

The Requirements

- Shelf registrations are limited to primary distributions made at the current market price of the security. Secondary issues do not qualify for shelf registration.
- Forms S-1-2-3- and S-8 (for employee benefit plans) can be shelf-registered, except that primary distribution "at the market" can be made only by S-3 qualified corporations.

(Note: At-the-market is defined by the SEC: "An offering into an existing trading market other than at a fixed price or through the facilities of a national securities exchange or to a market-maker otherwise than on an exchange.")

- There must be a reasonable expectation of selling shelf-registered shares within a two-year period. (The shares do not have to ever be sold, however.)
- The number of shares shelf-registered cannot exceed 10% of the float (outstanding stock) in the class of securities being shelf-registered.
- An underwriter(s) must be involved: 1) to provide an orderly distribution of the issue; 2) to ensure the accuracy of the Prospectus; 3) to assure compliance with the Prospectus delivery requirements.

Purpose

As noted, the registration process is expensive for the issuer. By permitting continuous registration, a corporation will incur the expense of only one registration for several new issues of the *same* class of security.

Formerly, corporations sold a new issue on the effective date of the registration, which involved an unknown price for the security until (literally) a few hours before the sale. With shelf registration the issuer can take advantage of favorable changes in the market price of the security, and withhold an issue if market conditions have turned unfavorable.

Updating the Shelf Registration

When necessary, a shelf registration is updated either by a supplement or amendment to the original registration. A supplement is simply a sticker attached to the Prospectus; it contains information relevant to the issue considered sufficiently material in nature by the issuer to be communicated to the public. Supplemental information is not passed upon by the SEC, nor is a part of the registration statement.

A post-effective amendment usually involves a revision of the original Prospectus. It is reviewed by the SEC, becomes a part of the registration statement, and must be declared effective by the SEC.

Rule 512 (a) (2) of regulation S-K:

" ... each such post-effective amendment shall be deemed to be a new registration statement relating to the securities offered therein ... "

Amendments are required:

- When anytime after nine months after the effective date of the registration statement the Prospectus contains information *more than* 16 months old.
- The Rule provides that anytime after nine months subsequent to the effective date of a registration statement, a Prospectus can no longer be used if any information in the Prospectus is over 16 months old. This requirement is usually triggered by the age of the certified financial statements. Assume year-end (any year) certified financial statements and assume a registration statement became effective on June 1. An updated Prospectus would have to be filed and become effective prior to April 30 of the following year.
- When any "facts or events arising after the effective date of the registration statement which, individually or in the aggregate, represent a fundamental change in the information set forth in the registration statement."
- When there is a material change in the original distribution plan of the issue.
- When there is a change in the managing underwriter.
- When false or misleading information is discovered after the effective date of the original registration statement.

The shelf-registration procedure is an experiment for which the SEC has set a time limit of two years ending December 31, 1983. The Commission will, during that time period, continuously appraise the results of the application of the shelf-registration approach before making a final determination with respect to its use.

The proponents of the Rule believe that it makes it easier for companies trying to deal with volatile markets to seize advantageous moments in the market to sell new security issues.

The opponents of the process believe the procedure can disrupt the stock market, after underwriting techniques, and is contrary to the interests of the investing public.

GOING PRIVATE

"Going Private" is a term applied to transactions that result in a reduction (or complete elimination) in the number of shareholders of a publicly-held corporation. In recent years there has been increasing activity in returning publicly-held corporations to private ownership.

The transactions are accomplished by open market purchases, cash tender offers, some type of exchange offer of one type of security for the outstanding securities, merger of the existing company with another company controlled by the issuer's principal shareholders, by reverse stock splits, and other types of transactions that alter the ownership of equity securities to a private ownership status.

Why go private?

While the stocks of many publicly-held corporations have increased greatly in value the past several years, the stocks of many companies, nevertheless, have continued to sell significantly below liquidating values. It is these companies that have been subject to corporate raiders, to shareholder pressures on management, have low returns on investment, have substantial cash positions, have consistently increased costs of public ownership and listing expenses on national securities exchanges, and have changed management attitudes toward the tangible and intangible benefits of public ownership.

Accountant's Participation

The accountant should know that the Securities and Exchange Commission requires valid reasons for "taking a company private," as current public shareholders must be dealt with fairly. The Exchange Act prohibits fraudulent, deceptive and manipulative acts or practices with respect to going private transactions. Rule 13E3, the controlling SEC rule governing going private transactions by public companies or their affiliates, requires filing with the SEC the disclosures and dissemination requirements to prevent unfair treatment of existing shareholders.

The primary question the accountant must ask is: Why go private? The answer includes such factors as reviewing the participation of the majority stockholders, the minority stockholders, management, directors, as well as the historic and recent financial and operating performance of the company.

The accountant must also consider whether private ownership will continue to manage the corporation on a "going concern" basis. This appraisal consists primarily of considering the various methods of going private and then developing *pro forma* projections of financial statements to determine which of the methods best protects the rights of the public shareholders.

Other considerations are an understanding of the company's industry and the company's position in that industry, the risk factors, the prospects of the company, the effects of the going private transaction on the current shareholders, comprehensive financial information, a history of the company, history of the prior price performance of the stock, and a detailed disclosure of the majority and minority interests. These and other factors that may be uniquely relevant to the corporation must be considered to ensure that a fair price is paid to the shareholders by the issuer.

One of the most significant problems that has developed in going private transactions is the interests of minority stockholders. Primarily, what is a fair price for their stock? The stockholders will lose the liquidity of a public marketplace and their investment position. For their protection, the regulations prohibit any sort of pressure, or coercion, to force minority stockholders to give up their investment.

The following is a list of the information required by Exchange Rule 13E-3 that must be disclosed to the shareholders on schedule 13E-3 of the corporation when they are solicited to approve a going private transaction.

The Income Statement:

- Net sales, operating revenues, and other revenues.
- Income before extraordinary items.
- Net income.

Balance Sheet:

- Working capital.
- Total assets.
- Stockholders' equity.

Per share Disclosure:

- Income per common share (before extraordinary items).
- Extraordinary items.

- Net income per common share, *and* per common share equivalents, if applicable.
- Net income per share on a *fully diluted* basis.
- Average number of shares of common stock outstanding for the two most recent fiscal years and adjusted for stock dividends or stock splits.
- Ratio of earnings to fixed charges for the two most recent fiscal years.
- Book value per share of the most recent fiscal year.
- *Pro Forma* data for the financial information that will disclose the effect of the method selected to complete the going private transaction.
- Audited financial statements for the past two years.
- Unaudited interim financial statements for the latest year-to-date interim period and corresponding interim period of the preceding year.

Additional information required:

1) The issuer must explicitly state the belief that the transaction is fair (or unfair) to unaffiliated security holders. The reasons for stating the belief that the offer is fair must be discussed.
2) Identity and background of the persons filing the controlling Schedule 13E3.
3) Past contracts, transactions or negotiations.
4) Terms of the transaction.
5) Plans or proposals of the issuer or affiliate.
6) Source and amounts of funds to finance the transaction.
7) Purpose, alternatives, reasons, and effects of the going private transaction.

(The relevant Rules and Schedules that should be referenced if responsible for a going private transaction are: Rule 13e3, *Going Private Transactions by Certain Issuers or their Affiliates*; Schedule 13E-3, *Transactions Statement*; Rule 13e4, *Tender Offers by Issuers*; Schedule 13E-4, *Issuer Tender Offer Statement*.)

84 ACCOUNTING AND FINANCIAL STATEMENTS DISCLOSURE DEFICIENCIES

The Securities and Exchange Commission has issued a list of 84 accounting and disclosure deficiencies commonly found by the Commission in the financial statements of corporations. The errors usually occur in the accountant's opinion, consolidated financial statements, balance sheet, liabilities, capital stock, surplus, income statement, and in various notes and schedules that supplement the statements.

The deficiencies that recur involve, for the most part, errors resulting from oversights in following accounting disclosure principles and presentation of financial data required in the financial statements.

It is the Commission's view that if accountants give careful attention to the requirements for completing the reports, corporations will avoid considerable expense and inconvenience to themselves. Properly completed statements (and annual reports to shareholders, where applicable), will facilitate user analysis of the statements, a factor to the reporting entity's interest from the point of view of prompt acceptance by users of the information in the financial reports.

1) Failure to state clearly an opinion with respect to the accounting principles and practices followed by the reporting entity.

2) Frequent use of equivocal phrases: i.e., "subject to the foregoing," "subject to comments and explanations in exhibits," "subject to accompanying comments," etc.

3) Failure to include in the opinion a comprehensive statement regarding the scope (the "scope paragraph") of the audit; i.e., restrictions by the company because of expense placed on the scope of the accountant's examination.

4) The accountant's failure to make a complete examination. The rules require that accountants must not omit any procedure that independent public accountants would ordinarily employ in the course of a regular annual examination.

5) Failure to certify *all* financial statements. For example, failure to certify the balance sheet and the income statements. Also, failure to certify the statements of the parent and subsidiaries consolidated.

6) Failure to identify clearly all supporting schedules, if any.

7) Certifying without explicit indication that the accounting practices of the company are in accordance with generally accepted accounting principles and procedures.

8) Failure either to comment upon or to clearly disclose the effect upon the financial statements of significant changes in accounting policies and practices.

9) Inadequate comment on the effect on the financial statements of the company's failure to follow GAAP.

10) Disclaiming responsibility for matters clearly within the certifying accountant's examination responsibilities.

11) Written reservation by the accountant with respect to matters not necessarily within his province, but with which the accountant was not satisfied.

12) Certificate undated. Certificate not manually signed.

13) Failure to footnote the accounting methods followed, clarifying the difference between the investment in subsidiaries on the parent's books, and the parent's equity in the net assets of the subsidiaries on the subsidiaries' books, as well as omitting the amount of the difference.

14) Failure to show in the balance sheet the amount of minority interest in the capital and surplus of the subsidiaries consolidated.

15) Failure to disclose the accounting principles followed for the inclusion and exclusion of subsidiaries in each consolidated balance sheet.

16) Improper treatment (in consolidation) of surpluses of subsidiary companies existing at the date of acquisition by the parent company.

17) Preparation of a consolidated income statement on a basis different from the consolidated balance sheet. For example, including income and expenses in the consolidated income statement of subsidiaries whose assets and liabilities are not reflected in the consolidated balance sheet, but for which separate balance sheets are furnished.

18) A failure to eliminate intercompany items, or to explain satisfactorily the reasons for not eliminating the items.

19) Failure to total current assets and to label the total.

20) Classification as current assets not realizable within one year. If recognized trade practices permit this procedure, an explanation should be footnoted.

21) Classifying receivables from subsidiaries as current assets in the parent's balance sheet, but classifying as noncurrent the subsidiary's obligations to the parent.

22) Failure to identify hypothecated (pledged) assets.

23) Failure to disclose or clearly explain conditionally held assets.

24) Classifying securities as "marketable" that are not in fact readily marketable.

25) Failure to disclose the basis for determining the balance sheet amounts of marketable securities and investments.

26) Failure to disclose the aggregate quoted value of investments and marketable securities when not shown on a current market basis.

27) Failure to reduce the carrying value of investments in subsidiaries by the amount of any dividends received out of the surplus of the subsidiaries.

28) Inclusion of improper accounts under trade receivables category.

29) Failure to disclose separately in the balance sheet, or to reference a schedule, the major classes of inventory; i.e., raw materials, work-in-process, finished goods, supplies.

30) Failure to show the basis for determining the amount of the inventories on the balance sheet.

31) Failure to provide a reserve for depreciation on the appreciate value of fixed assets.

32) Improper inclusion of expenditures in carrying value of fixed assets.

33) Failure to disclose the method used for amortizing debt discount and expense.

34) Failure to explain the method for writing off discounts and commissions on capital stock.

35) Failure to state the reasons for carrying treasury stock as an asset.

36) Failure to disclose separately the amount of reacquired debts.

37) Unexplained absence of an allowance for doubtful accounts.

38) Failure to total current liabilities and to label the total.

39) Inclusion in general reserves tax accruals that are actual liabilities.

40) Failure to segregate accounts and notes payable and accruals.

41) Deferred income not classified separately.

42) Failure to fully disclose all contingent liabilities.

43) Failure to disclose separately the aggregate capital stock liability of each class of stock.

44) Failure to show separately the number of authorized, treasury, and outstanding shares.

45) Failure to disclose in the balance sheet the division of retained earnings into various classes, if applicable.

46) Failure to disclose the par value, or a failure to show the assigned stated value of no par value stock.

47) Use of capital surplus to absorb writedowns in plant and equipment that should have been charged to retained earnings.

48) Failure to date earned surplus account after eliminating a deficit by a charge to capital surplus.

49) Failure to state the amount of retained earnings restricted because of the acquisition of a company's own stock. Also, failure to state amount of surplus restricted for the difference between par or stated value of preferred stock and the liquidating value of that class of stock.

50) Deficit not clearly designated in the balance sheet.

51) Treatment of surplus of subsidiary at date of acquisition of earned surplus.

52) Charges to surplus, rather than to earnings, for expenses or losses properly identified with current operations.

53) Crediting earnings instead of retained earnings for the proceeds of sale of assets previously written off by a charge to retained earnings.

54) Failure to disclose the basis for determining inventories when opening and closing inventories are used to determine the cost of goods sold.

55) Failure to indicate the omission of provisions for depreciation or depletion, and the effect on the income statement.

56) Failure to disclose the basis of conversion of all items in foreign currencies. Also, failure to state the amount and disposition of unrealized gains and losses in foreign currencies.

57) Failure to show gross sales net of discounts, and returns and allowances.

58) Failure to disclose gross sales and operating revenues separately, when the lesser of the two amounts exceeds 10 percent of the total of the two amounts.

59) Failure to segregate selling, general, and administrative expenses.

60) Failure to explain in footnotes the effect of changes in accounting practices in the compilation of the profit and loss statement.

61) Failure to disclose separately from other taxes a surtax on undistributed profits, or a failure to state explicitly that no liability for a surtax exists.

62) Failure to explain the method used to determine the cost of securities sold; i.e., average cost, first-in, first-out, specific certificate or bond or type of security.

63) Failure to show the basis for the recognition of profits on installment or other deferred sales.

64) Failure to reference appropriate schedules to the income statement when expense details are presented in supporting schedules.

65) Failure to list property by major classification; i.e., land, buildings, equipment, machinery, leaseholds, etc.

66) Failure to explain the nature of changes in property, plant, and equipment accounts.

67) Failure to disclose accounting policies with respect to amortization and/or depreciation of property, plant, and equipment when credited directly to asset accounts.

68) Failure to state accounting policies with respect to the provisions for depreciation, depletion, and amortization, or reserves created in lieu of appropriate provisions.

69) Failure to comply with the requirement that reserves should be disclosed to correspond with the classification of property in separating depreciation, depletion, and amortization.

70) Failure to explain charges to reserves, other than retirement, renewals, and replacement.

71) Failure to identify intangible assets by major classes.

72) Failure to state policy with respect to provisions for the amortization of intangible assets in cases where a clarifying schedule is not provided.

73) Failure to state the accounting policy with respect to the provisions for amortization of intangible assets, or reserves created in lieu of appropriate provisions.

74) Failure to explain all changes in reserves during the accounting period.

75) Failure to list each issue of capital stock of all the corporations in a consolidated group, whether or not eliminated in consolidation.

76) Improperly identifying unissued stock as treasury stock.

77) Failure to disclose division of retained earnings into classes; i.e., paid-in capital, capital surplus, earned surplus, appraisal surplus.

78) Failure to include an analysis of the retained earnings account, either in the balance sheet, or in a continuation of the income statement, or in a schedule referenced in the balance sheet.

79) Failure to describe precisely all miscellaneous retained earnings additions and deductions.

80) Failure to segregate amounts charged to costs, and amounts charged to other gain and loss items not segregated.

81) Failure to report all maintenance and repair expenses.

82) Failure to show items in schedules which are at variance or inconsistent with other statements or schedules.

83) Failure to disclose the amount of equity in net profit and loss for the fiscal year of affiliates, if dividends were received during the year from affiliates.

84) Failure to disclose separately for each affiliate the amount of dividends and the amount of equity in net profit and loss for the fiscal year. Corporations may report these items in total only when substantially all the stock and funded debt of the subsidiaries are held within the affiliated group.

Chapter 17

Business Combinations

BUSINESS COMBINATIONS AND ACQUISITIONS

This section deals with the *accounting* treatment of dealings involved with the following types of business combinations and acquisitions:

1) Those *combinations* occurring when a corporation and one or more *incorporated* or *unincorporated* businesses *are united into one* accounting entity, with that single entity then carrying on the activities of the prior separate entities. Two methods of accounting are applicable here:
   a) The Purchase Method, or
   b) The Pooling-of-Interests Method.

2) Those *stock acquisitions* (or stock investments) wherein one corporation *buys the voting common stock* of another corporation—sometimes acquiring voting control, sometimes not—with both entities continuing as separate, individual, distinct operating corporations. Three methods of accounting are applicable here:
   a) The Consolidation Method (or the alternate Combining Method),
   b) The Equity Method, or
   c) The Cost Method.

In each of these methods, the investment in the subsidiary's stock appears on the books of the owning company as an investment asset.

In order to clarify the distinctions involved—as a quick reference—these major points should be considered:

1) Consolidation, the Equity Method and the Cost Method all pertain to the acquisition of *voting stock* by the buying company.

   Pooling and Purchase pertain to the acquisition of *assets* and usually liabilities (inventory, plant, equipment, etc.).

2) How to distinguish between pooling and purchase:

   a) With *pooling*, the *acquiring* company uses its *own capital stock* to exchange for the capital stock of the acquired company. For example, a stockholder of Company B (the *acquired* company) will, after pooling, hold stock in Company A, the acquiring company. Company B's stock will have been cancelled. Or, a third Company C might be formed with both A and B companies folding into Company C. Pooling is usually a tax-free combination, provided all requirements are met.

   b) With *purchase*, the acquiring company buys the assets (usually net of liabilities), and the acquired company (the one selling the assets) must usually account for gain or loss on the sale of the individual assets, involving the recapture provisions of the tax law.

   c) Pooling involves the exchange of stock. Purchase can involve either stock, cash or property.

   d) In *purchase*, the assets are valued at *fair value*, usually creating goodwill. In *pooling*, there is no change in asset value, since they are picked up at net *book* value.

   e) Under both pooling and purchase, the acquired company is subsequently liquidated.

   f) A combination of *both* methods is unacceptable.

3) With *stock acquisitions*, all companies continue separate operations even though under new ownership or managerial control. Accounting records are maintained for each distinct company, and each company prepares financial statements independent of the other company. However, public release of those statements is guided by the rules of consolidation or the equity method.

4) With stock acquisitions:

   a) Use the *cost method* when owning less than 20% of the stock and exercising no effective managerial control.

   b) Use the *equity method* when owning 20% or more (influence is presumed)—or when owning less than 20% *but with substantial managerial* influence. Also, use the equity method when owning *over 50%* and *not using the consolidation method* .

   c) Use the *consolidation method* when ownership is *over 50%* (majority interest), *unless* conditions exist (described later) which constitute exception to the rules of consolidation and permit the use of the equity method.

d) An acquiring enterprise should account for contingencies that can be reasonably estimated and considered probable as an allocation to the purchase price of the acquired company.

Note that financial accounting (and the SEC) require consolidation for over 50% holdings, with exceptions noted, but the IRS requires a minimum 80% voting control for consolidated tax returns.

Consolidation must also be used for subsidiaries whose principal activity is leasing property or facilities to the parent or other affiliates.

FASB Statement 94, *Consolidation of All Majority-Owned Subsidiaries*, eliminates most of the exceptions from consolidation formerly permitted by Accounting Research Bulletin 51, *Consolidated Financial Statements*. The most significant exception that has been eliminated is the "nonhomogeneity exception," i.e., excluding majority-owned subsidiaries whose business is unrelated to either the business of the parent or of other members of the consolidated group. Essentially, Statement 94 permits only two exceptions: 1) subsidiaries under *temporary* control, and 2) subsidiaries *not* controlled by the majority owner. (Further discussion of FASB 94 appears at the end of this chapter.)

When *not* using consolidation, and the holdings are over 50%, the equity method must be used for all unconsolidated subsidiaries (foreign as well as domestic).

When holdings are 50% or under, down to 20%, you must use the equity method, since significant managerial voice is presumed (unless you prove the contrary).

Further details of each of these methods are now presented.

THE COST METHOD—STOCK ACQUISITIONS

The cost method: An investor records an investment in the stock of an investee at cost, and recognizes as income dividends received that are distributed from net accumulated earnings of the investee, since the date of acquisition by the investor.

Dividends from the investee's earnings are entered as income;

Dividends in *excess* of investee's earnings after date of investment reduce the cost of the investment;

Losses of the investee (after acquisition) should be recognized under the "marketable security" standards.

For the investor, under the *cost method*, dividends only are to be picked up as income (with cash being debited).

THE EQUITY METHOD—STOCK ACQUISITIONS

The equity method: An investor initially records an investment in the stock of an investee at cost and adjusts the carrying amount of the investment to recognize the investor's share of the earnings or losses of the investee after the date of the acquisition. The amount of the adjustment is included in the determination of net income by the investor, and such amount reflects adjustments similar to those made in preparing consolidated statements including adjustments to eliminate intercompany gains and losses, and to amortize, if appropriate, any difference between investor cost and underlying equity in net assets of the investee at the date of the investment.

Proportionate share of earnings, whether distributed or not, increases the carrying amount of the investment and is recorded as income;

Dividends reduce the carrying amount of the investment and are *not* recorded as income;

After investment, a series of losses by the investee may necessitate additional reduction in the carrying amount.

Under the equity method, the proportionate share of earnings (losses) of the investee (subsidiary) is picked up as income (loss), with the investment asset account being debited (or credited for a loss). Dividends, when received, are thus merely a conversion of part of that increased investment value to cash.

Both the investment and the share of earnings are recorded as single amounts. Market devaluation is *not* applicable.

The Equity Method Should Be Used (for Foreign or Domestic Subsidiaries):

1) When owning *20% or more* of the voting stock of the investee (significant control is presumed); or

2) When owning *less than 20%* and the investor can demonstrate the exercise of significant control; or

3) When not consolidating those investees in which more than 50% is owned; but the equity method should not be used if consolidation is justified; or

4) For participant's share of joint ventures.

The equity method *should not* be used:

1) When consolidation is proper for over 50% control; or

2) When ownership is below 20% and there is *no* demonstrable control (use the cost method); or

3) When the principal business activity of the subsidiary is leasing property or facilities to the parent or other affiliates (consolidate instead).

Voting stock interest is based on the *outstanding* shares without recognition of common stock equivalents.

Applying the Equity Method

1) Follow the rules of intercompany profit and loss eliminations as for consolidations;

2) At purchase of stock, adjust investment to reflect underlying equity and amortize goodwill, if any;

3) Show investment as a single amount, and show income as a single amount, except for (4) below;

4) Show share of extraordinary items separately, net of tax;

5) Any capital structure change of the investee should be accounted for as in consolidations;

6) When stock is sold, account for gain or loss based on the carrying amount then in the investment account;

7) Use the investee's latest financial statement;

8) Recognize non-temporary declines in the value of the investee's stock by adjusting the investment account;

9) Do not write investment account below zero; hold over any losses until future gains offset them;

10) Before picking up share of investee's income, deduct any cumulative preferred dividends (paid or unpaid) not already deducted by the investee;

11) If the level of ownership falls to the point which ordinarily calls for the cost method, stop accruing earnings undistributed, but apply dividends received to the investment account;

12) If changing from the cost method to the equity method for any one investment (because of change in ownership), make the necessary retroactive adjustments;

13) If goodwill is created in (12) above, it should be amortized.

Equity Method: A method of accounting by a parent company for investments in subsidiaries in which the parent's share of subsidiary income (or loss) is recorded in the parent company's accounts.

The accounting procedures for the equity method follow:

Investment—X Co.	275,000	
Cash		275,000
(To record the purchase of 25% of X Co. stock at cost; 25,000 shares @ $11.00)		
Investment—X Co.	40,000	
Goodwill		40,000
(Additional equity in X Co. at date of acquisition)		
Cash	5,000	
Investment—X Co.		5,000
(To record receipt of $20.00 per share cash dividend from X Co.).		
Investment—X Co.	27,500	
Investment from Parent share of X Co. undistributed earnings.		25,000
Income from Parent share of X Co. undistributed extraordinary item.		2,500
(To record 25% of X Co. net income of $100,000 from continuing operations and $10,000 extraordinary income; total income $110,000.)		
Income Tax Expense (on operation)	12,500	
Income Tax Expense (Extra. item)	1,250	
Deferred Taxes		13,750
(To record 50% of reported income as accrued taxes.)		

The following entry is made for the depreciation of the excess of fair value of assets less book value of the acquired assets:

Equity of Earnings of Investee	xxxx	
Investment in Investee		xxxx

Income Taxes

1) Set up a deferred tax based on the investor's proportion of the subsidiary's net income (after tax), based on the investor's rate of tax, *unless*: If it appears that the *undistributed earnings* of the investee meet the *indefinite reversal criteria* (see elsewhere in this text), do *not* accrue taxes, but make disclosure.

2) For dividends received, pull applicable tax out of deferred taxes and put in tax payable account;

3) Disclose applicable timing differences.

(See also Journal Entries in Appendix A, Timing Differences and Disclosures in this text.)

THE CONSOLIDATION METHOD—STOCK ACQUISITIONS

There is a presumption that consolidated statements are more meaningful than separate statements and that they are usually necessary for a fair presentation when one of the companies in the group directly or indirectly has a controlling financial interest in the other companies.

Assets, liabilities, revenues and expenses of the subsidiaries are combined with those of the parent company. Intercompany items are eliminated.

Earned surplus of a subsidiary company from prior to acquisition does not form part of the parent's consolidated earned surplus, and dividends therefrom do not constitute income.

The purpose of consolidated statements is to present the financial data as if it were one single unit.

Rule for Consolidation

The usual condition for a controlling financial interest is ownership of a majority voting interest and, therefore, as a general rule ownership by one company, directly or indirectly, of over 50% of the outstanding voting shares of another company is a condition pointing toward consolidation.

Do *not* consolidate:

1) When control is likely to be temporary; or

2) Where control does *not* rest with the *majority* holder (example: subsidiary is in reorganization or bankruptcy); or

3) Usually, for foreign subsidiaries (See later in this chapter); or

4) Where subsidiary is in a dissimilar business (manufacturer vs. financing); or

5) When the equity method or the cost method is more appropriate for the four conditions named above.

Note that the equity method should *usually* be used for all majority-held subsidiaries which are not consolidated, unless the cost method is necessitated by lack of influential control.

Foreign subsidiaries come under special standards and cost (with proper disclosure) may sometimes be used. (See later in this chapter.)

Other Considerations

A difference in fiscal period is no excuse for *not* consolidating. When the difference is no more than 3 months, use the subsidiary's fiscal-period report. Where greater than 3 months, corresponding period statements should be prepared for the subsidiary.

Intercompany items should be eliminated. (See later in this chapter.)

For partial years:

1) The year of acquisition: Consolidate for the year and, on income statement, deduct preacquisition earnings not applicable to the parent.

2) The year of disposition: do not consolidate income; show only equity of parent in the subsidiary's earnings prior to disposal as a separate line item.

Shares held by the parent should *not* be treated as outstanding stock in the consolidation.

When a subsidiary capitalizes retained earnings for stock dividends or split-ups effected as dividends, such transfer is not required for the consolidated balance sheet which reflects the accumulated earnings and capitalization of the group (not the subsidiary).

Combined Statements

This is the showing of the individual company statements *plus* the combined consolidation, which combination reflects all intercompany eliminations.

Examples of when to use combined statements:

1) Where one individual owns controlling interest in several related corporations; or

2) Where several companies are under common management; or

3) To present the information of a group of unconsolidated subsidiaries; or

4) When it is necessary to show the individual operations of parent as well as subsidiaries, as well as the consolidated results—for creditors usually. This type is also called a "Parent-Company" statement.

5) A subsidiary whose primary business is leasing to a parent should always be consolidated.

Limitations of Consolidated Statements

Along with their advantages, consolidated statements have certain limitations:

1) The separate financial position of each company is not disclosed.
2) The dividend policy of each company cannot be ascertained.
3) Any financial ratios derived from the consolidated statements are only averages and do not represent any particular company.
4) A consolidated income statement does not show which companies have been operating at a profit and which have been losing money.
5) Creditors who are concerned with the financial resources of individual companies would not get the information they desire.
6) Disclosing liens or other particulars of individual companies may require extensive footnotes.

(See Journal Entries, Appendix A, for example of Consolidating Entries.)

THE PURCHASE METHOD—BUSINESS COMBINATIONS

The Purchase Method accounts for a business combination as the acquisition of one company by another. The acquiring company records at its cost the acquired assets less liabilities assumed. A difference between the cost of an acquired company and the sum of the fair values of tangible and intangible assets less liabilities is recorded as goodwill. The reported income of an acquiring corporation includes the operations of the acquired company after acquisition, based on the cost to the acquiring corporation.

The financial statements should be supplemented after purchase with pro forma statements showing:

1) Results of operations for the current period as if the combination had occurred at the beginning of the period; and
2) Results for the immediately preceding period, presented as if they had combined.

The AICPA has listed some general guides for the assigning of values to certain individual items, as follows:

Receivables at present values of amounts to be received, less allowances for uncollectibles.

Marketable securities at net realizable values.

Inventories:

Finished goods at selling prices, less disposal costs and reasonable profit to the acquirer;

Work in process at selling price, less cost to complete, disposal cost and reasonable profit;

Raw materials at current replacement prices.

Plant and equipment at current replacement cost if to be used or, if to be disposed of, at net realizable value.

Intangibles (identifiable, excluding goodwill) at appraised values.

All other assets at appraised values (including land).

Accounts and notes payable, long-term debt and other claims payable at *present values*, using current rates.

Accruals at present values.

Other liabilities and commitments, at present values, determined by using appropriate current interest rates.

Goodwill should be amortized on a straight-line basis over a period not to exceed 40 years, and only to a shorter period if benefit can be pinpointed. Goodwill of the *acquired* company is not brought forward.

THE POOLING-OF-INTERESTS METHOD—BUSINESS COMBINATIONS

The pooling-of-interests method accounts for a business combination as the uniting of ownership interests of two or more companies by exchange of equity securities. No acquisition is recognized because the combination is accomplished without disbursing resources of the constituents. Ownership interests continue and the former bases of accounting are retained. The recorded assets and liabilities of the constituents are carried forward to the combined corporation at their recorded amounts. Income of the combined corporation includes income of the constituents for the entire fiscal period for which the combination occurs. The reported income of the constituents for prior periods is combined and restated as income of the combined corporations.

A pooling involves the combination of two or more stockholder interests which were previously *independent* of each other.

The AICPA has said that a business combination which meets *all* of the following 13 conditions should be accounted for as a pooling:

1) Attributes of the combining companies:

a) Each is autonomous and has not been a subsidiary or division of any other company for the prior two years; and

b) Each is independent (10 percent) of the other combining companies.

2. Manner of combining interests:

a) Effected within one year in a single transaction per a specified plan; and

b) The corporation issues only common stock identical with its majority outstanding voting stock in exchange for substantially all (90% or more) of the voting common stock of the acquired company at the date of consummation; and

c) None of the combining companies changes the equity interest of the voting common stock in contemplation of the combination within two years *before* the plan or between the dates the combination is initiated and it is consummated; and

d) No company re-acquires more than a normal number of shares and only for purposes other than for business combinations between the dates of initiation and consummation; and

e) Legal costs of pooling are expensed; and

f) The ratio of interest remains the same for each common stockholder, with nothing denied or surrendered, with respect to each person's proportion before the combination; and

g) Stockholder voting rights are neither restricted nor deprived of by the resulting combination; and

h) The plan is resolved at the planned date and no provisions remain pending or carried over after the combination.

3. There is the absence of the following planned transactions:

a) The combined corporation does not intend to retire or re-acquire any of the common stock issued to effect the combination; and

b) The combination does not enter any financial arrangements to benefit former stockholders (such as a guaranty of loans secured by stock issued in the combination); and

c) There is no intent or plan to dispose of any of the assets of the combination within two years after the combination other than those in the ordinary course of business or to eliminate duplicate facilities or excess capacity.

Financial statements of the current period, and of any prior period, should be presented as though the companies had been combined at the earliest dates presented and for the periods presented.

Disclosure should cover all the relevant details.

Purchase Method

Accounts Receivable	50,000	
Inventory	40,000	
Building	110,000	
Equipment	30,000	
Investments	5,000	
Goodwill	16,200	
Accounts Payable		25,000
Long-Term Debt		30,000
Unamortized discount on long-term debt		(3,800)
Common Stock (Par $10; 10,000 Shares)		100,000
Additional Paid-In Capital		100,000

Entry to apply the purchase method to account for the purchase of XYZ Co. assets and liabilities for 10,000 shares of common stock. Total purchase price $200,000 based on market price of the stock at date of consummation of $20 per share.

Amortization of Goodwill (1/40)	405	
Goodwill		405
Unamortized discount on long-term debt	760	
Discount Income		760
(Goodwill amortized on straight-line basis.)		

Pooling Method

It must be recognized that the two methods are not alternatives and it should not be inferred that there is a choice of one or the other method. Rather, the pooling-of-interests method can be applied only when 12 restrictive criteria as set forth in APB Opinion No. 16 "Accounting for Business Combinations" are met. GAAP requires *compliance* with *all* 12 of the conditions. If one or more of the criteria is not met, the purchase method of accounting for the combination *must* be applied.

The principal difference between the different methods of business combinations is the resulting corporate entity. In an *acquisition* both the acquired and acquiring companies remain as separate legal entities after the combination, with the acquiring company being the *parent* and the acquired company the *subsidiary*. In a *merger* two or more companies combine and one legal entity results, which can be any one of the combining companies. In a *consolidation*, the combining companies form a new legal entity.

Inventory	43,000	
Cash	5,000	
Accounts Receivable	60,000	
Allowance for Doubtful Accounts		7,000
Building	75,000	
Accu. Depreciation		15,000
Equipment	100,000	
Accu. Depreciation		60,000
Investments	4,000	
Accounts Payable		25,500
Long-Term Debt		30,000
Common Stock (Par, $10; 10,000 shares)		100,000
Additional Paid-In Capital		49,500

(Entries to reflect the pooling of XYZ Co. per the *book* value of the *items* on the date of *consummation*.) Note: *Goodwill cannot* be acquired by the *pooling* method.

APB Opinion No. 16 prohibits the use of treasury stock transactions for a business combination when a pooling of interest method is used. Treasury stock purchases are restricted to be used for purposes other than for business combinations for a period of two years before and during the period of the combination plan. Treasury shares acquired during this period are "tainted" and only a very small number of treasury shares can be used in a pooling. The restrictions on treasury stock purchased after the start of a plan are to prevent backdoor agreements to buy out certain stockholders.

FOREIGN SUBSIDIARIES

The following are the possible methods of providing information about foreign subsidiaries:

1) Exclude foreign subsidiaries from consolidation. Include a summary of their assets, liabilities, income and losses for the year and the parent's equity in such foreign subsidiary. The amount of investment in the foreign subsidiary and the basis by which it was arrived at should be shown. If the foreign subsidiary is excluded from consolidation, it is not proper to include intercompany profits (losses) which would have been eliminated by consolidating.

2) Consolidate domestic and foreign subsidiaries, furnishing information of the foreign subsidiaries' assets, liabilities, income and losses, as stated above.

3) Furnish complete consolidated statements:
   A) Including only domestic companies, *and*
   B) Including the foreign subsidiaries.

4) Consolidate domestic and foreign subsidiaries and furnish, in addition, parent company statements showing the investment in and income from foreign subsidiaries separately from those of domestic subsidiaries.

DISCS

A Domestic International Sales Corporation (DISC) is typically a 100%-owned domestic subsidiary corporation of a parent manufacturing or sales company, created especially for the purpose of benefiting from special tax provisions under IRS Code Section 991-997, and electing to be taxed thereunder.

The DISC income is derived predominantly (95% by tax law) from export sales and rentals. The primary accounting aspects are:

1) A DISC is a wholly owned domestic subsidiary and should be consolidated with the parent's financial statement. (The IRS prohibits it for tax purposes.)

2) Portions of the DISC's earnings are considered to be distributed by the IRS and taxable to the parent. Therefore, for accounting purposes, clear distinction should be made on the DISC's books setting up a "previously taxed dividend payable." The parent should set up a contra "previously taxed dividends receivable" until such time as the cash transfer is made.

3) For the remaining portion of the DISC's earnings, which are not deemed distributed but which will be picked up as part of the consolidated income, *no entry* should be made for the deferral of applicable income taxes, *unless* there is indication of impending distribution of those earnings. Since the main purpose of the DISC option is to *defer* taxability of those undistributed earnings, the presumption of non-distribution prevails, and the indefinite reversal criteria apply.

Changes in the Tax Law have replaced the DISC system with the Foreign Sales Corporation system (FSC) starting in 1985 (see Internal Revenue Code sections 921–927).

INTERCOMPANY TRANSACTIONS

In Consolidations

Since consolidated statements reflect the position and results of operations of what is considered a single economic entity, all intercompany balances and transactions must be eliminated. Some of these are obvious. Others are not.

Here are some of the items to be eliminated (done on worksheets which combine the company and its subsidiary figures):

1) The investment account in the subsidiary and its corresponding equity offset (capital stock and applicable retained earnings).

2) Intercompany open account balances, such as loans, receivables, payables arising from intercompany sales and purchases.

3) Intercompany security holdings, such as bonds, including related bond discount or premiums.

4) Intercompany profits where goods or services are exchanged for over cost, such as profits on transfers of inventory or fixed assets. Intercompany profits on fixed asset transfers might also involve adjustments to the accumulated depreciation account. Intercompany profits on inventory may affect both opening and closing inventories of raw materials, work in process and finished goods, as well as cost of sales.

5) Intercompany dividends.

6) Intercompany interest, rents, and fees.

7) Intercompany bad debts.

The amount of intercompany profit or loss eliminated is not to be affected by the existence of minority interests. Such items must be eliminated. However, in eliminating them, they may be allocated proportionately between the majority and minority interests.

If "bottom-line" accumulated losses occur to the extent of wiping out the minority interest, any excess losses should then be reflected against the *majority* interest, rather than showing a negative minority interest. However, future earnings should then first be applied to that excessive loss and the positive remaining earnings apportioned between the majority and minority interests.

In the Equity Method

Intercompany gains and losses should be eliminated in the same manner as if the subsidiary were consolidated. It is not necessary to eliminate intercompany gain on sales to such subsidiaries if the gain on the sales does *not* exceed the *unrecorded* equity in the *undistributed* earnings of the unconsolidated subsidiary. However, do *not* eliminate intercompany holdings or debt.

In Combined Statements

Intercompany transactions and intercompany profits and losses should be eliminated following the same manner as for consolidated statements.

Goodwill in Business Combinations

Goodwill arises only from the purchase method; no goodwill is created in the "pooling-of-interests" method of combining businesses, since assets and liabilities are carried forward to the combined corporation at their recorded amounts.

With respect to the purchase method and stock acquisitions treated under either the consolidation method or the equity method, accounting for goodwill requires its amortization over a period not in excess of forty years.

Goodwill is the amount assigned to the excess paid over the fair value of the identifiable net assets acquired.

Negative Goodwill

Negative Goodwill: When one company purchases another, negative goodwill arises where there is an excess of the assigned value of identifiable assets over the cost of an acquired company. The goodwill account has a credit balance. When the purchase price is less than the sum of the fair market value of the net assets acquired, the valuation of the noncurrent assets, except investments in Marketable Securities, must be reduced on a proportionate basis until the purchase price for the acquisition equals the adjusted valuation of the fair market value of the net assets acquired. If after the adjusted valuation of noncurrent assets is reduced to zero and the purchase price is still less than the net assets acquired, the difference is disclosed in the balance sheet as negative goodwill (a credit balance) and is amortized to income over a period not to exceed 40 years. (APB Opinion 16)

Summary

Consolidated Financial Statements: The combination of the financial positions and earnings reports of the parent company with those of various subsidiaries into an overall statement as if they were a single entity, i.e., the financial statements should reflect a group of affiliated companies as a single business enterprise—a single economic entity. The consolidated statements are in substance summations of the assets, liabilities, revenues, and expenses of the individual affiliates calculated on the basis of transactions with nonaffiliates. Intercompany transactions (transactions among the affiliates), intercompany investments, and account balances must be eliminated to avoid double-counting of resources, account balances, and operating results.

FASB Statement 94, *Consolidation of All Majority–Owned Subsidiaries*

FASB Statement 94 is designed to demonstrate the results of operations and the financial position of a parent company and its subsidiaries as if all the component companies were a single company with one or more branches or divisions. This objective is based on the position that, when one of the companies in a group has a controlling financial interest in the other companies, whether directly or indirectly, consolidated statements are more useful to shareholders and creditors than separate statements are necessary for a fair presentation. The normal requirement for a controlling interest revolves around a majority voting interest; in other words, one company claims ownership of more than 50 percent of the outstanding voting shares of the other company.

Statement 94 provisions add substantial amounts of debt on the balance sheets of many companies with unconsolidated subsidiaries in businesses entirely different from the parent. Companies in consumer products, auto, retail, and a number of other businesses have maintained finance, insurance, and real estate subsidiaries that were often more highly leveraged than the parent company.

In the past, this type of subsidiary could keep separate balance sheets when engaged in businesses substantially different from the parent corporation, or when the parent held less than a 50 percent interest. A real estate subsidiary, therefore, could develop an office building without the mortgage debt appearing on the parent company's balance sheet. However, FASB 94 requires companies to consolidate balance sheets even if the parent owns less than 50 percent of the subsidiary's stock as long as any degree of control is in the hands of the parent.

Companies can be expected to continue restructuring, repositioning, even divesting, in order to lessen the Rule's effect. Some companies may decide to sell subsidiaries affected by the Rule; other companies may devise more creative strategies than outright selling. They can separate the assets of their subsidiaries into separate and distinct entities over which they do not maintain control. For example, a company planning to develop existing real estate assets can form a partnership wherein it is the limited partner and the developer is the general partner.

Another approach enables a company to loan money to a subsidiary rather than take an equity position through stock ownership. Later the company can convert the debt into equity when the subsidiary's real estate project has been completed. The Rule makes it more difficult, but not impossible, for companies to buy, manage, or develop real estate through subsidiaries. The problem is to devise an approach for investing in real estate or other investments within the limits of the rule, while at the same time keeping as much debt as possible off the balance sheet.

However, these devices should not become so creative that they disguise the true financial status of the various components. The purpose of FASB 94 is to reveal the true picture of the whole. It may have been this type of creativity that made it necessary to adopt FASB 94 in the first place. A possible chance use of the word *heterogeneous* in paragraph 3 of ARB 51, *Consolidated Financial Statements*, resulted in an excuse, if not a valid reason, for avoiding consolidation of majority-owned subsidiaries as being *nonhomogeneous.* Under this paragraph, separate statements or combined statements would be considered preferable for a subsidiary or group of subsidiaries if it was believed that the presentation of financial information concerning the particular activities of such subsidiaries would be more informative to shareholders and creditors of the parent company than would the inclusion of these particular subsidiaries in the consolidation.

For example, separate statements were sometimes required for a subsidiary such as a bank, insurance company, or finance company when the parent and other subsidiaries were manufacturing companies. Nevertheless, abuses resulted and it was deemed necessary to stem the abuses in the interest of the investors and creditors. Therefore, Statement 94 requires companies to consolidate the balance sheets of the parent company and the company's subsidiaries. The Statement is intended to give a complete rundown of companies' assets and liabilities and to prevent corporate abuses in concealing debt through the use of subsidiaries.

The principal exception eliminated is the nonhomogeneity exception mentioned previously. Also eliminated as exceptions are large minority interests and foreign locations.

Only two exceptions remain allowable:

1) Subsidiaries under temporary control.
2) Subsidiaries that the majority owner does not actually control, as in the case of bankruptcy, a legal reorganization, or other governmental restriction.

Also eliminated is the use of only the parent company's financial statements as the primary financial statements of the reporting enterprise. It should be noted further that continuing disclosure of summarized financial information for subsidiaries consolidated as a result of FASB 94 is still required in the consolidated financial statements or notes, either for individual subsidiaries or in groups of similar types of enterprises.

Over a long period of time, business enterprises used nonhomogeneity as a basis for excluding from consolidation majority-owned (and even wholly owned) subsidiaries considered different in character from the parent company and its other affiliates. Subsidiaries most commonly not consolidated on that basis have been finance, insurance, real estate, and leasing subsidiaries of manufacturing and merchandising enterprises. However, some diversified

enterprises have consistently consolidated all of their majority owned subsidiaries despite differences in their operations. This resulted in similar enterprises using different consolidation policies. Excluding some subsidiaries from
consolidation resulted in the omission of significant amounts of assets, liabilities, revenues, and expenses from the consolidated statements of many enterprises. The omission of large amounts of liabilities, especially those of finance
and similar subsidiaries, led to the criticism that not consolidating those subsidiaries is an important factor for what has been termed off-balance-sheet
financing.

Statement 94 is important as a solution to the problem of off-balance-
sheet financing because unconsolidated majority-owned subsidiaries have
been a significant aspect of that problem. The growth in size and importance
over the years of finance and other unconsolidated majority-owned subsidiaries and the resulting amounts of assets, liabilities, revenues, and expenses that were not reflected in many consolidated financial statements resulted
in it being almost impossible to compare the economic health, or the lack of
it, of what should have been readily comparable companies.

Not only would this aspect of the "noncomparability" picture be of
interest to the investor or creditor, but also the internal user of the enterprise's financial statements has been affected. What useful information could
be obtained relating to differences in operational methods over a given period of time, or to financial status at comparison dates, if there were no basis for
comparison? Information that is most relevant to investors, creditors, and
other external and internal users of financial statements revolves around consolidated statements that are presented in a manner that clearly demonstrates
the result of operations and the financial position of a parent company and its
subsidiaries as if the group were a single company with one or more branches
or divisions. Therefore, consolidated financial statements that include all
majority-owned subsidiaries are significantly more informative than statements that exclude significant parts of an enterprise. Excluded parts would
presumably be the weak or atrophied parts that could actually be evidence of
a company's deteriorating financial condition.

Basic analytical tools are affected by whether a subsidiary was consolidated or accounted for by the equity method. One example is the debt-equity ratio, which is much lower if finance or other highly leveraged subsidiaries
were reported by the equity method rather than consolidated. Consolidation
of majority-owned subsidiaries results in significantly higher debt-equity
ratios for many companies and may have, or may still require, renegotiation
of loan covenants to avoid possible defaults. Affected companies can expect
to spend time reeducating creditors and examining alternatives for meaningful financial statement presentation. To encourage experimentation, FASB
does not outline specific rules for implementation, but leaves room for the
aforementioned creativity.

Use of the equity method for majority-owned subsidiaries that were significant parts of an enterprise provided less information about the enterprise. Consolidation of all majority owned subsidiaries greatly improves comparability between enterprises with similar information, especially quantitative information.

Consolidated financial statements that include all majority-owned subsidiaries result in more relevant information and comparable statements of cash flow. Although the equity method and consolidation may report the same net income and net assets, they do not report the same cash receipts and payments related to operating, investing, and financing activities. It is possible for significant information about how an enterprise generated cash to be omitted or obscured if subsidiaries are not consolidated.

Chapter 18

Management Principles

CAPITAL STRUCTURE

By capital structure we mean the division of the corporation's capital between debt and equity and the various classes within those categories.

Essentially, the capital structure is a means of allocating risk of loss, participation in profits and financial control by management. The final decision on the capital structure is usually governed by the kind of money available (debt or equity money) and the terms on which it can be obtained. Nevertheless, in organizing a new corporation, or in raising additional financing for an existing company, management should make an effort to formulate the financial structure which will be most desirable for the business in the long run.

Basic Principles to Follow

It is easier to obtain money from both equity and debt sources if the financial plan reflects basic economic principles. Generally, bonds are issued when future earnings of a corporation promise to be large and reasonably certain; preferred stock is issued when earnings are irregular but show promise of exceeding preferred stock dividend requirements; common stock is issued when earnings are uncertain and unpredictable. These principles are not automatic. Tax considerations may alter them. Debt financing has tax advantages.

Highest Return on Capital

The highest potential return on equity capital investment and the largest potential for capital appreciation are produced by the combination of the smallest possible proportion of equity investment—common stock—and the highest proportion of fixed amount debt. This is called trading on the equity, also commonly termed "leverage." A business borrows money in the hope that the borrowed funds will produce more earnings than the interest rate paid for the money. The danger is that failure to earn a rate of return higher than the interest cost of the borrowed money will consume basic capital and possibly result in creditors taking the business assets.

As an illustration, a business with $100,000 in capital stock can make 10% on capital. If it borrows another $100,000 and keeps its 10% earnings rate on the capital it uses, common stockholders will get a 14% return after paying 6% on the borrowed money. If the earnings rate can be increased to 15%, common stockholders will get a 24% return. But if the earnings rate on the capital employed declines to 5%, common stockholders will receive only 4%. If the corporation earns only 2% on its $200,000, 6% will still be payable on the $100,000 of borrowed money and the common stockholders' capital will be dissipated by 2% a year.

Increased earning power, inflation, or any other factor which operates to increase the dollar value of assets benefits common stockholders exclusively—not the holders of fixed-value notes or bonds, or of preferred stock. So the owners of the business will profit to a greater degree from appreciation in value and sustain any loss at a faster rate when there is a low proportion of common stock and a high proportion of fixed value obligations.

Taking Minimum Risks

Maximum safety calls for all common stock and no fixed obligations to pay interest and redeem loans. But debt may be advantageous to raise capital and to maximize income and capital gain possibilities. So a business may have to make a judgment on how far it can go into debt. Caution and prudence of lenders may, to a considerable extent, determine this factor. In general, a lender will want the borrower to have as much money at risk as the lender has; so this may restrict borrowing to no more than equal to the amount of invested capital. Often the owners will want to advance money to their business on a temporary basis, and this could increase the proportion of debt to equity.

Wise limits on the proportion of capital to debt vary in each situation, depending on the earnings prospects, stability of the business, and the financial position and skill of its management. The presence of one or more of the following factors, where a loan is required, would suggest caution before lending funds:

1) Instability of prices and volume.
2) Abnormally high percentage of fixed cost.
3) High rate of turnover.
4) Low ratio of profits to sales.

For example, a retail store should borrow proportionately less than an apartment house venture or a printing plant with a large fixed investment in heavy machines.

When expansion seems necessary or advantageous, good financing requires a high ratio of stocks to debt to provide borrowing power for future needs. However, if the owners are sure of their future earnings prospects and earning power and feel that a relatively short operating period will prove their judgment, they may borrow as much capital as they need—or can get—and hold off issuing stock until they can get a higher price for it. Because the capital requirements of a successful business can be expected to increase sharply, it may be wise to hold back enough stock for future expansion needs without heavy dilution of the owner's interest and control.

Maintaining Control of a Company

A financing plan that will bring in enough outside funds and also maximize control is often accomplished by giving sole voting power to a small common stock issue. The danger always exists that the owners' control will be lost and their interest diluted if they do not foresee and prepare for the rising financial requirements that successful operation brings. When further capital is needed, the owners may have to release too large a portion of their stock holdings to keep full control.

A preferred stock issue is usually used to secure the investor's money when some of the investing group contribute intangibles such as services, special skills, patent rights, etc., and so are entitled to a share of the profits over and above the normal return for cash investment. Again the owner of the underlying equity must anticipate and make sure that the financial requirements of a successful business can be obtained without loss of control and dilution of personal interest. The use of preferred stock allows the owner to retain a larger proportion of the common. As the business grows, issuance of additional voting stock may reinforce the owner's control by making it more difficult for another to purchase a controlling stock interest.

BUSINESS STRUCTURE CONSIDERATIONS

Any business enterprise is internally composed of two distinct human elements:

Employers—the owners of the business;

Employees—those employed by the owner.

(Sometimes an owner is an employee of his or her own firm, but the classification as an owner is unaffected.)

The owner (employer) of a business may be the founder—the one who initially organized and funded the operation—or a successor to that original founder. The founder, in starting the business, has several, but limited, options as to the *type* of legal business-structure format to be used for the operation. (Also, the founder or a successor may choose to change the structure from one type to another at a subsequent date.)

The primary considerations are:

1) The extent of personal liability should the business fail;
2) The comparative tax advantages offered by different methods of organization.

And the available options are:

1) Sole proprietorship
2) Partnership—in combination with one or more other owners
3) Corporation—in combination with others for legal formation, but there might in fact be subsequently a sole owner
4) Sub-chapter S Corporation—with others, or alone
5) Professional Corporation or Association—with others, or alone.

(A Joint Venture is merely a stop-gap entity from which profits flow to one of the above types of entity.)

If the owner places a priority on *tax-savings*, any format would be chosen in preference to the corporation format, which historically has been taxed on both the *earnings* and the *distribution (dividends)* of those same earnings. The Sub-S corporation and the Professional corporation (if electing the Sub-S option) do eliminate the double-taxation feature (and also offer the advantage of full corporate deductions for executive salaries, if paid timely), but they also involve personal taxation on all the undistributed earnings, which pass through to the individuals (with certain exceptions) effectively as in a partnership.

The owner who places priority on the *limitation* of personal liability will choose the corporate form (possibly with the Sub-S option). But he cannot choose the Professional corporation to limit liability, since most states prohibit this limitation by law (as for doctors, accountants, etc.).

Once the legal format is set, the method of financial accounting and reporting for that particular type of business is applied.

Most accounting textbooks and the guidelines seem to be directed toward the corporate method of accounting. The standards of maintaining records for most assets, liabilities and items of income and expense are generally applicable to any type of business structure. Whatever guidelines apply to the corporation also apply to most of the other forms of business entity, *except* in these areas:

1) The Capital or Equity section:
   A) Initial investment
   B) The sharing of profits/losses
2) Salaries/Drawings of owners
3) Income tax on the entity's profit
4) How to account for investments in subsidiaries or controlled nonsubsidiaries
5) Dissolution of the entity.

Here, in brief, are the major differences to recall or research for the various structures.

Clearly distinguish between *personal* expenditures and business expenditures. In proprietorships and partnerships, personal items are to be treated as drawings or withdrawals or as loans. In a corporation, treat as a loan or dividend.

In partnerships, the *partnership agreement* takes precedence and establishes all the rules, especially of distribution. The agreement should spell out: Capital contributions requirements and basis of assets or liabilities assumed, duties of the partners, time to be spent in the business, limitations on drawings, the ratio of sharing profits and losses, death provisions, insurance protection, loans and interest on loans. Salaries might, for example, be allotted to each working partner before the ratio-splitting of profits, but the salary plus the split-share of the remaining profit effactually go into that partner's capital account and are reduced by *actual drawings* (salary plus profit-withdrawal).

In *dissolution* of partnerships, liabilities to/from partners are paid before distribution, and *no* distribution is made in excess of each partner's just share needed for liquidation of liabilities.

Death usually dissolves a *partnership*, unless the agreement makes specific contingent provisions.

Financial statements for either a proprietorship or partnership should provide a "Statement of Capital Changes" (similar to a corporation's "Changes in Retained Earnings").

The valuation of assets (and/or liabilities) at original cost should be stated at fair value, in any structure. Goodwill is set up, if pertinent, and the Capital or Capital Stock section credited for the agreed ownership portion. (Law requires corporations sometimes to distinguish between "par value" and "excess of par.") "Negative goodwill" should be used to write down non-current (fixed) assets in an immediate proportion. Goodwill, if any, should be amortized for financial purposes over 40 years unless there is proof of a shorter benefit period. Goodwill is not deductible for tax purposes.

The *trade name*, if any, should be used on proprietorship or partnership statements, with disclosure of the type of business structure.

The "cash basis" of accounting is *not* a generally accepted accounting principle, and proper financial statements, when carrying an independent auditor's opinion, are either qualified ("subject to") or with a disclaimer, depending on the materiality of the difference had the accrual method been used.

Financial accounting for sole proprietorships and partnerships *should not* record accruals or deductions for the income tax which that owner or co-owner must pay on his or her respective share of the earnings. However, financial footnotes should make such a disclosure if the funds for such payment may deplete those belonging to the entity (as future "withdrawals").

The *equity method* of accounting for investments in subsidiaries or controlled non-subsidiaries is not permitted for sole proprietors, trusts or estates. Proprietors should carry investments *at cost*. Partnerships and joint-ventures should use cost adjusted for accumulated undistributed earnings.

Deferred taxes on undistributed earnings of subsidiaries or non-subsidiaries should *not* be set up for partnerships, because of the factor of "personal taxing" mentioned above.

Financial statements for sole proprietorships may show a "reasonable" salary allowance for the owner to arrive at a financial operating income. But the salary is still a withdrawal.

Consolidations are permitted a proprietorship (over 50% ownership):

1) If owning 100%, the investment is eliminated against equity;
2) If less than 100%, the minority interest is shown on the income statement before extraordinary items, and on the balance sheet between liabilities and net worth.

Other eliminations should be as in consolidations.

Joint ventures are usually not majority-controlled by any of the participants. Hence, consolidation is not in order. The equity method is used by partnerships or corporations that participate in a joint venture. Proprietors should use the cost method of investment. Sometimes, however, upon proper disclosure, "proportionate" consolidation is used. Here, a pro-rata share of assets, liabilities and income is consolidated.

LEASES AND LEASEBACKS

Leases today loom large in financing the acquisition of plant and equipment. The lease may be part of a sale-leaseback package or it may be the alternative to an outright purchase. A lease is preferred by some lessees because it does not usually require a large outlay of cash.

There are a number of terms in lease contracts that must be understood when considering a lease arrangement. These unique terms are defined below.

Bargain Purchase Option. A provision allowing the lessee, at his or her option, to purchase the leased property for a price that is sufficiently lower than the expected fair value of the property at the date the option becomes exercisable, provided that exercise of the option appears, at the *inception of the lease*, to be reasonably assured.

Bargain Renewal Option. A provision allowing the lessee, at his or her option, to renew the lease for a rental sufficiently lower than the fair rental value of the property at the date the option becomes exercisable. The exercise of the option must appear, at the inception of the lease, to be reasonably assured. ("Fair rental" means the expected rental for equivalent property under similar terms and conditions.)

Contingent Rentals. The increases or decreases in lease payments that result from changes occurring subsequent to the inception of the lease in the factors affecting the lease, other than the passage of time. Any factors that occur subsequent to the inception of the lease that materially affect the original minimum lease payments in the contract become contingent rentals, and must be considered in their entirety separately from the minimum lease payments.

Estimated Economic Life Of Lease Property. The estimated remaining period during which the property is expected to be economically usable by one or more users, with normal repairs and maintenance, for the purpose for which it was intended at the inception of the lease without limitation by the lease term.

Estimated Residual Value Of Leased Property. The estimated fair value of the leased property at the end of the lease term.

Executory Costs. Costs such as insurance, maintenance, taxes, and other costs associated with the lease property, whether paid by the lessor or lessee.

Fair Value Of Leased Property. The price for which the property could be sold in an *arm's-length transaction* between *unrelated* parties. Usually, the value is determined by the market price of similar property under market conditions prevailing at the time the lease is negotiated.

Inception Of The Lease. The date of the lease agreement, or commitment, if earlier. A commitment must be in writing, signed by the parties to the transaction, and specifically set forth the principal provisions of the transactions. No principal provision still to be negotiated qualifies for purposes of this definition.

Incremental Borrowing Rate. The rate of interest at the inception of the lease that the lessee would have had to pay to borrow the funds over a time period similar to the life of the lease for the funds necessary to have purchased the lease asset.

Initial Direct Costs. Costs incurred by the lessor that are directly associated with negotiating and consummating the completed transaction.

Interest Rate Implicit In The Lease. The discount rate applied to the minimum lease payments.

Lease Term. The fixed noncancelable term of the lease, plus all periods, if any, covered by bargain renewal options.

Minimum Lease Payments. The payments that the *lessee* is obligated to make for the leased property over the lease term. Also, any payments that the lessee must or can be required to make upon failure to renew or extend the lease at the expiration of the lease term, whether or not the payment would constitute a purchase of the leased property.

Related Parties. A parent company and its subsidiaries, an owner company, and joint ventures (corporate or otherwise), and partnerships, and an investor and its investees, provided that the parent company, owner company, or investor has the ability to exercise significant influence over operating and financial policies of the related party.

Renewal Or Extension Of A Lease The continuation of the original lease agreement beyond the original lease term, including a new lease under which the lessee continues to use the same property.

Unguaranteed Residual Value. The estimated residual value of the leased property exclusive of any portion guaranteed by the lessee or by any party related to the lessee or by a third party unrelated to the lessor.

Unrelated Parties. All parties that are not *related parties* as defined.

Lease or Buy?

This is a decision that many taxpayers are often faced with. And it cannot necessarily be made on the basis of lowest net-after-tax cost alone—although, of course, the net-after-tax cost is a big consideration. Often the scales may be tipped in favor of rental, because (1) the burden of maintenance is usually on the lessor, and (2) it's easier to switch to a new machine. The latter option may be of great importance where the possibility of a newer machine may make the previous one obsolete.

But the cost is undoubtedly a big factor. And in arriving at the net-after-tax cost, we have to take into account the impact of the various tax factors on each type of acquisition.

Before making the comparison, however, let's get straight just what we are comparing. On the one hand, we have a rental of a machine we do not own. On the other hand, we acquire ownership. What's more, we can acquire ownership by financing our purchase—a very large initial cash outlay of company funds may not be necessary. Most acquisitions today are made via the financing route. So, in a sense, in comparing rentals with purchases, we are comparing two different costs of money—the interest factor that's built into the rental structure and the interest that is paid for the equipment loan. And the tax factors have a considerable effect on determining the net cost.

Making the comparison.   Insofar as the rent paid is concerned, that's generally fully deductible for tax purposes. In addition, the lessor can pass through to the lessee the investment tax credit. Thus, the net cost is the gross rent less the tax benefit derived from both the deduction for rent and the investment credit.

On the purchase side, the buyer is paying both purchase price and interest. The interest is tax deductible. In addition, the buyer gets an investment credit and depreciation deductions. Thus, the net cost is the total of purchase price and interest, reduced by the tax benefits derived from the investment credit, the interest deductions and the depreciation deductions.

How to Set Up the Figures to Make the Comparison

There are a variety of rental arrangements available, and there are numerous financing arrangements available, as well. Rather than attempt to deal with a specific illustration that may or may not apply to the type of equipment you are likely to rent or buy, we have set forth two worksheets. One is for determining the first-year, after-tax cash cost of renting and the other for determining the first-year, after-tax cash cost of buying. Thus, you can insert your own figures on the worksheets and come up with a comparison that has meaning for you.

Worksheet for Determining First-Year, After-Tax Cost of Renting

1. Gross rent .... $ _____
2. Applicable tax rate .... _____
3. Tax saved via rent deduction (Line 1 × Line 2) .... $ _____
4. Net after-tax cost for first year (Line 1 minus Line 3) .... $ _____

Worksheet for Determining First-Year, After-Tax Cost of Buying

1. Total cost of acquired assets[1] .... $ _____
2. Cash down payment in first year .... $ _____
3. Other first-year installments paid .... $ _____
4. Interest paid on unpaid balance .... $ _____
5. Total cash outlay in first year (total of Lines 2, 3, and 4) .... $ _____
6. Regular depreciation .... $ _____
7. Interest paid (same as Line 4) .... $ _____
8. Total deductible items (total of Lines 6 and 7) .... $ _____
9. Total tax saved by deductions (Line 8 × tax rate) .... $ _____
10. Investment tax credit .... $ _____
11. Net after-tax, first-year cost (Line 5 minus Lines 9 and 10) .... $ _____

---

[1]Normally the total cost will be the contract price for the acquired assets. but if there is a trade-in, use adjusted basis—i.e., basis of the assets traded in plus balance paid or payable. If a trade-in is involved, substitute for the amount on Line 1 (for the purposes of this computation) the amount paid or payable for the equipment over and above the amount allowed by the seller for the trade-in.

PLANT FINANCING VIA LEASEBACKS

In a hypothetical example of a typical sale-leaseback deal by working through it, we can see how the figures affect both buyer and seller.

A corporation uses a plant in its business which it has owned for 15 years. Original cost was $1,000,000, of which $700,000 was allocated to the building and $300,000 to the land. It has taken $440,000 of depreciation, so its basis for the whole property is now $560,000. In January 1994, it decides to sell the property to an investor corporation if it can get a 15-year leaseback. The sale price is $760,000, with a net rental under the lease equivalent to a 15-year amortization of the $760,000 at a 9% return—or a rental of $77,225. Assume that the investor corporation can allocate $500,000 of its purchase price to the building for depreciation purposes.

The seller. The seller corporation has a $200,000 gain on the sale and pays a capital gains tax of $60,000. If it has borrowed $700,000 (the new amount it gets after the capital gains tax) at 9% interest payable over 15 years, on a constant payment basis, the yearly payment would have been $67,450. Over the 15-year period, the seller would have paid a total of some $1,012,000 instead of $1,158,000 (15 times $77,225) which it pays on the sale-leaseback. But in the case of the mortgage, the seller only gets a tax deduction for the $312,000 interest that it pays. This, together with the $260,000 depreciation that the seller had left on the property would have meant a total tax deduction of $527,000 or, at least 46% corporate rates, a saving of $263,000. The mortgage would have cost the seller $749,000 ($1,012,000 minus the tax saving). But, under the leaseback, the seller gets a tax deduction for the entire rental paid, so it gets a saving of $533,000 (46% of the entire 15-year rental), which would mean a cost to the seller of the leaseback of $625,000 ($1,158,000 minus $533,000). The result is that the sale-leaseback costs the seller $124,000 less than what the mortgage would have cost.

The buyer. The buyer, under the sale-leaseback, gets a deduction over the 15-year period of the lease of $500,000, the amount that it allocated to the building. This means that $500,000 of the rent income is protected from tax. The tax on the remainder is $302,000, so the net to the buyer on the sale-leaseback over the 15-year period is $856,000. If the buyer had taken a mortgage position in this particular property for $760,000 at 9% interest, it would have received $1,084,000 with $334,000 interest taxable to it (the remainder would have been mortgage amortization). This would have meant a total tax of $153,600 or a net after taxes to the buyer of $930,400. This is almost $74,400 more than the buyer's net in the case of the leaseback.

What the figures mean to both parties: Figures don't always tell the whole story. Here are some additional factors that can mean a great deal to one, or both, parties.

To the seller. The seller pays $124,000 less (net after tax deduction) than it would in the case of a mortgage. But to get this, the seller has given up its ownership of the property at the end of the lease. At present, the land is valued at $260,000. So, it appears, the seller actually loses $136,000. But this is deceptive. The seller's building wears out at the end of the lease and, because of the favorable aspects of the deal to the buyer, the buyer would be able, at the time of the sale-leaseback, to give the seller an option to renew for, say, another 10 or 15 years at a very low rental. Any improvements constructed by the seller during the renewal term would be depreciated by the seller. Also, the sale-leaseback provides the seller with the maximum amount of financing, since with the property worth $760,000, it would be hard (due to legal limitations on the amount of the mortgage in relation to market value and to the desire by the mortgagees for protection), in most states, to get a mortgage for the full market value.

To the buyer. In effect, the buyer has $74,400 of investment left in the property at the end of the original lease term. The buyer has gotten out a 9%

yield, plus the rest of the "principal" and will own the property worth at least $260,000, if land values don't change. The buyer can afford to give the seller a renewal lease at a rental of only $7,000 a year, and still get a 9% before-tax return on the $74,000. By this method, during the renewal lease term, the seller will have the land on a tax-deductible basis. And if the renewal lease is set up properly, any improvements will not be income to the buyer. At the end of the renewal term, or the original lease if the seller does not renew, the buyer still owns the land.

Special Forms of Sale-Leasebacks

Besides the conventional sale-leaseback between two unrelated parties, there are some specialized forms of setting up this type of transaction.

New construction.   Here a builder may arrange the financing of a new plant for a business corporation by getting that corporation to agree to lease the property, and by interesting an investor in the purchase of the property upon completion. In the meantime, the builder will obtain construction financing unless the investor is an insurance company or pension trust which can handle the financing from commencement of construction.

Exempt organizations.   Educational and charitable organizations and other tax exempts have been heavy buyers in these deals. They enjoy a favorable tax status and so can afford to offer the seller a good deal—the seller deducts the rent, but the charity is not ordinarily taxed on it as income unless it is unrelated to its exempt functions. Consequently, the charity will be able to charge less rent than an ordinary investor. Also a charity or educational institution is exempt from local realty taxes, usually.

When you sell to a tax-exempt organization, it will pay you to hold on to the furniture and equipment and any other depreciable property which the buyer doesn't want. The buyer gets no benefit from the depreciable deduction since the buyer pays no tax. You might as well keep these deductions for yourself.

FASB Statement 98, *Accounting for Leases (Sale–Leaseback Transactions Involving Real Estate, Sales–Type Leases of Real Estate, Definition of the Lease Term, Initial Direct Costs of Direct Financing Leases)*

Statement 98 specifies the accounting by a seller-lessee for a sale-leaseback transaction involving real estate or real estate with equipment. The Statement also modifies the lease-term provisions of FASB Statement 13 with respect to all leases, as well as the accounting by a lessor for sales-type leases of real estate that provide for the transfer of title, and the accounting for initial direct costs of direct financing leases.

The Statement clarifies that a seller-lessee can use sales-leaseback accounting for a transaction involving real estate or real estate with equipment only if the transaction qualifies for sales treatment under FASB Statement 66, *Accounting for Sales of Real Estate*. The Statement indicates that any continuing involvement with the property by the seller-lessee, other than a normal leaseback, would preclude accounting for the transaction as a sale. A "normal leaseback" would involve the active use of the property during the lease-term in the seller-lessee's trade or business.

Amended are the lease-term provisions of Statement 13 for all leases to include all renewal periods during which a loan related to the leased property from the seller-lessee to the buyer-lessor is expected to be outstanding. The definition of the lease term also is expanded to include all renewal periods for which a significant penalty, defined in the Statement, would be incurred by the lessee if the lease were cancelled. These amendments will result in lease terms that generally are longer than previously contemplated.

Statement 98 also amends the definition of a "sales-type" lease that involves real estate, including real estate with equipment. Under the amended definition, a sales-type lease involving real estate must transfer title to the property at or shortly after the end of the lease term. Otherwise, the lease would be classified and accounted for as an operating lease.

The Statement clarifies the amendment in FASB Statement 91 to specify that initial direct costs associated with direct financing leases are to be capitalized separately from the gross investment in the lease and amortized to income over the lease term so as to produce a constant periodic rate of return.

FORCES BEHIND BUSINESS SALES AND ACQUISITIONS

The accounting and financial officers of the company will be involved in any arrangements to buy a business or sell an existing business. Questions of value, technique (purchase or sale of assets or stock), accounting treatment (will the acquisition qualify as a "pooling-of-interest"?), tax consequences, desirability of the acquisition or sale all may be within the province of the chief financial officer and his or her staff.

Many businesses diversify and build up sales volume by acquiring other businesses. Capital values can be built by acquiring additional product lines, moving into new territory, etc. Financial statements may be improved. Taxes may be saved by acquiring companies with operating loss carry-forwards. This is done through tax-free exchanges.

We see an increasing use of a combination of methods that include leases, mortgage financing, and percentage and deferred purchase arrangements. They give a maximum retention of capital for regular business operations.

Benefits of Merging

Here's a list which will orient your own thinking and help you in any trade or negotiations with other firms:

1) *Many young companies just don't have the cash* to realize their potential. This is particularly true in areas which require nationwide merchandising, heavy development work, and expensive productive equipment.

2) *Diversification* is a major reason for acquisitions. The reasons for seeking diversification are numerous. For example, a company may be seeking to get into the so-called areas of today: e.g., electronics, chemicals, atomic energy. By picking up a company already in one of these fields, it may get into the desired area much more economically than otherwise. Diversification may also be sought where a company needs funds to expand into a new field. By first diversifying, it hopes to broaden its profit base and increase its growth, with the new funds generated by growth used to get into the areas the company originally sought to enter. Diversification may also be sought by companies in cyclical business by acquiring companies not subject to severe ups and downs. In this way, the acquiring company hopes to make its financial problems less burdensome in the periods when it needs substantial financing and to overcome periods of low revenue when business is contracted.

3) *Some firms merge with others to get into a new line because investors do not value the industry or its earnings very highly.* Unless such companies can substantially convert into another industry, they cannot realize a large mark-up in capital values.

4) *Many companies realize that they must have more volume to carry the research and overhead staff necessary to stay competitive today.* The volume required to carry necessary research will vary industry by industry. For example, one company doing about $12 million a year acquired enough additional lines of business to bring its volume up to $20 million. Anything less would have made the firm hard-pressed to carry on the research and staff services needed to compete with others in its industry.

5) *Plants become idle* as a result of a company's product lines becoming obsolete, or volume drops off for some other reason. The company finds itself with excess plant capacity. Where this plant capacity—e.g., machinery, equipment, etc.—is in good shape, and is not itself obsolete, acquiring a new business may be the best way of making use of this excess plant capacity. This may be a far better solution than a gradual shutdown and a contraction of the existing business.

6) *Companies are sometimes acquired to get their special attributes.* For example, it may be desirable to get the key personnel of a particular company, and the only way is to get the company as well. In other cases, an acquired company may have special machinery already available which might cost a considerable amount in dollars and time to reproduce. Sometimes the acquired company may have a sales organization which would be just what the acquiring company needs. It may be more economical to acquire the company than to try to build up a similar sales organization.

7) *Some new, successful companies are taxed so high that there's very little left for investors and expansion.* These make ideal buys for other firms with loss carryovers, which might be used to protect subsequent profits earned by the combined operation.

8) *Some companies have found that it doesn't pay to continue a product line which doesn't yield a specified volume.* One company decided to dispose of all subsidiaries and divisions which did less than $10 million a year. Many companies are trying to earn the premium which investors pay for stability of earnings. They seek diversification which will allow one line to hold up and balance off other lines which run through recessions.

9) *Many companies go on the block because their owners are faced by a personal estate tax squeeze* and aren't able to get money out of a profitable business to make their personal portfolio liquid. The only solution is to sell part or all the business at capital gains rates or merge with a publicly traded company.

10) *Many businesses don't want to distribute dividends* but would prefer to use accumulated earnings to acquire other products and expand into new territory or product lines.

11) *Closely-held companies, or companies with cash and mortgagable assets locked up in the corporation, offer a good buying opportunity*—(a) to companies with fairly marketable stock, which can acquire the locked-up assets by an exchange of stock, or (b) to companies with a cash surplus which permits them to buy stock or assets at a discount (likely because the original owner who taps the assets by taking a dividend distribution has to pay a heavy tax rate).

12) *Some companies with strong earnings position can reap big advantages by picking up a smaller company.* Suppose the market values a firm 15 times earnings. If the firm can then pick up a smaller company for 5 or 6 times earnings (frequently possible), it will realize an automatic profit for its stockholders and still be able to plow some earnings into building up the new acquisition.

13) *When two companies in the same business merge, they can often bring about a number of operating economies.* Bulk purchasing for both companies may cut the unit cost of purchases. In some cases, duplicating facilities may be eliminated—e.g., one warehouse may serve the purposes of both businesses and one warehouse may therefore be eliminated.

Buy-Sell Agreement for a Business Acquisition

When you sign on the dotted line. . . .
You are inflexibly obligated. . . .

What This Discussion Is About

This discussion concerns the negotiations and completed agreement for the sale-purchase of a business enterprise. Before an agreement of any kind is signed, the respective parties have freedom of choice and action. After a contract is signed, the principals are committed to perform precisely according to the terms of the agreement—options are no longer available.

What Is a Contract?

Before discussing the specifics of a business acquisition, it might be helpful to remind ourselves of the salient aspects of a contract generally, as a buy-sell agreement for a business is a contract.

A contract is simply a set of legal rules of a business transaction which two or more parties agree to live by. Buyers and sellers are adversaries, albeit friendly in most instances. Each one wants the best deal possible. That is why each side must be careful, because each side will strive for terms favorable to his or her own interests and objectives.

Two Common Pitfalls. Broadly, there are two common pitfalls that should be avoided:

- A contract may obligate you in ways you did not expect or intend when you signed.
- A contract may *not* obligate the other party in ways you expected him or her to be obligated.

Obligating yourself in unexpected ways can be avoided by careful scrutiny of the document before signing. (Details to watch out for will be covered in the next few pages.)

Failure to obligate the other party in proper ways is a more elusive pitfall. You tend to know more precisely what you are obligating yourself to do than what you think the other party should do. The inherent danger of this pitfall is that the failure to obligate the other party as you intended is not discovered until it is too late. Be mindful! You have no chance to make changes in a contract after you have signed on the dotted line. (Details concerning how to protect yourself against this pitfall will also be discussed in subsequent pages.)

Essential Ingredients of a Contract. Let's briefly examine the essential elements of any type of contract.

- A contract offers flexibility. That is to say, the law does not specify the exact wording of contracts. The parties concerned structure and furnish the wording for the agreed upon terms of a transaction.

- Contracts can be bilateral (two opposite parties), or multilateral (more than two parties involved).
- A contract starts from different positions of the parties; the signed contract brings the parties together because it represents agreement to the same set of *promises*.
- Note, again, the word "promises" above. A contract must contain promises of the parties concerned to do something: "I promise to do this if you promise to do that."
- A contract must be supported by *consideration*. Consideration is something of value received (or given) at the request of the promisor in reliance upon and in return for his or her promise.
- Most formal contracts have a uniform format consisting at least of: A heading, such as *Sale of Business Assets*.

  Date and geographic location of the agreement.

  The names of the parties involved.

  Recitals of facts.

  The promise clause(s).

  The body of the contract.

  Signatures of the contracting parties.

  Signatures of witnesses, with the calendar day and year.
- The law does not guarantee that every promise in a contract is enforceable. A contract to commit a crime, for example, is unenforceable because the commitment is an illegal act in the first place.

It should be noted that the general pattern of contracts developed more as a matter of practice than of any legal requirements for a set format. A contract can be valid and binding without any formal design. For example, an exchange of letters containing the agreed upon terms can be a valid and binding contract.

Negotiation

A contract is preceded by negotiations between the parties. What is negotiation? Negotiation can be thought of as the bargaining prelude to the final agreement, during which "opposite" parties become "alike." The negotiation process clarifies alternatives, resolves issues, establishes promises, determines future courses of conduct, and results in legally-enforceable obligations explicitly written into the document. Negotiation ends when the contract is signed.

In the course of negotiating the sale, the seller usually makes statements of fact to the buyer regarding the business and its assets. The buyer should verify the facts regarding such items as:

- The dollar amount of sales.
- Title to property being sold.
- Number and specific facts about the seller's customers.
- Manner of operation of the business.
- Validity of patents or other intangible rights.
- All contracts to which the seller is a party.
- Other material information.

Where such facts are important to the buyer, he or she should consult with an accountant for the financial aspects and with an attorney for the legal ramifications in order to incorporate the appropriate details into the contract.

Be Mindful. Protections that *might* have been included, possibilities that *might* have been considered, choices that *once* were available, all are foreclosed when you sign the contract at the completion of negotiations. Experience has demonstrated that most disputes relating to buy-sell agreements arise because significant details of the agreement were not precisely defined, or omitted entirely by oversight.

A Complex Transaction

The purchase and sale of an ongoing business is a complex transaction. It can involve the transfer from the seller to the buyer of many different kinds of items, commonly among which are:

- Inventory.
- Accounts receivable.
- Contracts of various sorts.
- Plant, machinery, equipment.
- Goodwill.
- Leaseholds.
- Patents and copyrights.
- Payables.
- Long-term liabilities.
- Equities.

Time-Lag Problem. The transaction usually involves a time-lag. There is a period of time between the date of agreement of the parties and the actual transfer of the business. It is not uncommon, for example, for payment to be not always entirely in cash. The manner of paying the deferred balance is a significant item in the negotiations, with final transfer to the buyer delayed until payment is completed. The basic problem is: Who runs the business until then?

Two Methods. When a going business is a corporation, two methods of sale and purchase exist. The corporation can sell the assets or the shareholders can sell their shares of stock. Under either method, the buyer gets a going business, but there are significant differences in results and tax consequences in these methods for both the buyer and seller.

The Buyer's Position. Ordinarily, the buyer prefers to purchase the assets of a going business, *net* of liabilities. The buyer then acquires only assets and none (or as few as possible) of the existing debt of the seller's company. The purchaser who buys all outstanding shares of stock acquires a corporation with all its known and unknown (beware!) liabilities.

The tax situation is different between the two methods. The cost of shares of stock is a capital expenditure, no part of which is depreciable. But when the net assets are purchased, the tax treatment of the cost of business assets depends upon the kinds of assets purchased. Capital items, like machinery, are depreciable. Inventory is part of the cost of goods sold. Generally, the tax statutes and regulations tend to favor purchase of business assets rather than shares of stock.

On the other hand, an important advantage in the purchase of corporate shares is the simplicity of the transaction. Only one item—the stock—is involved, which can be transferred with the stroke of a pen. When the assets are purchased, negotiations involve the complication of determining price, which in turn involves evaluation techniques of the business assets and liabilities. The latter tends to be the number one cause of breakdowns in the negotiations and withdrawal of the parties from the proposed acquisition, because of the extended negotiations and agreement on the value of such items as inventory, capital assets, real estate, goodwill, and other assets, tangible and intangible. In addition, there must be agreement regarding the valuation of liabilities, especially contingent liabilities, such as the outcome of ongoing litigation against (or for) the company, warranties outstanding, and the like.

The Seller's Position. The seller of a business usually wants to sell the corporation's stock when disposing of the business, primarily because of the simplicity, as noted, of a stock transaction compared to the complication of assets and liabilities valuation problems. The sale of assets leaves the owner-stockholder with a corporate entity, commonly termed a *corporate shell.* If the shell is the sole asset of the corporation, there is no reason for the corporation's continued existence after the assets are sold. But three problems still can remain for the seller:

- To convert any unsold assets, if any, to cash. Some assets might not have been sold—accounts receivable, for example.
- To dissolve the corporation and distribute remaining assets to the shareholders.
- Enter income taxes. The sale of corporate shares involves only one taxable event. The sale of assets is one taxable event, the disposition of

remaining assets, if any, is another taxable event, and corporate dissolution is still another taxable event.

Mechanics. The parties must reach agreement, not only upon the substance of the sale and purchase, but also upon the terms by which the deal will be consummated. It is possible that the consent of other persons may be required, for example, when the seller is a lessee and is assigning a leasehold interest. Documents in proper form must be prepared, signed, and ready for delivery by one party to the other.

There is frequently a lapse between the time the parties agree and the completion of the transaction. The time lapse is more critical in the sale of a going business than in most other routine sale-purchase transactions, simply because of the nature of the commodity being sold; i.e., an ongoing business. Does the seller continue the operation until the sale is final? Does the buyer want to take over promptly because he does not want others to operate the business that he will ultimately own?

Both parties usually want the business to continue during the transition period as it has been operated to date. The negotiations and final contractual agreement regarding the operation of the business during the transition period can be fully as complex as the negotiations for the sale price.

Professional Assistance

The seller and buyer of a business will become associated (presumably) with at least two odd species of advisors throughout the process of negotiating and closing a business acquisition. Who? An accountant and a lawyer! Who else?*

In a more serious context, both can perform services valuable to the principals. In fact, it would be foolhardy for a businessperson to attempt to sell (or buy) a business without accounting and legal services.

The Accountant—How to Use. The traditional habitat of an accountant has been that of a backroom office, with the accountant leaning over a long-legged desk, thick-rimmed glasses, pouring over an endless stack of accounting worksheets. Today accountants' responsibilities and services to clients have broadened considerably to include tax preparation and advisory and consultative services on financial matters.

Specifically, the accountant can:

- Determine the integrity of the financial statements. Even a simplified (but audited) balance sheet can be very informative. The explanatory footnotes to the financial statements can particularly be a gold mine of

---

*The authors once heard the following definitions of lawyers and accountants. "A lawyer is one who uses incomprehensible language." "An accountant is one who uses incomprehensible figures."

information. It is only half in jest to say that if business managers took the time to read the footnotes, they could avoid the distasteful task of analyzing and interpreting the inundation of numbers in the financial statements.

- Interpret audited statements which oftentimes represent long (and not always amicable) discussions between the company's independent auditor and executive management agreeing upon whether or not certain "material" matters, particularly negative financial information, should be disclosed in financial reports.
- Assist in the analysis of the financial data and other financial information furnished by the other side.
- Prepare *pro forma* financial information; i.e., financial statements based upon the assumption that the acquisition had already taken place.
- Assist in asset and liability valuations.
- Assist in income tax considerations, along with the attorney.
- Make a fundamental technical determination concerning the acquisition method—"pooling-of-interest" or "purchase" methods. (The technical considerations and consequences of the two methods are book-length in their aspects, far beyond the scope of this book. The accountant is familiar with the rules that must be applied to these choices.)
- Impartially apply "Generally Acceptable Accounting Principles" (acronym: GAAP). However, the accountant has broad leeway in the principles to be applied. Therefore, the accountant can advise entirely legitimate accounting methods which can, in fact, cause differences in results; i.e., differences in income, tax liabilities, capital (equity) changes.

The Lawyer—How to Use. Lawyers, too, have had their traditional habitat—the courtroom. But over the years legal services have expanded; in fact, many attorneys never see a courtroom, rather they specialize in different aspects of the law. As related to the substance of this chapter, sellers and buyers of a business could engage the services of a lawyer who specializes in the law of contracts, who actually makes a career solely of helping clients to negotiate and develop the terms of a buy-sell agreement for a business acquisition.

Specifically, the lawyer can:

- Draft a letter of intent, if utilized.
- Raise questions to be answered by the parties to the transaction (as well as questions for other professional advisors being retained).
- Suggest techniques for structuring the transaction.
- Develop the basic terms of the agreement as negotiations proceed.
- Advise on the form of the acquisition from the standpoint of legal considerations.

- Handle the preparation and closing of the acquisition documents (the final contract for signatures).

Two Common Errors. There are two common errors associated with the employment of accountants and lawyers in an acquisition.

- The first is to fail to use their services at all, or to give them a minor technical role, i.e., asking the accountant to check only if the financial statements make sense or asking the attorney only if the written agreement is legally binding as written.
- The second is a more common error—too much reliance on professional advisors. The business aspects of an acquisition are primary areas of responsibility for the managing officers of the seller's and buyer's respective companies. The parties concerned are in charge throughout the acquisition process, and should be totally independent of their professional advisors when making decisions along the way.

SUMMARY OF POINTS TO REMEMBER

- The sale of a business is a complicated transaction. Any number of items of material amounts of money are included in the sale of a business.
- Seller and buyer should agree at least on the items being sold and purchased, price, payment method, date and place of transfer of possession to the buyer, and the mechanics of continued operation of the business between the date of agreement and date when the sale is completed.
- Seller will usually prefer to sell shares of stock, rather than have the corporation sell its assets.
- Not all of the business assets will necessarily be sold.
- Both parties should understand clearly their obligation as set forth in the agreement. *Minds cannot be changed after the contract has been signed.*
- Seller should be secure with respect to deferred payment of any balance of the purchase price.
- Buyer should make certain to purchase the assets necessary to conduct the business.
- Buyer should be aware of all the obligations being assumed.
- Buyer should have explicit covenants (items) in the contract regarding future competition from the seller. A covenant for the seller not to compete, usually for some specified period of time or within the confines of a specified geographic area, is not uncommon in a sale-purchase contract of a business.
- Negotiate all the provisions you want before signing.

- Be certain the appropriate promises and consideration are in the terms of the contract.
- Both parties should recite all facts; all of the facts should be verified.
- Each party to the agreement should be clearly identified—no "hidden" principals.
- Take care to ascertain if possibly a trustee, incompetent, receiver, executor, or other parties might be involved.
- All signatures should be clearly legible.
- Preserve the completed and fully-signed contract, with all accompanying documents.
- There is no legal difference with respect to the format and design of a contract. A contract can be typed, printed, handwritten, or an exchange of letters.

Broadly. Both the seller and buyer of a business should:

- Ask the lawyer: "What is the worst that can happen?"
- Ask the accountant: "What financial information do I need?"

Conclusion of Buy-Sell Agreement

An agreement for the sale-purchase of a business should at least tell the seller of a business what he should do, when he should do it, and what will happen if he doesn't do it.

The acquisition contract should at least tell the buyer what he should do, when he should do it, and what will happen if he doesn't do it.

FINANCING—SHORT-TERM

Banks, finance companies and factors are the usual sources of short-term funds, although some finance company loans and bank term loans may run for a fairly long term or provide for a continuing line of credit.

Short-term credit may be available on the strength of the overall financial soundness of the borrower or for specific collateral—often accounts receivable.

ARRANGING FOR CREDIT LINES WITH BANKS

The most readily available and frequently used source of money for a business is a bank loan. For most businesses, banks are only a source of temporary short-term money. To qualify for an unsecured bank loan, a company has to be substantially established and adequately supplied with equity money. The exceptions are cases in which the bank is lending on the strength of the personal credit of the proprietor, or principal stockholder, or somebody else who underwrites the loan for the borrowing business.

In dealing with banks, it is important to understand the nature of a commercial banking operation. The money it lends is that placed with it by depositors plus its own capital. A portion of the deposited money is set aside in reserves, another portion is held to meet the depositors' regular demands for cash, and the remainder is available for loans. Neither banking laws nor banking practice permit investment in a business or making capital loans in lieu of equity capital.

Selecting a Bank

The choice of a bank is important in the development of proper credit facilities, and a good banking connection once made is a valuable asset. As a general rule, it is not necessary to shop around for a banking connection—a local bank can usually meet the company's banking needs in a satisfactory manner. Some companies deliberately patronize more than one bank with the idea that if one bank turns down a request for a loan, the other will grant the loan. But this may backfire. One bank may want quick repayment for fear that the other will get repayment first. Where the local bank has restrictions which make it unable to meet the company's requirements, it is wise to go to another bank. But ordinarily it pays to give one bank all your business, in the expectation that the bank will take care of a good customer in time of financial stress. Banks prefer the exclusive arrangement. In times of financial need the bank whose officials have a good working knowledge of a company's operations and financial background can take care of its credit needs more quickly and effectively.

How the Banker Judges a Borrower.   The banker will study the financial statements of the borrower, using many of the ratios described in this book.

In addition, the banker will want further information, obtainable partially from discussion with the prospective borrower, partially from checking the bank's credit files, and partially from checking with other creditors. The customer's or prospect's credit file, which contains the accumulated information about a particular business and its owner, is of tremendous importance in every loan decision. It is a marked trail which leads experienced lending officers back through the history of the organization and its officers and enables them to uncover and evaluate information that might not otherwise be made available.

The banker will want to know these things about the prospective borrower:

1) Its character, ability, and capacity.
2) What kind of capital resources does it have?
3) What kind of business organization is it? How good are its executives? What has been its sales trend?
4) Will the loan be a sound one? Are any of the following conditions present to an extent which would throw doubt on the financial soundness of the business:

   a) Heavy inventories in relation to sales.
   b) Excessive dividends and salary withdrawals.
   c) Heavy loans to officers of subsidiary organizations.
   d) Large past-due receivables.
   e) Top-heavy debt.
   f) Too much invested in fixed assets.
   g) An overextended position—i.e., scrambling to apply income and funds to pay the most insistent creditors.

Types of Bank Accommodations

A company should familiarize itself with the various kinds of loan accommodations a bank is willing to extend, the interest rates, terms, and security requirements of each.

A line of credit.   A line of credit is merely a declaration by a bank that, until further notice, it is prepared to lend up to a stated maximum amount on certain terms and conditions to the prospective borrower. Since the line of credit is only a declaration of intent, it can be canceled at any time. The availability of a line of credit is very valuable because, instead of fixed credits which call for continuing interest, only amounts of money actually used, plus a small commitment fee on any portion of the original commitment not actually borrowed, are charged, which add up to inexpensive financing.

The application for a line of credit is not an application for a loan but simply an arrangement under which the bank agrees to make loans if funds are needed. But even so, a bank conducts an intensive investigation before granting the line of credit.

Term loans.   A business loan which runs for a term of more than one year with provisions for amortization or retirement over the life of the loan is a term loan. Such a loan, even if secured, will depend upon the bank's appraisal of the long-range prospects of the company, its earning power and the quality of its management. The term is usually a maximum of ten years.

Short-term loans.   Short-term bank loans are obtained either by individual borrowing or by obtaining a *line of credit* against which advances may be obtained. Short-term borrowing is available to companies that have sufficient credit to minimize the bank's risk. The loan is granted on the basis of a study and analysis of the financial position of the company. The security for these loans is a series of promissory notes which evidence the cash advance. These notes have maturity dates calling for repayment within one year, at which time they are reviewed, repaid, reduced or extended. Short-term loans are particularly effective for seasonal financing and the financing of inventories, or to keep things running smoothly during spurts of seasonal activity. Before granting a short-term loan, the bank may require that between 10% and 20% of the loan actually made be kept on deposit (called a compensating balance), or that the loan be cleaned up at least once a year to prevent the use of bank credit as permanent funds.

Character loans.   These are short-term, unsecured loans, generally restricted to companies or individuals with excellent credit reputations.

Installment loans.   Large banks generally grant this type of loan. Installment loans are made for almost any productive purpose and may be granted for any period that the bank allows. Payments are usually made on a monthly basis; as the obligation is reduced, it often may be refinanced at more advantageous rates. The installment loan can be tailored to the seasonal requirements of the company.

Equipment loans.   An increasingly popular method of raising funds is to borrow money against machinery and equipment. There are two main ways of handling equipment loans. The first is to pledge equipment to which the company has an unencumbered title as security for the loan. The second method is via an installment financing plan.

Time purchase loans.   Many special types of time purchase loans are available to finance both retailer and consumer purchase of automobiles, household equipment, boats, mobile homes, industrial and farm equipment, etc., and are made for varying periods of time, depending on the product. This category also includes accounts receivable financing, indirect collections and factoring.

Inventory loans. These loans are available if the merchandise or inventory can qualify as collateral. The requirements are stiff and the loans are limited to certain classes of inventory.

Accounts receivable loans. Small banks are not usually equipped to offer this type of loan, and the majority of their business customers are too small to take advantage of it. Under this loan, the bank takes over the company's accounts and notes receivable as collateral for the loan.

Warehouse receipt loans. Under this plan, goods are stored in warehouses and the warehouse receipts are used as security for a loan to pay off the supplier. As fast as the company is able to sell the merchandise, it pays off the bank loan. This loan permits the company to get along without a large amount of working capital.

Collateral loans. A company may be able to obtain bank loans on the basis of such collateral as chattel mortgages, stock and bonds, real estate mortgages, and life insurance (up to the cash surrender value of the policy). Even with collateral, the bank will still give great weight to the company's ability to repay. The bank may turn down the application for a loan, no matter how good the collateral, if there is not a clear showing of ability to repay.

SHORT-TERM BORROWING FROM COMMERCIAL FINANCE COMPANIES

A commercial finance company will frequently step in where a commercial bank will not. Commercial finance companies charge a higher rate and will sometimes take more risk and almost always take on more clerical work to protect their money. Because many companies in the commercial finance field are also engaged in factoring, there is a tendency to confuse the two. Factoring is the service rendered through the assumption of the credit risk on sales purchased from the factored company and the acceptance of the bookkeeping and collection responsibilities for the resulting receivables. In contrast to factoring, the commercial finance company does not guarantee against credit losses on sales to customers.

Finance companies do not "lend" money—they provide revolving working capital. Perhaps this is a subtle distinction, but if a company requires borrowed money it should, if qualified, resort to the many commercial banks throughout the country to satisfy that need. Banks and commercial finance companies are not in competition with one another. Finance companies are among the largest borrowers of money from commercial banks, and commercial banks very frequently refer their customers to finance companies when the capital position of the prospective borrower is insufficient for the bank to grant the credit lines needed.

Funds advanced by commercial finance companies are secured by collateral—mainly accounts receivable—and the finance company has recourse to the borrowing firm. The decision to advance the necessary funds is based, among other things, upon the character and ability of the company's management, its diversification and performance, the quality of the assets pledged, and the ability of the company to operate at a profit if the funds are made available to it.

Commercial financing of accounts receivable and other collateral provides a flexible borrowing arrangement whereby a borrower will receive the funds needed, in the amounts needed, and at the time needed. The accounts receivable outstanding are self-liquidating through their collection. To keep interest charges at a minimum, the financed company may borrow only the funds it needs as and when needed. This method can be contrasted with the fixed-dollar loan, which carries a constant interest cost that must be met.

Accounts Receivable Financing

Accounts receivable are accepted by some banks and most commercial credit companies as collateral for a line of credit. Individual banking practices vary, however, and the borrower should become familiar with local banking requirements. The financing of accounts receivable involves the assignment by the borrower to the lender of the borrower's accounts receivable. These accounts receivable are security for advances which the lender makes to the borrower simultaneously with each assignment. As the proceeds of the assigned accounts are collected, they are turned over to the lender and applied to reduction of the indebtedness, the excess being returned by the lender to the borrower. The borrower remains responsible for the payment of the debt, even though the primary source of payment are the proceeds of the assigned accounts receivable. If the proceeds of the assigned accounts receivable are insufficient to repay the amount advanced, the borrower is liable for the deficiency. This is one important difference between accounts receivable financing and factoring. The factor purchases the accounts receivable from the borrower and assumes the risk of loss from any bad accounts.

Accounts receivable may be financed on a notification or a non-notification basis. Under a notification plan, the receivables are pledged and payment is made directly to the lender, but the borrower remains responsible for the payment. The lender notifies the borrower's customers that their accounts have been assigned and directs them to make payments directly to the lender. Under the more satisfactory and more commonly used non-notification plan, the borrower collects as agent for the lender. This method is preferable because the relationship between the borrower and his or her customers is not disturbed and the financing arrangement remains confidential.

Functions of Accounts Receivable Financing   The primary function of accounts receivable financing is to release funds tied up in these accounts, thereby giving a company working capital. Financing of receivables may put a borrowing company in a stronger position for sales expansion and may improve its credit standing by providing funds to discount its own payables.

Accounts receivable financing should be employed in conjunction with a cash forecast and financial plan. The financing will be used according to the plan's estimate of how much cash will be required before the expended cash comes back from customers. Whenever there is a shortage of working capital but available accounts receivable that are not yet due, the borrower is in a position to raise cash to meet any current needs. Of course, this financing aid is not the final answer to the problem of inadequate working capital; but it is a means of temporary relief, especially in seasonal industries where receivables are concentrated in a short period of the year and unacceptable collateral for long-term financing.

Mechanics of Accounts Receivable Financing   Before accepting accounts receivable as collateral, the lending agency will evaluate the risks and investigate the facts involved. Through analysis and investigation of the borrower's financial history and related factors, the lending agency can decide if it wants to assume the risk and how the risk can be minimized. At the outset it should be emphasized that certain types of businesses do not lend themselves to receivable financing. Most service enterprises fall into this category. This is because a serviceman may damage the customers' goods and offset any receivable that may be due. The same risk appears in businesses that furnish special orders. And generally factors do not look with favor on unstable industries.

Other considerations involve the accounts themselves. The lender will look to see if the accounts are acceptable for financing. Usually any account that represents a bona fide obligation owed to the borrower from a creditworthy customer, without the probability of setoff or the like, is available for financing. Under certain conditions, partial billings against unfinished contracts may be financed. The lender will have to be assured that these invoices are payable on regular terms and won't be unduly delayed. Under most circumstances, long-term dating will not disqualify the receivables unless there is undue hazard in their collection.

After the lender has satisfactorily completed an investigation, a basic contract between the lender and the borrower will be executed defining the rights and obligations of the parties. The contract is generally needed because accounts receivable financing contemplates a series of transactions rather than a single isolated loan. Many lenders require yearly contracts. While the agreements vary with the situations, a typical agreement might provide that the borrower assign all accounts receivable, or a selected group of them, to the lender as security. In return the lender agrees to advance funds up to 80% of the face value of the accounts receivable pledged, usually specifying a dollar maximum which can be borrowed. Periodically, schedules of customers' invoices are submitted to the lender to replenish borrowing power. Under this type of arrangement, the borrower, when cash is needed, simply lists the invoices being used to finance on the lender's standardized form and the lender advances the cash upon presentation of the form. The borrower should avoid arrangements where it is necessary to get clearance on each individual invoice. Blanket deals are much easier to administer, since invoice schedules are simply submitted periodically on accounts that have blanket approval and the lender worries about individual account limits.

Equity Adjustments   Upon the collection of the accounts, the financing company generally receives a larger amount than the percentage advanced. The excess, known as "equity," is credited to the client's accounts. (However, the full difference between the gross amount of the invoice and the percentage advanced is seldom realized upon payment because of returns, allowances and discounts.)

Cost of Accounts Receivable Financing   There are various methods of computing charges on open accounts receivable. The most common are:

1) Straight interest on the amount of funds advanced expressed either as a rate per annum, per month or per diem. The rate of interest is applied to the average daily balances;

2) A commission on the accounts assigned plus, in some cases, interest on the funds advanced. The logic behind the commission is that regardless of the amount of funds advanced against the assigned accounts, a major expense is incurred in handling the bookkeeping involved. The commission more accurately reflects the cost of maintaining the account;

3) Charges may be expressed as a percentage of the average balance of the collateral assigned;

4) A minimum charge may be required as assurance that the financing company will meet its expense in initiating and servicing the account;

5) Gradually decreasing rates may be applied in any of the above methods, reflecting the decreasing operating costs per dollar advanced as the account grows larger.

Rates on the accounts receivable loan vary widely. Commercial bank rates may range from prime to 2% over prime or higher per annum on the balance in the loan account. Some banks add a small service charge to cover the sizable amount of clerical work involved, such as one-half on one percent based on total receivables pledged or a flat amount for originally setting up the loan. As pointed out, banks do not often go into accounts receivable financing, so that the borrower will probably have to turn to a commercial finance company for the loan. The cost of financing accounts receivable through a finance company is high. This may cost the borrower 2% to 4% over prime on a loan where the advance is 75% of the face value of the receivables. The rates may range from 4% to 8% over prime, or higher, depending on the overall interest cost of money.

Split Loans

There may occasionally be a situation where a company's credit standing may no longer entitle it to unsecured borrowing, but its financial position may still be far better than that of the usual finance company client, and therefore the company may not be willing to pay the high finance company charge. In this case the finance company may be able to work a *split loan* with a bank at a reduced rate for the borrower. The finance company will approach the bank and do all the preliminary work of setting up the loan. The split loan is a three-way arrangement among the borrower, the finance company and the bank. Under this arrangement, the finance company advances half the needed funds and takes full charge of administering the accounts receivable, which are the security for the entire arrangement. The bank does no work except to lend the other half of the needed funds without guarantee by the finance company. The bank relies on the judgment of the finance company and is able to employ its funds at a good rate with no more expense than any unsecured loan would entail and with greater safety because both lenders are protected by the lien on the accounts receivable. The benefit to the borrower can be seen from the following figures:

Assume the finance company rate is 12%, the prime bank interest rate is 6% and the rate for a split loan is 9%. If the borrower had used the finance company exclusively, he would have paid 12%. Here, he pays 12% on half the loan and 6% on the other half, or a net rate of 9%.

FINANCING THROUGH A FACTOR

Factoring is primarily a credit business in which the factor checks credits and makes collections for a client. The factor also purchases a client's accounts receivable without recourse, thereby guaranteeing the client against credit losses. This is the basic service of a factor for which the factor receives a fee. Normally the account debtor is notified that the account was purchased by the factor and that payment thereon is to be made directly to the factor.

In this operation the factor checks the credits, makes the collections and assumes the loss in the event the accounts are not paid. Up to this point, however, the factor has passed no funds to the client, but has purchased the accounts and has agreed to pay for them on their net due dates.

Under the standard factoring contract, the factor buys the client's receivables outright, without recourse, as soon as the client creates them by shipping merchandise to customers whose credit the factor has investigated and approved. Cash is made available to the client immediately on shipment; thus, in effect, it is sold for cash and the receivables are turned into cash as fast as they are created. The arrangement is flexible, however, to the extent that the client may withdraw the full proceeds of the sale or leave the proceeds with the factor until their due date. She is charged interest only for money withdrawn prior to the due date. Thus the client has a 100% demand privilege on the funds available but pays interest only on funds actually used.

However, the factor will make cash advances to the client on the receivables prior to their maturity. For example, suppose that the factor purchases accounts receivable amounting to $40,000 from a client, without recourse, due in 60 days. In this case, the factor owes the client $40,000 which must be paid in 60 days. The factor, however, will advance, say, $35,000 to the client immediately, to make operating cash available. The other $5,000 will be paid when due. The factor will charge interest on the funds advanced to the client, and at current rates. If these advances are not enough to meet the needs of the client—and this occurs frequently in seasonal business—the factor will also make short-term, supplementary loans secured by inventory, fixed assets or other acceptable collateral.

Non-Notification Factoring

Non-notification factoring is now available to clients in many fields who sell directly to customers in the retail trade. In this type of factoring, the factor purchases the receivables outright without recourse but does not assume the collection function without specific request. The client makes collections himself, and the customer is not notified of the factoring arrangements. The fee for non-notification factoring may be less than that charged for notification factoring.

Bank and Factor in Combination

Frequently, a commercial bank cannot provide all the loan funds a growing company needs. Its balance sheet is not liquid enough or it can't clear off the bank debt every six or twelve months. A factor can provide funds to clear off bank loans periodically or make additional bank credit possible by guaranteeing accounts or replacing accounts receivable with cash.

When Should You Factor?

First, can you factor? Yes if:

1) You sell on normal credit terms;
2) 80 to 90% of your customers are rated;
3) Your annual volume is sufficiently large for profitable factoring.

What will factoring do for you? It converts your sales into cash sales. It can give you additional working funds to expand, modernize or do whatever will improve your business.

Now, what will it cost you? You pay a service charge and interest. Interest will be relatively high per annum on money actually used on a daily basis. The service charge, depending on the risk in your accounts and the amount of handling required, will be from three-quarters of one percent to one and one-half percent of the receivables purchased. But against this, you can credit savings:

1) On the salaries of credit and collection people;
2) On the elimination of bad debt writeoff;
3) On the interest on money borrowed to carry sales and accounts receivable.

What the Factor Wants to Know

The first points a factor considers are the type of sales and the selling terms of the borrower. The sales should be on open account, so as to create accounts receivable that can be sold. The terms of the sale determine the value of the account to the factor. The shorter the terms of payment, the faster the factor can expect to turn over his or her investment and the lower the rates. If payment terms are extended, the factor will have a long wait to realize any investment and will charge a higher rate, one that might be prohibitive.

Credit information on the accounts should be available. The credit rating determines the risk assumed by the factor upon purchase of the accounts without recourse. The factor will expect some credit losses and will include a loss reserve in the charges. A factor will not enter into a factoring agreement unless almost all of the borrower's regular customers seem to be good credit risks.

The arrangement should continue over an extended period of time—something more than a few months. Factors do not like to get involved in short-term deals.

The volume of accounts is important. Just as in any business the larger the earnings prospect, the more attractive the deal is. It does not pay a factor to handle a small volume. The size of the individual accounts controls the factor's costs. The greater the balance of the accounts, the smaller the percentage of fixed cost in its collection.

The factor will examine the records to determine if there is an abnormal percentage of returns and complaints. If the percentage of returns as compared with sales is too high, the factor may take this as a warning signal and back out of the transaction.

Provisions of Factoring Contract

The business of the present-day factor is to purchase accounts receivable upon much the same basis that tangible assets are bought and sold. The typical contract first provides that the client agrees to sell to the factor as absolute owner, and the factor agrees to purchase from the client without recourse to the client (with certain exceptions) all accounts receivables created by the client in the ordinary course of business. The factor usually has recourse to the borrower for returns or allowance for bad debts or errors in pricing.

INVENTORY LOANS

Inventories are not as liquid as accounts receivable, and a bank or finance company will generally want to secure its advances by accounts receivable and go to inventories only after the business has exhausted its ability to borrow on receivables. Receivables convert into cash automatically, they present fewer legal problems, and they don't go out of style or become technologically obsolete or suffer drastic price declines. But inventory financing is important, particularly to businesses that must build up a stock to meet a seasonal demand.

Inventory is acceptable as collateral usually if the following conditions are met:

1) The inventory is readily salable—that is, no great sales effort would be required to turn it into cash to satisfy the loan if that should become necessary;

2) The inventory consists of basic commodities that will not deteriorate or become obsolete within the period of the loan;

3) The necessary legal technicalities to protect the lender's position in the event of bankruptcy are available.

You will be able to borrow, if at all, only on your stock of raw materials or finished merchandise. Work in process has little value for borrowing purposes. No lender wants the responsibility for finishing up and selling work in process.

Here's what a lender will want to know about your inventory before deciding whether and how much to lend:

1) Is the price fairly stable or does it fluctuate sharply?
2) How broad a market is there for the commodity?
3) Are there any governmental restrictions on its sale?
4) Under what conditions may the commodity be stored and for how long?
5) Is the item closely graded by the trade?
6) How does the condition of the commodity affect its value?
7) Is the commodity usually sold in certain standard sizes, and does the commodity under consideration comply with those standards?
8) Is there any danger of obsolescence in the near future due to technological changes?
9) What should the costs of liquidation be, such as sales commissions, parking and transportation charges?
10) Can the commodity be hedged by the purchase of futures?

The Problem of Protecting the Lender

The Uniform Commercial Code, already adopted in most jurisdictions and all the leading commercial and industrial states, has eliminated a lot of legal problems that formerly existed in connection with inventory financing.

The Code rules relating to after-acquired property, future advances, dominion and control of the collateral by the debtor, commingling of goods, and transferring the lien on the collateral to the proceeds make possible so-called "floating liens." The concept of a floating lien is that of a lien on a shifting stock of goods or inventory, that is, a lien on collateral in more or less constant flux and undergoing quantitative and qualitative changes. It is a concept that responds to a long-felt need of businessmen for an effective device giving a lender a security interest on goods and materials which the debtor is permitted to retain, process, manufacture or otherwise change and sell, and also covering the proceeds of the sale and the new goods and materials bought by the debtor with the proceeds in a continuing cycle of business activity. The chattel mortgage has been unable to satisfy this need because of problems in connection with description of the property covered, after acquired property, and the power of the debtor to sell the collateral and to use the proceeds.

The fact that the Code makes legally possible a floating lien does not mean that the secured creditor's interest in collateral covered by the lien will necessarily be entitled to priority over all liens subsequently attaching or perfected in the same collateral. It may be subordinate to subsequent purchase money interests, and there will be problems of priority as against federal tax liens.

Also, a purchaser from the debtor in the ordinary course of business will get good title. However, the lender's lien may attach to the proceeds of the sale or the resulting account receivable.

In jurisdictions that have not adopted the Code, the lender will be looking for lien protection under a Factors' Lien Act or the Uniform Trust Receipt Act or by taking actual or constructive possession of the inventory. Actual possession of the goods is rarely feasible, and it will not be often that the lender can be given constructive possession by having the goods placed in a regular public warehouse and having the lender hold warehouse receipts. This can be cumbersome and expensive because it necessitates transferring the goods to and from the borrower's premises, plus storage charges. Field warehousing may be a more feasible alternative. Both of these continue to be used in Code jurisdictions, although the underlying legal requirements may vary somewhat from pre-Code law.

Field Warehouse Financing

A field warehouse is created by a warehouse company leasing, at a nominal rent, a portion of the buyer's premises where the pledged inventory is to be stored. This space is segregated from the rest of the buyer's premises by a partition, wire fence or other appropriate means. Separate locks are installed to prevent any person from entering the storage space without the consent of the warehouse company. Signs can be posted all about the leased premises indicating that the space is under the control of the warehouse company and not the borrower. The purpose of this is to assure that the borrower's creditors will not be misled into thinking that they can lay claim to this inventory, or that they are secured by the fact that this inventory is on the borrower's premises.

The warehouse company hires a custodian, usually putting on its payroll a stockman who has been looking after the inventory for the borrower. Warehouse receipts are issued to the lender.

Commercial finance companies have developed a method of handling the whole chain of transactions from the acquisition of raw material to finished inventory for accounts receivable. Withdrawals from the warehouse are replaced by a steady stream of new raw materials and finished goods going into the warehouse. The sales invoice goes into the hands of the commercial finance company to replace finished goods shipped out of the warehouse. The net effect is to add a substantial increment of working funds to the business. As the finance company furnishes funds to buy raw materials, it is repaid out of advances on the finished product and then gets repaid for these advances out of cash paid upon the collection of the accounts receivable created when the finished product is sold.

The Factor's Lien

The use of a field or other warehouse is usually not practical where the borrower must retain possession of the inventory for further processing. Field warehousing is unnecessary in states where there are factor's lien laws, because the procedure where a factor's lien is available can be much less cumbersome and less expensive than field warehousing.

The lien agreement between the borrower and the lender must be placed on public record and usually provides that the borrower will report to the lender at frequent intervals the nature and value of the inventory in the hands of the borrower at that time. The borrower agrees that it will, upon a reduction in its inventory, make payments to the lender on its loans equal to or greater than the amount of the inventory reduction. The law usually requires that a notice, in a specified form, of the existence of the factor's lien be posted in a conspicuous place at the principal entrance to the place of business of the borrower. For obvious reasons, the lending agency usually requires a liberal margin of inventory values against its advances, inspects the inventories at frequent intervals and follows loans of this kind with exceptional care.

This procedure gives the lender a good lien on practically every piece of inventory located on the premises. A factor's lien is not operative against bona fide purchasers for value of the merchandise, who purchase it from the borrower in the ordinary course of business without actual notice of the lien. These purchasers get good title to the merchandise free and clear of the lien, but the lien of the lender attaches to the account receivable created by the sale. It is very important that the lender adhere strictly to the notice, posting, and filing requirements of the statute which makes the factor's lien available.

The usual transaction involving the financing of inventory on a factor's lien contemplates a combined inventory and accounts receivable financing operation. The lender expects the inventory advances to be repaid out of the proceeds of the accounts receivable created by the sale of the inventory after it has been processed. The borrower expects to finance part of the cost of production by receiving additional advances on accounts receivable as they are created and assigned to the lender.

Trust Receipts

A trust receipt is a financing instrument in the form of an agreement between a bank (the lender), called the entruster, and a person, firm, or corporation (the borrower), called the trustee. It shows that certain goods or property, or evidence of title to these goods or property, having been acquired for financing purposes by the lender, are released by it under specified conditions to the borrower.

While the goods are in the borrower's possession, the lender retains ownership until the goods or property, or the evidence of title to goods or property, are properly accounted for by the trustee to the entruster. This accounting is through payment or otherwise, as set out in the instrument.

The trust receipt is used for interim financing of staple commodities when it is necessary to release pledged goods from a warehouse in order to sell or process them. Another use is in financing, under a "floor-planning" arrangement.

Floor planning. This term refers to the use of the trust receipt to finance the purchase by dealers or distributors of motor vehicles, household appliances and other products that may be readily identifiable as to specific units and that have other than a nominal unit value.

Under such a financing arrangement, the products are actually paid for by a bank or other lending agency, which obtains title through the payment of a draft with bill of lading attached, for the purchase price, or through a bill of sale or otherwise. In effect, the products are released by the lender to the borrower for inventory and sales purposes against the borrower's note and trust receipt. The trust receipt provides, in effect, that the borrower will hold the products in trust for the lender for the purpose of sale at not less than a specified minimum sale price per unit and will, pending sale, return the products to the lender upon demand. Or, upon sale, the borrower will keep the proceeds of sale segregated and deliver such proceeds to the lender immediately.

Floor plan terms. Frequently, the lender will advance for the original purchase no more than 90% or less of the invoice cost of the products to be financed. It will usually require the monthly curtailment of any advances outstanding at the end of three months, with complete liquidation required within six months after the date of purchase. Interest on daily loans outstanding is usually billed to the borrower at regular monthly intervals.

Floor plan procedures. During the period of outstanding advances, the lender will have a valid security interest (except against an innocent purchaser for value) in the products held by the borrower under trust receipt, provided they are clearly identifiable and the lender has observed all requirements of law surrounding trust receipt financing. These requirements may vary to some extent with the laws of each state but usually they include the necessity of placing on public record a "Statement of Trust Receipt Financing" which, in effect, is merely a notice that the borrower is engaged in trust receipt financing with a specified lender. At frequent but irregular intervals, the lender will make a detailed physical check of the products held by the borrower under trust receipt to establish their continued availability and to inspect their condition.

Observing floor plan terms and procedures.   The business using this method of inventory financing must take exceptional care to see that, when floor-planned products are sold, the proceeds of sale are delivered promptly to the lender to apply on outstanding advances. As the name implies, a trust receipt arrangement requires the trust of the lender in the integrity of the borrower. The latter must avoid any appearance of irregularities that might lead to the destruction of the confidence.

FINANCING—LONG-TERM

The basic distinction within a corporation's capital structure is that between equity (common and preferred stocks) and long-term debt. Short-term debt, even though it is anticipated that it will be renewed, is normally considered a current liability.

Long-term debt is generally shown as a separate category of liabilities and is distinguished from a stock issue in the following ways: (1) the corporation makes an absolute promise to pay the full amount at maturity; (2) the corporation promises to pay a fixed interest at periodic intervals; (3) the debt is frequently, but not necessarily, secured by specific assets of the corporation or by its assets generally; (4) the debt is frequently, but not necessarily, issued under an indenture under which a trustee is appointed to act as the creditors' representative in dealing with the corporation. Long-term debt is ordinarily in the form of bonds, although there is today a greater use of notes.

LONG-TERM BONDS

Long-term bonds are normally issued either in registered or coupon form. A coupon bond contains a coupon for each interest payable date during the life of the bond. When the interest date is reached, the bondholder clips the coupon and sends it to the corporation and subsequently receives an interest payment. Coupon bonds are transferable merely by delivery (like cash) and, hence, create a problem of safekeeping for the bondholder. A registered bond is registered with the corporation, and interest payments will be made directly to the registered owner until such time as the corporation is notified of a transfer. Registered bonds can only be transferred by negotiation (i.e., endorsement by the present owner) and are therefore less risky to hold.

Principal, Interest, and Maturity of Long-Term Bonds

A bond issue will normally be made up of a large number of bonds identical in all respects (except sometimes as to maturity). The usual denomination (par value) for a bond is $1,000, although in some cases "baby bonds" of $100 denominations have been issued to appeal to the smaller investor. The bond's stated, or "nominal", interest rate is selected on the basis of two considerations: (1) the current scale of money rates; (2) the quality of the company issuing the bonds. If the interest rate is set too low, the bond issue will be salable only at a substantial discount from par or may not be salable at all. If the interest rate is too high, the corporation will be paying more than necessary for money it obtains. Once the bonds have been issued, their price will fluctuate depending on changes in money rates and in the financial and operating condition of the company. It is unusual for a publicly traded bond to have the same market rate as the nominal rate—that is, it is unusual for the bond to be traded at exactly par value.

The current range of money rates plays a role in determining whether a long-term bond issue should be considered at all. Current interest rates are plotted on a graph according to the maturity of the various issues. This is called a "yield curve." An upsweeping yield curve means that the longer maturities yield the highest interest rates (the "normal" situation, since there must be some inducement for lenders to tie up their money for the longer periods). However, there are occasions when the yield curve will be downsweeping; i.e., interest rates for the shorter maturities will be higher than for the longer maturities. Obviously, the best time from the borrower's viewpoint for a long-term bond issue is when the yield curve is downsweeping, since long-term money is then cheaper than short-term money. On the other hand, if the yield curve is sharply upwards, short-term money may be so much cheaper that it would be wise to arrange the necessary financing through short-term loans (assuming they are available) with the intention of refinancing with long-term debt at some later date when the yield curve is more favorable.

The maturity of long-term debt may range anywhere from five years to 100 years. A bond issue may have a single maturity date for all the bonds or may be a serial issue, with a certain proportion of the bonds maturing at different dates. With a single maturity, the company must be prepared to pay off the entire issue at one time or refinance, called refunding. A serial issue spreads the corporation's obligation over a period of years and can be thought of as somewhat similar to a sinking fund.

Secured Bonds

For blue-chip corporations of the very highest quality, specific security for a bond issue is usually of little importance to the market because of the high credit standing of the company. But for other companies, the security underlying a bond may be an important factor in determining its marketability. Secured bonds can be divided into four classes:

1) Real property mortgage bonds. These are bonds secured by real estate owned by the corporation. The face amount of the bonds will normally not exceed two-thirds of the appraised value of the real estate in the case of first mortgage bonds. In addition, second or third mortgage bonds can be issued.

2) Equipment obligation bonds. These are bonds secured by chattel mortgages on personal property owned by the corporation. A special form of such bond is the equipment-trust certificate under which title to the property remains with the lender who leases it to the corporation until such time as the debt is paid. Equipment-trust certificates are most often used in the railroad industry.

3) Collateral trust bonds. These are bonds secured by investment securities in companies other than the borrower. The borrower is entitled to the interest or dividends from the securities, but they may be sold by the lender in case of the borrower's default.

4) General or blanket mortgage bonds. These are bonds secured by all of the corporation's assets. These bonds normally preclude any further issues of secured debt by the corporation unless they specifically provide that they may be subordinated to future bond issues secured by specified assets.

One major problem that frequently occurs in secured bonds is the inclusion of an after acquired property clause. This clause provides that the mortgage securing the bond issue will automatically be expanded to include all property or specified property subsequently acquired by the corporation. Sometimes this is limited to new property which is acquired to replace property originally included under the mortgage, but on other occasions the clause covers all new property acquired by the corporation and thus increases the security of the bondholders. If a corporation has such a bond indenture in existence and wishes to avoid subjecting new property to the outstanding mortgage, it may be able to proceed in one of the following ways:

1) Acquire the new property subject to a purchase money mortgage, which ordinarily has priority over the after-acquired property clause;
2) Organize a subsidiary company to hold the new property;
3) Lease instead of buy the new property;
4) Acquire the new property in connection with a merger or consolidation, which frequently renders the after-acquired clause inoperative;

5) As a last alternative, the outstanding bonds can be redeemed.

Guaranteed Bonds

The guarantee is a less common form of creating security for a bond issue. A guarantee differs from a mortgage in that the creditor is entitled to look to another person rather than to specified property as additional protection for a loan. The three most common types of guarantee bonds are:

1) Individual guarantees. These are most often used in closed corporations where all or some of the stockholders may sign the bonds or notes individually. They assume personal liability in addition to the corporate liability.

2) Guarantees by corporate parents. A corporation may decide to carry out some of its operations via subsidiary corporations. In that case, if the subsidiary sells a bond issue, the parent corporation by guaranteeing the bonds can sometimes make the bonds salable at a lower interest rate. Although corporations cannot, as a general rule, guarantee the obligations of others, most states make an exception for subsidiary corporations or for guarantees made within the scope of the corporation's business operations.

3) Joint guarantees. These are most common in the railroad industry where two or more railroad corporations may guarantee the bonds of a facility which is jointly used by them, such as a terminal building.

Debenture Bonds

These are unsecured bonds backed only by the general credit of the corporation. In the case of small and many medium-sized companies, debenture bonds are considerably riskier than either secured or guaranteed bonds. There are two primary categories of debentures:

1) Nonsubordinated debentures. These, on their face, make no provision for subordination to any future bond issues. However, if the bond indenture says nothing further, these bonds will automatically be junior in lien to any future bond issues which are secured by specific corporate assets. To prevent this from happening, the lender may insist that the indenture contains a provision limiting the total amount of future debt which the corporation may issue or a provision that the debenture bonds will have an equal status with the claim of any future mortgage bonds or secured bonds issued by the corporation.

2) Subordinated debentures. Of all the types of debt, these most resemble a stock issue. The subordination clause places the lender last among all the creditors of the company, past or future. The advantage to the corporation is that it preserves its future borrowing power, while at the same time creating deductible interest rather than nondeductible dividends. This type of bond issue will appeal to persons who are prepared to assume greater risk than the usual bondholder, but who also want a priority position as against the common stockholders. Debenture bonds are very similar, therefore, to preferred stock. In fact, the debentures will frequently carry a conversion privilege as a "sweetener," thus giving the bondholder the option to change an interest to stock in the event the company is successful.

Discount Bonds

Sometimes bonds may be issued at a discount instead of calling for interest. For example, a bond with a face of $1,000 may be issued at $850. At maturity, the bond will be redeemed for $1,000.

This type of bond is not usually used except by closely-held companies. But tax problems may be created by a discount bond.

For bonds issued on or before July 18, 1984, to the extent there is an "original issue discount" and the bondholders realize this discount, either on redemption or through sale to other holders, the gain realized is treated as ordinary income. Gain not attributable to the original issue discount—i.e., gain that might arise from purchasing a bond as between bondholders, at a further discount—is treated as capital gain. Note: There's a major law change for bonds issued after July 18, 1984 and purchased on resale at a discount. The gain is ordinary income to the extent of the accrued market discount.

From the corporation's point of view, discount should be amortized over the life of the bond, thereby increasing proportionately each year's interest expense. Where a premium is received, it too is amortized over the life of the bonds, thereby decreasing each year's interest expense.

Special Features of Bond Issues

Any or all of the following special types of provision may be found in a bond issue:

1) Sinking funds. A sinking fund requires the corporation to set aside a certain amount of cash each year so that, at the maturity of the bond issue, there will be sufficient funds to pay off the bondholders. The annual contribution may be set up in one of several different ways. For example, an increasing amount may be required each year on the theory that the underlying asset becomes more productive. Or, higher amounts may be required in the earlier years because increasing maintenance charges are anticipated as the asset grows older. If the sinking fund reserve is retained by the corporation until the maturity of the bond issue, the corporation may invest the funds in some form of investment which is both safe and liquid, such as Treasury obligations. On the other hand, the indenture may provide that the sinking fund cash is to be used to purchase bonds on the open market or from individual bondholders drawn by lot. Whatever the specific use of the sinking fund, it acts to increase the security of the remaining bondholders.

2) Restrictions on cash payments.   A bond indenture frequently prohibits the corporation from paying out cash dividends or using cash to reduce working capital unless a minimum amount of surplus is retained. Stock dividends, however, are normally not prohibited since they do not involve the flow of cash.

3) Convertibility to stock.   This has already been mentioned in connection with debentures. In setting conversion terms (the price of conversion), the corporation determines whether or not it wishes to force conversion. If it is issuing the bonds only as a temporary measure, it will give relatively easy conversion terms so that the bondholders are encouraged to take stock as soon as possible. On the other hand, if the corporation prefers the bonds (for example, because the interest is deductible), it may set the conversion terms to be attractive only after a period of years.

4) Call feature.   This is a provision frequently inserted in a bond indenture for the protection or benefit of the corporation issuing the bonds. It permits the corporation to redeem the entire bond issue by paying the call price, which usually is set somewhat above par. For example, if the bonds have a face value of $1,000, the corporation may be permitted to call (redeem) them at $1,050. The time at which the bonds may be called may begin either immediately or after a certain number of years. A callability provision has a disadvantage from the borrower's point of view since it puts a limit on the price potential of the bond. If interest rates decline, the bond price will rise as a consequence and, apart from the call price, may reach a level substantially above par. However, if the corporation has the call privilege, it will probably exercise it when bond prices begin to rise, because this means the corporation can refinance by issuing a new bond issue at lower interest rates.

TERM LOANS BY BANKS AND INSURANCE COMPANIES

Term loans are a common way of providing intermediate financing, i.e., from one to five years and sometimes up to ten years. The parties frequently proceed on the assumption that a term loan will be renewed each time it becomes due, provided of course that the financial condition of the business warrants such renewals. While such debt may therefore remain on the company's books for very long periods of time, it is nevertheless classified as intermediate because the lender has the option at relatively frequent intervals to terminate the loan.

There are numerous purposes for intermediate borrowing. One of the most common is to provide adequate working capital. A company may be undercapitalized from the start, or it may find that in times of prosperity more capital than anticipated is tied up in inventory and accounts receivables. In such a case, a term loan can supplement the firm's own equity investment. Another common use of the term loan is to acquire equipment with relatively short lives. Depreciation of the equipment affords tax-free cash which is available to pay off the loans; when new equipment is again required, the loan can be renewed. Finally, a term loan is often used when the company is actually seeking long-term funds but decides that the time is not propitious for floating long-term debt or for a public issue of stock. Typically, companies are reluctant to issue long-term debt when interest rates are very high, or to issue common stock when the market is quite weak.

Interest rates on term loans will, as befits their intermediate status, fall somewhere between the extremes of the maturity yield curve. They will tend to rise during periods of business expansion as the commercial banks are called upon to increase their business loans, and conversely term loans will be in less demand during times of economic recession. Commonly, the interest is in the form of a discount, whereby the bank deducts annual interest at the inception of the loan. This will make the actual interest rate higher than the nominal (contract) rate.

As regards repayment of principal, a term loan may be a standing loan, a fully amortized loan or a partially amortized loan. In the last case, the loan is called a balloon loan since a portion of the principal will remain due at maturity despite regular payments of principal. Generally, unsecured term loans will require some amortization, particularly if they run for more than one year. On the other hand, if the loan is secured by stocks or bonds or by other assets of the borrower, no or very little amortization may be required even though the loan is for a longer term.

Restriction in Term Loan Agreements

A term lender will be particularly interested in the borrower's cash flow rather than net income after taxes. The reason is that over a relatively short period, a company may be fully capable of paying off a term loan out of its cash flow, even though it may go through a temporary period of declining or nonexistent earnings. Or under opposite circumstances, a company may anticipate a large net income but may have a very small cash flow due to the need to purchase new equipment, pay off other loans, etc. Important provisions in the term loan agreement which act to restrict the borrower include the following:

Additional debt.   The lender may impose restrictions on the borrower's right to incur additional debt. This is more likely where the term debt is unsecured and new debt, by virtue of security provisions, may place the term loan in a subordinated position.

Restriction on dividends.   A common provision is one forbidding dividends unless net profits and/or cash flow and/or working capital reach designated amounts.

Restrictions of cash payments.   In addition to limiting dividend payments, the loan agreement may limit other cash payments. For example, surplus may not be used to retire existing stock or for investment in foreign subsidiaries.

Restrictions on salaries.   In the case of smaller companies, a lender may insist that salaries, bonuses and other compensation be restricted to stated amounts.

Minimum working capital.   The effect of the preceding restrictions is to insure that the company has sufficient working capital for its needs. In addition, the loan agreement may specifically provide for a minimum working capital position.

Barring merger or consolidation.   Finally, the lender may insist that no merger or consolidation take place while the term loan is outstanding. The reason is that such a combination may deprive the borrower of necessary cash or may place the term loan in a very subordinated position.

CONSERVING CASH

The amount of current assets which must be maintained by the business to sustain its working capital needs will vary, depending on such matters as the rapidity of inventory turnover, the length of the collection period, and the extent to which current assets are reduced by capital replacement, dividends and similar needs of the business.

Regardless of the absolute amounts needed by a particular business, it is a general principle of business finance that cash should be conserved whenever possible. In other words, the amount of inventory should be no higher than needed to sustain the normal sales volume of the business and every effort should be made to collect receivables as soon as possible.

Until quite recently, this principle of conserving cash led most financial officers to favor large cash balances in corporate checking accounts, since this represented 100% liquidity. The view was taken that any type of investment represented an unnecessary business risk. But this is now regarded as too conservative and, since it denies the business little or no return on its cash, too costly a practice to follow.

The Minimum Need for Cash

There are at least five reasons why a minimum cash balance must be maintained:

1) Immediate liabilities.   The company must have cash for its payroll and for other liabilities, such as tax payments or trade accounts which must be paid in the next few weeks.

2) Emergencies.   It is possible that the business will need a sum of cash for some emergency purpose, or perhaps even to make a highly advantageous purchase which must be consummated at once.

3) Purchase discount.   Companies like to have sufficient cash on hand to take advantage of all purchase discounts. While today many companies look upon the cost of merchandise or other items purchased as the net cost after discount, nevertheless failure to pay a bill within a discount period can be quite expensive. For example, merchandise purchased on a 2%/ten; net/30-basis will, in effect, pay 2% interest for the use of the money for 20 days if the bill is not paid within the 10-day period. This is the equivalent of a 36% annual interest rate. Hence it becomes important to pay all bills within the discount period, so it is important to have sufficient cash on hand to take advantage of the discounts.

4) Compensating bank balances.   Most commercial banks require that borrowers maintain a compensating deposit with them. For example, a company borrowing $100,000 may be required to maintain a continuing deposit of $20,000. This increases the actual interest cost because the borrower has the use of $80,000 instead of $100,000.

5) "Window-dressing."   This is a purely psychological factor but one which should not be overlooked. Even though a company has excellent reasons for maintaining an extremely low cash balance, such a figure on its balance sheet may prove disconcerting to stockholders and creditors, who may feel that the business is short of working capital, one of the most common reasons for business failure.

Nature of Risks in Investing Cash

In theory, conversion of cash into any other form of investment creates three possible kinds of risks: credit, money, and liquidity.

1) Credit risk.   This is the risk that the organization which issues the investment obligation will fail or will otherwise be unable to honor its obligation. Where the organization is the U.S. Government, this risk is almost nonexistent. The risk is small also for all practical purposes when the organization is a state, municipality or private organization which is insured by an agency of the government. Investors now, however, are more cautious of municipal obligations, after the experience of New York City and of Orange County, California. On the other hand, investing in common stock of a small enterprise obviously involves a high degree of risk.

2) Money risk.   This refers to the risk of loss due to changes in interest rates. For example, the price of a U.S. Government bond may fall (even though no credit risk is involved) because interest rates rise, which in turn reflects changes in the supply and demand for money. The existence of money risk precludes any investment of cash in long-term obligations. However, there are forms of short-term investments (Government bills and certificates and time deposits, called "near-money") which involve such a minimum degree of money risk that it can be ignored.

3) Liquidity risk.   This refers to the absence of a market for the investment. For example, a real estate mortgage may suffer no decline in price due to money risk or credit risk, but nevertheless may have no market at the time the holder wishes to sell it. To insure liquidity, corporate cash should be invested in obligations having an extremely active market, the most typical of which are U.S. Government securities.

Types of Investments for Corporate Cash

Having defined the basic type of risk, we may briefly indicate the types of investments which may be appropriate for the investment of corporate cash balances:

1) Ninety-day treasury bills.   Treasury bills are the shortest term obligation issued by the Federal Government and represent an obligation almost equal to actual cash in terms of the various risks outlined above. Treasury bills are issued for 91 or 182 days (there is normally a new issue every week), and their interest rate will vary depending on the degree of monetary ease which prevails. They are completely liquid, are sold by the government on a discount basis rather than on the basis of a face value plus accrued interest, and can be purchased only in minimum amounts.

2) Other federal obligations.   There are three other classes of Federal obligations: Treasury certificates (maturity of 6 to 12 months), Treasury notes (maturity of 1 to 5 years), and Treasury bonds (maturity of over 5 years). While these involve little credit risk or liquidity risk, they do involve a money risk as their prices will fluctuate in relation to the movement of interest rates.

3) Certificates of deposit.   The institutions which were hurt most by the transfer of corporate funds from demand deposits to income-bearing investments have been the commercial banks. In an attempt to win back some of the lost funds, commercial banks now offer certificates of deposit. These are issued to a corporation on deposit of a minimum amount of funds (e.g., $15,000–$100,000) for a minimum period of time (e.g., six months) and carry an interest rate which substantially exceeds the current rate on savings accounts. Although the money deposited must remain for the minimum period in order to earn interest, the certificates themselves are negotiable in the money market so that from the point of view of the corporation, there is no problem as to liquidity. Because of the short-term nature of the deposit, there is similarly less risk of loss from changes in interest rates.

4) Savings and loan association deposits.   Until commercial banks began issuing certificates of deposit, much of the corporate funds which were not invested in securities were placed in savings and loan associations. Here they could earn high interest and normally could be withdrawn upon 30-days' notice. While such deposits normally create little money risks or credit risks (since deposits are insured by an agency of the Federal Government), there is some possibility of nonliquidity in the event of a severe economic downturn which could result in a high foreclosure rate, which in turn might mean that some savings and loan associations (which invest primarily in mortgages) might not be in a position to pay their depositors upon demand.

5) Short-term commercial notes.   Finance companies and other monied corporations whose main assets are cash are constantly offering short-term notes to investors for the purpose of raising working capital. These notes, with maturities of from 90 days upwards, are suitable for many corporations since they provide a return slightly higher than that on Treasury obligations and, in the case of the largest finance companies, there is little risk.

6) Short-term corporate bonds.   One type of investment that is used by corporate treasurers is corporate bonds which have only a short time until maturity. In the case of the largest and strongest corporations, their bonds involve small risk. If their bonds are bought at a discount a short time prior to maturity, this also reduces the money risk since even if money rates rise (causing a decline in bond prices generally), the investor can count on at least par at the maturity of the bonds.

7) Municipal bonds.   This type of investment may yield slightly less than some others, but income is exempt from tax at the corporate level. Such income cannot be distributed as a tax-free dividend.

8) Commercial paper.   This is a short-term investment that usually pays interest at a rate higher than government obligations. The larger corporations borrow short-term funds in this manner with a 30-day maturity. If they are bought with discretion, the risk factor is moderate.

9) Repurchase agreements.   Many financial institutions now offer to sell investors a package of government securities at a discount, with an agreement to repurchase the package at some later date, 30 days to 89 days, at a specified price. The risk factor is small if purchased from solid institutions.

10) Money market funds.   Money-market funds are simply portfolios of money-market instruments put together by a manager and made available to investors. Such funds are highly liquid and can be bought and sold daily. In some cases the funds are set up so that you may withdraw funds by merely writing a check. Risk can be minimized by buying funds which hold only government securities.

FASB Statement 114: Accounting by Creditors for Impairment of a Loan

FASB 114 applies to all creditors and to all loans, both secured and unsecured, with the exception of loans with small balances which are collectively evaluated for impairment. Also excepted are loans measured at fair value or at the lower of cost or fair value, leases and debt securities, i.e., securities that represent a creditor relationship with an enterprise. Further, this Statement applies to all loans restructured in a troubled debt restructuring involving a modification of terms in accordance with the provisions set forth in the Statement.

The provisions must be applied to all financial statements prepared for fiscal years subsequent to December 15, 1994. These requirements will help the users of financial statements by providing a clearer picture of an enterprise's true financial situation.

As defined in the Statement, a loan becomes a contractual right to receive money on demand or on fixed or determinable dates, and becomes an asset in the creditor's statement of financial position. Impaired loans are required to be based on:

1) The present value of expected future cash flows discounted at the loan's effective interest rate.
2) The loan's observable market price.
3) The fair value of the security if the loan is security dependent.

If the latter approach is used, the effective interest rate used for discounting purposes is the original contractual interest rate. The effective rate for a restructured loan is based on the original contractual rate, not the rate in the restructuring agreement.

As previously noted, Statement 114 applies to all creditors. It covers the accounting by creditors for impairment of a loan by spelling out how allowances for credit losses pertaining to specific types of loans should be determined. In addition, the Statement covers the accounting by creditors for all loans that are restructured in a troubled debt restructuring where there is a modification of the terms of a receivable. However, it does not apply to restructurings of loans previously mentioned as excluded from the requirements of this Statement, including those where there has been a receipt of assets in partial satisfaction of a receivable.

Whenever the necessity for a loan accrual is decided upon, creditors need to consider the collectibility of both their contractual interest and the principal of all receivables. Statement 114 amends FASB 15, *Accounting by Debtors and Creditors for Troubled Debt Restructurings*, where a modification of terms takes place. Differences in an impaired loan's carrying value and its new valuation must be charged to income. Any later changes in valuation are accounted for in periodic income. Dependent on the circumstances, the income effect can be included in interest income or bad debt expense. The note of the impaired loan will need to be read by the creditor to determine the reporting company's policy and the changes in the accounts due to impaired loan accounting. As becomes obvious, measuring impaired loans requires judgments and estimates that may not be completely objective or accurate. The final outcome can differ widely from original estimates. Impaired loans and the risk factors therein fall into two basic categories:

1) Those impaired loans in which the risk factors are similar enough that they may be lumped together to measure the impairment. In these cases, the creditor may utilize historic statistics including, for example, average

amount recovered over an average recovery period, along with a composite effective rate.

2) Those impaired loans which display risk factors that are unique to an individual borrower and require more specific direction and application in measuring impairment.

It is imperative that the measurement methods detailed in Statement 114 be closely observed. If there is a significant change, whether it be from the borrower's improving or worsening condition, after measurement of recognized impairment has been made, the creditor should repeat the process to refigure the impairment and again adjust the valuation allowance. A changed condition can result from the amount or timing of an impaired loan's expected future cash flows, or from actual cash flows which are proving to be significantly different from the cash flows previously projected. It should also be taken into consideration that a creditor who measures impairment based on the observable market price of an impaired collateral dependent loan, must adjust the valuation allowance if significant increases or decreases occur in either of these bases. It must also be kept in mind, however, that the net carrying amount of the loan cannot exceed the recorded investment in the loan. The observable market price of an impaired loan or the fair value of the collateral of an impaired collateral dependent loan can very possibly change from one reporting period to the next. A creditor who measures impairment on either of those bases should report a decrease in the-impaired loan as bad debt expense in the same way that impairment was initially recognized. An increase in the measure of the impaired loan should be recorded as a reduction in the amount of bad debt expense that would otherwise be reported.

FASB STATEMENT 118: ACCOUNTING BY CREDITORS FOR IMPAIRMENT OF A LOAN—INCOME RECOGNITION AND DISCLOSURE

The Financial Accounting Standards Board had received requests for a delay in applying Statement 114's provisions which necessitated extensive accounting changes to comply with provisions regarding income recognition, measurement and disclosure related to certain impaired loans. Rather than delay the effective date, a majority of the Board agreed in adopting Statement 118 to eliminate the requirement for an entity to choose between two accounting methods spelled out in Statement 114, and to amend the Statement to allow creditors to continue using the existing method for recognizing interest income on impaired loans.

The Board also replaced the disclosure requirement section of Statement 114. The following are disclosures about impaired loans which are to be included in the body of the financial statements, or in the accompanying notes at the end of each period as spelled out in FASB 118:

1) The total investment in the impaired loans.
2) The amount of that investment for which there is a related allowance for credit losses and the amount.
3) The amount of the investment having no related credit losses allowance.
4) The creditor's policy for recognizing interest income and recording cash flow on impaired loans.
5) The average recorded investment in the impaired loans.
6) The related amount of interest income recognized during any given reporting time that the loans were impaired.
7) If practicable, the interest income amount recognized using a cash-basis method during that time.
8) The activity in the total allowance for credit losses related to the loans. The balance in the allowance at the beginning and end of each period, additions charged to operations, direct write-downs charged against the allowance, and recoveries of amounts already charged off.

Chapter 19

Employee Benefits

After over 12 years of studying the issue, the Financial Accounting Standards Board in December, 1985 issued FASB Statement No. 87 *"Employers' Accounting for Pension Plans,"* and Statement No. 88 *"Employers' Accounting for Settlements and Curtailments of Defined Benefit Pension Plans and for Termination Benefits."*

These two Statements, along with the more recently promulgated FASB Statement 106, *Employers' Accounting for Postretirement Benefits Other Than Pensions* and FASB Statement 112, *Employers' Accounting for Postemployment Benefits*, are the applicable GAAP for accounting for and disclosure about pension funds and related postemployment benefits.

PENSION FUND ACCOUNTING TERMS

The Statements have their own unique vernacular. The terminology used in the new rules should be reviewed as many familiar words and terms have shades of meaning in the pension fund accounting rules somewhat different from common, everyday usage, as well as the technical meaning of terms in a completely new vocabulary.

Definitions

Accumulated Benefit Obligation: The actuarial present value of benefits (whether vested or nonvested) attributed by the pension benefit formu-

463

la to employee service rendered before a specified date and based on employee service and compensation (if applicable) prior to that date. The accumulated benefit obligation differs from the projected benefit obligation in that it includes no assumption about future compensation levels. For plans with flat-benefit or non-pay-related pension benefit formulas, the accumulated benefit obligation and the projected benefit obligation are the same.

Actual Deferral Percentage: For the eligible highly compensated employee (top 1/3) and all other eligible employees (lower 2/3) for a plan year: the average of the ratio, calculated separately for each employee in such group, of the amount of employer contributions paid under the plan on behalf of each employee for such year to the employee's compensation for the same year.

Actual Return on Plan Assets Component of Net Periodic Pension Cost: The difference between the fair value of plan assets at the end of the period and the fair value at the beginning of the period, adjusted for contributions and benefits during the period.

Actuarial Funding Method: Any of several techniques that actuaries use in determining the amounts and incidence of employer contributions to provide for pension benefits.

Actuarial Gain or Loss: (See *Gain or Loss*)

Actuarial Present Value: The value, as of a specified date, of an amount or series of amounts payable or receivable in the future with each amount adjusted to reflect (1) the time value of money (through discounts for interest) and (2) the probability of payment by means of decrements for events such as death, disability, withdrawal, or retirement between the specified date and the expected date of payment.

Allocated Contract: A contrast with an insurance company under which payments to the insurance company are currently used to purchase immediate or deferred annuities for individual participants. (See *Annuity Contract*)

Amortization: In pension accounting, amortization is used to refer to the systematic recognition in net pension cost over several periods of previously unrecognized amounts, including unrecognized prior service cost and unrecognized net gain or loss.

Annuity Contract: A contrast in which an insurance company unconditionally undertakes a legal obligation to provide specified pension benefits to specific individuals in return for a fixed consideration or premium. An annuity contract is irrevocable and involves the transfer of significant risk from the employer to the insurance company. Annuity contracts are also called *allocated* contracts.

Assumptions: Estimates of the occurrence of future events affecting pension costs, such as mortality, withdrawal, disablement and retirement, changes in compensation and national pension benefits, and discount rates to reflect the time value of money.

Attribution: The process of assigning pension benefits or cost to periods of employee service.

Benefit Approach: One of two groups of basic approaches to attributing pension benefits or costs to periods of employee service. Approaches in this group assign a distinct unit of benefit to each year of credit service. The actuarial present value of that unit of benefit is computed separately and determines the cost assigned to that year. The accumulated benefits approach, benefit/compensation approach, and benefit/ years-of-service approach are benefit approaches.

Benefit Formula: (See *Pension Benefit Formula*)

Benefits: Payments to which participants may be entitled under a pension plan, including pension benefits, death benefits, and benefits due on termination of employment.

Benefit-Years-of-Service Approach: One of three benefit approaches. An equal portion of total estimated benefit is attributed to each year of service. The actuarial present value of the benefits is derived after the benefits are attributed to the periods.

Captive Insurance Subsidiary: An insurance company that does business primarily with related entities.

Career Average Pay Formula (Career Average Pay Plan): A benefit formula that bases benefits on the employee's compensation over the entire period of service with the employer. A career average pay plan is a plan with such a formula.

Contributory Plan: A pension plan under which employees contribute part of the cost. In some contributory plans, employees wishing to be covered must contribute; in other contributory plans, employee contributions result in increased benefits.

Cost Approach: One of the two groups of basic approaches to attributing pension benefits or costs to periods of service. Approaches in this group assign net pension costs to periods as level amounts or constant percentages of compensation.

Cost Compensation Approach: One of two cost approaches. Net pension costs under this approach are attributed to periods so that they are a constant percentage of compensation for each period.

Covered Employees: Those employees in any year whose accounts are credited with a contribution under the plan for that year.

Curtailment: (See *Plan Curtailment*)

Defined Benefit Pension Plan: A pension plan that defines an amount of pension benefit to be provided, usually as a function of one or more factors such as age, years of service, or compensation. Any pension plan that is not a defined contribution pension plan is, for purposes of Statement No. 87, a defined benefit pension plan.

Deferred Compensation Plan: A deferred compensation plan is a contractual agreement that specifies that a portion of the employee's compensation will be set aside and paid in future periods as retirement benefits.

Defined Contribution Pension Plan: A plan that provides pension benefits in return for services rendered, provides an individual account for each participant, and specifies how contributions to the individual's account are to be determined instead of specifying the amount of benefits the individual is to receive. Under a defined contribution pension plan, the benefits a participant will receive depend solely on the amount contributed to the participant's account, the returns earned on investments of those contributions, and forfeitures of other participants' benefits that may be allocated to such participant's account.

Eligible Employee: An employee who in any year is eligible for employer contributions under the plan for that year.

Employee Compensation: An employee's compensation is the amount taken into account under the plan prior to calculating the contribution made on behalf of the employee under the deferral election.

ERISA: The Employee Retirement Income Security Act of 1974.

Expected Long-Term Rate of Return on Plan Assets: An assumption as to the rate of return on plan assets reflecting the average rate of earnings expected on the funds invested or to be invested to provide for the benefits included in the projected benefit obligation.

Expected Return on Plan Assets: An amount calculated as a basis for determining the extent of delayed recognition of the effects of *changes* in the fair value of assets. The expected return on plan assets is determined based on the expected long-term rate of return on plan assets and the market-related value of plan assets.

Explicit Approach to Assumptions: An approach under which each significant assumption used reflects the best estimate of the plan's future experience solely with respect to that assumption. (See also Implicit Approach to Assumptions)

Fair Value: The amount that a pension plan could reasonably expect to receive for an investment in a current sale between a willing buyer and a willing seller (that is, other than in a forced or liquidation sale).

Final-Pay Formula (Final-Pay Plan): A benefit formula that bases benefits on the employee's compensation over a specified number of years near the end of the employee's service period or on the employee's highest compensation periods. For example, a plan might provide annual pension benefits equal to one percent of the employee's average salary for the last five years (or the highest consecutive five years) for each year of service. A final-pay plan is a plan with such a formula.

Flat-Benefit Formula (Flat-Benefit Plan): A benefit formula that bases benefits on a fixed amount per each year of service. A final-pay plan is a plan with such a formula.

401(k) Plan: An employee benefit plan, under which an employee can elect to defer current taxes on the portion of his/her taxable income contributed on his/her behalf by the employer.

Fund: Used as a *verb*, to pay over to a funding agency in order to fund future pension benefits or to fund pension cost. Used as a *noun*, fund means assets accumulated in the hands of a funding agency for the purpose of meeting pension benefits when they become due.

Funding Method: (See Actuarial Funding Method)

Funding Policy: The program regarding the amounts and timing of contributions by the employer(s), participants, and any other sources, e.g., state subsidies or federal grants, which will provide the benefits a pension plan specifies.

Gain or Loss: A change in the value of either the projected benefit obligation or the plan assets resulting from experience different from that assumed or from a change in an actuarial assumption. (See also Unrecognized Net Gain or Loss)

Gain or Loss Component of Net Periodic Pension Cost: The sum of (1) the difference between the actual return on plan assets and the expected return on the assets; (2) the amortization of the unrecognized net gain or loss from previous periods. The gain or loss component is the net effect of delayed recognition of gains and losses (the net change in the unrecognized net gain or loss) except that it does not include changes in the projected benefit obligation occurring during the period and deferred for later recognition.

Highly Compensated Employee: An eligible employee who receives more compensation than two-thirds of all other eligible employees.

Implicit Approach to Assumptions: An approach under which two or more assumptions do not individually represent the best estimate of the plan's future experience with respect to those assumptions. Instead, the aggregate effect of their combined use is presumed to be approximately the same as that produced by an explicit approach.

Interest Cost Component of Net Periodic Pension Cost: The increase in the projected benefit obligation due to passage of time.

Loss: (See *Gain or Loss*)

Market-Related Value of Plan Assets: A balance used to calculate the expected return on plan assets. Market-related value can be either fair market value or a calculated value that recognizes changes in fair value in a systematic and rational manner over not more than five years. Different ways of calculating market-related value may be used for different classes of assets, but the manner of determining market-related value shall be applied consistently from year to year for each asset class.

Measurement Date: The date as of which plan assets and obligations are measured.

Mortality Rate: The proportion of the number of deaths in a specified group to the number living at the beginning of the period in which the deaths occur. In estimating the amount of pension benefits that will become payable, actuaries use mortality tables, which show the death rates for each age.

Multi-Employer Plan: A pension plan to which two or more unrelated employers contribute, usually in compliance with one or more collective bargaining agreements. A characteristic of multi-employer plans is that assets contributed by one participating employer may be used to provide benefits to employees of other participating employers since assets contributed by each employer are not segregated in a separate account or restricted to provide benefits only to employees of that employer. A multi-employer plan is usually administered by a board of trustees composed of management and labor representatives and are referred to as a "joint trust" or "union" plan. Generally, many employers participate in a multi-employer plan, and an employer may participate in more than one plan. The employers participating in multi-employer plans usually have a common industry bond, but for some plans the employers are in different industries and the labor union may be their only common bond.

Multiple-Employer Plan: A pension plan maintained by more than one employer but not treated as a multi-employer plan. Multiple-employer plans are not as prevalent as single-employer and multi-employer plans, but some that do exist are large and involve many employers. Multiple-employer plans are generally not collectively bargained and are intended to allow participating employers, usually in the same industry, to pool their assets for investment purposes and reduce the costs of plan administration. A multiple-employer plan maintains separate accounts for each employer so that contributions provide benefits only for employees of the contributing employer. Some multiple-employer plans have features that allow participating employers to have different benefit formulas, with the employer's contributions to the plan based on the benefit formula selected by the employer.

Net Periodic Pension Cost: The amount recognized in an employer's financial statements as the cost of a pension plan for a period. Components of net periodic pension cost are service cost, interest cost, actual return on plan assets, gain or loss, amortization of unrecognized prior service cost, and amortization of the unrecognized net obligation or asset existing at the date of initial application of Statement No. 88. The Statement uses the term *net periodic pension cost* instead of *net pension expense* because part of the cost recognized in a period may be capitalized along with other costs as part of an asset, such as part of the cost of inventory.

Nonparticipating Annuity Contract: An annuity contract that does not provide for the purchaser to participate in the investment performance or in other experience of the insurance company. (See also Annuity Contract)

Nonpublic Enterprise: An enterprise other than one (1) whose debt or equity securities are traded in a public market, i.e., either on a stock exchange or in the over-the-counter market, or (2) whose financial statements are filed with a regulatory agency (federal or state) in preparation for the sale of any class of securities.

Participant: Any employee or former employee, or any member or former member of a trade or other employee association, or the beneficiaries of those individuals, for whom there are pension plan benefits.

Participating Annuity Contract: An annuity contract that provides for the purchaser to participate in the investment performance and possibly other experience (the mortality rate, for example) of the insurance company.

Participation Right: A purchaser's right under a participating contract to receive future dividends or retroactive rate credits from the insurance company.

PBGC: The Pension Benefit Guaranty Corporation.

Pension Benefit Formula (Plan's Benefit Formula or Benefit Formula): The basis for determining payments to which participants may be entitled under a pension plan. Pension formulas usually refer to the employee's service or compensation, or both.

Pension Benefits: Periodic, usually monthly, payments made pursuant to the terms of the pension plan to a person who has retired from employment or to that person's beneficiary.

Plan Amendment: A change in the terms of an existing plan or the initiation of a new plan. A plan amendment may increase benefits, including those attributed to years of service already rendered. (See also Retroactive Benefits)

Plan Assets: Assets—usually stocks, bonds, and other investments—that have been segregated and restricted, usually in a trust, to provide benefits. Plan assets include amounts contributed by the employer (and by employees for a contributory plan) and amounts earned from investing the contributions, less benefits paid. Plan assets cannot ordinarily be withdrawn by the employer except in certain circumstances when a plan has assets in excess of obligations and the employer has taken certain steps to satisfy existing obligations. Assets not segregated in a trust, or otherwise effectively restricted so that they cannot be used by the employer for other purposes, are not plan assets even though it may be intended that such assets be used to provide pensions. Amounts accrued by the employer as net periodic pension cost, but not yet paid to the plan, are not plan assets. Securities of the employer held by the plan are includable in plan assets provided they are transferable. If a plan has liabilities other than for benefits, the nonbenefit obligations are considered as reductions of plan assets.

Plan Assets Available for Benefits: (See *Plan Assets*)

Plan Curtailment: An event that significantly reduces the expected years of future service of present employees or eliminates for a significant number of employees the accrual of defined benefits for some or all of their future services.

Plan Suspension: An event in which the pension plan is frozen and no further benefits accrue. Future service may continue to be the basis for vesting of nonvested benefits existing at the date of suspension. The plan may still hold assets, pay benefits already accrued, and receive additional employer contributions for any unfunded benefits. Employees may or may not continue working for the employer.

Plan Termination: An event in which the pension plan ceases to exist and all benefits are settled by purchase of annuities or by other means. The plan may or may not be replaced by another plan. A plan termination with a replacement plan may or may not be in substance a plan termination for accounting purposes of accrued net pension cost.

Plan's Benefit Formula: (See Pension Benefit Formula)

Prepaid Pension Cost: Cumulative employer contribution in excess of accrued net pension cost.

Prior Service Cost: The cost of retroactive benefits granted in a plan amendment. (See also Unrecognized Prior Service Cost)

Projected Benefit Obligation: The actuarial present value as of a date of all benefits attributed by the pension benefit formula to employee service rendered prior to that date. The projected benefit obligation is measured using assumptions as to future compensation levels if the pension benefit formula is based on those future compensation levels, e.g., pay-related, final pay, final average pay, career average pay plans.

Retroactive Benefits: Benefits granted in a plan amendment that are attributed by the pension benefit formula to employee services rendered in periods prior to the amendment. The cost of the retroactive benefits is referred to as prior service cost.

Return on Plan Assets: (See Actual REturn on Plan Assets Component; Expected Return on Plan Assets)

Service: Employment taken into consideration under a pension plan. Years of employment before the inception of a plan constitute an employee's past service; years thereafter are classified in relation to the particular actuarial valuation being made or discussed. Years of employment, including past service, prior to the date of a particular valuation constitute prior service; years of employment following the date of the valuation constitute future service; a year of employment on the date of valuation, or in which such date falls, constitutes current service.

Service Cost Component of Net Periodic Pension Cost: The actuarial present value of benefits attributed by the pension benefit formula to services rendered by employees during that period. The service cost component is a portion of the projected benefit obligation and is unaffected by the funded status of the plan.

Settlement: An irrevocable action that relieves the employer (or the plan) of primary responsibility for a pension benefit obligation and eliminates significant risks related to the obligation and the assets used to effect the settlement. Examples of transactions that constitute a settlement include (1) making lump-sum cash payments to plan participants in exchange for their rights to receive specified pension benefits; (2) purchasing nonparticipating annuity contracts to cover vested benefits.

Single-Employer Plan: A pension plan that is maintained by one employer. The term also may be used to describe a plan that is maintained by related parties such as a parent and its subsidiaries.

Sponsor: A pension plan established or maintained by a single employer, the employer; a plan established or maintained by an employee organization, the employee organization; a plan established or maintained jointly by two or more employers or by one or more employers and one or more employee organization, the association, committee, joint board of trustees, or other group of representatives of the parties who have established or who maintain the pension plan.

Turnover: Termination of employment for a reason other than death or retirement.

Unallocated Contract: A contract with an insurance company under which payments to the insurance company are accumulated in an unallocated fund which is a fund not allocated to specific plan participants. An unallocated fund is to be used either directly or through the purchase of annuities to meet benefit payments when employees retire. Funds held by the insurance company under an unallocated contract may be withdrawn and otherwise invested.

Unfunded Accrued Pension Cost: Cumulative net pension cost accrued in excess of the employer's contributions.

Unfunded Accumulated Benefit Obligation: The excess of the projected benefit obligation over plan assets.

Unrecognized Net Gain or Loss: The cumulative net gain or loss that has not been recognized as a part of net periodic pension cost. (See *Gain or Loss*)

Unrecognized Prior Service Cost: That portion of prior service cost that has not been recognized as a part of net periodic pension cost.

Vested Benefit Obligation: The actuarial present value of vested benefits.

Vested Benefits: Benefits for which the employee's right to receive a present or future pension benefit is no longer contingent on remaining in the service of the employer. Other conditions, such as inadequacy of the pension fund, may prevent the employee from receiving the vested benefit. Under graded vesting, the initial vested right may be to receive in the future a stated percentage of a pension based on the number of years of accumulated credited service; thereafter, the percentage may increase with the number of years of service or of age until the right to receive the entire benefit has vested.

FASB STATEMENT 87, *Employers' Accounting for Pension Plans*

1) Companies using other than the prescribed plan-based benefit approach to attributing pension costs of periods were faced with a method change with potential significant effect on amounts recognized in the income statement.

2) Each significant assumption affecting the pension computation requires the best estimate of that factor alone. Under this explicit approach, the use of assumptions known to be inaccurate but with offsetting effect became unacceptable. Major assumptions that must be developed and continuously updated for significant changes include the discount rate (the current rate at which benefits could be effectively settled) used to measure pension obligations and portions of periodic pension cost; the expected long-term rate of return on plan assets necessary for the gain or loss calculation; and where determined by the plan's benefit formula, assumed future compensation levels.

3) Provided the accounting policy adopted is followed consistently, No. 87 allows a number of choices. The market-related value of plan assets, a factor in the gain or loss computation, may be either fair market value or a calculated value that recognizes changes in fair value of plan assets over not more than five years; different methods of calculating market-related value can be used for different classes of plan assets. Prior service costs may be amortized by the declining method prescribed for general use or by an alternative that reduces any unrecognized balance more rapidly. Subject to specified conditions, unrecognized net gains or losses may be amortized by any systematic method. The measurement date for requirements can be the date of the financial statements, or a date not more than three months earlier.

4) Calendar-year companies are required to report any minimum unfunded pension liabilities, offset by intangible assets and/or reductions in shareholders' equity in their balance sheets.

5) The income statement effects of adopting No. 87, which may include recording pension income instead of pension costs, may have unanticipated effects on bonus, profit-sharing, incentive, and similar plans. These effects should be estimated promptly and decisions made on whether the plans should be amended.

6) The rules for foreign plans are the same as the rules for domestic plans.

7) Compliance with rules for determining the tax deductibility of pension costs might require data for IRS different from that needed for reporting under No. 87. Supplemental actuarial valuations may be needed for tax purposes.

Of the several types of pension plans covered by these rules, the most significant impact of the new Standard is on single-employer defined benefit plans. (A single-employer plan is maintained by one employer. The term is also used to describe a plan that is maintained by related parties such as a parent and its subsidiaries.)

The main requirements of single-employer plans follow:

1) For calendar-year companies, balance sheet recognition of a minimum pension liability must be recognized. The "unfunded accumulated benefit obligation" equals the excess of the present value of benefits earned to date, calculated without reference to future compensation levels over the fair value of plan assets. Recording the minimum liability generates an intangible asset to the extent of unrecognized prior service cost; any excess is recorded as a reduction of equity.

2) Development of a standardized method for attributing pension cost to service periods. In requiring that the attribution method be based on the plan's benefit formula, the use of a "benefit" instead of a "cost" approach to determining periodic cost must be applied.

3) Recognition of future compensation levels in calculating the unrecognized net asset or obligation at the transition date, in determining net period cost and in disclosing the "projected benefit obligation" but not in calculating a minimum liability displayed in the balance sheet.

4) Linkage of current and delayed cost recognition to employee service periods. A liability must be recognized if net pension costs *exceeds* employer contribution. An additional minimum liability is recognized as an intangible asset. In limited circumstances, cost allocation is determined instead by the remaining life expectancy of inactive plan participants.

5) Prospective recognition of prior service cost and of the unrecognized net obligation or net asset determined at the transition date.

6) Delayed recognition of gains and losses. Those from all sources are aggregated and amortized by any systematic method consistently applied, subject to a floor set by the Standard's "corridor" approach. In an attempt to reduce volatility, the Board compounded the Standard's complexity by basing the gain or loss computation on the expected return on plan assets. That factor is determined by applying the expected long-term rate of return on plan assets to the market-related value of plan assets, which are defined as either fair value or a calculated value that spreads change in fair value over not more than five years.

7) Separate calculation of numerous components of net periodic pension cost and separate disclosure of four items: service cost, interest cost, actual return on plan assets, and the net total of all other components.

8) Disclosure requirements were significantly expanded from previous practice.

   a) There should be a brief description of the plan and the type of benefit formula applied.

b) Financial statements should disclose the nature and effects of significant changes in the factors affecting the computation of the net pension liability (or asset) and net periodic pension cost recognized in the financial statements.

c) The funding policy should be disclosed. (APB Opinion No. 8 and FASB Statement No. 36 can be helpful in understanding differences between funding pension plans and *accounting* for plans.)

d) Net periodic pension costs and their components should be disclosed.

e) The actual return on plan assets should be shown.

f) Disclosure of the components of the pension benefit obligation is required.

g) The plan assets should be described.

h) A reconciliation of the amounts included in the fund status of the plan's projected benefit obligation is essential to understanding the relationship between the accounting and the funded status of the plan.

i) An assumed weighted-average discount rate and rate of compensation increase should be disclosed.

j) The following disclosures are *suggested* by the Rule:

- The ratio of net periodic pension cost to covered payroll.
- The separate amounts of amortization of unrecognized prior service and amortization of unrecognized net gain or loss.
- Information about cash flows of the plan separately showing employer contributions, other contributions, and benefits paid during the period.
- The amounts of plan assets classified by major asset category.
- The amounts of the vested benefit obligation owed to retirees and to others.
- The change in the projected benefit obligation that would result from a one-percentage-point change in 1) the assumed discount rate and 2) the assumed rate of compensation increase.
- The change in the service cost and interest cost components of net periodic pension cost that would result from a one-percentage-point change in 1) the assumed discount rate and 2) the assumed rate of compensation increase.

9) Pension expense is reflected on the accrual basis.

10) Actuarial gains and losses applicable to a single event not related to the pension plan and not in the ordinary course of business are recognized immediately in earnings. (Examples are plant closing; segment disposal.)

FASB STATEMENT 88, EMPLOYER'S ACCOUNTING FOR SETTLEMENTS AND CURTAILMENTS OF DEFINED BENEFIT PENSION PLANS AND FOR TERMINATION BENEFITS

The reason for this separate Statement to be applied simultaneously with Statement 87 was the FASB's decision that a separate Statement on employer's accounting for a settlement of a pension obligation, or a curtailment of a defined benefit pension plan, or a termination of benefits, would provide a better understanding of the accounting procedures than to include them in the scope of Statement 87. This Statement applies to an employer that sponsors a defined benefit pension plan accounted for under the provisions of Statement 87 if all or part of the plan's pension benefit obligation is settled or the plan is curtailed. It also applies to an employer that offers benefits to employees in connection with their termination of employment.

The significant requirements of this Statement follow:

1) Statement 88 requires that recognized balances of prior service costs and net gains and losses computed under No. 87's delayed recognition model be considered to the extent specified in determining the effect on the income statement of a settlement or curtailment meeting the Standard's criteria.

2) Restatement of previously issued financial statements was prohibited, except for one provision that had a retroactive effect; e.g., at the time of transition to No. 87 companies having deferred gains resulting from previous asset reversions were required, subject to limitations, to recognize them as income.

3) A settlement and/or a curtailment may occur separately or together.

4) The maximum gain or loss subject to recognition in earnings when a pension obligation is settled is the unrecognized net gain or loss plus any remaining unrecognized net asset existing at the date of initial application of Statement 87.

5) The projected benefit obligation may be decreased (a gain) or increased (a loss) by a curtailment (see definition of *PLAN CURTAILMENT*). To the extent that a gain exceeds any unrecognized net loss, it is a curtailment gain. To the extent that a loss exceeds any unrecognized net gain, it is a curtailment loss.

6) An employer can provide benefits to employees in connection with their termination of employment. The benefits can be either *special termination benefits* offered only for a short period of time, or *contractual termination benefits* required by the terms of a plan only if a specified event (a plant closing, for example) occurs. The employer that gives special termination benefits must recognize a liability and a loss when the

employees accept the plan and the amount can be reasonably estimated. Termination benefits can take various forms including lump-sum payments, periodic future payments, a combination of both, paid directly from the employer's assets, from an existing pension plan, or from a new employee benefit plan.

7) The Statement sets forth the events that required previously unrecognized amounts to be recognized in earnings and as adjustments to assets and liabilities. The previously unrecognized net gain or net loss and the previously unrecognized prior service cost should be recognized in the period when *all* of the following conditions are met:

   a) All pension obligations are settled.

   b) Defined benefits are no longer accrued under the plan.

   c) The plan is not replaced by another defined benefit plan.

   d) No plan assets remain.

   e) The employees are terminated.

   f) The plan ceases to exist as an entity.

Disclosure Requirements

An employer recognizing a gain or loss must make the following disclosures:

1) A description of the nature of the event(s) associated with the gain or loss.

2) The amount of the gain or loss that is recognized.

"REASONABLE" COMPENSATION

Since all payments to compensate an employee for services which are ordinary and necessary to the operation of the business are deductible *provided* they are "reasonable," it is important to define the term.

What is "reasonable"? Not an easy task, the courts themselves have a hard time determining what is reasonable under certain facts. Nevertheless, following is a list of the several factors usually considered by the courts in dealing with this problem:

1) the employee's special qualifications

2) the nature, extent and scope of work

3) the size and complexities of the business

4) the prevailing general economic conditions

5) comparison of salaries to dividends

6) rates of compensation for comparable positions in comparable companies

7) the "arm's length" element in the compensation deal

8) consideration for past services and compensation in prior years

9) comparison of salaries paid with employee's stock ownership

Cash and Stock Bonuses

The cash bonus is used to assure the employee an immediate share of the company's profits over and above any regular compensation. In a non-contractual plan, answers to the questions concerning the amount of the bonus, who is to get it, and, in what proportions, are usually determined on a year-by-year basis—depending on the amount of profits.

Under a formal contractual basis, the employee knows beforehand exactly what to expect. If a certain profit is reached, the employee gets a definite amount.

The stock bonus plan is exactly like the cash bonus except, of course, that the payment is made in company stock. The big advantage of paying employee's bonuses in stock rather than cash is that the company can retain the cash to be used in the business. Furthermore, the corporation gets a compensation deduction for the market value of the stock.

Stock Options

An employee does not recognize any income upon the granting or exercise of an incentive stock option (ISO) provided that the option is exercised no later than three months after termination of employment and the employee does not dispose of the acquired shares within two years after the date of grant and one year after the date of exercise, whichever is later. Any gain realized upon disposition thereafter is treated as long-term capital gain. However, any difference between the option price and the market price must be recognized for alternative minimum tax purposes in the tax year the option is exercised.

These are the requirements for an incentive stock option.

1) The option must be granted in connection with employment and pursuant to a plan that includes:

   a) the aggregate number of shares that may be issued under the options and

b) the employees or class of employees eligible to receive options. The plan must be approved by the stockholders of the granting corporation within 12 months before or after the plan is adopted.

2) The option must be granted within 10 years after the plan is adopted or approved by the stockholders, whichever is earlier.

3) The option cannot be exercisable more than 10 years after the date of grant.

4) The option price cannot be less than the fair market value of the stock at the time of grant.

5) The option is nontransferable except by will or the laws of descent and distribution, and is exercisable only by the employee during his or her lifetime.

6) The employee does not own more than 10 percent of the voting stock of the employer corporation or of its parent or subsidiary.

DEFERRED COMPENSATION ARRANGEMENTS

With the fantastic growth of business over the years, the arrival of high corporate and individual tax rates, and the increased public interest in retirement planning, there has been evolved a mass of intricate and involved deferred compensation plans to attract new employees or retain old employees.

Under the deferred compensation plan, payment of compensation presently earned is postponed to a future period. If the plan qualifies as an exempt trust, the employer gets an immediate deduction for a contribution—even though the employee does not receive the sum until a later time. However, under a nonqualified deferred compensation contract, the employer gets a deduction only when the deferred compensation is actually paid to the employee (who is taxed at that time).

Under a nonqualified plan, the employer can pick and choose who will benefit and is not committed to a class of employees or any other rigid requirement as provided for in qualified deferred compensation plans. Generally, this arrangement is less ambitious than qualified plans and therefore more attractive to smaller organizations.

Most often the nonqualified deferred compensation plan is used for a key executive. The ordinary plan is to have the company accumulate funds for the benefit of the executive and then pay them out when the executive reaches post-retirement years and is in a lower tax bracket.

Deferred compensation contracts should be accounted for individually on an accrual basis, with the estimated amounts to be ultimately paid systematically, and rationally allocated over the period of active employment from the time the contract is effective until services are expected to end or the contract expires.

For annuity or lump-sum type settlements in these plans, the annual accrual should still be accrued over the time of active employment. Thus, the total expenses booked to the end of employment should equal the estimated present value of the money to be paid to the employee (or beneficiaries).

When payments extend beyond the period of active employment (such as annuity payments to a beneficiary), the present value of all said payments should be accrued and expensed.

Non-Compensatory Plans

A plan is considered to be non-compensatory when it possesses all four of the following characteristics:

1) Almost all full-time employees may participate
2) Stock is offered to employees equally based on a uniform percent of wages
3) The time for exercise is limited to a reasonable period
4) The discount from the market price of the stock is not greater than would be reasonable in an offer to stockholders or others.

Compensatory Plans

Stock issued to an employee under any plan *except* a non-compensatory plan (above) is considered to be a compensatory plan and calls for the recognition of *compensation expense* by the employer.

The time of earliest measurement (issuance, date of grant) is the determining factor as to when to record the compensation. The fact that the employee may not be able to receive or sell the stock for some years does *not* affect the compensation.

At the time of issuance (the date of the agreement), if the facts of the option price and a market price are known, the difference between a *higher* market price and the option price (the price at which the employee may buy the stock from the company) is considered to be compensation—at that time, not later. However, if the granting of the options is predicated upon the rendering of *future services*, the compensation calculated may be deferred to the period of future benefit (to be derived from those services). The excess (or bargain) is the theoretical benefit availed to the employee for services past, present or future.

For example, assume the employee's services would extend over two years (current and next year), the entry would be:

Current Year

Employees Compensation (current expense)		50.	
Unearned Compensation (holdover)		50.	
Paid-in Capital			100.
Market Price at issuance	$ 10.		
Option price	9.		
Excess per share	$ 1.		
100 shares@ $ 1	$ 100		

Next Year

Employees Compensation (expense)	50.	
Unearned Compensation		50.

Any "unearned compensation" should be shown as a separate reduction of stock options under the stockholders' equity.

No compensation is recognized if the option price equals or exceeds the market price at option issuance date.

Note again that the *exercise* date is not pertinent—yet.

For *tax* purposes, the amount deductible by the corporation is not applicable or determinable until the time the employee must pick up ordinary income, a factor which varies according to the plan as specified under IRS regulations. Thus, both the period and amount of expensing will probably differ for tax purposes, thus creating timing differences. Also, the difference between the compensation originally recorded and the tax-deductible amount goes to Capital Surplus.

The accounting for stock options follows:

Assume a stock option plan for an officer of the corporation which is for 1000 shares of $25 par value common stock. The stock can be purchased for $20 a share after 5 years. The market price on January 1, 1995, is $37.50 per share. January 1, 1995, is the measurement date, because the option price of $20 and the number of shares that can be acquired (1000) are both known. The compensation per share to be recognized is the difference between the market price ($37.50) and the option price ($20), as the officer is employed over the five-year period.

Entry at the End of Year 1

Dec. 31, 1995	Salary Expense	3,500	
	Stock Options		
	Excersisable		3,500

"To record portion of compensatory stock option plan earned as of 12/31/95. (1000 × $17.50=$17,500 × 1/5=$3,500)

This entry is repeated each year until the options are exercised.)

The options are exercised on December 31, 1999, and the officer remits the $20 per share option price.

Dec. 31, 1999	Cash	20,000	
	Stock Options		
	Exercisable	17,500	
	Common Stock ($25 par)		25,000
	Paid-in Capital in		
	Excess of Par Value		12,500

Effect Upon Earnings Per Share

All shares which could be issued under the arrangement are considered "as if" issued, and considered to be common stock equivalents and outstanding for earnings per share computations. If applicable, the treasury stock method is used to determine the incremental shares.

Compensatory stock options may thus affect *both* factors in the EPS formula: the numerator, for the compensation expense, and the denominator by the addition of the equivalent shares.

Both primary and fully diluted computations are affected, if three percent or more.

DEFINED CONTRIBUTION PLANS

These plans specify either:

1) Benefits will be based on defined *contributions*, or
2) Contributions will result in defined *benefits*.

In circumstance 1), the contribution is the pension cost for the year. Circumstance 2) requires the determination of pension cost in the same detailed manner just described.

PROFIT SHARING PLANS

Contributions are based upon independent action taken by the corporate Board of Directors, tied to the profit of the year, under a profit sharing agreement approved by both management and employees. The authority for the contribution is reflected in the minutes of the corporation. The IRS also approves the plan.

The IRS imposes a combined maximum tax-deductible limit for companies having *both* plans.

ACTUARIAL GAINS AND LOSSES

Reported gains or losses within the plans should be considered, generally on the average method, and only to the extent that they might necessitate a change in the contribution requirement. These gains or losses are usually reflected in the computations made by the fund administrator in the determination of the amount needed to be contributed by the corporation to keep the plan properly funded, subject to the minimum and maximum considerations.

INSURANCE PLANS

Insured plans.   Usually the amount of net premium payment determined by the insurance company is the proper pension cost for the employer, provided dividends, termination costs and other factors are handled properly by the insurance company.

Companies with more than one plan.   Actuarial methods may differ, but accounting for each plan should follow the stated standards.

Key-person insurance.   The acceptable method of accounting for premium costs incurred in buying key-person (non-term) life insurance is to first charge an asset account for the period's increase in the cash surrender value of the policy, and then expense the difference between that increase and the premium paid. The ratable charge method is not acceptable. This procedure applies only to those polices under which the corporation is the ultimate beneficiary. But the procedure also applies to those policies which may be taken on "debtor-corporation" officers.

A loan on a life insurance policy of an officer can be shown in either of two ways:

1) As a current liability if the company intends to repay it within the current year; or

2) As a deduction from the amount shown as cash surrender value if the company does *not* intend to repay it within a year. If it runs to the death of the insured, it is deducted from the proceeds if the corporation transmits them to the survivors.

Although the corporation is the beneficiary of these funds on a pay-out of the policy, the proceeds are usually used to pay benefits to the employee's family, to redeem stock, or for some other purpose beneficial to the employee.

Split-dollar insurance.   The employee pays a portion of the premium to the employer under this plan (life insurance), and that portion reduces the amount included in income (the includable amount would be, in effect, the employer's share of the premium). Any policy dividends received by the employee are also included in his or her income.

Group term life insurance.   This arrangement offers an employee an opportunity to acquire low-cost life insurance because it is purchased for a "group." Under a "group term" plan the employee can get insurance protection tax-free up to a specified amount; all premiums paid over that amount of insurance must be included in income. But the plan has to be a group *term* plan. Permanent insurance (whole life policy) does not qualify under this provision.

Group health.   This plan provides for the reimbursement of medical and hospitalization expenses incurred by an employee. Premiums are tax deductible by the employer and not taxable to the employee even though the plan provides for the protection of the employee's family. This plan is widely used by many employers to provide their employees with at least the basic health and accident protection. Of course, individual health plans for particular employees are also used.

Tax Advantages of Qualified Plans

Employer: The employer gets a current deduction for amounts contributed to the plan, within specified limits, although no benefits may have been actually distributed to the participating employees that year. This permits an employer to accumulate a trust fund for employees with before-tax dollars. The employer expense for the contribution to a qualified plan may be accrued at year-end, but it must be paid no later than the legal time of filing the return (including extensions).

Employees: The tax to the employee is deferred until the benefits under the plan are actually distributed or made available. If the employee receives a lump-sum distribution, a portion of it may be capital gains (based on years of participation prior to 1974) and the remaining taxable portion is subject to ordinary income rates, but there is a special 10-year averaging option available.

Trust Fund: The income and gains on the sale of trust property of the trust fund are exempt from tax—in effect, being postponed until distribution. Funds, which are compounded tax-free under a qualified plan, increase at a much greater rate than if such funds were currently distributed to employees and personally invested by them. In the latter case, the amount received by the employees is subject to two tax bites—upon receipt of the benefits and again on the investment income earned on what is left.

Choosing Between Pension and Profit Sharing

Profit Sharing

1) Generally favors younger employees.
2) Need not provide retirement benefits.
3) Contribution can be made only if profits exist.
4) Even in profitable years the amount of contributions, if any, can be left to discretion of management.
5) Contributed amounts generally cannot exceed 15% of year's payroll for participants.
6) Forfeitures may be allocated in favor of remaining participants.
7) No more than 50% of participant's account may be invested in life insurance.
8) Broad fringe benefits can be included (incidental accident and health insurance).
9) Employer may never recover any part of contribution or income therefrom.

Pension

1) Generally favors older employees.
2) Must provide retirement benefits.
3) Contributions must be made for profitable as well as for loss years.
4) Amount of contribution is not discretionary; it must be actuarially justifiable and tied to definitely determinable benefits.
5) No maximum limit on contributions as long as they are actuarially justifiable and total compensation is within IRS 162 limitations.
6) Forfeitures must be used to decrease future cost to employer.
7) May be completely funded by investment in life insurance.
8) Limited fringe benefits can be included (disability pension).
9) Employer on termination of plan may recover excess funds which arose as a result of actuarial error.

Miscellaneous Considerations

In a business combination, the rule for assigning an amount for the assumption of pension cost accruals should be the greater of:

1) The accrued pension cost computed in conformity with the accounting policies of the acquiring company, or
2) The excess, if any, of the actuarially computed value of the vested benefits over the amount of the fund.

In the disposal of a business segment, costs and expenses directly associated with the decision to dispose should include such items as:

1) Severance pay;
2) Additional pension costs;
3) Employee relocation expenses.

In pooling-of-interest, employee compensation and stock option plans, if reasonable, may carry over to the acquiring company without violating the precepts of pooling.

401(k) Plans

The main features of 401(k) plans follow:

1) Current tax savings for employers and employees.
2) Employees can accumulate a substantial retirement fund by putting a portion of their income into a tax-deductible plan.
3) Suitable for companies with a high percentage of employees who are willing to save a portion of their pay. 70 percent of all employees, or 80 percent of eligible employees, must choose to participate in the plan.
4) Companies contributing to a profit-sharing plan can also contribute to a 401(k) plan, as the plan can be combined with an existing pension or profit-sharing plan.
5) Employee's contribution can be a portion of pay, or in lieu of a pay increase.
6) All funds placed in the plan are deductible by the employer. And the employee's contribution and subsequent earnings on the plan's investments are tax-free to the employee until withdrawal.

7) Lump-sum withdrawals qualify for 10-year averaging.

8) Employer and employee's contributions can be as much as 15 percent of the employee's pay, up to an annual dollar limit on profit-sharing plans.

9) Employer's costs associated with establishing and administering the plan are deductible as ordinary business expenses.

10) 401(k) plan must be part of a qualified profit-sharing or stock bonus plan. A qualified plan must meet the following requirements:

    a) The plan must permit the employee to elect to have the employer's contribution made to an employee trust.

    b) The plan must prohibit a distribution of trust benefits attributable to employer contributions made merely because of the completion of a stated period of participation, or the lapse of a fixed number of years.

    c) The employee's right to the accrued benefit derived from employer contributions must be nonforfeitable.

    d) The plan must meet nondiscrimination rules pertaining to employee coverage.

A plan meets the nondiscrimination rule if:

    a) The plan prohibits contributions and benefits from discriminating in favor of employees who are officers, shareholders, or highly compensated employees.

    b) The plan either covers a certain minimum percentage of employees, or does not discriminate in its coverage.

    c) The plan must cover a certain minimum percentage of eligible employees.

    d) The contributions made to the plan must satisfy one of two *actual deferral percentage* tests:

        • The test for eligible highly compensated employees must not be more than the deferral percentage of all other eligible employees multiplied by 1.5; or

        • The excess of the actual deferral percentage for the highly compensated employees must not be more than the actual deferral percentage of all other eligible employees multiplied by 2.5.

11) Employees *may* borrow from the plan, but under strict guidelines set forth in the Code and in IRS regulations.

12) A 401(k) plan may impact other qualified plans. If an employee is a participant in a 401(k) plan and elects to defer a portion of pay into the plan, the reduction in compensation for federal income tax purposes may affect potential benefits under other plans in which the employee is a participant. For example, if the employee is in a profit-sharing plan under which employer contributions are geared to pay, a reduction in pay due to a 401(k) contribution may reduce the employer's contribution to the profit-sharing plan. The same is true with defined benefit pension plans in which potential benefits are based upon current compensation, and which could be affected by deferrals into a 401(k) plan.

13) Participation in a 401(k) plan does not affect an employee's right to set up an IRA.

14) The plan cannot discriminate in favor of "key" or highest paid officers, executives, the "highly compensated," or shareholders.

ERISA

The Employee Retirement Income Security Act of 1974, commonly called ERISA, substantially changed the rules and set new minimum standards for employees' trusts, most notably in the following areas:

1) Participation rules.
2) Vesting rights.
3) Funding requirements.

In addition, the tax and information forms which are required to be filed with the IRS (and in some cases with the Department of Labor) were changed and are constantly being revamped.

Arguments both for and against this law are being debated, and much confusion still surrounds its administration, regulation, interpretation and effect. Professional advice should be sought for updating old plans and for instituting new plans, as well as for assuring conformance with the required new regulations and reporting.

Social Security Benefits and Pension Plans

Some pension plans provide for reduced benefits to the extent of Social Security benefits. In estimating future benefits for present value purposes under the plan, estimate must also be made for the Social Security benefits applicable.

FASB STATEMENT 106, *Employers' Accounting for Postretirement Benefits Other Than Pensions*

FASB Statement 106 applies to all postretirement benefits other than pensions, sometimes referred to as OPEBs (other postretirement employee benefits), provided by employers to employees. The requirements of Statement 106 are similar in most respects to those in Statements 87 and 88. The product of nearly 11 years' work, Statement 106 requires large public companies to begin taking charges for the cash they expect to pay out in the future for medical and other nonpension benefits promised to retired employees and their families.

Previously, companies were given the option of using accrual accounting similar to that required under Standards 87 and 88 for the postretirement benefit plans. However, since so few employers availed themselves of the opportunity voluntarily, many were stunned by the arrival of 1993 and the concomitant necessity of facing up to the requirements of Statement 106. Private companies with fewer than 500 participants in a plan and non-U.S. plans had to be in compliance in 1995.

Until Statement 106, these costs had been recognized as expenses as they were paid each year. However, companies must now expense the costs associated with the benefits as they are earned by employees. In shifting from a pay-as-you-go cash basis to accrual accounting, companies must acknowledge a huge "catchup" liability: the total present value of future commitments already made to present retirees and employees.

Decisions about transition obligations relating to those benefits deemed earned at the time FASB 106 was adopted, but not yet expensed under cash-basis accounting, have now been weighed and considered. Subject to certain limitations, when a company converts to the accrual method, the transition obligation can be recognized immediately through a onetime charge to income. The other choice is to extend the transition obligations over succeeding years, using a straight-line method applied to the average remaining service period of active participants, or 20 years, whichever time is longer.

Regardless of which alternative has been selected, most companies have unquestionably had little awareness of the enormity of the obligations they were building up. If there were no other positive aspects, at last management has been forced to come face to face with the reality that lay ahead, particularly in relation to health care costs. However, other areas of benefits can also add substantial obligations: life insurance outside a pension plan, tuition assistance, day care, legal assistance, and housing subsidies, among other benefits.

The Statement covers both defined benefit and defined contribution-type plans. Underlying the new Statement is the assumption that postretirement benefits are a form of deferred compensation that should be recorded using the accrual method as a cost during the employee's active work life when the employer actually receives the benefits of the employee's services. The accrual of the cost under this method begins when an employee is hired, and continues until the employee becomes eligible for the full benefits under the terms of the particular plan.

In the case of defined contribution postretirement plans, the Rule requires that the postretirement cost be the annual contribution during the employee's active service period. If funding is delayed to retirement, the future estimated cost must be accrued over the employee's service life.

The estimate of the present value of an employer's postretirement benefit obligation is the principal determinant of postretirement benefit costs. An employer's postretirement obligation is the actuarial present value, as of a specific date, of the postretirement benefits expected to be provided by the employer in the future, that are attributable to current and retired employees.

Companies who must now separate the cost of retiree benefits from those of active workers could formerly combine them. To estimate future obligations in addition to current costs, company estimates will be required that could easily be far off the mark. The forward-looking estimates will necessitate a number of subjective considerations, including the projected cost of medical benefits. During the last decade, the number of retirees and the average life expectancy have increased appreciably, while the cost of health care has grown much faster than other sectors of the economy.

To add to the problem, a reduction of federal and state Medicare and Medicaid benefits has resulted in private companies having to absorb the increase in medical costs and has forced health care reimbursement plans to cover a larger share of these costs. As a result, earnings pressures may cause companies to consider reducing or canceling health care benefits, perhaps to the detriment of the company.

When taking into account years of benefit coverage, an important element in computing possible payouts, an estimate must include the number of retirees and dependents eligible for benefits, multiplied by the number of years each will be covered. These projections require using data on current employees and retirees, including age, gender, and number of dependents, as well as actuarial assumptions for retirement age, employee turnover, and life expectancy. As is readily apparent, these variables are subject to wide margins of error, but they are not the only element for errors in projections.

Another difficult determinant of plan payouts is the number of times each of the medical services covered under existing plans may be used by the retirees and their dependents and the net cost to the company. This can be projected by estimating plan variables, such as the deductible factor, level of participant contributions, number and length of hospital stays, and frequency of doctor visits by a similar sector of the population. Among important factors is the price paid by participants, net of relevant reimbursements such as Medicare. These costs must be estimated using actuarial projections of medical cost increases.

If a company changes its benefits and updates its assumptions, there will be an immediate effect on the annual service costs of employers' OPEB by producing actuarial gains and losses. Similar to pensions, a practice can be adopted that will either recognize or defer the changes. If deferral is used, amortization of the deferral is required only when the cumulative amount exceeds a prescribed minimum. The main effect of deferrals is to help eliminate volatility due to the need to use assumptions.

The major tax impact will arise from federal income taxes, although other taxes may also be affected for certain funding approaches. The deductions are governed by the tax code: "There shall be allowed as a deduction all the ordinary and necessary expenses paid or incurred during the taxable year in carrying on any trade or business, including a reasonable allowance for salaries or *other compensation* for personal services actually rendered." When postretirement benefits meet these requirements, they can be deducted when paid, as the tax code requires companies to use the pay-as-you-go method to compute their tax deduction for benefit payments. Federal tax deductions for OPEB are generally allowed only at the time the benefits are paid. Under limited conditions, deductions can be allowed when the obligation is prefunded.

Those who in the past have offered generous postretirement benefits and who have high ratios of retirees to active employees were probably already beginning to feel profit pressures even under cash-basis accounting. New, rapidly growing companies having low turnover, young workers, and few retirees may begin to feel the pressures under this rule.

However, Statement 106 does allow management, under certain circumstances, to assume it will be able to modify the company's current postretirement benefit plan to provide fewer future benefits, which will lower current obligations. Since plans with ceilings on benefits are usually less costly than plans without benefit limitations, a shift from unlimited to limited benefits appears to be one option a company faced with mounting benefits costs will consider. Such changes in the plan provisions to anticipate changes in the computation of the obligations and costs are permissible as long as the changes have been communicated to plan participants.

Not only is the employer required to adopt accrual accounting under FASB 106, but very specific and detailed *disclosure* is required relating to the employer's obligations and the accompanying costs.

Required disclosures include:

1) A description of the *substantive plan*, as opposed to merely presenting a copy of the *extant written* plan from the company's files, including:

   a) the nature of the plan,

   b) any modifications regarding cost-sharing provisions,

   c) any agreements for increase of monetary benefits,

   d) the employee groups covered,

   e) the nature and types of benefits covered,

   f) the funding policy,

   g) the types of assets and/or any significant nonbenefit liability, and

   h) the nature and effect of events, such as a business combination and divestiture, which could make it difficult to compare information of different accounting periods.

2) The amount of net periodic postretirement benefit costs with the following components shown separately:

   a) service cost,

   b) interest cost,

   c) actual return on plan assets for that period,

   d) amortization of any unrecognized transition obligations or assets,

   e) net total of other components.

3) A reconciliation of the funded status of the particular plan with the following amounts shown *separately* in the company's statement of financial position:

   a) the fair value of the plan assets,

   b) accumulated postretirement benefit obligations with separate identification of the portions attributable to the three distinct groups—retirees, other fully eligible plan participants, and other active plan participants,

   c) unrecognized prior service costs,

   d) unrecognized net gain/loss including plan asset gain/loss not yet reflected in the market-related value,

   e) any remaining unrecognized transition, obligation/asset, and

   f) the net result of combining the five items above to obtain the net postretirement benefit asset/liability.

4) The assumed health care cost trend rate utilized in measuring the anticipated costs for the next year, a general description of the direction and pattern of change in the following years, as well as the "ultimate" trend rate and when that rate is expected to be reached. (With the amount of

time, discussion, media coverage, and invective being devoted to health care costs at this juncture, this disclosure item will unquestionably be of the crystal ball variety.)

5) The weighted average of the assumed discount rate and rate of increase, if any, utilized in measuring the accumulated postretirement benefit obligation; the weighted average of the anticipated long-term rate of return on plan assets; and the estimated income tax rate included in that rate of return for plans in which the income is not included with the employer's investment income for tax purposes.

6) Based on the substantive plan with all other assumptions held constant, the effect of a one percent increase in the assumed health care cost trend rate for each future year relating to:

   a) the sum total of the service and interest cost items of net periodic postretirement health care benefit cost, and

   b) the accumulated postretirement benefit obligation for health care benefits.

7) The nature and amounts of any employer and related parties' securities held among plan assets; the approximate amount of annual benefits anticipated from insurance coverage issued by the employer and related parties.

8) Any alternative method used consistently in amortizing unrecognized prior service cost or unrecognized gain or loss more rapidly than required.

9) The amount of any gain or loss recognized with a description of the events leading to a settlement or curtailment during the year.

10) The cost of special or contractual termination benefits recognized including a description thereof during the given period.

FASB STATEMENT 112, *EMPLOYERS' ACCOUNTING FOR POSTEMPLOYMENT BENEFITS*

For fiscal years beginning after December 15, 1993, Statement 112 set standards for the financial accounting and reporting of the estimated costs incurred by employers who provide benefits to former or inactive employees after employment but before retirement. These postemployment benefits are of various types provided to former or inactive employees, their beneficiaries, and covered dependents.

Inactive employees are those who at a given time are not actively participating in company business or actually rendering service to the employer, but they have not been terminated. This group may consist of employees who have been laid off and those on disability leave, even though they may not be expected to return to active status. The benefits may include, but are not limited to, salary continuation, supplemental unemployment benefits, severance benefits, disability benefits including workers' compensation, job training and/or counseling, and continuation of benefits like health care and life insurance coverage.

These benefits can be provided in cash or in kind, and they can be paid as a result of death, or other event, as well as from temporary or permanent disability or layoff. They can be paid immediately upon cessation of active employment or over a specified period of time. Employees' rights to benefits may accumulate or vest as they render service.

The Statement should be considered an outgrowth, or more properly a continuation, of FASB work in developing Statement 106. While that project was underway, the members specifically declined to give consideration to the employers' accounting requirements for postemployment benefits other than pensions. They agreed to delay this specific aspect of the project and to deal with it as a separate phase. Thus, with the adoption of Statement 112, the Board's consideration of employers' accounting for pensions and all other postemployment benefits appears to be completed.

FASB 112 amends, but does not significantly alter, FASB Statement 5, *Accounting for Contingencies* and FASB Statement 43, *Accounting for Compensated Absences*. It affirms the view that generally accepted accounting principles require recognition of the cost of postemployment benefits on an accrual basis and amends the above mentioned Statements to include the accounting for these postemployment benefits.

It is necessary for employers to recognize the obligation to provide postemployment benefits in accordance with FASB Statement 43 if:

1) the obligation is attributable to employees' services already rendered
2) employees have the right to let those benefits accumulate or vest
3) payment of the benefits is probable
4) the amount of the benefits can be reasonably estimated.

If these four conditions are not met, the employer should account for postemployment benefits when it is probable that a liability has been incurred and the amount can be reasonably estimated in accordance with FASB 5. When an obligation for postemployment benefits has not been accrued in accordance with either of these FASB Statements because the company's management feels that the amount of the obligation cannot be reasonably estimated, the reasoning behind the inability to arrive at an estimate must be disclosed in the financial statement.

The accounting for postemployment benefits provided through a pension or postretirement benefit plan, as set forth in Statements 87, 88 and 106 are not affected by Statement 112.

Chapter 20

Tax Accounting

In a landmark case, the court ruled:

> "The essence of any effective system of taxation is the production of revenue ascertainable and payable to the Government at regular intervals. Only a system of ascertaining income and tax at regular intervals, i.e., years, could produce a regular flow of income to the Treasury and permit the application of methods of accounting, assessment and collection capable of practical application by both the government and the taxpayer."

The determination of the proper timing for reporting income and deductions for tax purposes is considered to be the most important function of accounting. The timing of income and deductions involves determining the proper year in which each item of income and each deductible item should be reported. In a Tax Court case, the court ruled:

> "The annual reporting period is a necessity in administering the tax law, and the cornerstone of our tax structure."

There is not complete conformity between tax accounting and financial accounting, primarily because many financial accounting decisions are based upon estimates and opinions, while tax accounting decisions are based upon completed transactions and clearly identifiable events. For example, it is proper financial accounting practice to establish a reserve for a contingent warranty expense, based upon a manufacturer's experience for the estimate of future warranty expense. This approach complies with the matching principle, i.e., the income from the sale of the product is matched with one of the

496

expenses of making the sale—the expense of fulfilling the warranty obligation. However, no tax deduction is allowed for tax accounting purposes until the estimated expense is actually incurred under the terms of the warranty.

Therefore, the main problem in tax accounting is the allocation of income and expense deductions to the maximum benefit of the taxpayer.

Accountant's Responsibility

Most everyone knows *something* about taxes; no one knows *everything* about taxes. Nonetheless, accountants are *presumed* to know taxes. Generally speaking, they probably are familiar with most of the overall, basic, more prominent features of the tax law—those sections which have been thoroughly tested in the courts and resolved into the traditional body of the law.

However, because of the intricate provisions and the relief loopholes provided and adjudicated, because of the often ambiguous legal wording and the necessity for interpretive regulations and further testing in the Tax Court, because of the very nature of the taxpayer/IRS adversary relationship, accountants, as well as others, merely serve as perhaps better-informed, but still "opinion-only" experts. Formerly, it was only the taxpayer who had to bear the burden—and the cost and the responsibility.

Now the Tax Reform Act of 1976, and subsequent amendments, subject preparers of tax returns to incur penalties if they do not comply with new standards and procedures. Accountants and others who prepare tax returns or give tax advice should be familiar with the preparer's liabilities for penalties. These penalties are incurred for the following simple omissions:

1) The failure to sign a tax return for which they were paid;
2) The failure to give a copy of the tax return to the taxpayer;
3) Failure to maintain a list of tax returns prepared.

A more serious problem has been created by subjecting a preparer to a penalty for other negligence or the willful understatement of income tax. This has been interpreted by some Districts of the Internal Revenue Service to mean the failure to follow all the rules and regulations of the Service. The highlights of tax methods, procedures and considerations presented in this section are timely reminders of certain features of the tax law to be considered when advising a client. In no way should they be considered all-inclusive or all-instructive.

Further research into the tax law, the regulations, the interpretations and the court decisions is advised. Extensive tax publication services are available, constantly updating the ever-changing features of Federal and State tax laws and regulations.

Tax *evasion* is illegal.

Tax *avoidance* is legal. It is statutory.

Tax avoidance is on the books, in the courts—for you to find.

Research all pertinent topics.

Tax Return Preparation

For many corporations, assembling and analyzing the information needed to prepare the corporate tax returns can be a considerable task. Most, if not all, of the company's accounts have to be analyzed; provision often must be made for various types of allocations for state tax purposes; in the case of a corporation the activities of many branches, subsidiaries, or affiliates have to be coordinated (and the accounting records may be dispersed over many locations). In addition, the accounting personnel responsible for keeping the corporate books are not likely to be tax men, and the tax department may have to review the accounts with an eye to the tax significance of the various transactions.

How the tax return information will be assembled will depend in large part on the organization of the company. In a small company with few employees, the "tax expert" may also be the one in charge of the books and may do all the analysis personally by direct examination of the company's books and records. In larger companies, the task of gathering the tax information may be more or less systematized, depending on the size of the company; the number and geographic location of the divisions, subsidiaries, or affiliates; the location and responsibilities for the accounting record; and the existence of a separate tax department.

In any event, however the information is put together, whether by direct examination of the books and records by the tax person, direct interviews of various accounting personnel by the tax department representatives, use of questionnaires (completed by the accounting personnel or by the tax department personnel after discussion with accounting personnel), some system should be developed to make sure all the pertinent information is gathered and analyzed in some systematic and usable form.

The accountant's task in finding tax opportunities (or pitfalls) may be greatly simplified by the use of a tax-planning checklist which points out some of the planning possibilities. The items on the checklist should be set up in financial audit format and should suggest the action to be taken which would bring the desired tax results.

An accountant performing preparer services must require a written statement from a client that the client has adequate records to support claimed travel and entertainment deductions.

A tax preparer who colludes with a client in a willful misstatement of the client's tax liability is liable to a $1,000 fine, and loss of the privilege to practice before the Internal Revenue Service. A taxpayer can be assessed a penalty for poor recordkeeping of deductions.

While it may not be necessary to analyze in detail each account for routine items, it probably is necessary to have some formal procedure for analyzing all items that have special tax significance. The checklists enumerate many of the items you may want to check (if they apply) and the reasons for wanting a special analysis of each. With these as starting points, you may readily find other areas of special significance that could be added.

The tax consequences of business transactions are usually determined by their legal status, the accounting treatment of such items, or both. It therefore becomes imperative to plan accounting techniques and legal opinions based upon legal requirements and generally accepted accounting principles and practices *before* entering into any transactions.

Once the transaction has occurred and the book entry has been made, it is usually too late to worry about the tax consequences. Even minor issues should be worked out in advance using proper procedures. For example, careful wording of purchase orders will often insure proper description on invoices, so that portions of work done that are deductible as repairs are properly described and billed separately from work done on permanent installations and improvements, that are required to be capitalized.

In order to plan properly, you must know the accounting techniques available to you. Here are the choices:

1) Taxable year.
2) Cash, accrual, or an approved hybrid accounting method.
3) Last-in-first-out (LIFO) or first-in-first-out (FIFO) inventory method.
4) Cost, or lower-of-cost-or-market, as method of evaluation of inventory.
5) Method of handling time sales.
6) Method of handling long-term contracts.

What the Tax Law Requires

Definitions

Gross Income: All income from whatever source derived, unless excluded by law. Includes income realized in any form whether in money, property, or services.

Income Taxes: Taxes based on income determined under the provisions of the U.S. Internal Revenue Code.

Taxable Income: For business, gross income reduced by all allowable deductions.

Income Tax Expense: The amount of income taxes (whether or not currently payable or refundable) allocable to a period in the determination of net income.

The law specifies only that you compute taxable income in accordance with the method of accounting you regularly employ in keeping your books; however, such method must clearly reflect your income.

Each taxpayer is authorized to adopt such forms and systems of accounting as judged best suited to his or her purpose. No uniform method is prescribed for all taxpayers. Nevertheless, the Regulations provide that:

1) All items of gross income and deductions must be treated with reasonable consistency;

2) In all cases in which the production, purchase, or sale of merchandise is an income producing factor, the accrual method of accounting must be used. Inventories of merchandise on hand (including finished goods, work in process, raw materials and supplies) must be taken at the beginning and end of the accounting period and used in computing taxable income of the period;

3) Expenditures made during the fiscal year should be properly classified as between capital and expense. Expenditures for items such as plant and equipment which have a useful life extending over a number of years must be charged to capital expenditures rather than to expense;

4) Where capital costs are being recovered through deductions for wear and tear, depletion, or obsolescence, expenditures (other than ordinary repairs) made to restore the property or prolong its useful life should be added to the property account or charged against the appropriate reserve, not to current expense;

Those who neither produce nor sell goods and consequently have no inventories can use either of the two regular methods of accounting, the cash or accrual. This includes artists; authors; artisans, such as carpenters and masons who either use their customers' materials or buy materials for specific jobs only; professionals, such as accountants, architects, attorneys, dentists, physicians and engineers; and brokers and agents rendering services of various kinds;

5) Special methods of accounting are also prescribed in the Code. Such methods include the crop method, the installment method and the long-term contract method. There are also special methods of accounting for particular items of income and expense;

6) A combination of methods (hybrid system) of accounting may also be used in connection with a trade or business, if consistently used;

7) The fact that books are kept in accordance with the requirements of a supervisory agency does not mean that income for tax purposes is computed in the same manner.

CHOOSING A TAXABLE YEAR

Taxable Year

The taxpayer's annual accounting period (including a 52- or 53-week year) which is the basis for which the taxpayer regularly computes an income in keeping the books.

The initial choice of an accounting period is generally within the control of the taxpayer. However, many taxpayers forfeit this right by giving the matter haphazard, last-minute consideration. The result is that they adopt an annual accounting period ill-suited to their business needs.

Four Possible Choices   There are four types of taxable years recognized by the Code. They are:

1) *Calendar Year.* A 12-month period ending on December 31;
2) *Fiscal Year.* A 12-month period ending on the last day of any month of the year other than December.
3) *52–53 Week Year.* This is a fiscal year, varying from 52 to 53 weeks in duration, which ends always on the same day of the week, which (a) occurs for the last time in a calendar month, or (b) falls nearest the end of the calendar month.
4) *Short Period.* A period of less than 12 months (allowed only in certain special situations such as initial return, final return, change in accounting period, and termination of taxable year by reason of jeopardy assessment).

Partnerships, S Corporations, and personal service corporations must use a taxable year that generally conforms to the taxable year of the owners. A partnership must use in order of priority: 1) the taxable year of the partners owning the majority of partnership profits and capital; 2) the taxable year of all of its principal partners; 3) a calendar year. S Corporations and personal service corporations must use the calendar year. If to the satisfaction of the Secretary of the Treasury it can be established that there is a business purpose for having a different taxable year, these three entities may be permitted an alternative choice.

Shift of Tax Year with Permission

In a first return a new taxpayer can select any taxable year permitted by the code. However, a taxpayer whose taxable year is a calendar year cannot adopt a fiscal year without the prior approval of IRS.

If a taxpayer does receive permission to change an accounting period, a return should be made for the short period beginning on the day after the close of the old taxable year and ending at the end of the day before the day designated as the first day of the new taxable year. Generally, if a return is made for a short period, it is necessary that the income for the period be annualized and then divided by the number of months in the short period. The tax is then computed on that amount.

To prevent inequities, the law provides that on the taxpayer's establishing the amount of taxable income for the 12-month period, computed as if the period were a taxable year, the tax for the short period shall be reduced to the greater of the following;

1) An amount which bears the same ratio to the tax computed on the taxable income for the 12-month period, as the taxable income computed on the basis of the short period bears to the taxable income for the 12-month period; or

2) The tax computed on the taxable income for the short period without placing the taxable income on an annual basis.

How to get permission: Application for permission to change must be made on Form 1128 by the 15th day of the second month following the short period needed to effect the change. The motive for the change must be a business reason and not one of tax avoidance.

CHANGE OF ACCOUNTING METHOD

What is a change in accounting method? This occurs when an accounting principle is used that is different from the principle used previously for reporting purposes. The term "accounting principle" includes not only accounting principles and practices, but also the methods of applying them. For example, a change in inventory valuation from LIFO to FIFO is a change in method.

It should be noted that the correction of an error in previously issued financial statements (computational errors, oversights, misapplication of an accounting principle) is not an accounting change or change in method.

A change in accounting method can be required either by IRS or initiated by the taxpayer. If the former, the change must conform to the method required by the law. If the latter, the taxpayer, with a few exceptions, must obtain IRS approval, irrespective of whether the changes conform to GAAP, or the tax law.

Changes requiring IRS approval:

• A change from cash to the accrual method for gross income and expenses.

- A change in depreciation method.
- A change in the basis for inventory valuation method.
- Changes in the reporting entity; e.g., a change in the subsidiary-parent organization because the statements are considered to be those of a different entity.
- Changes in the method for a material item. (A material item is defined in the Code to be "any item that involves the proper time for inclusion of an item in income or the taking of a deduction.")

Changes in method do not include:

- Correction of arithmetic errors.
- Correction of improper postings.
- Adjustments to the depreciation schedule.
- Changes made necessary by changes in the circumstances and facts governing the current method.

A special rule applies to dealers in personal property. A dealer can adopt at the time of a transaction (or a change *to*) the installment method of accounting without IRS consent. But a dealer cannot change *from* the installment method *to* any other method without IRS consent.

Under present procedure application for permission to change an accounting method or practice is filed on Form 3115 within the first 180 days of the year to which the change is to apply. Adjustments resulting from the change are taken ratably "over an approximate period, prescribed by the Commissioner, generally ten years," beginning with the year of change. Applications usually receive favorable consideration if the taxpayer agrees to the ten-year spread or any other approach suggested by IRS.

In the case of the taxpayer wanting to discontinue the LIFO method of inventory valuation, the readjustment period of ten years will usually be allowed; however, the taxpayer cannot apply LIFO again during the ten-year allocation period without IRS consent.

Income for tax purposes must be computed under the same method of accounting regularly used by you in keeping your books. If you have not used a method regularly or if the method regularly used does not clearly reflect income, the Commissioner can compute your income under a method which he considers clearly reflects your income.

Except for some special situations, you may not change your method of accounting without the prior consent of the Commissioner.

It becomes important, therefore, to know whether a change constitutes a change in accounting method or merely a correction of an error (not requiring consent).

Consent is *required* for the following changes:

1) From the cash to the accrual basis;
2) Method of valuing inventory;
3) From/to completed contract method, from/to percentage-of-completion method, or a change from/to any other method to the contract method;
4) Those involving special methods, such as the installment method or crop method;
5) Those specifically enumerated in the Code.

Consent is *not* required for the following changes:

1) Correction of mathematical, posting or timing errors;
2) Correction of bad debt reserves;
3) Changes in estimated useful lives of depreciable assets.

The 1984 tax bill clarified the Code with respect to changes in an accounting method. In the past, some taxpayers contended that there is no requirement to obtain IRS's permission to change from an *improper* to a proper accounting method; that a failure of IRS to consent to a change in this circumstance is a defense against an IRS charge of negligence and penalty assessment.

Congress in the new law has specifically provided that when a taxpayer fails to file a request to change its accounting method, the absence of IRS consent cannot be a defense to any penalty assessed for the taxpayer's failure to request a consent to the change.

Normally, a corporation is likely to use the accrual method of accounting. But some service companies will use the cash method. And in special types of businesses, specialized methods may be desirable.

(Note: APB Opinion No. 20, *Accounting Changes*, is the GAAP covering accounting changes.)

INCOME

The conflicts between tax accounting and generally accepted business accounting center around the questions: 1) *when* is it income? and 2) *when* is it deductible? To illustrate the differences that have existed in these two areas, we include the following list which was submitted by the American Institute of Certified Public Accountants to the House Committee on Ways and Means.

Form **3115** (Rev. April 1986) Department of the Treasury Internal Revenue Service	**Application for Change in Accounting Method** Note: *If you are applying for a change in accounting period, use Form 1128.* ▶ **See separate instructions.**	OMB No. 1545-0152 Expires 12-31-88

Name of applicant (if joint return is filed, show names of you and your spouse)	Identifying Number (See instructions)
Address (Number and street)	Applicant's area code and telephone number
City or town, state, and ZIP code	District Director's office having jurisdiction
Name of person to contact (Please type or print)	Telephone number of contact person

Check one: ☐ Individual ☐ Partnership; No. of Partners _____ ☐ Corporation ☐ S Corporation; No. of Shareholders_____
☐ Cooperative (Section 1381(a)) ☐ Ins. Co. (Sec. 801) ☐ Ins. Co. (Sec. 821) ☐ Ins. Co. (Sec. 831)
☐ Exempt organization; Enter code section _____
☐ Other (specify) ▶ _____

NOTE: *Are you making an election under section 458 or 466?* . . . . ☐ Yes ☐ No
If "Yes," see Specific Instructions for Section J. Do not fill in Section A. If "No," you must complete Section A.

Section A. Applicable to All Filers Other Than Those Answering "Yes" to "Note" Above

1 a Tax year of change begins (mo., day, yr.) ▶ _____and ends (mo., day, yr.) ▶ _____
  b Enter the 180th day of your tax year ▶ _____ If this date is earlier than date you signed this Form 3115 on page 6, see
    General Instruction for "Late Applications" before proceeding any further.

2 Nature of business and principal source of income (including type of business designated on your latest income tax return) ▶ _____

3 The following change in accounting method is requested (check and complete appropriate spaces):
  a ☐ Overall method of accounting : from ▶ _____ to_____
  b ☐ The accounting treatment of (identify item) ▶_____
    from (present method) ▶_____to (new method) ▶_____
    Attach a separate statement providing all relevant facts, including a detailed description of your present and proposed methods.
    See also item 14 of Section A on page 2 regarding the "legal basis" for the proposed change.

  c If a change is requested under 3b above, check the present overall method of accounting:
    ☐ Accrual   ☐ Cash   ☐ Hybrid (if a hybrid method is used, explain the overall hybrid method in detail in a
    separate statement)

		Yes	No
d	Is your use of your present method specifically not permitted by the Internal Revenue Code, the Income Tax Regulations, or by a decision of the U.S. Supreme Court? See sections 4, 5, and 6 of Rev. Proc. 84-74		
e	Are you currently under examination, or were you or any member of the affiliated group contacted in any manner by a representative of the Internal Revenue Service for the purpose of scheduling an examination of your Federal tax return(s) prior to the filing of this application, or do you have an examination under consideration by an appeals officer or before any Federal court, or is any criminal investigation pending? See sections 4 and 6 of Rev. Proc. 84-74. . . .		
f	Are you a manufacturer to whom Regulations section 1.471-11 applies? If "Yes," complete Section E-2 on page 4		
4	In the last 10 years have you requested permission to change your accounting period, your overall method of accounting, or the accounting treatment of any item? (Members of an affiliated group of corporations filing a consolidated return, see item 7d on page 2.)		
a	If "Yes," was a ruling letter granting permission to make the change issued? If "Yes," attach a copy of the letter. If "No," attach an explanation		
b	Regardless of your response to 4a, do you or an affiliated corporation have pending any accounting method or period ruling or technical advice request in the National Office?		

  c If 4b is "Yes," indicate the type of request (method, period, etc.) and the specific issue involved in each request ▶ _____
    _____

5 If engaged in a business or profession: **a** Enter your taxable income or (loss)* from operations for tax purposes for the five (5) tax years
preceding the year of change: (See Specific Instructions for Section A.)

1st preceding year ended: mo. yr.	2nd preceding year ended: mo. yr.	3rd preceding year ended: mo. yr.	4th preceding year ended: mo. yr.	5th preceding year ended: mo. yr.
$	$	$	$	$

b	Enter the amount of net operating loss to be carried over to the year of change, if any	$
c	Amount of investment credit carryover to year of change, if any	$
d	Other credit carryover, if any. (Identify) ▶	$

*Individuals enter net profit or (loss) from business; partnerships enter ordinary income or (loss); members of an affiliated group filing a consolidated
return, see item 7a on page 2.

For Paperwork Reduction Act Notice, see separate instructions.   Form **3115** (Rev. 4-86)

Form 3115 (Rev. 4-86)   Page **2**

	Yes	No

6 Do you have more than one trade or business? . . . .

  a If "Yes," do you account for each trade or business separately? . . . .

  b If "Yes," see Specific Instructions for Section A.

7 Is applicant a member of an affiliated group filing a consolidated return for the tax year of change? . . . .

  a If 7 is "Yes," state parent corporation's name, identifying number, address, tax year, and Service Center where return is filed and provide the information requested in item 5 on a consolidated basis ▶ _____

_____

  b If 7 is "Yes," do all other members of the affiliated group employ the method of accounting for which the change is requested? If "No," explain ▶ _____

  c If 7 is "Yes," are any of the items involved in the calculation of the net section 481(a) adjustment attributable to transactions between members of the affiliated group? . . . .

    If "Yes," attach explanation.

  d If 7 is "Yes," provide the information requested in items 4a, 4b, and 4c for each member of the affiliated group. Also, see General Instructions for "Signature."

8 Is applicant a member of an affiliated group not filing a consolidated return for the tax year of change? . . . .

  If "Yes," are any of the items involved in the calculation of the net section 481(a) adjustment attributable to transactions between members of the affiliated group or other related parties? (If "Yes," attach explanation.) . . . .

9 If change is granted, will the new method be used for financial reporting purposes? . . . .

  If "No," attach an explanation. Such explanation should include a discussion of whether your new method of accounting conforms to generally accepted accounting principles and how it will clearly reflect income.

10 Enter the net section 481(a) adjustment for the year of change, and the net section 481(a) adjustment that would have been required if the requested change had been made for each of the 3 preceding tax years preceding the year of change. (See Specific Instructions for Section A.)	At the beginning of the year of change ending, enter: mo. yr.	At the beginning of the 1st preceding year ended, enter: mo. yr.	At the beginning of the 2nd preceding year ended, enter: mo. yr.	At the beginning of the 3rd preceding year ended, enter: mo. yr.
	$	$	$	$

11 Has net adjustment under section 481(a) for the year of change been reduced in any way by a pre-1954 amount?

12 Number of tax years present method has been used for which the change is requested in item 3a or 3b. (See Specific Instructions for Section A.) ▶ _____

13 Has your present method been designated by Rev. Rul. or Rev. Proc. more than 2 years before filing this Form 3115 as a change in method of accounting to which section 5.12(2) of Rev. Proc. 84-74 applies? . . . .

14 State the reason(s) including the legal basis (statutes, regulation, published rulings, etc.) why you believe approval to make this change should be granted. See section 7 of Rev. Proc. 84-74. _____

Section B. Change in Overall Method of Accounting

1 The following amounts should be stated as of the end of the tax year **preceding** the year of change. If none, state "None." (Although some of the items listed below may not have been required in the computation of your taxable income due to your present method of accounting, it is necessary that they be entered here for this form to be complete. Show amounts attributable to long-term contracts on page 4, Section G-1.) Provide on a schedule the breakdown of the individual items which make up the "Amount" for lines 1a through 1h. See Rev. Proc. 85-36 and Rev. Proc. 85-37 for rules to make this change expeditiously.

	Amount	Show by (✓) how treated on last year's return	
		Included in income or deducted as expense	Excluded from income or not deducted as expense
a Income accrued but not received	$		
b Income received before the date on which it was earned. State nature of income. If discount on installment loans, see Section C below. For advance payments for goods and services, see Specific Instructions for Section B. ▶ _____			
c Expenses accrued but not paid			
d Other (specify) ▶ _____			
e Prepaid expense previously deducted			
f Supplies on hand previously deducted . . .			
g Inventory on hand . . . . . $ _____ Inventory reported on your return $ _____ Difference			
h Reserve for bad debts (See instructions) . .			
l **Net adjustment** (combine lines 1a through 1h)		$	

Form 3115 (Rev. 4-86)   Page **3**

2 Nature of inventory ▶ -

3 Method used to value inventory ☐ Cost ☐ Cost or market, whichever is lower ☐ Other (attach explanation)

4 Method of identifying costs in inventory ☐ Specific identification ☐ FIFO ☐ LIFO

5 Have any receivables been sold in the past

	1st preceding year ended, enter: mo. yr	2nd preceding year ended, enter: mo. yr.	3rd preceding year ended, enter: mo. yr.
three years? . . . . ☐ Yes ☐ No			
If "Yes," enter the amounts sold for each of the three years	$	$	$

6 Attach copies of Profit And Loss Statement (Schedule F (Form 1040) in the case of farmers) and Balance Sheet, if applicable, as of the close of the tax year preceding the year of change. State accounting method used when preparing balance sheet. If books of account are not kept, attach copy of the business schedule provided with your Federal income tax return or return of income for that period. If amounts in 1 above do not agree with those shown on profit and loss statement and balance sheet, explain on separate page.

Section C. Change in Method of Reporting Interest (Discount) on Installment and Other Loans

1 Change with respect to interest on ☐ Installment loans, ☐ Commercial loans, and ☐ Other loans (explain) ▶ - - - - - - - - - - - - - - - -

2 Do any of these loans cover a period in excess of 60 months? . . . . ☐ **Yes** ☐ **No**
If "Yes," please attach an explanation. (See Rev. Rul. 83-84 and Rev. Proc. 83-40.)
If you wish to change from the sum of the months digits method (rule of 78's) to the economic accrual of interest method for reporting interest (discount) under Rev. Rul. 83-84, see Rev. Procs. 84-27, 84-28, 84-29, and 84-30.

3 Amount of earned or realized interest that has not been reported on your return as of the end of the tax year preceding the year of change . . . . $

4 Amount of unearned or unrealized interest that has been reported on your return as of the end of the tax year preceding the year of change . . . . $

5 Method of rebating in event of prepayment of loans ▶

Section D. Change in Method of Reporting Bad Debts
(See Specific Instructions for Section D before completing item 2.)

1 If a change to the Reserve Method is requested and applicant has installment sales, are such sales reported on the installment method? ☐ **Yes** ☐ **No**
If "Yes," show whether change relates to: ☐ Installment sales, ☐ Sales other than installment sales, or ☐ Both.

2 If a change to the Reserve Method is requested, provide the following information for the five tax years preceding the year of change:

	1st preceding year	2nd preceding year	3rd preceding year	4th preceding year	5th preceding year
Total sales					
Deductions for specific bad debts charged off [1] . .					
Recoveries of bad debts deducted in prior years					
Year-end balances:					
Trade accounts receivable . . .					
Trade notes receivable [2]					
Installment accounts receivable [3] . .					
Other receivables (explain in detail) . .					

3 If a change to the method of deducting specific bad debt items is requested, enter the amount in reserve for bad debts at end of the year preceding the year of change . . . . $

[1] If your return was examined, enter amount allowed as a result of the examination.
[2] If loan company, enter only capital portion.
[3] Applicable only to receivables attributable to sales reported on installment method. Enter only the capital portion of such receivables.

Section E-1. Change in Method of Valuing Inventories. (See Specific Instructions for Section E-1.)

1 Nature of all inventories ▶ -

2 Method of identifying costs in inventory . . . . ☐ Specific identification ☐ FIFO ☐ LIFO
If "LIFO," attach copy of Form 970 adopting that method and copies of any Forms 970 filed to extend the use of the method.

3 Method used to value inventory: ☐ Cost ☐ Cost or market, whichever is lower ☐ Retail cost ☐ Retail lower cost or market ☐ Other (attach explanation)

4 Method of allocating indirect production costs: ☐ Standard cost method ☐ Burden method ☐ Other (attach explanation)

5 Show method and value of all inventories at the end of the tax year preceding the year of change under:
  a Present method ▶ - $
  b New method ▶ - $
  c If changing to cost method, are you going to elect LIFO for identifying costs? . . . . ☐ **Yes** ☐ **No**

Form 3115 (Rev. 4-86)   Page **4**

Section E-2. Change in Method of Inventory Costing by Manufacturers and Processors.
(See Specific Instructions for Section E-2.)

Please check (✓) the appropriate boxes showing which costs are included in inventoriable costs, under both the present and proposed methods, of all costs listed in Regulations sections 1.471-11(b)(2), (c)(2)(i), and (c)(2)(ii) for Federal income tax purposes, and all costs listed in or subject to Regulations section 1.471-11(c)(2)(iii) for tax and financial statement reporting purposes. If any boxes are not checked, it is assumed that these costs are excluded from inventoriable costs. If certain costs are not incurred , please mark "N/A" in the appropriate box.

		Federal income tax purposes	
		Present method	Proposed method
Part I Direct Production Costs (Regulations section 1.471-11(b)(2))		Included (✓)	Included (✓)
1	Material.		
2	Labor.		

Part II Indirect Production Costs:

		Present method	Proposed method
1	Category One Costs (Regulations section 1.471-11(c)(2)(i))		
a	Repairs		
b	Maintenance		
c	Utilities		
d	Rent		
e	Indirect labor and production supervisory wages		
f	Indirect materials and supplies		
g	Small tools and equipment		
h	Quality control and inspection		
2	Category Two Costs (Regulations section 1.471-11(c)(2)(ii) (See also Rev. Rul. 79-25))		
a	Marketing		
b	Advertising		
c	Selling		
d	Other distribution expenses		
e	Interest		
f	Research and experimental		
g	Section 165 losses		
h	Percentage depletion in excess of cost depletion		
i	Depreciation and amortization for Federal tax purposes in excess of financial report depreciation and amortization		
j	Local and foreign income taxes		
k	Past service costs of pensions		
l	Administrative (general)		
m	Other salaries (general)		

		Federal Income Tax Purposes		Financial Statements	
		Present method	Proposed method	Present method	Proposed method
3	Category Three Costs (Regulations section 1.471-11(c)(2)(iii)). (See also Rev. Proc. 75-40 and attach the data required by either section 5.02 or 5.03 of Rev. Proc. 75-40.)	Included (✓)	Included (✓)	Included (✓)	Included (✓)
a	Taxes under section 164 (other than local and foreign income taxes).				
b	Financial statement depreciation and cost depletion				
c	Employee benefits				
d	Costs of strikes, rework labor, scrap, and spoilage				
e	Factory administrative expenses				
f	Officers' salaries (manufacturing)				
g	Insurance costs (manufacturing)				

Section F. Change in Method of Treating Vacation Pay

1 Is the plan(s) fully vested as of the end of the tax year preceding the year of the change? ☐ **Yes** ☐ **No**
2 If "Yes," enter the amount of accrued vacation pay as of the end of the tax year preceding the year of change $ ....
3 Number of tax years plan(s) has been vested ▶

Section G-1. Change in Method of Reporting Income from Contracts

1 Are your contracts long-term contracts as defined in Regulations section 1.451-3? ☐ **Yes** ☐ **No**
2 Is the same method used for reporting all long-term contracts regardless of duration? If "No," explain ☐ **Yes** ☐ **No**
3 Do you have extended period long-term contracts as defined in Regulations section 1.451-3(b)(3)? ☐ **Yes** ☐ **No**
4 Net adjustment required under section 481(a) $ ....

Form 3115 (Rev. 4-86)   Page **5**

Section G-2. Change to the Completed Contract Method or Change in Allocation of Costs

Please check (✓) the appropriate boxes showing which costs are allocable to long-term contracts to the extent required by Regulations sections 1.451-3(d)(5) and (6) for Federal income tax purposes. Please mark "N/A" in boxes for costs that do not apply to the taxpayer.

	Tax Purposes			
	Non-Extended Period		Extended Period	
	Present Method	Proposed Method	Present Method	Proposed Method
	Included (✓)	Included (✓)	Included (✓)	Included (✓)
Direct Material				
Direct Labor				
Repairs				
Maintenance				
Utilities				
Rent				
Indirect labor and contract supervisory wages				
Indirect material and supplies				
Tools and equipment				
Quality control and inspection				
Taxes under section 164 (other than local and foreign income taxes)				
Financial statement depreciation and cost depletion				
Percentage depletion in excess of cost depletion				
Depreciation and amortization for Federal tax purposes in excess of financial report depreciation and amortization for equipment and facilities in use				
Administrative costs				
Other administrative, service, or support costs				
Officers' salaries attributable to long-term contract activities				
Insurance				
Employee benefits				
Research and experimental expenses attributable to extended period long-term contracts	░	░		
Other research and experimental expenses				
Rework labor, scrap, and spoilage				
Bidding expenses incurred in the solicitation of extended period long-term contracts	░	░		
Other bidding expenses				
Marketing, selling, and advertising				
Interest				
Other general and administrative costs				
Section 165 losses				
Income taxes				
Cost of strikes				

Section H. Change in Overall Method of Reporting Income of Farmers to Cash Receipts and Disbursements Method

Note: *Also complete Section B.*

1 Is the taxpayer a corporation? .... ☐ **Yes** ☐ **No**
2 Is the taxpayer a partnership with a corporation as a partner? .... ☐ **Yes** ☐ **No**
3 If either 1 or 2 is "Yes," has the taxpayer had gross receipts of $1,000,000 or less in each of its tax years beginning after 1975? .... ☐ **Yes** ☐ **No**
   If "No," attach a schedule showing which years the taxpayer's receipts were more than $1,000,000.
4 Provide the following information for the five tax years before the year of change:

	1st preceding yr.	2nd preceding yr.	3rd preceding yr.	4th preceding yr.	5th preceding yr.
a Gross receipts from farming					
b Inventory: Crops, etc.					
Livestock held for sale:					
Purchased					
Raised					
Livestock held for draft breeding, sport, or dairy purposes:					
Purchased					
Raised					
Total inventory					

Form 3115 (Rev. 4-86)   Page **6**

5   Method used to value inventory *(check appropriate block):*

☐ Cost   ☐ Cost or market, whichever is lower   ☐ Farm price   ☐ Unit livestock price   ☐ Other (explain on separate page)

Section I. Change in Method of Accounting for Depreciation

Applicants desiring to change their method of accounting for depreciation must complete this section. This information must be supplied for each account for which a change is requested. **Note:** *Certain changes in methods of accounting for depreciation may be filed with the Service Center where your return will be filed. See Rev. Proc. 74-11 for the methods covered.*

1   Date of acquisition ▶ ....

2   **a**   Are you the original owner or the first user of the property? . . . . ☐ **Yes**   ☐ **No**

     b   If residential property, did you live in the home before renting it? . . . . ☐ **Yes**   ☐ **No**

3   Is depreciation claimed under Regulations section 1.167(a)-11 (CLADR)? . . . . ☐ **Yes**   ☐ **No**

     If "Yes," the only changes permitted are under Regulations section 1.167(a)-11(c)(1)(iii). Identify these changes on the tax return for the year of change.

4   Is the property public utility property? . . . . ☐ **Yes**   ☐ **No**

5   Location of the property (city and state) ▶ ....

6   Type or character of the property ▶ ....

7   Cost or other basis of the property and adjustments thereto (exclude land) . . . . | $

8   Depreciation claimed in prior tax years (depreciation reserve) . . . . | $

9   Estimated salvage value . . . . | $

10   Estimated remaining useful life of the property ▶ ....

11   If the declining balance method is requested, show percentage of straight-line rate ▶ ....

12   Other information, if any ▶ ....

     ....

Section J. Change in Method of Accounting Not Listed Above *(See Specific Instructions for Section J.)*

....

....

....

....

....

Signature—All Filers *(See instructions.)*

Under penalties of perjury, I declare that I have examined this application, including accompanying schedules and statements, and to the best of my knowledge and belief, it is true, correct and complete. Declaration of preparer (other than applicant) is based on all information of which preparer has any knowledge.

Applicant's name	Signature and title	Date
Signing official's name (Please print or type)	Signature and title of officer of the parent corporation, if applicable	Date
Signature of individual or firm preparing the application		Date

Divergences Involving the Time of Recognition of Revenues

A) Revenues, deferred for general accounting purposes until earned, but reportable for tax purposes when received:

1) Revenues susceptible of proration on a fixed-time basis or on a service-rendered basis:

Rentals.

Commissions.

Revenues from maintenance and similar service contracts covering a specified period.

Warehousing and trucking fees.

Advertising revenues.

Advance royalties on patents or copyrights.

Transportation ticket and token sales.

Sales of coupon books entitling purchaser to services.

Theatre ticket sales.

Membership fees.

Tuition fees.

Laboratory fees.

2) Revenues susceptible of proration over average duration of demand:

Life memberships.

Revenues from service contracts extending over life of article serviced or period of ownership by original owner.

B) Revenues deferred for general accounting purposes until right to retain them is substantially assured, but reportable for tax purposes when received:

1) Receipts under claim of right.

C) Revenues accrued for general accounting purposes, but not reportable for tax purposes until collected:

1) Dividends declared.

2) Increase in withdrawal value of savings and loan shares.

Income Received in Advance

Frequently, a taxpayer receives payment for services not yet performed (e.g., club membership dues, magazine subscriptions). The question then is, in what year does the taxpayer have to report these payments as income?

Accounting rule.

The accountant says that you have no income until it is actually *earned*; that the mere receipt of cash or property does not result in a realization of income. The accountant treats the prepayment as a liability which obligates the recipient to perform services before the payment can be said to have been *earned*. (This problem applies to accrual-basis taxpayers; cash-basis taxpayers are considered to have *earned* a prepayment when it is received.)

Tax rule.

You have income when you have the *right to receive it*, even though it is not earned. Thus, cash payments received in advance, negotiable notes received as advance payments, and contract installments due and payable are taxable to the recipient as advance income, even though these payments are for services to be provided by the taxpayer in a subsequent tax year. Here is a composite tax picture.

Type of Income	Basis	Extent Taxable	Authority
Cash receipts	Cash or accrual	Full amount	*American Automobile Association*, 367 US 687; *Schedule*, 372 US 128.
Negotiable notes	Cash	Fair market value	*Pinellas Ice Co.*, 287 US 462; Reg. §1.61—2(d)(4).
	Accrual	Face Value	*Schedule*, 372 US 128; *Schedule*, TC Memo 1963-307; *Spring City Foundry Co.*, 292 US 182.
Unpaid contractual payments due and payable under terms of the contract	Cash	None—no fair market value	Est. of *Ennis*, 23 TC 799; *nonacq.*, 1956-2 CB 10; *Ennis*, 17 TC 465.
	Accrual	Face Value	*Schedule*, 32 TC 1271.
Unpaid contractual installments not due under the contract nor evidenced by notes	Cash	None	*Schedule*, 372 US 128.
	Accrual	None	*Schedule*, 372 US 128.

The tendency of the courts seems to be to require reporting prepaid receipts.

1) *Accrual-basis taxpayers* may defer prepaid income from service contracts or from the sale of goods.
2) *Publishers* may elect to spread prepaid subscription income.
3) *Membership organizations* organized without capital stock which do not distribute earnings to any members and do not report income by the cash receipts and disbursements method may spread their prepaid dues income ratably over the period (not to exceed 36 months) during which they are under a liability to render services.

Repayment of Income Received Under Claim of Right

Since the tax law requires the accrual-basis taxpayer to include payments received (although not yet earned) in taxable income when received, it obviously disagrees with good accounting practice on how to treat such payments if they must be repaid.

If you are required to repay money received under a claim of right, the tax law says you can deduct it in the year of repayment.

Premature Accruals*

Under the accrual method of accounting, an expense is generally deductible in the taxable year in which all the events have occurred that determine the fact of the liability, and the amount of the liability can be determined with reasonable accuracy (the so-called "all events test"). Whether an expense involving a future obligation can satisfy the all-events test in a year significantly earlier than the year in which the taxpayer must fulfill the obligation, has been the subject of controversy under present law. In general, the law provides that in determining whether an accrual method taxpayer has incurred an amount during the taxable year, all the events which establish the taxpayer's liability for such amount will not be deemed to have occurred any earlier than the time when economic performance occurs. If economic performance has occurred, the amount will be treated as incurred for purposes of the Code. Amounts incurred are deductible currently only if they are not properly chargeable to a capital account, and are not subject to any other pro-

---

*The use of the cash method of accounting by any C corporation, partnership that has a C corporation as a partner, tax-exempt trust with unrelated business income, or a tax shelter, is not allowable. The accrual method of accounting must be used. Qualified personal service corporations and entities, other than tax shelters, with average annual gross receipts of $5 million or less, are exempted from this requirement.

vision of the Code that requires the deduction to be taken in a taxable year later than the year when economic performance occurs.

The law provides criteria for determining when economic performance occurs in the case of two categories of liabilities: 1) liabilities arising from another person providing goods or services or the use of property to the taxpayer; 2) liabilities of the taxpayer to provide property or services. Economic performance occurs with respect to the first category as the property or services are provided to the taxpayer. Economic performance occurs with respect to the second category as the taxpayer provides the property or service.

In the case of interest, economic performance occurs with the passage of time; that is, it occurs as the borrower uses, and lender foregoes use of, the lender's money—rather than as payments are made. Interest incurred by accrual method taxpayers, with respect to debts, are deductible only on a constant interest basis.

INCOME TAXES—TIMING INCOME AND EXPENSES

There can be many reasons for shifting income and expenses. One year may have so many deductions already that additional income can be picked up tax-free. True, if the income were not picked up, the current year's loss could be carried back three years and forward 15 years. But perhaps the prior years were also loss years and no immediate benefit can be realized from the current year's loss (or if refunds will be available, the years may be subject to tax audit). On the other hand, the current year's deductions may be "light" but the following years' deductions are expected to be "heavy." Shifting income forward can match up the deductions with the income.

Similar results can be achieved by shifting expenses from one year to another. In a year when additional income is desirable, the same effect may be achieved by shifting expenses out of that year.

Where we have installment sales—whether the company is an installment dealer or makes a so-called casual sale of substantial property calling for payment over a number of years— the total tax paid on the income realized from the sale may be the same whether we use installment sale or accrual accounting. We may prefer to use the installment method of reporting the sale for tax purposes so as to match the actual tax payments with the receipt of income.

HOW TO HANDLE SALES

Gross sales are a decisive factor in determining the income level for a given year. The method of selling and the timing of shipments can control the tax year. In a cash-basis business, it is relatively simple to control the time of payment. Income can be increased for the year by accelerating collections; it can be reduced by either allowing payments to take their normal course or by a delay in billing. For accrual-basis businesses, a sale is taken into income when completed, which is when title has passed. As a general rule, title passes when delivery has been made, usually determined by reference to the invoice or bill of lading. Thus, an accrual-basis taxpayer can accelerate income by speeding up deliveries. Similarly, income can be reduced by holding off deliveries in the closing weeks of the year.

Long-term contracts. Taxpayer has the option of reporting on the percentage-completion method or the completed-contract basis.

Both the percentage-of-completion and the completed-contract methods of accounting are permitted for income tax purposes as long as more than one year elapses from the date of execution to the date of completion and acceptance of the contract.

Use of either of these methods is optional; the taxpayer may use the cash or accrual method for other operations although using the percentage-of-completion or completed-contract method for long-term contracts. But once the method of accounting is originally adopted, a change requires IRS approval.

Completed-Contract Method of Accounting

A corporation that accounts for income and expenses attributable to a long-term contract on the completed-contract method of accounting generally recognizes income and expense in the year in which the contract is completed. Under the 1984 law, a corporation that accounts for income and expense on this method is required to compute earnings and profits as if it were accounting for income and expense attributable to long-term contracts on a percentage of completion basis.

This provision is effective for contracts entered into after September 30, 1984, other than for binding contracts entered into on or prior to that date.

Construction Period Interest, Taxes, and Carrying Charges

For purposes of computing a corporation's earnings and profits, construction period interest, taxes, and carrying charges are required to be capitalized as a part of the asset to which they relate, and written off as is the asset itself. This rule applies to all corporations. Further, it applies with respect to both residential and nonresidential real property, and to personal property.

"Construction period interest and taxes" include: property taxes (real and personal); interest paid or accrued on debt incurred or continued, to acquire, construct, or carry property; and other carrying charges, but only to the extent such taxes, interest, and carrying charges are attributable to the construction period for such property.

This provision is applicable to the effect on earnings and profits of amounts paid or accrued in taxable years beginning after September 30, 1984.

INSTALLMENT SALES

Under prior laws a gain or loss from a sale of property generally is recognized in the taxable year in which the property is sold. Gain from certain sales of property in exchange for which the seller receives deferred payments is reported on the installment method, unless the taxpayer elects otherwise. Eligible sales include dispositions of personal property on the installment plan by a person who regularly sells or otherwise disposes of personal property on the installment plan and other dispositions of property, including publicly-traded property, where at least one payment is to be received after the close of the taxable year in which the disposition occurs. The installment method cannot be used where a sale results in a loss.

Under the installment method, a taxpayer recognizes income resulting from a disposition of property equal to an amount that bears the same ratio to the payments received in that year that the gross profit under the contract bears to the total contract price. Payments taken into account for this purpose generally include cash or other property, marketable securities, certain assumptions of liabilities, and evidences of indebtedness of the purchaser that are payable on demand or are readily tradable.

A portion of the receivables from sales of property sold under a revolving credit plan can be treated as installment receivables, and any income from the installment method should be reported. A revolving credit plan is an arrangement under which the customer agrees to pay a part of the outstanding balance of the customer's account during each period of time for which a periodic statement of charges and credits is rendered.

If an obligation is disposed of, a gain or loss is recognized equal to the difference between the amount realized and the basis of the obligation in the case of disposition at other than face value, or sale or exchange of the obligation. In the case of any other disposition, the difference is recognized between the fair market value of the obligation at the time of disposition and the basis of the obligation in the case of any other disposition.

For tax purposes, the books of account need not be kept on the installment basis; they can be kept regularly on the cash or accrual basis. But adequate records must be kept to provide the necessary information for computing the profit portion of the different installments.

The installment method applies only to *gains* from the sale of property. If the installment sale resulted in a *loss*, the loss must be deducted in the year of sale.

Expenses.   A *dealer* must deduct the expenses in the year when paid (on the cash basis) or when incurred (on the accrual basis). The expenses cannot be apportioned or spread over the years when the income from the installment sale is reported as collected.

Choice of Installment Method by a Dealer

What is meant by "installment method"? This method allows the taxpayer to report gains over the entire time period of the installment sales contract. This enables the taxpayer to avoid the burden of paying the tax before receiving the cash. The essential element of this method is for each dollar collected to be partly recovery of costs and partly taxable profit. (This method does not apply to losses; losses on an installment sale must be deducted in the taxable year of the sale.)

For tax purposes, a dealer can switch to installment reporting without prior approval by reflecting the proper figures, with appropriate supporting schedules, in the return. A dealer can use the installment method for reporting installment sales and the accrual method for reporting sales on open account.

Change of method.   The taxpayer who begins installment reporting needs the Commissioner's approval to switch to accrual reporting. (If changed within the first three years, the taxpayer can revoke an election automatically by filing amended returns for those years.) A dealer switching from accrual to installment reporting must report, when collected, the unrealized profit on receivables outstanding at the time of the switch. The fact that the entire profit was accrued and reported in the period the receivable arose doesn't change this.

The law largely eliminates the double tax that arises from reporting the same income twice. You take the gross profit in the current year attributable to collections of items accrued in a previous year and divide it by the total gross profits of the year of collection. You then apply that fraction to the year's tax to find what percentage of the current tax is attributable to that collection. Next, take that same gross profit attributable to the prior year's collection and divide it by the total gross profit of the year of accrual. This results in the percentage of the prior year's tax that was attributable to the amount accrued then but collected now. The lesser of the two figures is then applied to reduce the current year's tax.

Form **6252**	**Computation of Installment Sale Income**	OMB No. 1545-0228
Department of the Treasury Internal Revenue Service	▶ See instructions on back. ▶ Attach to your tax return. Use a separate form for each sale or other disposition of property on the installment method.	**1986** Attachment Sequence No. **79**

Name(s) as shown on tax return	Identifying number

A Description of property ▶ ....

B Date acquired (month, day, and year) ▶ ....   **C** Date sold (month, day, and year) ▶ ....

D Was property sold to a related party after May 14, 1980? (See instructions.) . . . . ☐ Yes ☐ No

E If the answer to D is "Yes," was the property a marketable security? . . . . ☐ Yes ☐ No

If you checked "Yes" to question E, complete Part III.

If you checked "No" to question E, complete Part III for the year of sale and for 2 years after the year of sale.

Part I **Computation of Gross Profit and Contract Price** *(Complete this part for the year of sale only.)*

1 Selling price including mortgages and other indebtedness. (Do not include stated or unstated interest.)		**1**
2 Mortgages and other indebtedness buyer assumed or took the property subject to, but not new mortgages the buyer got from a bank or other source . . .	**2**	
3 Subtract line 2 from line 1	**3**	
4 Cost or other basis of property sold	**4**	
5 Depreciation allowed or allowable.	**5**	
6 Adjusted basis (subtract line 5 from line 4)	**6**	
7 Commissions and other expenses of sale	**7**	
8 Income recapture from Form 4797, Part III. (See instructions.) . .	**8**	
9 Add lines 6, 7, and 8		**9**
10 Subtract line 9 from line 1. If zero or less, do not complete rest of form	**10**
11 If question A above, is a principal residence, enter the sum of lines 7 and 13 of Form 2119 . . .	**11**
12 Gross profit (subtract line 11 from line 10)	**12**
13 Subtract line 9 from line 2. If line 9 is more than line 2, enter zero	**13**
14 Contract price (add line 3 and line 13)	**14**

Part II **Computation of Taxable Part of Installment Sale**
(Complete this part for the year of sale and any year you receive a payment.)

15 Gross profit percentage (divide line 12 by line 14) (for years after the year of sale, see instructions) . .	**15**	
16 For year of sale only—enter amount from line 13 above; otherwise enter zero	**16**	
17 Payments received during year. (Do not include stated or unstated interest.)	**17**	
18 Add lines 16 and 17	**18**	
19 Payments received in prior years. (Do not include stated or unstated interest.).	**19**	
20 Taxable part of installment sale (multiply line 18 by line 15)	**20**	
21 Part of line 20 that is ordinary income under recapture rules. (See instructions.).	**21**	
22 Subtract line 21 from line 20. Enter on Schedule D or Form 4797	**22**	

Part III **Information and Computation for Related Party Installment Sale**
(Do not complete this part if you received the final installment payment this tax year.)

F Name, address, and taxpayer identifying number of related party ....

G Did the related party, during this tax year, resell or dispose of the property? . . . . ☐ Yes ☐ No

H If the answer to question G is "Yes," complete lines 23 through 30 below unless one of the following conditions is met (check only the box that applies).

☐ The first disposition was a sale or exchange of stock to the issuing corporation.

☐ The second disposition was an involuntary conversion where the threat of conversion occurred after the first disposition.

☐ The second disposition occurred after the death of the original seller or purchaser.

☐ It can be established to the satisfaction of the Internal Revenue Service that tax avoidance was not a principal purpose for either of the dispositions. If this box is checked, attach an explanation. (See instructions.)

23 Selling price of property sold by related party	**23**	
24 Enter contract price from line 14 for year of first sale	**24**	
25 Enter the smaller of line 23 or line 24	**25**	
26 Total payments received by the end of your 1986 tax year. Add lines 18 and 19	**26**	
27 Subtract line 26 from line 25. If line 26 is more than line 25, enter zero	**27**	
28 Multiply line 27 by the gross profit percentage on line 15 for year of first sale	**28**	
29 Part of line 28 that is ordinary income under recapture rules. (See instructions.).	**29**	
30 Subtract line 29 from line 28. Enter on Schedule D or Form 4797	**30**	

For Paperwork Reduction Act Notice, see back of form.   Form **6252** (1986)

General Instructions

(Section references are to the Internal Revenue Code, unless otherwise noted.)

Paperwork Reduction Act Notice

We ask for this information to carry out the Internal Revenue laws of the United States. We need it to ensure that taxpayers are complying with these laws and to allow us to figure and collect the right amount of tax. You are required to give us this information.

A Change You Should Note

The Tax Reform Act of 1986 provides new rules that apply to certain sales you make after August 16, 1986 if your tax year ends after December 31, 1986 and you use the installment method to report the following:

a. Real property used in your trade or business and sold for more than $150,000.

b. Real property held for the production of rental income and sold for more than $150,000.

For more information on figuring the amount of gain to report under the new law, see section 453C.

Purpose of Form

Form 6252 is used to report income from sales of real property and casual sales of personal property other than inventory if you will receive any payments (including payments from sales reported on the installment method prior to 1980) in a tax year after the year of sale.

Use Form 6252 unless you elect not to report the sale on the installment method. If you want to elect out, see the instructions for **Schedule D**, Capital Gains and Losses and Reconciliation of Forms 1099-B, or **Form 4797**, Gains and Losses From Sales or Exchanges of Assets Used in a Trade or Business and Involuntary Conversions. If you do not use the installment method, report the sale on your Schedule D or Form 4797.

You need not use this form for year-end stock sales where payment is received in the following year. Instead, report the sale directly on your Schedule D for the year of payment unless you elect out of the installment method by reporting it on Schedule D in the year of sale.

Report the ordinary income from sections 1245, 1250, 179, and 291 in full in the year of the sale even if no payments were received. Figure the ordinary income to be recaptured on Form 4797, Part III.

What Parts To Complete

For the Year of Sale—Complete questions A through E, Part I, and Part II.

For Years After the Year of Sale—Complete questions A through E, and Part II, for any year you receive a payment from an installment sale.

Related Party Sales—If you sold marketable securities to a related party, complete Form 6252 for each year of the installment agreement, even if you did not receive a payment. See **Installment Sales to Related Party** for the definition of a related party. For a year after the year of sale, complete questions A through E, and Part III. (If you received a payment, also complete Part II.) If you sold property other than marketable securities to a related party, complete the form for the year of sale and for 2 years after the year of sale, regardless of whether you received any payments. If during this 2-year period you did not receive a payment, complete questions A through E, and Part III. After this 2-year period, see "For Years After the Year of Sale" above.

Installment Sales to Related Party

A related party is your spouse, child, grandchild, parent, or a related corporation, S corporation,

partnership, estate, or trust. See **Publication 537,** Installment Sales, for related party rules which are in effect for sales after October 22, 1986.

If one of the exceptions in Part III applies, check the appropriate box and do not complete lines 23 through 30. If you can establish that tax avoidance was not a principal purpose for either disposition, attach an explanation. The following are some examples that are not tax avoidance:

● The second disposition is also an installment sale and the payment terms are equal to or longer than the first installment sale.

● The property sold is not real property or real property improvements, and it is used by the related purchaser as inventory for sale in the ordinary course of conducting a trade or business.

● The second disposition is a charitable contribution but not a bargain sale, and the property is capital-gain type property for which an election under section 170(b)(1)(C)(iii) is not in effect.

● Certain tax-free transfers, certain like-kind exchanges, and in some cases bankruptcy of the related buyer.

Sale of Depreciable Property to Related Party

If you sell depreciable property to a related party as defined in section 1239, installment sale rules do not apply, unless it is established to the satisfaction of the Internal Revenue Service that tax avoidance was not a principal purpose for the sale.

Get Publication 537 and the regulations under section 453 for more information, including single sales of several assets, disposition of installment obligations, like-kind exchanges, and change in selling price. Also see section 453(g) for new rules which apply to sales after October 22, 1986 if any of the payments are contingent as to amount and the FMV cannot be readily ascertained.

Specific Instructions

Do not include interest received, carrying charges received, or unstated interest on this form. Get Publication 537 for information on unstated interest.

Partnerships and S corporations that pass through a section 179 expense to their partners or shareholders should not include this amount on lines 5 and 8.

For the Year of Sale.—If this is the year of sale and you sold section 1245, 1250, 1252, 1254, or 1255 property, you may have ordinary income. Complete Part III of Form 4797 to figure the ordinary income and see Part IV of the Form 4797 instructions before starting Part I of Form 6252.

Line 1—Selling price.—Enter the sum of the money, face amount of the installment obligation, and the fair market value of other property, such as the buyer's note, that you received or will receive in exchange for the property sold. Include in line 1 any existing mortgage or other debt the buyer assumed or took the property subject to.

If there is no stated maximum selling price, such as in a contingent sale, attach a schedule showing the computation of gain, and enter the taxable part on lines 20 and 28, if Part III applies. See the regulations under section 453.

Line 2—Mortgage and other indebtedness.—Enter only mortgages (or other indebtedness) the buyer assumed from the seller or took the property subject to. Do not include new mortgages the buyer gets from a bank, the seller, or other source.

For information on wraparound mortgages, see regulations section 15A.453-1(b)(3)(ii).

Line 4—Cost or other basis of property sold.—Enter the original cost and other expenses you incurred in buying the property. Add the cost of improvements, etc., and subtract any casualty losses previously allowed. For more information, get Publication 551, Basis of Assets.

Line 5—Depreciation allowed or allowable.—Enter all depreciation or amortization you deducted or should have deducted from the date of purchase until the date of sale. Add any deduction you took under section 179 and the section 48(q)(1) downward basis adjustment, if any. Subtract 50% of any investment tax credit recaptured if the basis of the property was reduced under section 48(q)(1) and any section 179 or 280F recapture amount included in gross income in a prior tax year.

Line 7—Commissions and other expenses of sale.—Enter sales commissions, advertising expenses, attorney and legal fees, etc., you incurred in selling the property.

Line 8—Ordinary income recapture.— See Form 4797, Part III and Part IV of the instructions, to figure the recapture. Enter the part of the gain from the sale of depreciable property recaptured under sections 1245 and 1250 (including sections 179 and 291) here and on line 12 of Form 4797.

Line 15—Gross profit percentage.—Enter the gross profit percentage determined for the year of sale even if you did not file Form 6252 for that year.

Line 17—Payments received during the year.—Enter all money you received and the fair market value of any property you received in 1986. Include as payments any amount withheld to pay off a mortgage or other debt, such as broker and legal fees. Do not include the buyer's note or any mortgage or other liability assumed by the buyer. If you did not receive any payments in 1986, enter zero.

If in prior years, an amount was entered on the equivalent of line 25 of the 1986 form, do not include it on this line. Include it, however, on line 19.

Line 19—Payments received in prior years.— Enter all money and the fair market value of property you received before 1986 from the sale.

Lines 21 and 29.—Report on line(s) 21 and/or 29, any ordinary income recapture remaining from prior years on section 1245 and 1250 property sold before 6/7/84. Also report on these lines any ordinary income recapture on section 1252, 1254, and 1255 property regardless of when it was sold (that is, ordinary income recapture in the year of sale or any remaining recapture from a prior year sale). Do not enter ordinary income from the section 179 deduction. If this is the year of sale, see the instructions for Part IV of Form 4797.

The amount on these lines should not exceed the amount shown on line(s) 20 and/or 28.

Lines 22 and 30—Trade or business property.—Enter this amount on Form 4797, line 3 if the property was held more than 6 months. If the property was held 6 months or less or, if you have an ordinary gain from a noncapital asset (even if the holding period is more than 6 months), enter the amount on Form 4797, line 9 and write "From Form 6252."

Capital assets—Enter this amount on Schedule D as short-term or long-term gain. Use the lines identified as from Form 6252.

Line 23.—If in 1986 the related party sold part of the property from the original sale, enter the selling price of the part resold. If part was sold in an earlier year and part was sold this year, enter the cumulative selling price.

1) Adjustments in Tax on Change to Installment Method

	Taxable Years Prior to Change		Adjustment Years After Change	
	Year 1	Year 2	Year 3	Year 4
Gross profit from installment sales (receivable in periodic payments over 5 years)	$100,000	$ 50,000	$ 20,000[1] $ 10,000[2] 80,000[3]	$ 12,000[4] 8,000[5] 40,000[6] 90,000[7]
Other income	80,000	200,000	90,000	90,000
Gross income	$180,000	$250,000	$200,000	$240,000
Deductions	60,000	50,000	50,000	60,000
Taxable income	120,000	200,000	150,000	180,000
Tax rate assumed	30%	50%	40%	40%
Tax would be	$ 36,000	$100,000	$ 60,000	$ 72,000

	Computation of Adjustment in Year 3 Year 1 Items	Lesser Tax Portion
In Year 3		
Portion of tax	20,000/200,000 × 60,000 = $6,000	
In Year 1		
Portion of tax	20,000/180,000 × 36,000 = 4,000	$4,000
	Year 2 Items	
In Year 3		
Portion of tax	10,000/200,000 × 60,000 = 3,000	3,000
In Year 2	10,000/250,000 × 100,000 = 4,000	
Adjustment to tax of Year 3		$7,000
	Computation of Adjustment in Year 4 Year 1 Items	
In Year 4		
Portion of tax	12,000/240,000 × 72,000 = $3,600	
In Year 1		
Portion of tax	12,000/180,000 × 36,000 = 2,400	$2,400
	Year 2 Items	
In Year 3		
Portion of tax	8,000/240,000 × 72,000 = 2,400	2,400
In Year 2		
Portion of tax	8,000/250,000 × 100,000 = 3,200	
Adjustment to tax of Year 4		$4,800

[2] and [4] from Year 1 Sales

[5] and [6] from Year 2 Sales

[8] and [9] from Year 3 Sales

[7] from Year 4 Sales

2) Computation by Dealer Under Installment Method

	First Year		Second Year		Third Year	
	(a)	(b)	(a)	(b)	(a)	(b)
	Cash Sales	Installment Sales	Cash Sales	Installment Sales	Cash Sales	Installment Sales
(1) Unit sales	40	80	60	100	70	120
(2) Gross sales	$16,000	$40,000	$24,000	$50,000	$28,000	$60,000
(3) Cost of goods	12,000	24,000	18,900	31,500	20,300	34,800
(4) Gross profit	$ 4,000	$16,000	$ 5,100	$18,500	$ 7,700	$25,200
(5) Gross profit accrual basis	$20,000		$23,600		$32,900	
(6) Rate of gross profit		40%		37%		42%
(7) Receipts from installment sales:						
First year	$15,000		$24,000		$ 1,000	
Second year			15,000		27,500	
Third year	═══════		═══════		22,500	
(8) Gross profit from installment sales:						
First year 40%	$ 6,000		$ 9,600		$ 400	
Second year 37%			$ 5,550		10,175	
Third year 42%					9,450	
Total	$ 6,000		$15,150		$20,025	
Gross profit from cash and installment sales (4a) plus (9b)	$10,000		$20,250		$27,725	

3) Uncollected Installments and Unrealized Gross Profits

An example showing how the dealer computes his or her profit in using the installment method follows. Our dealer runs an appliance store and has been selling refrigerators on the installment plan. The price is $400 cash or $500 on an 18-month installment basis, $50 down and $25 a month thereafter. Average cost per unit sold is $300 for the first year, $315 for the second, and $290 for the third.

If an installment account becomes uncollectible, there is no deduction for uncollected gross profit; but the portion of the uncollected balance that represents unrecovered cost is a bad debt. To use an extreme case, suppose the entire $45,000 in the example below became uncollectible. There would be no deduction for the $18,525 of unrealized gross profit; however, the balance of $26,475 would be deductible as a bad debt. Repossessions would reduce the deduction by an amount equal to the fair market value of the repossessed items. If the value of the repossessions exceeds the basis for the installment obligation, the difference, in the case of a dealer, is ordinary income.

Here are the uncollected installments and unrealized gross profits at the end of the third year:

	Uncollected Installments	Rate	Unrealized Gross Profit
2nd year's sales	$ 7,500	37%	$ 2,775
3rd year's sales	37,500	42%	15,750
Total	$45,000		$18,525

Discounting Installment Receivables

There are two types of arrangements a dealer can make with banks or factors to obtain advances on installment receivables: 1) pledge them, that is, borrow against the receivables as collateral, or 2) discount them, that is, sell them at less than face value.

Proportionate disallowance rule. The law provides that if an installment obligation is pledged as collateral for a loan, the proceeds of the loan are treated as a payment on the obligation, and a proportionate amount of the gain that was deferred under the installment method must be recognized. The bill makes an exception with no payments treated as having been received on a portion of an installment obligation due within nine months of the receipt of the obligation, regardless of the maturity of any other payments on the obligation. If property is sold on a revolving credit plan, the amount eligible for the exception is that portion of the receivable balance that is determined to be paid within nine months of the related sale. Another exception to the rule exempts pledges of obligations for debt that by its terms is payable within 90 days, provided that the debt is not renewed or otherwise continued, and provided that the taxpayer does not issue additional debt within 45 days.

Use of the installment method is limited based on the amount of the outstanding indebtedness of the taxpayer. The limitation generally is applied by determining the amount of the taxpayer's "allocable installment indebtedness" (AII) for each taxable year and treating such amount as a payment immediately before the close of the taxable year on "applicable installment obligations" of the taxpayer that arose in that taxable year and are outstanding as of the end of the year. Applicable installment obligations are any installment obligations that arise from the sale after February, 1986, of 1) certain property held for sale to customers, and 2) real property used in the taxpayer's trade or business or held for the production of rental income, provided that the selling price of the property exceeds $150,000.

The AII for any taxable year is determined by dividing the face amount of the taxpayer's applicable installment obligations that are outstanding at the end of the year by the sum of the face amount of all installment obligations and the adjusted basis of all other assets of the taxpayer. The resulting quotient is multiplied by the taxpayer's average quarterly indebtedness, with any AII subtracted that is attributable to applicable installment obligations arising in previous years. (Depreciation can be deducted for purposes of computing the adjusted basis of the assets.)

In subsequent taxable years, the taxpayer is not required to recognize gain attributable to applicable installment obligations arising in prior years to the extent that any actual payments on the obligations do not exceed the amount of AII attributable to those obligations. On the receipt of the payments, the AII attributable to the obligation on which the payment is received is reduced by the amount of such payments. Payments on an applicable installment obligation in excess of the AII allocable to such obligations are accounted for under the ordinary rules for applying the installment method.

The taxpayer must compute average indebtedness for the year in order to calculate the amount of AII. The computation is made on a quarterly basis; all indebtedness of the taxpayer outstanding at the end of each quarter is taken into account. Indebtedness includes accounts payable and accrued expenses, as well as other amounts commonly considered as indebtedness, such as loans from banks and indebtedness in connection with the purchase of property by the taxpayer. If the taxpayer is a member of an affiliated group or a group under common control, all the members are treated as one taxpayer when making the calculations.

With respect to the installment method, the use of the method is disallowed in whole or in part for transactions in which the effect of the proportionate disallowance rule would be avoided through the use of related parties, pass-through entities, or intermediaries. Any corporation, partnership, or trust can be considered related to shareholders, partners, or beneficiaries.

The proportionate disallowance rule is effective for taxable years ending after December 31, 1986. Sales on a revolving credit plan are effective beginning after December 31, 1986. Any adjustment resulting from the change in accounting method must be taken into account over a period not exceeding four years; if a four year period is used, 15 percent of the adjustment is taken into account the first year, 25 percent the second year, and 30 percent in each of the following two years.

CONSIGNMENT SALES

Selling on consignment will defer income until sale by the consignee. Thus delivery to distributors on consignment postpones income. Instead of taking sales into account upon delivery, as where sales are made on open account, income on consignment sales is deferred while the goods are held on the distributor's floor.

Thus, a manufacturer can defer income by placing sales on a consignment basis, and, conversely, can accelerate income by shifting to an open-account basis. This might be done, for example, in order to use up an operating loss which is about to expire. Consigned goods (out) remain part of the manufacturer's inventory until sold.

Approval and return sales. Sales on approval aren't reflected in income until the buyer decides to take the goods. The parties agree the buyer is to take possession of the goods temporarily, with the understanding that if the goods aren't satisfactory, nothing is owed to the seller except their return. New and perishable products are frequently sold this way. Title does not pass until buyer approves.

Substantially the same business result, but different tax consequences can be achieved by a transaction known as "a sale or return." Seller and buyer agree that the goods will pass to the buyer on delivery but that they may be returned if they prove unsatisfactory. The income must be taken up immediately, even though the buyer may subsequently return the goods. Here, title passes on delivery. The form of the contract determines whether the transaction is a sale on approval or a sale with return privileges.

Application. If you have been using a contract which provides for sale with the privilege of return, you can defer a large slice of income simply by changing the contract to one for sale on approval. Or, if you have been selling on approval, you can bring a lot of additional sales into a given year by changing your contract to one providing for sale on delivery with the privilege of return.

Consignment and approval sales under the Uniform Commercial Code. Where the term *consignment sale* or its equivalent is used but nothing else is said, the UCC says the transaction is treated as a sale or return. Thus, if the parties want the income postponed until the buyer resells the goods, merely using the *consignment sale* designation is probably not enough; the contract should spell out the details of when the title is to pass. Whether this is desirable in view of other consequences under the UCC—e.g., rights in the goods of the buyer's creditors—is something to be decided by the parties.

OTHER FACTORS AFFECTING SALES

Here are some other areas involving sales where timing techniques may be employed for tax purposes.

Conditional sales.   In a conditional sale, the seller delivers merchandise to a buyer who contracts to pay for it over a period of time. The seller stipulates that title is not to pass until the price has been fully paid.

The sale is not legally complete until final payment is made and title has passed to the buyer. Nevertheless, for tax purposes, the sale price must be taken into income when the property has been transferred to the buyer.

Sales of specific goods on which work must be done.   When a contract for the sale of specific goods calls for the seller to do something to the goods to put them into a deliverable state, the property does not pass to the purchaser until such things are done unless the parties agree otherwise. Thus the accrual seller will realize no taxable income until the goods are placed in a deliverable state or title passes to the buyer, and to this extent receipt of taxable income can be controlled.

Sales on open account.   Where such goods, in a deliverable state, are "unconditionally appropriated" (i.e., "identified to," under the UCC) to the contract by either the buyer or seller with the consent of the other, the title in the goods passes to the buyer. Delivery of the goods to a *carrier* for shipment to the purchaser, even if such shipment is made C.O.D., constitutes an "unconditional appropriation." The seller who wants a larger taxable income in a particular year can realize it by simply increasing the rate of shipments. On the other hand, the seller who wants to postpone taxable income can slow up on the shipments or other acts of "unconditional appropriation."

Sales returns and allowances.   Where credits or refunds are made for damaged or unsatisfactory merchandise, the deduction becomes available when the liability is admitted.

OTHER ORDINARY INCOME

Dividend income.   Breakdown between foreign and domestic payors of dividends is necessary for federal tax purposes—e.g., domestic dividends are generally subject to an 80% dividend deduction; foreign dividends may be subject to credit for foreign taxes paid. Intercorporate dividends of affiliated corporations should be earmarked for elimination on consolidated returns. 100% deduction is now allowed for qualifying dividends received by affiliated corporations from other affiliates in the group, as long as consolidated returns are *not* filed.

Royalty and license income.   Allocation between foreign and domestic royalty or license income may be required for federal tax purposes (including foreign tax credit). It is important to have details about possible withholding of tax at the source. State allocations may also depend on source of the income.

Rental income. It is very important to keep location information of properties throwing off the rental income for state allocation purposes. In addition, rent paid by related taxpayers (e.g., subsidiaries) may be subject to reallocation by IRS on audit unless they have good substantiation for amounts paid.

Interest income. Source of payments is necessary for possible exemption of some of the income from either or both federal and state taxes.

Foreign income, blocked. In regard to income received or accrued in foreign currency which is not convertible into United States currency, a taxpayer has the election of deferring reporting the income until the restrictions are lifted or including it in the present year's income.

IMPUTED INTEREST

Seller-held financing is often a key ingredient in real estate deals. Taking back a note for part of the sales price helps the seller get top dollar for a property. From the buyer's viewpoint, seller financing is an attractive alternative to often hard-to-get bank financing.

Tax angle. The seller pays tax in the year of sale on the profit paid to him or her in the year of sale. Assuming there is no recapture of depreciation, the balance of the profit is taxed in later years upon receipt of payments on the note from the buyer. The interest payments the seller receives on the note are fully taxable ordinary income. Generally, the buyer's tax basis in the property—for all purposes, including depreciation—is the buyer's cost, including the seller-held mortgage. The interest paid on the note is deductible and not included in basis.

The 1984 Tax Law may have absolutely no effect on a seller-held financing deal. On the other hand, if a transaction is affected by the law, a seller may be required to pay more tax dollars sooner.

Background: Before 1985, a seller had to charge at least 9% interest on a note. If not, the transaction was refigured as if 10% interest had been charged. Result: A portion of the note principal was transformed into interest. For the seller, that resulted in a reduced sales price—and less low-taxed profit and more high-taxed ordinary income. For the buyer, it meant a lower cost basis and bigger interest deductions.

Beginning in 1985 there is a higher minimum interest rate. It's set at 110% of the rate paid on Treasury obligations with maturities similar to the seller-held note. If the seller charges a lower rate on his note, the transaction is refigured at a new, higher "imputed" interest rate—120% of the Treasury rate.

While these rates change every six months, the rate in effect when a transaction is closed governs the interest rate for the life of the note.

Still another change: In general, if the sales price exceeds $250,000 and the minimum rate isn't met, the transaction is covered by the complex original issue discount (OID) rules. And even if the stated note interest equals or exceeds the minimum rate, the OID rules apply if payment of part or all of the note interest payments is deferred. Here, the results are especially harsh: The seller is taxed on interest income each year even though not a penny in interest may be received for years. The buyer, on the other hand, can take current deductions for interest not yet paid.

Congress passed a measure that modifies the imputed-interest rules described above. Here are the highlights of the law: 1) For sales of real property and used personal property before July 1, 1985, involving seller financing of $2 million of principal or less, no interest will be imputed if the parties state at least 9% compound interest. If the parties fail to state an adequate interest rate, interest will be imputed at a 10% compound rate; 2) Transactions involving seller financing of more than $2 million will be subject to a blended interest rate, based on a weighted average between 9% and 10%, and 110% and 120% of the Treasury borrowing rate; 3) Assumptions of loans in connection with sales of principle residences, vacation homes, farms, ranches and small business property will be permanently exempt from '84 TRA provisions applying imputed interest rules to assumptions. And assumptions made before October 16, 1984 will be permanently exempt from new assumption rules, except for assumptions in connection with transactions involving a purchase price of $100 million or more; 4) For sales before July 1, 1985, of real property and used personal property used in the active business of farming or ranching, with seller financing of $2 million or less of principal, interest income and deductions will be accounted for by both the buyer and seller on the cash method; 5) Under the permanent rules of '84 TRA, sales of all principal residences, and farms or ranches costing $1 million or less, will be permanently exempt from original issue discount rules. The sale of a principal residence to the extent the cost is less than $250,000, and the sale of land in connection with the sale of a farm or ranch costing $1 million or less, will be permanently exempt from the requirement to state interest at 110% of the Treasury borrowing rate. These transactions will be subject to interest rates established by the IRS.

FASB Statement 109, Accounting for Income Taxes

Definitions.   There are a number of terms relevant only to FASB 109. The following definitions will aid the practitioner in implementing the rule.

Assumption—Reported assets that will be recovered and liabilities that will be settled.

Business Combinations—When the operations of two or more companies are brought under common control.

Current Tax Expense or Benefit—Income taxes paid or payable (or refundable) for a year.

Deferred Tax Asset—The amount of deferred taxes caused by temporary differences that will result in net tax deductions in future years.

Deferred Tax Expense or Benefit—The net change during the year in an enterprise's deferred tax liability.

Deferred Tax Liability—The amount of deferred taxes resulting from temporary differences that will result in future years.

Gains and Losses Included in Comprehensive Income but Excluded from Net Income— This category includes certain changes in the market value of investments in marketable equity securities classified as noncurrent assets, certain changes in adjustments from recognizing certain additional pension liabilities, and foreign currency adjustments. (Future changes in GAAP might modify what is included in this category.)

Income Tax Expense (Benefit)—The sum of current tax expense (benefit) and deferred tax expense (benefit).

Loss Carrybacks or Carryforwards—An excess of tax deductions over gross income during a specific year that may be carried back or forward to reduce taxable income in other years.

More Likely Than Not—There is better than a 50-50 probability that the potential deferred tax asset will be realized as an offset against future taxes.

More Than Likely—An event for which there is a better than 50-50 chance the event will occur.

Operating Loss Carryforward for Financial Reporting—The amount of an operating loss carryforward for tax purposes a) reduced by the amount of offsets for temporary differences that will result in net taxable amounts during the carryforward period, and b) increased by the amount of temporary differences that will result in net tax deductions.

Permanent Differences—Differences between pretax accounting income and taxable income which do *not* require tax allocation as compared to timing differences which *do* require tax allocation. Permanent differences arise from statutory provisions in the tax laws, such as tax-exempt securities; e.g., interest earned on municipal bonds that is excluded from federal taxes but included as revenue in accounting income.

Public Enterprise—An enterprise(s) a) whose debt or equity securities are traded in a public market, or b) whose financial statements are filed with a regulatory agency in preparation for the sale of securities.

Purchase Method—An accounting method to account for a business combination. The acquisition by one company of one or more other companies, with the combination recorded at cost. Cost is based on the fair value of the property acquired or on the fair value of the property given up. An asset acquired for cash is recorded at the amount disbursed for its acquisition, including expenses.

Statutory Limitations—Limits for the amount by which certain deductions or tax credits may reduce taxable income (or income taxes payable).

Tax Credit Carryback or Carryforward—Tax credits that exceed statutory limitations and may be carried back or forward to reduce taxes payable in other years.

Taxable Income—The amount of taxable revenue that exceeds tax-deductible expenses and exemptions for the year.

Temporary Differences—Differences between book and tax balances that will ultimately net out to zero. A *timing* difference exists when there is a difference between the period in which a transaction affects taxable income and the period in which the transaction enters into the determination of pre-tax accounting income. The taxes applicable to temporary timing differences are reversed as timing differences reverse. For example, a company might concurrently use the straight-line method of computing depreciation for accounting income and an accelerated method to calculate taxable income. Over the years, the cumulative depreciation will be identical, but depreciation amounts will differ during particular years over the life of the asset.

Timing Difference—A difference in income in which transactions affect taxable income and the accounting periods in which they enter into the determination of *pretax* accounting income.

Valuation Allowance—The difference between deferred tax assets and differences that pass the "more likely than not" test. The term *valuation* is used to convey the same meaning as *measurement*. A company's cash, for example, is valued (measured) as a certain amount on the balance sheet.

FASB Statement 109, *Accounting for Income Taxes* has been issued by the Financial Accounting Standards Board to supersede Statement 96, *Accounting for Income Taxes*. Statement 109 applies to fiscal years that began after December 15, 1992. Accounting for income taxes should address 1) the amount of taxes payable or refundable during the current year and 2) the deferred tax liabilities and assets for future tax consequences of entries that have been recognized in an enterprise's financial statements and/or tax returns.

Statement 109 is a marked departure from the manner in which companies have previously accounted for income taxes. Prior standards, including APB 11, *Accounting for Income Taxes*, failed to provide adequate simplified direction; Opinion 11 also failed to provide useful guidelines. In addition to being much too complicated and erring by being too specific, Statement 96 further failed to make provision for recognition of tax benefits expected to be realized in future years.

The FASB developed Statement 109 in an attempt to remedy the criticism of these earlier rulings. It is a further departure from APB 11, which related tax to pretax income. FASB 109, like FASB 96, utilizes the balance sheet as the focal point for tax determination. FASB 109 requires an asset and liability approach for financial accounting and reporting for income taxes. When employing a balance-sheet approach, deferred taxes represent the expected effects of existing book tax differences on those taxes that will be due in the future rather than the effects on taxes previously paid. Therefore, deferred taxes are to be adjusted for tax rate changes when the new rulings or laws become effective.

To further explain the Rule's approach to deferred taxes, a *deferred tax expense* (credit) *is the net change in deferred tax assets and liabilities during the accounting period. Deferred tax assets are tax credits recognized for book purposes, but not yet taken on the company's tax return.* Deferred tax liabilities *are taxes recognized for book purposes that have not yet been required by the IRS. Both are balance sheet accounts.*

A net deferred tax asset increase or a net deferred tax liability decrease results in a deferred tax credit in the income statement. A net deferred asset decrease or a net deferred tax liability increase results in a deferred tax charge on the income statement.

The accounting entry to recognize deferred tax credits is a debit to deferred tax assets and a credit to deferred tax expenses. The book tax expense or credit consists of two parts:

1) The current tax portion, which is the company's income taxes payable or refundable based on the company's tax returns;
2) The deferred tax portion, which is the tax effect of temporary differences (defined above) between the carrying values of assets and liabilities on the corporation's book and tax balance sheets.

Temporary differences.   Usually there are differences between a corporation's financial reporting and tax reporting balance sheets. Some of these differences, such as goodwill, are permanent. Goodwill will decline for book purposes as it is amortized, but it is not tax-deductible, so its tax book balance remains unchanged. Other differences between book and tax balance sheets are temporary and ultimately will net out to zero.

If a corporation uses straight-line depreciation on its tax returns, the net depreciable property balance on the book balance sheet will be higher than the comparable account on the tax balance sheet. The two net depreciable asset balances will be the same at the end of the asset's depreciable life.

The differences between the asset and liability balances on a corporation's financial reporting and tax reporting balance sheets give rise to deferred tax assets and liabilities. Temporary differences can be deductible and taxable. Deductible temporary differences are deferred tax assets and occur when a corporation reports higher income for tax returns than for financial reporting because it either recognized an expense for book purposes earlier than for tax purposes, or included income in its tax return earlier than for book purposes. Taxable temporary differences are deferred tax liabilities.

Book and tax warranty reserve accounting, for example, lead to a temporary deductible difference and a related deferred tax asset. GAAP requires that a warranty expense and an offsetting warranty reserve be recognized when a sale with a warranty is recorded for book purposes. The tax law only permits warranty costs to be deducted in the calculation of taxable income when the warranty expense is incurred. The financial reporting balance sheet, therefore, shows a warranty reserve and the tax balance sheet does not. Since it is anticipated that the amount shown as the warranty reserve will in the future be tax-deductible as the related warranty expenditures are made, a temporary deductible difference exists and a deferred tax asset must be recognized.

Taxable temporary differences occur when a corporation reports higher income for book purposes than it does on its tax return. This can occur because it either charges lower expenses in its financial report than in its tax return, or reports income earlier for financial reports than for tax purposes.

A taxable difference arises when a straight-line method is used in financial reports and accelerated methods for tax reporting. This results in the net depreciable asset balance being higher on the financial report than on the tax report. Since this difference is expected to net out to zero at the end of the asset's depreciable life, a temporary difference exists, making the temporary difference a taxable one.

The difference between the two asset balances represents future book depreciation that cannot be taken for future tax purposes. Future taxable income will be higher and a deferred tax liability must be recognized for the tax equivalent of the difference in carrying values.

FASB 109 requires a new approach in the manner in which tax consequences are accounted for in business combinations. Under the old purchase accounting rules, deferred tax assets and liabilities, due to the difference in book and tax bases, were not recognized at the time of acquisition. The difference in bases was handled by showing the fair value of assets and liabilities net of tax.

Statement 109 requires recognition at time of acquisition of acquired tax benefits. To the extent these meet the "more likely than not" test at acquisition, the recognized tax assets will reduce goodwill. Acquired tax benefits recognized after the combination date are treated as a reduction of goodwill. If the recognized acquired tax benefits are in excess of goodwill, the excess is treated as a reduction of intangibles. Any remaining excess is a credit to tax expense.

The *classification* of deferred tax assets and liabilities as current and noncurrent balance sheet items is changed by this Rule. Deferred assets and liabilities are now classified in the same category as the item that causes them to occur. If a tax asset or liability cannot now be related to a specific item, the old rule applies; i.e., deferred tax balances related to temporary differences that reverse over the succeeding 12-month accounting period are classified as current balance sheet items. The remaining are classified as noncurrent items.

Many companies are now forced into making difficult, rather subjective decisions in relation to assuming the likelihood of tax asset realization. The situation arises from the fact that, in line with Statement 109, tax assets that must be recorded are to be reduced by a reserve fund if impairment is apt to occur and the tax asset is never actually realized.

Several other aspects of the ruling are also instrumental in a specific enterprise's decisions regarding adoption options and the related effect on facets of the enterprise, including working capital, owners' equity. earnings trends, and various financial ratios, such as the current ratio, debt-equity ratio, and other balance sheet and income statement ratios.

Loss carryforwards and accruals for post retirement benefits, other than pensions (OPEBs) under FASB 106, derive the most advantage from the less stringent criteria for tax benefits in FASB 109. Benefits of loss carryforwards, according to this Statement, are subject to the same recognition criteria as other potential tax benefits where, according to the interpretations under FASB 96, it was not possible to recognize any benefits from book loss carryforwards.

Since accrual accounting for OPEBs became mandatory for most companies in 1993, and for foreign plans and some specific private companies in 1995, it is now easier to recognize the related tax benefits whether a particular company decides to record the entire transition liability immediately or amortize it over 20 years. Regardless, the greater the ability to recognize the related tax benefits under FASB 109, the more vital a factor this becomes in a company's decision.

It is fairly obvious that Statement 109 has brought about some changes in an enterprise's income statement. One change results from adjustments of deferred taxes for newly enacted tax rate changes, since these show up immediately in a company's continuing operations.

When a change in the corporate statutory tax rate is enacted, existing deferred tax asset and liability balances must be refigured to reflect the new rate. It should be noted that the remeasurement date is the *enactment date*, not the date the new rate goes into effect. For companies with deferred tax balances, the balance is increased to reflect that the future tax credits evidenced by the deferred tax assets will be higher because of the increased tax rate. The increase in the deferred tax asset balance is a debit entry and the offsetting credit entry is to income. If a company has a deferred tax liability balance, the deferred tax liability is increased to reflect the higher future deferred tax payments, and the offsetting entry is a charge to earnings.

Companies can now adopt deferred tax credits. Unrecognized tax benefits can now be recognized. Recognition of previously unrecognized deferred tax credits all at one time can result in higher book tax rates in future years and correspondingly lower profits. Possibly offsetting this effect would be an increase in the statutory tax rate. In the year of a tax rate increase announcement, the deferred asset must be increased to recognize the new higher tax rate and offset by a credit to income.

Companies may find that, after accrual accounting is adopted for OPEBs and the provisions of FASB 109, they have net deferred tax assets rather than net deferred tax liabilities. Additional income would result from an enacted increase in tax rates, while an expense would result from an enacted decrease in tax rates. Changes in the income statement could also be caused by reassessments of the valuation allowance for an enterprise's deferred tax assets.

If a company has not previously implemented the OPEB standard (FASB 106), it is beneficial to adopt it and the income tax rule, FASB 109, within the same fiscal year so that the Accounting Department (in particular) and management (in general) are faced with what could be fairly drastic accounting alterations within one year rather than in two different years. An additional advantage is that simultaneous adoption also increases the ability to record the tax benefit resulting from the OPEB charge.

If, for whatever reason, enterprises prefer to maintain the historical record rather than restate the financial statement for previous years, they will select prospective adoption. However, if for budgeting, planning, reporting, or other accounting reasons, it is important to make previous years' statistical results reasonably comparable to the current and future years, restatement will be the method selected. The number of prior years restated, if restatement is chosen, will depend to some extent on the availability of pertinent records and the value of the statistical data weighed against the time, effort, and cost involved.

Reporting the tax benefit of tax-deductible dividends paid on shares already earned by employees under an employee stock ownership plan (ESOP), according to requirements of Statement 109, is the same as for tax-deductible dividends paid to other shareholders and recorded in net income. The requirement for tax-deductible dividends paid on shares held by an ESOP, but not yet earned by employees, follows the same course under FASB 109 as laid down in Statement 96 and Opinion 25. An ESOP and a stock option plan are similar; the tax benefits of both are reported as a credit to shareholders' equity inasmuch as they are compensation methods which at times resulted in tax deductions that were not recognized as compensation expense in the financial statements.

The reasoning behind the differentiation is that tax deductions received for the payment of dividends, except for those paid on unallocated shares held by an ESOP, represent an exemption from taxation of an equivalent amount of earnings. Therefore, the tax benefit is to be shown as a reduction of tax expense and is not allocated directly to shareholders' equity. A tax benefit cannot be recognized, however, for tax deductions or for favorable tax rates related to future dividends on undistributed earnings for which deferred tax liability has not been recognized. For disclosure purposes, favorable tax treatment would be reflected in the unrecognized deferred tax liability.

Valuation allowance.   FASB 109 covers deferred tax asset data and a test for recognizing deferred tax assets and their related deferred tax credits to income. All of a company's potential deferred tax assets must be recorded. To the extent that it is "more likely than not" that all or part of the deferred tax assets will be realized in the future, they can be recognized. The valuation allowance must be reviewed at the end of each accounting period to determine if it needs adjusting because of changed circumstances, with any adjustments recorded in operating income. The impact of these adjustments on operating earnings and assumed future taxable assumptions must be determined. FASB 109 requires that a deferred tax asset be recognized for all potential tax credit carryforwards, with a valuation allowance as a possible offset to the deferred tax asset balance. The deferred tax asset should be reduced to the amount that it is "more likely than not" to be realized.

Companies that have deferred tax assets must record a charge to earnings when FASB 109 is adopted. If corporate tax rates have changed, companies have to adjust their deferred tax assets and liabilities to reflect the current corporate tax rate.

The Statement allows judgments with respect to anticipated future income levels and feasible tax strategies to generate future income. The related taxes payable required to recover the anticipated tax credits must be included. A valuation allowance should include the expectation of future losses, or give evidence that a deferred tax asset to be recognized includes a substantial appreciation in net assets and a strong earnings history.

When recording a valuation allowance for deferred tax assets, tax benefits are likely to be realized in the future under many circumstances. The judgment will also be difficult under other circumstances, because the judgments are especially critical and should involve top-level management as well as the accounting department.

Opportunities can develop to record the benefit of tax assets, especially for future deductions in jurisdictions where there are significant carryback/carryforward periods. Some enterprises may feel that, if a valuation reserve is recorded rather than the recognition of the full benefit, shareholders, financial analysts, and employees may consider this as grounds for concern about the company's viability in the future. Also, if the asset is not eventually realized, litigation could be forthcoming. When a valuation allowance is necessary, a full explanation of the reasoning behind it and an interpretation of the change in the accounting and reporting procedures should be made.

Liability method illustrated. The liability method of computation measures the future tax effects of existing timing differences awaiting reversal.

In the balance, sheet deferred taxes are assets or liabilities. They must present the estimated effects on taxes receivable or payable for the period in which the differences are expected to reverse.

The deferred tax expense for a tax period is derived from the changes for the period in the balance sheet's deferred tax receivables or payables.

Deferred taxes on existing timing differences are computed using tax rates expected to be in effect when the timing differences reverse. Existing deferred taxes are adjusted when tax rates change or future rate changes become known. If there are no legislative changes in the tax law or rates, current rates are used; that is, no estimate or prediction of rate changes is made.

The liability method is not too involved, as the cumulative timing differences are simply multiplied by the current tax rate. The result is a deferred tax liability or asset. The change in that amount for a year is the deferred tax expense for the year. The total tax currently payable plus deferred tax expense is the income tax expense for the year.

Assume a taxpayer has a deferred tax liability of $50,000 on a cumulative timing difference of $100,000 at the beginning of the year. Taxable income for the year is $200,000; the only timing difference is ACRS tax deductions over book depreciation. At year-end the net book value of depreciable assets is $500,000. The tax basis is $350,000. Pretax book income is $250,000.

Taxable income	$200,000
Tax rate	50%
Tax currently payable	$100,000
Book basis of depreciable assets	$500,000
Tax basis of depreciable assets	350,000
Cumulative timing differences	150,000
Tax rate	50%
Deferred tax liability at end of year	$ 75,000
Deferred tax liability at beginning of year	50,000
Deferred tax expense	25,000
Tax currently payable	100,000
Tax expense	$125,000

The following illustration compares the computations for the deferred method with the liability method, including a change in the tax rate in 1988.

Deferred Method

	1993	1994
Pretax book income	$1,000,000	$1,000,000
Taxable income	200,000	200,000
Tax rate	40%	50%
Taxes payable	$ 320,000	$ 400,000
Deferred tax		
($200,000 × 40%)	80,000	
($200,000 × 50%)		100,000
Tax expense	$ 400,000	$ 500,000
Cumulative deferred tax credit	$ 80,000	180,000

Applying the liability method and using the same data, the tax provisions and balance sheet amounts for the two years are calculated as follows:

Liability Method

	1993	1994
Taxes payable	$320,000	$400,000
Tax effects of		
timing differences		
($200,000 × 50%)	100,000	100,000
Tax expense	$420,000	$500,000
Cumulative liability		
for future taxes	$100,000	$200,000

To summarize, as stated earlier, compared to FASB 96, FASB 109 makes it easier to record deferred assets and their related deferred credits to income. As a result, there is the possibility that companies which in prior years could not record certain deferred credits under superseded FASB 96 could now record these period-related credits in 1993 income. Recording these credits in current income could lead to an overstatement of operating income, since it included credits that did not relate to the current period's operations. On the other hand, some companies have their tax credit reserve set up to confuse the picture at some later date. One thing that FASB 109 does *not* do is make it easier to compare various companies' financial statements.

The principal difference between the old Rule and the new Rule lies in when the accounting entry can be made and the dollar value of deferred tax credits recognized that arise from actual or potential future tax credits and loss carryforwards. Essentially, FASB 96 limited the recognition of future tax benefits to amounts that could be used currently or carried back to earlier periods. Obviously, this placed very restrictive restraints on companies. FASB 109 allows future tax benefits to be recognized if it is "more than likely" that the company will in fact realize these benefits in future periods.

Neither "more than likely" nor "better than a 50-50 chance" can be considered very restrictive requirements. It becomes evident that a great amount of leeway is afforded the decision makers. Nor is it likely that a company's auditors will question a judgmental decision made under such elastic guidelines. The decision for management has been when and how a company should account for the potential tax savings.

According to FASB 109, management is charged with gazing into its crystal ball. If management sees that the company will more than likely produce sufficient earnings in the future to warrant the use of the credit, then the company must book the value of the tax credit as income immediately and record it as a one-time accounting adjustment.

Among the companies that will probably recognize as much pain as possible early are those wanting to build their capital accounts, with the gain showing on the balance sheet as retained earnings. As mentioned earlier, other companies faced with huge charges against earnings to fund reserves for postretirement benefits under FASB 106 may want to show big gains immediately to lessen the negative effect of those charges on equity.

On the other hand, if management is hesitant to prognosticate a rosy earnings picture, the tax credit could be set aside in a reserve. This reserve can be doled out in the future at management's discretion to brighten the outlook on an otherwise disappointing earnings picture. Therefore, it would appear that the "hidden," but footnoted, reserves will provide a method for management to smooth out reported earnings in the future.

Computation of deferred tax liabilities or assets

- Compute all existing differences between the financial reporting basis of assets and liabilities. These are the temporary differences.
- Estimate the specific future years in which temporary differences will result in taxable or deductible amounts.
- Calculate the net taxable or deductible amount in each future year.
- Deduct operating loss carryforwards from net taxable amounts scheduled for future years and included in the loss carryforward period.
- Carryback or carryforward the net deductible amounts occurring in particular years to offset net taxable amounts scheduled for prior or subsequent years.
- Schedule the expected reversal of existing temporary differences.

- Calculate the tax effects of reversals based on existing tax laws and rates.
- Recognize a deferred tax asset for the tax benefit of net deductible amounts that could be realized by loss carryback from future years 1) to reduce a current deferred tax liability, and 2) to reduce taxes paid in the current or prior year.
- Calculate the tax for the remaining net taxable amounts scheduled to occur in future years. Apply current tax rates to the amount of net taxable amounts scheduled for each of those years.
- Deduct tax credit carryforwards from the amount of tax calculated for future years that are included in the carryforward periods.
- Recognize a deferred tax liability for the remaining amount of taxes payable for each future year.

The effects on deferred taxes of changes in tax rates and laws should be recorded when the changes occur as a component of tax expense for the period of the change. For accounting purposes, the change occurs the day the law is enacted.

Disclosure requirements.   Without regard for any particular sequence or organization, several salient features of the disclosure requirements are listed below.

1) The deferred tax consequences of temporary differences scheduled to reverse during the next year must be disclosed as current. The tax effects scheduled to reverse the following year are considered as noncurrent.

2) The amount of income tax expense for benefit from continuing operations is computed separately from any other category of earnings shown on the income statement. Income taxes are allocated among other categories, such as the cumulative effect of accounting changes, discontinued operations, and extraordinary items. The taxes are based on the incremental effect that each category has on income tax expense.

3) The tax benefits resulting from operating loss and tax credit carryforwards are categorized according to the type of income that results in the current period.

4) When the Statement is adopted, a cumulative catch-up adjustment occurs which can be disclosed by either:
   a) Actively restating financial statements for prior years; or
   b) Including the adjustment in net income as of the beginning of the year of adoption.

5) Amounts of refundable income taxes, income taxes currently payable, and deferred taxes must still be disclosed.

6) Deferred taxes continue to be categorized as current and noncurrent amounts, and the computing of current and noncurrent amounts must be consistent with the liability method.

7) The current amount is the net deferred tax asset or deferred tax liability caused by timing differences reversing in the year following the balance sheet date. Remaining net deferred taxes would be the noncurrent amounts. This results in a change from the old rule which required the current or noncurrent classification of most deferred taxes to follow the classification of the related asset or liability, if any.

8) A change caused by the liability method does not permit deferred tax liability and assets attributable to different tax jurisdictions to be offset.

9) For interim reporting, the entire effect of a change in tax rates is reported in the interim period in which the change is introduced. It should not be allocated over either prior or future interim periods.

10) The components of income tax expense or benefit resulting from continuous operations must be disclosed in the financial statement, or in footnotes. These include:

a) Current tax expense or benefit.

b) Deferred tax expense or benefit.

c) Investment tax credits and grants.

d) The benefit of operating loss carryforwards which result in a reduction of income tax expense.

e) Adjustments of a deferred tax liability or asset resulting from changes in the tax laws. or rates, or the status of the enterprise (for example, from nontaxable to taxable or vice versa).

f) SEC requirements are not affected by the new rule.

11) Disclosure is required for the amounts and expiration dates of operating loss and tax credit carryforwards for financial reporting purposes and for tax purposes.

12) a) Income tax expense or benefit allocated to other than continuing operations must be disclosed.

b) Included among these are extraordinary items and the foreign currency translation component of equity.

Chapter 21

Tax Terminology

Accountant's Report. When used regarding financial statements, a document in which an independent public or certified public accountant indicates the scope of the audit (or examination) which has been made and sets forth an opinion regarding the financial statements taken as a whole, or an assertion to the effect that an overall opinion cannot be expressed. When an overall opinion cannot be expressed, the reasons must be stated.

Accounting Method. A set of rules used to determine when and how income and expenses are reported.

Adjusted Issue Price. The issue price increased by any amount of discount deducted before repurchase, or, in the case of convertible obligations, decreased by any amount of premium included in gross income before repurchase.

Adjusted Sales Price. The amount realized, reduced by the aggregate for work performed on the old residence to assist in its sale. The reduction only applies to work performed during the 90-day period ending on the day on which the contract to sell the old residence is entered into.

Adverse Party. Any person having a substantial beneficial interest in the trust which would be adversely affected by the exercise or nonexercise of the authority which he/she possesses regarding the trust.

Affiliate. An affiliate of, or a person affiliated with, a specific person is one who directly or indirectly, through one or more intermediaries, controls, or is controlled by, or is under common control with, the person specified. (See **Person** below)

Affiliated Group. One or more chains of includable corporations connected through stock ownership with a common parent corporation which is an includable corporation. (See **Includable Corporation** below). The ownership of stock of any corporation means the common parent possesses at least 80 percent of the total voting power of the stock of such corporation and has a value equal to at least 80 percent of the total value of the stock of that corporation.

Alien. A foreigner is an alien who has filed his/her declaration of intention to become a citizen, but who has not yet been admitted to citizenship by a final order of a naturalization court.

American Aircraft. An aircraft registered under the laws of the United States.

American Vessel. Any vessel documented or numbered under the laws of the United States, and includes any vessel which is neither documented nor numbered under the laws of the Untied States nor documented under the laws of any foreign country, if its crew is employed solely by one or more citizens or residents of the United States or corporations organized under the laws of the United States or of any State.

Amount. When used regarding securities, the principal amount if relating to evidences of indebtedness the number of shares if relating to shares, and the number of units if relating to any other kind of security.

Amount Loaned. The amount received by the borrower.

Annual Accounting Period. The annual period, calendar year or fiscal year, on the basis of which the taxpayer regularly computes his/her income in keeping the books.

Annual Compensation. Includes an employee's average regular annual compensation, or such average compensation over the last five years, or such employee's last annual compensation if reasonably similar to his or her average regular annual compensation for the five preceding years.

Annuity Contract. A contract which may be payable in installments during the life of the annuitant only.

Applicable Installment Obligation. Any obligation which arises from the disposition of personal property under the installment method by a person who regularly sells or otherwise disposes of personal property of the same type on the installment plan. The disposition of real property under the installment method which is held by the taxpayer for sale to customers in the ordinary course of the taxpayer's trade or business, or the disposition of real property under the installment method which is property used in the taxpayer's trade or business, or property held for the production of rental income, but only if the sale price of such property exceeds $150,000.

Associate. Indicates a relationship with any person, and means 1) any corporation or organization of which such person is an officer or partner or is directly or indirectly the beneficial owner of 10 percent or more of any class of equity securities, 2) any trust or other estate in which such person has a substantial beneficial interest or for which such person serves as trustee or in a similar fiduciary capacity, and 3) any relative or spouse of such person, or any relative of such spouse, who has the same home as such person or who is a director or officer of the registrant or any of its parents or subsidiaries.

Audit (Examination). When used regarding financial statements, an examination of the statements by an accountant in accordance with generally accepted auditing standards for the purpose of expressing an opinion.

Balance. With respect to a reserve account or a guaranteed employment account, the amount standing to the credit of the account as of the computation date.

Bank. A bank or trust company or domestic building and loan association incorporated and doing business under the laws of the United States, including laws relating to the District of Columbia, or of any State, a substantial part of the business of which consists of receiving deposits and making loans and discounts, or of exercising fiduciary powers similar to those permitted to national banks under authority of the Comptroller of the Currency, and which is subject by law to supervision and examination by State or Federal authority having supervision over banking institutions.

Bank Holding Company. A person who is engaged, either directly or indirectly, primarily in the business of owning securities of one or more banks for the purpose, and with the effect, of exercising control. (See **Person** below)

Basis of Obligation. The basis of an installment obligation is the excess of the face value of the obligation over an amount equal to the income which would be returnable were the obligation satisfied in full.

Below-Market Loan. Any demand loan for which the interest is payable on the loan at a rate less than the applicable Federal rate, or in the case of a term loan (see **Term Loan** below) the amount loaned exceeds the present value of all payments due under the loan.

Bond. Any bond, debenture, note, or certificate or other evidence of indebtedness, but does not include any obligation which constitutes stock in trade of the taxpayer or any such obligation of a kind which would properly be included in the inventory of the taxpayer if on hand at the close of the taxable year, or any obligation held by the taxpayer primarily for sale to customers in the ordinary course of trade or business.

C Corporation. With respect to any taxable year, a corporation which is not an S corporation for such year.

Calendar Year. A period of 12 months ending on December 31. A taxpayer who has not established a fiscal year must make his/her tax return on the basis of a calendar year.

Capital Asset. Property held by a taxpayer, whether or not connected with a trade or business. The term does not include stock in trade of the taxpayer or other property of a kind which would properly be included in the inventory of the taxpayer if on hand at the close of the taxable year, or property held for sale to customers in the ordinary course of a trade or business.

Capital Expenditure. Any cost of a type that is properly chargeable to a capital account under general Federal income tax principles. Whether an expenditure is a capital expenditure is determined at the time the expenditure is paid with respect to the property. Future changes in law do not affect whether an expenditure is a capital expenditure. Capital expenditures do not include expenditures for items of current operating expense that are not properly chargeable to a capital account—so called *working capital* items.

Capital Gain. The excess of the gains from sales or exchanges of capital assets over the losses from sales or exchanges.

Carrier. An express carrier, sleeping car carrier, or rail carrier providing transportation.

Certified. When used regarding financial statements, examined and reported upon with an opinion expressed by an independent public or certified public accountant.

Charitable Contribution. A contribution or gift to or for the use of a corporation, trust, community chest, fund, or foundation operated exclusively for religious, charitable, scientific, literary, or educational purposes, or to foster national or international amateur sports competition if no part of its activities involves the provision of athletic facilities or equipment. A contribution or gift is deductible only if it is used within the Untied States or any of its possessions.

Charter. Articles of incorporation, declarations of trust, articles of association or partnership, or any similar instrument affecting, either with or without filing with any governmental agency, the organization or creation of an incorporated or unincorporated person (see **Person** below).

Child. Son, stepson, daughter, stepdaughter, adopted son, adopted daughter, or for taxable years after December 31, 1958, a child who is a member of an individual's household if the child was placed with the individual by an authorized placement agency for legal adoption pursuant to a formal application filed by the individual with the agency.

Child Care Facility. Any tangible property which qualifies as a child care center primarily for children of employees of the employer, except that the term does not include any property not of a character subject to depreciation, or located outside the United States.

Citizen. Every person born or naturalized in the United States and subject to its jurisdiction.

Collapsible Corporation. A corporation formed or availed of principally by the manufacture, construction, or production of property, for the purchase of property which is in the hands of the corporation, or for the holding of stock in a corporation so formed or availed of with a view to the sale or exchange of stock by its shareholders. The term includes distribution to its shareholders, before the realization by the corporation manufacturing, constructing, producing, or purchasing the property of 2/3 of the taxable income to be derived from such property, and by the realization by such shareholders of gain attributable to such property.

Common Equity. Any class of common stock or an equivalent interest including, but not limited to a unit of beneficial interest in a trust or a limited partnership interest.

Common Trust Fund. A fund maintained by a bank exclusively for the collective investment and reinvestment of moneys contributed thereto by the bank in its capacity as a trustee, executor, administrator, or guardian, or as a custodian of accounts which the Secretary determines are established pursuant to a State law, and which bank has established that it has duties and responsibilities similar to the duties and responsibilities of a trustee or guardian.

Company. Corporations, associations, and joint-stock companies.

Complete Liquidation. (See **Distribution** below)

Computation Date. The date, occurring at least once each calendar year and within 27 weeks prior to the effective date of new rates of contributions, as of which such dates are computed.

Constructive Sale Price. An article sold at retail, sold on consignment, or sold otherwise than through an arm's length transaction at less than the fair market price.

Contributions. Payments required by a State law to be made into an unemployment fund by any person on account of having individuals in his/her employ, to the extent that such payments are made without being deducted or deductible from the remuneration of the employed individuals.

Control. The ownership of stock possessing at least 80 percent of the total combined voting power of all classes of stock entitled to vote and at least 80 percent of the total number of shares of all other classes of stock of the corporation.

Controlled Foreign Corporation. Any foreign corporation if more than 50 percent of the total combined voting power of all classes of stock of such corporation entitled to vote, or the total value of the stock of such corporation, is owned, directly or indirectly, by and for a foreign corporation, foreign partnership, foreign trust, or foreign estate shall be considered as being owned proportionately by its shareholders, partners, or beneficiaries.

Controlled Group of Corporations. One or more chains of corporations connected through stock ownership with a common parent corporation if stock possessing at least 80 percent of the total combined voting power of all classes of stock entitled to vote or at least 80 percent of the total value of shares of all classes of stock of each of the corporations, and the common parent corporation is owned by one or more of the other corporations.

Convertible Obligation. An obligation which is convertible into the stock of the issuing corporation, or a corporation which, at the time the obligation is issued or repurchased, is in control of (see **Control** above) or controlled by the issuing corporation.

Cooperative Bank. An institution without capital stock organized and operated for mutual purposes and without profit, which is subject by law to supervision and examination by State or Federal authority having supervision over such institutions.

Cooperative Housing Corporation. A corporation having one and only one class of stock outstanding, each of the stockholders of which is entitled, solely by reason of ownership of stock in the corporation, to occupy for dwelling purposes a house, or an apartment in a building, owned or leased by the cooperative housing corporation. No stockholder of the housing corporation is entitled to receive any distribution that is not out of earnings and profits of the corporation except on a complete or partial liquidation of the corporation.

Corporate Acquisition Indebtedness. Any obligation evidenced by a bond, debenture, note, or certificate or other evidence of indebtedness issued by a corporation to provide consideration for the acquisition of stock in another corporation; or the acquisition of the assets of another corporation in accordance with a plan under which at least two-thirds in value of all the assets (excluding money) is used in trades and businesses carried on by the corporation.

Corporation. Includes associations, joint-stock companies, and insurance companies.

Currency Swap Contract. A contract involving different currencies between two or more parties to exchange periodic interim payments on or prior to maturity of the contract. The swap *principal amount* is an amount of two different currencies which, under the terms of the currency swap contract, is used to determine the periodic interim payments in each currency and which is exchanged upon maturity of the contract.

Date of Original Issue. The date on which the issue was first issued to the public, or the date on which the debt instrument was sold by the issuer. In the case of any debt instrument which is publicly offered, it is the date on which the debt instrument was issued in a sale or exchange.

Debt Instrument. A bond, debenture, note, or certificate or other evidence of indebtedness.

Deficiency. The amount by which the tax imposed exceeds the sum of the amount shown as the tax by the taxpayer upon his/her return, if a return was made by the taxpayer and an amount indicated as the tax. *Deficiency* includes the amounts previously assessed or collected without assessment as a deficiency over the amount of rebates.

Deficiency Dividends. The amount of dividends paid by the corporation on or after the date of the determination (see **Determination** below), before filing claims which would have been includable in the computation of the deduction for dividends paid for the taxable year with respect to which the liability for personal holding company tax exists, if distributed during such taxable year. No dividends are considered as *deficiency dividends* unless distributed within 90 days after the determination.

Deficiency Dividend Deduction. No deduction is allowed unless the claim therefore is filed within 120 days after the determination.

Demand Loan. Any loan which is payable in full at any time on the demand of the lender.

Dependent. Any of the following individuals *over half* of whose support for the calendar year in which the taxable year of the taxpayer begins was received from the taxpayer or treated as received from the taxpayer:

1) A son or daughter of the taxpayer, or a descendant of either.
2) A stepson or stepdaughter of the taxpayer.
3) A brother, sister, stepbrother, or stepsister of the taxpayer.
4) The father or mother of the taxpayer, or an ancestor of either.
5) A stepfather or stepmother of the taxpayer.
6) A son or daughter of a brother or sister of the taxpayer.
7) A brother or sister of the father or mother of the taxpayer.
8) A son-in-law, daughter-in-law, father-in-law, mother-in-law, brother-in-law, sister-in-law, of the taxpayer.
9) An individual, other than an individual who at any time during the taxable year was the spouse, who, for the taxable year of the taxpayer, has as his/her principal place of abode the home of the taxpayer and is a member of the taxpayer's household.

Depositary Share. A security, evidenced by an *American Depositary Receipt*, that represents a foreign security or a multiple of or fraction thereof deposited with a depositary.

Determination. A decision by the Tax Court or a judgment, decree, or other order by any court of competent jurisdiction, which has become final.

Development Stage Company. A company which is devoting substantially all its efforts to establishing a new business and either of the following conditions exists:

1) Planned principal operations have not commenced.
2) Planned principal operations have commenced, but there has been no significant revenue therefrom.

Distiller. Any person who produces distilled spirits from any source or substance.

Distribution. A *distribution* is treated as in complete liquidation of a corporation, if the distribution is one of a series of distributions in redemption of all of the stock of the corporation pursuant to a plan.

Dividend. Any distribution of property made by a corporation to its shareholders out of earnings and profits of the taxable year, or from the most recently accumulated earnings and profits, computed at the close of the taxable year, without regard to the amount of earnings and profits at the time the distribution was made.

Domestic. When applied to a corporation or partnership, created or organized in the United States or under the laws of the United States or of any State.

Domestic Building and Loan Association. A domestic building and loan association, a domestic savings and loan association, or a Federal savings and loan association.

Earned Income. Wages, salaries, or professional fees, and other amounts received as compensation for personal services rendered by an individual to a corporation which represent a distribution of earnings or profits rather than a reasonable allowance as compensation for the personal services actually rendered. *Earned income* includes net earnings from self-employment to the extent such net earnings constitute compensation for personal services actually rendered.

Educational Organization. An organization which normally maintains a regular faculty and curriculum and normally has regularly organized body of students in attendance at the place where its educational activities are carried on.

Employee. Any officer of a corporation; any individual who, under the usual common law rules applicable to determining the employer-employee relationship, has the status of an employee; any individual who performs services for remuneration for any person as an agent-driver engaged in distributing products; a full-time life insurance salesperson; a home worker performing work; a traveling or city salesperson.

Employee Stock Purchase Plan. A plan which provides that options are to be granted only to employees of the employer corporation, or of its parent or subsidiary corporation, to purchase stock in any such corporation; and such plan is approved by the stockholders of the granting corporation within 12 months before or after the plan is adopted.

Under the terms of the plan, no employee can be granted an option if the employee, immediately after the option is granted, owns stock amounting to 5 percent or more of the total combined voting power or value of all class-es of stock of the employee corporation or of its parent or subsidiary corpo-ration. Under the plan, options are to be granted to all employees of any cor-poration whose employees are granted any of such options by reason of their employment by such corporation, except employees who have been employed less than 2 years, or employees whose customary employment is 20 hours or less per week, or employees whose customary employment is for not more than 5 months in any calendar year.

Employer. With respect to any calendar year, any person who during any calendar quarter in the calendar year or the preceding calendar year, paid wages of $1500 or more, or on each of some 20 days during the calendar year or during the preceding calendar year (each day being in a different calendar week) employed at least one individual in employment for some portions of the day.

Employment. Any service of whatever nature performed by an employ-ee for the person employing him or her, irrespective of the citizenship or res-idence of either within the United States; or any service in connection with an American vessel or American aircraft under a contract of service which is entered into within the United States or during the performance of which and while the employee is employed on and in connection with such vessel or air-craft when outside the United States. The term also includes any service of whatever nature performed outside the United States by a citizen or resident of the United States as an employee of an American employer, or if it is ser-vice, regardless of where or by whom performed, which is designated as employment or recognized as equivalent to employment under an agreement entered into under the Social Security Act.

Endowment Contract. A contract with an insurance company which depends in part on the life expectancy of the insured, which may be payable in full during the insured's life.

Energy Property. Property that is described in at least one of 6 cate-gories:

1) Alternative energy property.
2) Solar or wind energy property.
3) Specifically defined energy property.
4) Recycling equipment.
5) Shale oil Equipment.
6) Equipment for producing natural gas from geopressured grime.

Property is not *energy property* unless depreciation or amortization is allowable and the property has an estimated useful life of 3 years or more from the time when the property is placed in service.

Enrolled Actuary. A person who is enrolled by the Joint Board for the Enrollment of Actuaries.

Equity Security. Any stock or similar security, or any security convertible, with or without consideration, into such a security, or carrying any warrant or right to subscribe to or purchase such security, or any such warrant or right.

Exchanged Basis Property. Property having a basis determined in whole or in part by reference to other property held at any time by the person for whom the basis is determined.

Executor. The administrator of the decedent, or, if there is none appointed, qualified, and acting within the United States, then any person in actual or constructive possession of any property of the decedent.

Farm. Includes stock, dairy, poultry, fruit and truck farms; also plantations, ranches, and all land used for farming operations.

Farmer. All individuals, partnerships, or corporations that cultivate, operate, or manage farms for gain or profit, either as owners or tenants.

Fiduciary. A guardian, trustee, executor, administrator, receiver, conservator, or any person acting in any fiduciary capacity for any person.

Fifty-Percent-Owned Person. A person approximately 50 percent of whose outstanding voting shares is owned by the specified person either directly or indirectly through one or more intermediaries (see **Person** below).

Financial Statements. Include all notes to the statements and all related schedules.

Fiscal Year. An accounting period of 12 months ending on the last day of any month other than December; the 52–53 week annual accounting period, if such period has been elected by the taxpayer. A fiscal year is recognized only if it is established as the annual accounting period of the taxpayer and only if the books of the taxpayer are kept in accordance with such fiscal year.

Foreign. A corporation or partnership which is *not* domestic.

Foreign Currency Contract. A contract which requires delivery of, or settlement of, and depends on the value of, a foreign currency which is a currency in which positions are also traded through regulated futures contracts. The contract is traded in the interbank market, and is entered into at arm's length at a price determined by reference to the price in the interbank market.

Foreign Earned Income. The amount received by any individual from sources within a foreign country or countries which constitutes earned income attributable to services performed by such individual. Amounts received are considered to be received in the taxable year in which the services to which the amounts are attributable are performed.

Foreign Estate (Foreign Trust). An estate or trust, as the case may be, the income of which comes from sources without the United States which are not materially connected with the conduct of a trade or business within the United States.

Foreign Insurer or Reinsurer. One who is a non-resident alien individual, or a foreign partnership, or a foreign corporation. The term includes a nonresident alien individual, foreign partnership, or foreign corporation which will become bound by an obligation of the nature of an indemnity bond. The term *does not include* a foreign government, or municipal or other corporation exercising the taxing power.

Foreign Investment Company. Any foreign corporation which is registered under the Investment Company Act of 1940, as amended, either as a management company or as a unit investment trust, or is engaged primarily in the business of investing, reinvesting, or trading in securities, commodities, or any interest in property, including a futures or forward contract or option.

FSC (Foreign Sales Corporation). Any corporation which was created or organized under the laws of any foreign country, or under the laws applicable to any possession of the United States, has no more than 25 shareholders at any time during the taxable year, does not have any preferred stock outstanding at any time during the taxable year, and during the taxable year maintains an office located outside the United States in a foreign country, or in any possession of the United States. The term *FSC does not include* any corporation which was created or organized under the laws of any foreign country unless there is in effect between such country and the United States a bilateral or multilateral agreement, or an income tax treaty which contains an exchange of information program to which the *FSC* is subject.

Foreign Trading Gross Receipts. The gross receipts of any FSC which are from the sale, exchange, or other disposition of export property, from the lease or rental of export property for use by the lessee outside the United States, or for services which are related and subsidiary to any sale, exchange, lease, or rental of export property by such corporation.

Foundation Manager. With respect to any private foundation, an officer, director, or trustee of a foundation responsible for any act, or failure to act, and for the employees of the foundation having authority or responsibility, and for their failure to act.

General Partner (see **Partner**). The person or persons responsible under state law for directing the management of the business and affairs of a partnership that are subject of a roll-up transaction (see **Roll-Up Transaction** below) including, but not limited to, a general partner(s), board of directors, board of trustees, or other person(s) having a fiduciary duty to such partnership.

General Power of Appointment. The power which is exercisable in favor of the decedent, his/her estate, his/her creditors, or the creditors of the estate.

Generation-Skipping Transfer. A taxable distribution, a taxable termination, and a direct skip. The term does not include any transfer to the extent the property transferred was subject to a prior tax imposed; and such transfers do not have the effect of avoiding tax.

Gift Loan. Any below-market loan where the forgoing of interest is in the nature of a gift (see **Below-Market Loan** above).

Gross Income. All income derived from whatever source; income realized in any form, whether in money, property, or services; income realized in the form of services, meals, accommodations, stock, or other property, as well as in cash. Gross income, however, is not limited to the items enumerated.

Head of Household. An individual is considered a head of a household if, and only if, such individual is *not* married at the close of his/her taxable year, is not a surviving spouse, (see **Surviving Spouse** below) maintains as his/her home a household which constitutes more than one-half of such taxable year the principal place of abode as a member of such household.

Holder. Any individual whose efforts created property held; any other individual who has acquired an interest in such property in exchange for consideration in money or money's worth paid to such creator of the invention covered by the patent, if such individual is neither the employer of the creator, nor related to the creator.

Housing Expenses. The reasonable expenses paid or incurred during the taxable year by or on behalf of an individual for housing in a foreign country for the individual, spouse and dependants.

Includable Corporation. Any corporation except those exempt from taxation, foreign corporations, insurance companies subject to taxation, regulated investment companies, and real estate investment trusts subject to tax.

Income Recognition. Dividends are included in income on the ex-dividend date; interest is accrued on a daily basis. Dividends declared on short positions existing on the record date are recorded on the ex-dividend date and included as an expense of the period.

Income Tax Return Preparer. Any person who prepares for compensation, or who employs one or more persons to prepare for compensation, any return of tax or any claim for refund of tax. The preparation of a substantial portion of a return or claim for refund is treated as if it were the preparation of such return or claim for refund.

A person is *not* an *income tax return preparer* merely because such person furnishes typing, reproducing, or other mechanical assistance, or prepares a return or claim for refund of the employer, or of an officer or employee of the employer, by whom the person is regularly and continuously employed.

Indian Tribal Government. A governing body of a tribe, band, pueblo, community, village, or a group of native American Indians, or Alaska Native.

Individual Retirement Account. A trust created or organized in the United States for the exclusive benefit of an individual or his/her beneficiaries, but only if the written governing instrument creating the trust meets the following requirements:

1) The trustee is a bank, or such other person who demonstrates that the manner in which such other person will administer the trust will be consistent with the requirements of this section.
2) No part of the trust funds will be invested in life insurance contracts.
3) The interest of the individual in the balance of the account is non-forefeitable.
4) The assets of the trust will not be commingled with other property except in a common trust fund or common investment fund.

Individual Retirement Annuity. An annuity contract, or an endowment contract issued by an insurance company which meets the following requirements:

1) The contract is not transferable by the owner.
2) Under the contract, the premiums are not fixed.
3) Any refund of premiums will be applied before the close of the calendar year following the year of the refund toward the payment of future premiums or the purchase of additional benefits.
4) The entire interest of the owner is nonforfeitable.

Influencing Legislation. Any attempt to have an effect on legislation by trying to impact the opinions of the general public or any segment thereof through communication with any member or employee of a legislative body, or with any government official or employee who may participate in the formulation of the legislation. It does not include any communication with a government official or employee *other than* one whose *principal purpose* is to affect legislation.

Insurance Company. A company whose primary and predominant business activity during the taxable year is the issuing of insurance or annuity contracts, or the reinsuring of risks underwritten by insurance companies. It is the character of the business actually done in the taxable year which determines whether a company is taxable as an insurance company. Insurance companies include both stock and mutual companies, as well as mutual benefit insurance companies. A voluntary unincorporated association of employees, including an association formed for the purpose of relieving sick and aged members, and the dependants of deceased members, is an insurance company.

Interest. Return on any obligation issued in registered form, or of a type issued to the public, but does not include any obligation with a maturity (at issue) of not more than 1 year which is held by a corporation.

International organization. A public international organization entitled to the privileges, exemptions, and immunities as an international organization under the *International Organizations Immunities Act.*

Investment in the Contract. As of the annuity starting date, the aggregate amount of premiums or other consideration paid for the contract, minus the aggregate amount received under the contract before such date, to the extent that such amount was excludable from gross income under prior income tax laws.

Itemized Deductions. Those allowable other than the deductions allowable in arriving at adjusted gross income and the deduction for personal exemptions.

Joint Return. A single return made jointly by a husband and wife.

Life Insurance Contract. An *endowment contract* which is not ordinarily payable in full during the life of the insured.

Lobbying Expenditures. Amounts spent for the purpose of influencing legislation (see **Influencing Legislation** above).

Local Telephone Service. Any telephone service not taxable as long distance telephone service; leased wire, teletypewriter or talking circuit special service, or wire and equipment service. Amounts paid for the installation of instruments, wire, poles, switchboards, apparatus, and equipment, are not considered amounts paid for service.

Long Distance Telephone Service. A telephone or radio telephone message or conversation for which the toll charge is more than 24 cents and for which the charge is paid within the United States.

Long-Term Capital Gain. A gain from the sale or exchange of a capital asset held for more than 1 year, if and to the extent such gain is taken into account in computing gross income.

Long-Term Capital Loss. A loss from the sale or exchange of a capital asset held for more than 1 year, if and to the extent that such loss is taken into account in computing taxable income.

Long-Term Contract. A building, installation, construction or manufacturing contract (see **Manufacturing Contract** on next page) which is not completed within the taxable year in which it is initiated.

Lottery. A numbers game, policy, and similar types of wagering (see **Wager** on page 564).

Lowest Price. Determined without requiring that any given percentage of sales be made at that price, and without including any fixed amount to which the purchaser has a right as a result of contractual arrangements existing at the time of the sale.

Majority-Owned Subsidiary Company. A corporation, stock of which represents in the aggregate more than 50 percent of the total combined voting power of all classes of stock of such corporation entitled to vote, is owned wholly by a registered holding company, or partly by such registered holding company and partly by one or more majority-owned subsidiary companies, or by one or more majority-owned subsidiary companies of the registered holding company.

Managing Underwriter. An underwriter(s) who, by contract or otherwise, deals with the registrant, organizes the selling effort, receives some benefit, directly or indirectly, in which all other underwriters similarly situated do not share in proportion to their respective interests in the underwriting, or represents any other underwriters in such matters as maintaining the records of the distribution, arranging the allotments of securities offered, or arranging for appropriate stabilization activities, if any.

Manufacturing Contract. A long-term contract which involves the manufacture of unique items of a type which is not normally carried in the finished goods inventory of the taxpayer, or of items which normally require more than 12 calendar months to complete regardless of the duration of the actual contract.

Material. Information required for those matters about which an average prudent investor ought reasonably to be informed.

MATHEMATICAL OR CLERICAL ERROR:

1) An error in addition, subtraction, multiplication, or division shown on any return.
2) An incorrect use of any table provided by the IRS with respect to any return, if such incorrect use is apparent from the existence of other information on the return.
3) An entry on a return of an item which is inconsistent with another entry of the same or another item on the return.
4) An omission of information which is required to be supplied to substantiate an entry on the return.
5) An entry on a return of a deduction or credit in amount which exceeds a statutory limit, if such limit is expressed as a specified monetary amount, or as a percentage, ratio, or fraction, and if the items entering into the application of such limit appear on the return.

Municipal Bond. Any obligation issued by a government or political subdivision thereof, if the interest on such obligation is excludable from gross income. It does not include such an obligation if it is sold or otherwise disposed of by the taxpayer within 30 days after the date of its acquisition.

Net Capital Gain. The excess of the net long-term capital gain for the taxable year over the net short-term capital loss for that year.

Net Capital Loss. For corporations, the excess of the losses from sales or exchanges of capital assets only to the extent of gains from such sales or exchanges. For taxpayers other than a corporation, losses from sales or exchanges of capital assets are allowable only to the extent of the gains from such sales or exchanges, plus the lower of $3,000 ($1,500 in the case of a married individual filing a separate return), or the excess of such losses over such gains.

Net Earnings from Self-Employment. The gross income derived by an individual from any trade or business carried on by such individual, less the deductions allowed which are attributable to such trade or business.

Net Long-Term Capital Gain. The excess of long-term capital gains for the taxable year over the long-term capital losses for such year.

Net Long-Term Capital Loss. The excess of long-term capital losses for the taxable year over the long-term capital gains for such year.

Net Operating Loss. The excess of the deductions allowed over the gross income. In the case of a taxpayer other than a corporation, the amount deductible on account of losses from sales or exchanges of capital assets cannot exceed the amount includable on account of gains from sales or exchanges of capital assets.

Net Short-Term Capital Gain. The excess of short-term capital gains for the taxable year over the short-term capital losses for such year.

Net Short-Term Capital Loss. The excess of short-term capital losses for the taxable year over the short-term capital gains for such year.

Nonadverse Party. Any person who is not an adverse party (see **Adeverse Party,** above).

Nonrecognition Transaction. Any disposition of property in a transaction in which gain or loss is *not* recognized in whole or in part.

Notional Principal Contract. A contract that provides for the payment of amounts by one party to another at specified intervals calculated by reference to a specified index upon a *notional principal amount* in exchange for a specified consideration or a promise to pay similar amounts.

Obligation. Any bond, debenture, note, certificate, or other evidence of indebtedness.

Operating Foundation. Any private foundation which makes distributions directly for the conduct of the activities constituting the purpose or function for which the foundation is organized and operated, equal to substantially all of the lesser of its adjusted net income, or its minimum investment return.

Option. The right or privilege of an individual to purchase stock from a corporation by virtue of an offer of the corporation continuing for a stated period of time, whether or not irrevocable, to sell such stock at a price determined under an option price, or price paid under the option. *Option Price* means the consideration in money or property which, pursuant to the terms of the option, is the price at which the stock subject to the option is purchased.

The individual owning the option is under no obligation to purchase, and the right or privilege must be evidenced in writing. While no particular form of words is necessary, the written option should express, among other things, an offer to sell at the option price and the period of time during which the offer will remain open. The individual who has the right or privilege is the *optionee* and the corporation offering to sell stock under such an arrangement is referred to as the *optionor*.

Organizational Expenditures. Any expenditure which is incident to the creation of a corporation, chargeable to capital accounts, and is of a character which, if expended incident to the creation of a corporation having a limited life, would be amortizable over such life.

Overpayment. Any payment of an Internal Revenue tax which is assessed or collected after the expiration of the period of limitation properly applicable thereto.

Owner-Employee. An owner of a proprietorship, or, in the case of a partnership, a partner who owns either more than 10 percent of the capital interest, or more than 10 percent of the profits interest, of the partnership.

Paid or Incurred (Paid or Accrued). Defined according to the method of accounting upon the basis of which the taxable income is computed.

Parent. Of a specified person, (see **Person** below) is an affiliate controlling such person directly, or, indirectly, through one or more intermediaries.

Parent Corporation. Any corporation, other than the employer corporation, in an unbroken chain of corporations ending with the employer corporation if each of the corporations other than the employer corporation owns stock possessing 50 percent or more of the total combined voting power of all classes of stock in one of the other corporations in the chain.

Partially Pooled Account. A part of an unemployment fund in which all contributions thereto are mingled and undivided. Compensation from this part is payable only to individuals to whom compensation would be payable from a reserve account or from a guaranteed employment account but for the exhaustion or termination of such reserve account or of a guaranteed employment account. (See **Pooled Fund** below)

Partner. A member of a partnership.

Partner's Interest, Liquidation Thereof. The termination of a partner's entire interest in a partnership by means of a distribution, or a series of distributions, to the partner by the partnership. A series of distributions means distributions whether they are made in one year or in more than one year. Where a partner's interest is to be liquidated by a series of distributions, the interest will not be considered as liquidated until the final distribution has been made. One which is not in liquidation of a partner's entire interest is a *current distribution*. Current distributions, therefore, include those in partial liquidation of a partner's interest, and those of the partner's distributive share.

Partnership. A syndicate, pool, group, joint venture or other unincorporated organization through or by means of which any business, financial operation, or venture is carried on, and is not a corporation, trust, or estate.

Partnership Agreement. Includes the original agreement and any modifications thereof agreed to by all the partners or adopted in any other manner provided by the partnership agreement. The agreements or modifications can be oral or written.

Payroll Period. A time frame for which a payment of wages is ordinarily made to the employee by the employer. The term *miscellaneous payroll period* means one other than a daily, weekly, biweekly, semimonthly, monthly, quarterly, semiannual, or annual period.

Pension Plan Contracts. Any contract entered into with trusts which at the time the contracts were entered into were deemed to be trusts and exempt from tax. Includes contracts entered into with trusts which were individual retirement accounts, or under contracts entered into with individual retirement annuities.

Person. Includes an individual, a trust, estate, partnership, association, company, or corporation, an officer or employee of a corporation or a member or employee of a partnership, who is under a duty to surrender the property or rights to property to discharge the obligation. The term also includes an officer or employee of the United States, of the District of Columbia, or of any agency or instrumentality who is under a duty to discharge the obligation.

Personal Holding Company. Any corporation if at least 60 percent of its adjusted ordinary gross income for the taxable year is personal holding company income, and at any time during the last half of the taxable year more than 50 percent in value of its outstanding stock is owned, directly or indirectly, by or for not more than 5 individuals. To meet the gross income requirement, it is necessary that at least 80 percent of the total gross income of the corporation for the taxable year be personal holding company income (see **Personal Holding Company Income** below).

Personal Holding Company Income. The portion of the adjusted ordinary gross income which consists of dividends, interest, royalties (other than mineral, oil, or gas royalties or copyright royalties), and annuities.

Political Organization. A party, committee, association, fund, or other organization, whether or not incorporated, organized and operated primarily for the purpose of directly or indirectly accepting contributions or making expenditures for an exempt function activity. A political organization can be a committee or other group which accepts contributions or makes expenditures for the purpose of promoting the nomination of an individual for an elective public office in a primary election, or in a meeting or caucus of a political party:

1) **Exempt Function Activity.** Includes all activities that are directly related to and support the process of influencing or attempting to influence the selection, nomination, election, or appointment of any individual to public office, or office in a political organization.

2) **Segregated Fund.** A fund which is established and maintained by a political organization or an individual separate from the assets of the organization or the personal assets of the individual. The amounts in the fund must be for use only for an exempt function, or for an activity necessary to fulfill an exempt function. A segregated fund established and maintained by an individual may qualify as a political organization.

Pooled Fund. An unemployment fund or any part thereof other than a reserve account (see **Reserve Account** below) or a guaranteed employment account, into which the total contributions of persons contributing thereto are payable, in which all contributions are mingled and undivided, and from which compensation is payable to all eligible individuals.

Predecessor. A person from whom another person acquired the major portion of the business and assets in a single succession, or in a series of related successions. In each of these successions the acquiring person received the major portion of the business and assets of the acquired.

Previously Filed or Reported. Previously filed with, or reported in, a definitive proxy statement or information statement, or in a registration statement under the Securities Act of 1933.

Principal Holder of Equity Securities. Used regarding a registrant or other person named in a particular statement or report, a holder of record or a known beneficial owner of more than 10 percent of any class of equity securities of the registrant or other person, respectively, as of the date of the related balance sheet filed.

Principal Underwriter. An underwriter in privity of contract with the issuer of the securities as to which he or she is underwriter.

Promoter. Any person who, acting alone or in conjunction with others, directly or indirectly, takes initiative in founding and organizing the business or enterprise of an issuer. Any person who in so doing received in consideration of services or property, or both services and property, 10 percent or more of any class of securities of the issuer or 10 percent or more of the proceeds from the sale of any class of securities. However, a person who receives such securities or proceeds with or solely as underwriting commissions or solely in consideration of property will not be deemed a promoter within the meaning of this paragraph if such person does not otherwise take part in founding and organizing the enterprise.

Property Used in the Trade or Business. That property used in a trade or business of a character which is subject to an allowance for depreciation, held for more than 1 year, and *real* property used in a trade or business, held for more than 1 year, and which is not a copyright, a literary work, musical, artistic composition, or similar property. Also *not* included in the definition is property of a kind which would properly be includable in the inventory of the taxpayer if on hand at the close of the taxable year, nor property held by the taxpayer primarily for sale to customers in the ordinary course of the trade or business.

Qualified Assets. The nature of any investments and other assets maintained, or required to be maintained, by applicable legal instruments in respect of outstanding face-amount certificates. If the nature of the qualifying assets and amount thereof is not subject to the provisions of the Investment Company Act of 1940, a statement to that effect should be made.

Qualified Individual. An individual whose tax home is in a foreign country and who is a citizen of the United States and establishes that he/she has been a bona fide resident of a foreign country (or countries) for an uninterrupted period which includes an entire taxable year, or a citizen or resident of the United States and who, during any period of 12 consecutive months, is present in a foreign country (or countries) during at least 330 full days in such period.

Qualified Pension, Profit-Sharing, Stock Bonus Plans and Annuity Plans. Compensation is paid under a deferred payment plan, and bond purchase plan. The plan is a definite written program and arrangement which is communicated to the employees and which is established and maintained by an employer.

In the case of a *pension plan*, to provide for the livelihood of the employees or their beneficiaries after the retirement of such employees through the benefits determined without regard to profits.

In the case of a *profit-sharing plan*, to enable employees or their beneficiaries to participate in the profits of the employer's trade or business, or in the profits of an affiliated employer who is entitled to deduct any contributions to the plan pursuant to a definite formula for allocating the contributions and for distributing the funds accumulated under the plan.

In the case of a *stock bonus plan*, to provide employees or their beneficiaries benefits similar to those of profit-sharing plans, except that such benefits are distributable in stock of the employer, and that the contributions by the employer are not necessarily dependent upon profits.

Real Estate Investment Trust (REIT). A corporation, trust, or association which meets the following conditions:

1) Is managed by one or more trustees or directors. A trustee means a person who holds legal title to the property of the *real estate investment trust*, and has such rights and powers as will meet the requirement of centralization of management. The trustee must have continuing exclusive authority over the management of the trust, the conduct of its affairs, and the disposition of the trust property.

2) Has beneficial ownership which is evidenced by transferable shares or by transferable certificates of beneficial interest and must be held by more than 100 persons determined without reference to any rules of attribution.

3) In case of a taxable year beginning before October 5, 1976, does not hold any property, other than foreclosure property, primarily for sale to customers in the ordinary course of its trade or business.

4) Is neither a financial institution, nor an insurance company.

5) Beneficial ownership of the REIT is held by 100 or more persons.

6) The REIT would not be a personal holding company if all of its gross income constituted personal holding company income.

Recomputed Basis. With respect to any property, its adjusted basis recomputed by adding to it all adjustments reflected on account of deductions allowed or allowable to the taxpayer or to any other person for depreciation or amortization.

Recovery. Regarding the recovery of tax benefit items, gross income does not include income attributable to the recovery during the taxable year of any amount deducted in any prior taxable year to the extent such amount did not reduce the amount of tax imposed.

Recovery Exclusion. Regarding a bad debt, prior tax, or delinquency amount, it is the amount determined in accordance with regulations of the deductions or credits allowed, on account of such bad debt, prior tax, or delinquency amount, which did not result in a reduction of the taxpayer's tax under corresponding provisions of prior income tax laws.

Registrant. The issuers of the securities for which an application, a registration statement, or a report is filed.

Related Parties. All affiliates of an enterprise, including its management and their immediate families, its principal owners and their immediate families, its investments accounted for by the equity method, beneficial employee trusts that are managed by the management of the enterprise, and any party that may, or does, deal with the enterprise and has ownership of, control over, or can significantly influence the management or operating policies of another party, to the extent that an arm's-length transaction may not be achieved.

Reorganization, A Party To. Includes a corporation resulting from a *reorganization*, and both corporations in a transaction qualifying as a reorganization where one corporation acquires stock or properties of another corporation. A corporation remains a *party to* the reorganization although it transfers all or part of the assets acquired as a controlled subsidiary. A corporation controlling an acquiring corporation is a party to the reorganization when the stock of the controlling corporation is used in the acquisition of properties.

Repurchase Premium. the excess of the repurchase price paid or incurred to repurchase the obligation over its adjusted issue price (see **Adjusted Issue Price** above).

Reserve Account. A separate account in an unemployment fund, maintained with respect to a person, or group of persons, having individuals in his, her, or their employ, from which account (unless such account is exhausted) is paid all and only compensation payable on the basis of services performed for such person, or for one or more of the persons comprising the group.

Restricted Securities. Investment securities which cannot be offered for public sale without first being registered under the Securities Act of 1933.

Return. Any return, statement, schedule, or list, and any supplement thereto, filed with respect to any tax imposed by the law.

Roll-Up Transaction. Any transaction or series of transactions that, directly or indirectly, through acquisition or otherwise, involve the combination or reorganization of one or more partnerships and the offer or sale of securities by a successor entity, whether newly formed or previously existing, to one or more limited partners of the partnerships to be combined or reorganized.

Rules and Regulations. All needful *rules and regulations* approved by the Commissioner for the enforcement of the Code. Includes all rules and regulations necessary by reason of the alterations of the law in relation to Internal Revenue.

S Corporation. Regarding any taxable year, a small business corporation for which an election is in effect for such year (see **Small Business Corporation**).

Section 1245 Property. Any property, other than livestock, which is or has been property of a character subject to an allowance for depreciation or subject to an allowance for amortization and is personal property, or other property if such property is tangible, but not including a building or its structural components.

Section 1250 Property. Any *real* property, other than Section 1245 property, which is or has been property of a character subject to an allowance for depreciation.

Self-Employment Income. The net earnings from self-employment derived by an individual during any taxable year, except if such net earnings for the taxable year are less than $400.

Share. A *unit* of stock in a corporation, or unit of interest in an unincorporated person.

Short-Term Capital Gain. A gain from the sale or exchange of a capital asset held for not more than 1 year, if and to the extent such gain is taken into account in computing gross income.

Short-Term Capital Loss. A loss from the sale or exchange of a capital asset held for not more than 1 year, if and to the extent that such loss is taken into account in computing gross income.

Significant Subsidiary. A *subsidiary*, including its subsidiaries, which meets any of the following conditions:

1) The registrant's and its other subsidiaries' investments in and advances to the subsidiary exceed 10 percent of the total assets of the registrant and its subsidiaries consolidated as of the end of the most recently completed fiscal year for a proposed business combination to be accounted for as a pooling-of-interests. This condition is also met when the number of common shares exchanged by the registrant exceeds 10 percent of its total common shares outstanding at the date the combination is initiated.

2) The registrant's and its other subsidiaries' proportionate share of the total assets, after intercompany eliminations, of the subsidiary exceeds 10 percent of the total assets of the registrant and its subsidiaries consolidated as of the end of the most recently completed fiscal year.

3) The registrant's and its other subsidiaries' equity in the income from continuing operations before income taxes, extraordinary items and cumulative effect of a change in accounting principle of the subsidiary exceeds 10 percent of such income of the registrant and its subsidiaries consolidated for the most recently completed fiscal year.

Small Business Corporation. A domestic corporation which is not an ineligible corporation, e.g., a member of an affiliated group, and which does not have more than 35 shareholders, does not have as a shareholder a person, other than an estate or trust, who is not an individual, and does not have a nonresident alien as a shareholder.

Standard Deduction. The sum of the basic standard deduction and the additional standard deduction.

Straight Debt. Any written unconditional promise to pay on demand or on a specified date a sum certain in money if the interest rate and interest payment dates are not contingent on profits or the borrower's discretion, not convertible into stock, and the creditor is an individual, an estate, or a trust.

Subsidiary Corporation. (see **Parent Corporation** above)

Substituted Basis Property. Property which is transferred basis property, or exchanged basis property.

Summarized Financial Information. The presentation of summarized information as to the assets, liabilities and results of operations of the entity for which the information is required.

Support. Includes food, shelter, clothing, medical and dental care, education, etc. The amount of an item of *support* will be the amount of expense incurred by the one furnishing such item. If the item of *support* furnished an individual is in the form of property or lodging, it is necessary to measure the amount of such item of support in terms of its fair market value.

Surviving Spouse. A taxpayer whose spouse died during either of his/her two taxable years immediately preceding the taxable year, and who maintains as his/her home a household which constitutes for the taxable year the principal place of abode as a member of such household.

Tax Court. The United States Tax Court.

Tax-Exempt Obligation. Any obligation if the interest on such obligation is not includable in gross income.

Taxable Gifts. The total amount of gifts made during the calendar year, less the deductions provided.

Taxable Income. Gross income minus the deductions allowed, other than the standard deduction (see **Standard Deduction** above). For individuals who do not itemize deductions for the taxable year, it is adjusted gross income, minus the standard deduction, and the deductions for personal exemptions.

Taxable Transportation. Transportation by air which begins and ends in the United States or in the 225-mile zone. The term *225-mile zone* means that portion of Canada and Mexico which is not more than 225 miles from the nearest point in the continental United States. The term *Continental United States* means the District of Columbia and the States other than Alaska and Hawaii.

Taxable Year. The taxpayer's annual accounting period if it is a calendar year or a fiscal year, or the calendar year if the taxpayer keeps no books or has no accounting period. (See **Annual Accounting Period** and **Calendar Year** above.)

Term Loan. Any loan which is not a demand loan (see **Demand Loan** above).

Tips. Wages received while performing services which constitute employment, and included in a written statement furnished to the employer.

Toll Telephone Service. A telephonic quality communication for which there is a toll charge which varies in amount with the distance and elapsed transmission time of each individual communication.

Totally Held Subsidiary. A subsidiary substantially all of whose outstanding equity securities are owned by its parent and/or the parent's other totally held subsidiaries, and which is not indebted, in an amount which is material in relation to the particular subsidiary, excepting indebtedness incurred in the ordinary course of business which is not overdue and which matures within 1 year from the date of its creation whether evidenced by securities or not. Indebtedness of a subsidiary which is secured by its parent by guarantee, pledge, assignment, or otherwise, is excluded.

Tract of Real Property. A single piece of real property, except that two or more pieces of real property should be considered a tract if at any time they were contiguous in the hands of the taxpayer, or if they would be contiguous except for the imposition of a road, street, railroad, stream, or similar property.

Trade or Business. Includes the performance of personal services within the United States at any time within the taxable year. Includes the performance of the functions of a public office.

Transferred Basis Property. Property having a basis determined in whole or in part by reference to the basis in the hands of the donor, grantor, or other transferor.

Trust. As used in the Internal Revenue Code, an arrangement created either by a will or by an *inter vivos* declaration whereby trustees take title to property for the purpose of protecting or conserving it for the beneficiaries under the ordinary rules applied in chancery or probate courts. Usually the beneficiaries of such a trust do no more than accept the benefits thereof and are not the voluntary planners or creators of the trust arrangement.

Undistributed Foreign Personal Holding Company Income. The taxable income of a *foreign personal holding company*.

Undistributed Personal Holding Company Income. The amount which is subject to the personal holding company tax.

United States Property. Any property which is a tangible property located in the United States, stock of a domestic corporation, an obligation of a United States resident, or any right to the use in the United States of a patent or copyright, an invention, model, or design (whether or not patented).

Unrealized Receivables. Any rights, contractual or otherwise, to payments for goods delivered, or to be delivered, to the extent that such payment would be treated as received for property other than a capital asset. Includes services rendered, or to be rendered, to the extent that income arising from such right to payment was not previously includable in income under the method of accounting employed. The basis for unrealized receivables includes all costs or expenses attributable thereto paid or accrued, but not previously taken into account under the method of accounting employed.

Unrecognized Gain. Any position held by the taxpayer as of the close of the taxable year, the amount of gain which would be taken into account with respect to such position if such position were sold on the last business day of such taxable year at its fair market value.

Valuation of Assets. The balance sheets of registered investment companies, other than issuers of face-amount certificates, which reflect all investments at value, with the aggregate cost of each category of investment and of the total investments reported shown parenthetically.

Voting Shares. The sum of all rights, other than as affected by events of default, to vote for election of directors; the sum of all interests in an unincorporated person (see **Person** above).

Wager. Any *bet* with respect to any sporting event or a contest placed with a person engaged in the business of accepting such bets. Includes any bet placed in a wagering pool with respect to a sports event or a contest, if such pool is conducted for profit, and any bet placed in a lottery (see **Lottery** above) conducted for profit.

Wages. All remuneration for services performed by an employee for an employer, including the cash value of all remuneration, including benefits.

Welfare Benefits Fund. Any fund which is part of a plan of an employer, and through which the employer provides welfare benefits to employees or their beneficiaries.

Wholly Owned Subsidiary. A subsidiary substantially all of whose outstanding voting shares (see **Voting Shares** above) are owned by its parent and/or the parent's other wholly owned subsidiaries.

Year. Any 12 *consecutive* months.

Chapter 22
Tax Regulations

The objective of this chapter is to make the tax requirements as understandable as possible by simplifying the verbiage as written in the Code and IRS Regulations manuals. Care is taken not to change the meaning of any of the Code or Regulations. The highlights of the major topics commonly used in tax preparation work by qualified tax preparers are covered, and they are listed in the Index for ready reference in the book.

CORPORATIONS

Tax Rate Schedule

Over	But not over	Tax is	Of the amount over
$0	$50,000	15%	$0
50,000	75,000	7,500 + 25%	50,000
75,000	100,000	13,750 + 34%	75,000
100,000	335,000	22,250 + 39%	100,000
335,000	10,000,000	113,900 + 34%	335,000
10,0000	15,000,000	3,400,000 + 35%	10,000,000
15,000,000	18,333,333	5,150,000 + 38%	15,000,000
18,333,333	—	35%	0

Forming a corporation requires a transfer of money, property, or both by prospective shareholders in exchange for capital stock in the corporation. If one or more individuals transfer money or property to a corporation solely in exchange for stock of that corporation, and immediately after the exchange they control the corporation, neither the transferors nor the transferee corporation recognize gain or loss. The transferors must be in control of the corporation immediately after the exchange. To be in control, the transferors must, as a group, own:

1) At least 80% of the combined voting power of all classes of stock entitled to vote.
2) At least 80% of the total number of shares of all other classes of stock.

Basis of Stock

The basis of stock received for property transferred to a corporation is the same as the basis of property transferred with certain adjustments. The basis is decreased by:

1) The FMV of any other property, except money, received by the transferor.
2) Any money received by the transferor.
3) Any loss recognized by the transferor on the exchange.

The basis is increased by:

1) Any amount treated as a dividend.
2) Any gain recognized on the exchange.

The basis of property received, other than money or stock, is its FMV.
The basis of property a corporation receives from the transferor in exchange for its stock:

1) In an 80% control transaction.
2) As paid-in surplus.
3) As a contribution to capital.

which has the same basis the transferor had in the property increased by any gain the transferor recognized on the exchange.

Start-Up Expenses

A corporation starts business when it starts the activities for which it was organized. This usually occurs after the charter is issued; however, a corporation is considered to have begun business when its activities reach the point necessary to establish the nature of its business operations, even though it has not received its charter. If a corporation acquires the assets to operate its business, it is considered to have begun business activities.

A corporation cannot take a deduction for start-up expenses unless it treats them as deferred expenses and amortizes them. When they are amortized, they should be deducted in equal amounts over a period of 60 months, or more. The amortization period starts in the month the organizers start or acquire the active business. A start-up expense is one that is paid for:

1) Creating an active trade or business.
2) Investigating the possibility of creating or acquiring an active trade or business.

To be amortizable, the expenses must be deductible if paid or incurred in the operation of an existing trade or business in the same field.

Start-up expenses include amounts paid or incurred in any activity engaged in for profit and for the production of income in anticipation of the activity becoming an active trade or business. Start-up expenses, those incurred before business operations begin, should not be confused with organizational expenses (discussed below). They include expenses both for investigating a prospective business and getting the business started; they do not include interest, taxes, or research and experimental expenses allowable as deductions.

If start-up expenses are to be amortized, a statement is attached to the corporation's tax return showing their total amount, with a description of what the expenses were for, date incurred, month the corporation began business, and months in the amortization period which cannot be fewer than 60 months.

Organizational Expenses

A newly organized corporation can treat its organizational expenses as deferred expenses and amortize them. To amortize, the expenses should be deducted in equal monthly amounts over a period of 60 months, or more. The period starts with the first month the corporation is actively in business. If the corporation does not use the amortization method, these expenses are capitalized and deducted only in the year the corporation finally liquidates. The corporation must incur these expenses before the end of the first tax year it is in business.

Organizational expenses are those used directly for the creation of a corporation that would be chargeable to the capital account. If spent for the creation of a corporation having a limited life, they are amortizable over that limited life. The expenses include those of temporary directors, organizational meetings of directors and shareholders, fees paid to a state for incorporation, and accounting and legal services incident to the organization. These services include drafting the charter, the bylaws, minutes of organizational meetings, and terms of the original stock certificates. A corporation cannot deduct or amortize expenses for issuance or the sale of stock or securities, such as commissions, professional fees and printing costs. No deduction or amortization is allowable for the expenses of transferring assets to the corporation.

Dividends Received Deduction

A corporation can deduct a percentage of certain dividends received during its tax year. It can deduct 70% of the dividends received from domestic corporations if the corporation receiving the dividends owns less than 20% of the distributing corporation. If a corporation owns 20% or more of the dividend-paying domestic corporation, it can deduct 80% of the dividends received or accrued.

Accrual Accounting Method

A corporation can claim a limited deduction for any charitable contributions made in cash or other property. If it uses the cash method of accounting, it can deduct contributions only in the tax year paid; if it uses an accrual method of accounting, it can choose to deduct unpaid contributions for the tax year in which the board of directors authorizes them if paid within 2 1/2 months after the close of that tax year. The choice is made by reporting the contribution on the corporation return for the tax year.

A corporation cannot deduct contributions that total more than 10% of taxable income. Taxable income for this purpose is calculated without the following:

1) Deductions for contributions.
2) Deductions for dividends received and dividends paid.
3) Deductions for contributions to a capital construction fund.
4) Any net *operating* loss carryback to the tax year.
5) Any *capital* loss carryback to the tax year.

Any contributions made during the year that are more than the 10% limit can be carried over to each of the following 5 years. Any excess not used within that period is lost.

A corporation can deduct capital losses only up to its capital gains. If a corporation has a net capital loss, it cannot deduct the loss in the current tax year; rather it must carry the loss to other tax years and deduct it from capital gains that occur in those years. The first step is to carry the net capital loss back 3 years where it is deducted from any total capital gain which occurred in that year. If the full loss is not deducted, it may be carried forward 1 year (2 years back) and then 1 more year (1 year back). If any loss remains, it may then be carried over to future tax years, 1 year at a time for up to 5 years. Any net capital loss carried to another tax year is treated as a short-term loss.

A corporation cannot carry a capital loss from, or to, a year for which it is an S corporation.

Related Taxpayers

The related party rules apply to:

1) An individual and a corporation an individual controls.
2) Two corporations that are members of the same controlled group.
3) A partnership and a corporation owned by the same person.
4) An S corporation and a C corporation if owned by the same person.

The rules do not allow the deduction of losses on the sale or exchange of property between related parties. Also not allowed is the deduction of certain unpaid business expenses and interest on transactions between the related parties. Losses on the sale or exchange of property between members of the same controlled group of corporations are deferred rather than not allowed.

An accrual basis taxpayer cannot deduct expenses owed to a related cash basis person until payment is made and the amount is includable in the gross income of the person paid. This rule applies even if the relationship ceases before the amount is includable in the gross income of the person paid. The disallowance of losses from the sale or exchange of property between related parties does not apply to liquidating distributions. It does not apply to any loss of either the distributing corporation or a distributee for a distribution in complete liquidation.

PERSONAL SERVICE CORPORATIONS

The tax rate for personal service corporations for tax years beginning on or after January 1, 1993, is 35% of taxable income. A corporation is a qualified personal service corporation if at least 95% of its stock is held by employees, or their estates or beneficiaries, and its employees perform services at least 95% of the time in health, law, engineering, architecture, accounting, actuarial sciences, veterinary services, performing arts, consulting.

ALTERNATIVE MINIMUM TAX

Special tax treatment is allowed for some kinds of income and for special deductions and credits for some kinds of expenses. In order that taxpayers who benefit from these laws will pay at least a minimum amount of tax, a special tax was enacted named the *alternative minimum tax* (AMT) for corporations. The AMT rate for corporations is 20%. There is an exemption up to $40,000, which is reduced by 25% of the amount by which AMT exceeds $150,000. The calculation for the AMT begins *with taxable income before any net operating loss deduction* on the return. The following formula is used to figure AMT:

Add or Subtract

Adjustments and preferences

Equals

Preadjustment alternative minimum taxable

Income

Add or Subtract

Adjusted current earnings (ACE)

Equals

Tentative alternative minimum taxable income

Subtract

Alternative tax net operating loss deductions

Equals

Alternative minimum taxable income

Subtract

Exemption Amount

Multiply by 20%

Subtract

Alternative minimum tax foreign tax credit

Equals

Tentative Minimum Tax

Subtract

Regular Tax

Equals

Alternative Minimum Tax (AMT)

Accelerated Depreciation on Property

This adjustment applies to property placed in service after 1986. The depreciation deduction used for AMT is the amount calculated under the alternative depreciation system (ADS) under the modified accelerated cost recovery system (MACRS). For real property, the straight-line method is used with a 40-year recovery and the mid-month convention. For most property other than real property, the 150% declining-balance method is used switching to the straight-line method when it gives a larger allowance. The following types of property are not considered in figuring the adjustment item:

1) Property that was excluded from MACRS that is depreciated under the unit-of-production method, or most other methods of depreciation not expressed in terms of years.
2) Certain public utility property.
3) Any motion picture film or video tape.
4) Any sound recording.

The adjustment is the difference between the total depreciation for all property for AMT purposes and the total depreciation for regular income tax purposes.

DISTRIBUTIONS

Any distribution to shareholders from earnings and profits is a dividend. Corporate distributions can be ordinary dividends, stock dividends, or a return of capital. Distributions can be made in money, stock, or property. A distribution is not a taxable dividend if it is a return of capital to the shareholder. A $10 or more dividend paid to a shareholder must be reported to the IRS.

The amount of a distribution received by a shareholder is the money plus the FMV on the distribution date of other property received by the shareholder. The distribution of the liabilities of the corporation assumed by the shareholder and the liabilities to which the property is subject should be reduced, but not below zero. Property means any property, including money, securities, and indebtedness to the corporation, except stock of the distributing corporation, or rights to acquire such stock.

ACCUMULATED EARNINGS TAX

A corporation can accumulate its earnings for a possible expansion or for other bona fide business reasons. However, if a corporation allows earnings to accumulate beyond the reasonable needs of the business, it can be subject to an accumulated earnings tax of 39.6%. This is an extra tax, in the nature of a penalty, imposed if a corporation is formed for the purpose of preventing the imposition of income tax upon its shareholders, or the shareholders of any other corporation, by permitting earnings or profits to accumulate instead of being distributed. If the accumulated earnings tax applies, interest is charged for an underpayment of the tax from the date the corporate return was originally due, without extensions. An accumulation of $250,000 or less is treated as being within the reasonable needs of a business; however the limit is $150,000 or less for a business whose principal function is performing services, e.g., law, engineering, accounting, etc.

In determining if the corporation has accumulated earnings and profits beyond its reasonable needs, the listed and readily marketable securities owned by the corporation and purchased with its earnings and profits are figured at net liquidation value, not at cost. The reasonable needs of a business include:

1) Specific, definite, and feasible plans for use of the earnings accumulation in the business.

2) The amount necessary to redeem the corporation's stock included in a deceased shareholder's gross estate, if the amount does not exceed the reasonably anticipated total estate and inheritance taxes, funeral, and administration expenses incurred by the shareholder's estate.

If a corporation with accumulated earnings of more than $250,000 does not make regular distributions to its shareholders, it should be prepared to show a bona fide business reason for not doing so in order to avoid liability. It must show that tax avoidance by its shareholders is not one of the purposes of the accumulation; the simple existence of a tax avoidance purpose is insufficient.

INDIVIDUAL

Inasmuch as accounting practitioners include individual income tax services, and prior editions of this Desk Book have focused upon corporate tax laws, the tax section of this Tenth Edition includes some of the highlights of tax information for individual returns that have been passed by Congress since the major, comprehensive changes made by the Tax Reform Act of 1986.

Information that is provided *supplements* that in the Taxpayers Instruction booklet furnished by the IRS. Some of the topics explained in this Section are the standard deduction, the kinds of expenses an individual can deduct, and the various kinds of credits that can be taken to reduce the taxpayer's payment. This includes the rules for the earned income credit and the advance earned income credit, as well as coverage of a number of other topics.

The rules explained in this Section are based upon Federal tax laws, which may differ from the tax requirements of the state in which the practitioner's client may be subject to income taxes.

Since the individual tax rate schedules for 1994 are on the tax return forms, they are omitted from this discussion because the schedules are not stable from year-to-year.

Exemptions

The amount that can be deducted in 1994 is $2,400, an increase from $2,350. The amount that can be claimed as a deduction for exemptions is phased out once a taxpayer's adjusted gross income (AGI) goes above a certain level for the taxpayer's filing status.

These levels are:

Filing Status	AGI Level Which Reduces Exemption Amount
Married filing separately	$ 83,500
Single	111,800
Head of household	139,740
Married filing jointly	167,700
Qualifying widow(er)	167,700

The dollar amount of the exemptions must be reduced by 2% for each $2,500, or part of $2,500 ($1,250 if married filing separately), that the AGI exceeds the amount shown above for the filing status. If the AGI exceeds the amounts shown in the tables by more than $122,500 ($61,250 if married filing separately), the amount of the deduction for exemptions is reduced to zero.

The member of a household or relationship test requires that a person must live with the taxpayer for the entire year as a member of the household, or be related to the taxpayer. A person is considered to occupy the taxpayer's house despite a temporary absence due to special circumstances which include those due to illness, education, business, vacation, and military service. If a person is placed in a nursing home for an indefinite period of time to receive constant medical care, the absence is considered temporary.

A person who died during the year, but was a member of the taxpayer's household until death, meets the member of household test. Also, a child who was born during the year and was a member of the taxpayer's household for the rest of the year meets the test. A person who is related to the taxpayer in any of the following ways does not have to live with the taxpayer for the entire year as a member of the household:

1) A child, grandchild, great-grandchild, a legally adopted child, and a stepchild.
2) A brother, sister, half-brother, half-sister, stepbrother, or stepsister.
3) The taxpayer's parent, grandparent, or other direct ancestor, but not foster parent.
4) A son or daughter of the taxpayer's brother or sister; a brother or sister of the taxpayer's father or mother.
5) The taxpayer's father-in-law, mother-in-law, son-in-law, daughter-in-law, brother-in-law, sister-in-law.

Any of the above relationships that were established by marriage are not ended by death or divorce.

Before *legal adoption*, a child is considered to be the taxpayer's child if the child was placed for adoption by an authorized agency. Also, the child must have been a member of the household if the child was not placed with the taxpayer by such an agency, but the child will meet the relationship test only if the child was a member of the household for the *entire* tax year. If a joint return is filed, it need not be shown that a dependant is related to both the taxpayer and spouse.

To meet the *citizenship* test, a person must be a U.S. citizen or resident, or a resident of Canada or Mexico, for some part of the calendar year in which a tax year begins.

Gross Income Test

An exemption cannot be taken for a dependant if that person had gross income of $2,450 or more for the year. This test does not apply if the person is the taxpayer's child and is either under age 19 at the end of the year or a student under age 24. To qualify as a student, the child must be during some part of 5 calendar months during the calendar year (not necessarily consecutive) a full-time student at a school that has a regular teaching staff, course of study, and regularly enrolled body of students in attendance. A full-time student is a person who is enrolled for the number of hours or courses the school considers to be full-time attendance. The term *school* includes elementary schools, junior and senior high schools, colleges, universities, and technical, trade and mechanical schools, It does not include on-the-job training courses, correspondence schools, and night schools.

Support Test

A taxpayer must provide more than half of a person's total support during the calendar year to meet the support test. The *more-than-half* is figured by comparing the amount contributed to the person's support with the entire amount of support the person received from all sources. The sources include the person's own funds used for support; however, the person's own funds are not support funds, unless they are actually spent for support. The total cost, not the period of time the support is provided, determines whether more than half of the support is provided.

Earned Income Credit

Earned income is salaries, wages, tips, professional fees, and other amounts received as pay for work actually performed.

The earned income credit is a special credit for certain persons who work. The credit reduces the amount of tax owed and is intended to offset some of the increases in living expenses and Social Security taxes. If the taxpayer wishes, the IRS will figure the credit for the taxpayer.

The earned income credit now includes some persons who work and earn under $9,000, and do not have a qualifying child. The credit can be as much as $306. If the taxpayer has one qualifying child, the maximum credit has increased from $1,434 in 1993 to $2,038 in 1994. If a taxpayer has two or more qualifying children, the maximum credit has been increased from $1,511 in 1993 to $2,528 in 1994. The amount of income that can be earned and still get the credit has increased. With one qualifying child, the taxpayer can earn up to less than $23,756; with two or more qualifying children, up to less than $25,296. Beginning with 1994 tax returns, the earned income credit is available to persons both with and without a qualifying child. A child is a qualifying child if it meets three tests:

1) Relationship.
2) Residency.
3) Age.

The *relationship* test includes son, daughter, or adopted child, or a descendant of the taxpayer's son, daughter, or adopted child, stepson or stepdaughter, or eligible foster child who is a child that has lived with the taxpayer and was a member of the household for the whole year and receives the same care as if the foster child were the taxpayer's own child. To meet the *residency* test the child must have lived with the taxpayer for more than half of the year, except a whole year if a foster child. The home must be in the United States. To meet the *age* test the child must be under age 19 at the end of the year; must be a full-time student; must be permanently and totally disabled at any time during the tax year regardless of age.

The *standard deduction* for taxpayers who do not itemize deductions is higher in 1994 than in 1993. The amount that can be deducted for itemized deductions is limited if the taxpayer's adjusted gross income is more than $111,800; $55,900 if married filing separately. If itemized deductions are subject to the limit, they are reduced by the *smaller* of 3% of the amount by which the AGI exceeds the limits, or 80% of the itemized deductions that are affected by the limit. The amount of the itemized deductions should be compared with the taxpayer's standard deduction, and the greater deduction can be used.

Medical and dental expenses must be itemized. Only the amount of medical and dental expenses that is more than 7.5% of AGI can be deducted. Medical expenses include amounts paid for the diagnosis, cure, mitigation, treatment, or prevention of disease, and for treatments affecting any part or function of the body.

Rental Income

Is any payment received for the use or occupation of property. All amounts received as rent must be included in gross income, as well as other amounts that can be rental income, such as a security deposit to be used as a final payment of rent, payments received for tenant's canceling a lease, expenses paid by the tenant, property or services received instead of money, and any rental income received from a part interest in rental property.

Rental Expenses

If the taxpayer owns a part interest in rental property, part of the expenses paid can be deducted in the year in which the expenses were paid or incurred. If vacant rental property is held that is for rental purposes, ordinary and necessary expenses for managing, conserving, or maintaining rental property can be deducted. The cost of repairs, advertising, janitor and maid service, utilities, fire and liability insurance, taxes, interest, commissions for the collection of rent, ordinary and necessary travel and transportation, and rental payments made for property used for rental purposes are deductible expenses.

An improvement made to rental property cannot be deducted as an expense because the costs are added to the basis of the property and are recovered by taking depreciation. Depreciation is a tax deduction each year of a portion of the cost of the property; depreciation reduces the basis for figuring gain or loss on a later sale or exchange of the property. The depreciation amount should be taken each tax year; if in an earlier tax year the depreciation deduction was not taken, the basis of the property must, nevertheless, be reduced by the amount of depreciation that should have been deducted. The unclaimed deprecation deduction cannot be taken in the current or later tax year; however, the depreciation amount can be claimed on an amended return for the earlier year.

To deduct the proper amount of depreciation each year, the *basis* of the property should be determined. The basis used for depreciation is the original basis, which usually is the taxpayer's cost, in the property increased by any improvements made to the property.

PARTNERSHIPS

This section explains how the tax law applies to partnerships and to partners. A partnership does not pay tax on its income but passes through any profits or losses to its partners who are required to include partnership items on their tax returns. The rules cited apply to both general and limited partnerships.

Definition

A partnership is the relationship between two or more persons who join together to carry on a trade or business. Each person contributes money, property, labor, or skill, and each expects to share in the profits and losses. "Person" when used to describe a partner means an individual, a corporation, a trust, an estate, or another partnership.

For income tax purposes, the term "partnership" includes a syndicate, group, pool, joint venture, or similar organization that is carrying on a trade or business, and that is not classified as a trust, estate, or corporation. *A joint undertaking* to share expenses is not a partnership. Mere co-ownership of property that is maintained and leased or rented is not a partnership. However, if the co-owners provide services to the tenants, a partnership exists. If spouses carry on a business together and share in the profits and losses, they might be partners whether or not they have a formal partnership agreement.

Partnership Agreement

The partnership agreement includes the original agreement and any modifications of it. The modifications must be agreed to by all the partners or adopted in any other manner provided by the partnership agreement. The agreement or modifications can be oral or written.

Partners can modify the partnership agreement for a particular tax year after the close of the year but not later than the date for filing the partnership return for that year. The filing date does not include any extensions of time. A partner's share of income, gains, losses, deductions, or credits is usually controlled by the partnership agreement. However, the partnership agreement or any modification of it will be disregarded if the allocation of income, gains, losses, deductions, or credits to a partner under the agreement does not have substantial economic effect.

If the partnership agreement or any modification is silent on any matter, the provisions of local law are treated as a part of the agreement.

Some partnerships may be completely or partially *excluded* from being treated as partnerships for federal income tax purposes if all the partners agree. The exclusion applies only to certain investing or operating agreement partnerships where there is no active conduct of a business. It applies to the joint production, extraction, or use of property, but not to the sales of services or sales of property produced or extracted. The members of such an organization must be able to figure their income without having to figure partnership taxable income.

The partners of excluded partnerships are not exempt from partnership provisions that limit a partner's distributive share of a partnership loss, or the requirement of a business purpose for the adoption of a tax year for the partnership which is different from its required tax year. In certain circumstances, even though a choice for exclusion was not made, it will be considered to have been made if the members can show that at the time of the organization's formation, they intended to be excluded from partnership treatment. To choose *complete exclusion*, the partnership must file a partnership return for the first year it chooses to be excluded. The return must be filed by the due date for filing the return. The return needs to contain only the name, or other identification, and the address of the organization. The return or a separate statement attached to the return must contain all of the following:

1) The names, addresses, and identification numbers of all members of the organization.
2) A statement that the organization is an investing or operating agreement partnership.
3) A statement that all the members have chosen the exclusion from partnership treatment.
4) A statement indicating where a copy of the operating agreement is available.

Required Tax Year

A partnership generally must conform its tax year to its partners' tax years as follows:

1) If one or more partners having the same tax year owns an interest in partnership profits and capital of more than 50 percent (a majority interest) the partnership must use the tax year of that (those) partner(s) (the *majority tax year*). The partnership determines if there is a majority interest tax year, usually the first day of the partnership's current tax year. If a partnership is required to change to a majority interest tax year, it will not be required to change to another year for two years following the year of change.

2) If there is no majority interest tax year, the partnership is required to use the tax year of all its principal partners. A *principal partner is* one who has a 5 percent or more interest in the profits or capital of the partnership.

3) If there is no majority interest tax year or the principal partners do not have the same tax year, the partnership must generally use a tax year that results in the least aggregate deferral of income to the partners. This will almost always be the same as the tax year of at least one of the partners.

The least aggregate deferral of income is determined by comparing the deferral that all the partners would get if the partnership used the tax year of one of its partners. A computation must be made for each partner whose tax year is different from the other partners as follows:

1) Determine the number of months of deferral using one partner's tax year. The months of deferral are found by counting the months from the end of the partnership's tax year forward to the end of that partner's tax year.

2) Multiply the deferral period found in step 1) by each partner's share of his or her interest in the partnership profits for the year.

3) Add the amounts figured in step 2) to get the aggregate which is the total amount of deferral.

4) Repeat steps 1) through 3) for each partner's tax year that is different from the other partners' years.

The partner's tax year that results in the lowest aggregate total number is the tax year that must be used by the partnership. If more than one year qualifies as the tax year that has the least aggregate deferral of income, the partnership may choose any year that qualifies. However, if one of the tax years that qualifies is already the partnership's existing year, the partnership must retain that year.

Example: X and Y have equal shares in a partnership that uses a fiscal year ending June 30. X uses a calendar year while Y has a fiscal year ending

November 30. The partnership must change its tax year to a fiscal year ending November 30 because this results in the least aggregate deferral of income to the partners.

There are exceptions to the required tax year rule. One exception allows a partnership to use its natural business year. Another exception allows a partnership to make a Section 444 election.

Natural Business Year

If a partnership establishes an acceptable business purpose for having a tax year that is different from its required tax year, the different tax year can be used. The deferral of income to the partners is not considered a business purpose.

Section 444 Election

Under Section 444 of the Code, certain partnerships may elect to use a tax year that is different from their required tax year. A partnership is eligible to make a Section 444 election if it meets all of the following conditions:

1) It is not a member of a tiered structure. (A tiered structure, for this purpose, occurs when a partnership directly owns any part of another partnership, S corporation, or personal service corporation, or any part of the partnership itself is owned by one of these entities.) If the tiered structure consists only of partnerships, S corporations, or both, the partnership can make a Section 444 election if all the entities have the same tax year.

2) It has not made a Section 444 election before.

3) It does not choose a tax year where the deferral period is more than 3 months, or the deferral period of the tax year being changed if this period is shorter.

A partnership should not make a Section 444 election when it wants to establish a business purpose for having a tax year different from its required year. If a Section 444 election is made, the deferral period is the number of months between the end of the elected tax year and the close of the required tax year.

A partnership is *not* a taxable entity, but the partnership must figure its total income and file Form 1065 which provides information on partnership income or losses for the year. A partnership computes its income and files a return in the same way as an individual does, except that a partnership must state certain items of gain, loss, income, etc., separately.

The partnership, not the partners, makes the choices about how to compute income. These include choices for: general accounting methods; depreciation methods; accounting for specific items, such as depletion or installment sales; nonrecognition of gain on the involuntary conversion of property; and amortization of certain organization fees and business start-up costs of the partnership.

A partnership does not make estimated tax payments. However, the partners may have to make payments of estimated tax as a result of partnership distributions. If the partnership uses the accrual method of accounting, its deductions for expenses may depend on economic performance.

Neither the partnership nor any partner can deduct amounts paid or incurred to organize a partnership or to promote the sale of, or to sell, an interest in the partnership. It can choose to amortize certain organization fees over a period of not less than 60 months. The 60-month period starts with the month the partnership begins business. If it is liquidated before the end of the 60-month period, the remaining balance in this account can be deductible as a loss, but only if the 60-month amortization election has been made. Amortization applies to expenses that:

1) Are incident to the creation of the partnership.
2) Are chargeable to a capital account.
3) Would be amortized over the life of the partnership if they were incurred for a partnership having a fixed life.

Amortization does not apply to expenses connected with the issuing and marketing of interests in the partnership, such as commissions, professional fees, and printing costs. These expenses are capitalized. Syndication fees can never be deducted by the partnership even if the syndication is unsuccessful. If a partnership begins or acquires a business, it can elect to amortize certain start-up expenses over a period of at least 60 months. To make this election, attach a statement to the partnership return for the tax year in which the amortization period begins, which is the month the partnership begins or acquires the business. The statement must include a description of and amount of the expenses, the date the expenses were paid or incurred, the month in which the partnership began or acquired the business, and the number of months in the amortization period.

Start-up expenses are amounts paid or incurred in connection with creating an active trade or business or for investigating the creation or acquisition of an active trade or business. They must be of a type that could be deducted in the tax year they were paid or incurred, if they were paid or incurred to expand an existing trade or business in the same field. Once the partnership chooses a period of time for amortizing start-up expenses and files the election, it cannot change to a different time period.

The original basis of an interest is *increased* by:

1) Additional contributions to the partnership.
2) The partner's distributive share of both taxable and nontaxable partnership income.
3) The excess of the deductions for depletion over the basis of the depletable property.

The original basis is *decreased*, but never below zero, by:

1) The amount of money and the adjusted basis of property distributed to the partner by the partnership.
2) The partner's distributive share of the partnership losses, including capital losses.
3) Nondeductible partnership expenses that are not capital expenditures.
4) The amount of any deduction for depletion for oil and gas wells.
5) The partner's share of any section 179 expenses, even if the partner cannot deduct the entire amount on his or her individual tax return. (Section 179 allows a deduction of up to $10,000 for the cost of depreciable property placed in service during the year.)

Partnership Liabilities

A partner's basis includes a partnership liability only if, and to the extent that, the liability:

1) Creates or increases the partnership's basis in any of its assets.
2) Gives rise to a current deduction to the partnership.
3) Decreases the partner's basis in the partnership because it *relates* to a nondeductible partnership expense that is not a capital expenditure.

The term *assets* includes capitalized items allocable to future periods, such as organizational expenses. Partnership liabilities do not include accrued but unpaid expenses or accounts payable of a cash basis partnership. If the liabilities of a partnership are increased, resulting in an increase in a partner's share of the liabilities, this increase is treated as a contribution of money by the partner to the partnership.

If the liabilities of a partnership are decreased resulting in a decrease in a partner's share of the liabilities, this decrease is treated as a distribution of money to the partner by the partnership.

Example 1: X and Y are equal partners and their partnership borrows $1,000. The basis of the partnership interest of each is increased by $500 since each is considered to have contributed that amount to the partnership. Partners increase their basis regardless of the partnership's method of accounting.

Example 2: X and Y are equal partners and their partnership repays a $10,000 note. The basis of the partnership interest of each is decreased by $5,000 since each is considered to have received a distribution of that amount from the partnership.

Partner's share. A partner's share of partnership liabilities depends on whether the liability is a recourse or nonrecourse liability. A liability is a *recourse liability* of the partnership to the extent that any partner has an economic risk of loss for that liability. A partner's share of such liability equals that partner's share of the economic risk of loss. A *limited partner* generally has no obligation to contribute additional capital to the partnership and, therefore, does not have an economic risk of loss in partnership liabilities.

A liability is a *nonrecourse liability* of the partnership if no partner has an economic risk of loss for that liability. A partner's share of such liability generally is determined by the partner's ratio for sharing partnership profits.

A partner has an economic risk of loss if obligated (whether by agreement or operation of law) to make a net payment to the creditor or a contribution to the partnership with respect to the liability if the partnership is constructively liquidated. A partner that is the creditor for a liability that would otherwise be a nonrecourse liability has an economic risk of loss in that liability.

Generally, in a constructive liquidation, all partnership assets (including cash) are assumed to become worthless and all partnership liabilities are assumed to become due and payable in full. Therefore, the partnership lacks the assets needed to pay off the liability and the partner or partners who have to pay it off have an economic risk of loss.

Example: X and Y form a general partnership with cash contributions of $20,000 each. Under the partnership agreement, they share all partnership profits and losses equally. They borrow $60,000 to purchase business equipment. This indebtedness qualifies as a partnership liability.

If neither partner has an economic risk of loss in the liability, it is a nonrecourse liability. Each partner's basis would include a share of the liability, $30,000 each.

If X, under the agreement, had to pay the creditor if the partnership defaulted, X would have an economic risk of loss in the liability. His or her basis in the partnership would be $80,000, while Y's basis would be $20,000 (the amount of Y's original contribution to the partnership).

Liquidation of Partner's Interest

When payments are made by the partnership to a retiring partner or to a successor in interest of a deceased partner in return for the partner's entire interest in the partnership, the payments may have to be allocated between payments in liquidation and other payments.

For income tax purposes, a retired partner or a successor in interest to a deceased partner is vested as a partner until his or her interest in the partnership has been completely liquidated.

Payments in liquidation of a partner's entire interest, to the extent that they are made in exchange for the interest in partnership property, are treated as distributions to the partner by the partnership. Amounts paid for unrealized receivables, or for goodwill, are not treated as distributions. However, if the partnership agreement provides for payments for goodwill, these payments are treated as distributions.

Generally, the partners' valuation of a partner's interest in partnership property in an arm's length agreement will be treated as correct. If the valuation reflects only the partner's net interest in the property (total assets less liabilities), it must be adjusted so that both the value of and the basis for the partner's interest include the partner's share of partnership liabilities.

The remaining partners' distributive shares are not reduced by payments in exchange for a retired partner's interest in partnership property.

Deceased partner.   If a partner dies, the partner's estate or other successor in interest reports in its return the decedent's distributive share of the partnership items for the partnership year ending after the death occurred. If the partnership year terminates with the death of the partner, the deceased partner's share of income for that year will be included in the deceased partner's final return.

Closing of Partnership Year

Generally, the partnership's tax year is not closed because of the sale, exchange, or liquidation of a partner's interest; the death of a partner; or the entry of a new partner. If a partner sells, exchanges, or liquidates his or her entire interest, the partnership's tax year is closed for that partner.

If a partner disposes of his or her entire interest in a partnership, the partner must include his or her distributive share of partnership items in taxable income for the tax year in which membership in the partnership ends. To compute the distributive share of these items, the partnership's tax year is considered ended on the date that the partner disposed of the interest. To avoid an interim closing of the partnership books, the partners can agree that the distributive share can be estimated by taking a prorated part of the amount of the items the partner would have included in income if he or she had remained a partner for the entire partnership tax year.

A partner who sells or exchanges only part of an interest in a partnership, or whose interest is changed (whether by entry of a new partner, partial liquidation of a partner's interest, gift, or otherwise), reports his or her distributive share of partnership items by taking into account his or her varying interests during the partnership year.

Example: XYZ is a calendar year partnership with three partners, A, B, and C. Under the partnership agreement, profits and losses are to be shared in proportion to their contributions. As of January 1, this was 90 percent for A, 5 percent for B, and 5 percent for C. On December 1, B and C each contributed additional amounts so that the new profit and loss sharing ratios were 30 percent for A, 35 percent for B, and 35 percent for C. For its tax year ended December 31, the partnership had a loss of $1,200. This loss occurred equally over the partnership's tax year. The loss is divided among the partners as follows:

Partner	Profit or Loss Percent		Part of Year Held		Total Loss		Share of Loss
A	90	×	11/12	×	$1,200	=	$990
	30	×	1/12	×	1,200	=	30
B	5	×	11/12	×	1,200	=	55
	35	×	1/12	×	1,200	=	35
C	5	×	11/12	×	1,200	=	55
	35	×	1/12	×	1,200	=	35

If any partner's interest in a partnership changes during the tax year, each partner's share of certain cash basis items of the partnership must be determined by prorating the items on a daily basis. Then that daily portion is allocated to the partners in proportion to their interests in the partnership at the close of each day. This rule applies to the following items for which the partnership uses the cash method of accounting.

1) Interest.
2) Taxes.
3) Payments for services or for the use of property.
4) Any other item for which it is appropriate to use this rule in order to avoid significant misstatements of the partners' income.

Filing Requirements   Every partnership must file a return showing its income, deductions, and other information required. This is an information return and must be signed by one partner. The return must be filed for every tax year of the partnership even though it has no income for the year. However, the first return is not required to be filed before the first tax year in which the partnership has income or deductions.

Form 1065 must be filed on or before April 15 following the close of the partnership's tax year if the accounting period is the calendar year. A fiscal year partnership generally must file its return by the 15th day of the 4th month following the close of its fiscal year.

Partner's Income

1) Gains and losses from sales or exchanges of capital assets.

2) Gains and losses from sales or exchanges of certain property used in a trade or business and from involuntary conversions (for example, casualties, thefts, or condemnations).

3) Charitable contributions.

4) Dividends for which corporate partners can claim a deduction.

5) Certain taxes paid or accrued to foreign countries and to possessions of the United States.

6) Depletion allowances for partnership oil and gas properties.

7) Intangible drilling and development costs.

8) Recoveries of tax benefit items.

9) Gains and losses from wagering.

10) Soil and water conservation expenses.

11) IRA, Keogh, or SEP payments; alimony payments; medical insurance for a partner, a partner's spouse, and dependants; and any penalty on early withdrawal of savings.

12) Interest and taxes paid to cooperating housing corporations.

13) Any item of income, gain, loss, deduction, or credit that is allocated under the partnership agreement in a way that differs from the partnership's usual allocation of taxable income or loss.

14) Interest expense allocated to debt-financed distributions.

15) Amounts paid by the partnership that would be an itemized deduction on a partner's income tax return if paid by the partner, such as medical and dental expenses; dependant care expenses; and meal, travel, and entertainment expenses.

16) Any amount that would result in a different income tax liability for a partner if it were taken into account separately rather than as part of the total income or loss.

17) Taxable income or loss of the partnership, determined without the items requiring separate computations.

To determine the allowable amount of any deduction or exclusion that is limited, a partner must combine the amounts of any separate deductions or exclusions on his or her income tax return with the distributive share of partnership deductions or exclusions before applying the limit.

Basis of Partner's Interest

The adjusted basis of a partner's partnership interest is ordinarily computed at the end of a partnership's tax year. However, if there has been a sale or exchange of all or a part of the partner's interest or a liquidation of his or her entire interest in a partnership, the adjusted basis is computed on the date of the sale, exchange, or liquidation.

The adjusted basis of a partner's interest is determined without considering any amount shown in the partnership books as a capital, equity, or similar account.

Example: X contributes property to a partnership that has an adjusted basis of $400 and a fair market value of $1,000. His partner contributes $1,000 cash. While under the partnership agreement each has a capital account in the partnership of $1,000, which will be reflected in the partnership books, the adjusted basis of X's interest is only $400 and the partner's basis is $1,000.

Original basis. The original basis of a partnership interest is the money a partner contributed plus the adjusted basis of any property contributed. If the property contribution results in taxable income to the partner, the income generally will be included in the basis of the partner's interest. Any increase in a partner's individual liabilities because of an assumption of partnership liabilities is also treated as a contribution of money to the partnership by the partner.

If the property contributed is subject to indebtedness or if a partner's liabilities are assumed by the partnership, the basis of that partner's interest is reduced by the liability that is assumed by the other partners. This partner must reduce his or her basis because the assumption of the liability is treated as though a contribution of money had been made to the partnership.

Example 1: John acquired a 20 percent interest in a partnership by contributing property that had an adjusted basis to him of $8,000 and was subject to a $4,000 mortgage. Payment of the mortgage was assumed by the partnership. The adjusted basis of John's interest is:

Adjusted basis of the property contributed	$8,000
Minus: Part of mortgage assumed by his partners that must be treated as a distribution of money to him, 80% of $4,000	3,200
Basis of John's partnership interest	$4,800

Example 2: If, in the above example, the property John contributed had a $12,000 mortgage, the adjusted basis of his partnership interest would be zero. The difference between the amount of the mortgage assumed by the other partners, $9,600 (80 percent × $12,000), and his basis of $8,000 would be treated as a gain to him from the sale or exchange of a capital asset. However, this gain would not increase the basis of John's partnership interest.

The original basis of an interest is *increased* by:

1) Additional contributions to the partnership.
2) The partner's distributive share of both taxable and nontaxable partnership income.
3) The excess of the deductions for depletion over the basis of the depletable property.

The original basis is *decreased*, but never below zero, by:

1) The amount of money and the adjusted basis of property distributed to the partner by the partnership.
2) The partner's distributive share of the partnership losses, including capital losses.
3) Nondeductible partnership expenses that are not capital expenditures.
4) The amount of any deduction for depletion for oil and gas wells.
5) The partner's share of any Section 179 expenses, even if the partner cannot deduct the entire amount on his or her individual tax return. (Section 179 allows a deduction of up to $10,000 for the cost of depreciable property placed in service during the year.)

Distributions of Marketable Securities to a Partner

Gain is not recognized to a partner in a distribution except to the extent that money distributed exceeds the basis of the partner's interest. The law is amended to provide that money includes marketable securities based on the fair market value on the date of distribution. The term *marketable securities* includes financial instruments, foreign currencies actively traded, and certain interests in trust funds, mutual funds, financial instruments based on marketable securities, and interests in precious metals.

Special rules are provided for investment partnerships. The basis of marketable securities is increased for any gain realized on a distribution. An exception is provided for certain distributions of marketable securities contributed to the partnership by the partner.

S CORPORATIONS

An eligible domestic corporation can avoid double taxation (once to the corporation and again to the shareholders) by electing to be treated as an S corporation under the rules of Subchapter S of the Internal Revenue Code. In this way, the S corporation passes its items of income, losses, deductions, and credits through to its shareholders to be included on separate returns. Individual shareholders may benefit from a reduction in their taxable income during the first years of the corporation's existence when it may be operating at a loss.

The following information discusses how to start an S corporation, how an S corporation is taxed, how income is distributed to shareholders, and how to terminate an S corporation.

Starting an S Corporation

A corporation can become an S corporation if:

1) It meets the requirements of S corporation status.

2) All its shareholders consent to S corporation status.

3) It uses a permitted tax year, or elects to use a tax year other than a permitted tax year.

4) It files to indicate it chooses S corporation status.

Requirements of an S Corporation.   To qualify for S corporation status, a corporation must meet *all* of the following requirements:

1) It must be a domestic corporation. The term *corporation* includes joint-stock companies, insurance companies, and association.

2) It must have only one class of stock.

3) It must have no more than 35 shareholders.

4) It must have only individuals as shareholders, trusts, estate, and including estates of individuals in bankruptcy.

5) All of its shareholders must be citizens or residents of the United States.

Certain domestic corporations are ineligible to elect S corporation status. They are:

1) A member of an affiliated group of corporations. An affiliated group means one or more chains of corporations connected through stock ownership with a common parent corporation that is also part of the group.

2) A DISC corporation, or a former DISC.

3) A corporation that takes the Puerto Rico and possessions tax credit for doing business in a United States possession.

4) A financial institution that is a bank, including mutual savings banks, cooperative banks, and domestic building and loan associations.

5) An insurance company taxed under Subchapter L of the Internal Revenue Code.

A corporation is treated as having only one class of stock if all outstanding shares of stock of the corporation give identical rights to distribution and liquidation proceeds. Stock can have differences in voting rights and still be considered one class of stock. The determination of whether stock has identical rights to distribution and liquidation proceeds is made based on the governing provisions of the corporate charter, articles of incorporation, bylaws, applicable state laws, and binding agreements relating to distribution proceeds.

When counting shareholders to comply with the 35 shareholder limit, the following rules apply:

1) Count the individual, estate, or other person who is considered the shareholder if the stock is actually held by a trust.

2) Count a husband and wife, and their estates, as one shareholder, even if they own stock separately.

3) Count everyone who owns any stock, even if the stock is owned jointly with someone else.

A corporation's election of S corporation status is valid only if *all* shareholders consent to the election. A shareholder's consent is binding and cannot be withdrawn after a valid election is made by the corporation. Each co-owner, tenant in common, and joint tenant must consent, if stock is owned as community property, or if income from the stock is community property, both husband and wife must consent.

Tax Year

A *permitted tax year* is a calendar year, or any other accounting period for which the corporation establishes for the IRS a substantial business purpose. An S corporation also can elect to have a tax year other than the permitted tax year if the deferred period of the taxable year elected is not longer than 3 months; or if a *change* in the tax year is made, the deferral period cannot be longer than the shorter of 3 months or the deferral period of the taxable year which is being changed. Significant consideration in permitting the use of a different tax year is whether it would create a substantial distortion of income. Examples are:

1) Deferring a substantial portion of income, or shifting a substantial portion of deductions from one year to another in order to reduce tax liability.
2) Causing a similar deferral or shifting to any other person.
3) Creating a short period in which there is a substantial net operating loss.

S Corporation Income and Expenses

Shareholders must report their *pro rata* share of an S corporation's income, losses, deductions, and credits on their returns. *Separately and nonseparately stated items* concern the passing through to the shareholders income, losses, deductions, and credit items which are reported on the shareholders' individual returns. Any items whose separate treatment could affect a shareholder's tax liability must be passed through separately. These items are referred to as separately stated items. All others are combined and referred to as nonseparately stated income or loss. Both the separately stated items and the nonseparately stated income or loss are passed through to the shareholders in proportion to their shareholdings. The list of items that must be separately stated includes, but is not limited to:

1) Net income or loss from rental real estate activities.
2) Net income or loss from other rental activities.
3) Interest income, dividend income, royalty income, short-term capital gain or loss, long-term capital gain or loss.
4) Charitable contributions.
5) Expenses related to portfolio income or loss.
6) Low income housing credits; qualified rehabilitation expenses; and other credits.
7) Investment interest expense, e.g., money borrowed by an S corporation to carry investment property.
8) Tax preference and adjustment items needed to figure shareholders' alternative minimum tax.

Tax Preference Items.   If an S corporation or any predecessor was a regular corporation for any of the 3 immediately preceding tax years, the S corporation must adjust its tax preference items. In determining its taxable income, these items, which are also items subject to an alternative minimum tax and are considered tax preference items, must be adjusted. If an adjustment is made to a tax preference item, the adjusted amount must be shown as a tax preference item for the shareholder.

An S corporation, like any other business, pays its own excise and employment taxes; it is subject to the following taxes:

1) The tax on excess net passive investment income.
2) The tax on certain capital gains.
3) The tax from recomputing a prior year's investment credit.
4) LIFO recapture tax.

Shareholder Taxable Income. Each shareholder reports a *pro rata* share of each item of income, loss, deduction, or credit that is separately stated and a *pro rata* share of nonseparately stated income or loss on his/her income tax return. When it is reported on the shareholder's income tax return, the character of any item included in a shareholder's *pro rata* share is determined as if the item were realized directly from the source from which the S corporation realized it, or incurred from the same manner in which the corporation incurred it. Any time it is necessary to determine a shareholder's gross income, include the shareholder's *pro rata* share of the gross income of the corporation.

The tax treatment of any S corporation item is determined at the corporate level. Shareholders must treat S corporation items the same way on their tax returns as they are treated on the S corporation return. If an item on a shareholder's return is treated differently from the way it is treated on the corporation's return, the IRS can assess taxes and penalties. It can take action to immediately collect any deficiency and penalties that result from an adjustment to the shareholder's individual return to make that treatment consistent with the amount or treatment of the item on the S corporation's return.

These rules do not apply to an S corporation with five or fewer shareholders if each shareholder is a natural person or an estate unless the corporation chooses to have them apply. There cannot be more than five shareholders at any time during the year. For S corporations, a husband and wife, and their estates, are treated as one shareholder. For stock owned by tenants in common or joint tenants, each individual is considered a shareholder.

Self-Employment Tax. A shareholder's share of the corporation's taxable income is not self-employment income, even though it is included in gross income of the shareholder. If a shareholder is an officer of the corporation and performs substantial services, the person is considered an employee. Reasonable compensation for these services is subject to FICA, FUTA, and income tax withholding, no matter how the corporation calls the payments.

If an officer of the corporation who is responsible for the withholding of taxes willfully fails to withhold, the person can be held liable for a penalty equal to the unpaid tax, plus interest.

Limits on Shareholder's Losses and Deductions.   S corporation shareholders who hold stock at anytime during the year can claim their share of corporate losses and deductions on their individual tax returns. The amount of losses and deductions a shareholder can take is limited to the shareholder's stock plus any loans the shareholder makes to the corporation. To arrive at the adjusted basis of a shareholder's stock or loans, the shareholder's basis must first be determined. If the stock was purchased, the basis is its cost. If money was loaned to the corporation, the basis is the amount of the loan. If the shareholder received stock in exchange for property, the basis in the stock is the same as the basis of the property transferred.

During the time the corporation is an S corporation, shareholders will increase or decrease the basis of their stock, but not below zero.

Increases:

1) All income items including tax-exempt income, that are separately stated.
2) Any nonseparately stated income.
3) The amount of the deduction for depletion that is more than the basis of the property being depleted.

If the amount described in 1 or 2 must be included in income, a shareholder can increases the basis of the stock only by the amount actually included as gross income on the individual income tax return.

Each shareholder's *pro rata* share of the following items decreases the basis of the stock.

Decreases:

1) Distributions that were not included in the shareholder's income.
2) Any nonseparately stated loss.
3) All loss and deduction items that are separately stated.
4) Any expense that is not deducted in determining the S corporation's taxable income and not properly chargeable to capital accounts.

How S corporation's distributions to a shareholder are taxed depends on whether the corporation has earnings and profits. An S corporation is not considered to have earnings and profits for tax years beginning after 1982. The corporation can have accumulated earnings and profits from years before 1983 or from tax years before an S corporation's election was made. The existence of earnings and profits is important to an S corporation if it has passed investment income or makes distributions. The presence of earnings and profits can mean that a distribution is a taxable dividend or the corporation is liable for a tax on its excess net passive income. An S corporation is not considered to have earnings and profits for tax years beginning after 1982 in which it was an S corporation; however, it can have earnings and profits from tax years in which it was not an S corporation, from any of the corporation's tax years that began before 1983, or from a corporate acquisition that results in a carryover of earnings and profits.

For purposes of determining the limit, the adjusted basis of the shareholder's stock is figured at year-end and includes the increases, but not the decreases, for that year. The adjusted basis of any loans is figured before any of the adjustments are made for the tax year. If the amount of the loss or deductions of a shareholder is limited, the excess is treated as incurred by the corporation in the next tax year for that shareholder; it can be carried over until used by the shareholder.

Terminating S Corporation Status

A corporation's status as an S corporation is terminated by revoking the election to be an S corporation; or ceasing to qualify as an S corporation; or by violating the passive investment income restrictions on S corporations with pre-S corporation earnings and profits for three consecutive tax years. If a corporation's status as an S corporation has been terminated, it must wait 5 years before it can again become an S corporation. If it gets the permission of the IRS, the waiting period can be less than 5 years.

BANKRUPTCY TAXATION

When an individual taxpayer files for bankruptcy under Chapter 7 or Chapter 11 of the Bankruptcy Code a separate *estate* is created consisting of property that belonged to the debtor before the filing date. The bankruptcy estate is a new taxable entity, completely separate from that of the individual taxpayer.

The estate, under a Chapter 7 proceeding, is represented by a trustee who is appointed by the bankruptcy court to administer the estate and liquidate the assets of the debtor. In a Chapter 11 proceeding, the debtor remains in control of the assets as a debtor-in-possession. However, the bankruptcy court can if necessary appoint a trustee in a Chapter 11 case and the debtor-in-possession must turn over to the trustee control of the debtor's assets.

The estate can produce its own income a well as incur its own expenses. The gross income of the bankruptcy estate includes any of the debtor's gross income to which the state is entitled under the bankruptcy law. The estate's gross income also includes any income the estate is entitled to and receives or accrues after the beginning of the bankruptcy case. Gross income of the bankruptcy estate does not include amounts received or accrued by the debtor before the bankruptcy petition date. The bankruptcy estate can deduct or take as a credit any expenses it pays or incurs, the same way that the debtor would have deducted or credited them had he or she continued in the same trade, business, or activity and actually paid or accrued the expenses. The bankruptcy estate figures the estate's taxable income the same way as individuals figure taxable income.

The creation of a separate bankruptcy estate allows the debtor to earn wages and acquire property after the bankruptcy case has begun without their becoming a part of the bankruptcy estate. If the bankruptcy case began and was later dismissed by the bankruptcy court, the estate is not treated as a separate entity, and the debtor is treated as if the bankruptcy petition had never been filed in the first place. Amended returns can be filed to replace any returns previously filed and would include items of income, deductions, or credits that were or would have been reported by the bankruptcy estate on its returns and were not reported on returns the debtor might have previously filed.

Debtor's Responsibilities

The individual debtor must file income tax returns during the period of the bankruptcy proceedings. The return should not include the income, deductions, or credits belonging to the separate bankruptcy estate, nor include as income the debts canceled because of bankruptcy, because the bankruptcy estate must reduce certain losses, credits, and the basis in property by the amount of canceled debt. Deductions and credit carryovers and decisions that the debtor made in earlier years are taken over by the bankruptcy estate when the bankruptcy petition is filed. These include carryover of deductions, losses, and credits, the debtor's accounting method, and the basis and holding period of assets. These are termed *tax attributes*. When the estate is terminated, the debtor assumes any remaining tax attributes that were taken over by the estate as well as any attributes arising during the administration of the estate. The bankruptcy estate treats its tax attributes the same way that the debtor would have treated them. These items must be determined as of the first day of the debtor's tax year in which the bankruptcy case begins.

The bankruptcy estate gets the following tax attributes from the debtor:

1) Net operating loss carryovers.
2) Carryovers of excess charitable contributions.

3) Recovery of tax benefit items.
4) Credit carryovers.
5) Capital loss carryovers.
6) Basis, holding period, and character of assets.
7) Method of accounting.
8) Passive activity loss and credit carryovers.
9) Unused at-risk deductions.
10) Other tax attributes as provided in the regulations.

If the estate has any tax attributes at the time it is terminated, they are assumed by the debtor.

The bankruptcy law determines which of the debtor's assets become part of the bankruptcy estate. Usually, all of the debtor's legal and equitable interests become property of the estate. A transfer, other than by sale or exchange of an asset by the debtor to the bankruptcy estate, is not treated as a *disposition for income tax purposes*, which means that the transfer does not result in gain or loss, recapture of deductions or credits, or acceleration of income or deductions.

The trustee for Chapter 7 cases, or the debtor-in-possession for Chapter 11 cases, is responsible for preparing and filing the estate's tax returns and paying its taxes. The debtor remains responsible for filing returns and paying taxes on any income that does not belong to the estate. If a bankruptcy case begins, but later is dismissed by the bankruptcy court, the estate is not treated as a separate taxable entity. If tax returns have been filed for the estate, amended returns must be filed to move income and deductions from the estate's returns to the debtor's returns.

Income, Deductions, and Credits

The gross income of the bankruptcy estate includes any of the debtor's gross income to which the estate is entitled under the bankruptcy law. It also includes any income the estate is entitled to and receives or accrues after the beginning of the bankruptcy case. Gross income of the estate does not include amounts received or accrued by the debtor before the bankruptcy petition date. The bankruptcy estate can deduct or take as a credit any expenses it pays or incurs, the same way that the debtor would have deducted or credited them had the debtor continued in the same trade, business, or activity and actually paid or accrued the expenses.

The bankruptcy estate figures its taxable income the same way as individual taxpayers figure their taxable income. The estate can take one personal exemption and other individual, itemized deductions, or the basic standard deduction for a married individual filing a separate return. The estate cannot take the higher standard deduction allowed for married persons filing separately who are 65 or older or blind. The estate uses the rates for a married individual filing separately to figure the tax on its taxable income.

Administrative Expenses

The bankruptcy estate is allowed a deduction for administrative expenses and any fees or charges assessed. These expenses are deductible as itemized deductions subject to the 2% floor on miscellaneous itemized deductions. However, administrative expenses attributable to the conduct of a trade or business by the bankruptcy estate or the production of the estate's rents or royalties are deductible in arriving at adjusted gross income. Expenses are subject to disallowance under other provisions of the Internal Revenue Code, such as disallowing certain capital expenditures, taxes, or expenses relating to tax-exempt interest. These expenses can only be deducted by the estate, never by the debtor.

If the administrative expenses of the estate are more than its gross income for the tax year, the excess amount can be carried back 3 years and forward 7 years. The amounts can only be carried back or forward to a tax year of the estate, never to other debtor's tax year. The excess amount to be carried back or forward is treated like net operating loss and must first be carried back to the earliest year possible. If the estate itself has a net operating loss separate from any losses passing to the estate from the debtor under the attribute carryover rules, the bankruptcy estate can carry the loss back not only to its own earlier tax years, but also to the debtor's tax years before the year the bankruptcy case began. The estate can also carry back excess credits to the post-bankruptcy years.

The trustee, or debtor-in-possession, must withhold income and Social Security taxes and the *employment tax* returns for any wages paid by the trustee or debtor, including wage claims paid as administrative expenses. Until these employment taxes are deposited as required by the Internal Revenue Code, they should be set apart in a separate bank account to ensure that funds are available to satisfy the liability. If the employment taxes are not paid as required, the trustee can be held personally liable for payment of the taxes.

Disclosure of Tax Return Information

The debtor's income tax returns for the year the bankruptcy case begins and for earlier years are, upon written request, open to inspection by, or disclosure to, the trustee. If the bankruptcy case was not voluntary, disclosure cannot be made before the bankruptcy court has entered an order for relief, unless the court rules that the disclosure is needed for determining whether relief should be ordered.

Partnerships and Corporations

A separate taxable estate is not created when a partnership or corporation files a bankruptcy petition. The court-appointed trustee is, however, responsible for filing the regular tax returns. The filing requirements for a partnership in bankruptcy proceedings do not change; the filing of required returns becomes the responsibility of an appointed trustee, receiver, or a debtor-in-possession rather than a general partner. A partnership's debt that is canceled because of bankruptcy is not included in the partnership's income. It may or may not be included in the individual partner's income.

Corporations

Corporations in a bankruptcy proceeding or insolvency generally follow the same rules for debt cancellation and reduction of tax attributes as an individual or individual bankruptcy estate would follow. The earnings and profits of a corporation do not include income from the discharge of indebtedness to the extent of the amount applied to reduce the basis of the corporation's property. Discharge of indebtedness income, including amounts excluded from gross income, increases the earnings and profits of the corporation, or reduces a deficit in earnings and profits.

Tax-Free Reorganizations

The tax-free reorganization provisions of the Internal Revenue Code apply to a transfer by a corporation of all or part of its assets to another corporation in a Title 11 or similar case, but only if stocks or securities of the corporation to which the assets are transferred are distributed in a transaction qualifying under Section 354 of the Internal Revenue Code, *Exchanges of Stock and Bonds.*

Securities in Reorganizations. Section 354 provides that no gain or loss is recognized if a corporation's stock is exchanged solely for stock or securities in the same or another corporation under a qualifying reorganization plan. In this case, shareholders in the bankrupt corporation would recognize no gain or loss if they exchange their stock only for stock or securities of the corporation acquiring the bankrupt's assets.

No gain or loss is recognized by a shareholder if a corporation distributes stock or securities of another corporation that the distributing corporation controls immediately before the distribution. In an exchange that qualifies under Section 354, except when other property or money besides the permitted stock or securities is received by the shareholder, gain is recognized by the shareholder only to the extent of the money and the fair market value of the property received. No loss is recognized.

Corporate Filing Requirements and Tax Procedures

The filing of required returns is the responsibility of an appointed trustee, receiver, or a debtor-in-possession, rather than of a corporate officer. The person responsible for filing can apply to the IRS for relief from filing federal income tax returns for the corporation. To qualify, the corporation must have ceased business operations and must have neither assets nor income. The request must show why relief is needed from filing requirements by including statements and supporting documents. The first step in the determination of the tax due is the preparation and filing of the return. The individual bankrupt debtor files a Form 1040 for the tax year involved, and the trustee of the bankruptcy estate files a Form 1041. A bankrupt corporation, or a receiver, trustee, or assignee having possession of, or holding title to, substantially all the property or business of the corporation, files a Form 1120 for the tax year.

After the return is filed, the IRS can redetermine the tax liability shown on the return. When the IRS corrections have been made, any issues concerning the return that remain can be litigated either in the bankruptcy court or in the U.S. Tax Court. The trustee of the bankruptcy estate can request a determination of any unpaid liability of the estate for tax incurred during the administration of the case by filing a tax return and a request for such a determination with the IRS:

1) As determined by the IRS.
2) As determined by the bankruptcy.
3) As shown on the return if the IRS does not:
   a) Notify the trustee within 60 days after the request for the determination that the return has been selected for examination.
   b) Complete the examination and notify the trustee of any tax due within 180 days.

The IRS will notify the trustee within 60 days whether the return filed has been selected for examination, or has been accepted as filed. If the return is selected for examination, it will be examined as soon as possible. The bankruptcy court has authority to determine the amount or legality of any tax imposed on the debtor or the estate, including any fine, penalty, or addition to the tax, whether or not the tax was previously assessed or paid. The bankruptcy court does not have authority to determine the amount or legality of a tax, fine, penalty, or addition to tax that was contested before and decided by a court, nor can the bankruptcy court decide the right of the bankruptcy estate to a tax refund until the trustee of the estate requests the refund from the IRS. The IRS will notify the trustee of its decision within 120 days from the date of filing the refund claim. The debtor must include in gross income for tax purposes a debt that is canceled or forgiven other than as a gift or bequest. A debt includes any indebtedness for which the debtor is liable or which attaches to property the debtor holds.

VARIOUS FORMS OF STATE TAXATION

Virtually all states impose some form of franchise and/or income tax on corporations. The basis for either or both taxes varies from state to state, as does the definition of the terminology. For the corporation involved in interstate commerce, these state taxes can present some onerous burdens. You need detailed records in order to work out the various allocation or apportionment formulas called for by the states involved (so as to avoid imposing a tax on more than what is applicable to that state). Sometimes with proper planning, taking into account the needs of the business, it is possible to avoid completely the taxes of some of the states with which your company has contact.

In addition to an income or franchise tax, some states impose a capital values tax, and a large number have a sales and use tax. This can become a burden when the states insist that you collect the use tax from customers to whom you sell in that state, even though you have no office or other permanent contact within that state. In the paragraphs that follow, we consider these taxes, when they apply, and what you can do about them in some situations.

Corporate Income Taxes

There are three basic types of state corporate income taxes:

1) A state may impose a tax on all income arising out of, or derived from, property located within the state. Often these taxes will be imposed without regard to whether business is conducted within the geographical confines of the state. Where a company has a manufacturing plant or real property located in a state which imposes taxes upon income from property located within the geographical confines of the state, it will be subject to the tax on the income which can be traced to that property.

2) Some states which impose a corporation income tax, base it on income from business conducted in the state. If that is the state basis, it might be that investment-type income derived from property in the state would not be reached. The applicability of a tax imposed upon income from a business conducted within a state to income from real estate or other tangible proper-ty located within the state would generally depend upon the use to which the property is put, the language of the particular statute, and its administration.

3) Some states impose a tax upon income attributable to, or derived from, sources within the state. This probably affords the widest possible tax base for a state attempting to tax foreign corporations.

Some states do not permit the filing of consolidated returns.

Apportionment of Tax

Normally the federal taxable income is a starting point for determining the state income tax. The federal income is usually then modified by eliminating the deduction for local and state franchise and income taxes. There are other adjust-ments according to the state laws that are made to the federal income before allocating a portion of that income to the state. The most commonly used appor-tionment formula (or a variant of such) is:

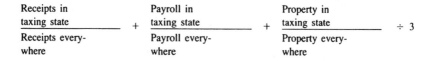

$$\frac{\text{Receipts in taxing state}}{\text{Receipts every-where}} + \frac{\text{Payroll in taxing state}}{\text{Payroll every-where}} + \frac{\text{Property in taxing state}}{\text{Property every-where}} \div 3$$

Often the formula will provide for a separate allocation of items like capital gains income, rents, royalties, and dividends. Income of this type may be allocated to the situs of the property, the place of its use, the domicile of the owner, or the source of the income.

Unitary and separate businesses. Some states which impose an appor-tioned corporate income tax on foreign corporations apply the apportionment formulas only to unitary businesses. A unitary business is one which has basi-cally one income-producing activity and its separate divisions are connected with, and directed toward, this activity. Thus, a company which both manu-factured and sold its products, even though it operated through separate departments or divisions, would be a unitary business. Where two or more businesses of different types are conducted independently of each other, they are sometimes entitled to use their own separate accounting for purposes of apportioning income under state apportionment formulas.

What Is a Sufficient "Nexus"?

A foreign corporation will have sufficient nexus or connection with the taxing state where it has assets or property within the borders of the taxing state. Similarly, where a foreign corporation qualifies to do business within a particular state by complying with the provisions of the state "qualification" statute, the corporation will be deemed to have established a domicile or residence within the state, giving that state a sufficient nexus for taxing that corporation.

Merely deriving income from within a state may be a sufficient nexus, unless:

1) The corporation is engaged in truly minimal operations within the taxing state.

2) The state's tax statute is not sufficiently broad to reach, in whole or in part, the particular type of activity which the foreign corporation is engaged in.

3) The tax, although described as a corporate income tax, is not really a corporate income tax but essentially a privilege tax, so it may not be imposed upon a corporation which is engaged solely in interstate commerce as to the taxing state.

How to Avoid a State's Income Tax

There are situations when a corporation can plan its operation so as to avoid all or part of the taxes imposed in one or more states from which it derives income.

Planning Activities Within a State

Where a state taxes only companies doing business within the geographical confines of a state, the state's taxing authority may be avoided if you avoid activities which will bring your corporation within the definitions of the state tax law. Often this will mean that you cannot maintain an office in the state, maintain servicemen in the state, sell on consignment to in-state agents, or execute or perform contracts.

Withdrawing from a State

Where your contacts with a state are reduced to the point that qualification is no longer required under the state's corporate statutes, you should consider withdrawing from the state. Most state corporate statutes have provisions whereby companies which have qualified under the laws of the state can subsequently withdraw.

Taking Advantage of Apportionment Formulas

Often by carefully planning your activities and locating property, payroll, or other factors which enter into apportionment formulas in states which do not consider those factors in apportioning income, or minimize those factors in their allocation formulas, you can reduce the over-all tax bite.

Capital Values Tax

Many states impose a tax upon the capital value of corporations. A capital values tax imposed on domestic corporations will generally tax the entire capital value of the corporation. However, apportionment is required when a capital values tax is imposed upon the property of a foreign corporation doing business in the state. The capital values taxes are generally based on the following factors: (a) actual value, (b) debt capital, and (c) capital stock.

Actual value.   A foreign corporation may be taxed on the entire property which it employs in a particular state. This would include physical property located in the state even though it is used primarily in interstate commerce. However, a state's authority to tax the intangible property of a foreign corporation is restricted. A state may tax the entire property—tangible and intangible—of a domestic corporation.

In some states credits are given in calculating the actual value on which the capital values tax is imposed for property which is reached by the state's property tax.

Debt capital.   In some states the amount of debt can be a factor in determining the basis for the capital values tax. Where a state seeks to use "debt capital" as a basis for a tax imposed upon foreign corporations, it must be apportioned. A foreign corporation's tax liability will be limited to the proportion of the debt capital which may be apportioned to the state.

Capital stock.   A capital values tax can be based upon the capital stock of the corporation. Most states levy a tax of this form on domestic corporations (in the form of a franchise tax) and on foreign corporations which are qualified to do business within the state. Where a tax or fee based on the capital stock of the corporation is levied upon the stock of a foreign corporation, there is generally either a reasonable floor or minimum or provision whereby it is apportioned—i.e., a foreign corporation is required to pay the tax on only that portion of its authorized capital stock which would be apportioned to the activities or capital employed within the geographic confines of the state.

Apportioning Intangible Property for Capital Values Tax

Intangible property presents a special problem for a capital values tax. Where a capital values tax on foreign corporations must be apportioned, it is necessary to establish a situs of the intangible property owned by a foreign corporation. Several basic theories have been developed as to the situs of intangible property:

Domicile.   The traditional theory is that corporate intangible property has a situs in the state where the corporation is incorporated. This is known as the domicile theory of situs. A few states have provided by statute that intangible property has a situs in the state where the principal office of the corporation is located, rather than the state of incorporation. Tangible property would have a situs where it is physically located.

Business situs.   In some states a doctrine of "business situs" for intangible property has developed. Under the business situs theory, intangible property may be taxed in the state where it has its situs or the intangible property came into existence. For example, an account receivable—a typical example of business intangible property—would have a situs in the state where the account arose. Other forms of business intangible property would have a situs where the business out of which they arose was conducted.

Sales and Use Taxes

Where a corporation makes sales to consumers within a state (i.e., not for resale) from goods located within the state, or it otherwise retains places of business within the state from which the sales are made, it is required to collect sales taxes in those states which impose this tax.

The big problem arises for companies engaged in interstate commerce which make interstate sales to customers in states imposing a sales tax. Usually, there is no basis for the state to impose the sales tax. But to "protect" the sales tax, the state imposes a "compensating use" tax which is imposed on the buyer located in the state, on goods acquired from without the state and not subject to the sales tax, but which would have been subject to the sales tax had they been purchased within the state. Although the tax is imposed on the user within the state, the state in most cases would have difficulty enforcing the tax. The state attempts to find some basis for having the *seller* (who is located outside the state) collect the use tax from the buyer and remit it to the buyer's state.

It is very important that the corporation obtain and preserve the documentation where it is not required to collect sales tax. For example, if the buyer has an exemption certification because it resells the goods, the corporation should have a copy of the exemption certificate in its files.

Chapter 23

Business Topics

Definitions

The following terms defined are frequently used in the personal tax laws covering the deductibility of nonbusiness and noninvestment kinds of interest expense.

Acquisition Debt—Any loan secured by a main or second home and used to buy, build, or improve a home.

Allocation of Interest—The method of tracing the use of loan proceeds to determine how much interest can be deducted for federal income tax purposes.

Amortization of Interest—A deductible expense allowed by spreading the cost of an asset over a period of time.

Below-Market Interest Rate Loan—A loan on which no interest is charged or on which interest is charged at a rate below the federal rate.

Capitalized Interest—Interest added to the cost of personal property, rather than deducting it on the taxpayer's return.

Debt—An obligation to pay a sum of money by certain and express agreement.

Demand Loan—A loan payable in full at any time upon the lender's demand.

Eligible Debt—Includes all debt *except* any debt with:

1) Permanently nondeductible interest, such as tax-exempt interest.

607

2) Personal interest.

3) Qualified home mortgage interest.

4) Interest incurred by a tax-exempt organization.

5) Interest attributable to a debt between a taxpayer and certain related parties, or between the parties themselves, if the rate of interest is less than the applicable federal interest rate.

Foregone Interest—The amount of interest that would be payable on a loan if the interest were figured at the applicable federal rate over the amount of interest actually paid on the loan.

Gift Loan—A loan where the foregoing of interest is treated as a gift.

Graduated Payment Mortgage (GPM)—Monthly mortgage payments that increase each year for a certain number of years, then remain at the same level.

Home Acquisition Debt—Any loan secured by a person's main or second home and used to buy, build, or improve the home.

Home Equity Debt—Any loan secured by a person's main or second home that is not acquisition debt. The interest on home equity debt is fully deductible on indebtedness of $100,000 or less ($50,000 or less if married filing a separate return). The debt may not exceed the fair market value of the main or second home reduced by any acquisition debt on that home.

Installment Plan Purchase—The purchase of an item on credit that allows the taxpayer to pay a portion of the amount owed every month, or other specified period. The amount owed is the cost of the item plus interest on the credit purchase.

Interest—The amount paid for the use of borrowed money.

Investment Interest Expense—The interest paid or accrued on a loan the funds from which were allocable to investment property.

Main Home—A taxpayer has only one main home, which is the property lived in most of the time. It may be a house, condominium, cooperative, mobile home, boat or similar property. It must provide basic living accommodations including sleeping space, toilet, and cooking facilities.

Mortgage Prepayment Penalty—An amount charged to a borrower who pays off a mortgage early.

Passive Activity Interest—Interest on a loan used to invest in a passive activity. (A passive activity, generally, is any activity involving the conduct of any trade or business in which the taxpayer does not *materially* participate.)

Personal Interest—Any interest paid on a loan the proceeds of which are used for personal reasons; for example, to pay for a car, boat, furniture, or a vacation.

Points (paid by the borrower)—A general term used to describe the charges paid by a borrower when getting a home mortgage. Points are also known as loan origination fees, maximum loan charges, or premium charges.

Points (paid by the seller)—Also known as loan placement fees. The seller sometimes must pay this fee to the lender to arrange financing for the buyer.

Portfolio Expenditure Interest—Interest on a loan, the proceeds of which are generally used to purchase stocks or bonds.

Production Period—For real property, the production period begins when physical activity is first performed on the property.

Reverse Mortgage Loan—A loan in which the lender pays the borrower the loan proceeds in installments over a period of time. If the borrower is a cash method taxpayer, only the interest actually paid on this type of loan can be deducted.

Second Home—Property which has been selected to be a home in which the owner spends less time than in a main home. It may be a house, condominium, cooperative, mobile home, boat or similar property. It must provide basic living accommodations, including sleeping space, toilet and cooking facilities.

Shared Appreciation Mortgage (SAM)—This type of loan involves the borrower paying a fixed rate of interest as well as a contingent interest. The contingent interest is based on the appreciation in the value of the home.

Term Loan—A loan whose maturity is usually longer than 5 years.

Traced Debt—Debt allocated to a particular cost by tracing payments made from the debt's proceeds to that cost.

Unstated Interest (imputed interest)—Interest that is treated as paid on certain loans that do not provide adequate stated interest payments.

Allocation of Interest

The rules for deducting interest vary, depending on whether it is used for business, personal home, mortgage, investment or passive activities. If the proceeds of a loan are used for more than one expense, an allocation must be made to determine the amount of interest for each use of the loan's proceeds.

The most advantageous way to allocate interest is to keep the proceeds of a particular loan separate from any other funds. If the proceeds are deposited in an account containing other funds, or received in cash, the loans should generally be used for a specific purpose within 15 days if they are not intended to allocate interest.

In general, the interest on a loan is allocated in the same way as the loan itself is allocated. This is true even if the funds are paid directly to a third party. Loans are allocated by tracing disbursements to specific uses. If the interest expense must be allocated, use the following categories:

1) A loan is allocated according to the use of its proceeds. The interest on a loan is allocated in the same way as the loan is allocated for the same time period. Loan proceeds and the related interest are allocated only by reference to the use of the proceeds. The allocation is not affected by the use of property that secures the loan.

For example, when property is used in a trade or business as security for a loan and the proceeds used to buy an auto for personal use, the interest expense on the loan must be allocated to the personal expenditure for the auto even though the loan is secured by business property.

2) A loan is allocated to a particular use from the date the proceeds are used to the earlier of either the date the loan is repaid or the date the loan is reallocated to another use.

3) If at the time any part of a loan is repaid, and the loan is allocated to more than one use, the loan is treated as repaid in the following order:

   a) Amounts allocated to personal use.

   b) Amounts allocated to investments and passive activities (other than those included in c) below).

   c) Amounts allocated to passive activities in connection with a rental real estate activity in which the taxpayer actively participates.

   d) Amounts allocated to former passive activities.

   e) Amounts allocated to a trade or business use and to expenses for certain low-income housing projects.

Special rules apply to the allocation of interest expense in connection with debt-financed acquisition of, and distributions from, *Partnerships and S Corporations*. These rules will not apply if the partnership or S corporation is formed or used for the principal purpose of avoiding the interest allocation rules.

Debt-financed Acquisitions is the use of loan proceeds to purchase an interest in an entity or to make a contribution to the capital of the entity. If an interest in an entity is purchased, the loan proceeds and the interest expense are allocated among all the assets of the entity. The allocation can be based on the fair market value, book value, or adjusted basis of the assets, reduced by any debts allocated to the assets.

If the taxpayer contributes to the capital of an entity, the allocation is based on the assets or by tracing the loan proceeds to the entity's expenditures. A purchase of an interest in an entity is treated as a contribution to capital to the extent the entity receives any proceeds of the purchases.

For example, an interest in a partnership is purchased for $20,000 using $75,000 of borrowed funds. The partnership's only assets include machinery used in its business valued at $60,000, and stocks valued at $15,000. The loan proceeds are allocated based on the value of the assets. Therefore, $16,000 of the loan proceeds ($60,000/$75,000 × $20,000) and the interest expense on that part are allocated to trade or business use. $4,000 ($15,000/$75,000 × $20,000) and the interest on that part are allocated to investment use.

If *debt-financed distributions* are allocated to partners or shareholders, the distributed loan proceeds and related interest expense must be reported to the partners and shareholders separately. This is because the loan proceeds and the interest expense must be allocated depending on how the partner or shareholder uses the proceeds. For example, if a shareholder uses distributed loan proceeds to invest in a passive activity, that shareholder's portion of the entity's interest expense on the loan proceeds is allocated to a passive activity use.

If the lender pays a *third party* for the borrower, the borrower allocates the loan based on the reason the third party received the funds. If the loan proceeds are not given directly to the borrower, the loan is allocated based on the use of the funds. This would apply if the borrower pays for property, services, or anything else by incurring a loan, or if the borrower takes property subject to debt.

For example, John Smith, a calendar year taxpayer, borrows $100,000 on January 4 and immediately uses the proceeds to open a checking account that pays no interest. No other amounts are deposited in the account during the year, and no part of the loan principal is repaid during the year. On April 1, John uses $20,000 of the loan proceeds held in the account for a passive activity expenditure. On September 1, John uses an additional $40,000 of the loan proceeds held in the account for a personal expenditure.

Under the interest allocation rules, the entire $100,000 loan is allocated to an investment expenditure for the period January 4 through March 31. From April 1 through August 31, John must allocate $20,000 of the loan to the passive activity expenditure, and $80,000 of the loan to the investment expenditure. From September 1 through December 31, he must allocate $40,000 of the loan to the personal expenditure, $20,000 to the passive activity expenditure, and $40,000 to the investment expenditure.

The *order of funds spent from an account* that are loan proceeds deposited in an account generally are treated as used (spent) *before* any unborrowed amounts in the same account and before any amounts deposited after the loan proceeds.

If the proceeds of a loan are received in *cash*, any expenditure up to the amount of the loan is treated as being paid from the loan's proceeds, if the expenditure is made within *30 days* before or after the proceeds of the loan are received. The expenditure can be made from any account or from cash. Also the expenditure can be treated as made on the date the cash is received. Otherwise, loan proceeds received in cash are treated as personal loans.

If the borrower has a line of credit or similar arrangement for *continuous borrowings*, all borrowings on which interest accrues at the same fixed or variable rate are treated as a single loan, and borrowings or parts of borrowings on which interest accrues at different fixed or variable rates are treated as different loans. These loans are treated as repaid in the order in which they are treated as repaid under the loan agreement.

Interest capitalization.   Under the uniform capitalization rules, interest on debt must generally be capitalized if used to finance the production of real or tangible personal property. The property must be used in a trade or business or held for sale to customers. Interest on a debt on property that was acquired and held for resale does not have to be capitalized. Interest paid or incurred during the product period must be capitalized if the property produced is *qualified property*. Qualified property is:

1) Real property.
2) Personal property with a class life of 20 years or more.
3) Personal property with an estimated production period of more than two years.
4) Personal property with an estimated production period of more than one year, if the estimated cost of production is more than $1,000,000.

Property is considered to be *produced property* if constructed, built, installed, manufactured, developed, improved, created, raised, or the property is grown.

Capitalized interest is treated as a cost of the property produced. This interest is recovered when the property is sold, used, or otherwise disposed of under the rules that apply to such transactions. Capitalized interest is recovered through cost of goods sold, an adjustment to basis, depreciation, or other method.

Interest capitalization applies to interest paid or incurred on any debt allocable to the costs of producing qualified property that must be capitalized. For example, these costs would include planning and design activities which are generally incurred before the production period begins, as well as the costs of raw land and materials acquired before the production period begins. Also included are any costs incurred under a contract for property produced by a third party.

Interest on a debt incurred to finance any asset used in the production of property (for example, manufacturing equipment and facilities) must also be capitalized to the extent the interest is paid or incurred during the production of the property. If an asset is used in the production of property and for other purposes, only the portion of the interest associated to the production activity is capitalized.

CORPORATION NET OPERATING LOSSES

A *net operating loss (NOL)* is defined as the deductions for a taxable year exceeding income for that year. A NOL can be used by deducting it from income either in the year that it occurs or in other preceding or following years. To have a NOL deduction, a loss must be caused by a) deductions from a trade or business or b) deductions for casualty and theft losses.

A NOL is calculated in the same way as taxable income. It starts with the corporation's gross income, and the deductible expenses from income are subtracted. If the deductions are more than the gross income, the corporation has a NOL. There are rules that either limit what can be deducted or permit deductions not ordinarily allowed:

1) NOL carrybacks or carryovers from other years cannot be deducted.

2) A corporation can take a deduction for dividends received without limiting it to a percentage of its taxable income.

3) A corporation can figure the deduction for dividends paid on certain preferred stock of public utilities without limiting it to its taxable income for the year.

The amount of a corporation's deduction for dividends received from domestic corporations—70% or 80% of the dividends—is limited to 70% or 80% of its taxable income. If a corporation sustains a NOL for a tax year, the limit of 70% or 80% of taxable income does not apply. In determining if a corporation has a NOL, the corporation figures the dividends-received deduction without regard to the 70% or 80% of taxable income limit.

Example: A corporation has $250,000 gross income from business operations and $312,500 of allowable business expenses. It received $75,000 in dividends from a domestic corporation, for which it can take an 80% deduction, limited to 80% of its taxable income before the deduction.

Income from the business	$250,000
Dividends	75,000
Gross income	$325,000
Deductions, expenses	312,500
Taxable income before special deductions	$ 12,500
Minus: Deduction for dividends received not limited to 80% of taxable income (80% of $75,000)	$ 60,000
Net operating loss	($47,500)

If a corporation has a NOL available for a carryback or carryforward year that is greater than the taxable income for that year, the corporation must modify its taxable income to figure how much of the NOL it will use in that year and how much it can carry to the next tax year. The carryover is the excess of the NOL deduction over the modified taxable income for the carry-back or carryforward year.

A corporation figures its *modified taxable income* in the same way as its taxable income. But NOLs can be deducted only from years before the NOL year when carryover is being calculated. A deduction for charitable contributions must be figured without considering any NOL carrybacks.

Modified taxable income is used only to figure how much of a NOL the corporation uses in the carryback or carryover year and how much it carries to the next year. It is not used to fill out the corporation's tax return or figure its tax.

Worksheet for Calculating an NOL Carryover

PART I

A. Carryback or carryforward year—Enter the year from which the NOL is being carried . . . .

B. NOL year—Enter the year in which the NOL occurred (the loss year). If the corporation has more than one NOL, see the instructions . . . .

C. NOL amount—Enter the amount of the NOL from year B that was carried to year A . . . .

D. If the corporation has more than one NOL, enter the total of all—
1. Carryovers from NOL years before both years A and B . . . .
2. Carrybacks from NOL years before year B . . . .

PART II

1. Taxable income for year A before the NOL deduction and special deductions:
   a. Enter the amount from line 28, Form 1120 (line 24, Form 1120-A) . . . .
   b. If year A is a carryforward year, enter the amount from line 19, Form 1120 or Form 1120-A. Otherwise, enter zero . . . .
   c. Subtract line 1b from line 1a . . . .

2. Enter the amount from line D1 of Part I . . . .

3. Subtract line 2 from line 1c . . . .

4. If year A is a carryforward year, enter the deduction for charitable contributions figured by using the amount on line 3 as taxable income. Otherwise, enter zero . . . .

5. Enter the amount from line D2 of PART I . . . .

6. Dividends received deduction:
   a. Subtract line 4 from line 1c . . . .
   b. Dividends received deduction figured by using the amount on line 6a as taxable income . . . .

7. Add lines 4, 5, and 6b . . . .

8. Modified taxable income—Subtract line 7 from line 3. (If line 7 is more than line 3, enter zero.) . . . . .

9. Carryover—Subtract line 8 from line C, PART I . . . .

DEDUCTING BUSINESS EXPENSES

Business expenses are the normal and current costs of carrying on a trade, business, or profession, and are usually deductible, provided that the business is operated to make a profit.

This review covers the kinds of expenses that can be deducted, the year in which the expenses can be deducted, and the limits on how much can be deducted. It is important to distinguish costs that are capital expenses from costs that are deductible expenses. Otherwise, the entire amount spent may be required to be capitalized, even if part of the cost can be deductible as an expense.

To be deductible, a business expense must be both ordinary and necessary. An *ordinary* expense is one that is common and accepted in the particular field of business, trade, or profession claiming the expense deduction. A *necessary* expense is one that is helpful and appropriate for the specific trade, business, or profession. An expense does not have to be indispensable to be considered necessary.

It is important to separate business expenses from 1) the expenses used to figure the cost of goods sold, and 2) capital expenses. In addition, business expenses must be kept separable from personal expenses. If an expense is partly for business and partly personal, the expense must separate the personal part from the business part.

Cost of Goods Sold

If the business manufactures products or purchases them for resale, some of the expenses are for the products that are sold. These expenses are used to figure the cost of the goods sold during the taxable year. Cost of goods sold is subtracted from the total amount the business takes in to figure its gross profit for the year. If an expense is used to figure cost of goods sold, it cannot be deducted again as a business expense. Among the expenses that go into figuring cost of goods sold are:

1) The cost of products or raw materials in inventory, including the cost of having them shipped to the business.
2) The cost of storing the products that are sold.
3) Direct labor costs (including contributions to pension or annuity plans) for workers who produce the products.
4) Depreciation on machinery used to produce the products.
5) Factory overhead expenses.

Under the uniform capitalization rules, all indirect costs incurred because of production and resale activities are required to be included in cost of goods sold. Indirect costs include rent, interest, taxes, storage, purchasing, processing, repackaging, handling, and general and administrative costs. This rule on indirect costs does not apply to personal property acquired for resale if the average annual gross receipts for the business for the preceding three tax years are not more than $10 million.

Capital Expenses

Some costs must be capitalized rather than deducted. These costs in general, three types, are considered a part of the investment in the business and are called *capital expenses*.

1) Going into business.
2) Business assets.
3) Improvements.

The costs of *getting started in business* and before actual business operations are begun are all capital expenses. These expenses are treated as capital expenses and are a part of the investor(s) basis in the business. Capital expenses become a part of the *basis* in the business and its assets. Basis is a way of measuring an investment in an asset for tax purposes. The basis is used to figure depreciation deductions, casualty losses, and gain or loss on an eventual sale of an asset.

What is spent for any asset for use in the business for more than one year is a *capital expenditure*. There are many different kinds of business assets, i.e., land, buildings, machinery, furniture, trucks, patents and franchise rights. The full cost of an asset, including freight and installation charges, must be capitalized. Under the uniform capitalization rules, direct and indirect costs incurred in producing real or tangible personal property for use in the trade or business must be capitalized.

The cost of making *improvements* to a business asset are capital expenses, if the improvements add to the value of the asset, appreciably lengthen the time the asset can be used, or adapt the asset to a different use. Ordinarily, the cost of the improvement is added to the basis of the improved property. Improvements include such items as new electric wiring, a new roof, a new floor, new plumbing, strengthening for a wall, and lighting improvements.

How Much Can Be Deducted?

A business cannot deduct more for an expense than the amount actually spent. There is no other limit on how much can be deducted provided that the amount is reasonable. If deductions are large enough to produce a net business loss for the year, the amount of tax loss may be limited. If the deductions for an investment or business activity are more than the income it brings in, a net loss results. There may be limits on how much, if any, of the loss can be used to offset income from other sources. If a business activity is carried on with the intention of not making a profit, the loss from the activity cannot be used to offset other income. In general, a deductible loss from a business or investment activity is limited to the amount of investment that is *at-risk* in the activity. Any money invested in the business is considered to be at-risk. Amounts borrowed for use in the business are considered to be at-risk. Deductions from passive activities can be used only to offset the income from the passive activities. Any excess deductions cannot be deducted against other income. A passive activity can be defined as any activity that involves the con-

duct of any trade or business, and in which the investor(s) does not materially participate. (Any rental activity is a passive activity even if the owner(s)
materially participates in the activity.)

When Can an Expense Be Deducted?

Under the cash method of accounting, business expenses are deducted
in the tax year they are actually paid—even if they were incurred in an earlier year. Under the accrual method of accounting, business expenses are
deductible when the business becomes liable for them—whether or not they
are paid in the same year that they are incurred. All events that set the
amount of the liability must have happened, and the expense must be figured
with reasonable accuracy.

Not-For-Profit Activities

If a business activity, or an activity which an individual has invested in,
is not carried on to make a profit, the deductions for it are limited and no loss
will be allowed to offset other income. Activities done as a hobby, or mainly
for sport or recreation, come under this limit. So would an investment activity that is intended only to produce tax losses for the investors.

The limit on not-for-profit losses applies to individuals, partnerships,
estates, trusts, and S corporations. It does not apply to corporations other
than S corporations.

In determining whether an activity is carried on for profits, all the facts
in regard to the activity are taken into account. No one factor alone is decisive. Among the factors to be considered are:

1) Whether you carry on the activity in a businesslike manner.
2) Whether the time and effort the taxpayer puts into the activity indicate
   that the intent is to make the activity profitable.
3) Whether the income from the activity is used for the livelihood of the
   owner of the business.
4) Whether the losses from the activity are due to circumstances beyond
   the owner's control, or are normal in the start-up phase of the business.
5) Whether the methods of operation are changed in an attempt to
   improve the profitability of the activity.
6) Whether the organizers of the activity have the knowledge needed to
   carry on the activity as a successful business.
7) Whether the organizers of the activity have been successful in making a
   profit in similar activities in the past.

8) Whether the activity makes a profit in some years, and how much profit it makes.

9) Whether future profit can be expected from the appreciation of the assets used in the activity.

Limits on Deductions and Losses

If the activity is not carried on for profit, deductions are allowed only in the following order, only to the extent stated in the three categories, and only if the deductions are itemized on Schedule A of Form 1040.

Category 1. Deductions that can be taken for personal as well as for business activities are allowed in full. All nonbusiness deductions, such as those for interest, taxes, and casualty losses, belong in this category and are deducted on the appropriate lines of Schedule A, Form 1040.

Category 2. Deductions that do not result in an adjustment to the basis of property are allowed next, but only to the extent that the taxpayer's gross income from the activity is more than the deductions he/she has taken, or could take for it, under Category 1. Most business deductions belong in this category.

Category 3. Business deductions that decrease the basis of property are allowed last, but only to the extent that the gross income from the activity is more than deductions taken, or could be taken, under the first two categories. The deductions for depreciation, amortization, and the portion of a casualty loss not deductible in Category 1 belong in this category. Where more than one asset is involved, depreciation and these other deductions must be divided proportionally among those assets.

Example:

Gross Income...............................		$3,200
Less Expenses:		
Real estate taxes	$700	
Interest on mortgage	$900	
Insurance	$400	
Utilities........................	$700	
Maintenance.....................	$200	
Depreciation on auto..............	$600	
Depreciation on machine	$200	
Total Expenses............................		$3,700
Loss.....................................		$ 500

The interest on the mortgage is deductible in full. The deductions are limited to $3,200, the amount of gross income earned from the activity. The limit is reached in category 3), as follows:

Limit on Deduction............................		$3,200
Category 1. Taxes and Interest	$1,600	
Category 2. Insurance, utilities,		
maintenance......................	1,300	2,900
Available for Category 3.........................		$ 300

The $300 for depreciation is divided between the automobile and the machine as follows:

$600/$800 × $300 = $225 automobile depreciation.

$200/$800 × $300 = $ 75 machine depreciation.

The basis of each asset is reduced accordingly.

Employees' Pay

Salaries, wages, and other forms of pay given to employees are deductible business expenses. However, a deduction for salaries and wages must be reduced by any jobs credit determined for the tax year.

Employees' wages and salaries paid to produce real or tangible personal property or to acquire property for resale generally must be capitalized or included in inventory. Personal property acquired for resale is not subject to this rule if average annual gross receipts are $10,000,000 or less. Salaries and other expenses incurred for constructing capital assets cannot be deducted. They should be included in the basis of the constructed asset and covered through depreciation allowances.

Mining and manufacturing businesses include most of their salaries, wages, or other compensation expenses as part of cost of goods sold. They cannot deduct such items as current business expenses. To be deductible, employees' pay must meet four tests, i.e., ordinary and necessary, reasonable, for services performed, paid or incurred. Employers can be asked to prove that salaries, wages, and other payments for employees' services are ordinary and necessary expenses directly connected with the trade or business. What is reasonable to pay is determined by the facts. Usually, it is the amount that ordinarily would be paid for these services by similar enterprises under similar circumstances.

The employer must prove that the payments were made for services actually performed. The payments must actually have been made or incurred during the tax year. If the cash method of accounting is used, the expense for salaries and wages can be deducted only during the tax year.

Vacation Pay

Vacation pay is any amount paid or to be paid to an employee while the employee is on vacation. Vacation pay also includes amounts paid an employee when the employee chooses not to take a vacation. Vacation pay does not include amounts for sick pay or holiday pay. If the cash basis of accounting is used, vacation pay can be deducted when the employee is paid. If an accrual basis of accounting is used, vacation pay earned by employees can be deducted in the year earned only if the amount is paid at the close of the tax year, or if the amount is vested within two months after the close of the year. If it is paid later than this, it is deducted in the year actually paid.

Meals and Entertainment

A business generally can deduct 50% of business-related meal and entertainment expenses. This limit applies to employers even if they reimburse their employees for 100% of the expenses.

The 50% limit applies to meal expenses incurred while traveling away from home on business, in entertaining business customers at the place of business or a restaurant, or in attending a business convention or reception, business meeting, or business luncheon at a club. The limit may apply to meals furnished on the premises to employees. Taxes and tips relating to a meal or entertainment activity are included in the amount subject to the 50% limit. However, the cost of transportation to and from a business meal or entertainment activity that is otherwise allowable is not subject to the 50% limit.

The 50% limit on meal and entertainment expenses applies if the expense is otherwise deductible. The limit applies to trade or business expenses, to expenses incurred for the production of income including rental or royalty income, and to deductible education expenses.

It must be shown that meal and entertainment expenses are directly for, or associated with, the conduct of the trade or business, or are covered by one of the exceptions. (Some of the exceptions to the 50% limit must still meet other restrictions.) To be deductible, the expense must be an ordinary and necessary expense of carrying on the trade or business, and the taxpayer must be able to prove the expense.

Costs Chosen to Deduct or to Capitalize

There are certain costs that a business can choose *either* to deduct or to capitalize. The choice usually depends upon when it is best for the business to recover the costs. If a cost is deducted as an expense, it is recovered in full, i.e., recovered from income. If a cost is capitalized it can be recovered through a

Section 179 deduction or periodic deductions for depreciation, amortization, or depletion. The costs that can be deducted or capitalized include:

1) Certain carrying charges on property.

2) Research and experimental costs.

3) *Intangible* drilling and development costs for oil, gas, and geothermal wells.

4) Exploration costs for new mineral deposits.

5) Mine development costs for a new mineral deposit.

6) Costs of increasing the circulation of a newspaper or other periodical.

7) Costs of making public transportation vehicles, buildings, and other facilities more accessible.

The decision to capitalize or to deduct belongs to the business entity—the sole proprietor, partnership, corporation, estate, or trust. Individual partners, shareholders, and beneficiaries do not make the choice themselves (except for exploration costs for a new mineral deposit).

Amortization

A *part* of certain capital expenses can be deducted each year as amortization. Amortization allows these certain expenses to be recovered in a way that is similar to straight-line depreciation. Only certain specified expenses can be amortized for federal income tax purposes.

Since amortization sometimes allows a write-off of costs that are not ordinarily deductible, a taxpayer may want to recover eligible costs by electing to take amortization deductions. Business start-up costs, pollution control facilities, and research and experimental costs are costs that are commonly amortized. (They must be amortized over a period of *not less than 60 months*.)

If a taxpayer owns mineral property, an oil, gas, or geothermal well, or standing timber, a deduction can be taken for *depletion*. The taxpayer must have an economic interest in the mineral deposits or standing timber.

RICs, REITs, REMICs

- RIC—regulated investment company
- REIT—real estate investment trust
- REMIC—real estate mortgage investment conduit

RIC

A *regulated investment company* is any domestic corporation

1) Which at all times during the taxable year is registered as an investment company under the Investment Company Act of 1940 as a management company or unit investment trust, *or* has in effect an election under such Act to be treated as a business development company; *or*
2) Which is a common trust fund or similar fund excluded by the Act from the definition of "investment company" and is not included in the definition of a *common trust fund* by Section 584(a).

A regulated investment company's (RIC) income from a partnership or trust will be treated as derived from RIC business only when it can be shown to qualify as income. Here, the 30% test can be applied to specified sales or dispositions not specifically involved with the company's principal business. Any profits occurring after the adoption of a plan of complete liquidation are not taken into account under this test when the RIC liquidation comes about in the year when the plan was adopted. In some instances, a fund belonging to a series would not be disqualified under the 30% test on sales resulting from, and occurring within, five days of abnormal redemptions.

REIT

The term *real estate investment trust* means a corporation, trust, or association which meets the qualifying conditions. In order for a REIT to qualify, it must be an organization:

1) Which is managed by one or more trustees or directors.
2) The beneficial ownership of which is evidenced by transferable shares or by transferable certificates of beneficial interest.
3) Which would be taxable as a domestic corporation but for the provisions of Section 856, Chapter 1, Subchapter M, Part 11 of the Code.
4) Which in the case of a taxable year beginning before October 5, 1976, does not hold any property, other than foreclosure property, primarily for sale to customers in the ordinary course of its trade or business.
5) Which is neither a financial institution to which Section 585, 586, or 593 apply, nor an insurance company to which Subchapter L applies.
6) Beneficial ownership of which is held by 100 or more persons.
7) Which would not be a personal holding company as defined in Section 542, if all of its gross income constituted personal holding company income as defined in Section 543.

8) Which is not closely held as determined under Section 856(h).

The IRS may waive a real estate investment trust (REIT) dividend distribution quota for a year if the REIT is not in a position to meet the quota because distribution was made to get around Code Sec. 4981 excise tax on undistributed income. Additionally, when specific conditions are satisfied, sums received or accrued from a tenant could be treated as rents from real property. A similar rule relates to interest.

A REIT may reduce its capital gain net income by the amount of REIT net ordinary losses. Computation of REIT taxable income includes the net income resulting from the sale of foreclosed property.

REMIC

The term *real estate mortgage investment conduit* means any entity:

1) To which an election to be treated as a *REMIC* applies for the taxable year and all prior taxable years.

2) In which all of the interests are regular interests or residual interests.

3) Which has one (and only one) class of residual interests and all distributions, if any, with respect to such interests are *pro rata*.

4) Of which substantially all of the assets consist of qualified and permitted investments as of the close of the third month beginning after the start-up day and at all times thereafter.

5) Which has a taxable year that is a calendar year.

6) With respect to which there are reasonable arrangements designed to ensure that:

a) Residual interests in such entity are not held by disqualified organizations as defined in Section 860E(e)(5);

b) Information necessary for the application of Section 860E(e) will be made available by the entity.

When applied to real estate mortgage investment conduits (REMIC), the asset test for a business electing REMIC status is continuous after the end of the third month after its startup, but not applicable during the qualified liquidation period.

CHANGE IN ACCOUNTING METHODS

Either the IRS or the taxpayer may require a change in the accounting method utilized. If the IRS requires the change, the altered approach must conform to the method required by law. The taxpayer, with a few exceptions, must obtain IRS approval whether the changes conform to GAAP (APB Opinion 20) or to the tax law.

Following are examples of changes requiring IRS approval:

1) Gross income and expenses, switched from cash to accrual method.
2) Altered basis for inventory valuation.
3) A change in depreciation method.
4) Changes in the reporting entity. Realignment of subsidiary-parent organizations may result in the creation of different entities for accounting purposes.
5) Changes in method for a material item. Any items that involve the proper time for inclusion of said items in income or the taking of a deduction are considered material items.

Following are items not considered to be changes in method.

1) Correction of mathematical errors.
2) Improper posting corrections.
3) Depreciation schedule adjustments.
4) Alterations in circumstances and facts governing the current method.

A special rule applies to dealers in personal property. A dealer may adopt the installment method of accounting at the time of a transaction, or make a change to the installment method without IRS consent. However, a dealer may *not* change from the installment method to any other method without IRS consent.

Under present procedure, Form 3115 application for permission to change an accounting method or practice is filed within the first 180 days of the year to which the change is to apply. Resulting adjustments are generally apportioned over a ten-year period as prescribed by the Commissioner. When the taxpayer agrees to the ten-year spread, or whatever time frame is suggested by IRS, the application is usually approved.

When a taxpayer desires to discontinue the LIFO method of inventory valuation, the ten-year readjustment period is normally allowed; however, the taxpayer may *not* revert to LIFO during the previously approved readjustment without IRS consent.

BASIS OF ASSETS

Basis of assets is the amount of investment (equity) in property for tax purposes. Use the basis of property to figure the deductions for depreciation, depletion, and casualty losses. Also use it to figure gain or loss on the sale or other disposition of property.

The following are the meanings of the terms used in the tax regulations to report the basis of assets.

Agreement Not to Compete—An agreement (intangible property) made by the seller of a business not to be in competition with the buyer.

Amortization—A ratable deduction for the cost of certain intangible property over the period specified by law. Research and mining costs are examples of costs that can be amortized.

Business Assets—Property used in the conduct of a trade or business, such as business machinery and office furniture.

Capital Assets—Generally, everything owned for personal purposes or investment is a capital asset. This includes a home, personal car, or stocks and bonds. It does not include inventory or depreciable property.

Capital Expenses—Costs that must be added to (increase the basis of) business investments or capital assets.

Capitalization—Adding costs, such as improvements, to the basis of assets.

Depletion—Yearly deduction allowed to recover investments in minerals, in-place or standing timber. To take the deduction, the business must have the right to income from the extraction and sale of the minerals or from the cutting of timber.

Goodwill—Intangible property that represents the advantage or benefit acquired in a business beyond the value of its other assets. It is not confined to a name but can be attached to a particular area where business is transacted, to a list of customers, or to other elements of value in a business as a going concern.

Intangible Property—Property such as goodwill, patents, copyrights, etc.

Like-kind Property—Items of property with the same nature or character. The grade or quality of the properties does not matter. An example of like-kind properties are two vacant plots of land.

Nonbusiness Assets—Property used for personal purposes, such as a home or family car.

Personal Property—Property, such as machinery, equipment, or furniture, that is not real property.

Real Property—Land and generally anything erected on, growing on, or attached to land; i.e., a building.

Recapture—Amount of depreciation that must be reported as ordinary income when property is sold at a gain.

Section 179 Deduction—A special deduction allowed against the cost of certain property purchased for use in the active conduct of a trade or business.

Tangible Property—Property that can be seen or touched, such as furniture and buildings.

Unstated Interest—The part of the sales price treated as interest when an installment contract provides for little or no interest.

The *basis of property* is usually its *cost*. The basis in some assets cannot be determined by cost, such as property received by a gift or inheritance. It also applies to property received in an involuntary exchange, and in certain other circumstances. If the asset is used in a trade or business or an activity conducted for profit, many direct and indirect costs must be capitalized (added to the basis) as part of the cost basis.

The original basis in property, whether cost or other, is increased or decreased by certain events. If improvements to the property are made, the basis is increased. The basis is reduced if deductions for depreciation or casualty losses are taken.

The basis of property is usually its cost, as stated above; the *cost* is the amount paid in cash or in other property or services. Cost also includes amounts paid for sales tax charged on the purchase, freight charges to obtain the property, and installation and testing charges. In addition, the cost basis of real property and business assets will include other items.

Loans with Low or No Interest

If business or investment property is bought on any time-payment plan that charges little or no interest, the basis of the property is the stated purchase price, less the amount considered to be unstated interest. Unstated interest is an interest rate less than the applicable federal rate.

The cost basis of *stocks and bonds* is the purchase price plus the costs of purchase, such as commissions and recording or transfer fees. There are other ways to determine the basis of stocks or bonds depending on how they are acquired. Some ways in which stock can be acquired are by automatic investment programs, dividend reinvestments, and stock rights. An average basis of shares in a regulated investment company can be used if the shares are acquired at different times and prices, and the shares are kept by a custodian or agent.

When *real property* is bought and the buyer agrees to pay certain taxes the seller owed on it, the taxes are treated as part of the cost of the property. These payments cannot be deducted as taxes. If the seller is reimbursed for taxes paid for the buyer, the buyer can deduct that amount. That amount cannot be included in the cost of the property.

Settlement fees and other costs, such as legal and recording fees, are some of the costs included in the basis of property. Some others are abstract fees, charges for installing utility services, surveys, transfer taxes, title insurance, and any amounts the seller owes that are paid by the buyer, such as back taxes or interest, recording or mortgage fees, charges for improvements or repairs, and sales commissions.

These fees and costs must be allocated between land and improvements, such as buildings, to figure the basis for depreciation of the improvements. The fees are allocated according to the market values of the land and improvements at the time of purchase. Settlement fees do not include amounts placed in escrow for the future payment of items such as taxes and insurance.

Fair market value (FMV) is the price at which the property would change hands between a buyer and a seller, neither being required to buy or sell, and both having reasonable knowledge of all necessary facts. Sales of similar property, on or about the same date, may be helpful in figuring the FMV.

If the buyer of property becomes liable for an existing mortgage on the property, the basis is the amount paid for the property plus the amount to be paid on the assumed mortgage. If a building, for example, is bought for $40,000 and the mortgage on it to be paid is $60,000, the cost basis is $100,000.

Business Assets

If property is purchased to use in a business, the basis is usually the actual cost. If property is constructed, built, or otherwise produced, the business may be subject to the uniform capitalization rules to determine the basis of the property. The *uniform capitalization* rules specify the costs to be added to basis in certain circumstances. A business is subject to the uniform capitalization rules if it:

1) Produces real property or tangible personal property for use in a trade or business.
2) Produces real property or tangible personal property for sale to customers.
3) Acquires property for resale.

Property is produced if it is constructed, built, installed, manufactured, developed, improved, created, or anything raised or grown on the property. Property produced under a contract is treated as produced to the extent that payments are made or otherwise are incurred for the property. Tangible personal property includes films, sound recordings, videotapes, books, and other similar property.

Under the uniform capitalization rules, direct costs and an allocable part of most indirect costs that benefit or are incurred because of production or resale activities must be capitalized. This means that certain expenses incurred during the year will be included in the basis of property produced or in inventory costs, rather than claimed as a current deduction. These costs are recovered through depreciation, amortization, or cost of goods sold when the property is used, sold, or otherwise disposed of.

Any cost which is not used in figuring taxable income for any tax year is not subject to the uniform capitalization rules. The uniform capitalization rules also do not apply to:

1) Property produced that is not used in the trade or business or an activity conducted for profit.

2) Costs paid or incurred by an individual other than as an employee, or a qualified employee-owner of a corporation in the business of being a writer, photographer, or artist.

3) Certain developments and other intangible costs of oil and gas, or geothermal wells, or other mineral property allowable as a deduction.

4) Property produced under a long-term contract.

5) Research and developmental expenses allowable as a deduction.

6) Cost incurred for the production of property for use in a trade or business if substantial construction of the property occurred before March 1, 1986.

7) Costs for personal property acquired for resale if the average annual gross receipts do not exceed $10 million.

8) Costs of raising, growing, or harvesting trees (including costs associated with the land under the trees) other than ornamental trees or trees bearing fruit, nuts, or other crops. Ornamental trees do not include evergreens over 6 years old when severed from the roots.

9) Costs, other than circulation expenses, subject to ten-year amortization under the alternative minimum tax.

Direct Costs

Direct material costs and direct labor costs incurred for production or resale activities must be capitalized. Direct material costs include the cost of materials that become an integral part of the asset plus the cost of materials used in the ordinary course of the activity.

Direct labor costs include the cost of labor that can be identified or associated with a particular activity. This includes all types of compensation: basic; overtime; sick; vacation; etc.; as well as payroll taxes and payments to a supplemental unemployment plan.

Indirect Costs

Indirect costs include all costs other than direct material and labor costs. Certain types of costs may directly benefit, or be incurred because of a particular activity even though the same costs also benefit other activities. These costs require allocation to determine the part for each of the activities.

Indirect costs that must be capitalized for production or resale activities include but are not limited to amounts incurred for:

1) Repair and maintenance of equipment or facilities.
2) Utilities related to equipment or facilities.
3) Rent of equipment, facilities, or land.
4) Indirect labor and contract supervisory wages including payroll taxes and payments to supplemental unemployment benefit plans.
5) Indirect materials and supplies.
6) Tools and equipment not otherwise capitalized.
7) Quality control and inspection.
8) Taxes otherwise allowable as a deduction (other than state, local, and foreign income taxes) that relate to labor, materials, supplies, equipment, land, or facilities. Taxes as part of the cost of property are not included.
9) Depreciation, amortization, and cost recovery allowance on equipment and facilities to the extent allowable as a deduction.
10) Depletion, whether or not in excess of cost.
11) Administrative costs, whether or not performed on a job site, but not including any cost of selling, or any return on capital.
12) Insurance on plant, machinery, or equipment; or insurance on a particular activity.

If materials, labor, or services are provided by a *related person* for a price less than the arm's-length charge for the items, special rules apply.

Interest

Interest must be capitalized for all items produced but not for property acquired for resale. Interest paid or incurred during the production period must be capitalized if the property produced is:

1) Real property.
2) Personal property with a class life of 20 years or more for determining depreciation.
3) Personal property with an estimated production period of more than two years.

4) Personal property with an estimated production period of more than one year if the estimated cost of production is more than $1 million.

The production period begins on the date the production of the property begins, and ends on the date the property is ready to be placed in service or is ready to be held for sale.

Costs Not Capitalized

Costs which are not required to be capitalized for production or resale activities include amounts incurred for:

1) Marketing, selling, advertising, and distribution expenses.

2) Bidding expenses incurred in the solicitation of contracts not awarded to the bidding company.

3) General and administrative expenses, and compensation paid to officers for the performance of services not directly benefiting, or not incurred, because of a particular production activity.

4) Research and experimental expenses.

5) Casualties, thefts, and other losses allowed by Section 165 of the Internal Revenue Code.

6) Depreciation, amortization, and cost recovery allowances on equipment and facilities that have been placed in service but are temporarily idle.

7) Income taxes.

8) Costs attributable to strikes.

9) Repair expenses that do not relate to the manufacture or production of property.

Intangible Assets

Intangible assets include goodwill, copyrights, trademarks, grade names, and franchises. The basis of an intangible asset is usually its cost. If a number of assets are acquired for a lump-sum price, for example, a going business, the basis of the individual assets is determined by allocating the total purchase price among the individual assets.

Goodwill

The basis of goodwill usually is its cost if it is bought. However, if a going business is bought with the intent to continue the business, goodwill can be included in the price.

Patents

If the individual gets a patent for an invention, the basis is the cost of development, such as research and experimental expenditures, drawings, working models, and attorneys and government fees. If the research and experimental expenditures are deducted as current business expenses, they cannot be included in the cost of the patent. The value of the inventor's time spent on an invention is not a part of the basis.

Copyrights

When a copyright is bought, the basis is the amount paid for it. However, if the person is an author, the basis usually will be the cost of getting the copyright plus copyright fees, attorneys' fees, clerical assistance, and the cost of plates that remain in the author's possession. The basis does not include the value of the author's time.

Franchises, Trademarks, and Trade Names

The basis is the cost of the franchise, trademark, or trade name.

Trade or Business Acquired

If a group of assets is acquired that is a trade or business to which goodwill or going concern value is attached, the following method must be used to allocate the purchase price to the various assets:

1) Cash, demand deposits, and similar accounts.
2) The remaining purchase price to the following assets is allocating to each asset an amount proportionate to, but not in excess of, its fair market value in the following order:
   a) Certificates of deposit, U.S. government securities, readily marketable stock or securities, and foreign currency.
   b) All other assets except goodwill and going concern value.

Any remainder of the purchase price, after making these allocations, is the basis for goodwill and going concern value.

If the buyer and seller agree *in writing* to the allocation of any consideration, or on the fair market value of any asset, the agreement is binding on both the buyer and seller unless the IRS determines the allocation, or fair market value, is not appropriate.

Land and Buildings

If buildings and the land on which they stand are bought for a business and a lump-sum price is paid for them, the basis of the whole property is allocated among the land and buildings in order to figure the depreciation allowable on the buildings. When the cost between land and buildings is allocated, the part of the cost that is used as the basis of each asset is the ratio of the FMV of that asset to the FMV of the whole property at the time of purchase. If there is uncertainty about the FMV of the land and buildings, the cost is allocated among them based on their assessed values for real estate tax purposes.

Demolition of Building

The costs of demolition and other losses incurred for the demolition of any building are added to the basis of the land on which the demolished building was located, rather than claimed as a current deduction.

Subdivided Lots

If a tract of land is bought and subdivided into individual lots, the basis is allocated to the individual lots based on the FMV of each lot to the total price paid for the tract. This allocation is necessary because the gain or loss on the sale of each individual lot must be figured. If a mistake is made in figuring the cost of subdivided lots that were sold in previous years, the mistake cannot be refigured for years for which the statute of limitations has expired. The cost basis of any remaining lots is figured by allocating the correct original cost basis of the entire tract among the original lots.

Example: A tract of land is bought for $15,000 and is subdivided into 15 building lots of equal size. The cost basis of each lot is divided equally to $1,000. The sale of each lot is treated as a separate transaction and gain or loss figured separately on each sale.

Several years later it is determined that the original cost basis in the tract was $22,500 instead of $15,000. Eight of the lots have been sold using $8,000 of basis in years for which the statute of limitations has expired. Only a basis of $1,500 can be taken into account for figuring gain or loss on the sale of each of the remaining seven lots ($22,000 basis divided among all 15 total lots). The basis of the eight lots sold in tax years barred by the statute of limitations cannot be refigured.

Before figuring a gain or loss on a sale, exchange, or other disposition of property, or to figure depreciation, depletion, or amortization, certain adjustments must usually be made that increase or decrease the basis of the property. The result of these adjustments to the basis is the *adjusted basis.*

Increases to Basis

The basis of any property is increased by all items added to a capital account. This includes the cost of any improvements having a useful life of more than 1 year and amounts spent after a casualty to restore the damaged property. Rehabilitation expenses also increase the basis, but any rehabilitation credit allowed for these expenses must be subtracted before adding them to the basis. If any of the credit has to be recaptured, the basis is increased by the amount of the recapture.

If additions or improvements are made to business property, separate accounts must be kept for these and depreciated on the basis of each according to the depreciation rules in effect when the addition or improvement is placed in service. Some items that are added to the basis of property are:

1) The cost of extending utility service lines to the property.
2) Legal fees such as the cost of defending and protecting title.
3) Legal fees for obtaining a decrease in an assessment levied against property to pay for local improvements.
4) Zoning costs.
5) The capitalized value of a redeemable ground rent.

Assessments for Local Improvements

Assessments for items such as streets and sidewalks, which tend to increase the value of the property assessed, are added to the basis of the property and not deducted as taxes. Assessments for maintenance, repair, or meeting interest charges on the improvements are deductible.

Example: If the city changes the street in front of an owner's store into an enclosed pedestrian mall, and assesses the owner for the cost of the conversion, add the assessment to the basis of the property. The amount of the assessment is a depreciable asset.

Deducting vs. Capitalizing Costs

Costs that are deductible as current expense cannot be added to the basis of property. There are certain costs that can either be deducted or capitalized. If capitalized, these costs are included in the basis. If deducted, they cannot be included in the basis. Costs which may be chosen to deduct or to capitalize are:

1) Carrying charges, such as interest and taxes, that are paid to own property.

2) Research and expenditure costs.

3) Intangible drilling and development costs for oil, gas, and geothermal wells.

4) Exploration costs for new mineral deposits.

5) Mine development costs for a new mineral deposit.

6) The cost of increasing the circulation of a newspaper or other periodical.

7) The cost of removing architectural and transportation barriers to the handicapped and elderly.

Decreases to Basis

1) Election to expense certain depreciable business assets.

2) Nontaxable dividends.

3) Deductions previously allowed, or allowable, for amortization, depreciation, and depletion.

Casualty and theft losses decrease the basis of property by the amount of any insurance or other reimbursement. The basis is increased for amounts spent after a casualty to restore the damaged property.

The amount received for granting an easement is usually considered to be from the sale of an interest in real property. It reduces the basis of the affected part of the property. If the amount received is more than the basis of the part of the property affected by the easement, the basis is reduced to zero and the excess is recognized as a gain.

The basis of property is decreased by the *depreciation* that could have been deducted on the tax returns under the method of depreciation selected. If less depreciation is taken than could have been taken under the method selected, the basis is decreased by the amount that could have been taken under that method. If a depreciation deduction is not taken, the adjustments to basis for depreciation that could have been taken are made using the accelerated cost recovery system (ACRS) or the modified accelerated cost recovery system (MACRS). The straight-line method is used for property not depreciable using ACRS or MACRS.

If more deductions are taken than permissible, the basis is decreased by the amount that should have been deducted, plus the part of the excess deducted that actually resulted in a decrease in the tax liability for any year.

In decreasing a basis for depreciation, not only the amount deducted on the tax return as depreciation, but also any depreciation required to be capitalized under the uniform capitalization rules must be taken into account.

Nontaxable Exchanges

A nontaxable exchange is an exchange in which any gain is not taxed and any loss cannot be deducted. If property is received in a nontaxable exchange, its basis is usually the same as the basis of the property exchanged. An exchange must meet the following conditions to be nontaxable:

1) The property must be business or investment property. The property exchanged and the property received must be held for business or investment purposes. Neither a home nor family car can be exchanged for personal purposes.

2) The property must be *like-kind property*. For exchanges after April 10, 1991, depreciable tangible property can be either "like-kind" or "like-class." The exchange of real estate for real estate or personal property or similar property is a trade of like property. The exchange of an apartment house for a store building, or a panel truck for a pickup truck, is a like-kind exchange. The exchange of a piece of machinery for a store building is not a like-kind trade. The exchange of real property located in the United States for real property located outside the United States is not a like-kind exchange. The exchange of a personal computer for a printer is a *like-class exchange.*

3) The property may be either tangible or intangible. The exchange rules do not apply to exchanges of stocks, bonds, notes, certain other intangible property, or interests in a partnership.

4) The property must not be property held for sale. The property exchanged and the property received must not be property for sale to customers, such as merchandise. It must be property held for use in a business or for investment.

5) The property received must meet identification requirements. The property to be received in the exchange must be identified on or before the day that is 45 days after the date of transfer of the property that is exchanged.

6) The trade must meet the completed transaction requirement. The property to be received in the exchange must be received the earlier of the 181st day after the date of transfer of the property exchanged, or the due date, including extensions, for the tax return of the tax year during which the property exchanged is transferred.

If property is traded in a nontaxable exchange and an additional amount is paid, the basis of the property received is the basis of the property exchanged, increased by the additional amount paid.

Related persons are ancestors, lineal descendants, brothers and sisters of whole and half blood, a spouse, two or more corporations, an individual and a corporation, and a grantor and fiduciary. Generally, when related persons exchange like-kind property the nontaxable exchange rules apply. For exchanges made directly or indirectly between related persons after July 10, 1989, the exchange is disqualified from nontaxable exchange rules if either party disposes of the like-kind property within two years after the exchange. Each related person must report any gain or loss not recognized on the original exchange on a tax return filed for the year in which the later disposition occurred. The basis in the property received in the original exchange will be its fair market value. These rules generally do not apply to dispositions due to the death of either related party, involuntary conversions, or exchanges whose main purpose is not the avoidance of federal income tax.

Exchange of Businesses

The exchange of assets of one business for the assets of another business is an exchange of multiple assets and cannot be treated as a disposition of a single property. The various assets that comprise each business must be checked to determine which are like-kind exchanges. The assets treated as transferred in exchange for like-kind property are excluded from the allocation rules. Property that is not like-kind property is subject to the allocation rules.

To figure the basis of property *received as a gift*, the adjusted basis to the donor must be known just before it was given to the recipient of the gift. Its FMV at the time it was given and the amount of the gift tax paid on it must also be known. If the FMV of the property was less than the donor's adjusted basis, the basis for depreciation, depletion, and amortization, and for gain on its sale or other disposition, is the same as the donor's adjusted basis. The basis for loss on its sale or other disposition is its FMV at the time the gift is received. If the donor's adjusted basis is used for figuring a gain and results in a loss, and then the FMV basis is used for figuring a loss that results in gain, there is neither gain nor loss on its sale or disposition.

Example: An acre of land is received as a gift. At the time of the gift, the acre had a FMV of $8,000. The donor's adjusted basis was $10,000. If the recipient later sells the property for $12,000, the gain is $2,000 because the donor's adjusted basis at the time of the gift was $10,000, which is used as the basis for reporting the gain. If the property is sold for $7,000, the recipient has a loss of $1,000 because the FMV of $8,000 at the time of the gift is used to report a loss.

If the sale price is between $8,000 and $10,000, the taxpayer has neither a gain or a loss. For instance, if the sale price was $9,000 and a gain was computed using the donor's adjusted basis of $10,000, there would be a loss of

$1,000. If a loss was computed using the FMV of $8,000, there would be a gain of $1,000.

PASSIVE ACTIVITY AND AT-RISK RULES

In applying the *Passive Activity and At-Risk Rules*, the at-risk rules must be applied before the passive activity rules. The following activities are subject to the at-risk rules:

1) Exploring for oil and gas as a trade or business or for the production of income.
2) Holding, producing, or distributing motion picture films or video tapes.
3) Farming.
4) Equipment leasing Section 1245, including personal property, and certain other tangible property that is depreciable or amortizable.
5) Exploring for geothermal deposits for wells started after September 1978.
6) Holding mineral property.
7) Holding real property placed in service after 1986.
8) Any other activity not included in 1) through 7) that is carried on as a trade or business or for the production of income.

If a closely held corporation is actively engaged in equipment leasing, the equipment leasing is treated as a separate activity not covered by the at-risk rules. A closely held corporation is actively engaged in equipment leasing if 50% or more of its gross receipts for the tax year are from equipment leasing. *Equipment leasing* means the leasing, purchasing, servicing, and selling of equipment that is Section 1245 property. Section 1245 property is any depreciable or amortizable property that is:

1) Personal property.
2) Other tangible property, other than a building or its structural components that is:
   a) used in manufacturing, production, or extraction or in furnishing transportation, communications, energy, water, or sewage disposal;
   b) a research facility used for the activities in a);
   c) a bulk storage facility used for the activities in a).
3) A single-purpose agricultural or horticultural structure.
4) A storage facility, other than a building or its structural components, used for the distribution of petroleum.

Real property is treated as a separate activity to which the at-risk limits apply after 1986. Personal property and services that are associated with making real property available as living accommodations are included in the activity of holding real property.

A qualified corporation is not subject to the at-risk limits for any qualifying business carried on by the corporation. Each qualifying business is treated as a separate activity. A qualified corporation is a closely held corporation that is *not* a personal holding company, a foreign personal holding company, or a personal service corporation. A qualifying business is any active business if *all* of the following apply:

1) During the entire 12-month period, the corporation had at least one full-time employee whose services were in the active management of the business, and three full-time nonowner employees whose services were directly related to the business. A nonowner employee does not own more than 5% in value of the outstanding stock of the corporation at any time during the tax year.

2) The business is not an *excluded business*. An excluded business involves the use, exploitation, sale, lease, or other disposition of tangible or intangible assets associated with literary, artistic, musical, or similar properties.

An individual is considered at risk in an activity to the extent of cash and the adjusted basis of other property contributed to the activity. An at-risk amount also includes a share of partnership net income that is not withdrawn and certain amounts borrowed for use in that activity.

Passive activity losses can be deducted only from passive activity income; any excess is carried forward to the following year or years until used or until the owner(s) disposes of an entire interest in the activity in a fully taxable transaction. Passive activity credits can be taken only from the tax on net passive income.

For the passive activity rules, a corporation is a *personal service corporation* if it meets *all* of the following requirements:

1) It is a corporation other than an S corporation.

2) Its principal activity during the testing period is performing personal services. The *testing period* for any tax year is the previous tax year. If the corporation has just been formed, the *testing period* begins on the first day of its tax year and ends on the earlier of the last day of the tax year, or the last day of the calendar year in which its tax year begins. The services in 2) must be substantially performed by the employee-owners.

3) The employee-owners own more than 10% of the fair market value of the outstanding stock on the last day of the testing period.

Personal services are those in the fields of health, law, engineering, architecture, accounting, actuarial science, performing arts, and consulting. A person is an employee-owner of a personal service corporation if he or she is an employee or performs personal services for or on behalf of the corporation as an independent contractor during any day of the testing period, and the person owns any stock in the corporation at any time during the testing period.

To determine passive losses, one or more trade or business activities or rental activities can be treated as a single activity if those activities form an *appropriate economic unit* for measuring gain or loss under the passive activity rules. To determine if more than one activity forms an appropriate economic unit, all the relevant facts and circumstances must be considered. The following factors have the greatest weight in determining whether activities are treated as an appropriate economic unit. (It is not necessary to have all the factors to treat more than one activity as a single activity.) The factors are:

1) The similarities and differences in types of business.
2) The extent of common control.
3) The extent of common ownership.
4) The geographical location.
5) The interdependencies between the activities.

Interdependencies between activities means the extent to which the activities purchase or sell goods among themselves, involve products or services that are generally provided together, have the same customers, have the same employees, use a single set of books and records to account for the activities.

There are two kinds of passive activities: 1) trade or business activities in which the taxpayer does not materially participate during the tax year, and 2) rental activities regardless of taxpayer participation. A *trade or business* activity is an activity that involves the conduct of a trade or business, is conducted in anticipation of starting a trade or business, involves research or experimental expenditures that are either deductible or capitalized.

A *rental activity* is a passive activity if tangible property, real or personal, is used by customers and the gross income from the activity represents amounts paid mainly for the use of the property.

The following are *not* passive activities:

1) Trade or business in which the taxpayer materially participated for the tax year.

2) A working interest in an oil or gas well.

3) The rental of a dwelling unit used as a residence.

4) An activity of trading personal property for the account of those who own interests in the activity.

5) Low-income housing activities. Losses from certain investments in low-income housing after 1983 are not treated as losses from a passive activity for a period up to seven years from the date of the original investment.

A trade or business activity is *not* a passive activity if an individual materially participates in the activity. Participation for a tax year in a trade or business activity is *material participation:*

1) If an individual participates in the activity more than 500 hours.

2) If an individual participated in the activity for any five of the ten preceding tax years, whether or not consecutive years.

3) If based on all the facts and circumstances, an individual participated in the activity on a regular, continuous, and substantial basis.

Losses from passive activities can offset only income from passive activities which *does not* include:

1) Income from activity that is not a passive activity.

2) Gain from the disposition of substantially appreciated property that had been used in a nonpassive activity.

3) Portfolio income that includes interest, dividends, annuities, and royalties not derived in the ordinary course of a trade or business.

4) Personal service income that includes salaried wages, commissions, self-employment income from trade or business activities in which the individual materially participated, deferred compensation, taxable Social Security and other retirement benefits, and payments from partnerships to partners for personal services.

5) Any income from intangible property if the taxpayer's personal efforts significantly contributed to the creation of the property.

Appendix A
Index to Journal Entries

SAMPLE JOURNAL ENTRIES

OPENING INVESTMENT — Sole Proprietorship:
[1]

Cash	5,000	
Building (fair value)	45,000	
A. Able, Net Worth		50,000

OPENING INVESTMENT — Partnership:
[2]

Cash	30,000	
Inventory	30,000	
B. Baker (50%), Capital		30,000
C. Charles (50%), Capital		30,000

PARTNERSHIP INVESTMENT — with Goodwill:
[3]

Building (fair value)	45,000	
Goodwill	15,000	
A. Able (50%), Capital		60,000

Able contributes building for
½ share of partnership.

PARTNERSHIP INVESTMENT — Skill, no funds:
[4]

A. Able, Capital	3,000	
B. Baker, Capital	3,000	
C. Charles, Capital	6,000	
D. Dog, Capital		12,000

Dog gets 10% of partnership
for the skill he'll contribute.
Ratios will now be:

Able	(25% less 10%)	22.5%
Baker	(same)	22.5%
Charles	(50% less 10%)	45.0%
Dog	(as granted)	10.0%
		100.0%

PARTNERSHIP INCORPORATES:
[5]

Cash	30,000	
Inventory — Raw Material	30,000	
Building (fair value)	45,000	
Capital Stock (par $10; 10,000		
shares issued; 100,000 auth.)		100,000
Additional Paid-in Capital		5,000

Shares issued: A. 2250; B. 2250;
C. 4500; D. 1,000. Note that
partnership goodwill is not carried
over to corporation.

CORPORATE INVESTMENT — with Goodwill:
[6]

Machinery & Equipment (fair value)	9,000	
Goodwill	1,000	
Capital Stock (1,000 shares)		10,000

Issuing 1,000 shares to E. Easy
@ $10 par for machinery contributed.

CORPORATION MONTHLY ENTRIES — The corporation

records all entries into the general ledger *through* summary entries
made in the general journal from the books and sources of original
entry:

[7] *Summary of Purchase Journal,* where all vendor invoices
are entered:

Purchases — Raw Material	10,000	
Shop Supplies	2,000	
Office Supplies	1,000	
Office Equipment	3,000	
Utilities	1,000	
Freight Out	2,000	
Advertising	1,000	
Accounts Payable		20,000

[8] *Summary of Cash Disbursement, Regular Cash A/C:*

Cash — Payroll A/C	13,000	
Petty Cash	200	
Accounts Payable	14,500	
Federal Tax Deposits Made	5,100	
Bank Charges	2	
Cash — Regular A/C		32,602
Cash Discounts Taken		200

[9] *Summary of Cash Disbursements, Payroll A/C:*

Direct Labor — Shop	12,500	
Indirect Labor — Shop	1.500	
Salaries — Sales Dept.	2,000	
Salaries — G & A	4,000	
Cash — Payroll A/C (net pay)		13,000
W/H Tax Pay — Federal		4,400
FICA Tax Withheld		1,200
SUI & Disability W/H		300
State Income Taxes W/H		600
Savings Bonds W/H		500

[10] *Summary of Sales Book:*

Accounts Receivable	35,000	
Sales Returns & Allowances	500	
Sales — Product L		18,000
Sales — Product M		16,600
Sales Taxes Payable		900

[11] *Summary of Cash Receipts Book:*

Cash — Regular A/C	30,500	
Cash Discounts Allowed	500	
Accounts Receivable		30,000
Machinery and Equipment		1,000

[12] *Summary of Petty Cash Box:*

Postage	40	
Entertainment	60	
Travel Expense	30	
Misc. Expense	20	
Petty Cash		150

[13] *General Journal Entries during month:*

Depreciation — M & E	10	
Machinery and Equipment	400	
Gain on Sale of Machinery		410

To correct entry from cash receipts:

Basis	$ 600	
Deprec.	10	(1/60th)
	590	
S.P.	1000	
Gain	$ 410	

[14]

Depr.— Bldg (1/40x45,000x1/12)	94	
Depr.— M&E (1/5 x 8,400x1/12)	140	
Depr.— OE (1/5 x 3,000x1/12)	50	
Amortization (1/40x1,000x1/12)	2	
Accum Depr.— Bldg		94
Accum Depr.— M&E		140
Accum Depr.— OE		50
Goodwill		2

[15]

Real Estate Taxes	300	
Accrued Taxes — RE		300

1/12th of estimated $3,600 for yr

[16]

Direct Labor (3125)	2,500	
Indirect Labor (375)	300	
Salaries — Selling (500)	400	
Salaries — G & A (1000)	800	
Accrued Salaries (5000)		4,000

To accrue 4/5 of last payroll in month.

[17]

W/H Tax Payable — Federal	3,300	
FICA Tax Withheld	900	
FICA Tax Expense — employer	900	
Federal Tax Deposits Made		5,100
FICA Tax Expense — employer	300	
SUI & DISAB Expense	600	
FUI Expense	100	
Accrued Taxes — Payroll		1,000

To zero deposit account against
withholding accounts and to book
employer FICA expense and estimated
unemployment tax for month.

[18]

Overhead	6,106	
Depr.— Bldg (60% of 94)		56
Depr.— M&E (all)		140
Indirect Labor (all)		1,800
Payroll Tax Exp (70% of 1900)		1,330
Shop supplies (all considered used)		2,000

Utilities (60% of 1000)		600
Taxes — RE (60% of 300)		180

To allocate expenses to overhead.
Taxes based on payroll proportion.
Other allocations based on space occupied.

[19]

Inventory — Raw Materials	(15,000)	
Inventory — Work in Process	none	
Inventory — Finished Goods	15,369	
Cost of Production — Inventory Change		369

To increase or (decrease) inventory
accounts to reflect new month-end
inventory as follows:

Raw Material:

Opening Inventory	$ 30,000
Purchases	10,000
Less used in production	(25,000)
Closing inventory	15,000
To adjust opening	$ (15,000)

Finished Goods:

Materials used (above)	$ 25,000
Direct labor costs	15,000
Overhead costs	6,106
3 units produced	46,106
1 unit unsold (⅓)	$ 15,369

(none at hand at beginning)
No work in process this month.

(The entries through here are all related with respect to the dollars shown. From here on,
they are independent with respect to each CAPITAL HEADING, but related within the
headed area.)

CUSTOMER'S CHECK BOUNCES
[20]

Accounts Receivable (Mr. A.)	100	
Cash (Disbursements)		100

To record bank charge for
Mr. A's check return — insufficient
funds.

[21]

Cash (Receipts)	100	
Accounts Receivable (Mr. A.)		100

For re-deposit of above, per
customer's instructions.

NOTES RECEIVABLE DISCOUNTED

[22]

Cash	9,900
Interest Expense	250

Notes receivable Discounted		10,000
Interest Income		150

For proceeds from customer note discounted,
due 90 days @ 6%, discount rate 10%.

[23]

Notes Receivable Discounted	10,000	
Notes Receivable		10,000

To offset. Customer note paid,
per bank notice.

FIRST-YEAR DEPRECIATION

[24]

Depreciation Expense — M & E	2,000	
Accumulated Depr — M & E		2,000

For maximum first-year depreciation
taken on 6/30 purchase of extruder.
See next entry for regular deprec.

[25]

Depreciation — M & E	400	
Accumulated Depr — M & E		400

To take straight-line on above:

Cost	$	10,000
Less 1st yr. Depr		(2,000)
S/L basis		8,000
Over 10 yrs — per yr	$	800
Six months this yr (no salvage value).	$	400

TAX LOSS CARRYBACK

[26]

FIT Refund and Interest Receivable	106,000	
Income Tax (Current Yr. Income Statement)		100,000
Interest Income		6,000

To set up receivable for carryback tax
refund due, plus interest.

SUBCHAPTER S EQUITY ENTRIES

End of Year 1:

[27]

Net income for Current Year	30,000	
Undistributed Earnings — Post-Election		30,000

To close year's net income into
new Sub-S undistributed earnings
Equity account.

[28]

Retained Earnings	55,000	
Retained Earnings — Pre-Election		55,000

To retitle opening retained earnings
account and keep it separate from
earnings after Sub-S election.

[29]

Post-Election Dividends	10,000	
Cash		10,000

For cash distributions made of current earnings. (NOTE: State law may require a *formal* declaration of a dividend for corporations. If this is true, and there is no such declaration, this must be treated as a *loan receivable* from stockholders.)

INSTALLMENT SALES METHOD

[30]

Accounts Receivable	1,000	
Cost of Installment Sale		700
Deferred Gross Profit on Installment Sales		300

For original sale. (GP% is 30%)

[31]

Cash	300	
Accounts Receivable		300

For payment on account.

[32]

Deferred Gross Profit on Installment Sales	90	
Realized Gross Profit		90

To amortize 30% of above collection
to realized income.

VOIDING YOUR OWN CHECK (Issued in a prior period)

[33]

Cash (Ck # 1601)	1,500	
Rent Expense		1,500

To void check #1601 (last month).
Check reported lost. Payment
stopped. Replaced with this month's
check #1752. (See CD book)

INVESTMENT TAX CREDIT — THE DEFERRAL METHOD

[34]

Taxes Payable	7,000	
Deferred Investment Tax Credits		7,000

To set up investment tax credit under
the deferred method. *Note:* The tax
expense for this year on the income
statement does *not* reflect the use
of this credit.

Year 2:

[35]

Deferred Investment Tax Credits	700	
Income Tax Expense		700

To amortize 1/10th, based on 10-year
life of asset to which applicable.

ACCUMULATED PREFERRED STOCK DIVIDENDS
[36]

Dividends (Income Statement)	30,000	
Dividends Payable (Liability)		30,000

To accrue this year's commitment,
6% of $500,000. *Note:* There was
no "only as earned" provision attached
to this issue.

DIVIDEND DECLARATION — COMMON STOCK
[37]

Retained Earnings	100,000	
Common Stock Extra Dividend		
Declared — (show in Equity Section)		100,000

To segregate common stock extra dividend
from accumulated earnings (until paid),
10¢ per share, 1,000,000 shares.

PAYMENT OF ABOVE TWO DIVIDENDS
[38]

Dividends Payable	30,000	
Common Stock Extra Dividend Declared	100,000	
Cash		130,000

For payment of dividends.

APPROPRIATION OF RETAINED EARNINGS
[39]

Retained Earnings	50,000	
Reserve Appropriation for Inventory		
Declines (Equity Section)		50,000

To set aside retained earnings for possible
inventory losses — per Board resolution.

[40]

Retained Earnings — (1/1 opening)	150,000	
Accounts Payable (XYZ Co.)		150,000

To record prior year billing error made
by supplier, XYZ Co., on invoice #____,
dated 12/10. Error not discovered by
XYZ until after closing of our books and
issuance of statements. Error is considered
material enough to treat as prior period
adjustment. Item was not in inventory
at 12/31.

STOCK DIVIDEND

    Usually:

[41]

Retained Earnings (at market)	45,000	
Common Stock (par $10, 3,000 shares)		30,000
Additional Paid-in Capital		15,000

For 3% stock dividend distributed on
100,000 shares — 3,000 shares issued.
Market value $15 at dividend date.

Sometimes:

[42]

Additional Paid-in Capital	30,000	
Common Stock (par $10, 3,000 shares)		30,000
For non-taxable distribution out of		
Paid-in Capital.		

SPLIT-UP EFFECTED IN THE FORM OF A STOCK DIVIDEND
[43]

Retained Earnings (at par)	1,000,000	
Common Stock (par $10, 100,000 shs)		1,000,000
For split in the form of a stock dividend		
(to conform with state law). One share		
issued for each share outstanding.		
100,000 shares at par of $10.		

STOCK SPLIT-UP
[44]

Common Stock (100,000 shares @ $10.)	memo	
Common Stock (200,000 shares @ $5.)		memo
Memo entry only. To record stock split-up		
by showing change in par value and in		
number of shares outstanding. One share		
issued for each outstanding. Par changed		
from $10 to $5.		

STOCK OPTIONS FOR EMPLOYEES AS COMPENSATION

PARTNERSHIP WITHDRAWALS
[45]

S. Stone, Withdrawals	15,000	
T. Times, Withdrawals	5,000	
Cash		20,000
For cash withdrawals.		

PARTNERSHIP PROFIT ENTRY
[46]

Net Income — P & L a/c	100,000	
S. Stone, Capital (50%)		50,000
T. Times, Capital (50%)		50,000
To split profit as follows:		
Per P & L closing account	$ 80,000	
Add back above included		
in P & L account	20,000	
Profit to distribute	$100,000	

[47]

S. Stone, Capital	15,000	
T. Times, Capital	5,000	
S. Stone, Withdrawals		15,000
T. Times, Withdrawals		5,000
To close withdrawal accounts		
to capital accounts.		

IMPUTED INTEREST (ON NOTES RECEIVABLE)

[48]

Notes Receivable (Supplier A — 6 yrs)	1,000,000	
Cash		1,000,000

For loan made to supplier. Received
non-interest bearing note, due 6 yrs.

[49]

Cost of Merchandise (from supplier A)	370,000	
Unamortized Discount on Notes Receiv.		370,000

To charge imputed interest of 8% on
above note, due in 6 years, to cost
of merchandise bought from A.

Year 2:

[50]

Unamortized Discount on Notes Receiv.	50,000	
Interest Income		50,000

To amortize this year's applicable
imputed interest on note.

BOND DISCOUNT, PREMIUM AND ISSUE COSTS

[51]

Cash	2,025,000	
Unamortized Bond Issue Costs	15,000	
Bonds Payable (8%, 10 yrs)		2,000,000
Unamortized Premium on Bonds		40,000

To set up face value of bonds, issue
costs and net cash proceeds received.

Year 2:

[52]

Unamortized Premium on Bonds	4,000*	
Unamortized Bond Issue Cost		1,500*
Interest Expense (difference)		2,500

To set up approximate amortization.
(*Should actually be based on present
values.)

[53]

Interest Expense	160,000	
Cash		160,000

To record actual payment of bond
interest. 8% of $2,000,000.

FEDERAL INCOME TAX — INTERIMS —
AND EXTRAORDINARY ITEM

[54]

Income Tax (on continuing operations)	350,000	
Extraordinary Loss (tax effect)		50,000
Taxes Payable		300,000

To set up FIT at end of First Quarter
based on full year's 50% rate and
to segregate tax applicable to
extraordinary item.

Statement should show:

Net from continuing operations	$700,000
Less FIT	(350,000)
	350,000
Extraordinary loss	
(net of $50,000 tax effect)	50,000
Net Income	$300,000

CAPITALIZING A LEASE (LESSEE)

At contracting:

[55]

Capitalized Leases	1,920,000	
Long-Term Lease Liability		3,600,000
Unamortized Discount on Lease		(1,680,000)

To capitalize lease of $25,000 per
month for 12 years @ 12% imputed
interest rate. Estimated life of asset
is 15 years. Present value used, since
fair value is higher at $2,000,000.

(Note: The two credit items shown are
netted and shown as *one net liability*
on the balance sheet. The liability
(at present value) should always equal
the asset value, also at present value.
Future lease payments are broken out,
effectively, into principal and interest.)

Month-end 1:

[56]

Long-Term Lease Liability	25,000	
Cash		25,000

First payment on lease.

[57]

Interest Expense	18,950	
Unamortized Discount on Lease		18,950

For one month's interest.
1% of $3,600,000 less $1,680,000,
less initial payment on signing of
contract of $25,000 *(entry not shown)* or
$1,895,000.

[58]

Depreciation Expense	10,667	
Accumulated Depr of Capitalized Lease		10,667

One month:
$1,920,000 x 1/5 x 1/12

CASH SURRENDER VALUE — OFFICER LIFE INSURANCE

[59]

Officer Life Insurance — expense	1,500	
Cash		1,500

For payment of premium. *Note:* Expense

is not deductible for tax purpose and
is a *permanent* difference.

[60]

Cash Surrender Value-Officer Life Ins.	1,045	
Officer Life Ins. expense		1,045
To reflect increase in C.S.V. for year		

[61]

Cash	5,000	
Loans Against Officer Life Insurance		5,000
(Displayed against the asset "C.S.V.")		
To record loan against life policy. No intent		
to repay within the next year.		

STANDARD COST VARIANCES

[62]

Purchases — Raw Mat (at stand)	200	
Accounts Payable — actual		188
Variance — material price		12

[63]

Direct Labor — at standard	50	
Variance — Direct Labor rate	10	
Payroll — actual direct labor		58
Variance — Labor Time		2

[64]

Overhead — at Standard	75	
Variance — overhead	15	
Overhead itemized actual accounts		90

Adjusting Inventories:

[65]

Inventory — Raw Materials at standard	100	
Finished Goods — at standard	75	
Cost of Production — at standard		175
To adjust inventory accounts to reflect		
end-of-month on-hand figures at standards.		

[66]

Variance — material price	xx	
Variance — labor time	xx	
Variance — direct labor rate		xx
Variance — overhead		xx
Contra Inventory Asset a/c (variances		
to offset standard and reflect cost)		xx

To pull out of variance accounts that
portion which is applicable to inventory,
in order to keep an isolated contra account,
which in offset to the "standard" asset
account, reflects approximate cost.
The portion is based on an overall ratio
of variances to production and inventory
figures (at standard). (If normal, apply
to cost of sales for interims.)

ADJUSTING INVENTORY FOR SAMPLING RESULTS

[67]

Cost of Sales	50,000	

Inventory		50,000

To reduce inventory by $50,000 based
on sampling results:

Inventory per computer run	$ 1,000,000	
Estimated calculated		
inventory per sample	950,000	
Reduction this year	$ 50,000	

Year 2:

[68]

Inventory	10,000	
Cost of Sales		10,000

To adjust inventory to actual
based on actual physical count
of entire inventory. Last year-end
sample error proved to be 4%,
not 5%.

ADJUSTING CLOSING INVENTORY FROM CLIENT'S STANDARD COST TO
AUDITOR'S DETERMINED (AND CLIENT AGREED) ACTUAL COST, AND TO
REFLECT PHYSICAL INVENTORY VS. BOOK INVENTORY DIFFERENCES

[69]

Inventory — Finished Goods (Standard)	25,000	
Cost of Sales		25,000

To adjust general ledger inventory
(at standard) to actual physical
inventory count, priced out at
standard. Actual is $25,000 more.

[70]

Cost of Sales	80,000	
Inventory — Finished Goods		
(Asset Contra Cost account)		80,000

To set up a contra account reducing
asset account, which is at standard
costs, effectively to audited actual
cost or market, whichever lower.

Year 2: (End of Year)

[71]

Inventory — Finished Goods (Asset		
Contra Cost account)	50,000	
Cost of Sales		50,000

To reduce the contra account to
the new year-end difference between
the "standard" asset account and the
actual cost determined for this new
year-end inventory.

PARTNERSHIP DISSOLUTION:

Balance Sheet

Cash	$ 20,000	
Assets other	35,000	

Liabilities	(25,000)	
A Capital (50%)	(20,000)	
B Capital (30%)	(14,000)	
C Capital (20%)	4,000	
	-0-	

[72]

Cash	15,000	
Assets other		15,000

For sale of some assets at book value.

[73]

A Capital (⅝)	2,500	
B Capital (⅜)	1,500	
C Capital		4,000

C cannot put in his overdraw —
to apportion his deficit.

[74]

Liabilities	25,000	
Cash		25,000

To pay liabilities

[75]

Cash	10,000	
Loss on Sale of Assets other	10,000	
Assets other		20,000
A Capital (⅝)	6,250	
B Capital (⅜)	3,750	
Loss on Sale of Assets other		10,000

Selling remaining assets and apportioning loss

[76]

A Capital (remaining balance)	11,250	
B Capital (remaining balance)	8,750	
Cash		20,000

To distribute remaining cash
and zero capital accounts.

NOTE THE SHARING OF C'S DEFICIT
AND OF THE LOSS ON ASSET SALE
BEFORE DISTRIBUTING REMAINING
CASH.

MARKETABLE SECURITIES

Shown as Current Assets:

[77]

Unrealized Loss — to P & L	1,500	
Valuation Allowance — Current		1,500

To write down 100 U.S. Steel:

Cost 1/1	$10,000	
Market 12/31	8,500	
Unrealized Loss	$ 1,500	

Year 2:

[78]

Cash	4,500	
Realized Loss — P & L	500	

Marketable Securities — Current   5,000

Sold 50 @ 90	$ 4,500	
Cost 50 @ 90	5,000	
Realized Loss	$ 500	

[79]

Valuation Allowance — Current   1,250

Valuation Adjustment — Current (P&L Gain)   1,250*

To adjust valuation allowance a/c
(current) for remaining securities
left in portfolio:

50 US Steel — cost 100	$ 5,000	
Market, this year end — 95	4,750	
Bal. should be	250 Cr.	
Balance in valuation a/c	1,500 Cr.	
Debit valuation a/c	$ 1,250 Dr.	

*Note: Unrealized *gains* are called
"valuation adjustments." Unrealized
losses are called "unrealized losses."

Shown as Noncurrent Asset:

[80]

Unrealized Noncurrent Loss (Equity section)   1,000

Valuation Allowance — Noncurrent   1,000

To write down 100 shares GM
from cost of 60 to market
value at 12/31 of 50.

Year 2:

[81]

Cash	2,900	
Realized Loss — P & L	100	
Marketable Securities — Noncurrent		3,000

Sold 50 GM @ 58	$ 2,900	
Cost 50 GM @ 60	3,000	
Realized loss	$ 100	

[82]

Valuation Allowance — Noncurrent   1,000

Unrealized Noncurrent Loss (Equity Section)   1,000

To adjust valuation allowance a/c
(Noncurrent) as follows:

Cost 50 GM @ 60	$ 3,000	
Market now @ 65	N/A	
(Higher than cost)		
Valuation a/c should be	-0-	
(Because market is higher		
than cost)		
Balance in valuation a/c	1,000 Cr.	
Debit to correct	$ 1,000 Dr.	

TREASURY STOCK

Purchase of:

[83]

Treasury Stock — at Cost	125,000	
Cash		125,000

Purchase of 1,000 shares @ 125
market. Par value $50.
No intent to cancel the stock.

Sale of:

[84]

Cash	140,000	
Treasury Stock — at Cost		125,000
Additional Paid — in Capital		15,000

For sale of treasury stock @ 140.

APPRAISAL WRITE-UPS
[85]

Building	350,000	
Appraisal Capital (Equity Section)		350,000

To raise building from cost of $400,000 to
appraised value of $750,000 per require-
ment of the lending institution.

Year 2:
[86]

Depreciation — Building	21,667	
Accumulated Depreciation — Building		21,667

To depreciate based on appraised value:
(400,000 for 40 years; 350,000 for 30 yrs)
Building was 10 years old at appraisal.

FOREIGN CURRENCY EXCHANGE
[87]

Unrealized Loss (balance sheet)	10,000	
Accts Payable — Foreign		10,000

To adjust liabilities payable in
Swiss Francs to US Dollars at 12/31:

Exchange rate at 12/31 .40	$40,000
Booked at (100,000 frs) .30	30,000
More dollars owed	$10,000

[88]

Deferred Taxes	5,000*	
Unrealized Loss		5,000*

To show deferred tax effect (50% rate
times $10,000 above)
*Less Foreign or Domestic Dividend
Credits, if Applicable

Year 2:
[89]

Accounts Payable — Foreign	20,000	
Cash		19,000
Realized gain (Books, not Tax)		1,000

For payment of 50,000 Swiss Francs at exchange rate of .38

[90]

Accounts Payable — Foreign	500	
Balance Sheet		500

To restate liability at year-end:

50,000 Frs @ .39	$ 19,500	
Booked to last yr.	20,000	
(Gain)	$ (500)	

[91]

Taxes Payable	2,000	
Income Tax Expense	500	
Deferred Taxes		2,500

To transfer to actual taxes payable (from
deferred) that portion applying to the payment of $19,000. Original debt in dollars
was $15,000. 50% tax rate on $4,000 or
$2,000, plus $500 — to offset 2,500
booked to last 12/31.

[92]

| Income Tax Expenses | 250 | |
| Deferred Taxes | | 250 |

To adjust deferred taxes to equal ½ of
4,500 (19,500 liability now, less original
liability of 15,000) for $2,250 tax deferral.

THE EQUITY METHOD
[93]

| Investment — Oleo Co. | 275,000 | |
| Cash | | 275,000 |

Purchase of 25% of Oleo's stock,
at cost (25,000 shares @ $11).

[94]

| Investment — Oleo Co. | 40,000 | |
| Deferred Good Will in Oleo | | 40,000 |

To set up additional underlying equity in
Oleo Co. at date of acquisition — to
write-off over 40 years.

[95]

| Cash | 5,000 | |
| Investment — Oleo Co. | | 5,000 |

For receipt of 20¢ per share cash dividend
from Oleo.

[96]

Investment — Oleo Co.	27,500	
Income from Equity Share of Undistributed Earnings of Oleo continuing operations		25,000
Income from Equity Share of Undistributed Extraordinary Item of Oleo		2,500

To pick up 25% of the following
reported Oleo annual figures:

Net income after taxes, but before Extraordinary item	$100,000
Extraordinary Income (net)	10,000
Total net income reported	$110,000

[97]

| Income Tax Expense — Regular | 12,500* |
| Income Tax Expense — Extra Item | 1,250* |

Deferred Taxes   13,750*
To set up 50% of above income as accrued
taxes. Expectation is that Oleo will
continue paying dividends.

*Dividend Tax Credit, if any, should reduce
these Amounts

[98]

Deferred Taxes   2,500*
   Income Taxes Payable   2,500*
To set up actual liability for tax on cash
dividends received.

*Dividend Tax Credit, if any, should reduce
these Amounts

CONSOLIDATION

Trial Balances
Now-at
*12/31-*End of Year

	A Co.	B Co.	Fair Value Excess at Acquisition
Cash	10,000	6,000	
A/R	20,000	10,000	
Inventory	30,000	5,000	
Equip	50,000	30,000	5,000
Investment Cost	40,000		
Liabilities	(30,000)	(5,000)	(1,000)
Common Stock	(20,000)	(10,000)*	
Retained Earnings	(50,000)	(20,000)*	
Sales	(80,000)	(40,000)	
Costs of Sale	20,000	14,000	
Expenses	10,000	10,000	
	-0-	-0-	
	(Parent)	(Sub)	

*Unchanged from opening balances.

At year-end there were $5,000 intercompany receivables/payables. The parent had sold $5,000 worth of product to the subsidiary. The inventory of the subsidiary was $1,000 over the parent's cost.

Consolidating
Entries:

[99]

Excess Paid over Book Value   10,000
   Investment Cost   10,000

To reduce investment cost to that of the
subsidiary's equity at time of purchase (unchanged at 12/31).

[100]

Equipment	5,000	
Liabilities		1,000
Excess Paid over Book Value		4,000

To reflect fair value corrections at time of
consolidation for the combination of current year-end trial balances.

[101]

B Co. Equity	30,000	
Investment Cost		30,000
Sales	5,000	
Costs of Sale		5,000
Costs of Sale	1,000	
Inventory		1,000
Liabilities	5,000	
Accounts Receivable		5,000
Excess paid over book value (expense)	150	
Goodwill		150

To eliminate intercompany dealings, debt,
investment, and to amortize goodwill.

Consolidated figures will then be:

Cash	16,000	
A/R	25,000	
Inventories	34,000	
Equipment	85,000	
Investment cost	—	
Goodwill	5,850	
Liabilities	(31,000)	
Common Stock	(20,000)	(Opening)
Ret. Earnings	(50,000)	(Opening)
Sales	(115,000)	
Cost of sales	30,000	
Expenses	20,150	
	-0-	

The year's consolidated net income (before
provision for income taxes) is $64,850.

PURCHASE METHOD OF BUSINESS COMBINATION

[102]

Accounts Receivable (present value)	50,000	
Inventory (current cost or market, lowest)	40,000	
Building (fair value)	110,000	
Equipment (fair value)	30,000	
Investments, non-current securities-market	5,000	
Goodwill	16,200	
Accounts Payable — (present value)		25,000
Long-term Debt — (face value)		30,000
Unamortized discount on long-term debt		

(to reflect present value)		(3,800)
Common Stock (Par $10; 10,000 shares)		100,000
Additional Paid-in Capital		100,000

To reflect, by the purchase method, the purchase of Diablo Company assets and liabilities for 10,000 shares of common stock; total purchase price of contract $200,000 based on market price of stock at date of consummation of $20 per share (1/1).

[103]

Amortization of Goodwill (1/40)	405	
Goodwill		405
Unamortized discount on long-term debt	760	
Discount Income (approx 1/5th)		760*

To amortize pertinent Diablo items, first yearend. Goodwill on straight-line basis — 40 years. *Should be calculated present value computation.

POOLING METHOD OF BUSINESS COMBINATION
[104]

Inventory	43,000	
Cash	5,000	
Accounts Receivable	60,000	
Reserve for Doubtful Accounts		7,000
Building	75,000	
Accumulated Depreciation — Building		15,000
Equipment	100,000	
Accumulated Depreciation — Building		60,000
Investments — non-current securities	4,000	
Accounts Payable		25,500
Long-Term Debt		30,000
Common Stock (10,000 shs @ par $10)		100,000
Additional Paid-in Capital		49,500

To reflect the pooling of Diablo items, per *their book value* on date of consummation.

FUND ACCOUNTING

Initial transactions:

[105]

Cash	100,000	
Dues Income		100,000

For initial membership dues received.

[106]

Building	50,000	
Mortgage Payable		40,000
Cash		10,000

Purchase of building for cash and mortgage.

[107]

Interest Expense	2,400	
Mortgage Payable	2,000	

Cash		4,400

For first payment on mortgage.

[108]

Net income (100,000 less 2,400)	97,600	
Current Fund Balance		97,600

To close year's income

[109]

Mortgage Payable	38,000	
Current Fund Balance	12,000	
Building		50,000

To transfer building and mortgage to plant fund.

Plant Fund Entry:

[110]

Building	50,000	
Mortgage Payable		38,000
Plant Fund Balance		12,000

To set up building in plant fund.

Note that interest expense is to be
borne by the current fund every year
as a current operating expense used
in the calculation of required dues
from members. Also, the principal
sum-payments against mortgage are
to come out of current fund assets,
with no interfund debt to be set up,
until such time as a special drive is
held for plant fund donations for improvements and expansion.

MUNICIPAL ACCOUNTING — CURRENT
OPERATING FUND

To book the budget:

[111]

Estimated Revenues	600,000	
Appropriations		590,000
Fund Balance		10,000

Actual year's transactions:

[112]

Encumbrances	575,000	
Reserve for Encumbrances		575,000

To enter contracts and purchase orders issued.

[113]

Expenditures — itemized (not here)	515,000	
Vouchers Payable		515,000
Reserve for Encumbrances	503,000	
Encumbrances		503,000

To enter actual invoices for deliveries received and service contracts performed and
to reverse applicable encumbrances.

[114]

Taxes Receivable — Current	570,000	
Revenues		541,500
Estimated Current Uncollectible Taxes		28,500

To enter actual tax levy and to estimate uncollectibles at 5%.

[115]

Cash	55,000	
Revenues		55,000

For cash received from licenses, fees,
fines and other sources.

[116]

Cash	549,500	
Estimated Current Uncollectible Taxes	8,000	
Taxes Receivable		549,500
Revenues		8,000

For actual taxes collected for this year.

To close out budget accounts:

[117]

Revenues	604,500	
Appropriations	590,000	
Estimated Revenue		600,000
Expenditures		515,000
Encumbrances		72,000
Fund Balance		7,500

To zero budget accounts and adjust
fund balance.

DISCS — DEEMED DISTRIBUTIONS (Parent's Books)

1975 — under old law

[118]

DISC Dividends Receivable (previously taxed)	110,000	
Deemed Distribution from DISC (income)		110,000

To pick up ½ of DISC's net of $220,000.

1976 — under the new law.

[119]

DISC Dividends Receivable (previously taxed)	189,375	
Deemed Distribution from DISC (income)		189,375

As follows:

Facts:

Gross export receipts average for 1972-1975	$1,100,000
Gross export receipts - 1976	$1,300,000
Net DISC income - 1976 only	$ 250,000

Since the 1976 net income is over
$150,000, the graduated relief in the 1976
law does not apply, and the calculation is:

67% of 1,100,000 = 670,000

670,000 ÷ 1,300,000 = 51.5%

51.5% × 250,000 = $ 128,750

250,000 − 128,750 = 121,250

121,250 × 50% =   60,625

Total Deemed Distribution $ 189,375

[120]

Capitalization of Interest Costs
Qualifying Asset   10,000
    Accrued Interest   10,000

[121]

Employee Compensation   50,000
    Accrued Vacation   50,000

Appendix B

The Going Concern Concept

The concept that financial statements are prepared on the basis of a "going concern" is one of the basics relating to financial accounting. There is an underlying presumption in the standards set for financial accounting that a business, once started, will continue functioning and operating. For example, the use of historical costs for building and property, which are currently more valuable, presupposes that the *use* of that property will generate more advantages than would present disposition. Deferrals to future periods through systematic allocations also indicate a presumption of longevity.

This presumption of continuance as a going concern is never stated by the independent auditor—never worded in his or her own opinion. On the *contrary*, it is when there appears to be danger of the firm's *not* being able to continue as a going concern that the auditor makes the assertion that "the statements have been prepared on the basis of a going concern," and that he or she is *unable* to express an opinion because of major uncertainties, then described. Therefore, the actual use of the terminology, "going concern," in the auditor's opinion indicates trouble.

Two types of problems may dictate against an entity's continuation as a going concern:

1) Operational uncertainties which may present two different types of situations giving cause for concern:
   a) Progressive deterioration of a firm's financial stability resulting from changing markets, outmoded or inefficient plant and facilities, inept management. This, in turn, leads to declining earnings or actual loss-

es, reduced cash balances and eventually an inability to meet current liabilities. Such uncertainties may result in gradual deterioration or, less frequently, in a very sudden turnaround of a previously profitable firm.

b) A start-up business that may never get off the ground. This is the enterprise that begins with high hopes but has not yet met with success nor achieved a solid financial footing. In the event of even a minor setback at this juncture, the firm's continuation may be open to question particularly in relation to the liquidity of its assets. What assets it has are probably tied up in inventories, specialized plant and equipment and deferred charges.

2) External difficulties beyond the control of an entity. These may be as a result of governmental controls, natural disasters such as earthquakes or floods, mandatory product recalls or devastating lawsuits. Any of these or other potential catastrophes could drain an entity beyond its financial capacity to recover.

Following is a random listing of factors which could be indicative of *possible* failure to continue as a going concern:

1) Inability to satisfy obligations on due dates.
2) Inability to perform contractual obligations.
3) Inability to meet substantial loan covenants.
4) A substantial deficit.
5) A series of continued losses.
6) The presence of major contingencies which could lead to heavy losses.
7) Catastrophes which have rendered the business inoperable.
8) Negative cash flows from operations.
9) Adverse key financial ratios.
10) Denial of usual trade credit from suppliers.
11) Necessity of finding new sources of financing.
12) Loss of key personnel.
13) Loss of a principal customer.
14) Work stoppage and labor disputes.

Appendix C
Goodwill

Goodwill is intangible property that represents the advantage or benefits acquired in a business in excess of the value of other certain assets. It does not have a specific name, but it can be associated with a particular area where business is transacted, with a list of customers, or with other elements of value in a business as a going concern. The basis of goodwill usually is its cost, if it is bought. However, if a going business is bought with the intent to continue the business, goodwill can be included in the price. Goodwill can be internally generated as a result of earnings, or it can be purchased as part of the cost of acquiring a group of assets, such as a business combination.

Goodwill can be related to future expected profits. For accounting and tax purposes, there are no uniform accepted rules for the determination of goodwill or for its valuation thereafter. The circumstances and history of the business must be considered. The taxpayer has the right to value the goodwill, if any, under the methods and accounting and tax rules which have been generally accepted for a valuation of goodwill. Expert opinions will be given consideration and weight in the determination of whether goodwill exists and the value thereof. The opinion, however, must be by qualified persons whose qualifications are proved before they testify and whose reasoning is sound and logical, based upon the facts at the time, and founded on actual knowledge of the situation or the property involved.

Goodwill is not necessarily the difference between cost and the book value of an investment, unless the book value is equal to the fair value of the underlying assets. The underlying assets represented by an investment must be individually assigned a fair value at the date of acquisition, and if the assigned fair value is less than the amount of the investment, the difference is goodwill. If after assigning values to the underlying assets of an investment there is resulting goodwill, it must be amortized over a period of 40 years or less, starting from the date of the acquisition of the investment. Goodwill is amortized by the straight-line method.

In cases where the values assigned to the net assets exceed the cost, the result is *negative goodwill*. Excess of net assets over negative goodwill is not recorded in the financial statements unless all the identifiable noncurrent assets (excluding long-term investments in marketable securities) have been reduced to zero.

Goodwill is not necessarily the difference between cost and the book value of an investment, unless the book value is equal to the fair value of the underlying assets. The underlying assets represented by an investment must be individually assigned a fair value at the date of acquisition, and if the assigned values are less than the amount of the investment, the difference is goodwill.

Appendix D
Guidelines for Interim Reporting

Guidelines for interim reporting by publicly traded companies have been established by the AICPA (and the SEC). For those private companies which do not bear the same responsibility for full and adequate disclosure to public shareholders, the guideline for public disclosure should be studied and followed, where feasible and relevant, for possible selfprotection against insurgent parties, since adherence to standards would probably be more defensible than nonadherence.

Following are the standards for determining applicable information and the appropriate guidelines for minimum disclosure:

1) Results should be based on the same principles and practices used for the latest annual statements (subject to the modifications below).
2) Revenue should be recognized as earned for the interim on the same basis as for the full year. Losses should be recognized as incurred or when becoming evident.
3) Costs may be classified as:
   a) Those associated with revenue (cost of goods sold);
   b) All other costs expenses based on:
      1) Those actually incurred, or
      2) Those allocated, based on: time expired, or benefits received, or other period activity.
4) Costs or losses (including extraordinary times) should not be deferred or apportioned unless they would be at year end. Advertised costs may be apportioned in relation to sales for interims.

5) With respect to inventory and cost of sales:

   a) LIFO basis should not be liquidated if expected to be replaced later, but should be based on expected replacement factor;

   b) Inventory losses should not be deferred because of cost or market rule; and conversely, later periods should then reflect gains on market price recoveries. Inventory losses should be reflected if resulting from permanent declines in market value in the interim period in which they occur; recoveries of such losses would be gains in a later interim period. If a change in inventory value is temporary, no recognition is given.

   c) With standard costs, variances which are expected to be absorbed by year end should be deferred for the interim, not expensed. Unplanned purchase price or volume variance, not expected to turn around, is to be absorbed during the period;

   d) The estimated gross profit method may be used, but must be disclosed.

6) The seasonal nature of activities should be disclosed, preferably including additional 12-month-to-date information with prior comparative figures.

7) Income taxes:

   a) Effective yearly tax rate (including year-end applicable tax-planned advantages) should be applied to interim taxable income;

   b) Extraordinary items applicable to the interim period should be shown separately net of applicable tax and the effect of the tax not applied to the tax on ordinary net income.

8) Extraordinary and unusual items including the effects of segment disposals should be disclosed separately, net of tax, for the interim period in which they occur, and they should not be apportioned over the year.

9) Contingencies should be disclosed the same as for the annual report.

10) Changes in accounting practices or principles from those allowed in prior periods should be disclosed and, where possible, those changes should be made in the first period of the year.

11) Retroactive restatement and/or prior period adjustments are required under the same rules applying to annual statements.

12) The effect of a change in an accounting estimate, including a change in the estimated effective annual tax rate, should be accounted for in the period in which the change in estimate is made. No restatement of previously reported interim information should be made for changes in estimates, but the effect on earnings of a change in estimate made in a cur-

rent interim period should be reported in the current and subsequent interim periods, if material in relation to any period presented, and should continue to be reported in interim financial information of the subsequent year, for as many periods as necessary to avoid misleading comparisons.

MINIMUM DATA TO BE REPORTED ON INTERIM STATEMENTS :

1) Sales or gross revenues, provisions for income taxes, extraordinary items (including related tax), cumulative effect of changes in accounting principles or practices, and net income;
2) Primary and fully diluted earnings per share data for each period presented;
3) Seasonal revenue, costs and expenses;
4) Disposal of business segments and extraordinary items, as well as unusual or infrequent items;
5) Contingencies;
6) Changes in estimates, changes in accounting principles or practices;
7) Significant changes in balance sheet items;
8) Significant changes in tax provisions;
9) Current year-to-date, or the last 12 months, with comparative data for prior periods;
10) In the absence of a separate fourth-quarter report, special fourth-quarter adjustments and extraordinary, infrequent or unusual items which occurred during that fourth quarter should be disclosed in a note to the annual financial statement;
11) Though not required, condensed balance sheet data and funds flow data are suggested to provide better understanding of the interim report.
12) If a fourth quarter is not presented, any material adjustment to that quarter must be commented upon in the annual report.

Interim reports are usually prepared by management and issued with that clear stipulation.

Accounting firms which issue reports for interim periods are to be guided by auditing standards set for "Reports on a Limited Review of Interim Financial Information" in Section 722 of Statements on Auditing Standards, April, 1981.

ACCOUNTING CHANGES IN INTERIM STATEMENTS

FASB 3, *Reporting Accounting Changes in Interim Financial Statements* amended APB Opinion No. 28, *Interim Financial Reporting* with respect to reporting an accounting change in interim financial reports that have a *cumulative effect*.

The following disclosures of accounting changes that have cumulative effects on income from continuing operations, net income, and related per share amounts for the interim period in which the change is made must be included in interim reports:

1) In the interim period in which the new accounting principle is adopted, disclosure should explain the nature and justification for the change.

2) Disclosure should be made of the effect of the change in the interim period in which the change is made.

3) The effect of the change for each pre-change interim period of that fiscal year should be disclosed.

4) The cumulative effect of the change should be shown on retained earnings at the beginning of that fiscal year, if the change is made in other than the first interim period of the company's fiscal year.

5) In the interim period in which a change is made, disclosure must include amounts computed on a *pro forma* basis for the interim period in which the change is made and for any interim periods of prior fiscal years for which financial information is being presented.

6) In financial reports for a subsequent interim period of the fiscal year in which a new principle is adopted, disclosure must include the effect of the change on income from continuing operations, net income, and related per share amounts for the post-change interim period.

Appendix E
Segment Reporting

As a result primarily of the conglomerate movement, which is essentially an approach to corporate diversification, the users of financial statements (particularly financial analysts) needed more detailed information about the financial condition of affiliated companies underlying consolidated reports, as well as about business activities in foreign countries. Accordingly, in 1976 the FASB issued Statement No. 14, *Financial Reporting for Segments of a Business Enterprise.* The purpose of the Statement is to provide revenue and income data and additional significant information about the individual subsidiaries, divisions, and affiliates which contribute to the total income reported on the consolidated statements.

(FASB 14 has also since been amended by FASBs 18, 21, 24, 30.)

It should be noted that FASB 21 eliminates the original requirement that *all* companies, large and small, nonpublic or public, must disclose segment information. Now only publicly-held corporations are required to comply with FASB 14.

The following are the essential requirements for reporting by segments. (Any user of this book who may have to comply with the segment rules should have access to the above Statements, as they are technically complex rules and long in substance.)

1) Segment information (termed "disaggregated information") must be disclosed using the same accounting principles as those applied to the consolidated statements.

676

2) The revenues, operating gains (or losses), and identifiable assets of each segment (or related segments) must be reconciled to the consolidated statements.
3) Depreciation, depletion, and amortization expense must be reported by segment.
4) Capital expenditures must be disclosed by segment.
5) Transactions between segments must be included in segment information, even though eliminated in the preparation of consolidated statements.
6) The effect on operating profits of a segment resulting from a change in an accounting principle must be disclosed.
7) When prior information about a segment is reported in the *current* period, the *prior* period information must be retroactively restated.

What is a segment?   A segment must be determined by management; it is a judgment decision. The FASB *suggests* three broad factors to be considered in identifying a segment:

1) The type of product or service. Principally, this means products that are similar in character with reasonably comparable rates of profitably.
2) The production process, which means products or services that share the same production facilities, sales efforts, equipment and labor.
3) Markets and/or marketing policies and methods, which mean similar geographic markets, types of customers, and other marketing factors common to the enterprise's products or services.

The Statement suggests the following quantitative guidelines for disclosure:

1) If the revenue generated by a segment (or related segments) is 10 percent or more of the enterprise's total revenue, the product or service should be considered a segment.
2) The operating profit (or loss) is 10 percent or more of the greater of
   a) the combined operating profit of all the segments in the enterprise that *did not* have an operating loss, or
   b) the operating loss of all industry segments that *did* have an operating loss. (Operating profit, or loss, excludes general corporate revenue, expenses, interest expense, and income taxes.)

3) The identifiable assets of a segment (or related segments) are 10 percent or more of the combined identifiable assets of all of the enterprise's segments.

There is an additional percentage to be applied; i.e., the segmented results must be 75 percent or more of the combined sales of the enterprise to unaffiliated customers. This requirement prevents a company from reporting on only a few segments and combining the results of a large number of segments, defeating the objective of Statement 14. However, the FASB recognized there should be a reasonable limit to the number of segments that should be reported to avoid what might result in excessive accounting costs. The Statement suggests a guideline limit of 10 reportable segments (or a few more if necessary to comply with the 75 percent test).

The statement sets forth three broad bases for reporting segmented results:

1) service or product line in different industries,
2) foreign operations and export sales by absolute amounts and significant geographic areas
3) major customers' classifications.

Additional reporting requirements include:

1) Foreign operating income, revenues and identifiable assets are reported when sales of this type which are 10 percent or more of consolidated revenues, or identifiable assets are 10 percent or more of the total assets of the business.
2) Export sales must be reported when a company gets 10 percent or more of its revenues from sales from this source.
3) A "major" customer is one that accounts for 10 percent or more of a company's total sales and requires separate disclosure.

Segment Presentation

Segment information can be included in the financial statements in any of the following ways:

1) Included directly in the statements with explanatory footnotes.
2) All of the information can be presented in footnotes.
3) The information can be disclosed in separate schedules.

Appendix F
Rule of 78s

APPLICATION TO INSTALLMENT LOAN TRANSACTION

The Rule of 78s can be used to account for realized interest income on certain types of loan transactions. It is also used by retail merchants who sell on an installment basis. The Rule is a computational procedure used to determine the portion of precomputed income charges earned as of a particular date over the life of an installment loan transaction. It is also used to compute interest rebates on installment loans paid in full prior to maturity. Further, it is applied to transactions where interest is computed on the basis of an Add-On rate, where such a rate is equivalent to the stated rate per dollar amount of the loan per number of years the loan will be outstanding, e.g., 12% per $100 per year. When Add-On is used, the interest is charged as if the loan were to be repaid in one lump sum on the maturity date, even though it will actually be systematically amortized over the life of the loan. However, a deficiency exists with respect to recognizing revenue since an Add-On rate, *per se*, gives no consideration to the principal amount outstanding at various points over the course of the loan. To overcome this deficiency, the Rule of 78s is employed to account systematically for the interest earnings.

An explanation of the basic concepts and operational procedures for the Rule of 78s shows that it has wide application, and is a valid approach to recording interest revenue as long as certain guidelines are observed.

Even though revenue is usually considered a flow process in accounting, revenue can also be realized by permitting others to use certain resources. A case in point is the interest which accrues over a period of time in a lending transaction. For banks and other lending institutions, as well as those retail outlets that customarily deal in extended credit, interest on installment loans may well constitute an important source of current income. Such income must be accounted for in an approved manner. In the case of some savings institutions, this may be the main source of current income, and in the case of retail outlets, it may make the difference between operating at a break-even point or making a profit.

Explanation of the Concept. The Rule of 78s involves the following two steps:

1) Determination or computation of the appropriate income factor.
2) Multiplication of this factor by the loan's total precomputed interest charge to yield the dollar amount of realized income.

The factor takes the form of a fraction and ranges between a value greater than zero but less than one. To compute the correct value, separate steps must be taken to determine the denominator and the numerator of the fraction. The denominator is equal to the sum of the values of the number of months in the original term of the loan where the first month carries a value of one, through the last month which carries a value equal to the number of months in the original term of the loan. For example, with a 12-month loan, the denominator would equal the number which gives its name to the Rule:

$$1+2+3+4...+11+12 = 78.$$

The numerator of the factor is arrived at by determining the sum of the values of the number of months that the loan has been outstanding beginning with the highest value for the series, where this value equals the number of months in the original term of the loan, plus the next highest value for each additional month the loan has been outstanding.

For example, with an 18-month loan that has been outstanding for 12 months, the numerator equals:

$$18+17+16+....+9+8+7 = 150$$

and the realized income factor equals:

$$\frac{18+17+16+...+9+8+7}{1+2+3...+16+17+18} = \frac{150}{171} = 87.72\%$$

The figure of 87.72 represents the percent of total precomputed interest charges earned by the twelfth month of an 18-month loan. The percentage figure will change according to the length of the loan and the number of months that have expired. However, the factor itself is not affected by the size of the loan or the applicable Add-On rate. These variables are considered in the amount of total recomputed interest charges. In Add-On loans, the total amount of interest charges is figured on the basis of 1) the interest rate used, 2) the total amount loaned, 3) the length of the loan. For example, the pre-computed interest charges for a 12%, $2,000, 18-month loan would be:

$$12 \times 2,000 \times 1.5 = \$360.00.$$

It is to this that the interest factor is applied to determine the dollar amount of interest income earned. For the above series of illustrations, the amount of recognized income would equal $.8772 \times 360 = \$315.79$.

These examples illustrate the way two of the basic applications of the Rule of 78s are figured. The interest earned over a period of time is actually equal to the sum of individual monthly realized income where the monthly income declines over time.

This principle is illustrated below:

For an 18-month loan that has been outstanding for 12 months, the interest earned equals:

$$\frac{18 + 17 + 16 + \ldots + 9 + 8 + 7}{1 + 2 + 3 + \ldots + 16 + 17 + 18} = \frac{150}{171} = 87.72\%$$

This is equivalent to:

$$\frac{18}{171} + \frac{17}{171} + \frac{16}{171} + \ldots + \frac{9}{171} + \frac{8}{171} + \frac{7}{171} = \frac{150}{171}$$

In turn, this equivalency can be restated as:

$$10.53\% + 9.94\% + 9.36\% + \ldots + 5.26\% + 4.68\% + 4.09\% = 87.72\%$$

where 18/171 or 10.53% equals realized income in the first month, 17/171 or 9.94% equals realized income in the second month, and so on down to 7/171 or 4.09% as realized income in the twelfth month of this 18-month loan.

It now becomes evident that the Rule of 78s provides the amount of interest earned at interim stages over the course of a loan. Furthermore, the greatest monthly income is recognized in the early stages of the loan when the amount of the principal balance outstanding is greatest.

The preceding discussion and procedures apply to installment loans that are amortized on a monthly basis. While this is the most common type of installment loan, with slight adjustments, the Rule of 78s can also be used to compute realized income where the credit is not repaid on a monthly basis. When quarterly amortization schedules are used, the accuracy and the effects of interest rates, size of the loan and maturity are identical to those which appear with monthly schedules.

Three conditions need to exist in order to justify the use of the Rule of 78s:

1) Interest charges must be computed on an Add-On basis.
2) The loan must be amortized in equal dollar installments.
3) The installment payments must be made in equal intervals.

The third condition *implies* that there are 12 thirty-day months in a 360-day-year. The inference arises directly from the mathematical procedures used to compute the income factors. Regardless of whether the payment interval is one month, two months, or three months, it is impossible to obtain exactly equal intervals unless the payment date changes every month. However, the effects of this practical feature are very slight and certainly are not sufficient to negate use of the rule.

When all of the above conditions exist, the use of the Rule can be utilized in accounting for installment credits amortized in whatever manner. The factor computational procedures associated with non-monthly repayment schedules, quarterly, for example, are similar to those outlined above. The basic difference is that instead of working with the values of the number of months in the loan, the procedure depends on working with the values of the number of payment periods in the loan. For example, with a two-year loan that is amortized on a quarterly basis, the computation of the denominator would be dependent upon the number of payment periods over the original term of the loan. Since there are eight intervals in this particular loan, the denominator would be 1+2. . .+7+8 = 36. Again, working in payment periods, the numerator is computed along the same lines as explained above. The numerator of the realized income factor after the fourth payment would equal 8+7+6+5 = 26. The realized income factor would be 26/36 = 72.22%.

Validity of the Rule

Since Add-On interest rates fail to recognize the fact that the principal balance of an installment loan is reduced over time, it is necessary to use a method such as the Rule of 78s to determine realized income. The Rule attempts to relate the amount of monthly interest income to the outstanding principal balance of the loan. One important question remains unsolved: How well does the Rule of 78s accomplish this function? To judge the validity of the Rule, it is necessary to go beyond mere computations and take into consideration the principles upon which the Rule is based. What the rule undertakes to accomplish is the recognition of interest earnings in a manner which approximates that which would accrue on an equivalent simple interest basis without the complication. However, certain conditions must be fulfilled.

The Rule of 78s accounts for interest income in the manner described. However, given certain conditions, this method actually results in earnings which are comparable to those which accrue with the use of an equivalent simple interest rate. Figure 1 provides an illustration of the interest income recognized through the Rule vs. that realized on the basis of simple interest. In this illustration, the borrower is assumed to have taken out a $1,000 one-year, 12% Add-On loan with equal monthly payments of $93.33. This is equivalent to a similar 21.45% simple interest loan requiring equal monthly payments of $93.33 and would involve total precomputed interest charges of $120.00.

This figure also shows that the use of the Rule can result in interest earnings that are similar to those recorded on a simple interest basis, i.e., where the interest income is relative to the unpaid principal of the loan. The two methods are not perfect substitutes for each other, nor can they be as long as use of the Rule results in an accelerated recognition of earnings as illustrated in the tables below. But since the absolute dollars and relative percentage earnings' differentials are so small, the above illustration suggests a high degree of accuracy and considerable justification for use of the Rule of 78s.

FIGURE 1
Monthly Earnings From a $1,000, One-year Installment Loan Transaction Earnings As Realized From Application of the Rule of 78s vs. Simple Interest

	12% Add-On 93 Mon. Pmts.		21.45% Simple 93.3 Mon. Pmts.		Monthly Diff. in Earnings		Cum. Diff. in Earnings	
Pmt.	Prin.	Int. (1)	Prin.	Int. (2)	$	% (3)	$	% (4)
1	$74.87	$18.46	$75.46	$17.88	0.58	3.28%	0.58	3.28%
2	$76.41	$16.92	$76.81	$16.53	0.40	2.42%	0.99	2.87%
3	$77.95	$15.38	$78.18	$15.15	0.23	1.55%	1.22	2.46%
4	$79.48	$13.85	$79.58	$13.76	0.09	0.68%	1.31	2.07%
5	$81.02	$12.31	$81.00	$12.33	-0.02	-0.19%	1.29	1.71%
6	$82.56	$10.77	$82.45	$10.89	-0.11	-1.04%	1.18	1.36%
7	$84.10	$9.23	$83.92	$9.41	-0.18	-1.89%	1.00	1.04%
8	$85.64	$7.69	$85.42	$7.91	-0.22	-2.74%	0.78	0.75%
9	$87.18	$6.15	$86.95	$6.38	-0.23	-3.57%	0.55	0.50%
10	$88.71	$4.62	$88.50	$4.83	-0.21	-4.39%	0.34	0.30%
11	$90.25	$3.08	$90.08	$3.25	-0.17	-5.19%	0.17	0.15%
12	$91.79	$1.54	$91.69	$1.64	-0.10	-5.91%	0.08	0.06%
Totals	$999.96	$120.00	$1,000.04	$119.96	0.08			

Situation. Borrower repays loan in 12 equal ($93.33) monthly install-ments; payments being made on regularly scheduled payments dates; the first payment one month from the date of the transaction; the 21.45% simple inter-est rate is equivalent to the 12% Add-On.

1) Interest earned as computed on the Rule of 78s.
2) Interest earnings as computed on principle of simple interest.
3) Relative % diff. = a dollar amount of difference relative to amount charged on simple interest basis.
4) Cum. % diff. = cum. dollar amount of difference relative to cumulative amount of interest as charged on simple basis.

This example is just one of a wide range of possible loan transactions; as a result the effects of the interest rate size, and maturity have not been con-sidered thus far. When the effect of the interest rate feature is examined with the Add-On rate being changed as the size of the loan and the maturity are held constant, it becomes evident that both the absolute and relative earnings' differentials are directly related to the Add-On rate. In other words, a higher Add-On rate results in more acceleration of earnings and, therefore, provides monthly income figures that are less comparable to those generated from equivalent simple interest. This principle holds regardless of the original amount of the cash advance or the term-to-maturity of the loan.

Relative to the effects of the size feature, the size of the loan affects only the absolute dollar amount of the earnings' differential. The spread between the earnings recorded on the basis of simple vs. Add-On is a multiple of the relative difference in the size of the loan; for example, for any given month, the dollar amount of the earnings' differential would be three times greater for a $3,000 loan than for a $1,000 loan. Conversely, the size factor has no effect when the earnings difference is measured on a relative basis; i.e., the difference is 3.25% in the first month for any one-year 12% Add-On loan, regardless of the amount of the cash advance. In contrast to the size factor, the maturity of the loan does affect both the absolute and relative amounts of the earnings difference; as the term-to-maturity lengthens, the absolute and rela-tive differences become greater. In effect, the spread in earnings, in both dol-lar and percentage terms, is more in the early stages of longer lived loans and less in the final stages. The cross-over point where the interest from the sim-ple basis first exceeds that accruing from application of the rule of 78s is equal to approximately one-third the maturity of the loan, regardless of the amount of the loan or the Add-On rate being used.

The monthly interest income recognized with the Rule vs. that recog-nized on the basis of simple interest is greater during the first third of the life of the loan and less during the last two-thirds. Thus the accuracy of the Rule of 78s declines as maturity lengthens and rate of acceleration increases. To the extent that the relative differential is the most, or only important criterion, the precision of the Rule is unaffected by the size of the loan, but is adversely affected with longer loans and/or with loans carrying higher Add-On interest rates.

With acceptable maturities and interest rates, the use of the Rule of 78s with Add-On installment loans provides a valid method for computing interest income. There is some acceleration in recognizing earnings and it is not precisely accurate in relation to simple interest; however, it does account for interest income in a manner similar to that which accrues from use of an equivalent simple interest. Since the Rule of 78s is basically a shortcut in computing interest earned, in all but the most atypical situations, the deviation is too slight to affect the validity of the results.

The Rule of 78s cannot be used to figure interest income or expenses, unless the loan qualifies as a short-term consumer loan. A short-term consumer loan is self-amortizing and requires level payments at regular intervals at least annually over a period of not more than five years, with no balloon payment at the end of the loan term. If the taxpayer has short-term consumer loans, the Rule of 78s method can be used for these loans to change the method of accounting for interest income or expense.

Appendix G

The SEC Electronic Data Gathering, Analysis, and Retrieval System

The Securities and Exchange Commission electronic computer system has been developed during the past ten years to receive, accept, analyze, store, retrieve and disseminate SEC disclosure documents in electronic format.

The system was developed with three specific aims in mind:

1) To bring some relief to the SEC personnel who were having to deal with the enormous volume of paper filings that the Commission receives annually. (The volume has increased rapidly over the years; it now exceeds 13 million pages annually.)

2) To provide more readily available access to the public portions of the disclosure filings for the benefit of investors and others interested in financial matters.

3) To reduce the cost and the time required for registrants submitting filings to the SEC—and even more importantly, receiving acknowledgement back from the SEC of the receipt of those filings.

Initially, a trial use of the system by filers of registration statements was on a voluntary basis by corporations and investment companies. Subsequently, in 1993 the SEC mandated four groups of registrants to begin electronic filing, and by the end of 1993 over 2,000 large corporations and nearly a thousand large investment companies were filing electronically on the system. The SEC established a final set of rules for the use of the electronic system in December 1994. Unless otherwise exempted, all SEC registrants who were not yet using the system in the test phase of the program have had to begin filing electronically.

The system uses about 300 types of forms, including correspondence and cover letters. The forms cover nearly all of the filing requirements under the 1993 Act, the 1934 Act, the Trust Indenture Act, and the Investment Company Act. Not all of the different SEC requirements have to be electronically filed—the annual report to shareholders, for example, that is required by the SEC for information purposes need not be electronically filed.

There is no limit on the number of documents nor on the number of pages that can be included in a single document that can be submitted electronically. Further, they may appear in any order as long as exhibits follow the filing document that contains the exhibit index. Each document, including exhibits, cover letters and correspondence, has its own document header, which identifies the document. The headers for submissions must identify the filing type, the filer, the subject company if there is one, and the number of documents in the submission. A submission contact person should be noted in case the system has difficulty receiving or processing a filing.

When upon receipt a registration filing has been accepted, it is forwarded electronically to the SEC branch chief responsible for its review. The branch chief then assigns the filing to one or more examiners, usually an accountant and an attorney, for detailed review. When the examiners are notified of an assignment on their own workstation screens, they can print a copy of any filing or portion of a filing they want to review off-line. There is no need for them to request a hard copy from the filer.

All public documents filed electronically are available to the public and to private system subscribers as soon as a filing is accepted. The public has access to the filings through the system terminals in the SEC Public Reference Rooms in Washington, New York, and Chicago. Those who have on-line service can access an accepted filing immediately, or on the following business day if they have a tape service.

Appendix H
Financial Planning Tables

The following tables, involving the effects of interest factors, are useful in various forms of future business planning.

SIMPLE INTEREST TABLE

SIMPLE INTEREST TABLE

__Example of use of this table:__
      Find amount of $500 in 8 years at 6% simple interest.
      From table at 8 yrs. and 6% for $1   1.48
      Value in 8 yrs. for $500 (500 x 1.48) $740

Number of Years	Interest Rate							
	3%	4%	5%	6%	7%	8%	9%	10%
1	1.03	1.04	1.05	1.06	1.07	1.08	1.09	1.10
2	1.06	1.08	1.10	1.12	1.14	1.16	1.18	1.20
3	1.09	1.12	1.15	1.18	1.21	1.24	1.27	1.30
4	1.12	1.16	1.20	1.24	1.28	1.32	1.36	1.40
5	1.15	1.20	1.25	1.30	1.35	1.40	1.45	1.50
6	1.18	1.24	1.30	1.36	1.42	1.48	1.54	1.60
7	1.21	1.28	1.35	1.42	1.49	1.56	1.63	1.70
8	1.24	1.32	1.40	1.48	1.56	1.64	1.72	1.80
9	1.27	1.36	1.45	1.54	1.63	1.72	1.81	1.90
10	1.30	1.40	1.50	1.60	1.70	1.80	1.90	2.00
11	1.33	1.44	1.55	1.66	1.77	1.88	1.99	2.10
12	1.36	1.48	1.60	1.72	1.84	1.96	2.08	2.20
13	1.39	1.52	1.65	1.78	1.91	2.04	2.17	2.30
14	1.42	1.56	1.70	1.84	1.98	2.12	2.26	2.40
15	1.45	1.60	1.75	1.90	2.05	2.20	2.35	2.50
16	1.48	1.64	1.80	1.96	2.12	2.28	2.44	2.60
17	1.51	1.68	1.85	2.02	2.19	2.36	2.53	2.70
18	1.54	1.72	1.90	2.08	2.26	2.44	2.62	2.80
19	1.57	1.76	1.95	2.14	2.33	2.52	2.71	2.90
20	1.60	1.80	2.00	2.20	2.40	2.60	2.80	3.00
21	1.63	1.84	2.05	2.26	2.47	2.68	2.89	3.10
22	1.66	1.88	2.10	2.32	2.54	2.76	2.98	3.20
23	1.69	1.92	2.15	2.38	2.61	2.84	3.07	3.30
24	1.72	1.96	2.20	2.44	2.68	2.92	3.16	3.40
25	1.75	2.00	2.25	2.50	2.75	3.00	3.25	3.50
26	1.78	2.04	2.30	2.56	2.82	3.08	3.34	3.60
27	1.81	2.08	2.35	2.62	2.89	3.16	3.43	3.70
28	1.84	2.12	2.40	2.68	2.96	3.24	3.52	3.80
29	1.87	2.16	2.45	2.74	3.03	3.32	3.61	3.90
30	1.90	2.20	2.50	2.80	3.10	3.40	3.70	4.00
31	1.93	2.24	2.55	2.86	3.17	3.48	3.79	4.10
32	1.96	2.28	2.60	2.92	3.24	3.56	3.88	4.20
33	1.99	2.32	2.65	2.98	3.31	3.64	3.97	4.30
34	2.02	2.36	2.70	3.04	3.38	3.72	4.06	4.40
35	2.05	2.40	2.75	3.10	3.45	3.80	4.15	4.50
36	2.08	2.44	2.80	3.16	3.52	3.88	4.24	4.60
37	2.11	2.48	2.85	3.22	3.59	3.96	4.33	4.70
38	2.14	2.52	2.90	3.28	3.66	4.04	4.42	4.80
39	2.17	2.56	2.95	3.34	3.73	4.12	4.51	4.90
40	2.20	2.60	3.00	3.40	3.80	4.20	4.60	5.00

COMPOUND INTEREST TABLE

Example of use of this table:

Find how much $1,000 now in bank will grow to in 14 years at 6% interest.

From table 14 years at 6%   2.2609

Value in 14 years of $1,000 $2,260.9

Interest Rate

Number of Years	6%	6 1/2%	7%	7 1/2%	8%	8 1/2%	9%	9 1/2%
1	1.0600	1.0650	1.0700	1.0750	1.0800	1.0850	1.0900	1.0950
2	1.1236	1.1342	1.1449	1.1556	1.1664	1.1772	1.1881	1.1990
3	1.1910	1.2079	1.2250	1.2422	1.2597	1.2772	1.2950	1.3129
4	1.2624	1.2864	1.3107	1.3354	1.3604	1.3858	1.4115	1.4376
5	1.3332	1.3700	1.4025	1.4356	1.4693	1.5036	1.5386	1.5742
6	1.4135	1.4591	1.5007	1.5433	1.5868	1.6314	1.6771	1.7237
7	1.5030	1.5539	1.6057	1.6590	1.7138	1.7701	1.8230	1.8875
8	1.5938	1.6549	1.7181	1.7834	1.8509	1.9206	1.9925	2.0668
9	1.6894	1.7625	1.8384	1.9172	1.9990	2.0838	2.1718	2.2632
10	1.7908	1.8771	1.9671	2.0610	2.1589	2.2609	2.3673	2.4782
11	1.8982	1.9991	2.1048	2.2156	2.3316	2.4531	2.5804	2.7136
12	2.0121	2.1290	2.2521	2.3817	2.5181	2.6616	2.8126	2.9714
13	2.1329	2.2674	2.4098	2.5604	2.7196	2.8879	3.0658	3.2537
14	2.2609	2.4148	2.5785	2.7524	2.9371	3.1334	3.3417	3.5628
15	2.3965	2.5718	2.7590	2.9588	3.1721	3.3997	3.6424	3.9013
16	2.5403	2.7390	2.9521	3.1807	3.4259	3.6887	3.9703	4.2719
17	2.6927	2.9170	3.1588	3.4193	3.7000	4.0022	4.3276	4.6777
18	2.8543	3.1066	3.3799	3.6758	3.9960	4.3424	4.7171	5.1221
19	3.0255	3.3085	3.6165	3.9514	4.3157	4.7115	5.1416	5.6087
20	3.2075	3.5236	3.8696	4.2478	4.6609	5.1120	5.6044	6.1416
21	3.3995	3.7526	4.1405	4.5664	5.0338	5.5465	6.1088	6.7250
22	3.6035	3.9966	4.4304	4.9089	5.4365	6.0180	6.6586	7.3639
23	3.8197	4.2563	4.7405	5.2770	5.8714	6.5295	7.2578	8.0635
24	4.0489	4.5330	5.0723	5.6728	6.3411	7.0845	7.9110	8.8295
25	4.2918	4.8276	5.4274	6.0983	6.8484	7.6867	8.6230	9.6683
26	4.5493	5.1414	5.8073	6.5557	7.3963	8.3401	9.3991	10.5868
27	4.8223	5.4756	6.2138	7.0473	7.9880	9.0490	10.2450	11.5926
28	5.1116	5.8316	6.6488	7.5759	8.6271	9.8182	11.1671	12.6939
29	5.4183	6.2106	7.1142	8.1441	9.3172	10.6527	12.1721	13.8998
30	5.7434	6.6143	7.6122	8.7549	10.5582	11.5582	13.2676	15.2203
31	6.0881	7.0442	8.1451	9.4115	10.8676	12.5407	14.4617	16.6662
32	6.4533	7.5021	8.7152	10.1174	11.7370	13.6066	15.7633	18.2495
33	6.8408	7.9898	9.3253	10.8762	12.6760	14.7632	17.1820	19.9832
34	7.2510	8.5091	9.9781	11.6919	13.6901	16.0181	18.7284	21.8816
35	7.6860	9.0622	10.6765	12.5688	14.7853	17.3796	20.4139	23.9604
36	8.1479	9.6513	11.4239	13.5115	15.9681	18.8569	22.2512	26.2366
37	8.6360	10.2786	12.2236	14.5249	17.2456	20.4597	24.2538	28.7291
38	9.1542	10.9467	13.0792	15.6142	18.6252	22.1988	26.4366	31.4583
39	9.7035	11.6582	13.9948	16.7853	20.1152	24.0857	28.8159	34.4469
40	10.2857	12.4160	14.9744	18.0442	21.7245	26.1330	31.4094	37.7193

Compound Interest Table (Con't.)

Number of Years	10%	11%	12%	13%	14%	15%	16%	17%
1	1.1000	1.1100	1.1200	1.1300	1.1400	1.1500	1.1600	1.1700
2	1.2100	1.2321	1.2544	1.2769	1.2996	1.3225	1.3456	1.3689
3	1.3310	1.3576	1.4049	1.4428	1.4815	1.5208	1.5606	1.6016
4	1.4647	1.5180	1.5735	1.6304	1.6389	1.7490	1.8106	1.8738
5	1.6105	1.6350	1.7623	1.8424	1.9254	2.0113	2.1003	2.1924
6	1.7715	1.8704	1.9738	2.0819	2.1949	2.3130	2.4363	2.5651
7	1.9487	2.0761	2.2106	2.3526	2.5022	2.6600	2.8262	3.0012
8	2.1435	2.3045	2.4759	2.6584	2.8525	3.0590	3.2784	3.5114
9	2.3579	2.5580	2.7730	3.0040	3.2519	3.5178	3.8029	4.1084
10	2.5937	2.8394	3.1058	3.3945	3.7072	4.0455	4.4114	4.8068
11	2.8531	3.1517	3.4785	3.8358	4.2262	4.6523	5.1172	5.6239
12	3.1384	3.4984	3.8959	4.3345	4.8179	5.3502	5.9360	6.5800
13	3.4522	3.8832	4.3634	4.8980	5.4924	6.1527	6.8857	7.6986
14	3.7974	4.3104	4.8871	5.5347	6.2613	7.0757	7.9875	9.0074
15	4.1772	4.7845	5.4735	6.2542	7.1379	8.1370	9.2655	10.5387
16	4.5949	5.3108	6.1303	7.0673	8.1372	9.3576	10.7480	12.3303
17	5.0544	5.8950	6.8660	7.9860	9.2764	10.7612	12.4676	14.4264
18	5.5599	6.5435	7.6899	9.0242	10.5751	12.3754	14.4625	16.8789
19	6.1159	7.2633	8.6127	10.1974	12.0556	14.2317	16.7765	19.7483
20	6.7274	8.0623	9.6462	11.5230	13.7434	16.3665	19.4607	23.1055
21	7.4002	8.9491	10.8038	13.0210	15.6675	18.8215	22.5744	27.0335
22	8.1402	9.9335	12.1003	14.7138	17.8610	21.6447	26.1863	31.6292
23	8.9543	11.0262	13.5523	16.6266	20.3615	24.8914	30.3762	37.0062
24	9.8497	12.2391	15.1786	18.7880	23.2122	28.6251	35.2364	43.2972
25	10.8347	13.5854	17.0000	21.2305	26.4619	32.9189	40.8742	50.6578
26	11.9181	15.0793	19.0400	23.9905	30.1665	37.8567	47.4141	59.2696
27	13.1099	16.7386	21.3248	27.1092	34.3899	43.5353	55.0003	69.3454
28	14.4209	18.5799	23.8838	30.6334	39.2044	50.0656	63.8004	81.1342
29	15.8630	20.6236	26.7499	34.6158	44.6931	57.5754	74.0085	94.9270
30	17.4494	22.8922	29.9599	39.1158	50.9501	66.2117	85.8498	111.0646
31	19.1943	25.4104	33.5551	44.2009	58.0831	76.1435	99.5858	129.9456
32	21.1137	28.2055	37.5817	49.9470	66.2148	87.5650	115.5195	152.0363
33	23.2251	31.3082	42.0915	56.4402	75.4849	100.6998	134.0027	177.8825
34	25.5476	34.7521	47.1425	63.7774	86.0527	115.8048	155.4431	208.1226
35	28.1024	38.5748	52.7996	72.0685	98.1001	133.1755	180.3140	243.5034
36	30.9128	42.8180	59.1355	81.4374	111.8342	153.1518	209.1643	284.8990
37	34.0039	47.5280	66.2318	92.0242	127.4909	176.1246	242.6306	333.3319
38	37.4048	52.7561	74.1796	103.9874	145.3397	202.5433	281.4515	389.9983
39	41.1447	58.5593	83.0812	117.5057	165.6872	232.9248	326.4837	456.2980
40	45.2592	65.0008	93.0509	132.7815	188.8835	267.8635	378.7211	533.8687

Compound Interest Table (Con't.)

Number of Years	18%	19%	20%	21%	22%	23%	24%	25%
1	1.1800	1.1900	1.2000	1.2100	1.2200	1.2300	1.2400	1.2500
2	1.3924	1.4161	1.4400	1.4641	1.4884	1.5129	1.5376	1.5625
3	1.6430	1.6851	1.7280	1.7715	1.8158	1.8608	1.9066	1.9531
4	1.9387	2.0053	2.0736	2.1435	2.2153	2.2888	2.3642	2.4414
5	2.2877	2.3863	2.4883	2.5937	2.7027	2.8153	2.9316	3.0517
6	2.6995	2.8397	2.9859	3.1384	3.2973	3.4628	3.6352	3.8146
7	3.1854	3.3793	3.5831	3.7974	4.0227	4.2592	4.5076	4.7683
8	3.7588	4.0213	4.2998	4.5949	4.9077	5.2389	5.5895	5.9604
9	4.4354	4.7854	5.1597	5.5599	5.9874	6.4438	6.9309	7.4505
10	5.2338	5.6946	6.1917	6.7274	7.3046	7.9259	8.5944	9.3132
11	6.1759	6.7766	7.4300	8.1402	8.9116	9.7489	10.6570	11.6415
12	7.2875	8.0642	8.9161	9.8497	10.8722	11.9911	13.2147	14.5519
13	8.5993	9.5964	10.6993	11.9181	13.2641	14.7491	16.3863	18.1898
14	10.1472	11.4197	12.8391	14.4209	16.1822	18.1414	20.3190	22.7373
15	11.9737	13.5895	15.4070	17.4494	19.7422	22.3139	25.1956	28.4217
16	14.1290	16.1715	18.4884	21.1137	24.0855	27.4461	31.2425	35.5271
17	16.6722	19.2441	22.1861	25.5476	29.3844	33.7587	38.7408	44.4089
18	19.6732	22.9005	26.6233	30.9126	35.8489	41.5233	48.0385	55.5111
19	23.2144	27.2516	31.9479	37.4043	43.7357	51.0736	59.5678	69.3889
20	27.3930	32.4294	38.3375	45.2592	53.3576	62.8206	73.8641	86.7361
21	32.3237	38.5910	46.0051	54.7636	65.0963	77.2693	91.5915	108.4202
22	38.1420	45.9233	55.2061	66.2640	79.4175	95.0413	113.5735	135.5252
23	45.0076	54.6487	66.2473	80.1795	96.8893	116.9008	140.8311	169.4065
24	53.1090	65.0319	79.4968	97.0172	118.2050	143.7880	174.6306	211.7582
25	62.6686	77.3880	95.3962	117.3908	144.2101	176.8592	216.5419	264.6977
26	73.9488	92.0918	114.4754	142.0429	175.9363	217.5368	268.5120	330.8722
27	87.2597	109.5892	137.3705	171.8719	214.6423	267.5703	332.9549	413.5903
28	102.9665	130.4112	164.8446	207.9650	261.8636	329.1115	412.8641	516.9878
29	121.5005	155.1893	197.8135	251.6377	319.4736	404.8072	511.9515	646.2348
30	143.3708	184.6753	237.3763	304.4816	389.7578	497.9128	634.8199	807.7935
31	169.1773	219.7636	284.8515	368.4227	475.5046	612.4328	787.1767	1009.7419
32	199.6292	261.5187	341.8218	445.7915	580.1156	753.2923	976.0991	1262.1774
33	235.5625	311.2072	410.1862	539.4077	707.7410	926.5496	1210.3629	1577.7218
34	277.9638	370.3366	492.2235	652.6834	863.4441	1139.6560	1500.8500	1972.1522
35	327.9972	440.7006	590.6682	789.7469	1053.4018	1401.7769	1861.0540	2465.1903
36	387.0368	524.4337	708.8018	955.5938	1285.1502	1724.1855	2307.7069	3081.4879
37	456.7034	624.0761	850.5622	1156.2685	1567.8833	2120.7482	2861.5566	3851.8598
38	538.9100	742.6505	1020.6746	1399.0849	1912.8176	2608.5203	3548.3302	4814.8248
39	635.9138	883.7542	1224.8096	1692.8927	2333.6375	3208.4800	4399.9295	6018.5310
40	750.3783	1051.6675	1469.7715	2048.4002	2847.0377	3946.4304	5455.9126	7523.1638

PERIODIC DEPOSIT TABLE

Example of use of this table:
How much is $1,000 a year invested at 6% worth in 20 years?
At 6% for 20 years, the figure is   38.993
For $1,000 a year, the amount is $38,993

Interest Rate

Number of Years	6%	7%	8%	9%	10%	11%	12%	13%
1	1.060	1.070	1.080	1.090	1.100	1.110	1.120	1.130
2	2.183	2.215	2.246	2.278	2.310	2.342	2.374	2.407
3	3.375	3.440	3.506	3.573	3.641	3.710	3.779	3.850
4	4.637	4.751	4.867	4.985	5.105	5.228	5.353	5.480
5	5.975	6.153	6.336	6.523	6.716	6.913	7.115	7.323
6	7.394	7.654	7.923	8.200	8.487	8.783	9.089	9.405
7	8.897	9.260	9.637	10.028	10.436	10.859	11.300	11.757
8	10.491	10.978	11.488	12.021	12.579	13.164	13.776	14.416
9	12.181	12.816	13.487	14.193	14.937	15.722	16.549	17.420
10	13.972	14.784	15.645	16.560	17.531	18.561	19.655	20.814
11	15.870	16.888	17.977	19.141	20.384	21.713	23.133	24.650
12	17.882	19.141	20.495	21.953	23.523	25.212	27.029	28.985
13	20.015	21.550	23.215	25.019	26.975	29.095	31.393	33.883
14	22.276	24.129	26.152	28.361	30.772	33.405	36.280	39.417
15	24.673	26.888	29.324	32.003	34.950	38.190	41.753	45.672
16	27.213	29.840	32.750	35.974	39.545	43.501	47.884	52.739
17	29.906	32.999	36.450	40.301	44.599	49.396	54.750	60.725
18	32.760	36.379	40.446	45.018	50.159	55.939	62.440	69.749
19	35.786	39.995	44.762	50.160	56.275	63.203	71.052	79.947
20	38.993	43.865	49.423	55.765	63.002	71.265	80.699	91.470
21	42.392	48.006	54.457	61.873	70.403	80.214	91.503	104.491
22	45.996	52.436	59.893	68.532	78.543	90.148	103.603	119.205
23	49.816	57.177	65.765	75.790	87.497	101.174	117.155	135.831
24	53.865	62.249	72.106	83.701	97.347	113.413	132.334	154.620
25	58.156	67.676	78.954	92.324	108.182	126.999	149.334	175.850
26	62.706	73.484	86.351	101.723	120.100	142.079	168.374	199.841
27	67.528	79.698	94.339	111.968	133.210	158.817	189.699	226.950
28	72.640	86.347	102.966	123.135	147.631	177.397	213.583	257.583
29	78.058	93.461	112.283	135.308	163.494	198.021	240.333	292.199
30	83.802	101.073	122.346	148.575	180.943	220.913	270.293	331.315
31	89.890	109.218	133.214	163.037	200.138	246.324	303.848	375.516
32	96.343	117.933	144.951	178.800	221.252	274.529	341.429	425.463
33	103.184	127.259	157.627	195.982	244.477	305.837	383.521	481.903
34	110.435	137.237	171.317	214.711	270.024	340.590	430.663	545.681
35	118.121	147.913	186.102	235.125	298.127	379.164	483.463	617.749
36	126.268	159.337	202.070	257.376	329.039	421.982	542.599	699.187
37	134.904	171.561	219.316	281.630	363.043	469.511	608.831	791.211
38	144.058	184.640	237.941	308.066	400.448	522.267	683.010	895.198
39	153.762	198.635	258.057	336.882	441.593	580.826	766.091	1012.704
40	164.048	213.610	279.781	368.292	486.852	645.827	859.142	1145.486

COMPOUND DISCOUNT TABLE

This table shows the present or discounted value of $1 due at a given future time. For example, assume property which will revert to a lessor in 10 years will then be worth $1,000. The present value of this reversion, computed at an assumed rate of 4% on the investment, is found by finding the factor on the 10-year line in the 4% column. The factor .6756 is multiplied by 1000 to obtain the answer of $675.60.

Years	4%	4-1/2%	5%	5-1/2%	6%	6-1/2%	7%	7-1/2%	8%	9%	10%	11%
1	0.9615	0.9569	0.9524	0.9479	0.9434	0.9390	0.9346	0.9302	0.9259	0.9174	0.9091	0.9009
2	.9246	.9157	.9070	.8985	.8900	.8817	.8734	.8653	.8573	.8417	.8264	.8116
3	.8890	.8763	.8638	.8516	.8396	.8278	.8163	.8050	.7938	.7722	.7513	.7312
4	.8548	.8386	.8227	.8072	.7921	.7773	.7629	.7488	.7350	.7084	.6830	.6587
5	.8219	.8025	.7835	.7651	.7473	.7299	.7130	.6966	.6806	.6499	.6209	.5935
6	.7903	.7679	.7462	.7252	.7050	.6853	.6663	.6480	.6302	.5963	.5645	.5346
7	.7599	.7343	.7107	.6874	.6651	.6435	.6227	.6027	.5835	.5470	.5132	.4816
8	.7307	.7032	.6768	.6516	.6274	.6042	.5820	.5607	.5403	.5019	.4665	.4339
9	.7026	.6729	.6446	.6176	.5919	.5673	.5439	.5216	.5002	.4604	.4241	.3909
10	.6756	.6439	.6139	.5854	.5584	.5327	.5083	.4852	.4632	.4224	.3855	.3522
11	.6496	.6162	.5847	.5549	.5268	.5002	.4751	.4514	.4289	.3875	.3505	.3173
12	.6246	.5897	.5568	.5260	.4970	.4697	.4440	.4199	.3971	.3555	.3186	.2858
13	.6006	.5643	.5303	.4986	.4688	.4410	.4150	.3906	.3677	.3262	.2897	.2575
14	.5775	.5400	.5051	.4726	.4423	.4141	.3878	.3633	.3405	.2992	.2633	.2320
15	.5553	.5167	.4810	.4479	.4173	.3888	.3624	.3380	.3152	.2745	.2394	.2090
16	.5339	.4945	.4581	.4246	.3936	.3651	.3387	.3144	.2919	.2519	.2176	.1883
17	.5134	.4732	.4363	.4024	.3714	.3428	.3166	.2924	.2703	.2311	.1978	.1696
18	.4936	.4528	.4155	.3815	.3503	.3219	.2959	.2720	.2502	.2120	.1799	.1528
19	.4746	.4333	.3957	.3616	.3305	.3022	.2765	.2531	.2317	.1945	.1635	.1377
20	.4564	.4146	.3769	.3427	.3118	.2838	.2584	.2354	.2145	.1784	.1486	.1240
21	.4388	.3968	.3589	.3249	.2942	.2665	.2415	.2190	.1987	.1637	.1351	.1117
22	.4220	.3797	.3418	.3079	.2775	.2502	.2257	.2037	.1839	.1502	.1228	.1007
23	.4057	.3633	.3256	.2919	.2618	.2349	.2109	.1895	.1703	.1378	.1117	.0907
24	.3901	.3477	.3101	.2766	.2470	.2206	.1971	.1763	.1577	.1264	.1015	.0817
25	.3751	.3327	.2953	.2622	.2330	.2071	.1842	.1640	.1460	.1160	.0923	.0736
26	.3607	.3184	.2812	.2486	.2198	.1945	.1722	.1525	.1352	.1064	.0829	.0663
27	.3468	.3047	.2678	.2356	.2074	.1826	.1609	.1419	.1252	.0976	.0763	.0597
28	.3335	.2916	.2551	.2233	.1956	.1715	.1504	.1320	.1159	.0895	.0693	.0538

Compound Discount Table (Con't.)

Years	4%	4-1/2%	5%	5-1/2%	6%	6-1/2%	7%	7-1/2%	8%	9%	10%	11%
29	0.3207	0.2790	0.2429	0.2117	0.1846	0.1610	0.1406	0.1228	0.1073	0.0822	0.0630	0.0485
30	.3083	.2670	.2314	.2006	.1741	.1512	.1314	.1142	.0994	.0754	.0573	.0437
31	.2965	.2555	.2204	.1902	.1643	.1420	.1228	.1063	.0920	.0691	.0521	.0394
32	.2851	.2445	.2099	.1803	.1550	.1333	.1147	.0988	.0852	.0634	.0474	.0354
33	.2741	.2340	.1999	.1709	.1462	.1251	.1072	.0919	.0789	.0582	.0431	.0319
34	.2636	.2239	.1904	.1620	.1379	.1175	.1002	.0855	.0730	.0534	.0391	.0288
35	.2534	.2142	.1813	.1535	.1301	.1103	.0937	.0796	.0676	.0490	.0356	.0259
36	.2437	.2050	.1727	.1455	.1227	.1036	.0875	.0740	.0626	.0449	.0323	.0234
37	.2343	.1962	.1644	.1379	.1158	.0973	.0818	.0688	.0580	.0412	.0294	.0210
38	.2253	.1878	.1566	.1307	.1092	.0914	.0765	.0640	.0537	.0378	.0267	.0189
39	.2166	.1797	.1491	.1239	.1031	.0858	.0715	.0596	.0497	.0347	.0243	.0171
40	.2083	.1719	.1420	.1175	.0972	.0805	.0668	.0554	.0460	.0318	.0221	.0154
41	.2003	.1645	.1353	.1113	.0917	.0756	.0624	.0515	.0426	.0292	.0201	.0139
42	.1926	.1574	.1288	.1055	.0865	.0710	.0583	.0480	.0395	.0268	.0183	.0125
43	.1852	.1507	.1227	.1000	.0816	.0667	.0545	.0446	.0365	.0246	.0166	.0112
44	.1780	.1442	.1169	.0948	.0770	.0626	.0509	.0415	.0338	.0225	.0151	.0101
45	.1712	.1380	.1113	.0899	.0726	.0588	.0476	.0386	.0313	.0207	.0137	.0091
46	.1646	.1320	.1060	.0852	.0685	.0552	.0445	.0359	.0290	.0190	.0125	.0082
47	.1583	.1263	.1009	.0807	.0647	.0518	.0416	.0334	.0269	.0174	.0113	.0074
48	.1522	.1209	.0961	.0765	.0610	.0487	.0389	.0311	.0249	.0160	.0103	.0067
49	.1463	.1157	.0916	.0725	.0575	.0457	.0363	.0289	.0230	.0147	.0094	.0060
50	.1407	.1107	.0872	.0688	.0543	.0429	.0339	.0269	.0213	.0134	.0085	.0054
51	.1353	.1059	.0831	.0652	.0512	.0403	.0317	.0250	.0197	.0123	.0077	.00488
52	.1301	.1014	.0791	.0618	.0483	.0378	.0297	.0233	.0183	.0113	.0070	.00440
53	.1251	.0970	.0753	.0586	.0456	.0355	.0277	.0216	.0169	.0104	.0064	.00396
54	.1203	.0928	.0717	.0555	.0430	.0333	.0259	.0201	.0157	.0095	.0058	.00357
55	.1157	.0888	.0683	.0526	.0406	.0313	.0242	.0187	.0145	.0087	.0053	.00322
56	.1112	.0850	.0651	.0499	.0383	.0294	.0226	.0174	.0134	.0080	.0048	.00290
57	.1069	.0814	.0620	.0473	.0361	.0276	.0211	.0162	.0124	.0073	.0044	.00261
58	.1028	.0778	.0590	.0448	.0341	.0259	.0198	.0151	.0115	.0067	.0040	.00235
59	.0989	.0745	.0562	.0425	.0321	.0243	.0185	.0140	.0107	.0062	.0036	.00212
60	.0951	.0713	.0535	.0403	.0303	.0229	.0173	.0130	.0099	.0057	.0033	.00191

PRESENT WORTH TABLE — SINGLE FUTURE PAYMENT

Example of use of this table:
Find how much $10,000 payable in 12 years is worth now at an interest rate of 6%.
From table for 12 years 6%
Present value of $10,000 in 12 years (10,000 × .4970)

.4970
$4.970

Interest Rate

Number of Years	6%	7%	8%	9%	10%	11%	12%	13%
1	0.9434	0.9346	0.9259	0.9174	0.9091	0.9009	0.8929	0.8850
2	0.8900	0.8734	0.8573	0.8417	0.8264	0.8116	0.7972	0.7831
3	0.8396	0.8163	0.7938	0.7722	0.7513	0.7312	0.7118	0.6931
4	0.7921	0.7629	0.7350	0.7084	0.6830	0.6587	0.6355	0.6133
5	0.7473	0.7130	0.6806	0.6499	0.6209	0.5935	0.5674	0.5428
6	0.7050	0.6663	0.6302	0.5963	0.5645	0.5346	0.5066	0.4803
7	0.6651	0.6227	0.5835	0.5470	0.5132	0.4816	0.4523	0.4251
8	0.6274	0.5820	0.5403	0.5019	0.4665	0.4339	0.4039	0.3762
9	0.5919	0.5439	0.5002	0.4604	0.4241	0.3909	0.3606	0.3329
10	0.5584	0.5083	0.4632	0.4224	0.3855	0.3522	0.3220	0.2946
11	0.5268	0.4751	0.4289	0.3875	0.3505	0.3173	0.2875	0.2607
12	0.4970	0.4440	0.3971	0.3555	0.3186	0.2858	0.2567	0.2307
13	0.4688	0.4150	0.3677	0.3262	0.2897	0.2575	0.2292	0.2042
14	0.4423	0.3878	0.3405	0.2992	0.2633	0.2320	0.2046	0.1807
15	0.4173	0.3624	0.3152	0.2745	0.2394	0.2090	0.1827	0.1599
16	0.3936	0.3387	0.2919	0.2519	0.2176	0.1883	0.1631	0.1415
17	0.3714	0.3166	0.2703	0.2311	0.1978	0.1696	0.1456	0.1252
18	0.3503	0.2959	0.2502	0.2120	0.1799	0.1528	0.1300	0.1108
19	0.3305	0.2765	0.2317	0.1945	0.1635	0.1377	0.1161	0.0981
20	0.3118	0.2584	0.2145	0.1784	0.1486	0.1240	0.1037	0.0868
21	0.2942	0.2415	0.1987	0.1637	0.1351	0.1117	0.0926	0.0768
22	0.2775	0.2257	0.1839	0.1502	0.1228	0.1007	0.0826	0.0680
23	0.2618	0.2109	0.1703	0.1378	0.1117	0.0907	0.0738	0.0601
24	0.2470	0.1971	0.1577	0.1264	0.1015	0.0817	0.0660	0.0532
25	0.2330	0.1842	0.1460	0.1160	0.0923	0.0736	0.0588	0.0471
26	0.2198	0.1722	0.1352	0.1064	0.0829	0.0663	0.0525	0.0417
27	0.2074	0.1609	0.1252	0.0976	0.0763	0.0597	0.0470	0.0369
28	0.1956	0.1504	0.1159	0.0895	0.0693	0.0538	0.0420	0.0326
29	0.1846	0.1406	0.1073	0.0822	0.0630	0.0485	0.0374	0.0289
30	0.1741	0.1314	0.0994	0.0754	0.0573	0.0437	0.0334	0.0256
31	0.1643	0.1228	0.0920	0.0691	0.0521	0.0394	0.0298	0.0226
32	0.1550	0.1147	0.0852	0.0634	0.0474	0.0354	0.0266	0.0200
33	0.1462	0.1072	0.0789	0.0582	0.0431	0.0319	0.0238	0.0177
34	0.1379	0.1002	0.0730	0.0534	0.0391	0.0288	0.0212	0.0157
35	0.1301	0.0937	0.0676	0.0490	0.0356	0.0259	0.0189	0.0139
36	0.1227	0.0875	0.0626	0.0449	0.0323	0.0234	0.0169	0.0123
37	0.1158	0.0818	0.0580	0.0412	0.0294	0.0210	0.0151	0.0109
38	0.1092	0.0765	0.0536	0.0378	0.0267	0.0189	0.0135	0.0096
39	0.1031	0.0715	0.0497	0.0347	0.0243	0.0171	0.0120	0.0085
40	0.0972	0.0668	0.0460	0.0318	0.0221	0.0154	0.0107	0.0075

PRESENT WORTH TABLE — PERIODIC FUTURE PAYMENTS

Example of use of this table:
To find the cost now of $1,000 of income per year for 20 years at 7%.
From table for 20 years at 7%   10.5940
Cost of $1,000 per year ($1,000 × 10.5940) $10,594

Interest Rate

Number of Years	6%	7%	8%	9%	10%	11%	12%	13%
1	0.9434	0.9346	0.9259	0.9174	0.9091	0.9009	0.8929	0.8850
2	1.8334	1.8080	1.7833	1.7591	1.7355	1.7125	1.6901	1.6681
3	2.6730	2.6243	2.5771	2.5313	2.4869	2.4437	2.4018	2.3612
4	3.4651	3.3872	3.3121	3.2397	3.1699	3.1024	3.0373	2.9745
5	4.2124	4.1002	3.9927	3.8897	3.7908	3.6959	3.6048	3.5172
6	4.9173	4.7665	4.6229	4.4859	4.3553	4.2305	4.1114	3.9975
7	5.5824	5.3893	5.2064	5.0330	4.8684	4.7122	4.5638	4.4226
8	6.2098	5.9713	5.7466	5.5348	5.3349	5.1461	4.9676	4.7988
9	6.8017	6.5152	6.2469	5.9952	5.7590	5.5370	5.3282	5.1317
10	7.3601	7.0236	6.7101	6.4177	6.1446	5.8892	5.6502	5.4262
11	7.8869	7.4987	7.1390	6.8052	6.4951	6.2065	5.9377	5.6869
12	8.3838	7.9427	7.5361	7.1607	6.8137	6.4924	6.1944	5.9176
13	8.8527	8.3577	7.9038	7.4869	7.1034	6.7499	6.4235	6.1218
14	9.2950	8.7455	8.2442	7.7862	7.3667	6.9819	6.6282	6.3025
15	9.7122	9.1079	8.5595	8.0607	7.6061	7.1909	6.8109	6.4624
16	10.1059	9.4466	8.8514	8.3126	7.8237	7.3792	6.9740	6.6039
17	10.4773	9.7632	9.1216	8.5436	8.0216	7.5488	7.1196	6.7291
18	10.8276	10.0591	9.3719	8.7556	8.2014	7.7016	7.2497	6.8399
19	11.1581	10.3356	9.6036	8.9501	8.3649	7.8393	7.3658	6.9380
20	11.4699	10.5940	9.8181	9.1285	8.5136	7.9633	7.4694	7.0248
21	11.7641	10.8355	10.0168	9.2922	8.6487	8.0751	7.5620	7.1016
22	12.0416	11.0612	10.2007	9.4424	8.7715	8.1757	7.6446	7.1695
23	12.3034	11.2722	10.3711	9.5802	8.8832	8.2664	7.7184	7.2297
24	12.5504	11.4693	10.5288	9.7066	8.9847	8.3481	7.7843	7.2829
25	12.7834	11.6536	10.6748	9.8226	9.0770	8.4217	7.8431	7.3299
26	13.0032	11.8258	10.8100	9.9290	9.1609	8.4881	7.8957	7.3717
27	13.2105	11.9867	10.9352	10.0266	9.2372	8.5478	7.9426	7.4086
28	13.4062	12.1371	11.0511	10.1161	9.3066	8.6016	7.9844	7.4412
29	13.5907	12.2777	11.1584	10.1983	9.3696	8.6501	8.0218	7.4701
30	13.7648	12.4090	11.2578	10.2737	9.4269	8.6938	8.0552	7.4957
31	13.9291	12.5318	11.3498	10.3428	9.4790	8.7331	8.0850	7.5183
32	14.0840	12.6466	11.4350	10.4062	9.5264	8.7686	8.1116	7.5383
33	14.2302	12.7538	11.5139	10.4644	9.5694	8.8005	8.1354	7.5560
34	14.3681	12.8540	11.5869	10.5178	9.6086	8.8293	8.1566	7.5717
35	14.4982	12.9477	11.6546	10.5668	9.6442	8.8552	8.1755	7.5856
36	14.6210	13.0352	11.7172	10.6118	9.6765	8.8786	8.1924	7.5979
37	14.7368	13.1170	11.7752	10.6530	9.7059	8.8996	8.2075	7.6087
38	14.8460	13.1935	11.8289	10.6908	9.7327	8.9186	8.2210	7.6183
39	14.9491	13.2649	11.8786	10.7255	9.7569	8.9357	8.2330	7.6268
40	15.0463	13.3317	11.9246	10.7574	9.7791	8.9511	8.2438	7.6344

SINKING FUND REQUIREMENTS TABLE

Example of use of this table:
　To find the amount of money which must be deposited at the end of each year to grow to $10,000 in 19 years at 8%.
　　From table for 19 years at 8%　　　　　.02413
　　Amount of each deposit ($10,000 × .02413)　$241.30

Interest Rate

Number of Years	6%	7%	8%	9%	10%	11%	12%	13%
1	1.00000	1.00000	1.00000	1.00000	1.00000	1.00000	1.00000	1.00000
2	.48544	.48309	.48077	.47847	.47619	.47393	.47169	.46948
3	.31411	.31105	.30803	.30505	.30211	.29921	.29635	.29352
4	.22859	.22523	.22192	.21867	.21547	.21233	.20923	.20619
5	.17740	.17389	.17046	.16709	.16379	.16057	.15741	.15431
6	.14336	.13979	.13632	.13292	.12961	.12638	.12323	.12015
7	.11913	.11555	.11207	.10869	.10541	.10222	.09912	.09611
8	.10104	.09747	.09401	.09067	.08744	.08432	.08130	.07839
9	.08702	.08349	.08008	.07679	.07364	.07060	.06768	.06487
10	.07587	.07238	.06903	.06582	.06275	.05980	.05698	.05429
11	.06679	.06336	.06008	.05695	.05396	.05112	.04846	.04584
12	.05928	.05590	.05269	.04965	.04676	.04403	.04144	.03899
13	.05296	.04965	.04652	.04357	.04078	.03815	.03568	.03335
14	.04758	.04434	.04129	.03843	.03575	.03323	.03087	.02867
15	.04206	.03979	.03683	.03406	.03147	.02907	.02682	.02474
16	.03895	.03586	.03298	.03030	.02782	.02552	.02339	.02143
17	.03544	.03243	.02963	.02705	.02466	.02247	.02046	.01861
18	.03236	.02941	.02670	.02421	.02193	.01984	.01794	.01620
19	.02962	.02675	.02413	.02173	.01955	.01756	.01576	.01413
20	.02718	.02439	.02185	.01955	.01746	.01558	.01388	.01235
21	.02500	.02229	.01983	.01762	.01562	.01384	.01224	.01081
22	.02305	.02041	.01803	.01590	.01401	.01231	.01081	.00948
23	.02128	.01871	.01642	.01438	.01257	.01097	.00956	.00832
24	.01968	.01719	.01498	.01302	.01129	.00979	.00846	.00731
25	.01823	.01581	.01368	.01181	.01017	.00874	.00749	.00643
26	.01690	.01456	.01251	.01072	.00916	.00781	.00665	.00565
27	.01570	.01343	.01145	.00973	.00826	.00699	.00590	.00498
28	.01459	.01239	.01049	.00885	.00745	.00626	.00524	.00439
29	.01358	.01145	.00962	.00806	.00673	.00561	.00466	.00387
30	.01265	.01059	.00883	.00734	.00608	.00502	.00414	.00341
31	.01179	.00979	.00811	.00669	.00549	.00451	.00369	.00301
32	.01100	.00907	.00745	.00609	.00497	.00404	.00328	.00266
33	.01027	.00841	.00685	.00556	.00449	.00363	.00292	.00234
34	.00960	.00779	.00630	.00508	.00407	.00326	.00260	.00207
35	.00897	.00723	.00580	.00464	.00369	.00293	.00232	.00183
36	.00839	.00676	.00534	.00424	.00334	.00263	.00206	.00162
37	.00786	.00624	.00492	.00387	.00303	.00236	.00184	.00143
38	.00736	.00579	.00454	.00354	.00275	.00213	.00164	.00126
39	.00689	.00539	.00419	.00323	.00249	.00191	.00146	.00112
40	.00646	.00501	.00386	.00296	.00226	.00172	.00130	.00099

Index

B